Java™ GUI Development

Vartan Piroumian

A Division of Macmillan Computer Publishing
201 West 103rd St., Indianapolis, Indiana, 46290 USA

Java™ GUI Development

Copyright© 1999 by Sams Publishing

International Standard Book Number: 0-672-31546-7

Library of Congress Catalog Card Number: 99-62247

Printed in the United States of America

First Printing: August 1999

01 00 99   4   3   2   1

Trademarks

Warning and Disclaimer

EXECUTIVE EDITOR
Tim Ryan

ACQUISITIONS EDITOR
Steve Anglin

DEVELOPMENT EDITOR
Jon Steever

MANAGING EDITOR
Jodi Jensen

SENIOR EDITOR
Susan Ross Moore

COPY EDITOR
Mary Lagu

INDEXER
Kevin Fulcher

PROOFREADER
Megan Wade

TECHNICAL EDITOR
Jeff Perkins

SOFTWARE DEVELOPMENT SPECIALIST
Aaron Price

TEAM COORDINATOR
Karen Opal

INTERIOR DESIGN
Anne Jones

COVER DESIGN
Alan Clements

COPY WRITER
Eric Borgert

LAYOUT TECHNICIANS
Brian Borders
Susan Geiselman
Mark Walchle

Overview

Introduction **1**

1   UI Programming Concepts **7**

2   Introducing the Java Foundation Classes **15**

3   Program Structure **47**

4   AWT Concepts and Architecture **73**

5   The AWT Components **101**

6   Swing Concepts and Architecture **139**

7   The Swing Components **177**

8   Layout Managers **295**

9   Events and Event Handling **361**

10   Models **501**

11   Graphics **537**

12   Fonts and Colors **591**

Index **615**

Contents

Introduction   **1**

1   UI Programming Concepts   **7**

Designing for the Target Audience 8

Creating Abstraction in Engineering Design 9

The Model-View-Controller Idiom...10

Summary 13

2   Introducing the Java Foundation Classes   **15**

The Big Picture 16

The Abstract Windowing Toolkit 16

Platform-Independence 18

AWT Components 20

The AWT Component Class 21

AWT Containers 22

Layout Managers 23

The Java Foundation Classes 23

Lightweight Components 26

Swing's Pluggable Look-and-Feel 29

The Delegation Event Model 32

The JFC Containment Model 33

Layered Panes 38

Glass Panes 39

The JFC and Swing Class Hierarchies 40

The JFC Model Architecture 41

Summary 46

3   Basic Program Structure   **47**

Program Building Blocks 48

Creating an Application 51

Subclassing java.awt.Frame...54

Subclassing java.awt.Panel 60

Starting and Stopping Your Application 63

Using Lightweight Containers 63

Creating an Applet 64

Programs That Are Both Applications and Applets 67

Summary 71

4   AWT Concepts and Architecture   **73**

AWT Components 74

The java.awt.Component Class..75

Component Appearance...78
Component Location..78
Component Sizing...78
Component Visibility...79
Component Responsiveness to Events 79
Component Cursors...80
Rendering Components 81
The java.awt.Container Class 82
Adding Components to a Container 85
Using Nested Containers for Organization 92
How AWT Containers Store Children...97
Front-to-Back Component Ordering in Containers.........................98
Summary 99

5   The AWT Components   101
The AWT Components 102
Buttons..102
Check Boxes 105
Choices 108
Dialogs...110
Labels...114
Lists 117
Menus 121
Text Areas and Text Fields 131
Summary 137

6   Swing Concepts and Architecture   139
The Swing Component Tool Set...140
The javax.swing.JComponent Class 143
Making Swing Components Lightweight...145
Abstractions Encapsulated by the JComponent Class 146
Swing Containers 148
Limitations of the AWT Containment Model 149
The Swing Container Abstraction...149
The JRootPane Container 151
The JLayeredPane Class 159
Lightweight and Heavyweight Containers 162
Configuring Look-and-Feel 166
Summary 174

7   The Swing Components   177
The Swing Lightweight Component Tool Set 178
Buttons..181
Check Boxes 189

Radio Buttons 192

Combo Boxes 196

File Choosers...201

Labels...208

Lists 215

Menus and Menu Bars...223

Progress Indicators 234

Sliders 238

Split Panes 244

Tabbed Panes 250

Text Components...255

Text Fields 260

Password Fields 263

Text Area 265

Editor Panes..269

Text Panes 273

ToolTips 282

Trees 284

Summary 294

8   Layout Managers   295

The Role of the Layout Manager 296

The FlowLayout Class 303

The GridLayout Class...308

The BorderLayout Class 313

The CardLayout 318

The BoxLayout 322

The GridBagLayout Class 334

gridx and gridy 341

gridwidth and gridheight 343

fill...347

anchor 348

insets 351

ipadx and ipady 353

weightx and weighty 354

Collaboration Between Containers and Layout Managers.................359

Summary 360

9   Events and Event Handling   361

Events 362

Event Type Hierarchy 362

Event Types...363

AWT Event Types 365

Swing Event Types 368

Handling Events 371

Delivering Events 371

Event Listeners 372

AWT and Swing Events Are Complimentary 377

A Sample Event Handler...378

Adapters 386

Inner Classes...388

Named Inner Classes..389

Anonymous Inner Classes 391

Combining Event Sources and Listeners 401

Notifying Multiple Listeners 402

Using AWT Events 402

Component and Container Events...403

Focus Events 407

Key Events...410

Mouse Events 415

Consuming Input Events 419

Paint Events...422

Window Events 422

Item Events 425

Text Events 427

Adjustment Events...429

Using Swing Events 433

Ancestor Events..434

Caret Events..435

Change Events...437

Hyperlink Events 440

Internal Frame Events 444

List Data Events 449

List Selection Events 455

Menu Events 458

Pop-up Menu Events 464

Tree Expansion Events 468

Tree Selection Events 476

Tree Model Events...478

Menu Key Events 482

Menu Drag Mouse Events...486

Swing Action Objects 488

Summary..499

10   Models   501

Identifying and Targeting Abstractions..502

Utilizing the MVC Paradigm 503

The Swing Model Architecture...504

    Integrating the View and Controller 505

Swing Model Anatomy...506

    Swing Component Support for MVC 507

    Supporting Events and Event Handling 508

    Two Kinds of Models 512

    Distinguishing Between Types of Models......................................512

    Dual Context Models...517

    Where and When To Use Models 519

Swing Models and Their Related Types..521

Swing Models 525

    ButtonModel 525

    ComboBoxModel and MutableComboBoxModel 526

    SingleSelectionModel 528

    TableModel and TableColumnModel 528

    TreeModel and TreeSelectionModel...529

Defining Your Own Models 534

Summary...534

11   Graphics   537

The AWT Graphics Model 538

    Obtaining Graphics Objects for Drawing 539

    Disposing of Graphics Instances...548

The Graphics Class...549

Using Graphics for Basic Drawing..551

    Drawing Lines 557

    Drawing Ovals..558

    Drawing Polygons 558

    Drawing Rectangles..559

    Drawing Arcs..560

    Drawing Text 561

Clipping 562

Translating the Graphics Origin 569

Graphics Modes 574

How Components Are Painted 581

    Events Trigger Painting..582

    The AWT Paint Model..582

    The Swing Paint Model..584

Summary...590

12   Fonts and Colors   591

Organization of Color Support Classes 592

Color Models 593

The Index Color Model 593

The Direct Color Model 596

Using Colors 597

Using the java.awt.Color Class 597

Using System Colors 600

Fonts 602

Font Metrics..606

Summary 612

Index   615

Preface

The purpose of this book is simply to teach the reader to program graphical user interface applications using Java.

It attempts to accomplish this singular goal by giving the reader a conceptual and pragmatic foundation on which to build whatever knowledge is necessary to make him/her an accomplished Java GUI programmer.

This book assumes that you have fluency with the Java programming language. It does not, however, require any experience with GUI programming. In fact, it does not target readers with any particular level of GUI programming knowledge. Rather, it starts from the beginning, presenting the knowledge that all Java GUI programmers must have, and builds a foundation upon which all other advanced Java GUI programming skills must be based. Experienced GUI programmers new to Java GUI programming, and beginners alike can benefit from this book.

It focuses on teaching the concepts and paradigms around which the Java GUI platform was designed and built. The idea behind focusing on concepts is to show how the platform manifests support for commonly used paradigms and capabilities.

In order to program effectively with any platform, one must understand its "personality." Knowing how to accomplish a task "the right way" allows you to write more efficient and effective programs. For example, understanding conceptually to which feature category a certain function belongs can help you find where, in an overwhelmingly large tool kit, to discover the class or method that helps you accomplish the task at hand. Regardless of your experience with other GUI platforms, the concepts and paradigms that apply to the Java GUI environment will be a necessary weapon in your arsenal.

If you understand the conceptual framework, you can easily gain fluency with the concrete details needed to use any of the classes in the JDK. Conversely, it is unreasonable to expect you to figure out the paradigms of a platform or the subtle semantics of a class or method by simply examining sparse API documentation or source code. Like learning a programming language, learning to use a platform involves learning the patterns and idioms around which the designers built the platform.

Of course, the purpose of learning concepts is to apply them. Therefore, this book also gives many pragmatic examples that show how to utilize the concepts you learn. The examples focus on the topic at hand, instead of overwhelming you with a plethora of features that distract you from concentrating on the particular feature being presented.

Topics are presented in the order that you need to learn and understand them to be able to create a program from scratch. This approach helps develop your conceptual understanding of why you must write your programs a certain way. It also reduces interdependencies of technical know-how as much as possible.

This approach is based on my professional experience writing Java GUI programs. I have seen cases where others have struggled to get relatively simple parts of a GUI up and running because they never formally learned the concepts and organization of the GUI tool kit.

As a professional programmer, it is important to understand concepts. If you just take existing code and "tune" it to your needs, you will not understand what is really going on. Eventually, you will reach a limit to the kinds of things you can do. But if you learn why you are doing certain tasks, you will soon be crafting your own sophisticated Java GUIs.

No book can show you every aspect of every API, and certainly, no book can stay current with the explosion of information for even one specialized area like Java GUI development. However, the number of concepts and paradigms are fairly manageable. You can easily learn these concepts, and recognize when and how they are applied throughout the JDK. Thus, you can easily figure out how to use an API after you recognize the patterns involved.

I personally enjoy working with Java and GUI programming. I find it rewarding to see the fruits of one's labor reflected back from the screen. May you, too, derive pleasure from your experience writing Java GUI programs.

V.P.
May 1999
Palo Alto, CA

About the Author

Vartan Piroumian is an independent consultant in his native California. He has 16 years of professional software engineering experience. He first started learning about object-oriented programming in 1980 using Lisp.

Vartan specializes in object-oriented technology, Java, and internationalization. He works with various companies in the San Francisco Bay and the Los Angeles areas. He works frequently with Sun Microsystems' Solaris and Java Software divisions, where he created the first Japanese localized version of the Hot Java Views MailView application.

Vartan also teaches object-oriented technology and Java courses for the University of California Santa Cruz in the Santa Clara Valley.

In his free time he enjoys athletics, photography, playing the mandolin, and spending time with his family.

Dedication

To my father...

Frederic Albert Piroumian

*He is a man of immense raw intelligence,
talent, and knowledge,*

a man with true wisdom and class,

*a scientist, musician, philosopher, photographer, historian,
humanitarian*

*with an incredible, voracious love for
knowledge, learning, and truth,*

*a man with charisma, power, ability,
principle, responsibility, and integrity.*

*His vast love,
used only in selfless devotion and commitment to his family,*

*taught us to question and wonder,
to recognize the importance of thinking independently
and analyzing the world around us,*

and to always learn, in order to appreciate the beauty in this world.

*With unspeakable respect, gratitude, and humility,
I dedicate this book to him.*

Acknowledgments

Many people participated in this book project, and I would like to thank them all for their effort and involvement.

First of all, I would like to mention Steve Anglin, the Acquisitions Editor at Macmillan Publishing who first approached me with an offer to write this book. Without his resourcefulness, I might never have embarked upon this journey. I also want to acknowledge Steve's work throughout the project as the liaison between me and the staff at Macmillan. He coordinated all communication and often shielded me from the demands of the publisher when my deadlines were looming.

Steve and I also commiserated on the pitfalls of being called for jury duty three weeks before the deadline for a completed manuscript.

Tim Ryan, the Executive Editor, made the final decision to give me the chance to write this book. I would like to thank him for his faith in my ability, for championing my proposal, and for making sure that this project came to fruition.

Jon Steever, the Development Editor, played a huge role in every phase of this project.

Jon really bent over backwards to make my life easier and allow me to focus on the technical aspects of the book. Jon is involved with many projects, and somehow manages to handle them all gracefully.

I would also like to thank Susan Moore, the Project Editor. Susan is one of those individuals who works behind the scenes to ensure that many tasks get accomplished. The fact that I almost never had to communicate with Susan directly proves that she did her job admirably.

I would also like to recognize the work of Jeff Perkins, the technical editor, for his accurate review of my code examples and manuscript and for suggesting ways in which I could make this book more useful to readers.

Karen Opal was the Team Coordinator, and Katie Robinson and Mandie Rowell were the formatters. I would like to thank them for their extra effort in preparing the original manuscript.

I would like to give special acknowledgment to the copy editors, Rhonda Tinch-Mize and, in particular, I want to thank Mary Lagu for all her help and patience. The work of copy editors is seldom publicized. They are the ones who ensure that what starts out as a confused jumble of technical expression ends up as an organized, comprehensible work.

And, last, but certainly not least, I would like to acknowledge my family. My mother Edith is the other half of our wonderful parents who deserve more acknowledgment than I can possibly give them. Her love and fierce support for her children is humbling. I also want to acknowledge the life-long love and support of my sister Lisa, and my brother Fred. They never cease to encourage me, and believe that nothing is out of my reach. Ironically, I think they are far more talented than I.

They are the people who have made our family special, one which has always fostered a tremendous amount of generosity, kindness, love, and faith. Without them, not much would seem meaningful in this life.

Notwithstanding my professional interest in computer science and software engineering, the catalyst that resulted in the genesis of this book was my desire to honor them.

V.P.
Palo Alto, CA
May 1999

Tell Us What You Think!

As the reader of this book, *you* are our most important critic and commentator. We value your opinion and want to know what we're doing right, what we could do better, what areas you'd like to see us publish in, and any other words of wisdom you're willing to pass our way.

As an executive editor for Sams Publishing, I welcome your comments. You can fax, email, or write me directly to let me know what you did or didn't like about this book—as well as what we can do to make our books stronger.

When you write, please be sure to include this book's title and author as well as your name and phone or fax number. I will carefully review your comments and share them with the author and editors who worked on the book.

Fax: 317-581-4770

Email: `java@mcp.com`

Mail: Tim Ryan
Executive Editor
Sams Publishing
201 West 103rd Street
Indianapolis, IN 46290 USA

Introduction

The subject of this book is writing graphical user interface software using the Java Foundation Classes (JFC). It is organized to teach you how to write a GUI program in Java, assuming you have never done so. Therefore, it starts from the beginning.

This book attempts to present concepts and show how to apply them. Therefore, each chapter first introduces one or more related concepts that pertain to a particular aspect of Java GUI programming. The conceptual discussion includes how the Java toolkit manifests support for the concept. This is followed by examples that show how the concept is applied.

Book Content and Organization

This book covers the skills that are fundamental to all Java GUI programming. Understanding the concepts, and acquiring fluency with the APIs that manifest support for them is important for all levels of Java GUI programs.

This book takes a comprehensive approach to organization. Topics are organized in the order you would learn them to actually design and construct a real Java GUI program. Therefore, it is probably best to read the chapters in order if you are new to either GUI programming or GUI programming in Java.

If you have some experience writing Java GUI programs, and want to read about a particular topic, the chapter title will lead you there. Chapter titles indicate the conceptual category to which the chapter material belongs.

In particular, Chapter 2, "Introducing the Java Foundation Classes," is a conceptual overview of the JFC. It defines JFC and discusses the new features in Swing. This chapter is intended to give experienced AWT programmers an understanding of the tools available to them in the JFC. Each of the topics in Chapter 2 is covered later in the book with code examples.

In each chapter, concepts are explained as they are introduced, and followed with concrete examples of code that demonstrate use of the concepts or the preferred toolkit paradigm or idiom that manifests support for those concepts.

Topics are introduced from a high level and gradually delve into more detail. The order in which topics are introduced attempts to eliminate interdependencies of skills as much as possible.

The primary focus of the book is on the Java Foundation Classes (JFC) defined in the latest release, version 2 of the Java Development Kit (JDK). Wherever possible, concepts and examples are presented in the context of the JFC packages and classes.

However, the Abstract Windowing Toolkit (AWT) is the foundation for all GUI programming in Java; the JFC does not obsolete the AWT. Therefore, the AWT concepts that form the foundation for all JFC programming are also discussed. Additionally, basic AWT classes are introduced to accommodate those readers who still need to work with strictly AWT programs.

The Java Foundation classes are comprised of four APIs: AWT, the Java 2D API, Swing, and the Accessibility API. This book discusses the AWT and Swing.

This book does not discuss the original AWT 1.0.x releases. Many fundamental architectural elements have changed since release 1.1 of the JDK such as the original inheritance-based event model. Java developers are strongly encouraged to use the latest JDK release.

The topics chosen for this book are those that will enable you to create full GUI applications. This book gives you enough information to produce complex Java GUI applications.

You will learn about the following topics:

- Chapter 1, "UI Programming Concepts," presents a short review of basic concepts of user interface programming. Here, I discuss important design principles and architectural approaches that are useful in many programming environments. This is a good review or introduction to the Java GUI platform, which is well-designed and employs these architectural principles. Understanding these principles will make it much easier for the reader to grasp the design of the Java platform and the individual packages and classes.

- Chapter 2, "Introducing the Java Foundation Classes," gives an overall perspective of the JFC by introducing its organization and presenting a conceptual discussion of its overall architecture and features.

  The chapter first introduces the organization of the JDK 2 packages that provide support for GUI programming in Java. This discussion is useful to both newcomers and experienced AWT programmers. Newcomers will be able to navigate through the many packages that comprise the JFC, and experienced AWT programmers will be able to easily determine what features are implemented in the new packages.

  This chapter also highlights the general concepts and capabilities supported by the JFC, such as platform independence, peer classes and the Model-View-Controller architecture.

  The material in this chapter is intentionally conceptual, with no code examples. The idea is to give an overall, high-level perspective, without showing examples that require the inclusion of other technical areas.

- Chapter 3, "Program Structure," begins a more concrete treatment of Java GUI programming. It introduces components, containers, and layout managers, which are the primary building blocks of all Java GUI programs. It starts by showing how programs are structured and built, and how to get a simple GUI to show on screen.

This chapter also defines, discusses, and compares applets and applications. It shows how to make your program behave as either an applet or an application, and highlights security and compatibility issues.

- Chapter 4, "AWT Concepts and Architecture," takes a closer look at the way AWT components and containers work. These topics are very important in building a foundation for all programs. The chapter discusses in depth the new JFC container architecture implemented in Swing, and compares it to the original AWT containment architecture. It also discusses the relationship between different components and how to use them.

- Chapter 5, "The AWT Components," introduces the concrete AWT components. This chapter also uses full code examples to show you how to build applications using only AWT components. This chapter is included for those programmers who still need to program with only the AWT and not the Swing components.

- Chapter 6, "Swing Concepts and Architecture," introduces the Swing API. This chapter introduces the new concepts and architectural features that the Swing packages add to the JFC.

- Chapter 7, "The Swing Components," introduces the concrete Swing components. This chapter uses working code examples to show you how to build programs using only Swing components.

- Layout Managers are one of the fundamentally important building blocks of any Java GUI. All the JFC (AWT and Swing) layout managers are discussed in depth in Chapter 8, "Layout Managers," and related to components and containers.

- Event handling is critical to every application. Chapter 9, "Events and Event Handling," starts with a conceptual overview, and then discusses events and event handlers in great detail, highlighting all the classes that implement this mechanism in the JDK. It also covers the context of components and containers, and how events and event handling combine all components in your application.

- Swing introduces built-in support for the Model-View-Controller paradigm. Chapter 10, "The Swing Model Architecture," discusses the MVC paradigm and how the Swing tool kit manifests support for it.

- The AWT defines support for basic graphical drawing operations on components. Chapter 11, "Graphics," introduces the AWT graphics support, which is also available to Swing components.

- Java nicely supports the use of multiple fonts and colors. In Chapter 12, "Fonts and Colors," you will learn how to enhance your application with fonts and colors. This chapter does not cover the Java 2D API.

Audience

This book is intended for Java programmers who already have a solid understanding of the Java programming language and runtime environment. Although you don't need to be an object-oriented programming expert, readers should feel comfortable reading references to object-oriented concepts and how they are supported by the Java language.

Readers need not have any prior experience either to GUI programming or to GUI programming using Java. In fact, Chapter 1, "UI Programming Concepts," is written to accommodate those programmers who have never used any GUI programming APIs.

Conventions Used in This Book

Throughout this book the conventions shown in Table I.1 will be used to indicate various types of program data or source code components.

TABLE I.1   Method and Class Naming Conventions Used Throughout the Book

Type of Data	Example Print for that Type of Data
Java method names and variable names have an initial lowercase first word; each subsequent component word has an initial capital letter.	`public void doSomething()`
Java Class names have initial capital for each component word.	`public class AnExampleClass`

New terms and source code will use the following typographic conventions shown in Table 0.2:

TABLE I.2   Typographic Conventions

Description of Data	Typography Used
Java source code	`Fixed width font looks like this.`
Terms	*Italic font.*

NOTE

Notes present interesting or useful information that isn't necessarily essential to the discussion. This secondary track of information enhances your understanding of Java GUI Development

TIP

Tips present advice on quick or often overlooked procedures. These include shortcuts that save you time.

CAUTION

Cautions serve to warn you about potential problems that a procedure may cause, about unexpected results and mistakes to avoid.

Finding the Code Examples From the Book

To get the code examples from this book's support page on the Web, go to the following URL in your browser: `http://www.mcp.com`. Click on the "Product Support" link. On the Product Support page, enter this book's ISBN (0672315467) in the "Book Information and Downloads" field and click "Search." The book's support page will then load, giving you access to the code examples from the book, support files, and errata.

UI Programming Concepts

IN THIS CHAPTER

- **Designing for the Target Audience   8**
- **Creating Abstraction in Engineering Design   9**
- **The Model-View-Controller Idiom   10**

Most programs have a user interface (UI) of some kind. In fact, depending on exactly how you define *user interface*, you could say that all programs have a user interface.

For instance, if the program is one that executes as a daemon process, the user interface is the set of command line options available for the user to start the daemon, either manually or through an automated script. The program's error message reporting mechanism is also part of the interface; does it log messages to a file, print them on the console, or beep at the user?

Nowadays, we tend to think of user interfaces as interfaces that are at least screen-oriented, limited to drawing simple alphabetic characters in fixed rows and columns. A Graphical User Interface (GUI) is one that controls a bit-mapped graphics display device. These devices are capable of addressing individual picture elements (pixels). This resolution enables programs to render arbitrary shapes, images, and so forth on the screen.

GUI programming is about creating a medium through which a user—most likely a human—can effectively communicate with the underlying program logic and affect its state and behavior. The user must be able to understand the interface, its functions, its messages, and its logical flow.

Possibly the greatest advantage of graphic bit-mapped displays is that they give GUI programs the power to create more meaningful icons, images, and components that represent real-world entities. The program creates an *abstraction* of these entities. Humans can easily recognize the abstraction and grasp the nature and purpose of the interface.

Designing for the Target Audience

The user's background, knowledge, experience, and perspective define a usage context. The user forms expectations that the program will present the right information and perform in a certain way based on what the program is advertised to do.

Naturally, then, different classes of users will have different expectations. The GUI interface should clearly convey the proper perspective and level of detail appropriate for the background of the target audience.

For instance, a medical doctor has domain knowledge of the medical field, and, therefore, expects a program to present abstractions that represent concepts and terminology used by doctors, not lay people. The icons in such a program, for example, should represent concepts that a doctor would recognize. It is irrelevant whether a lay person could make sense of the user interface designed for a doctor.

Similarly, the graphical display of a bank ATM machine presents abstractions of entities and behavior with which users are familiar. For example, the information display may represent the state of your bank account. In order to be useful, the ATM must represent your bank account information in a way that allows you to recognize and properly interpret it.

The first step, therefore, toward creating a meaningful interface is to identify your target audience. Who will be using your program? What do they want to do? How do they expect a GUI program to help them? What real-world process or entity are they trying to simulate by using the program? These questions are important because programs simulate processes or workflow with which the user is already familiar.

The design of an application's workflow should also adhere to the usage patterns suggested by the user's domain knowledge. Your program should preserve the user's expectations regarding the organization and flow of information. We all have some notion of the basic sequence of events that will transpire when we use some entity or object. A GUI that represents the object should preserve its behavior as well as its attributes. If it doesn't present the same sequence of steps and states as the real object, the user might have trouble figuring out how to use it.

NOTE

When designing a GUI application, address the user's needs first. The application should be comprehensible, meaningful, and appealing to the target audience. Don't simplify the implementation issues at the expense of the intuitiveness or organization of the GUI.

Creating Abstraction in Engineering Design

When designing user interface software, the primary goal of the software engineer should be to place the needs of the user first. The user interface's clarity, organization, and applicability to the target audience should take top priority.

The software engineer should not choose a design because it is convenient to implement. On the contrary, the design should first and foremost support an interface that creates the most meaningful abstractions, and organizes functions, data, and workflow in the most intuitive way *for the user*. This is one of the challenges of creating good GUI software.

Another challenge to crafting good GUI software is that the engineer must use the available tools of the trade to create these abstractions. For software engineers and programmers these tools are programming languages, compilers, class libraries, operating systems, and window systems.

The Java Foundation Classes (JFC), the foremost subject of this book, is one such set of class libraries. The JFC contains implementations of visual components that represent familiar entities with which the user can interact. Elements, such as dialogs, buttons, text fields, and so forth, are the building blocks that the software engineer can use to create the visual abstractions of the user interface.

Underneath an application's GUI is a lot of application logic that gives life to the user interface. The application logic takes care of doing all the work that makes the UI capable of supporting user interaction, such as interpreting mouse clicks and key strokes, organizing, storing and retrieving application data, and so forth.

The internal logic must provide a framework that supports the GUI. This implies that the states of the GUI and application logic must be synchronized. They represent the same information. Therefore, the application must internally abstract the same entities and concepts that are presented by the UI.

Even though the internal logic conceptually addresses the same elements, it must do so in a different manner. The application logic must present abstractions that are meaningful to the software engineer, not the end user.

So the software engineer must work with two orthogonal sets of abstractions. The first set must be meaningful to users, whereas the second set must be meaningful to engineers. The challenge for the software designer is bridging these abstractions so that the two major parts of the application, namely the GUI and application logic, can work together.

The Model-View-Controller Idiom

Java is an object-oriented programming language. The JFC visual components are defined by Java classes. In order to bridge the gap between the two sets of abstractions mentioned in the previous section, each component must have a corresponding data structure in the application logic. These, too, must be defined by classes, which are the primary building block of Java programs.

Because the internal logic and its corresponding GUI component implement different abstractions of the same entity, it is useful to define each with their own class. This approach supports the object-oriented design principle that a class should represent one entity.

If a single class definition tries to accommodate two abstractions it becomes cluttered, and its purpose becomes muddled. Nevertheless, the software engineer still has the challenge of relating the two definitions so that object instances can communicate and keep their states synchronized.

One approach that has proven useful in other systems, such as Smalltalk, is the *Model-View-Controller* or MVC paradigm. It is a central architectural feature of the Java Foundation Classes.

When a program uses the MVC paradigm, it employs three constituents to help it bridge the application data and visual models that it uses. The program must create and manage an association between three collaborating elements:

- View: This comprises the visible GUI that the user sees.
- Model: This is the abstraction used in the application logic to represent the nature and state of the visual objects that are presented on the screen to the user.
- Controller: This component enables the model and view components to communicate. It also allows the model to be updated to reflect changes incurred by interaction with the user.

Figure 1.1 shows the relationship between these three constituent parts of an application.

The job of the view object is to manage GUI issues such as rendering of the display components, layout, redrawing, event handling, and so on. These tasks are heavily focused on presenting a meaningful representation of the internal state of the application to the user.

The application model has a different job. It must create and maintain the internal application logic state associated with whatever entities the program represents or simulates. The GUI represents a visual analog of the nature and internal state of the model.

The controller is really the part of the application that forms a communication path between the model and view. It allows the view and model to communicate changes in their state to one another.

An external entity other than the GUI can initiate a change to the state of the model. In that case, the model makes a request to update the view object. Another scenario is that the user performs some action that requires a change to the model's state. The GUI reflects this change, but it is really the model that tracks the change.

In either case, the controller is the medium through which the model and view communicate. The view translates the abstraction employed by the model into to a form suitable for the user. The model, therefore, is the heart of the application logic and state. For the software engineer who designs, architects and implements the application, the primary focus will be on the model.

NOTE

Application logic design should center around the model, not the view. When designing a GUI application, the software engineer should first formulate and design the abstractions that support the application logic. Then he designs the view that visually represents these abstractions.

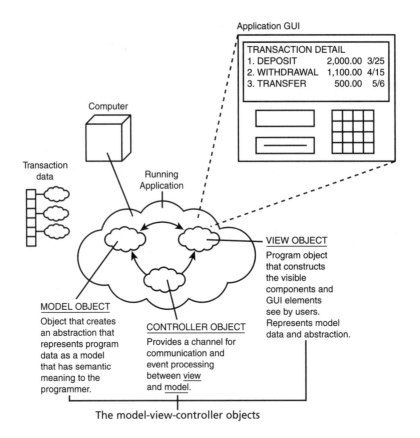

The model-view-controller objects

FIGURE 1.1

Model, view, and controller objects communicate in order to maintain synchronized states. The controller can be designed to enable unidirectional or bidirectional communication.

The description of the MVC architecture presented thus far suggests that the software engineer should partition the whole application into model, view, and controller components. Practically, however, the MVC paradigm is applied to smaller subsets of the overall application.

As mentioned earlier, the JFC components are entities like buttons, scroll bars, text fields, and so forth. Each such component used in a GUI comprises some subset of the overall view. Each represents an entity in itself, and, therefore, has a corresponding model that stores the state of the application data it represents.

The JFC components each reference a model object. The component and its model create a logical and visual representation, respectively, of the same entity. That is, they create different, albeit related, abstractions. Abstractions are created by type definitions. Every type defined by the programmer is really an abstraction of an entity.

In the JFC, the type employed by a component is congruent with the abstraction represented by the JFC component. This built-in support for MVC makes the JFC much more powerful. Many common abstractions are available for your use. The JFC classes essentially implement the MVC paradigm for you at this component level.

Nevertheless, it is still important to recognize the abstractions that they implement in order to be able to use them effectively. Identifying the application of the concepts will also enable you to extend the use of the MVC paradigm when designing your own classes.

The JFC MVC implementations exist in JDK 2. Their definitions capitalize extensively on Java's interface mechanism. You will see an in-depth discussion of the Swing model architecture in Chapter 10, "Models."

Interfaces allow the programmer to identify behavior, and they separate specification from implementation. This notion of capturing the conceptual nature of an entity's behavior is crucial to formulating an appropriate abstraction. In fact, the critical task for the engineer is to bridge the differences in the abstractions of the model and view by identifying the interface that describes the common nature of the objects being represented. This enables the two parts to communicate and maintain synchronization.

NOTE

When identifying the conceptual nature of an entity, give highest priority to understanding its behavior. This enables you to define an interface that creates an abstraction for the entity's type without committing you to an implementation.

Using interfaces to define the nature of a type gives flexibility to an MVC collaboration. A component accesses its view by referring to the interface type. This enables the programmer to use any implementation that adheres to the interface specification, without affecting the implementation of the view.

Summary

This chapter has highlighted some of the important concepts of GUI design. In particular, it discussed the challenges of GUI programming, where applications become internally more complex as they attempt to match the abstractions of higher level entities and concepts created by the visual GUI components. The MVC architecture helps simplify the complexity of such abstractions by separating the task of creating the visual abstraction from the task of creating the internal abstraction that serves the needs of the application logic.

This chapter prepares you to pay particular attention to the MVC concept because it is used heavily throughout the design of the JFC. The next chapter will discuss new architectural features in JFC that support construction of complex visual GUIs and a mechanism for managing them. These features enable the application logic to keep pace with the demands of presenting data to the user in meaningful ways.

Introducing the Java
Foundation Classes

CHAPTER

2

IN THIS CHAPTER

- The Big Picture   16
- The Abstract Windowing Toolkit   16
- Platform-Independence   18
- AWT Components   20
- The AWT Component Class   21
- AWT Containers   22
- Layout Managers   23
- The Java Foundation Classes   23
- Lightweight Components   26
- Swing's Pluggable Look-and-Feel   29
- The Delegation Event Model   32
- The JFC Containment Model   33
- The JFC and Swing Class Hierarchies   40
- The JFC Model Architecture   41

This chapter introduces the Java Foundation Classes (JFC). You will learn the concepts and architectural features around which the platform was designed and built. The chapter first introduces general concepts related to all Java GUI programming. This includes concepts upon which the JFC is built.

The Big Picture

The Java Foundation Classes (JFC) are a set of APIs that together comprise an application development environment for GUI programming with Java. The APIs that comprise the JFC are the Java 2D Graphics and Imaging API, the Accessibility API, the Drag-and-Drop API, and the Swing tool set as implemented in AWT version 1.1 of the Java Development Kit. These APIs are implemented in several packages that comprise release 2 of the JDK.

The Swing tool kit is a part of the JFC—perhaps the most significant part—but, technically, it is not considered an API by its creators. Rather, it is considered an architecture that implements a framework upon which GUI components can be built. Nevertheless, the JFC is built upon the foundation provided by the Swing tool set, so the Swing tool set is necessary for building JFC applications.

Swing really is a set of new architectural features that extend the capabilities of the original AWT architecture. The Swing components are a new set of components built upon this architecture.

The Swing architecture was originally introduced in the JDK release 1.1, and it is implemented in the packages that comprise the AWT in JDK release 1.1 and beyond.

Because Swing extends the architecture and capabilities of the AWT classes, I will first discuss some concepts, embedded in the design of the AWT, which are applicable to all JFC programs. I introduce them first, and then follow with a discussion of the features of Swing.

NOTE

Throughout this book, I only discuss the JDK after release 1.1. Any terms used herein refer to JDK releases 1.1 and beyond.

The Abstract Windowing Toolkit

The Abstract Windowing Toolkit (AWT) is the primary toolkit for GUI programming in Java. In fact, it is the foundation for all GUI program development in Java. Release 1.1 of the JDK implements many features upon which later releases are built. It provides support for most of the standard tasks of GUI programs, such as creating basic visual components, supporting event-handling, and constructing and rendering images.

These features and many others are implemented in quite a few packages that come with the JDK. Table 2.1 lists the AWT packages and their basic features in alphabetical order. To be complete, I also include the packages that define the Java 2D and Input Method Framework, even though these APIs are not discussed in this book.

TABLE 2.1 The AWT Release 1.1 Packages

AWT package	*Description*
java.applet	Support for creating applets
java.awt	Defines all the classes for basic AWT UI components and for painting and drawing images
java.awt.color	Defines classes for manipulating colors
java.awt.datatransfer	Provides support for transferring data between different applications and between components within the same application
java.awt.dnd	Defines classes to support drag-and-drop
java.awt.event	Defines all the event types for GUI programs
java.awt.font	Supports multiple fonts and font handling
java.awt.geom	Defines the Java 2D API
java.awt.im	Defines the input method editor API
java.awt.image	Supports creating and manipulating images
java.awt.image.renderable	Provides support for manipulating images independently of their rendering
java.awt.print	Defines types for a platform-independent printing API
java.beans	Defines the Java Beans framework, which supports a component parameterization model
java.beans.beancontext	Defines support types related to Java Beans programming

The Java Beans-related packages are listed in the preceding table because Java Beans are primarily intended to be a component architecture aimed at visual components. Technically, it is not part of the AWT, but is built upon the AWT event model and other AWT architectural features.

The Java Beans API is not discussed in this book. It is a specialized topic that is best visited after the programmer has some experience writing JFC programs. For example, it requires a thorough understanding of the JFC event model.

Platform-Independence

The AWT, like all of Java, is designed and built upon the notion of platform-independence. GUI programs, like all other Java programs, can run unaltered on multiple operating system platforms.

In fact, the AWT classes that define components—the widget-like buttons, check boxes, and menus—are themselves written in Java, as might be expected. This means that not only are your programs platform-independent, but so is most of the AWT.

The AWT accomplishes this by enlisting the help of *native peer objects* that represent the visual components your program constructs. For each AWT class that defines a visual component, there exists a corresponding native peer definition which can be rendered on the screen by the native window system.

AWT components like windows, frames, dialog boxes, and menus must each have an associated native window object that is created and managed by the native window system. These native window objects are called peers, and are implemented as rectangular, opaque windows.

The Java platform does not have its own window system, so, at some level, every Java GUI program must have some help to display GUI components on the screen. Neither the Java VM nor the AWT know how to display objects on the screen. This is the job of the native platform's window system, which, at some level, manipulates a physical graphics device, accessed via system code.

It is the native window system that must actually construct and render these native objects on the screen. The AWT components that your program uses make calls to construct their native peer object. The actual peer object created is based on the current execution platform, enabling your program code to maintain its platform-independence.

Since the native platform window system is rendering your components, they will adopt the look-and-feel of that platform. A button will be rendered to look like a Windows button on Windows NT, a Motif button on UNIX, and a Mac button on the Macintosh.

With the advent of Swing's Pluggable Look-and-Feel API, you can specify the look and feel of your program independently of the platform on which it is running. Chapter 6 on Swing concepts, "Swing Concepts and Architecture," discusses how to use the Swing pluggable look-and-feel API, however, this volume does not go into detail about its design or architecture.

Java programs are insulated from the outside world by the Java VM. To maintain the portability achieved by this platform-independence, programs should not make calls to native platform window system libraries. Accessing the underlying native platform window system would make the program non-portable.

The AWT classes are responsible for creating native peer objects that map to the visual components in your program. Your program rarely, if ever, needs to deal directly with native peer objects. A native peer is a platform-dependent object or data structure that can be managed and rendered by the window system.

Figure 2.1 shows how native peer objects allow your GUI components to be rendered on the screen without exposing your program to native platform libraries. The AWT component definitions call routines in the native platform window system libraries. These calls enable the AWT to request the construction of a native window that represents your program component. Because AWT components create a corresponding native platform window, they are called *heavyweight*.

2
INTRODUCING THE
JAVA FOUNDATION
CLASSES

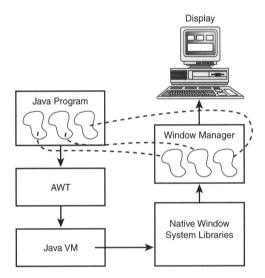

FIGURE 2.1

Each heavyweight visual component has a corresponding native peer object that is created and managed by the platform's native window system.

NOTE

The AWT 1.1 visual components require the construction of a native peer object. For this reason they are called *heavyweight components*, a term which refers to the extra memory used by the peer. Peer objects significantly increase the memory usage of AWT programs. In Chapter 6 you will see how Swing alleviates this problem.

Although this scheme allows your program to be platform-independent, it relies on the underlying native platform window system to provide a consistent look-and-feel among all component implementations. It is difficult for the AWT to promise consistency in look-and-feel when it has no control of the underlying platform libraries. There can be variations in the behavior of applications that are caused by inconsistencies in the features supported by the peers on different platforms.

AWT Components

The components mentioned above are the basic building blocks of every Java GUI program. The following table shows you some of those basic components.

Table 2.2 lists the most common AWT components defined in AWT 1.1. These are still valid when programming in JFC. In fact, some of them are required.

TABLE 2.2   Common AWT Component Classes

Component name	Description
Component	An abstract class that is the parent of all AWT components
Container	The parent of all container classes, which can aggregate other components
Button	A button that can be the source of events such as mouse clicks
Canvas	A component on which to draw geometric shapes
Checkbox	An item that can be selected or unselected
Choice	A pop-up menu of different elements, one of which can be selected
Dialog	A window that can be displayed to request input from the user
Frame	A top-level or outermost program window that contains the visible elements of a GUI program
Label	A component for placing a text string in a container
List	A scrolling list of items that can be placed in a container
Menu	A menu on a frame which defines actions that users can perform on an application-wide context
MenuBar	A special kind of container that can contain menus
MenuItem	An item inside a menu
Panel	A type of container
Scrollbar	A horizontal or vertical scrollbar to attach to containers
TextArea	A potentially multi-line area for writing text
TextComponent	The superclass of text-based components
TextField	A single-line area for text

Perhaps the two most important classes in the AWT are `java.awt.Component` and `java.awt.Container`.

All visible components in Java are subclasses of the abstract class `java.awt.Component` class. Components, like buttons, text areas, panels, and so forth, are all subclasses of `java.awt.Component`.

Containers are the specialized components that enable us to aggregate other components in order to manage the organization and layout of your GUI. The AWT defines several container objects, which are all subclasses of `java.awt.Component` and, therefore, are also components.

Any class that must have the capability to contain other objects must subclass `java.awt.Container`. Both `java.awt.Component` and `java.awt.Container` are abstract classes. They have no implementation; you cannot instantiate an instance of them. You shall see that this definition—by design—has important implications related to the JFC visual classes.

The AWT Component Class

You will now take a closer look at the concept of components. All AWT components have certain basic capabilities and attributes. Most of them are defined in the `java.awt.Component` class itself. It's an abstract class, but nevertheless lays the foundation for all concrete components, including containers.

All AWT components have the following attributes:

- `Graphics` object
- Foreground and background color
- Minimum and maximum layout sizes
- Preferred layout size
- Dimension (or size)
- Font
- Cursor
- Locale context
- Screen location
- Parent container
- Peer object

These attributes enable the AWT tool kit to manipulate and manage components on the screen. In subsequent chapters, I will discuss these attributes in detail.

AWT Containers

The second most important AWT class is `java.awt.Container`.

Because containers are also components, they have all the attributes listed in the previous list. Containers also have additional attributes and behavior.

Containers can contain other objects. Therefore, they are responsible for laying out those objects—positioning them relative to one another on the screen according to some policy.

Containers also have to support adding and removing components from their contained set.

Containers have the additional features which are listed here:

- Layout manager object
- List of child components
- Insets object

AWT containers have only one way to store child components. When a child is added to a container, it will be displayed within the visible bounds of the container's opaque window. There is only one repository in which to lump all the children. As you will see shortly, this model changes in the new JFC class definitions.

Some of the common AWT container classes are listed in Table 2.3.

TABLE 2.3   COMMON AWT COMPONENT CLASSES

Container class	Description
Applet	The superclass of all applet programs
Container	Superclass of all containers
Dialog	The class used for creating dialog boxes for user interaction
FileDialog	Dialog box to query user to specify a file
Frame	A top-level container with a visible frame and a menu bar
Panel	Basic and most commonly used container for aggregating visual components in a program
ScrollPane	Container that can scroll the view of its contents
Window	A top-level container with no border or menu bar

The various containers serve different purposes. What they all share is the same policy and mechanism for containing children. They all internally maintain one list to which all children are added. That is, they have only one mechanism for containing children.

Layout Managers

As mentioned previously, containers are responsible for laying out their children. This means they must manage how the graphical representation of the components they contain are displayed on the screen. This task is accomplished by a layout manager object.

Layout managers are objects that adhere to a specific interface which identifies the notion of laying out components in a container. Different implementations can define different layout policies, but they all obey the same interface.

The AWT defines most of the layout managers available in JFC. You will cover the topic of layout managers in Chapter 8, "Layout Managers." Table 2.4 lists the AWT `Layout Manager` classes.

TABLE 2.4 The AWT `Layout Manager` Classes

AWT `Layout Manager` *class*	*Description of layout policy*
`BorderLayout`	Lays out children according to compass points; North, South, East, West, or Center.
`FlowLayout`	Lays out components from left-to-right, top-to-bottom, like text filled in a paragraph.
`CardLayout`	Lays out components as a stack of cards, where only the top component is visible at any one time.
`GridLayout`	Lays out components in a grid whose row and column dimensions are MONO. All grid squares have the same size.
`GridBagLayout`	Lays out components using a complex policy. Allows flexibility in alignment, size, weighting, and resizing.

Besides new components classes, the JFC defines at least one new layout manager class, `BoxLayout`. The `javax.swing.Box` class is a container that uses the `BoxLayout` layout manager. I will cover this in detail in Chapter 8.

The Java Foundation Classes

You know that Java GUI programs consist of components, containers and layout managers collaborating to manage the GUI display. The Java Foundation Classes (JFC) are the subset of classes and packages in the JDK that support GUI programming in Java.

Viewed from a functional (feature) perspective, the JFC consists of a set of APIs. Table 2.5 lists these APIs and their primary functions.

TABLE 2.5   The JFC APIs

API	Features supported
Accessibility	Support for assistive technologies, such as interfaces for physically impaired users, for example, a voice-recognition interface for components
Drag-and-Drop	Support for transferring data between applications or transferring data between components within the same application
Java 2D	Graphics package for creating sophisticated two-dimensional imaging and graphics applications
Swing	Support for basic GUI platform features, such as drag-and-drop, the delegation event model, lightweight components, and printing and mouseless operation
Input Method Framework	Support for construction of input method editors that can parse multilingual character input

The JFC is really several packages that implement an enhanced GUI programming environment with new features built upon the Swing architecture defined by the AWT in release 1.1 of the JDK.

The Swing architecture, or tool set, is only one part of the JFC that extends the AWT; it does not replace the AWT. On the contrary, it is the AWT that contains the basic architectural framework for all Java GUI programming, such as graphics, imaging, data transfer, clipboard operations, drag-and-drop, and printing. The foundation of the Swing tool set is completely implemented in the AWT release 1.1, that is, JDK release 1.1.

The term Swing really refers to the organization of the packages that implement new features not found in the original AWT. Swing adds support for new features and capabilities, and remedies the shortcomings of the original AWT 1.0 implementation. The original AWT design had problems with support for sophisticated commercial application development.

As mentioned earlier, the Swing tool set is technically not an API in the JFC. The purpose behind the creation of Swing is to provide implementations for the following abstractions:

- A set of lightweight components which have a pure Java implementation; Swing components don't use any native platform code
- Multiple look-and-feels without using native peer objects
- The advantages of the existing AWT (without obsoleting it)
- The advantages of the MVC architecture

The Swing tool set implements the following features:

- Lightweight component support
- Pluggable look-and-feel architecture
- Delegation event model
- Localization support
- Accessibility support
- Mouseless operation and pop-up menus
- Adherence to the Java Beans component specification

Possibly the three most visible parts of the Swing tool set are

- A new set of sophisticated, lightweight visual GUI components. Their definitions descend from the AWT component definitions. Lightweight components are rendered on screen without the help of a native peer object.
- A new set of non-visual classes to support the new component classes.
- A new set of support interfaces. These help define a new conceptual programming paradigm, called the Swing model architecture, which is a manifestation of the MVC paradigm implemented by the new component classes.

One of the most recognized parts of Swing is its set of new lightweight components. This feature is discussed in the upcoming section entitled *The Swing Lightweight Components*.

But before you learn about lightweight components, you need to complete your overall view of organization of the JFC. Table 2.6 lists the packages that comprise the JFC.

TABLE 2.6 The JFC Packages

Swing package	*Description*
`javax.swing`	Defines all the basic Swing lightweight visual components
`javax.swing.border`	Defines classes that draw specialized borders around arbitrary Swing components
`javax.swing.colorchooser`	Defines support classes used by the `JColorChooser` class
`javax.swing.event`	Defines new Swing event types
`javax.swing.plaf`	Defines types used by the pluggable look-and-feel architecture
`javax.swing.plaf.basic`	Defines the `basic` look-and-feel types
`javax.swing.plaf.metal`	Defines the `metal` look-and-feel, which is Java's signature look-and-feel

continues

2

INTRODUCING THE
JAVA FOUNDATION
CLASSES

TABLE 2.6   Continued

Swing package	Description
javax.swing.plaf.multi	Defines classes that allow combining different look-and-feels
javax.swing.table	Defines support classes and interfaces for working with the JTable class, which is a Swing component
javax.swing.text	Defines an extensive package for manipulating components that handle text
javax.swing.text.html	Defines specialized handling for components that can manipulate HTML data
javax.swing.text.html.parser	Defines types that encapsulate the nature of a general HTML parser
javax.swing.text.rtf	Defines types that parse rich-text format
javax.swing.tree	Defines types that support the JTree class
javax.swing.undo	Defines types that support an undo function as it might be used in a text editor kit

Lightweight Components

The original AWT components are all heavyweight, which, as you know, mean that each instance has a corresponding native platform peer object. This implementation scheme supports platform-independent programs, but results in severe resource usage problems. GUI programs that use AWT components require a huge amount of memory. Native peer objects take up a lot of memory as do the VM and your program.

This, in turn, affects scalability. Building a non-trivial GUI interface requires designing a complex nesting organization of containers, which contain components and even other containers. With the original AWT implementation, this results in the creation of a native peer for every component, including containers that are not visible, but whose only purpose is to provide a way of aggregating other components. Panels are often used for the purpose of nesting components this way.

The AWT in JDK 1.1 devises a new scheme that allows Java GUI programs to retain their platform-independence, and also cuts down on the amount of memory required. This is achieved by implementing support for lightweight components.

A *lightweight component* is by definition one which has no native peer. All lightweight component definitions must be direct subclasses of either java.awt.Component or java.awt.Container.

At some point, of course, each lightweight component must be associated with a heavyweight component somewhere in its containment hierarchy, because this is the only mechanism that the native window system supports for drawing on the physical screen.

The visual screen representation of a lightweight component is created by drawing in the lightweight component's heavyweight parent container. So, even in a program that uses only the new Swing components, there must be at least one heavyweight component. However, you can now eliminate almost all of the heavyweight components that were used previously. Figure 2.2 shows a comparison between AWT and Swing labels and buttons.

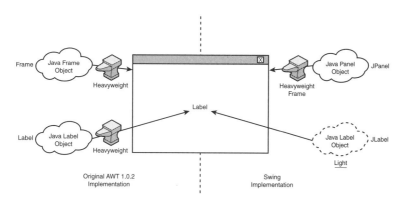

FIGURE 2.2

The original AWT component implementations are all heavyweight; each component constructs a native peer object. The Swing component implementations are all lightweight, except for four Swing heavyweight container classes. The panel in this figure shows the difference between AWT heavyweight labels and buttons, and Swing lightweight labels and buttons.

Swing defines a few basic heavyweight containers (as shown in Table 2.7). These are the classes that define windows, frames, dialog boxes, and pop-ups, which represent top-level windows that cannot be contained by other containers. The rest of the Swing visual component implementations are all lightweight.

TABLE 2.7 The JFC Heavyweight Containers

JFC container	Description
javax.swing.JApplet	The root of all Swing applets
javax.swing.JDialog	The class that defines dialog boxes
javax.swing.JFrame	The outermost container of any application, with a border and usually with a menu bar
javax.swing.JWindow	A container like a frame but with no borders and no menu bar

Except for the classes listed in Table 2.7, all the Swing visual component implementations are lightweight. Note that none of these new component definitions obsolete the AWT components; they simply add to them.

The following table lists some of the JFC component classes and their AWT equivalents. Although the AWT version of these components are all heavyweight, the JFC versions are implemented as lightweight components, except where noted.

TABLE 2.8   Common JFC Visual Components

AWT component	*Equivalent JFC component*
Applet	JApplet (heavyweight)
Component	JComponent
Container	no equivalent
Button	JButton
Canvas	no equivalent
Checkbox	JCheckBox
Dialog	JDialog (heavyweight)
Frame	JDrame (heavyweight)
Label	JLabel
List	JList
Menu	JMenu
MenuBar	JMenuBar
MenuItem	JMenuItem
Panel	JPanel
Scrollbar	JScrollBar
TextArea	JTextArea
TextComponent	JTextComponent
TextField	JTextField

The JFC lightweight components give programmers the option of using implementations that use system resources more efficiently. Additionally, the JFC defines new visual component classes that have no AWT equivalent.

The JFC visual component classes are all lightweight because they directly subclass either `java.awt.Component` or `java.awt.Container` (see Table 2.9).

TABLE 2.9   Common JFC Component Classes with No AWT Equivalent

JFC class name	Description
Box	A new container that uses a `BoxLayout` layout manager
JColorChooser	A control pane for defining and selecting colors
JComboBox	A typical combo box with drop-down list and text items
JDesktopPane	A container that can be used as a desktop manager
JEditorPane	A container that can be used as an editor of various kinds of content
JInternalFrame	A lightweight frame that supports native frame functions such as iconification, moving, and resizing
JLayeredPane	A lightweight component that allows visual components to be overlapped
JRadioButton	JFC's radio button
JSeparator	A separator to add space between menu items
JSlider	A implementation of a slider bar
JSplitPane	A pane that can show two views
JTable	A container that can contain arbitrarily complex components in a two-dimensional table view
JTextPane	A pane built for displaying and marking up text
JToggleButton	A two-state button, for example, In or Out
JToolBar	A toolbar that can contain buttons that represent frequently accessed functions
JToolTip	A component for displaying ToolTip text, such as the thin banners displayed when moving the over a button
JTree	An implementation of a graphic that represents a set of hierarchical data
JViewport	A pane that can be moved to create an abstraction of moving a view window over some content

Swing's Pluggable Look-and-Feel

Besides memory consumption, the biggest challenge created by the heavyweight AWT component implementations is trying to maintain a consistent look and feel across platforms.

Each component must have an associated native peer implementation for *each* AWT platform supported. Besides being a huge maintenance challenge, it is difficult to make components look and act the same on different platforms because the facilities and APIs supported by the different underlying window systems are widely disparate. Thus, the same Java program looks and feels quite differently if run on Windows, Motif, Mac, or some other platform.

The Swing designers had two goals related to solving these problems:

- To eliminate the maintenance overhead of heavyweight components.
- To devise a way to create a consistent look and feel across platforms.

The JFC accomplishes this using its lightweight component architecture and the new configurable UI architecture, or *Pluggable Look-and-Feel* architecture.

The JFC lightweight components delegate the job of actually rendering the component to an associated look-and-feel object. JFC lightweight components (the Swing components) maintain a reference to a *UI delegate* object, which is an instance of javax.swing.plaf.ComponentUI. The UI delegate is responsible for creating and maintaining the component's look-and-feel.

Figure 2.3 shows the UML diagram that defines the relationship between a Swing lightweight component and its component UI object.

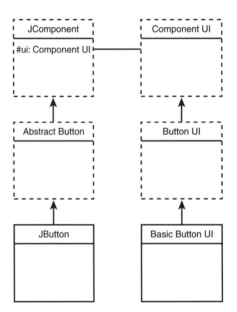

FIGURE 2.3

UML diagram showing how the JFC components delegate the job of look-and-feel management to a plaf *module, or pluggable look-and-feel module. This UI delegate is an object that knows how to paint its corresponding component appropriately for the current look-and-feel context.*

Plaf modules eliminate the look-and-feel consistency problems exhibited by the AWT heavy-weight peer components. They render the look-and-feel of a lightweight Swing component by drawing into the graphics context of their heavyweight parent. The plaf module uses all the low-level Java graphics drawing routines that allow it to render the exact desired look of the component.

Thus, the plaf module implementation does not rely on the native window system facilities for rendering. It can, therefore, always remain the same for a given lightweight component, regardless of the platform. Essentially, only the five heavyweight Swing containers still require separate heavyweight implementations for each supported platform.

The point is that the look-and-feel of a lightweight component no longer relies on the facilities and APIs of the underlying native window system. Only the heavyweight component definitions rely on the native platform facilities.

Certainly this design eliminates the consistency problems mentioned earlier. But the name of this architecture, *Pluggable Look-and-Feel* implies something more—some configurable look-and-feel capabilities.

So far you know that each lightweight component references a UI delegate that implements a specific look-and-feel policy. It seems, then, that a different UI delegate, that implements a different look-and-feel policy, could be employed by each lightweight component.

In fact, this is exactly the case. The Pluggable Look-and-Feel architecture allows you to plug in different UI delegates that each implement their own look-and-feel. This capability is accomplished with the implementation of classes in several new packages, listed in Table 2.10.

The pluggable look-and-feel implementation is comprised of four packages in JDK 2. The `javax.swing.plaf` package implements the primary support for the pluggable look-and-feel architecture.

Look-and-feel modules for all the standard platforms come with the JDK. Of course, as you might expect, you can define your own look-and-feel and use that in a Swing program.

The `basic` package defines ways to draw all the building blocks that components need, such as borders, menu bars, panes, sliders, and so on. The `metal` look-and-feel is the name given to the generic Java look-and-feel. The `multi` package defines look-and-feels for the popular computing platforms such as Motif, Windows, and Mac.

The design and architecture of this API is itself an involved topic, and we don't go into detail in this book. The point is for you to just understand its presence and use. A future volume will present a more in-depth treatment of the architectural issues.

TABLE 2.10   The JFC Pluggable Look-and-Feel Packages

JFC Plaf package	Description of contents
javax.swing.plaf	Defines types used by the pluggable look-and-feel architecture
javax.swing.plaf.basic	Defines the basic look-and-feel types
javax.swing.plaf.metal	Defines the metal look-and-feel, which is the Java's signature look-and-feel
javax.swing.plat.multi	Defines classes that allow combining different look-and-feels

The Delegation Event Model

Arguably, two of the most important features in Swing are the Lightweight Component Framework and the Delegation Event Model. You already learned about lightweight components and their advantages in flexibility and extensibility.

The delegation event model is the event model that allows Java GUI programs to perform effective and efficient event handling. It, too, offers a design that is flexible and extensible.

Program events are objects that correspond to occurrences of asynchronous actions that occur externally to your program, such as a mouse click on part of the GUI, a mouse motion, a typed keystroke, or the selection of an item in a pick list. Programs need to be able to respond to events and do something appropriate semantically.

Presumably, it's best to allow flexibility in defining which part of the program can do the event handling. It should be the code that can most easily access other collaborating objects such as those in an MVC organization; or the part of the program that yields the cleanest separation of functionality; or simply the code which can most effectively handle the event.

In the delegation event model, usually several objects communicate to perform event handling in programs. An *event source* is any component on which an event occurs. The *event handler or event listener,* as it is often called in Java GUI contexts, is the object that receives notification of the event and responds to it.

Typically, when an event occurs, the event handler will update the view of the event source, as well as the corresponding data model object that represents that view. In fact, the event handler function can even be included in the design of your object that acts as a data model or view object.

Besides the source and listener objects, there may be *an event target*, which might be another object that requires modification as a result of an event occurrence; the event handler may also own the job of modifying this object when events occur.

The delegation event model allows you flexibility in designing the objects that respond to events and how they communicate with the event sources. This flexibility was a major design goal, in part to make the model amenable for use in MVC designs. The collaborating event sources and handlers are aware of each other and work together to maintain consistent states. You have the power of choice when designing which objects will do a task.

Swing's event model enables components to register objects that are interested in being notified when a certain type of event (or events) occurs on the component.

It makes sense for certain events to occur on certain types of components. Those component classes must present, as part of their public API, methods to allow listeners to register as interested parties in those event types. Event sources notify listeners of events by calling a method and passing it an event object.

The classes that implement listeners must implement interfaces for handling certain types of events. When the event occurs the source notifies all listeners.

The event source is satisfied that, if it notifies a listener by calling a certain method, that listener in fact has an implementation for that method, because it was specified in the interface implemented by the listener.

Components must also allow listeners to remove themselves from registration. This function is part of the API implemented by objects that can be event sources.

The JFC Containment Model

Container objects are responsible for managing tasks like the layout and delivery of events to their children in certain cases. The AWT container classes are containers, and, therefore, have the inherent ability to contain other components. They simply maintain a list of children for which they are responsible.

On the other hand, the JFC heavyweight container classes define and implement a new containment architecture, which creates a nested structure for containers to organize the components they contain and the types of components that they are able to contain.

These JFC heavyweight containers have a more complex containment hierarchy than lightweight containers—those that directly subclass either `java.awt.Component` or `java.awt.Container`. Heavyweight containers maintain more than one list of related components. That is, they have one primary container to which they add actual children, but other containers to which they delegate the job of maintaining and managing the components that make up the whole aggregation of pieces that define the nature of all heavyweight containers.

The set of containers maintained defines the containment capabilities of that container; that is, it defines what types of objects it can contain. For instance, a frame object that encapsulates a whole GUI application probably has a menu bar. An internal frame could also have a menu bar, but may not in certain cases; and dialog boxes, too, can have menu bars. However, arbitrary containers inside the application's frame are not allowed to install a menu bar.

This new approach creates a much more flexible strategy to deal with common GUI programming challenges like layering pop-ups and dialogs so they appear on top of other elements; or drawing the outline of a frame or component while dragging and repositioning it, so that it is visible during the whole move operation.

The JFC heavyweight containers are the classes that define this new nested containment architecture (illustrated in Figure 2.4). You could call it a hierarchy, but don't confuse the use of that term with an inheritance hierarchy.

Table 2.11 shows the four heavyweight containers, and the one lightweight container defined by the JFC that implement this new containment model. The heavyweight components are the ones that have a corresponding native peer object. The JFC containers that implement the new containment model are shown in the following table.

TABLE 2.11   The JFC Containers Using the New Containment Model

JFC heavyweight container	Description
javax.swing.JApplet	Class for creating applets.
javax.swing.JDialog	Class used for dialog boxes.
javax.swing.JFrame	Class used as the outermost container for Swing applications.
javax.swing.JInternalFrame	Used to simulate the capabilities of a native, heavyweight frame. This class actually defines a lightweight component.
javax.swing.JWindow	Class used to create a window without a frame or menu bar.

When you program using the JFC classes, you must be aware of the new policy that the JFC heavyweight containers implement for adding components to containers. Otherwise, it's difficult to get even the simplest GUI to display properly.

Unlike the regular AWT containers, which are the containers that contain other objects, these JFC/Swing containers do not actually directly contain components. Rather, they contain other specialized containers to which they delegate the job of containing child components.

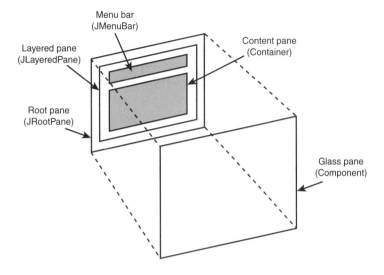

FIGURE 2.4
This diagram shows the physical components that comprise the nested-container hierarchy used by the JFC heavyweight container classes.

The following list shows the names of these new containers, called *panes*.

- Root pane—A container which manages a glass pane, content pane, and menu bar.
- Content pane—The pane which performs the normal AWT style function of containing the child components.
- Layered pane—A pane which manages the content pane. This pane creates the abstraction of a z-ordering of its components (front-to-back layering) levels, but all children are in the content pane. It allows flexible stacking components such as pop-ups, dialog boxes, and so on.
- Glass pane—An arbitrary component that can be used, for instance, to intercept events before they are delivered to other components in a JFC heavyweight container.
- Menu bar—The lightweight component that contains menu items.

All the JFC heavyweight containers do not necessarily maintain an instance of all the panes in the list. For example, `javax.swing.JWindow` components do not have a menu bar or visible frame; menu bars are optional in this scheme.

When adding a component to a JFC heavyweight, you no longer simply add a child component to the JFC container. You always add child components to the container's content pane, which is the container that actually manages the child components.

Whereas you previously added child components directly to a container using AWT, now you add those children to the Swing container's content pane. Of course, you should do this using the available API provided by the container class. This API is important, because it hides the details of the complex hierarchy with which the panes are organized. They are structured in a cascading containment hierarchy shown by the following diagram.

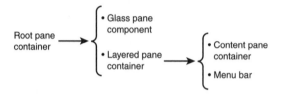

FIGURE 2.5

The Swing heavyweight containers delegate their containment duties to another container, called a root pane container, which in turn delegates various containment and layout responsibilities to other containers. All these containers are arranged in a cascading, nesting hierarchy.

Earlier I said that you now add children to a JFC/Swing container's content pane. But the Swing heavyweight containers do not directly manage or reference a content pane.

All the primary containers, such as a JFrame, delegate the job of containing children to a root pane. The root pane is responsible for managing all matters of layout, layering, and containment of elements for its heavyweight container, such as the menu bar.

The root pane, in turn, passes on the responsibility of specific tasks to the other panes. As the diagram shows, the root pane contains a glass pane and a layered pane. For the children that you add, the root pane actually passes on the responsibility of managing them to its layered pane.

The layered pane contains a content pane and menu bar. It, in turn, delegates the job of actually containing the children to the content pane. It also manages the heavyweight container's menu bar.

This structure enables internal containers to have menu bars, for instance. In the original AWT model, only the outermost container, such as a frame, could have a menu bar. This new model allows new class definitions that can contain a menu bar.

Whatever panes are supported and available for users of the class must, of course, be supported in the class's API. The class's API essentially defines what containment capability a container provides for your use. So, for example, you won't see any public API in window classes to add a menu bar; windows differ from frames in that they don't have menu bars.

It is important to note that this containment hierarchy only exists in the JFC classes since JDK release 1.2. The primary AWT container classes, like `java.awt.Frame`, `java.awt.Window` and `java.awt.Panel`, do not create this multilevel containment abstraction.

The containment abstraction has nothing to do with the inheritance hierarchy defined by the Swing classes; so it is really not part of Swing. It is a new abstraction implemented specifically by the JFC heavyweight classes. It is only a reflection of the container instances defined as fields of the Swing heavyweight containers.

Table 2.12 indicates which containers maintain the panes discussed in the preceding paragraphs.

TABLE 2.12   The JFC Heavyweight Containers and Their Panes

JFC container	*Member panes*
`JApplet`	Root pane
`JComponent`	None
`JDialog`	Root pane
`JFrame`	Root pane
`JInternalFrame`	Root pane
`JLayeredPane`	Content pane, menu bar
`JRootPane`	Glass pane, layered pane
`JWindow`	Root pane

If you take a look at these panes, you can see that inheritance has nothing to do with determining which containers have what containment capabilities. Only the JFC heavyweight containers listed in the previous table conceptualize this containment hierarchy. The derivation of the JFC heavyweight containers does not determine their containment abstraction. This is accomplished by the references they maintain to other container objects.

The root of the JFC components that implement the JFC containment model is the `javax.swing.JComponent` class. Remember that all JFC component classes are direct subclasses of `javax.swing.JComponent`.

It, in turn, is a direct subclass of `java.awt.Container`. So all Swing components are themselves containers. You can, for instance, store an image in a button, or a menu in the field of a table widget.

This delegation of containment responsibilities appears to belie a different type of container class definition. In fact, there is no new definition for what a container is. The JFC heavyweight container simply maintains references to more than one container, all used for aggregating children into separate groups.

The following table shows the JFC/Swing container panes and their defined types. The existing container types provide the containment capabilities needed to implement the containment abstraction.

TABLE 2.13   The JFC Container Panes and Their Types

Container	Type of object
Root pane	`javax.swing.JRootPane`
Glass pane	`java.awt.Component`
Layered pane	`javax.swing.JLayeredPane`
Content pane	`java.awt.Container`
Menu bar	`JMenuBar`

The mechanics of how the component gets stored in any one of the given panes is the same as in the AWT model, because the storage panes are each really AWT containers according to their derivations (inheritance).

Now that you know what these panes are and their relationship to one another, you will learn why these multiple panes are needed.

They each serve a different function, so let's look at the purpose for their existence.

Layered Panes

The layered pane mentioned previously is the container that actually does the work of containing children added to the `container` object that your program constructs.

The layered pane enables you to specify the z-order depth at which a component lies. This allows components to be displayed in a manner which allows visible overlapping.

Basically, the only real difference between the original AWT containers sub-classed from `java.awt.Container` and a `javax.swing.JLayeredPane` is that the latter creates the abstraction of having multiple layers. But it still maintains a list of children that it must manage.

The `JLayeredPane` class defines five layers for you to use, as shown in Table 2.14.

TABLE 2.14   `JLayeredPane` Layers

Layer name	Description
Default layer	The default layer for child components.
Palette layer	The layer immediately above the default layer. It is useful for floating toolbars and palettes.

Layer name	Description
Modal layer	The layer intended to contain modal dialog boxes.
Pop-up layer	The layer intended to contain pop-up windows or frames.
Drag	The layer to which components are added when dragged.

The default layer is the layer to which components are normally added, unless specified otherwise by the user. The palette layer enables you to add things like floating toolbars, and ensure the toolbar will display above the other components.

Similarly, dialog boxes need to display above other components so the user can read the message or prompt. Modal boxes are ones which require the user to respond and dismiss the box before he/she can do anything else.

Components like combo boxes and modal dialog boxes can themselves contain elements that should display over everything else, such as ToolTips or Help text. These need to display even over the component that generated them. They can be placed in the pop-up layer.

The drag layer is designed for components that are being repositioned inside their container. If you drag a window or dialog box, it is nice to be able to see the exact borders of the new location. Placing the component at this topmost drag layer ensures that it is visible while being dragged.

The `JLayeredPane` enables you to reposition any component at any time. For instance, you can place a component in the drag layer just before the drag motion begins and replace it in its normal layer when the repositioning is completed.

Glass Panes

The glass pane is an optional component in a root pane. It can be any component, in fact, because the root pane defines the type of its glass pane member to be a `java.awt.Component`.

The glass pane always fills the extents of its container. This makes it useful for doing things like intercepting events or drawing over the surface of more than one component in the container.

For instance, you may wish to toggle a mode of operation where all mouse events are intercepted by the glass pane and not delivered to the underlying child components in the container. You can do this by raising the glass pane to be positioned on top of all other panes.

Similarly, if it is on top, you can draw lines, shapes, and so forth that will appear to the user to transcend the individual component borders. For instance, this is sometimes useful in GUI applications.

The JFC and Swing Class Hierarchies

Understanding the relationship between the AWT, Swing, and JFC classes is important in helping you find the right classes for your job.

As a JFC programmer, however, you will find yourself more concerned with the exact definitions of classes, their derivations, features, and so forth, so that you can figure out which one is appropriate for the task at hand.

You now know that JFC is really a set of APIs. The Swing visual components defined in AWT 1.1 components are basically lightweight versions of the AWT 1.0.2 component classes. Swing implements an architectural framework via its API that adds power and capabilities to the applications you develop.

The JFC visual components are also really a set of mostly lightweight components. However, there are a few major differences between the lightweight Swing components and the lightweight JFC components.

These JFC lightweight visual components are derived from the lightweight `javax.swing.JComponent` class. These classes which define the JFC visual components all begin with `J`.

They add some new abstractions, features, and capabilities to the standard Swing components. One major feature that they implement is the hierarchical container abstraction discussed previously. They also implement half of the JFC model architecture. The other half is implemented by the JFC support classes and interfaces.

The JFC also defines many support classes and interfaces that support abstractions like the MVC architecture. The containment model that you were introduced to previously and the model architecture are other such powerful abstractions.

At first it's a bit difficult to keep all these classes, packages, and APIs straight. The following diagram helps delineate all these pieces.

The derivation hierarchy is a good way for us to see the relationships between classes. You can see that all the JFC visual components derive from `java.awt.Container`, which makes them true Swing components.

Because `JComponent` is the root of the JFC visual classes, it is the first place that you see evidence of the new abstractions introduced by the JFC classes that are not implemented in the Swing API.

It's also clear how four of the JFC containers are heavyweight. They derive directly from their AWT heavyweight counterparts (see Table 2.15).

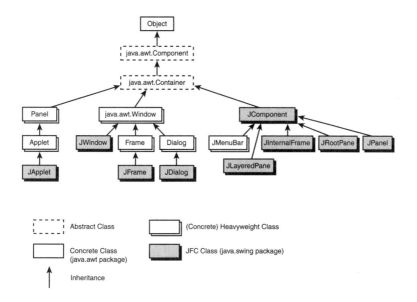

FIGURE 2.6
The Swing API is implemented by the AWT 1.1 classes. The JFC classes extend these, adding new abstractions and features for the user, via the architectural elements that they build on top of Swing.

TABLE 2.15   The JFC Heavyweight Containers and Their Parents

JFC heavyweight container	*Derived from*
javax.swing.Japplet	java.awt.Applet
javax.swing.Jframe	java.awt.Frame
javax.swing.Jdialog	java.awt.Dialog
javax.swing.Jwindow	java.awt.Window

The JFC Model Architecture

The JFC model architecture is designed to address the MVC architecture at the class level. Essentially, it is the mechanism by which the JFC classes and interfaces manifest support for the MVC paradigm at the class level. You were introduced to the MVC paradigm in Chapter 1, "UI Programming Concepts."

Swing's model architecture is a mechanism that enables designers to separate the different functional abstractions of GUI programs identified by the MVC model. Components with a visual representation are called *views*. Objects that implement a data model are called *models*. Model objects implement a particular data abstraction.

Models collaborate with views to present to the user a visual representation of the abstraction being maintained by the program. These two objects collaborate via a *controller*. Controllers trap events that occur on either the view or the model and send messages to update the other object so that the two maintain consistent states.

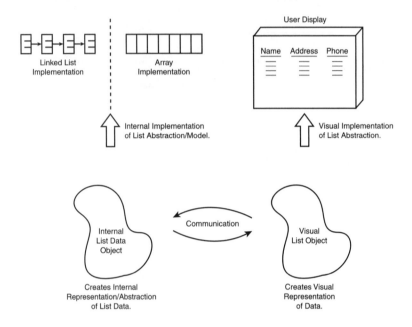

FIGURE 2.7

The MVC paradigm represents data abstractions using different perspectives. The view presents an abstraction that users can project; the model implements the abstraction appropriate for the programming language and data-structure design.

In the JFC, the controller and view objects are usually collapsed into one object, which presents as part of its public interface all the methods needed for the object to function in either capacity.

The model architecture is really an abstraction built into the JFC's lightweight classes. It supports the MVC abstraction and is manifested by features defined by the JFC lightweight component classes, as well as by a few other classes that do not have visual representations.

The abstraction is, of course, built on top of the classes that define the Swing architecture. It is not supported merely by the parts of Swing defined in AWT 1.1. The parts of Swing defined by the AWT 1.1 know nothing of Swing's model architecture.

This model architecture is actually different—albeit closely related to—the MVC architecture paradigm. In fact, it is the mechanism that Swing employs to support designs that use the MVC paradigm.

Basically, the definition of various classes and interfaces—their public interface and implementation—enable them to act like either a model, view, or controller object. Some of the JFC classes can function in more than one of these roles.

The model, view, and controller delineate the responsibilities and tasks required of a program which uses the MVC paradigm. Together, these three conceptual pieces give elements of GUI applications the capability to manage complexity. Separating the model, view, and component functions makes a program more manageable.

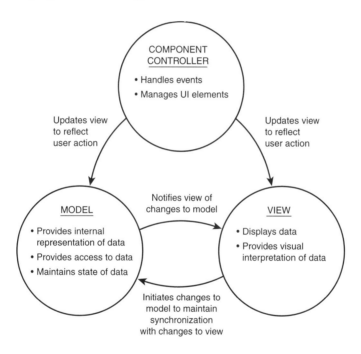

FIGURE 2.8

In a traditional MVC implementation, three objects collaborate to create and manage a data abstraction and its visual presentation to the user.

When implementations are readily available for the programmer, it helps give perspective to the paradigm and how to use it. Some of the JFC classes implement one or more interfaces which encapsulate a particular data abstraction. These classes can support a data model or a particular view of a data model. They implement a concrete mechanism for supporting the abstraction that the data model defines.

The JFC defines many classes that can be used as models, views, controllers, and even some that function as both views and controllers. This gives you the programmer predefined components that can be assembled together in a program that is built around the MVC paradigm.

The interface(s) that define the model or view nature of a particular class is just one subset of the public interface supported by classes that function as models or views. They still have other methods that comprise the nature of what they are.

Whether this interface defines a model, view, or controller interface depends on the nature of the class. It is certainly possible for a class to collapse support for the model and view parts of a data abstraction into one implementation. It's also possible to collapse the view and controller parts together.

The JFC classes mostly do just that. The view and controller are realized in the same implementation. This implementation decision in no way affects the conceptual nature of the MVC paradigm. It is often easier to do, because the controller object often responds to events that require updating a data model's view.

Table 2.16 presents a list of some of the JFC model types and their purpose. It gives you a more concrete definition of some of these interfaces.

TABLE 2.16 Standard JFC Data Abstraction Models

JFC model name	Abstraction
BoundedRangeModel	Defines the abstraction for objects whose state can be specified as a bounded range of values, for instance, sliders and progress bars
ButtonModel	Defines the states of a button
ComboBoxModel	Defines the abstraction of selecting an element from a list of values
ListModel	Defines a list, an ordered set of values with a length
MutableComboBoxModel	Defines a combo box model that may be changed or edited
SingleSelectionModel	Defines data structures that can have only one element selected at any given time

Notice that the interface names end in the word Model. This consistent naming makes it easy to identify and understand the models. You are welcome to provide your own implementations of these interfaces to suite the needs of your classes.

The JFC provides default implementations for these model interfaces. These may be sufficient for your purposes. You can even extend these to define more complex models. Table 2.17 associates the names of the models with the default implementations provided for you.

TABLE 2.17 Standard JFC Models and Their Default Implementing Classes

JFC model name	Default implementing class
BoundedRangeModel	DefaultBoundedRangeModel
ButtonModel	DefaultButtonModel
ComboBoxModel	DefaultComboBoxModel
ListModel	DefaultListModel
MutableComboBoxModel	DefaultComboBoxModel
SingleSelectionModel	DefaultSingleSelectionModel

The JFC model architecture defines a standard policy for creating implementations of abstract data models. Using this policy enables classes to support a consistent approach to implementing models. All the JFC classes employ the same canonical structure to providing a manifestation the models that they implement. This is true for classes that implement data models and views of the data models.

Using a consistent policy makes it easy for you to write your own classes and provide a congruent interface that will be recognized by others. It also makes it easy for you to understand the interfaces available for your use in the predefined JFC classes when you are looking for a class to perform a particular function.

Of course, the details of the methods comprising the model interfaces will vary according to the nature of the abstraction encapsulated by the model. However, the methods that identify ways at getting and setting the data that defines the abstraction are consistent (see Table 2.18).

TABLE 2.18 The `javax.swing.ListModel` Interface

Method name	Purpose
getElementAt(int index)	Retrieve a specific list element
getSize()	Get the size of the list
AddListDataListener(ListDataListener l)	Add an event listener
RemoveListDataListener(ListDataListener l)	Remove an event listener

Notice that there are two parts to this interface. The first two methods address the details of the data abstraction itself. The latter two support the delegation event model mentioned previously. You will meet both of these architectural issues in great detail in subsequent chapters.

You are certainly welcome to define your own models. Whenever a component creates a new data abstraction, it may be useful to create an associated model if an appropriate one does not exist.

A new class may define the view of this data abstraction, and it may need an interface to identify how it supports use of your new model. Similarly, the corresponding model will need to specify how it supports implementation of the model.

If you build in this support in a standard way, it will be easy to use and easy for others to recognize your MVC support, because it will be consistent with the JFC model architecture guidelines.

Summary

The Java Foundation Classes are a plethora of Java class definitions, organized in several packages, that constitute a foundation for GUI program development in Java.

The JFC is comprised of two parts, the Swing architecture and a new set of classes that implement new abstractions relevant to GUI programming.

These two parts are implemented via four APIs that comprise the JFC. The four APIs are the AWT in release 1.1 of the JDK, the Java 2D API, the Accessibility API, and the Drag-and-Drop API.

The AWT 1.1 provides the delegation event model, support for lightweight components, clipboard and datatransfer, and support for printing and mouseless operation.

Although the JDK 1.1 AWT implements the Swing architecture, all the AWT 1.1 visual component implementations are heavyweight. The JFC does include a new set of visual component classes that descend from `javax.swing.JComponent`. These classes are all lightweight implementations. They are defined in the Swing packages.

The JFC classes implement such new abstractions as a model architecture and a new model for containers to contain child components. The model architecture supports easy adoption of the MVC paradigm at the class level in application development. Many JFC classes are provided that can behave as a model, view, or controller object in the MVC architecture.

This chapter has intentionally given you a conceptual description of the features and capabilities of JFC. Now that you have this conceptual foundation, it will be easier to identify when and where concrete parts of the JFC manifest these concepts.

You are now ready to dive into writing code. Chapter 3, "Program Structure," begins a concrete explanation of how to start organizing and writing JFC programs.

Basic Program Structure

IN THIS CHAPTER

- **Program Building Blocks**   48
- **Creating an Application**   51
- **Using Lightweight Containers**   63
- **Creating an Applet**   64
- **Programs That Are Both Applications and Applets**   67

This chapter discusses high-level program structure and organization, which is the first step in building a GUI application. After the basic structure is laid out, you can define your program's user interface, its structure, and organization.

In this chapter, you will explore your options for high-level program structure and how it lays the framework for building a complicated GUI application. The topics discussed in this chapter are germane to every Java GUI program. For the first time, you will learn what you have to do to get a GUI to display on your screen.

This chapter introduces the approach to defining a new class which represents your application. It considers alternative ways of defining your class—from where it derives—and what this implies about how it can be used.

It explains the different approaches that you can take in organizing your application, and the implications, pros, and cons of choosing one approach over another.

Program Building Blocks

All Java GUI programs consist primarily of three types of elements: components, containers, and layout managers. Together these three building blocks give you, the programmer, great flexibility to create the visual interface that implements your application's abstractions.

Primarily, Java GUI programs consist of a set of visual and non-visual *components*. In Java parlance, components are objects that have some graphical or visual representation. Components, of course, are defined by classes; components that exist in an executing program are object instances of these classes. They are the primary building blocks of all Java GUI programs.

Typically, a large number of the components in your program primarily define those elements that comprise the "view" part of the Model-View-Controller paradigm that was introduced in the previous chapter.

Many of the visual objects in your program will be instances of component classes that are predefined in the JDK. The `java.awt` and `javax.swing` packages contain these predefined visual component classes. These classes are the foundation of all Java GUI programs. Your applications will use many of these classes.

Components are GUI elements like buttons, text fields, text areas, panels, and canvases on which you can draw graphics, scrolling lists, combo boxes, and so on. These are the typical components available to programs in all popular graphical user interface programming environments. Table 3.1 lists some of these common component classes and their descriptions.

TABLE 3.1 Common AWT Visual Components and Their Functions

Class name	Description
java.awt.Applet	The ancestor of all Java applet definitions
java.awt.Button	A standard push button
java.awt.Checkbox	A checkbox that can be selected
java.awt.CheckboxMenuItem	A checkbox that can be contained by a menu
java.awt.Component	An abstract class that defines common attributes and behavior of all components
java.awt.Container	The ancestor of all container classes, which defines components that can contain other components
java.awt.Dialog	A standard dialog box for message display
java.awt.FileDialog	A dialog box that prompts for a file name
java.awt.Frame	A window with a border and a menu bar
java.awt.Label	A fixed textual label
java.awt.Menu	A standard menu on a menu bar
java.awt.MenuBar	A container of menus on a frame
java.awt.MenuItem	An element of a menu
java.awt.Panel	A container that can contain other elements
java.awt.PopupMenu	A typical pop-up menu
java.awt.Scrollbar	A scrollbar that can attach to a panel
java.awt.ScrollPane	A pane that can scroll the view of its contents
java.awt.TextField	A field that stores a single line of text
java.awt.TextArea	A component that defines a field that stores multiple lines of text
java.awt.Window	A window with no border or menu bar

3

BASIC PROGRAM STRUCTURE

Figure 3.1 shows what some of these common AWT GUI components look like.

Components are not just haphazardly placed on the screen. They are aggregated and organized by *containers*, which are the second major building block of Java GUI programs. Containers basically contain components. A Java GUI program will have many components and many containers that organize the components by aggregating them in several nested levels.

Containers are the mechanism by which you contain and organize arbitrary components and give structure to your applications. However, containers themselves are a special kind of component. This relationship between components and containers permits containers to contain other containers, thereby enabling the programmer to nest components and create a multilevel containment model for all the visual objects that the user sees on the display.

FIGURE 3.1

Some of the standard AWT visual components.

Figure 3.2 shows a UML diagram that defines the relationship between components and containers that supports this kind of recursive composition.

A container that contains arbitrary components is called a *parent*, and the components it contains are called its *children*. Since containers are components, a container can contain other containers. A container can be a child of another container. And, of course, such a container can itself be a parent that contains other children—including other containers. This relationship between components and containers allows multiple levels of nesting.

Nesting enables you to organize your GUI's visual components in a nested hierarchy. This capability gives you great flexibility in defining how components are organized and managed. Components can be grouped into manageable sets, enabling you to group functionally or semantically related screen elements.

The AWT basically allows limitless levels of nesting. In addition to organizational and logistic benefits, nesting enables each container to employ a separate policy for managing and organizing the layout of the components it contains.

This brings us to the third type of major building block at your disposal for creating GUIs. The third basic building block for building the visual part of your GUI is the *layout manager*. Layout managers are objects with no visual representation. Containers reference a layout manager object to which they delegate the job of visually laying out their children.

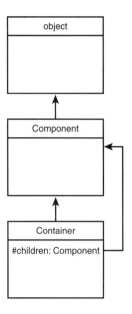

FIGURE 3.2

UML diagram showing the relationship between components and containers. A container object can be specified anywhere that a component is valid.

Each container can use a separate layout manager and can customize the way its child components are visually organized. This mechanism, coupled with the ability to nest containers inside other containers, gives you the capability to define very complex GUIs.

Layout managers are an involved topic. Chapter 8, "Layout Managers," is completely devoted to this topic. I just introduce them here to complete your exposure to the different conceptual building blocks of Java GUI programs.

Creating an Application

When you create a new Java GUI application, you must define a class that encapsulates the structure and organization of the whole application. This new class defines your application. How you define this class is the topic of this section.

Conceptually, there are basically four steps that are involved in creating and displaying the actual visual part of a Java GUI application. Every application must take the responsibility to ensure that these steps occur, or the program's visual user interface won't even display on the console.

These four steps are the responsibility of the class that you create to define your new application. Conceptually, every GUI program must do the following upon startup:

1. Create the outermost container that contains every other component and object in your application. This container essentially defines the context of your application. Shortly you will see that the type of container you choose defines the nature of your application.

2. Create the visual components that the user sees on the screen. These are all of the components contained by the outermost container from the first step. These components essentially create your application's user interface.

3. Create the aggregation of the visual components. Define and implement the nesting structure of all of your application components. This aggregation defines and implements the organization and positioning of components that the user sees. This step is accomplished by creating the nesting hierarchy introduced earlier.

4. Display the actual GUI. That means you will cause the outermost container to display on the user's screen. This in turn displays all of the components contained therein—all the components that comprise your total UI.

The outermost container that contains the whole GUI must be a heavyweight container. Every Java GUI application, therefore, must have at least one heavyweight container that contains every other visual component in the application. Chapter 2, "Introducing the Java Foundation Classes," discussed heavyweight components.

Your first step is to decide how to define the container object that will serve as your application's outermost container. The decision essentially centers on the notion of what type of container will best serve the needs of your application and how it will be used.

Essentially, you have two choices:

- The class you define to represent your new application is itself a subclass of a heavyweight window class. Windows and frames are heavyweight containers, so an instance of either class can act as the outermost container that contains all elements of your GUI.

- The class you define is a container, but not a window. It is an arbitrary container that contains all elements of your GUI. Your program creates an instance of your class, and ensures that it becomes a child of some instance of a window or frame. The program requests the window to be displayed on the screen.

You know that every Java GUI application must create an outermost heavyweight window that contains every other component in the application. Because your program is the only entity executing, it is responsible for creating both the heavyweight container and the GUI that represents your application.

This must be done in the `main()` method of your new class that defines your application. Your `main()` method will take one of two approaches that coincide with the two choices just outlined.

Using the first approach, your application's `main()` method creates an instance of your application. Because you derived this definition from one of the JFC heavyweight container classes, you already have your outermost container and the balance of your GUI components.

Using the second approach, your `main()` method can create an instance of your application—an instance of the class that defines your application. It can then create a heavyweight container and pass the application instance to the heavyweight.

Your program creates the necessary elements, and then it simply requests that the heavyweight container be displayed on the screen.

The one requirement you cannot escape is that the `main()` method in the class you define is the entry point of your program execution. How it works reflects how you defined your class—either as a subclass of a window container or as a subclass of some arbitrary container. This determines the nature of your application.

> **NOTE**
>
> Any class that defines an intended entry point for your GUI program must define a `main()` method, just as with non-GUI Java programs. Your `main()` method should, at the very least, create an instance of your class. In the typical paradigm, your constructor invocation sequence constructs the visible GUI and makes it visible onscreen.
>
> Alternatively, you can invoke a method on the newly created object instance that constructs and displays the visible portion of your GUI. Do not, however, invoke the `main()` method on an object instance after it is constructed. This will result in an infinite loop.

Either way, all component instances in your application end up contained in an outermost container. In Chapter 2, "Introducing the Java Foundation Classes," you learned that every program must have at least one native platform window to display on screen.

Heavyweight containers are the only containers that create a peer object, which creates the native platform window. By definition then, this means that your program must create *at least one* heavyweight container—the outermost container for your whole application.

In fact, your application's outermost heavyweight container must be an instance of `java.awt.Window` or one of its concrete subclasses. Typically it will be a frame, which is a type of window with a border and menu bar. However, it could be a simple window with no frame or menu bar. Regardless, your Java program constructs a heavyweight container.

Earlier you learned that you must define at least one class in order to build a GUI program. The two choices you have are to subclass one of the AWT window containers, or to subclass a non-window container class.

Stating it more concretely, you can define your application's class in one of the following two ways:

- Your class subclasses the heavyweight `java.awt.Window` or `java.awt.Frame` classes. Your program creates an instance of your class, which is the frame that contains everything else. The AWT creates the corresponding native platform peer window. Your `main()` method then displays your application instance, which is already the required window or frame.

- Your class subclasses an arbitrary container class such as `java.awt.Panel` that is not a window or frame. This container holds all the elements of your program. Your program also creates a `java.awt.Window` or `java.awt.Frame` instance and asks it to contain the instance of your class. Your `main()` method then displays the window or frame.

Table 3.2 shows the AWT container classes. Typically, your application will subclass either `Frame` or `Panel`.

If you choose to subclass `Panel`, you are opting to use the second approach, where your application is just an arbitrary container that still must have a heavyweight container that can contain and display it.

If you subclass `Window` or `Frame`, then you are choosing to use the first approach to define your application—your instance is itself the heavyweight container that contains your whole application. This model still requires you to explicitly create an instance of your class. It doesn't happen automatically.

TABLE 3.2   Container Names and Types

Container name	Container type
java.awt.Applet	Heavyweight; subclass of `Panel`.
java.awt.Container	Heavyweight; ancestor of all containers.
java.awt.Frame	Heavyweight; a window with a border and menu bar.
java.awt.Panel	Heavyweight; not a type of window but a type of container.
java.awt.Window	Heavyweight; no border or menu bar. It is not a visible container.

Subclassing `java.awt.Frame`

Listing 3.1 shows a very simple starter application that defines a new class which subclasses `java.awt.Frame`.

LISTING 3.1 Creating an Application Using a Class That Subclasses One of the AWT Window Classes

```
import java.awt.BorderLayout;
import java.awt.Dimension;
import java.awt.Frame;
import java.awt.Label;
import java.awt.Panel;

/**
    Defines simple frame objects with no child components.
    This class subclasses java.awt.Frame and
    is therefore a type of frame.
*/
class FrameOnly extends Frame
{
    /**
        No-arg constructor.
    */
    public FrameOnly()
    {
        super("An empty frame");
    }

    /**
        Specifies the preferred size of the component.

        @return the preferred size as a Dimension object.
    */
public Dimension getPreferredSize()
{
    return new Dimension(300, 300);
}


    /**
        Main function.  Creates an instance of the application,
        which is already the frame necessary for display on the
        screen.  Calculates the required minimum size of the
        frame, and displays it.
    */
    public static void main(String [] args)
    {
```

continues

3

BASIC PROGRAM
STRUCTURE

LISTING 3.1   Continued

```java
        FrameOnly f = new FrameOnly();
        f.pack();
        f.setVisible(true);
    }


}



import java.awt.Dimension;
import java.awt.Frame;
import java.awt.Label;

/**
   This class creates a subclass of java.awt.Frame.
   It demonstrates how to build an application
   Whose elements are all contained in the heavyweight
   Container it creates.
   */
class FrameOnly extends Frame
{
  /**
     Constructor.
     */
  public FrameOnly()
  {
    super("An empty frame");
  }

  /**
     Indicates the preferred size for all
     Instances of this class. Sizes are
     Width and height in pixels.

     @return the preferred layout size of this frame.
     */
  public Dimension getPreferredSize()
  {
    return new Dimension(300, 300);
  }

  public static void main(String [] args)
  {
    // Create the frame.
```

```
    FrameOnly f = new FrameOnly();

    // Request the frame to calculate its
    // preferred size, based on the size
    // requirements of its children, if any.
    f.pack();

    // Make the frame visible so it shows on
    // screen.
    f.setVisible(true);
  }
}
```

To execute this application you must first compile it. GUI programs compile no differently than any other Java program.

```
$ javac FrameOnly
```

You then execute this application by typing

```
$ java FrameOnly
```

on the command line. Of course, just as with any non-GUI application, you should set your CLASSPATH environment variable correctly. At the very least you will need to include in the classpath the location of the JDK installation on your system.

For development, it is a good idea to also include the "current directory" in the CLASSPATH. This allows you to compile and run programs in the same directory without having to move the .class file to a directory that is in the CLASSPATH after each compilation.

Figure 3.3 shows what you will see on the screen when the application starts up.

There are several important points to note about how you structure this very simple application. First of all, your application is a subclass of java.awt.Frame. Every instance you create is, therefore, a frame that is capable of displaying your GUI on the screen via the help of its native peer object. This must be the case. You cannot subclass java.awt.Window, because window objects have no visual representation.

It is important that your class actually subclass the Frame class. You could not have simply created a frame and tried to add things to it. For example, You could not have done the following:

```
class FrameOnly
{
  public FrameOnly()
  {

  }
```

```
...

public static void main(String [] args)
{
  FrameOnly app = new FrameOnly();

  Frame f = new Frame();
  f.add(app);
  f.pack();
  f.setVisible(true);
}
}
```

FIGURE 3.3
The simplest GUI consists of an empty frame and contains no components.

This looks like it might be okay; you create a frame and add your class's instance to it. But because your class doesn't subclass any AWT component it *is not* any kind of component. So the frame object doesn't know how to deal with it. Looking at the formal parameters of the add() methods in the Container class or any of its subclasses will give this away; you must pass in a Component and not an arbitrary Object.

The second point is that you must indicate the preferred size for your application. Basically, the frame must specify how big it should be—how big the native peer window must be. In a frame with no components, if you don't specify a size, the AWT will calculate that it requires no screen real estate and not render it onscreen. You will see in Chapter 4, "AWT Concepts and Architecture," that all components must specify a preferred size in one way or another.

The `Component.getPreferredSize()` method allows the frame's layout manager to query your object about its size requirements. You can also specify minimum and maximum sizes for all components.

> **NOTE**
>
> Every component must indicate a preferred size either explicitly or implicitly. To explicitly indicate the preferred size for its instances a class should override the `Component.getPreferredSize()` method to return the actual preferred size. Containers don't have to provide an explicit value by overriding `getPreferredSize()` because their preferred size can be calculated by summing the size requirements of their children.

The next task is to make sure the frame displays on the screen. You first call `pack()`, which basically "packs" the children in the frame and performs the size calculations for the frame—its preferred layout size. Next, you set its visible state. All components can be specified as visible or non-visible. Even though a component exists, it may not be visible. You must tell the container to cause your component's peer object to be created and displayed.

So far, you have outlined the basic program structure that all Java GUI applications must support. You must create the application object, initiate its size calculation, and make it visible. Each of these steps is always required.

> **NOTE**
>
> You must call `setVisible(true)` on your outermost window or frame in order for it to appear onscreen. Furthermore, you must explicitly initiate a size calculation for your window or frame. You can do this in one of two ways.
>
> The first approach is to explicitly specify the desired size for the window or frame. You can call one of the two overloaded versions of the `Component.setBounds()` method on your window instance, or you can override the `Component.getPreferredSize()` method to return the desired size of the window.
>
> The second approach is to explicitly call the `Window.pack()` method on your window instance, which results in the window calculating its required size based on the sizes of the components that it contains.
>
> *continues*

3

BASIC PROGRAM STRUCTURE

If you call pack() on a window that contains no components, you will see only the frame created by the native window system shrunk to its smallest possible size. Even if you explicitly set the dimensions of your window by using the setBounds() method, calling pack() on a window that contains no components will create a window with the minimum possible size. However, providing a getPreferredSize() method will render the window with its desired size.

Subclassing `java.awt.Panel`

In the first example, the application's defining class chose to subclass java.awt.Frame, essentially making your application a type of frame. This approach is well suited for programs that will be run as standalone applications. When they are started, they will always have their own window or frame.

The drawback to defining your application as a frame is that you cannot insert your application as a component in another container. For example, another application cannot include an instance of your application as one of its components. Therefore, if you plan to create an application that can be used as part of another, you will not define it this way.

Fortunately, the second approach available to you solves this problem. The next example shows how to use the second approach. The class in the following example subclasses java.awt.Panel, which is a different kind of container that is not a type of window. Thus, the logic in your class must create a frame somewhere and add the instance of your class as a contained component. The frame that you create is the outermost container that you need to encapsulate everything in your application. It will have a corresponding native peer window that encompasses your whole application.

LISTING 3.2 Creating a Class that Defines a Container that Encompasses All of Your GUI but Is not a Standalone Window

```
import java.awt.BorderLayout;
import java.awt.Dimension;
import java.awt.Frame;
import java.awt.Panel;

/**
    This class defines a panel that does not contain any
    children.  Instances of this class need to be placed in a
    separately created frame object in order to be displayed
    on screen.
*/
class PanelOnly extends Panel
```

```
{
    /**
        No-arg constructor.
    */
    public PanelOnly()
    {
        super();
    }


    /**
        Specifies the preferred size of the component.

        @return the preferred size as a Dimension object.
    */
    public Dimension getPreferredSize()
    {
        return new Dimension(300, 300);
    }


    /**
        Creates an instance of this class.  Also creates the
        frame that must contain the instance.  Packs the frame
        and displays it.
    */
    public static void main(String [] args)
    {
        PanelOnly app = new PanelOnly();

        Frame f = new Frame("An empty panel in a frame"); f.add(app);
        f.pack();
        f.setVisible(true);
    }
}


import java.awt.Dimension;
import java.awt.Frame;
import java.awt.Panel;

/**
  This class creates an empty container.  The
  Container is not a standalone window, so it
  Must be placed in a window.
  */
```

continues

LISTING 3.2   Continued

```
class PanelOnly extends Panel
{
  /**
    No-arg constructor.
    */
  public PanelOnly()
  {
    super();
  }

  /**
    Indicates the preferred size of the
    Panel.

    @return the preferred layout size of this panel.
    */
```

There are only two real differences between this version of the application and the previous one. First of all, notice that you now subclass java.awt.Panel. Your application instance is really a panel, not a frame. Panels are containers, but they are not standalone windows of any kind. Therefore, you must create a window which will create the native peer that you need to render your application on the screen.

Secondly, in your main() method you now create a separate Frame object. Now you have the frame, but you need to make sure it contains your application object—your panel—which is a component. You use the add() method to do this. In Chapter 4, you will see that the add() method is defined in the Container class.

The advantage of this second approach to structuring your applications is flexibility. You can see how simple it is to construct a frame and add your panel to it. Moreover, another application can easily instantiate your class and add it as a component to its structure. This is valid anywhere that a panel object is allowed.

If you think you need the flexibility to include your container as a component in another application context, define your class to be a panel. Of course, if you want to prohibit this for some reason, simply make your application a frame.

In this last example, the main() method creates a frame and adds the instance of the application class to it. Although it is necessary to create the frame, it need not be done in your class's main.

You can define a second class which essentially sports nothing but a main() method. The main() method would simply create a frame, instantiate your other class, and place it in the frame. There is no real advantage to this approach, and it clutters your application by defining a second class that only utilizes its main() method. Nevertheless, this option is available.

Starting and Stopping Your Application

Java *applications* are always executed from the command line. If you compile and run the programs in Listing 3.1 and 3.2 you will notice that there is no way to stop them. You must kill or abort their execution by typing Ctrl-C at the console.

Java programs do provide a mechanism on the GUI to terminate execution in a more responsible way. This capability involves adding event handling to your program. You will learn about event handling in Chapter 9, "Events and Event Handling." There you will learn how to add an event handler that listens for requests to dispose the outermost window of an application.

Using Lightweight Containers

By using the Swing container and component classes, your program can consist mostly of lightweight components, meaning that the native platform does not create corresponding native peer windows for each visual component. But, alas, you still need at least one native peer window, and, therefore, at least one heavyweight container. The heavyweight container must be one that can stand alone without requiring another container in which to reside.

The Swing tool set defines four heavyweight containers which create native peer objects when they are instantiated by your program. If you use only Swing components, your outermost container must be one of these four heavyweight components. Table 3.3 lists the Swing container classes.

> **NOTE**
>
> You can also put your Swing program into an outermost AWT container. This is an exception to the rule that you should not mix AWT and Swing components. If you use an AWT container, you will notice that its look-and-feel will be different than that of your Swing components, but it will work just fine.

TABLE 3.3   Swing's Container Classes

Container	Superclass	Heavy or light
javax.swing.JApplet	java.awt.Applet	Heavyweight
javax.swing.JDialog	java.awt.Dialog	Heavyweight
javax.swing.JFrame	java.awt.Frame	Heavyweight
javax.swing.JInternalFrame	javax.swing.JComponent	Lightweight
javax.swing.JWindow	java.awt.Window	Heavyweight

Swing defines heavyweight containers, which allow you to create applications that use exclusively Swing components. Your program will have a consistent look-and-feel because the Swing heavyweight containers implement the same look-and-feel as the other Swing components.

If you create an all-Swing program, typically, your class will subclass either `JFrame` if it is an application, or `JApplet` if it is an applet. Any of the heavyweight containers will do.

Swing also gives you one container, `JInternalFrame`, that is lightweight but can be used to simulate an outermost frame. This is useful, for example, if your application creates a separate application-level frame internally. An example of such an application is one whose GUI creates a desktop.

Such an application, however, cannot use a `JInternalPane` as its outermost container; that is, your class cannot subclass `JInternalPane` because it is not a heavyweight container. `JInternalPane` is useful, nevertheless, as an internal container. It has the advantages of simulating an outermost container without the burden of being heavyweight. You will see examples that use `JInternalPane` in Chapter 7, "The Swing Components."

You will delve into this area of heavyweight versus lightweight components in more detail in Chapter 4. There are many more issues related to components and containers than simply displaying the initial GUI.

Creating an Applet

Applets are a second type of GUI program that are specifically designed to be executed under the control of a web browser. That is, the browser executes a VM and runs the applet for you.

An HTML page can specify an applet to be part of its content by the inclusion of a special applet tag. The applet tag indicates the applet program to execute, and the location and size of the area on the page to reserve for the applet. When the HTML page is loaded, the browser loads and starts the applet. The applet executes and uses the reserved space for its graphical output. When the page is dismissed, the browser stops the applet.

Listing 3.3 shows an HTML page that contains an applet specification. The HTML page indicates the inclusion of an applet. The `code` parameter indicates the name of the class file to execute. In this case it is a file called `SimpleApplet.class`, which tells you that there is a class called `SimpleApplet` that defines this applet via a special applet tag.

The `codebase` parameter indicates the path to the executable class file, that is, the directory in which it is found. The `width` and `height` parameters specify the amount of screen real estate to reserve for the applet.

Applets are organized on the page like other HTML elements. The position of the applet tag in the HTML file indicates where it is located relative to other page elements.

LISTING 3.3   An HTML Page That Contains an Applet Specification

```
<!DOCTYPE HTML PUBLIC "-//IETF//DTD HTML//EN">
<html>
    <head>
        <title>A Simple HTML Page With an Applet</title>
    </head>

    Here is some arbitrary text before the applet. <hr>

<applet code="SimpleApp.class"
        codebase=/home/vartan/dev/book/ch3
        width=350 height=200>
</applet>

<hr>
Perhaps some more arbitrary text comes after the applet.
This text will not appear if you run this applet with the
appletviewer program.  However, it will appear if you load
this page in a web browser.

</html>
```

When the browser parses the HTML file and detects an applet tag it takes the necessary steps to create an environment in which the applet can execute. First, it starts a VM that will execute the applet.

It then starts the applet running by requesting that the VM call the method that defines the entry point for all applets. Applets define a different interface for controlling their execution. There is no `main()` method. Instead, applets define the methods detailed in Table 3.4.

TABLE 3.4   Methods That Control Applet Execution

Applet method	*Description*
`init()`	Called to initialize the applet when the page containing the applet is loaded in the browser.
`start()`	Called after the `init()` method to start applet execution.
`stop()`	Called to stop execution when the user leaves the HTML page containing the applet.
`destroy()`	Called after the `stop` method. This method should contain code to clean up any resources used by the applet.

3

BASIC PROGRAM
STRUCTURE

Applets are not quite executed in the same manner as applications. Instead, the browser tells the VM to first call an `init` method. You can place any initialization code in this method.

The applet's `start` method is invoked next. Your `start` method is the counterpart to an application's `main()` method. It really starts the execution of the applet that the user sees, for instance, displaying the visible elements of the GUI.

When the user leaves the page containing your applet, the browser calls your applet's `stop` method and then your `destroy` method. The `stop` method stops execution of your applet. The `destroy` method lets you define any cleanup that should reclaim resources used by your applet.

Although it is a VM started by the browser that executes the actual code, it is the browser that controls when these methods are called. Only the browser knows when pages are loaded and unloaded, so it must request the VM to help it do the necessary tasks. This is done through an API supported by the VM.

Listing 3.4 shows an example applet. Note that the applet class defined in the listing extends the `JApplet` class. All applets must extend either `java.applet.Applet` or `javax.swing.JApplet`. The `Applet` class defines default definitions of the `init`, `start`, `stop`, and `destroy` methods that are empty. Your subclass must override these methods to define the context and behavior of your applet.

Recall from Table 3.2 that `JApplet` is a heavyweight Swing container. In fact, `JApplet` directly extends `Applet`, which, of course, is also heavyweight as you know. The `Applet` class in turn extends `java.awt.Panel`, which, as you know, is heavyweight because it is an AWT `JApplet` container.

However, the `Panel` class is not any type of window or frame. You still don't have the heavyweight window container you need. Your applet object must be contained by such a heavyweight container—a window or frame—just like any other Java GUI application. Figure 3.4 shows the inheritance hierarchy of the applet support classes. You can see that applets are not any kind of window or frame object which could have a corresponding native peer window.

Yet even though an applet instance has no heavyweight container, your applet programs should never create the required frame or window. One will be created for you by the browser.

Before the browser asks the VM to start executing your applet, it first creates a heavyweight frame for you and adds your applet instance to it. It then passes the whole structure to the VM, which controls its execution.

When you are writing applets, you really have only one choice for structuring your program, instead of the two choices you have when creating standalone applications: You must define a class that extends either `Applet` or `JApplet`. This is not a restriction, however, because applets were specifically designed to be programs that execute inside a browser environment.

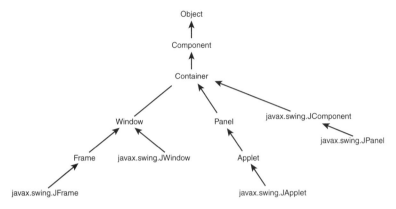

FIGURE 3.4

The two applet support classes derive from non-window containers, which means that they do not create a heavyweight frame or window. Subclasses, therefore, also do not have a frame when they are instantiated.

Programs That Are Both Applications and Applets

Applets and applications behave differently. The VM invokes an application's main() method as the program entry point, whereas it invokes an applet's init method as the applet entry point.

It would be nice if you could create one class definition that will run your program as either an applet or an application. In fact, you can.

If your class defines a main() method and the required init(), start(), stop(), and destroy() methods, you can use it as both an applet and an application.

The idea is to reuse the same code to construct your program, instead of duplicating it to accommodate two different entry points, namely main() for the application and init() for the applet.

As an applet, an instance of your class inherently has a heavyweight frame object. That is, a heavyweight container is always created for you by the browser.

When you run your program as an application, you can create the heavyweight frame in your main() method. This suggests that your class should be a Panel.

Listing 3.4 shows a program that can be run both as an applet and an application. Notice that the code in the start() method gets called either way. When run as an applet, the browser calls the start() method. When run as an application, the code in the main() method calls it.

LISTING 3.4   A Program That Can Be Run as an Applet or Application

```java
import java.applet.Applet
import java.awt.BorderLayout;
import java.awt.Dimension;
import java.awt.Frame;
import java.awt.Insets;
import java.awt.Label;
import java.awt.Panel;

/**
    A class that can be used as either an applet or
    application.

    <p>To use as an applet the init method creates the
    instance of the SimpleApp class to the applet panel.

    <p>To use as an application, the main function creates
    the necessary frame in which to place the SimpleApp
    instance.
*/
public class SimpleApp extends Applet
{
    // Don't need a constructor.  Instead we build the applet
    // contents in the start() method.

    /**
        Specify the preferred size of this instance.

        @return the preferred size as a
        <code>java.awt.Dimension</code> object.
    */
    public Dimension getPreferredSize()
    {
        return new Dimension(350, 200);
    }

    public void init()
    {
        // Don't need to do anything here.  There is no browser
        // to call init() and start() for us when we run this as
        // an application.  Instead of building the contents of
        // the applet in the init() method, and calling both
        // init() and start(), we can simply put initialization
        // code in start() and call it, which is a simpler
        // approach.
    }
```

```
/**
    Construct the contents of the applet.  This method can
    also be called explicitly in the main() function when
    running as an application.  This the reason we place
    the code here instead of in a constructor: we don't
    have to duplicate the same code.
*/
public void start()
{
    setLayout(new BorderLayout());

    Label label = new
        Label("A program that's both an application and an applet.");

    add(label, BorderLayout.CENTER);
}


public void stop()
{
    // Don't need to do any cleanup.
}


public void destroy()
{
    // Don't need to do any cleanup.
}


/**
    Specifies the minimum amount of space between the edges
    of this container and the layout of any of its
    children.

    @return the Insets for this container.
*/
public Insets getInsets()
{
    return new Insets(5, 20, 5, 20);
}


/**
    Creates the <code>Frame</code> needed to contain the
    instance of this class for running as an application.
```

3

BASIC PROGRAM STRUCTURE

continues

LISTING 3.4 Continued

```
    */
    public static void main(String [] args)
    {
        // Because SimpleApp extends Applet, which is a Panel,
        // we can add it to a Frame.
        //
        SimpleApp app = new SimpleApp();

        // Call the applet's start() method, which builds its
        // contents.
        //
        app.start();

        // Create the Frame to hold the Applet, which is a type
        // of Panel.
        //
        Frame f = new Frame("A Simple Application"); f.add(app);
        f.pack();
        f.setVisible(true);
    }


    SimpleApplet app;
}
```

Notice that you have to define your application to be a subclass of a non-window container class like Panel or JPanel. Simply defining the init, start, stop and destroy methods is not sufficient to make your class an applet.

If instead you subclass Frame, then your class definition conflicts with the requirements for executing as an applet. The browser cannot add a window or frame instance to another window. Top-level components like windows and frames cannot be children of another window or frame.

Figure 3.5 shows the program in Listing 3.6 when run as an application. Figure 3.6 shows the program when run as an applet.

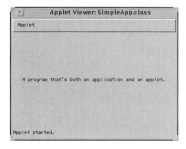

FIGURE 3.5

Program from listing 3.6 being run as an application.

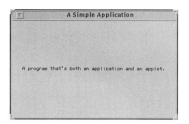

FIGURE 3.6

Same program being run as an applet.

Summary

In this chapter you've been introduced to the basic structure of a Java GUI program. You learned the three primary building blocks: components, containers, and layout managers, and you were shown how they are related.

Components are objects that represent the visual elements used to construct your GUIs. Containers are special components that can contain other components. They enable you to organize your GUIs more effectively by nesting the components in a hierarchy of containers. Layout managers are objects with no visual attribute that maintain the way components are arranged by a container.

To get even a simple window to show up on the screen, your program must create at least one heavyweight container, which acts as your application's outermost container that contains all other components.

Your application must create a heavyweight container to realize the creation of a corresponding native peer window. The native peer is necessary because it is the window that you see on your display. Only the AWT's peer classes know anything about displaying and managing actual objects on the native platform windowing system. The AWT component classes you use in your program know nothing about rendering components on the native windowing platform.

Although the AWT architecture in JDK 1.1 supports the definition and use of lightweight component classes, all of the AWT component classes have heavyweight implementations. The Swing component set, however, defines a set of the standard GUI components with lightweight implementations, including some new types of containers.

Nevertheless, Swing's primary containers are heavyweight for the same reason that the AWT containers are. An application written completely using Swing component classes must still be able to ensure that a native peer is instantiated that can "contain" all of your application's visual components. This requires a heavyweight container.

Applets are the second type of GUI program. They use a different interface to define their standard-execution entry point. Applets subclass an applet class. The browser that controls the applet's execution creates the heavyweight frame needed to display on the screen.

Your program can serve as both an application and an applet by defining a `main()` method, as well as the methods `init()`, `start()`, `stop()`, and `destroy()`.

Now that you understand the conceptual organization and structure of Java GUI programs, you are ready to build some concrete, working applications by applying these concepts. Chapter 4 introduces you to the application of the concepts you have learned in this chapter.

AWT Concepts and Architecture

IN THIS CHAPTER

- AWT Components   74
- The java.awt.Component Class   75
- The java.awt.Container Class   82
- Adding Components to a Container   85

This chapter takes a closer look at AWT components and containers. Whether you plan to program in AWT or Swing, understanding the way components and containers work together is crucial to writing a Java program of any substance. Even if you plan to use only Swing components, you need to understand the AWT foundation upon which all the Swing tool set is build.

This chapter focuses on the attributes and capabilities that are characteristic of all components, and discusses how they work. I will examine in detail the `java.awt.Component` class, which is the ancestor of all component types in Java, and I will discuss the concepts that relate to the use of all component classes.

I will also take a closer look at the `java.awt.Container` class, its definition, interface, and behavior. Containers are also components, and their ability to contain arbitrary components gives you the primary mechanism you need to organize complex GUIs.

After I discuss the conceptual issues of components and containers, I will show you how to move on to the next step in building applications, namely, adding components to containers to build complex GUIs. I will expand upon the simple empty frame that you produced in the previous chapter.

AWT Components

By now you know that Java GUI programs are made up of many components. Some of these component classes define widgets with which you are undoubtedly already familiar—buttons, check boxes, menus, lists, text fields, labels, and so forth.

Containers are another kind of component with the special capability to contain and manage other components. Many containers are not visible; their sole function is to contain other components, giving the GUI a more organized overall structure. However, containers certainly can have a visible appearance if they are so defined.

All the AWT component classes have heavyweight implementations. This means that for every instance of an AWT component in your program, there is a corresponding native window peer object that is essentially a native platform window object. This scheme is the way that your Java GUI components are actually rendered on the screen.

The native peer approach was Java's first implementation of a platform-independent GUI programming platform. Native window peer objects are defined by peer classes. Changing the peer class associated with the AWT components in the Java program allows you to obtain a look-and-feel that matches the look-and-feel of the platform on which your program is executing.

All AWT components use native peers. But the AWT 1.1 does more. The `java.awt` package in AWT 1.1 and beyond implements the architecture that supports lightweight components. But it doesn't actually define any such lightweight implementations for you.

In the previous chapter, Table 3.1 lists some of the common AWT component classes and their functions. Each of those classes are concrete implementations of specific AWT components. All these AWT component classes have one thing in common—their common ancestor is the `java.awt.Component` class. Figure 4.1 shows an inheritance hierarchy involving some of these common AWT component classes.

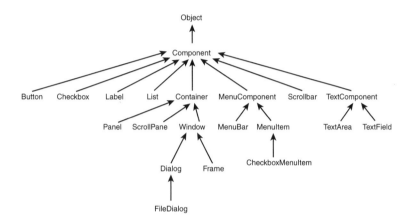

FIGURE 4.1

All the AWT component classes descend from `java.awt.Component`, *allowing them to take advantage of common attributes and behavior.*

This class is the cornerstone of GUI programming in Java. It defines all the properties that are common to all components. Moreover, it implements certain policies that make the rich set of component subclasses adhere to a common standard of attributes and behavior. Therefore, a good place to start is with an examination of the attributes, properties, and behavior defined by the `java.awt.Component` class.

The java.awt.Component Class

All visual component class definitions in both the AWT and Swing descend from the `java.awt.Component` class. It's worthwhile to take a closer look at this class. You need to understand what it offers before you can understand how containers and the `java.awt.Container` class behave.

The `java.awt.Component` class is an abstract class; you cannot instantiate it. Its primary purpose is to capture the nature and behavior of all GUI components.

As good design would dictate, the `java.awt.Component` class implements all the functionality that is common to all its descendants. It also defines all the attributes that every type of component has. This ensures consistency between components.

All AWT components have the attributes, or properties, that are listed in Table 4.1.

TABLE 4.1   Properties Defined by `java.awt.Component`

Attribute	Description
Background color	The component's background color.
Foreground color	The component's foreground color.
Cursor	The glyph used when the mouse is in this component.
Bounds	The screen coordinates of the component.
Enabled	Responsive/not responsive to events.
Font	The font used for text displayed by this component.
Locale	A representation of the language environment that determines how the component displays certain data.
Relative location	Position of the component's upper-left corner relative to its parent container.
Screen location	The location of the component's upper-left corner on the screen, relative to the physical screen dimensions.
Size	The height and width of this component.
Visibility	Whether the component is showing on screen or not.
Name	A String name for the component.

Access to these attributes and properties are supported by a public interface that essentially defines the nature of the `Component` class, and, therefore, all other components. Table 4.2 lists the public methods that are presented by the public interface of the `Component` class.

Table 4.2 lists a good many—but not all—of the methods defined by the `Component` class, and relates them to the property that is modified or retrieved by their invocation.

I will go through many of these methods. Some of the methods defined in `Component` will not be discussed now, however. I will save the balance not discussed here for the chapters that discuss the specific conceptual areas addressed by those methods, such as layout management and event handling.

TABLE 4.2   Component Methods Related to Component Properties

Property/Attribute	Related `java.awt.Component` methods
Background color	`void setBackgroundColor(Color)`
	`Color getBackgroundColor()`
Bounds	`void setBounds(Rectangle)`
	`void setBounds(int, int, int, int)`
	`Rectangle getBounds()`

Property/Attribute	*Related* java.awt.Component *methods*
Cursor	void setCursor(Cursor)
	Cursor getCursor()
Enabled	void setEnabled(boolean)
	boolean isEnabled()
Font	void setFont(Font)
	Font setFont()
Foreground color	void setForegroundColor()
	Color getForegroundColor()
Locale	void setLocale(Locale)
	Locale getLocale()
Name	void setName(String)
	String getName()
Relative location	void setLocation(Point)
	void setLocation(int, int)
	Point getLocation()
Screen location	Point getLocationOnScreen()
	int getX()
	int getY()
	float getAlignmentY()
	float getAlignmentX()
Size	void setSize(Dimension)
	Dimension getSize()
	int getWidth()
	int getHeight()
Visibility	void setVisible(boolean)
	boolean isVisible()
	boolean isShowing()

Any component instance in an executing program can set the values of its attributes. This is done by using the public methods available to all components, defined in the java.awt.Component class. There are get and set methods for most of these properties.

I can loosely classify the aforementioned component properties in a few different groups, each of which I will now discuss.

Component Appearance

Every component instance can independently specify a foreground and background color. The foreground color is used to draw text that appears on component lettering. The background color sets the background of components.

Figure 4.2 shows some components with different foreground and background colors set.

FIGURE 4.2
Components can each set their foreground and background colors.

Component Location

Every component must have a location on the screen when your GUI is displayed. The location value of a component is an instance of the `java.awt.Point` class. It specifies the location of the component's upper-left corner as an x-y coordinate, relative to its container's upper-left corner.

For instance, if you query a component for its location, and the value returned indicates a value of 23 for x and 52 for y, the upper-left corner of your component is 23 pixels to the right and 52 pixels down from the upper-left corner of its container.

You can also determine the absolute position of your component on the display. The `getLocationOnScreen()` method returns the actual screen coordinates of the upper-left corner of your component. For example, a component with relative position of (23, 52) might have an absolute screen position of (62, 101).

You can also obtain information about a component's *bounds*. Instead of identifying the position of the component's upper-left corner, the bounds are specified as an instance of a `java.awt.Rectangle`, which represents the actual area covered by your component. The x and y values of the rectangle are still relative to the upper-left corner of the container, however.

Component Sizing

Components can override the three methods `getPreferredSize()`, `getMinimumSize`, and `getMaximumSize` to specify the quantities *preferred size*, *minimum size*, and *maximum size*, respectively. A component class implements these methods to always return the same value.

A component's preferred size indicates the size that the component would like to take on, assuming its container can accommodate that size. The maximum size indicates the maximum size that makes sense for the component, no matter how large the container is. The minimum size indicates the minimum size that a container should shrink the component when it is rendered onscreen.

Sizes make a difference when visual attributes like a component's font is changed. For instance, if you shrink a component too much, its text might not be visible because the size is too small to accommodate the size of characters in that font.

Layout managers frequently query components about their size preferences. A layout manager needs to know how big to make a container based upon the space required to display all its children.

You saw in the empty frame program in Chapter 3, "Program Structure," that you had to specify a preferred size to get anything to display. The reason was that no children were in the frame. Therefore, there was no way to determine how much space the frame needed. In fact, it didn't need any, but you still wanted it to be displayed. Specifying a preferred size or a minimum size forces the component to get some screen real estate.

You can also use the `setSize(Dimension)` method to specifically set the size of a component. And, or course, there is a corresponding `getSize()` method that returns the current size of a component.

Component Visibility

A component's visibility attribute determines if the component is visible on screen or not. You can set this attribute to show or hide each component independently by using the `setVisible(boolean)` method.

Component Responsiveness to Events

You can also enable or disable a component's ability to respond to user input events. For instance, if you disable a text field, the user will no longer be able to type into the text field. If you disable a button, the user can no longer activate the button.

When a component is disabled, it will be rendered differently on the screen. Each native platform toolkit has its own way of indicating the component's state. In other words, the visual representation is platform dependent. If you create custom components, one alternative is to provide two different images to use for the component's enabled and disabled state, respectively.

I don't say how a component responds to user input events yet; I just note that you can enable or disable a component's ability to respond to input. I will cover event handling in great detail in Chapter 9, "Events and Event Handling."

Component Cursors

When the mouse is inside a component's bounds, a cursor is displayed. The glyph displayed corresponds to the cursor that is set to be the current cursor for that component. You can specify the current cursor, or determine the current cursor, via the setCursor(Cursor)/getCursor() methods.

Several default cursors are available for your use. They are specified by constants defined in the java.awt.Cursor class. Table 4.3 lists the Cursor class constants that you can use.

TABLE 4.3   Predefined Constants for Cursor Class Cursors

Cursor identifier	Description
DEFAULT_CURSOR	Normal cursor.
CROSSHAIR_CURSOR	Cross hair.
TEXT_CURSOR	Standard text component cursor.
WAIT_CURSOR	Stopwatch-like cursor.
SW_RESIZE_CURSOR	Lower-left corner resize.
SE_RESIZE_CURSOR	Lower-right corner resize.
NW_RESIZE_CURSOR	Upper-left corner resize.
NE_RESIZE_CURSOR	Upper-right corner resize.
N_RESIZE_CURSOR	Northern component edge resize.
S_RESIZE_CURSOR	Southern component edge resize.
W_RESIZE_CURSOR	Western component edge resize.
E_RESIZE_CURSOR	Eastern component edge resize.
HAND_CURSOR	Hand-like cursor image.
MOVE_CURSOR	Move image cursor.

You can define each component to have a different cursor. But the normal approach is to change the cursor to reflect a certain state of either the component or the container or the whole application. This helps increase the effectiveness and clarity of your GUI.

> **NOTE**
>
> Cursors are not components. The java.awt.Cursor class is a direct subclass of java.lang.Object. The Cursor class basically defines some constants that represent particular cursor concepts. It is up to the AWT components to render the cursor that visually corresponds to the predefined cursor types. Cursors may look different on different platforms. For example, the WAIT_CURSOR is a wristwatch under Motif, but it is rendered as an hour glass on Windows.

Rendering Components

In addition to certain attributes and properties, the Component class defines some basic behavior that is shared by all components. One of the most important areas of behavior is the manner in which a component's visual representation is rendered on the screen.

All components have a visual representation. We say that a component is *painted* to render its visual representation. Heavyweight components will be rendered by their native peer object. Lightweight components will be rendered in the native peer that corresponds to their closest heavyweight container.

A heavyweight container that contains a lightweight component is responsible for reserving part of its peer's screen area to render the representation of the component. The peer essentially renders the pixels that correspond to the component's defined visual appearance. I will discuss this more in Chapter 6, "Swing Concepts and Architecture."

A component can be painted as a result of two types of events.

- The system issues a request to repaint the component in response to some event, such as the window being raised after it was occluded by another window.
- The application requests to repaint a component.

The Component class defines three methods that collaborate to render a component's visual state. Table 4.4 lists the methods defined in java.awt.Component that define the standard policy for painting components.

TABLE 4.4   Component Rendering Methods

Component *class method*	*Description*
paint(Graphics g)	Responsible for defining the visual appearance of the component. Each component class redefines this method.
update(Graphics g)	Clears the component's background and calls the paint() method.
repaint()	Schedules an asynchronous call to update() to repaint this component as soon as possible.
repaint(int x, int y, int w, int h)	Repaints the specified rectangle, which is a subset of the component's area.
repaint(long ms)	Repaints within this many milliseconds.
repaint(long ms, int x, int y, int w, int h)	Repaints the sub-area within this many milliseconds.

4

AWT
CONCEPTS AND
ARCHITECTURE

Each component class overrides the `paint()` method to draw the component's unique visual appearance. How you do this and what goes inside the `paint()` method is the subject of Chapter 11, "Graphics."

Components get painted as a result of either a system request to paint the component, or a request from the application to paint the component. In either case, the `repaint()` method is called. This causes the system's AWT event dispatching thread to issue a request to invoke the component's `repaint()` method.

The default definition of `repaint()` in the `Component` class simply calls the component's `update()` method, which clears the background and then calls the component's `paint()` method. When the `paint()` method executes, the component is redrawn. The actual screen display is updated when the peer object is redrawn.

Often, component classes do not have to alter the inherited definitions of the `repaint()`, `update()`, or `paint()` methods. However, sometimes it is necessary to do so. If you want to avoid flicker, you can override your `update()` method to call `paint()` directly, without clearing the background. This is useful if you have a component that is updated continuously.

A custom component definition can be one that subclasses an existing component definition, or subclasses the component directly. A custom component that wishes to define a new look must override the `paint()` method to draw the graphics that result in the component's desired look.

> **NOTE**
>
> All calls to graphics drawing routines that customize a component's look *must* go in the `paint()` method of the defining class, or in a method called from the `paint()` method. *Never* put drawing code in any other method. A component's `paint()` method needs to override its parent's definition only if it performs custom drawing.

The java.awt.Container Class

I said earlier that containers are special types of components. Like components, they have a superclass that encapsulates attributes, properties, and behaviors that are common to all containers. The class that defines these common features is the `java.awt.Container` class.

Unlike the `Component` class, the `Container` class is concrete, not abstract. It inherits all the features that make it a bona fide component, and defines new features that also make it capable of containing other components.

Containers essentially add the ability to contain other components, including other containers, to the Component class. Because containers are valid components, they can be treated as such by any container that contains them. Referring once more to Figure 4.1 shows us the inheritance hierarchy that makes this possible.

Table 4.5 shows the methods in the Container class that set the foundation for the capabilities of all containers.

TABLE 4.5 Container Class Methods

Container *class method name*	*Description*
void add(Component comp)	Adds a component to this container
void add(Component comp, int index)	Adds a component to this container at the specified index position
void add(Component comp, Object constraints)	Adds the specified component to this container such that its layout is subject to the specified constraints
void add(Component comp, Object constraints, int index)	Adds a component with the specified constraints at the specified index position
void add(String name, Component comp)	Adds the component with the given name to this container
Component findComponentAt (int x, int y)	Finds the component that contains the specified position
Component findComponentAt (Point p)	Finds the component that contains the specified point
Component getComponent(int n)	Gets the nth component added to this container
Component getComponentAt (int x, int y)	Gets the component that contains the specified position
Component getComponent (Point p)	Gets the component that contains the specified point
Component getComponentCount()	Returns the number of components in this container
Component [] getComponents()	Returns all this container's children
boolean isAncestorOf (Component c)	Determines if the component is a child of this container
void remove(Component comp)	Removes the specified component from this container
void remove(int index)	Removes the nth child from this container
void removeAll()	Removes all child components

The `Container` class also has many other methods that aren't shown in Table 4.5. These address event handling and layout management, and I will discuss them in detail in Chapter 9, "Events and Event Handling."

The methods in Table 4.1 comprise the public interface that lets you add components to containers. Of course, containers inherit all the methods in the `Component` class too, and you can still use these to manipulate containers as components.

A container's primary responsibility is to contain children. The various `add()` methods in Table 4.4 give you several ways to add components to a container. Components are stored in the same order in which they are added to their container. However, you can essentially insert a component in a particular slot by specifying its index using the `add(Component c, index int)` method.

After you've added a component to a container, you can determine its position with the `Component getComponent(int index)` method. And, naturally, you can remove components from a container using the `void remove()` methods or the `void removeAll()` method.

A few of the `add()` methods take a constraint object. This is an object that specifies the manner in which the layout manager should constrain the placement of the component within the container. The component is subject to the restrictions of this object. I will discuss this more in Chapter 8, "Layout Managers."

Often, a container will want to determine the component whose bounds include a specific x-y coordinate or a specific point. This is the purpose of the `Component getComponentAt()` methods. These methods will determine the container's child component whose bounds include the location. If the container has two or more children that overlap in the x-y plane, it will return the topmost child, that is, the front-most one in a front-to-back stacking.

You undoubtedly noticed that there are two `Component findComponentAt()` methods in Table 4.4 also. Their names seem to indicate that they do the same thing as the `getComponentAt()` methods. Actually, they do a bit more work. Like their `getComponentAt()` cousins, they find the topmost component whose bounds include the specified location. However, if that component is a container, the method will continue searching its children. In this manner, the method will return the most deeply nested component that is not a container.

Sometimes you need to determine if a given component is really a child of a container. The `boolean isAncestorOf(Component c)` method tells you if a component is a child of the container invoking the method.

Adding Components to a Container

Now that you know more about what containers are, what they do for you, and how components and containers are related, you are ready to proceed with building a more involved GUI. In Chapter 3, I showed the simplest possible GUI—just a frame with nothing inside. The frame was a container.

You know that every Java GUI application must have at least one container. At least the outermost component of every GUI application must be a container. Actually, it must be a heavyweight container.

Of course, you must use concrete container classes to create actual container instances in your programs. Table 4.6 lists the AWT container classes. They are all defined in the `java.awt` package.

TABLE 4.6 The AWT Container Classes

Class name	Superclass	Description
java.awt.Container	Component	An abstract class; ancestor of all container classes
java.awt.Frame	Window	A window with a border and menu bar
java.awt.Panel	Container	A general container for use inside windows
java.awt.Window	Container	A window with no border or menu bar

As you recall from the AWT inheritance hierarchy, a frame is a container. You should be able to add components to it; the frame will then have some children, and will be responsible for managing those children.

To add children to an AWT container, you simply use one of the `add()` methods described earlier. Listing 4.1 shows how you do this by simply adding a label to your container.

LISTING 4.1 Adding Components to a Container by Using Any of Several Overloaded `add()` Methods Defined by the `Component` Class

```
import java.awt.BorderLayout;
import java.awt.Dimension;
import java.awt.FlowLayout;
import java.awt.Font;
import java.awt.Frame;
```

continues

LISTING 4.1 Continued

```java
import java.awt.Label;
import java.awt.Panel;

class FrameWithComponents extends Frame
{
  /**
     No-arg constructor.  This constructor builds the GUI
     before it returns.  It sets the layout manager object
     used by this container.
     */
  public FrameWithComponents()
  {
    super("A frame with some components");
    setLayout(new FlowLayout());

    // This container contains a single component, the
    // label below.
    Label l = new Label("A simple label in a frame");
    add(l);
  }

  /**
     Specifies the preferred layout size for this
     container. This class prefers its instances
     to always be 300 by 300 pixels.

     @return the preferred size as a Dimension object.
     */
  public Dimension getPreferredSize()
  {
    return new Dimension(300, 300);
  }

  public static void main(String [] args)
  {
    FrameWithComponents f = new FrameWithComponents();
    f.pack();
    f.setVisible(true);
  }
}
```

Now instead of an empty frame, you have a frame that contains a simple label. If you run this application, it now looks like the picture in Figure 4.3.

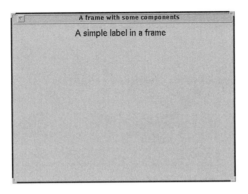

FIGURE 4.3
A frame that contains a label.

It's worthwhile taking a closer look at the structure of this example. It's an application so it has a `main()` method. The `main()` method is quite simple; it instantiates an object of your class and displays it.

The class that defines your application is essentially a container. By that I mean that you subclass one of the container types when you create a new class as the entry point of a new application. When your application starts, your `main()` method creates an instance of your class—which is a container. To that container you must add all the components you want to display.

The brunt of the work is done when the object instance is constructed. At that time, your code must build the whole visible GUI—at least the part that you want to appear when the GUI is rendered on screen for the first time.

Basically, your constructor(s) must do the work. Your constructor(s) can call upon other methods to help with the work, but the task must be completed before the object construction completes.

Notice in the example that your constructor indeed does contain the code that builds your component objects. This is typically the idiom that you will need to follow to build the visible GUI part of your application.

Of course you can add many components to a container. This is how you build up the visual appearance of your GUI application. In fact, you can add other components and other containers that themselves contain some components.

Listing 4.2 shows a more complicated GUI that contains several components.

LISTING 4.2   A Container With Multiple Child Components

```java
import java.awt.BorderLayout;
import java.awt.Button;
import java.awt.Dimension;
import java.awt.FlowLayout;
import java.awt.Font;
import java.awt.Frame;
import java.awt.Label;
import java.awt.List;
import java.awt.Panel;
import java.awt.TextField;

/**
   This class demonstrates how to add a component to a
   container.
*/
class MultipleComponents extends Frame
{
  /**
     No-arg constructor.  Builds the container and places
     several components in it.
  */
  public MultipleComponents()
  {
    super("A frame with some components");
    setLayout(new FlowLayout());

    Font font14 = new Font("SansSerif", Font.PLAIN, 14);
    Font font18 = new Font("SansSerif", Font.PLAIN, 18);

    // A Label component.
    label = new Label("A simple label in a frame");
    label.setFont(font18);

    // A Button component.
    button = new Button("Push me");
    button.setFont(font14);

    // A TextField component.
    textField = new TextField("A text field");
    textField.setFont(font14);

    // A List component.  Create a list object and populate
    // it with string items.
    //
```

```
    list = new List(7);
    list.setFont(font14);
    list.add("Button");
    list.add("Canvas");
    list.add("Checkbox");
    list.add("Label");
    list.add("List");
    list.add("Scrollbar");
    list.add("ScrollPane");
    list.add("TextField");
    list.add("TextArea");

    // Add the four components created above to the container.
    //
    add(label);
    add(button);
    add(textField);
    add(list);
  }

  public Dimension getPreferredSize()
  {
    return new Dimension(300, 300);
  }

  public static void main(String [] args)
  {
    MultipleComponents f = new MultipleComponents();
    f.pack();
    f.setVisible(true);
  }

  Button button;
  TextField textField;
  Label label;
  List list;

}

import java.awt.BorderLayout;
import java.awt.Button;
import java.awt.Dimension;
import java.awt.FlowLayout;
import java.awt.Font;
import java.awt.Frame;
```

continues

4

AWT
CONCEPTS AND
ARCHITECTURE

LISTING 4.2   Continued

```java
import java.awt.Label;
import java.awt.List;
import java.awt.Panel;
import java.awt.TextField;

class FrameWithMultipleComponents extends Frame
{
  public FrameWithMultipleComponents()
  {
    super("A Frame With Multiple Components");
    setLayout(new FlowLayout());

    label = new Label("A simple label in a frame");

    button = new Button("Push me");

    textField = new TextField("A text field");

    list = new List(7);
    list.add("Button");
    list.add("Canvas");
    list.add("Checkbox");
    list.add("Label");
    list.add("List");
    list.add("Scrollbar");
    list.add("ScrollPane");
    list.add("TextField");
    list.add("TextArea");

    add(label);
    add(button);
    add(textField);
    add(list);
  }

  public Dimension getPreferredSize()
  {
    return new Dimension(300, 300);
  }

  public static void main(String [] args)
  {
    FrameWithMultipleComponents f = new FrameWithMultipleComponents();
    f.pack();
```

```
    f.setVisible(true);
  }

  Button button;
  TextField textField;
  Label label;
  List list;
}
```

When you run this version, you can see that your frame now contains more components. Figure 4.4 shows what it looks like now.

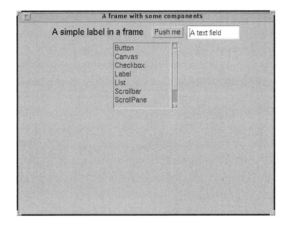

FIGURE 4.4
Sequentially adding components to a container inserts the components in the order they were added to the container.

The container doesn't do a very nice job of organizing its children. In fact, there doesn't seem to be much rhyme or reason to the structure. Organizing the layout of a container's components is the job of the container's layout manager object. I intentionally gloss over this issue here. Layout management is a complex topic and is discussed in Chapter 8.

One more item is noteworthy about the previous example. Notice that your component references are now defined in the class scope. The components you add to your container are not defined in the constructor. The reason for doing this is so that you can reference them later. Defining them in the class scope means they are accessible to all the methods in your class. If you kept their definition in the constructor, they would not be accessible to any other methods in your class.

This is important because you will later need these references to the elements of your GUI. As you will see in Chapter 9, after you create and display your GUI, it will typically receive events and respond to those events. Part of responding to events usually involves modifying the state of the visual components on the GUI. In order to do this, whatever code is handling the event and modifying the GUI needs to have access to a reference to the affected visual component. Therefore, programs should define variables that will be so affected in the class scope.

Using Nested Containers for Organization

The way it stands now, your GUI is not very well organized. It's difficult to see any rhyme or reason to the way the components are laid out in the container. Consequently, it's difficult to grasp the purpose of this GUI, what it's supposed to do, or what abstraction it attempts to create. Moreover, it doesn't look very aesthetically pleasing. Somehow you need to add better organization and structure to your GUI.

Furthermore, as I mentioned in the previous section, managing the components in a container quickly becomes a daunting task as you add more and more components. It's difficult to remember which component is where in the container.

This is where you can benefit from the fact that containers are components; you are able to include other containers as part of a container's set of children. You can use this capability as a tool to help you organize your GUI. By nesting containers inside other containers, you can create a *logical hierarchy* of containers, each of which contains its own subset of the components that comprise your GUI. You can logically *nest* the components into subsets and manage the organization and arrangement of each of the subsets individually.

In Chapter 1, "UI Programming Concepts," I introduced some concepts regarding good GUI design. Its central theme is that the visual GUI should make sense to the user. It must be well organized so that what it does and how one should use it are relatively self-evident. Effective organization of your GUI's visual components plays an important role in achieving this clarity.

If you simply continue to add components to your GUI's single container, it will not only look ugly and disorganized, but also it will be difficult for you to keep track of what's where and how to modify the look and organization if you want to make changes or add components.

Listing 4.3 shows your previous GUI restructured to have a more organized, cleaner layout. It uses some additional containers to produce a nested hierarchy of components.

LISTING 4.3   Using Nested Containers To Organize Child Components

```
import java.awt.BorderLayout;
import java.awt.Button;
import java.awt.Dimension;
import java.awt.FlowLayout;
import java.awt.Font;
```

```
import java.awt.GridLayout;
import java.awt.Frame;
import java.awt.Label;
import java.awt.List;
import java.awt.Panel;
import java.awt.TextField;

/**
   A class that demonstrates the use of multiple nested
   containers to organize the location of its components.
*/
class MultipleContainers extends Frame
{
  /**
     No-arg constructor.
  */
  public MultipleContainers()
  {
    super("A frame with some components");
    setLayout(new GridLayout(4,1));

    Font font14 = new Font("SansSerif", Font.PLAIN, 14);
    Font font18 = new Font("SansSerif", Font.PLAIN, 18);

    // A Label component.
    //
    label = new Label("A simple label in a frame");
    label.setFont(font18);

    // Create a new container.  This is an internal
    // container nested inside the main application
    // container (the Frame).
    //
    Panel panel1 = new Panel();

    // Add the Label component to this container.
    panel1.add(label);

    // A Button component.
    //
    button = new Button("Push me");
    button.setFont(font14);

    // Create a second internal container.  Add the button
    // to this second panel.
    //
```

continues

LISTING 4.3   Continued

```
Panel panel2 = new Panel();
panel2.add(button);

// A TextField component.
//
textField = new TextField("A text field");
textField.setFont(font14);

// Create a third internal container.  Add the text
// field to it.
//
Panel panel3 = new Panel();
panel3.add(textField);

// Create and populate a List component.
//
list = new List(4);
list.setFont(font14);
list.add("Button");
list.add("Canvas");
list.add("Checkbox");
list.add("Label");
list.add("List");
list.add("Scrollbar");
list.add("ScrollPane");
list.add("TextField");
list.add("TextArea");

// Create a fourth nested container.  Add the list to it.
//
Panel panel4 = new Panel();
panel4.add(list);

// Now add the four internal panels to our class instance.
// This step creates the nesting.
//
add(panel1);
add(panel2);
add(panel3);
add(panel4);

// Notice that we create and add these two buttons to panel2
// after we've added the other components to their panels.
// The buttons still show up on top of the text field and list
// components on the GUI because they are added to a different
// container, panel2, which is added to the application container
```

```
    // ahead of the panel that contains the text field.
    //
    Button button2 = new Button("Push me too");
    button2.setFont(font14);
    panel2.add(button2);

    Button button3 = new Button("Me first");
    button3.setFont(font14);
    panel2.add(button3);
  }

  public Dimension getPreferredSize()
  {
    return new Dimension(300, 300);
  }

  public static void main(String [] args)
  {
    MultipleContainers f = new MultipleContainers();
    f.pack();
    f.setVisible(true);
  }

  Button button;
  TextField textField;
  Label label;
  List list;
}


import java.awt.BorderLayout;
import java.awt.Button;
import java.awt.Dimension;
import java.awt.FlowLayout;
import java.awt.Font;
import java.awt.GridLayout;
import java.awt.Frame;
import java.awt.Label;
import java.awt.List;
import java.awt.Panel;
import java.awt.TextField;

class MultipleContainers extends Frame
{
  public MultipleContainers()
  {

    super("A frame with some components");
    setLayout(new GridLayout(4,1));
```

Now your GUI looks different because the additional containers you use enforce a certain nesting of the components. You now have more than one container in your program, and not all your components are in the container defined by your class instance. Your class instance contains the other containers, which contain the components.

Figure 4.5 shows your new GUI. Notice that even though you added the second and third buttons *after* you added the text field and list components, they are still grouped adjacent to the first button. The reason is that you didn't add them to your original container—your class instance itself. You added them to one of the nested containers, called `panel2` in your source code.

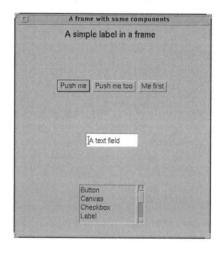

FIGURE 4.5

Using nested containers makes it easy to organize complex GUIs that contain many components. This GUI contains six containers, four of which are used only for nesting.

Your new GUI has no less than six containers. The top-level frame is the outermost container. The instance of your class is a panel. And you created four internal panels that are all nested—contained—in your class instance. You can't see them, but they are there. In cases like this where you use additional panels for organization, you often don't want them to be visible. It's not important to the user *how* you create the GUI, just that it looks organized and logical.

The grouping and arrangement of each set of components are done by the container to which they are added. You can now add components to any of your internal containers without affecting the arrangement of components in any other container. This is how nesting containers helps you organize your GUI's visual layout. It also helps you organize your application logically. Components can be grouped in the way that makes the most sense in terms of the application. Nesting containers also makes this process more manageable.

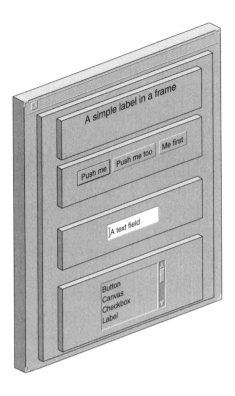

FIGURE 4.6

Nesting containers in containers produces a containment hierarchy that allows easier management of your GUI components.

Theoretically, this nesting can go on indefinitely, limited only by your system memory, performance issues, and your ability to now keep track of all the containers and the nesting abstraction you've created!

In Chapter 8, you will learn that each of these containers has its own layout manager object. Each container has an associated layout manager object that manages the layout of the container's components. Each container can use a separate layout manager, and, thus, lay out its children independently of all other containers. Each container can choose the layout policy that is most suitable for it, and that allows you to organize the container's children in the arrangement you desire.

How AWT Containers Store Children

There is one very important point that you should remember about the preceding examples. When you are programming with the AWT containers, you simply add components to the container directly. All AWT containers implement the same model; they have only one way of storing children. The children are maintained as a list of references. (Implementation details should not concern you at this time!) The point is that there is only one "place" where an AWT container can store its child components.

In Chapter 7, "The Swing Components," I will introduce the Swing components and containers, and you will see that those container classes implement a different containment model. It is important to delineate the abstractions manifested by the two models. Adding components to Swing containers is not as straightforward. It is important not to confuse the differences in the containment abstractions manifested by the two toolkits.

Front-to-Back Component Ordering in Containers

When a container is repainted, all of its children are also repainted; for instance, if the container window is exposed after being hidden by another screen element. The order in which components are added to a container affect the order in which they are rendered and the resulting appearance of the components.

As you saw in the previous examples, components are added to containers one by one. The container classes maintain an ordered list of their children. Components that are added first are referred to as being closer to the front of the list than components added later, which are closer to the back of the list.

The order that components are painted corresponds to the order in which they are added to a container. The AWT in Release 1.1 of the JDK guarantees this behavior. This results in a *z-ordering* or front-to-back ordering of the components in a container. The term z-order refers to the apparent stacking of components along the z axis, which protrudes outward perpendicularly from the screen's x-y plane.

Thus, the first component added to a container is painted first, the second next, and so on. This means that if components overlap in the z direction, the component that comes later in the container's list will be rendered visibly over any components that are in a position closer to the beginning of the list. Components overlap if their bounds intersect.

The AWT containers don't really define a containment model that abstracts the notion of stacking along the z axis. Only if the bounds of two or more components overlap do we think that components can be stacked. Actually, this is just an abstraction interpreted by the person viewing the GUI.

Nevertheless, it can be a problem. If you intentionally have components with overlapping bounds, and you want to ensure that they are painted in a certain way, you must alter the order in which they are added to their container. By altering the order in which they are placed in the container, you can achieve the correct apparent stacking.

The standard layout managers, however, always lay out a container's children so that they never overlap. Nevertheless, you can define your own layout managers that do allow overlapping.

Summary

In this chapter, I've introduced the AWT components and containers. Components are the visual building blocks of all Java GUI programs. All component definitions derive from the `java.awt.Component` class, and thus share a common set of attributes and behaviors.

Containers are defined by the `java.awt.Container` class, which is a direct subclass of `Component`. Containers are, therefore, a special kind of component. They add the capability to contain other components.

Java GUI programs are a collection of components and containers. Every Java GUI must have at least one heavyweight container that contains all of the program's components.

You can choose one of two schemes to organize the structure of your GUI. Your class can subclass a non-window container, and then explicitly create the window in which to place the container. Alternatively, you can subclass a window class that directly holds the contents of your GUI.

At this point you have a conceptual understanding of the role of components and containers. You understand how the AWT works, and you also know how to structure your GUI application or applet to fit the AWT organizational and behavioral models.

The next step is to build a more complicated GUI. To do this, you need some facility with the elements that make up a GUI, namely, the concrete AWT components. Chapter 5, "The AWT Components," introduces you to the AWT component set, and teaches you how to use these basic building blocks to help you create more sophisticated GUIs.

The AWT Components

IN THIS CHAPTER

- The AWT Components   102

So far, I've emphasized more concepts than pragmatic programming. You've become familiar with the concepts and ideas upon which Java GUI programming, and the Swing architecture in particular, are built.

At this point, you know how to organize a GUI program and get it to display. The sample GUI screens did not have much on them, however. It's now time to introduce some actual components—real widgets—that you can use to build more functional GUIs.

This chapter introduces the AWT component set. You will look at the basic visual components, how to construct them and add them to a GUI, and how to use their basic features. It is still possible to build complete GUI applications using only the original AWT components. Therefore, it is useful to examine the contents of the AWT package.

This chapter is presented to aid those who must still build Java GUI programs using only the AWT components and not Swing's new lightweight components. However, you are strongly encouraged to use the new lightweight components if you are starting fresh.

The Personal Java platform for embedded programming does not support Swing so you need to use the AWT for that environment.

The AWT Components

The AWT components are defined in the `java.awt` package. Table 2.2 lists the AWT components defined in the `java.awt` package. By now you know that this package is part of the JFC since the JDK 1.1 release. All AWT components are JFC components. However, they are implemented as heavyweight components. Each AWT component instance creates a corresponding native platform peer object.

Components appear on the GUI display, so users can interact with them. User actions such as clicking a button, scrolling a scrollbar, typing in a text field, and so on generate events. Even though events are related to components, I do not cover events or how to handle them in this chapter. I devote Chapter 9, "Events and Event Handling," to this topic.

Without further ado, let's look at the basic AWT components.

Buttons

Buttons are simple components that can be clicked. A button can be created with a text label. In Chapter 9, you'll see that clicking a button creates an event to which your program can respond.

Listing 5.1 shows the source code that displays the GUI shown in Figure 5.1. Figure 5.1 shows three buttons with different visual states that represent the different possible visual states of all AWT buttons.

Notice that this application creates its third button with no label, but sets the label with the setLabel() method. There is also a complementary getLabel() method defined in the Button class.

LISTING 5.1   The Different Possible States of a Button

```java
import java.awt.Button;
import java.awt.Component;
import java.awt.Font;
import java.awt.Frame;
import java.awt.Panel;

public class Buttons extends Panel
{
  /**
     No-arg constructor. Builds the entire visible GUI before
     it returns.
  */
  public Buttons()
  {
    Font f18 = new Font("SansSerif", Font.PLAIN, 18);

    Button b1 = new Button("Enabled button");
    Button b2 = new Button("Disabled button");

    Button b3 = new Button();
    b3.setLabel("Depressed button");

    b1.setFont(f18);

    // The second button is initially disabled.
    //
    b2.setFont(f18);
    b2.setEnabled(false);

    b3.setFont(f18);

    add(b1);
    add(b2);
    add(b3);
  }

  public static void main(String [] args)
  {
    Buttons app = new Buttons();
```

continues

LISTING 5.1   Continued

```
    Frame f = new Frame("Buttons");
    f.add(app);
    f.pack();
    f.setVisible(true);
  }
}
```

FIGURE 5.1

Buttons are rendered differently depending on their state.

Table 5.1 lists the methods in the Button class that pertain to manipulating the button.

TABLE 5.1   Button Constructors and Methods

Button *constructors and methods*	*Description*
Button()	No-arg constructor. Creates a button with no label.
Button(String label)	Constructor. Creates a button with the specified label.
String getLabel()	Gets this button's label.
void setLabel(String label)	Sets this button's label.

Also note that you did not have to set the visibility of your buttons so that they would appear on screen. Back in Chapter 3, you had to call setVisible(true) and pack() on your frames so that the application would appear on screen. To set a component's visibility to true means that the component should be visible when its parent is visible.

You only have to set visibility for top-level components such as frames. Other components, such as the ones I discuss in this chapter, are visible by default. They will appear on screen when their parent is made visible.

When a component is enabled, it can accept events. In Figure 5.1, the disabled button cannot accept events because it has been disabled.

Check Boxes

A check box is a component that can be either on or off, that is, either selected or not. You toggle a check box's state by clicking on it. Listing 5.2 shows how you can add some check boxes to a panel, and initialize them to be selected or not.

LISTING 5.2   Standalone Check Boxes and Grouped Check Boxes

```java
import java.awt.Checkbox;
import java.awt.CheckboxGroup;
import java.awt.Font;
import java.awt.Frame;
import java.awt.GridLayout;
import java.awt.Panel;

public class Checkboxes extends Panel
{
  /**
     No-arg constructor.  Builds the complete visible GUI
     before it returns.
  */
  public Checkboxes()
  {
    setLayout(new GridLayout(2, 3));
    Font f18 = new Font("SansSerif", Font.PLAIN, 18);
    Font f14 = new Font("SansSerif", Font.PLAIN, 14);

    Checkbox c1 = new Checkbox("Checkbox 1");
    Checkbox c2 = new Checkbox();
    c2.setLabel("Checkbox 2");
    c2.setEnabled(false);

    Checkbox c3 = new Checkbox("Checkbox 3");

    // Create a CheckboxGroup object to manage the states of
    // the second row of check boxes.
    //
    CheckboxGroup group = new CheckboxGroup();

    Checkbox c4 = new Checkbox("Checkbox 4", group, true);
    Checkbox c5 = new Checkbox("Checkbox 5", group, true);
    Checkbox c6 = new Checkbox("Checkbox 6", group, true);

    // Make the text more readable.
    //
```

continues

LISTING 5.2   Continued

```
    c1.setFont(f18);
    c2.setFont(f18);
    c3.setFont(f18);
    c4.setFont(f18);
    c5.setFont(f18);
    c6.setFont(f18);

    add(c1);
    add(c2);
    add(c3);
    add(c4);
    add(c5);
    add(c6);
  }

  public static void main(String [] args)
  {
    Checkboxes app = new Checkboxes();

    Frame f = new Frame("Checkboxes");
    f.add(app);
    f.pack();
    f.setVisible(true);
  }
}
```

Figure 5.2 shows what this program's GUI looks like. The first row contains three check boxes that exist independently of each other. Any combination of them can be selected. The example shows numbers one and three selected, while number two is disabled.

The three checkboxes in the second row are part of a CheckboxGroup. You can see from Listing 5.2 that we added all of them to the group in their enabled state. CheckboxGroup objects are not visible; they serve only an organizational role. In the AWT, a group of check boxes can only have one member selected at any given time.

Also notice that the glyph for the two types of check boxes are different. The independent check boxes have square glyphs, whereas the check boxes that are part of a group have diamond shaped glyphs. This helps you determine their organization and membership.

The actual glyphs used may vary from platform to platform. It is the native peer which dictates the actual look of an AWT component. For example, Windows does not use the diamond glyph to display check boxes.

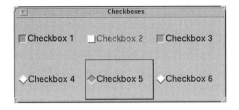

FIGURE 5.2

Check boxes can be organized in groups that allow only one to be selected at once.

Table 5.2 shows the methods in the Checkbox class.

TABLE 5.2   Checkbox Constructors and Methods

Checkbox *constructors and methods*	*Description*
Checkbox()	No-arg constructor. Constructs a check box with no label.
Checkbox(String label)	Constructs a check box with this label.
Checkbox(String label, boolean state)	Constructs a check box with this label and the specified enabled/disabled state.
Checkbox(String label, boolean state, CheckboxGroup group)	Constructs a check box with this label and the specified enabled/disabled state, and belonging to the check box group.
CheckboxGroup getCheckboxGroup()	Gets the group to which this check box belongs.
String getLabel()	Gets this check box's label.
Object [] getSelectedObjects()	Gets an array containing the label of this check box's label, or null if it's not selected.
boolean getState()	Gets the enabled/disabled state.
void setCheckboxGroup (ChecboxGroup g)	Sets the group to which this check box belongs.
void setLabel(String label)	Sets the label for this check box.
void setState(boolean state)	Sets the enabled/disabled state.

Choices

The Choice class gives you a way to create a pop-up menu of selections. A choice component looks somewhat like a button, but has a distinctive face. Clicking on a choice component drops down a type of menu (in appearance, but not the same as a real menu). You can select one of the elements in the choice object.

Listing 5.3 shows code that builds such a choice component and Figure 5.3 shows what a choice component looks like. Figure 5.4 shows the choice element when it is expanded.

LISTING 5.3   Constructing a Choice Component and Adding Elements to It

```java
import java.awt.Choice;
import java.awt.Dimension;
import java.awt.Font;
import java.awt.Frame;
import java.awt.GridLayout;
import java.awt.Panel;

public class Choices extends Panel
{
  public Choices()
  {
    Font f18 = new Font("SansSerif", Font.PLAIN, 18);
    Font f14 = new Font("SansSerif", Font.PLAIN, 14);

    // Create a choice object and add the string items to it.
    //
    Choice c = new Choice();

    c.addItem(new String("Albinoni"));
    c.addItem(new String("Bach"));
    c.addItem(new String("Beethoven"));
    c.addItem(new String("Brahms"));
    c.addItem(new String("Chopin"));
    c.addItem(new String("Debussey"));
    c.addItem(new String("Gluck"));
    c.addItem(new String("Kachaturian"));
    c.addItem(new String("Mahler"));

    c.setFont(f18);

    add(c);
  }
```

```
public Dimension getPreferredSize()
{
  return new Dimension(175, 300);
}

public static void main(String [] args)
{
  Choices app = new Choices();

  Frame f = new Frame("Choices");
  f.add(app);
  f.pack();
  f.setVisible(true);
}
}
```

FIGURE 5.3
Choice components let you choose one of a list of choices.

FIGURE 5.4
A choice component after the user has clicked on it.

Table 5.3 shows the constructor and methods of the `Choice` class.

TABLE 5.3   Choice Class Constructors and Methods

Choice *constructors and methods*	*Description*
`Choice()`	No-arg constructor.
`void add(String item)`	Adds an item to this choice.
`void addItem(String item)`	Adds an item to this choice.
`String getItem(int index)`	Gets the name of the item at the specified index.
`int getItemCount()`	Gets the number of items in this choice.
`int getSelectedIndex()`	Gets the index of the selected item.
`int getSelectedItem()`	Gets the name of the selected item.
`Object [] getSelectedObjects()`	Gets an array of length one that contains the selected item.
`void insert(String item, int index)`	Inserts a new item with the string name indicated at the specified index.
`void select(int pos)`	Selects the item in the indicated position.
`void select(String str)`	Sets the selected choice item to be the one whose name matches the string.

Dialogs

So far the components you've seen have been direct subclasses of `java.awt.Component`. Dialogs, however, are direct subclasses of `java.awt.Window`. A dialog is a window that can be displayed independently of the main window of your application. Dialogs, like frames, have a border and menu bar.

There are some differences between dialogs and frames. Each dialog must have an associated frame, which is its owner. For instance, the main frame of your application might be the owner of any dialog it pops up.

If the associated frame is made into an icon or terminated, any associated dialogs will disappear from the screen. Redisplaying (restoring) the main window will also redisplay any dialogs that were open when the window was minimized.

Dialogs can be *modal*, which means that the user must dismiss the displayed dialog before interacting with any other part of the application that owns the dialog. Typically, a dialog will have a do and cancel button or equivalents.

Listing 5.4 shows a dialog box in action. Clicking on the button in the main frame of the application will bring up a dialog box. Notice that a reference to the main application frame is passed to the `Dialog` constructor, specifying the dialog's owner.

Don't worry about any event handling code in this application that looks foreign right now. You will learn about event handling in Chapter 9.

LISTING 5.4   Creating a Dialog from a Parent Frame

```java
import java.awt.BorderLayout;
import java.awt.Button;
import java.awt.Dialog;
import java.awt.FlowLayout;
import java.awt.Font;
import java.awt.Frame;
import java.awt.Dimension;
import java.awt.GridLayout;
import java.awt.Label;
import java.awt.Panel;

import java.awt.event.ActionEvent;
import java.awt.event.ActionListener;

/**
   Defines a simple frame.  The dialog created by this
   example must have an associated frame.  An instance of
   this class provides that frame.

   <p> We don't need to specify a getPreferredSize() method
   because we are adding a button to the frame.  The size
   required by the button will be the minimum size allocated
   for the frame.
*/
public class DialogExample extends Frame implements ActionListener
{
  /**
     Constructor. Creates an instance of a frame with a
     button. Pressing the button brings up a dialog.

     @param title the title of the frame, not the dialog.
  */
  public DialogExample(String title)
  {
    super(title);
```

continues

LISTING 5.4   Continued

```
   Font f18 = new Font("SansSerif", Font.PLAIN, 18);
   Font f14 = new Font("SansSerif", Font.PLAIN, 14);

   Button b = new Button("Bring up dialog");
   b.setFont(f18);
   b.addActionListener(this);

   Panel p = new Panel();
   p.add(b);

   add(p);
 }

 public void actionPerformed(ActionEvent e)
 {
   d = new CustomDialog(this, "Make a decision", true);
   d.setVisible(true);
 }

 public static void main(String [] args)
 {
   DialogExample app = new DialogExample("Dialog Example");

   app.pack();
   app.setVisible(true);
 }

 Dialog d;
}


/**
   Creates a dialog box.  Dialog boxes must be associated
   with a frame.
*/
class CustomDialog extends Dialog
{
 /**
    Constructor.  Builds a dialog box.  A reference to a
    frame is required to create a dialog.

    @param parent the associated parent frame of this dialog.

    @param title this dialog's title.

    @param modal the behavior of the
```

```
        dialog. <code>true</code> means modal, otherwise it's
        non-modal.
    */
    CustomDialog(Frame parent, String title, boolean modal)
    {
        super(parent, title, modal);

        Panel p1 = new Panel(new FlowLayout(FlowLayout.LEFT));
        Label question = new Label("And now what?");
        question.setFont(new Font("SansSerif", Font.PLAIN, 18));
        p1.add(question);

        add(p1, BorderLayout.CENTER);

        Panel p2 = new Panel(new FlowLayout(FlowLayout.RIGHT));

        dontknow = new Button("Don't know");
        dontknow.setFont(new Font("SansSerif", Font.PLAIN, 18));
        cancel = new Button("Cancel");
        cancel.setFont(new Font("SansSerif", Font.PLAIN, 18));

        p2.add(dontknow);
        p2.add(cancel);

        add(p2, BorderLayout.SOUTH);
        pack();
    }


    Button dontknow;
    Button cancel;
}
```

Figure 5.5 displays the main frame and the dialog box that appears after clicking the frame's button. Table 5.4 lists the methods of the `Dialog` class.

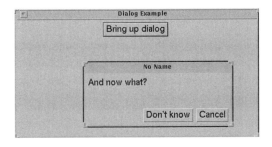

FIGURE 5.5

Dialogs appear in their own native platform frame.

TABLE 5.4   Dialog Class Constructors and Methods

Dialog *constructor* *or method name*	*Description*
`Dialog(Dialog owner)`	Constructs a dialog with another dialog as its owner.
`Dialog(Dialog owner,` `String title)`	Constructs a dialog with the specified title and the dialog as its owner.
`Dialog(Dialog owner,` `String title, boolean modal)`	Constructs a dialog with the specified modal behavior and name, and the specified dialog as its owner.
`Dialog(Frame owner)`	Constructs a dialog with the specified frame as its owner.
`Dialog(Frame owner,` `boolean modal)`	Constructs a dialog with the specified frame as its owner and the given modal behavior.
`Dialog(Frame owner,` `String title)`	Constructs a dialog with the frame as owner and the specified title.
`Dialog(Frame owner,` `String title, boolean modal)`	Constructs a dialog with the specified modal behavior and title, and the specified frame as its owner.
`String getTitle()`	Gets the dialog's title.
`boolean isModal()`	Indicates if this dialog is modal.
`boolean isResizable()`	Indicates if this dialog is resizable.
`void setModal(boolean modal)`	Sets the dialog's modal behavior as specified.
`void setResizable` `(boolean resizable)`	Sets the dialog's resizing behavior as specified.
`void setTitle(String title)`	Sets the dialogs title.
`void show()`	Must be called to make the dialog visible.

Labels

Labels are components that contain a simple text string that can appear in a container. Labels are not selectable like the text in text fields or text areas, which I will introduce in the following section. However, because labels are bona fide components, they can be placed in containers like any other component.

You can set the lateral alignment of a label's text to specify that it be anchored at the left, center, or right of the area allocated for the label's layout. The valid values for specifying the label's anchor position are the constants `Label.LEFT`, `Label.CENTER`, or `Label.RIGHT`.

Listing 5.5 shows the source code for the program that creates Figure 5.6. Figure 5.6 shows the GUI produced by the program in Listing 5.5. The left column labels are right justified and the right column labels are left justified. The position of the label text doesn't represent the extent of the area allocated for the label component. Most likely, the bounds of the label extend beyond the left edge of the text for right-justified text, and beyond the right edge for left-justified text.

LISTING 5.5   Program That Demonstrates Labels with Different Alignments

```
import java.awt.Choice;
import java.awt.Font;
import java.awt.Frame;
import java.awt.GridLayout;
import java.awt.Label;
import java.awt.Panel;

/**
   Creates a panel of labels with various alignments.  No
   getPreferredSize() method is needed.  The layout manager
   will call the inherited version.  The size of the panel
   will be at least the size required to lay out all of the
   labels that are children of the panel.
*/
public class Labels extends Panel
{
  /**
     No-arg constructor.
  */
  public Labels()
  {
    Font f18 = new Font("SansSerif", Font.PLAIN, 18);
    Font f14 = new Font("SansSerif", Font.PLAIN, 14);

    // This label's text is aligned to the right edge of its
    // display area.
    Label name = new Label("Name :   ");
    name.setAlignment(Label.RIGHT);
    name.setFont(f14);

    // This label's text is aligned to the left edge of its
    // display area.
    Label nameVal = new Label("Jim Morrison");
    nameVal.setAlignment(Label.LEFT);
    nameVal.setFont(f14);

    Label address = new Label("Address :   ");
    address.setAlignment(Label.RIGHT);
    address.setFont(f14);
```

continues

LISTING 5.5   Continued

```java
        Label addVal = new Label("Cimetiere Pere LaChese");
        addVal.setAlignment(Label.LEFT);
        addVal.setFont(f14);

        Label city = new Label("City/State/Zip :   ");
        city.setAlignment(Label.RIGHT);
        city.setFont(f14);

        Label cityVal = new Label("Paris, France Cedex 01432");
        cityVal.setAlignment(Label.LEFT);
        cityVal.setFont(f14);

        Label phone = new Label("Phone :   ");
        phone.setAlignment(Label.RIGHT);
        phone.setFont(f14);

        Label phoneVal = new Label("213-555-1212");
        phoneVal.setAlignment(Label.LEFT);
        phoneVal.setFont(f14);

        Panel p = new Panel();
        p.setLayout(new GridLayout(0, 2));
        p.add(name);
        p.add(nameVal);
        p.add(address);
        p.add(addVal);
        p.add(city);
        p.add(cityVal);
        p.add(phone);
        p.add(phoneVal);

        add(p);
    }

    public static void main(String [] args)
    {
        Labels app = new Labels();

        Frame f = new Frame("Labels");
        f.add(app);
        f.pack();
        f.setVisible(true);
    }
}
```

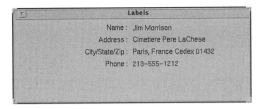

FIGURE 5.6
Labels are simple components that display a string of text. They can be manipulated just like other components.

Table 5.5 shows the constructors and methods of the Label class.

TABLE 5.5   Dialog Class Constructors and Methods

Label *constructor or method name*	*Description*
Label()	Constructs an empty label.
Label(String text)	Constructs a label with the specified text.
Label(String text, int alignment)	Constructs a label with the specified text and alignment.
int getAlignment()	Gets the label's alignment.
String getText()	Gets the label's text.
void setAlignment(int alignment)	Sets the label's alignment
void setText(String text)	Sets the label's text.

Lists

Lists are groups of items that are formatted inside a kind of scrolling pane. The list can be scrolled up and down in order to see all its elements. The list gives you a window in which to view some subset of the list elements.

Lists can be single selection or multiple selection, which means, respectively, that only one, or multiple items can be selected simultaneously. Selected elements can be retrieved from a list component and used for various purposes by your application.

Listing 5.6 shows a program that creates a list in a container. Don't worry about any code that looks unfamiliar; I will get to it soon enough.

The GUI created by this program is shown in Figure 5.7. The left list of Figure 5.7 uses a single selection model, while the right list uses a multiple selection model.

LISTING 5.6   Program That Demonstrates Single and Multiple Selection Lists

```java
import java.awt.Choice;
import java.awt.Font;
import java.awt.Frame;
import java.awt.GridLayout;
import java.awt.GridBagLayout;
import java.awt.GridBagConstraints;
import java.awt.Insets;
import java.awt.Label;
import java.awt.List;
import java.awt.Panel;

/**
   A class that creates two juxtaposed lists.  The left-hand
   list only supports the selection of a single item.  The
   right-hand list supports the selection of multiple items.
   Again, no getPreferredSize() method is needed.
*/
public class Lists extends Panel
{
  /**
     No-arg constructor.
  */
  public Lists()
  {
    Font f18 = new Font("SansSerif", Font.PLAIN, 18);
    Font f14 = new Font("SansSerif", Font.PLAIN, 14);

    Label single = new Label("A single selection list");
    single.setFont(f14);

    // The single selection list.
    //
    List singleList = new List(6, false);
    singleList.setFont(f14);

    singleList.add(new String("Ludwig von Beethoven"));
    singleList.add(new String("Lee Ritenaur"));
    singleList.add(new String("Thelonious Monk"));
    singleList.add(new String("Elton John"));
    singleList.add(new String("Julio Eglesias"));
    singleList.add(new String("Benny Goodman"));

    Label multiple = new Label("A multiple selection list");
    multiple.setFont(f14);
```

```
    // The multiple selection list.
    //
    List multipleList = new List(6);
    multipleList.setMultipleMode(true);
    multipleList.setFont(f14);

    multipleList.add(new String("Classical"));
    multipleList.add(new String("Pop"));
    multipleList.add(new String("Rock"));
    multipleList.add(new String("Swing"));
    multipleList.add(new String("Jazz"));

    GridBagLayout gbl = new GridBagLayout();
    GridBagConstraints gbc = new GridBagConstraints();
    setLayout(gbl);

    gbl.setConstraints(single, gbc);
    add(single);

    gbc.insets = new Insets(5, 5, 5, 5);
    gbc.gridx = GridBagConstraints.RELATIVE;
    gbl.setConstraints(multiple, gbc);
    add(multiple);

    gbc.gridx = 0;
    gbc.gridy = GridBagConstraints.RELATIVE;
    gbl.setConstraints(singleList, gbc);
    add(singleList);

    gbc.gridx = GridBagConstraints.RELATIVE;
    gbc.gridy = 1;
    gbl.setConstraints(multipleList, gbc);
    add(multipleList);
  }

  public static void main(String [] args)
  {
    Lists app = new Lists();

    Frame f = new Frame("Lists");
    f.add(app);
    f.pack();
    f.setVisible(true);
  }
}
```

Figure 5.7 shows an example of a list.

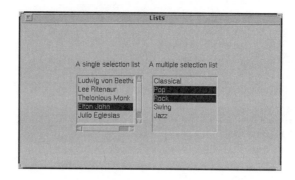

FIGURE 5.7

Lists give you a way to aggregate strings. They can support both single and multiple selection behavior.

Table 5.6 lists most of the methods in the `List` class. Again, I omit methods related to event handling at this time.

TABLE 5.6   List Constructors and Methods

List *constructor or method name*	*Description*
`List()`	Creates a new scrolling list.
`List(int rows)`	Creates a new list with the number of visible rows specified.
`List(int rows, boolean multipleMode)`	Creates a new list with the number of visible rows and the specified selection mode behavior.
`void add(String item)`	Adds a new item to the list.
`void add(String item, int index)`	Adds a new item at the specified position.
`void addItem(String item)`	Adds a new item to the list.
`void addItem(String item, int index)`	Adds a new item at the specified position.
`void deselect(int index)`	Deselects the item at the specified index.
`String getItem(int index)`	Gets the item at the specified index.
`int getItemCount()`	Gets the number of elements in the list
`String [] getItems()`	Gets an array of the element names.
`int getRows()`	Gets the number of lines that are currently visible.
`int getSelectedIndex()`	Gets the index of the selected item.

List *constructor or method name*	*Description*
`int [] getSelectedIndexes()`	Gets a list of items that are all selected.
`String getSelectedItem()`	Gets the string that represents the text of the selected item.
`String [] getSelectedItems()`	Gets a list of the strings that represent the selected items.
`Object [] getSelectedObjects()`	Gets a list of selected strings as `Objects`.
`int getVisibleIndex()`	Gets the index of the item that was last made visible by the `makeVisible()` method.
`boolean isIndexSelected (int index)`	Indicates if the specified index represents a selected element.
`boolean isMultipleMode()`	Indicates if multiple elements can be simultaneously selected.
`void makeVisible(int index)`	Makes the item at the specified index visible.
`void remove(int position)`	Removes the item at the specified position.
`void remove(String item)`	Removes the first occurrence of the item that matches the string.
`void removeAll()`	Removes all items from this list.
`void replaceItem(String newValue, int index)`	Replaces the item at the specified position with the new item.
`void select(int index)`	Selects the item at the specified position.
`void setMultipleMode (boolean b)`	Makes this list use a multiple selection policy.

Menus

Menus are elements that are included as members of menu bars. A menu bar can be placed on a frame. The frame manages its location and layout.

Menus display a list of member menu items when clicked. Selecting the menu item usually results in some action performed by the application. These components behave as their counterparts in other window programming environments.

Menus contain menu items. These two elements are defined by the `Menu` and `MenuItem` classes. Menu bars are defined by the `MenuBar` class.

Menu items can be either simple labels, separators—simply horizontal lines that separate menu items—or other menus. Listing 5.7 shows the program that creates some menus on a menu bar. The menu bar is attached to a frame. The GUI is shown in Figure 5.8.

You can see examples of all the types of menu items, simple labels, separators, and other menus that produce walking menus.

LISTING 5.7   Program That Demonstrates How to Use Menus and Menu Items

```java
import java.awt.Choice;
import java.awt.Dimension;
import java.awt.Font;
import java.awt.Frame;
import java.awt.GridLayout;
import java.awt.GridBagLayout;
import java.awt.GridBagConstraints;
import java.awt.Insets;
import java.awt.Label;
import java.awt.List;
import java.awt.Menu;
import java.awt.MenuBar;
import java.awt.MenuItem;
import java.awt.Panel;

/**
   A class that creates a frame with three menus.
*/
public class Menus extends Frame
{
  /**
     Constructor.  Builds the menus and attaches them to the
     frame.  This constructor builds the entire visible GUI.

     <p>Constructors can call other methods to help them do
     the construction job.  For example, each menu could
     have been constructed by a helper method.

     @param title the title of the frame that contains the
     menus.
  */
  public Menus(String title)
  {
    super(title);

    Font f18 = new Font("SansSerif", Font.PLAIN, 18);
    Font f14 = new Font("SansSerif", Font.PLAIN, 14);

    // The "File" menu.  This menu appears to the far left
    // of the menu bar. This menu contains three menu items.
    //
    Menu file = new Menu("File");
```

```
file.setFont(f14);

// Create the three menu items for the "File" menu.
//
MenuItem open = new MenuItem("Open...");
open.setFont(f14);
MenuItem openOW = new MenuItem("Open in other window...");
openOW.setFont(f14);
MenuItem openOF = new MenuItem("Open in other frame...");
openOF.setFont(f14);

// Add the three menu items to the menu.
//
file.add(open);
file.add(openOW);
file.add(openOF);

// The "Edit" menu.  This menu appears immediately to
// the right of the "File" menu.
//
Menu edit = new Menu("Edit");
edit.setFont(f14);

// Create the menu items for the "Edit" menu.
//
MenuItem undo = new MenuItem("Undo");
undo.setFont(f14);
MenuItem cut = new MenuItem("Cut");
cut.setFont(f14);
MenuItem copy = new MenuItem("Copy");
copy.setFont(f14);
MenuItem paste = new MenuItem("Paste");
paste.setFont(f14);

// Add the "Edit" menu items to the menu.
//
edit.add(undo);
edit.add(cut);
edit.add(copy);
edit.add(paste);

// The "Help" menu.
//
Menu help = new Menu("Help");
help.setFont(f14);
MenuItem about = new MenuItem("About...");
```

continues

5

THE AWT
COMPONENTS

LISTING 5.7   Continued

```
about.setFont(f14);

// Create the menu items for the "Help" menu.  Notice
// that the "Help" menu's menu items are themselves
// menus.
//
Menu basics = new Menu("Basics");
basics.setFont(f14);

// Create the menu items for the "Basics" submenu of the
// "Help" menu.
//
MenuItem b1 = new MenuItem("Tutorial");
b1.setFont(f14);
MenuItem b2 = new MenuItem("News");
b2.setFont(f14);
MenuItem b3 = new MenuItem("Packages");
b3.setFont(f14);
MenuItem b4 = new MenuItem("Splash");
b4.setFont(f14);

// Add the menu items to the "Basics" submenu.
//
basics.add(b1);
basics.add(b2);
basics.add(b3);
basics.add(b4);

MenuItem faq = new MenuItem("FAQ");
faq.setFont(f14);
MenuItem sample = new MenuItem("Sample");
sample.setFont(f14);

help.add(about);
help.add(basics);

// The following method call adds a textured horizontal
// line between the last menu item added to the menu,
// and the next item that will be added.
//
help.addSeparator();
```

```
    // Add the remaining two menu items.  These come after
    // the separator added previously.
    //
    help.add(faq);
    help.add(sample);

    MenuBar mb = new MenuBar();
    mb.add(file);
    mb.add(edit);

    // The "Help" menu is added to the menu bar as "the help
    // menu". The "help" menu always appears to the far
    // right of the menu bar.
    //
    mb.setHelpMenu(help);

    setMenuBar(mb);
  }

  /**
     Returns the preferred size of this frame.  Because the
     frame doesn't contain any children, the inherited
     version of getPreferredSize() would be called by the
     layout manager if this method is not defined here. This
     method dictates the preferred size for the frame.

     @return the preferred size of this frame as a Dimension
     object.
  */
  public Dimension getPreferredSize()
  {
    return new Dimension(250, 250);
  }

  public static void main(String [] args)
  {
    Menus app = new Menus("Menus");

    app.pack();
    app.setVisible(true);
  }
}
```

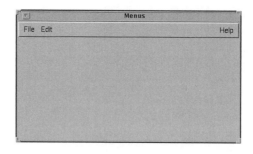

FIGURE 5.8

Menus can contain menu items which include other menus. This allows menus to be organized in a cascading or walking menu structure.

The program that displays this frame and its menus is shown in Listing 5.7.

In this example, I created three menus and added some menu items to the help menu. The help menu contains another menu, which contains additional menu items.

The capability for menus to contain other menus allows you to create walking or cascading menus. In order for this to be possible, menus must be a type of menu item. The relationship between the Menu and MenuItem classes makes this possible. This relationship follows a pattern that you've seen before. The relationship between the Component and Container classes is conceptually the same.

NOTE

Notice the similarity between the relationship shared by the Menu and MenuItem classes, and the relationship shared by the Component and Container classes. Both relationships exhibit the same *pattern*, namely, one that defines a recursive structure.

In fact, this pattern has been given the name *Composite* in a popular text that identifies and names patterns that occur commonly in object-oriented design and programming. See Gamma, E. et al, *Design Patterns*, Addison-Wesley, C. 1995.

Chapter 10, "The Swing Model Architecture," will discuss how to recognize patterns by identifying the underlying abstraction.

Figure 5.9 shows the UML static class diagram for the relationship between the Menu and MenuItem classes.

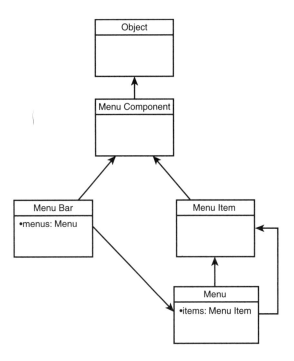

FIGURE 5.9

Menus are menu items, allowing menus to include other menus as their items.

From Figure 5.9 you can see that menus and menu items are somewhat different from other components. Technically, they are not components because they do not extend the Component class. Yet, effectively, they are components in terms of their behavior.

Notice in Figure 5.9 the MenuComponent class. Its presence defines both menus and menu items to be a type of menu component. This class defines attributes and behavior common to all types of menu components.

The reason that the menu classes don't belong to the normal component hierarchy is that they cannot always be treated as true components. For instance, you cannot add a menu to an arbitrary container in your program. So, even though they appear to function like components, they are different in some important ways. In Chapter 7, "The Swing Components," you will see that menus are defined much more flexibly in Swing.

CAUTION

Beware that the model for menus and menu items changes in Swing. You should anticipate this if you plan to program in AWT now but later convert your program to use Swing menu components.

Unlike the AWT menu components, Swing menu components are true components. This makes it much more flexible for you to use them in more places within your GUI.

Table 5.7 lists the constructors and methods of the Menu class.

TABLE 5.7   The Menu Class Constructors and Methods

Menu *constructor or method name*	*Description*
`Menu()`	Creates a menu.
`Menu(String label)`	Creates a menu with the specified name.
`Menu(String label, boolean tearOff)`	Creates a tear-off menu with the specified name.
`void add(MenuItem mi)`	Adds a menu item to this menu.
`void add(String label)`	Adds a simple menu item with the specified label to this menu.
`void addSeparator()`	Adds a horizontal line separator as a menu item.
`int getItem(int index)`	Gets the menu item with the specified name.
`int getItemCount()`	Gets the number of items in this menu.
`void insert(MenuItem, int index)`	Inserts the specified menu item in the indicated position.
`void insert(String label, int index),`	Inserts a new menu item with the given label in the indicated position.
`void insertSeparator(int index)`	Inserts a separator at the specified position.
`boolean isTearOff()`	Indicates if this menu is capable of being "torn-off", that is, displayed in a separate frame.
`void remove(int index)`	Removes the menu item at the indicated position from this menu.
`void remove (MenuComponent item)`	Removes the specified menu item from this menu.
`void removeAll()`	Removes all menu items from this menu.

Menus support adding, removing, and inserting menu items that include other menus and separators that help make the menus more readable. You can define a menu to be a "tear-off" menu, which means it will be rendered in a window detached from the frame that contains the menu bar to which the menu belongs.

Table 5.8 lists the constructors and methods of the `MenuItem` class.

TABLE 5.8 The `MenuItem` Class Constructors and Methods

MenuItem *constructor or method name*	*Description*
`MenuItem()`	Constructs a new menu item.
`MenuItem(String label)`	Constructs a new menu item with the specified label.
`MenuItem(String label, MenuShortcut s)`	Constructs a new menu item with the specified label and shortcut.
`void deleteShortcut()`	Deletes the shortcut item associated with this menu item.
`String getActionCommand()`	Gets this menu item's string that represents a command name.
`String getLabel()`	Gets this menu item's text label.
`MenuShortcut getShortcut()`	Gets the menu shortcut item associated with this menu item.
`boolean isEnabled()`	Indicates if this menu item is enabled.
`void setActionCommand (String command)`	Sets the action command string for this menu item.
`void setEnabled()`	Enables this menu item.
`void setLabel(String label)`	Sets this menu item's text label to the specified string.
`void setShortcut (MenuShortcut s)`	Sets the shortcut for this menu item.

Most of the behavior that you will use is defined in the `Menu` and `MenuItem` classes. However, the `MenuComponent` class defines the common behavior for all menu related types, including `MenuBars`.

Table 5.9 lists the constructors and methods of the `MenuComponent` class.

TABLE 5.9 The `MenuComponent` Class Constructors and Methods

MenuComponent *constructor or method*	*Description*
`MenuComponent()`	Constructor.
`Font getFont()`	Gets the font used for this menu component's text.

continues

TABLE 5.9   Continued

MenuComponent *constructor or method*	*Description*
String getName()	Gets the name of this menu component.
void setFont()	Sets the font used for this menu component's text.
void setName(String name)	Sets the name of this menu component.

The MenuComponent class is abstract, so you can't instantiate it. It's purpose is to define common attributes and methods related to all menu classes. From Figure 5.9, you can see that Menus, MenuItems, and MenuBars are all subclasses of MenuComponent.

From Table 5.10, and from the source code in Listing 5.7, you can see that help menus are treated differently from other menus. The MenuBar class interprets a help menu as the menu to be placed to the far right side of the menu bar. You need to specify such a menu by using the setHelpMenu() method. Simply adding menus by using the add() method will add the menus from left to right, always starting at the left hand side, and treat them like regular menus.

TABLE 5.10   The MenuBar Class Constructors and Methods

MenuBar *constructor or method name*	*Description*
MenuBar()	Creates a new menu bar.
Menu add(Menu m)	Adds the specified menu to this menu bar.
int deleteShortcut (MenuShortcut s)	Deletes the specified shortcut.
Menu getHelpMenu()	Gets the Help menu from this menu bar.
Menu getMenu(int i)	Gets the menu at the specified index on this menu bar.
int getMenuCount()	Gets the number of menus on this menu bar.
MenuItem getShortcut MenuItem()(MenuShortcut s)	Gets the menu item identified by the specified menu shortcut.
void remove(int index)	Removes the menu at the specified index.
void remove(MenuComponent c)	Removes the specified menu component from this from this menu bar.
void setHelpMenu(Menu m)	Adds the specified menu as this menu bar's Help menu.
Enumeration shortcuts()	Gets all the short cuts for this menu bar.

Text Areas and Text Fields

Text components are components that store and display text which can be selected and altered. Text components support a number of features including text insertion, editing, selection, and deletion.

The text component classes are subclasses of the `TextComponent` class, which defines attributes and behavior that is applicable to all text components. The `TextComponent` class supports text selection, caret positioning, text setting, and toggling of the component's editable state because these features are common to both text fields and text areas.

The AWT defines two types of text components. A text area is a multi-line, multicolumn component that supports typing in its display area. Text fields are similar except that they support only one line of text. Because these two types are so closely related, I will discuss them together.

The `TextField` and `TextArea` classes define an *echo character*. An echo character can be specified as the one that is echoed when the user types in the text field or text area. This is useful for fields such as password fields that want to hide the user's key strokes. For example, a password field could set the echo character to a space or asterisk.

Listing 5.8 shows a program that creates a container that includes various text components. Figure 5.10 shows some text fields and a text area created by the program in Listing 5.8.

Notice in Figure 5.10 that the *name* text field is gray instead of white like the others. The program disables this field. When a field is not editable, the peer component changes the color to gray. This behavior, of course, is dictated by the peer class and not by the text field. Another peer implementation could define a different policy for representing disabled fields. Text areas work the same way incidentally.

LISTING 5.8   Program That Demonstrates Use of the Different Text Component Classes

```
public class Text extends Panel
{
  public Text()
  {
    setLayout(new GridLayout(0, 1));

    GridBagLayout gbl = new GridBagLayout();
    GridBagConstraints gbc = new GridBagConstraints();

    Panel addressPanel = new Panel();
    addressPanel.setLayout(gbl);

    gbc.anchor = GridBagConstraints.EAST;
```

continues

5

THE AWT COMPONENTS

LISTING 5.8 Continued

```
Label name = new Label("Name :   ");
gbl.setConstraints(name, gbc);

gbc.gridx = 0;
gbc.gridy = GridBagConstraints.RELATIVE;

Label address = new Label("Address :   ");
gbl.setConstraints(address, gbc);

Label city = new Label("City/State/Zip :   ");
gbl.setConstraints(city, gbc);

Label phone = new Label("Phone :   ");
gbl.setConstraints(phone, gbc);

addressPanel.add(name);
addressPanel.add(address);
addressPanel.add(city);
addressPanel.add(phone);

gbc.gridx = 1;
gbc.anchor = GridBagConstraints.WEST;
TextField nameVal = new TextField("Confucius");
nameVal.setEditable(false);
gbl.setConstraints(nameVal, gbc);

TextField addVal = new TextField("Kong miao");
gbl.setConstraints(addVal, gbc);

TextField cityVal = new TextField("Shan dong, Shan dong province, China");
cityVal.select(3, 9);
gbl.setConstraints(cityVal, gbc);

TextField phoneVal = new TextField("011 86 56 33 23 54 91");
gbl.setConstraints(phoneVal, gbc);

addressPanel.add(nameVal);
addressPanel.add(addVal);
addressPanel.add(cityVal);
addressPanel.add(phoneVal);
```

```
        add(addressPanel);

        Panel bioPanel = new Panel();
        bioPanel.setLayout(gbl);

        gbc.gridx = 0;
        Label favorite = new Label("Favorite proverb:");
        favorite.setFont(f14);
        gbl.setConstraints(favorite, gbc);
        bioPanel.add(favorite);

        TextArea proverb = new TextArea();

        StringBuffer str = "Better for one to remain silent ";
        str.append("and be thought a fool, \n");
        str.append("than to open one's mouth ");
        str.append("and remove all doubt.");
        proverb.setText(str.toString);

        proverb.setEditable(false);

        gbl.setConstraints(proverb, gbc);
        gbc.gridheight = 3;
        bioPanel.add(proverb);

        add(bioPanel);
    }

    public static void main(String [] args)
    {
        Text app = new Text();

        Frame f = new Frame("Text Components");
        f.add(app);
        f.pack();
        f.setVisible(true);
    }
}
```

Figure 5.10

Text areas and text fields are text components that support a variety of text entry and editing functions.

From Tables 5.11–5.13, you can see which classes define which methods.

Table 5.11 shows the constructors and methods of the TextComponent class. You can tell that these methods do represent functions that are common to both `TextArea` and `TextField` objects.

TABLE 5.11   The `TextComponent` Class Constructors and Methods

TextComponent *constructor or method name*	*Description*
`int getCaretPosition()`	Gets the position of the text insertion caret for this component.
`String getSelectedText()`	Gets the text that is currently selected in this component.
`int getSelectedEnd()`	Gets the position that marks the beginning of the selected text.
`int getSelectedStart()`	Gets the position that marks the end of the selected text.
`String getText()`	Gets all the text in this text component.
`boolean isEditable()`	Indicates if editing is currently allowed on this text component.
`void select(int selectionStart, int selectionEnd)`	Marks as selected the text region indicated by the specified begin and end marks.
`void selectAll()`	Marks all text in this component as selected.
`void setCaretPosition (int position)`	Sets the caret to be at the specified position.
`void setEditable (boolean b)`	Sets this text component to be editable or not.

TextComponent *constructor* or method name	*Description*
void setSelectedEnd (int selectionEnd)	Marks the end of the selected region for this text component.
void setSelectedStart (int selectionStart)	Marks the beginning of the selected region for this text component.
void setText(String t)	Sets the text that is presented by this text component.

Among other things, the `TextField` and `TextArea` classes must present methods to set and get their minimum and preferred sizes, based on the number of columns for text areas, and the number of rows and columns for text fields. This behavior is specific to each type of component and is, therefore, overridden from the `TextComponent` class.

TABLE 5.12   The TextArea Class Constructors and Methods

TextArea *constructor* or method name	*Description*
TextArea()	Constructs a new text area.
TextArea(int rows, int columns)	Constructs a new text area with the specified number of rows and columns.
TextArea(String text)	Constructs a new text area with the specified initial text.
TextArea(String text, int rows, int columns)	Constructs a new text area with the specified initial text, and the specified rows and columns.
TextArea(String text, int rows, int columns, int scrollbars)	Constructs a new text area with the specified initial text, the specified number of rows and columns, and the specified policy for displaying scrollbars.
void append(String str)	Appends the specified text to the contained text of this text area.
int getColumns()	Gets the number of columns of this text area.
Dimension getMinimumSize()	Determines the minimum size of this text area.
Dimension getMinimumSize (int rows, int columns)	Determines the minimum size of an area with the specified number of rows and columns.
Dimension getPreferredSize()	Determines the preferred size of this text area.
Dimension getPreferredSize (int rows, int columns)	Determines the preferred size of a text area with the specified number of rows and columns.
int getRows()	Gets the number of rows in this text area.
int getScrollbar Visibility()	Gets a value that determines which scrollbars this text area uses.

continues

TABLE 5.12   Continued

TextArea *constructor or method name*	*Description*
`void insert(String str, int pos)`	Inserts the specified text starting at the indicated position in this text area.
`void replaceRange(String str, int start, int end)`	Replaces with the specified string the range of text indicated by the start and end positions in this text area.
`void setColumns(int columns)`	Sets the number of columns for this text area.
`void setRows(int rows)`	Sets the number of rows for this text area.

TABLE 5.13   The `TextField` Class Constructors and Methods

TextField *constructor or method name*	*Description*
`TextField()`	Constructs a new text field.
`TextField(int columns)`	Constructs a new text field with the specified number of columns.
`TextField(String text)`	Constructs a new text field that initializes the specified text.
`TextField(String text, int columns)`	Constructs a new text field with the initial text and the number of columns specified.
`boolean echoCharIsSet()`	Indicates if this text field has an echo character that is currently set.
`int getColumns()`	Gets the number of columns of this text field.
`char getEchoChar()`	Gets the echo character currently set on this text area.
`Dimension getMinimumSize()`	Gets the minimum dimension for this text field.
`Dimension getMinimumSize (int columns)`	Gets the minimum dimension for this text field with the specified number of columns.
`Dimension getPreferredSize()`	Gets the preferred size of this text field.
`Dimension getPreferredSize(int columns)`	Gets the preferred size of a text field with the specified number of columns.
`void setColumns(int columns)`	Sets the number of columns for this text field.
`void setEchoChar(char c)`	Sets the echo character to be used by this text field.
`void setText(String t)`	Sets the text presented by this text field *TextField* to the specified string.

Summary

The `java.awt` package contains the AWT component classes. Many of these have visual representations and define standard metaphors such as buttons, lists, text fields, and so on.

All the AWT components have heavyweight implementations, which means each instance creates a native peer window object.

You can use these components to build GUI applications. Components can be organized in a variety of configurations to meet the needs of each application. Additional containers, such as `Panels`, can be used to nest components so that it becomes easier for you to organize and manage the components in your GUI.

Although you can write non-trivial applications using only the AWT components, you are encouraged to use the Swing set of visual components instead. Chapter 7 introduces the Swing components.

Before you look at the Swing components, you need to understand the concepts that surround the Swing component set. The Swing components introduce some new abstractions not found in the AWT components. Therefore, the next chapter introduces the concepts that surround Swing. You will then be ready to tackle the Swing components.

Swing Concepts and Architecture

IN THIS CHAPTER

- The Swing Component Tool Set   140

- The javax.swing.JComponent Class   143

- Making Swing Components
  Lightweight   145

- Abstractions Encapsulated by the
  JComponent Class   146

- Swing Containers   148

- The Swing Container Abstraction   149

- The JRootPane Container   151

- The JLayeredPane Class   159

- Lightweight and Heavyweight
  Containers   162

- Configuring Look-and-Feel   166

In this chapter, I discuss the concepts and architecture underlying the Swing tool set, which is the foundation upon which the Swing component set is built. Just as I did for the AWT component architecture, I will discuss the attributes, properties, behavior, and abstractions shared by all Swing components.

You will see the importance of studying and understanding the AWT components before examining the Swing components. Although the Swing components define new abstractions, they are built upon the AWT foundation. All Swing components are bona fide AWT components first.

In Chapter 4, "AWT Concepts and Architecture," you learned how to bring up a simple GUI and populate it with some components. Here you will continue learning how to do the same thing, this time using the Swing components. As usual, you start with a conceptual grounding. In this chapter, you will concentrate on examining only those Swing abstractions that pertain to getting a simple Swing application up and running.

After you understand the basic Swing abstractions related to components and containers, I will delve into some programming examples that show you how to create the basic architecture of a Swing GUI.

The Swing Component Tool Set

The Swing tool set is really comprised of a few different parts:

- An architecture that supports implementation of a new set of abstractions, features, and functionality.

- A new set of visual components that implements these new abstractions, features, and functionality, which enhance the standard AWT component set. The Swing visual components have lightweight implementations.

- A set of classes that does not define visual components, but helps support the abstractions used by Swing's visual components.

The AWT in Release 1.1 of the JDK is the foundation for all Swing programming. It is an integral part of Swing. But Swing also includes a whole new set of packages found under the `javax.swing` package hierarchy. You can see from the package-naming convention that Swing is considered to be a standard extension to the JDK; it is not placed under the standard `java` hierarchy. The Swing tool set is not part of the standard Java release.

This organization shows that it is possible to write Java GUI programs without using any of the Swing packages—that is, without using any of the components defined by classes in the Swing packages. Therefore, Swing is treated as an extension to standard Java. It is important, however, to understand that much of the support for the abstractions defined by the Swing tool set is built into the AWT in release 1.1 of the JDK.

Swing Concepts and Architecture

CHAPTER 6

141

6

SWING CONCEPTS
AND
ARCHITECTURE

In Chapter 5, "The Basic AWT Components," you saw that the AWT provides a standard set of visual components for GUI programming. In addition to these AWT Components, the Swing tool set defines its own set of visual components that are available for your use. All these Swing components, which are defined in the `javax.swing` package, can be used in a program along with the AWT components.

CAUTION

It is generally a bad idea to mix AWT and Swing components in the same program. You are strongly discouraged from doing so.

There are a few compatibility issues that appear when you mix the two types of components. Heavyweight components are always rendered on top of lightweight components.

In this chapter, I will discuss those Swing abstractions that relate to the definition and nature of Swing's components and containers. Table 6.1 highlights the new abstractions and features that relate to Swing's component hierarchy.

TABLE 6.1 Swing Abstractions and Features

Abstraction	Implemented in	Description
Lightweight components	`java.awt`	Provides support for the creation of lightweight component definitions.
New containment model	`javax.swing`	Defines a new containment abstraction for container classes, used by Swing containers.
Models	`javax.swing`	Provide predefined data model definitions and implementations that are used by the Swing components as part of their MVC paradigm implementation.
Custom UI Look-and-Feel Pluggable Look-and-Feel	`javax.swing`	Defines a framework for creating a uniform component API that is separate from the API that supports multiple look-and-feel implementations.
Model architecture	`javax.swing`	Defines a framework that supports the MVC paradigm. Swing components have a built-in implementation of MVC.
ToolTips	`javax.swing`	Supports the use of fly-over text by components.

continues

TABLE 6.1   Continued

Abstraction	Implemented in	Description
Internationalization	`javax.swing`	Supports locale-sensitive operations by Swing components.
Commands	`javax.swing`	An object that defines an action associated with a component. This action object can be executed whenever the component receives certain types of events.

NOTE

Swing consists of other packages that define many nonvisual classes that support the abstractions defined by Swing and the JFC. However, these address issues like events and event handling, which are discussed later (in Chapter 9, "Events and Event Handling").

These abstractions provide a foundation for a set of capabilities above and beyond those provided by AWT components. The Swing components implement these abstractions and create a tool set whose classes contain capabilities not found in the implementation of the standard AWT components.

However, the support for some of these features is actually implemented in the AWT Release 1.1 classes in the `java.awt` package. The other features and abstractions are implemented completely by the classes in the `javax.swing` Swing extension packages proper. Therefore Swing is actually implemented in both the AWT packages and the Swing extension packages.

This is sometimes confusing to programmers who are newcomers to Java or to the JDK since Release 1.1. The AWT Release 1.1 and beyond supports an essential part of the architecture—or framework if you prefer—used by Swing. Therefore, the standard AWT 1.1 is required in order to support programming in Swing. However, the Swing component classes that implement Swing's new abstractions are defined in the Swing packages.

The most noticeable example of this symbiosis between the AWT and Swing packages is in the area of lightweight components, which are a new feature of Swing. Although the Swing tool set defines a set of concrete lightweight component implementations in its `javax.swing` package, the architecture that really supports the lightweight component abstraction—the capability to create lightweight component definitions—is built into the AWT 1.1 classes, not the classes in the `javax.swing` package. Specifically, it is the `java.awt.Component` and `java.awt.Container` classes that provide the brunt of the framework for defining any concrete lightweight component implementations.

This support does not exist in versions of the AWT prior to JDK Release 1.1. Prior to AWT 1.1, if you subclassed `Component` or `Container`, your class would be heavyweight. Using the AWT 1.1 (or subsequent releases), if you subclass a concrete AWT component class, your class will have a heavyweight implementation; but if you subclass `Component` or `Container` your class will have a lightweight implementation.

The javax.swing.JComponent Class

Just as the `java.awt.Component` class lays the foundation for all AWT components, the `javax.swing.JComponent` class lays the foundation for all Swing's lightweight component classes.

Swing components inherit all the properties and methods defined by the `Component` class, and, therefore, exhibit the same basic behavior as the AWT components, making them true components in every sense of the word. The Swing tool set also defines new containers, and these, too, are bona fide AWT components.

Swing components are essentially a special kind of AWT component that have some added features, and which support some new programming abstractions. In particular, their implementations are lightweight, which means they do not realize a native window peer when they are instantiated.

This support for the creation of lightweight component class implementations is one of the most important new features in Swing.

It may surprise you that concrete Swing component implementations can derive from the AWT, whose components are heavyweight. You know that the concrete AWT component classes have heavyweight implementations, which means they do realize a native window peer object when they are instantiated. Examining the inheritance hierarchy of the AWT and Swing will shed light on what's really going on.

Figure 6.1 shows the inheritance hierarchy of the Swing components. The Swing components do not derive from the concrete AWT component implementations. Instead, they derive from the `java.awt.Component` and `java.awt.Container` classes. The `Component` class is abstract and, therefore, does not accept responsibility for defining native peers for any particular concrete subclass.

The `Component` class generally encapsulates the abstraction of what all components are. However, it is up to specific concrete subclasses to define their individual behavior and onscreen appearance. In the case of the heavyweight AWT components, it is up to the concrete subclasses to specify how their corresponding native peers are created. Only a concrete implementation can know what peer object appropriately represents it onscreen.

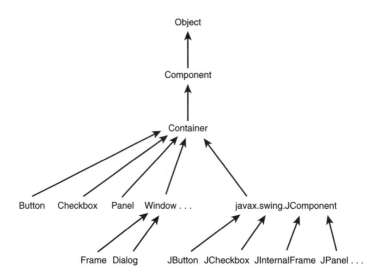

FIGURE 6.1

Swing's lightweight components derive from `java.awt.Container` *and not from AWT concrete components. All Swing's lightweight component classes begin with* `J`. *They enjoy an additional set of abstractions supported by* `JComponent`, *whose ancestry enables all Swing lightweight components to inherit the capabilities and properties enjoyed by the AWT components. In this way, they maintain consistency between the AWT and Swing components.*

Because the `Component` class is abstract, the concrete Swing component classes do not inherit an implementation that is heavyweight; their ancestors do not specify details or policy for creation of native peers. Only the concrete AWT component subclasses do this.

The Swing tool set also defines containers, which can also have lightweight implementations. In order to support creation of lightweight Swing containers, the Swing container classes must also derive from ancestors that do not impose any policy for creation of heavyweight native peers.

So Swing components and containers are true AWT components. Where, then, are the new Swing tool set abstractions introduced and defined?

Figure 6.1 gives you the answer. The concrete Swing component classes don't derive directly from the `java.awt.Component` and `java.awt.Container` classes. All Swing lightweight components descend directly from a new component class, `javax.swing.JComponent`, which is an abstract class that is a direct subclass of `java.awt.Container`. It is the instrument that defines the basic abstractions shared by all Swing components—both components and containers. It enables the Swing components to define these new attributes and behavior that are not found in the standard AWT components.

Swing Concepts and Architecture

CHAPTER 6

145

6

SWING CONCEPTS
AND
ARCHITECTURE

In Figure 6.1 you can see that `JComponent` derives from the `java.awt.Component` and `java.awt.Container` classes, giving Swing components their capability to act like generalized components and containers.

If you look carefully at the hierarchy in Figure 6.1 you see that all Swing components are also containers because `JComponent` derives directly from `Container`. This inheritance hierarchy creates a very flexible containment model. For instance, because any Swing component can be a container, a button object can store an associated image to display on the button's face, or a cell in a table can store a combo box. This gives you the capability to design very sophisticated user-interface structures.

Note that the Swing lightweight components do not derive from any of the AWT heavyweight component classes. This is the key to their lightweight implementation. The new `JComponent` root in the hierarchy is the place from which all the abstractions new to Swing's lightweight component classes stem.

Making Swing Components Lightweight

You can see from Table 6.1 that most of Swing's new abstractions are defined in the `JComponent` class, including support for ToolTips, support for easy use of Swing components in MVC designs, and customizable look-and-feel. However, it is the standard AWT that lays the groundwork for one of Swing's most important new abstractions—lightweight components.

Unlike the AWT components, the concrete components in the Swing tool set are implemented as lightweight components instead of as heavyweight components such as those in the AWT. But make no mistake, regardless of their implementation, Swing components are components in every sense of the word.

You know that Swing's new `JComponent` class is the root of all Swing's lightweight component implementations. Remember that `JComponent` directly extends `java.awt.Container`.

With that definition in mind, take a closer look at the inheritance hierarchy. I have said several times already that the concrete AWT component classes, which directly extend `java.awt.Component` or `java.awt.Container`, are heavyweight. How, then, can Swing's `JComponent` class—the ancestor of all Swing's lightweight components—subclass these AWT classes and build a foundation for a set of lightweight components?

The answer is that the `java.awt.Component` class is abstract. And although `java.awt.Container` is concrete, neither it nor `java.awt.Component` specify behavior related to native peers. There is no native nature of `java.awt.Component` or `java.awt.Container` that the `JComponent` class must overcome.

In fact, it is precisely the definitions of these two classes that support the lightweight component framework introduced in Swing. The AWT `Component` and `Container` classes were rewritten in Release 1.1 of the JDK to support the lightweight component model. Their abstract nature and some details of their attributes and implementation are the elements that form the foundation of the lightweight component framework.

This is a prime example of how the definition and implementation of Swing is really distributed across the AWT and the Swing packages, namely the `java.awt` and `javax.swing` package hierarchies. This is why AWT Release 1.1 is required in order to use the Swing tool set.

> **NOTE**
>
> The AWT framework is required to program in Swing. Besides supporting the implementation of lightweight components, the AWT defines the foundation for layout management and event handling, as you will see in Chapters 8, "Layout Managers," and 9, "Events and Event Handling," respectively.

The `java.awt.Component` and `java.awt.Container` classes are not responsible for determining the appropriate native peer of a concrete class. However, they do provide methods that support this function. This function is the responsibility of the concrete subclass that implements each component. Each concrete subclass must request that the platform instantiate the right native peer object when the component is instantiated, possibly enlisting the help of methods defined in the `Component` or `Container` classes.

The `JComponent` class is also abstract. It is technically neither heavyweight nor lightweight; these terms refer to the creation of native peer objects for concrete component classes. Basically, as an abstract class, `JComponent` enables the creation of lightweight implementations for its concrete subclasses.

This approach enables the Swing components to take on the properties and behavior defined by the AWT component set and also define their lightweight nature, among other things. It also enables the Swing components to maintain backward compatibility with the AWT 1.1 class implementations.

Abstractions Encapsulated by the JComponent Class

The `javax.swing.JComponent` class is the cornerstone of the Swing tool set. It is the ancestor of all Swing's lightweight component classes. It defines and implements the foundation upon which all Swing lightweight components are built, and it provides several new abstractions not found in the AWT components. As a result, the Swing components are more fully featured than their AWT counterparts.

These abstractions are implemented via `JComponent`'s attributes, properties, and public interface. `JComponent`'s specification allows all Swing components to benefit from the consistency and uniformity of a single root class that serves as the lynch pin for the whole component set.

Like the AWT `Component` and `Container` classes, it defines all the attributes and behavior that are common to all the Swing lightweight components.

Its presence in the hierarchy allows Swing to introduce abstractions that do not exist in the regular AWT. The `JComponent` class is precisely the place that introduces these abstractions via new attributes, properties, and a public interface that is a superset of that inherited from the AWT classes.

Table 6.2 lists the properties defined in `JComponent` that are shared by all the Swing lightweight components. These properties comprise the mechanism used to implement the Swing abstractions listed in Table 6.1.

TABLE 6.2 New Component Properties Defined by the Swing Component Tool Set

Property	Abstraction	Description
Data model	Model architecture	An object that implements a data model (implements a data abstraction) for which the GUI component is a view. It manifests support for MVC.
Custom UI	Pluggable L&F	A user interface object that implements a particular look-and-feel. An application's look-and-feel is dynamically configurable.
ToolTip	ToolTips	Implements fly–over text, which is text that pops up when the mouse "flies over" (is placed over) the component; it can describe the component's function or use.
Root pane	Container architecture	A container to which Swing visual containers delegate their duties of containing and managing children. It is used primarily by the Swing heavyweight containers.
Locale	Internationalization	A locale context that conforms to the behavior, attributes, and characteristics of a certain language and geographical context.
Action object	Action commands	An object that defines an action associated with the component. This action object can be executed whenever the component receives certain types of events.

continues

TABLE 6.2   Continued

Property	Abstraction	Description
Double buffering	Smooth component painting	Paints images in a separate buffer before displaying in the screen buffer, thereby avoiding flicker. It is implemented by all Swing components.
Accessible content	Support for accessibility APIs	A framework that allows Java programs to interface uniformly with special devices for disabled persons.

Table 6.3 lists the public methods in the JComponent class that provide access to the properties listed in Table 6.2.

TABLE 6.3   JComponent's Public Interface

Property	Related methods
Data model	`void setModel(Model model)` `Model getModel()`

Custom UI	`ComponentUI getUI()`
	`void setUI(ComponentUI ui)`
	`void updateUI()`

ToolTip	`JToolTip createToolTip()`
	`Point getToolTipLocation(MouseEvent event)`
	`String getToolTipText(MouseEvent event)`
	`setToolTipText(String text)`

Root pane container	`JRootPane getRootPane()` `Container getContentPane()`
Locale	`Locale getLocale()` `void setLocale(Locale locale)`
Accessibility	`AccessibleContext getAccessibleContext()`
Double buffering	`boolean isDoubleBuffered()` `void setDoubleBuffered(boolean aFlag)`

Swing Containers

One of the most noticeable changes to the Java GUI programming model found in Swing is the new containment model used by Swing heavyweight containers. The Swing heavyweight containers utilize a new containment abstraction that is defined as part of the Swing tool set. This

Swing Concepts and Architecture

CHAPTER 6

149

6

SWING CONCEPTS
AND
ARCHITECTURE

new abstraction is quite different from the flat containment abstraction implemented by the standard AWT containers and the Swing lightweight containers. If you build a GUI using only Swing components you must use at least one heavyweight Swing container.

To build even the simplest Swing GUI you must understand how this model works; otherwise, it may be difficult to get even the simplest container to work as expected.

Limitations of the AWT Containment Model

All the AWT components have the same, relatively simple, containment policy. In addition to implementing the AWT containment policy, each container class, such as `Frame`, may want to define attributes such as the presence of a menu bar. Unfortunately, each class must define and implement support for the attributes they desire, independently of the other containers. For example, unlike `Frames`, `Windows` have no menu bar.

You can see that every new container class that wants to have access to features like a menu bar would need to implement that behavior on its own, while retaining its basic container nature. Therefore, the knowledge of how to manage properties like menu bars must spread throughout the JDK, duplicating implementations.

AWT containers basically inherit their capability to contain children from the `Container` class from which they all derive. Therefore, if a `Container` subclass wants to implement a more complex containment abstraction, in order to implement some feature like the z-ordering of its children, it must define and implement that policy on its own, independently of other `Container` classes. It might then have a new, more complex and feature-rich containment model, but might lose compatibility or consistency with other AWT containers.

The Swing Container Abstraction

The Swing container model defines a new abstraction that

- Creates a more complex and facile model for containing children.
- Provides a more scalable model that retains consistency and eliminates re-implementation efforts by each container class.
- Separates arbitrary class attributes and design issues from the containment abstraction.

This new model enables different kinds of containers to adopt the same capabilities. For example, both heavyweight and lightweight containers can adopt the same containment policy. It offers a flexible way to specify and implement a new containment abstraction that doesn't rely on the nature of the container itself.

Basically, Swing's new containment abstraction defines two major features:

- Standard organization and policy for containers to manage menu bars and glass panes, in addition to the child components they contain.
- Z-ordering of child components. It creates the abstraction of a front-to-back layering of child components as well as pop ups and graphic drawing that transcend container bounds.

A heavyweight container's children can be placed in any of five different layers, creating the illusion or abstraction of front-to-back ordering. The new containment abstraction also allows arbitrary containers to manage elements like a menu bar. In the AWT containers, only frames could contain a menu bar, and any container type that wanted to do so had to implement the behavior on its own.

The new Swing container model achieves this flexibility and uniformity across all containers by requiring that its containers delegate their container duties to another specialized container object.

By requiring Swing containers to delegate their duties, the new, complex containment abstraction can be implemented by a specialized, dedicated class. This implementation can then be used by any container that wishes to advertise this abstraction, regardless of any other attributes that dictate the nature of the container. It also relieves all the containers from re-implementing the same abstraction and possibly losing the canonical nature of one standard policy.

The Swing containment model provides quite a few capabilities. In fact, because of its robustness, its implementation requires the help of more than one specialized container. One container defines a policy for managing a menu bar and a secondary container that is hidden from the programmer. This secondary container, in turn, enlists the help of yet another container to actually contain the original container's child components. This model is quite different from the AWT model in which each container does its own work.

In the AWT containment model, containers like `Frame`, `Panel`, `Applet`, and `Window` are themselves the actual objects that hold the child components. The exact implementation mechanism is unimportant now, but remember that the container object you instantiate is the actual container to which you add your children. There is only one container doing the work of containing children.

There are five Swing containers that use a delegate container to support this new complex containment model. Typically, containers that adopt this model will be those that are used as top-level application containers. The Swing containers that use this new model are Swing's equivalent of the AWT `Frame`, `Applet`, `Window`, and `Dialog` containers.

Table 6.4 shows the Swing containers that use the new containment model.

TABLE 6.4 The Swing Containers That Use the Swing Container Model

Swing Container class	Superclass	Description
javax.swing.JApplet	java.awt.Applet	The base class for defining Swing applets. All Swing applets must subclass this class.
javax.swing.JDialog	java.awt.Applet	The base class for all Swing dialog boxes.
javax.swing.JFrame	java.awt.Frame	A basic Swing frame, which is used as an application's outermost container.
javax.swing.JInternalFrame	javax.swing.JComponent	A frame that can manage all the same elements of an outermost application frame, but can be used internally in an application, that is, in another container.
javax.swing.JWindow	java.awt.Frame	A window with no border or menu bar.

The JRootPane Container

The five Swing containers in Table 6.4 delegate their containment duties to a special root pane container. The class that defines the root pane is the javax.swing.JRootPane. Every instance of these five container types defined in Table 6.4 maintains a reference to a root pane instance to which it delegates its containment duties. It is the JRootPane class that implements Swing's containment abstraction.

Actually, JRootPane doesn't do all the work itself. It, in turn, delegates some of the job of creating the containment abstraction to some other helper classes that are also specialized types of containers, each with its own capabilities and abstraction that meet its responsibilities.

Each JRootPane instance has a set of other containers that each do part of the job of containing all constituent components of the original container—that is, those listed in Table 6.4. Each of the containers and components used by a container's JRootPane instance specialize in implementing part of the overall Swing containment abstraction.

Table 6.5 lists the elements of the JRootPane class that help it carry out its duties. Together, these objects collaborate with each other to complete the containment abstraction.

TABLE 6.5   The Conceptual Parts of a `JRootPane` Container

Container member	Abstraction
Content pane	A container that provides the abstraction for containing the children of the primary container (the container that uses the content pane).
Glass pane	A special component that can be placed above all the other children of the primary container. It enables the primary container to intercept events targeted for its children. It also allows drawing across the boundaries of multiple children of the container.
Layered pane	A container that implements a z-ordering abstraction. It gives the primary container the capability to simulate a z-ordering for its children. By default, it initially places all the children in the content pane.
Menu bar	Implements a menu bar. It is used by Swing containers that utilize a root pane.

Each of the elements in Table 6.5 collaborate to implement the Swing containment model. Each container or component has a specific responsibility, also described in Table 6.5. Together, all these containers and components enable the primary swing containers in Table 6.4 to offer sophisticated handling of child components and elements such as menu bars. The new policy essentially implements a new abstraction for how and where it stores components in the primary container.

You know that the five primary Swing containers of Table 6.4 delegate their containment duties to a `JRootPane` object. This container, in turn, delegates some of these duties to other containers and components. However, `JRootPane` does perform some of the duties itself.

The `JRootPane` container itself manages the primary container's menu bar. In fact, it uses a proprietary layout policy to ensure that the content pane doesn't occlude the menu bar in any way. JRootPane uses a special layout manager class to implement its layout policy. Containers that rely on a root pane must always have a root pane instance. Otherwise, there will be no container to manage the holding and layout of the menu bar and content pane. You cannot set a JRootPane's layout manager to `null`.

The content pane is the pane that actually stores the primary container's children initially. For the same reason, a container's content pane cannot be null. There must be a container to manage the container's content—its children.

Figure 6.2 shows schematically how all these components are arranged.

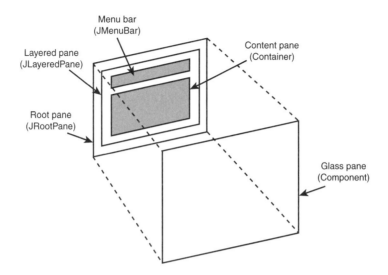

FIGURE 6.2

The JRootPane *container manages the container's menu bar, content pane, layered pane, and glass pane. It lays out these objects as shown.*

Table 6.5 only gives conceptual names to JRootPane's cronies. The names hint at their function, but you still don't know what these containers are or what classes define them.

Table 6.6 lists the specialized containers and components that collaborate with JRootPane to create the complete Swing containment abstraction. Let's discuss their exact function.

TABLE 6.6 JRootPane's Container Delegates

Container	*Class*	*Superclass*
Root pane	javax.swing.JRootPane	javax.swing.JComponent
Content pane	java.awt.Container	java.awt.Component
Layered pane	javax.swing.JLayeredPane	javax.swing.JComponent
Glass pane	java.awt.Component	java.lang.Object
Menu bar	javax.swing.JMenuBar	javax.swing.JComponent

The glass pane can be any component. It can be used to intercept events generated by user actions before they are delivered to the other components in the primary container. In Chapter 9 I discuss some situations in which this is desirable.

Having a glass pane gives you more flexibility to change the behavior of your GUI during its execution. You can add or remove a glass pane at will. Unlike the content pane and layered pane, your primary container is not required to maintain a glass pane.

The root pane ensures that the glass pane sits on top of all the other elements that it manages. This enables you to do a few things that are normally difficult. For example, you can draw graphics that cross the bounds of the components in the layered pane. Normally, you cannot draw outside a container's bounds, making it difficult to do things like draw a rectangular border that follows the motion of the mouse while you are dragging a component.

The JRootPane is not visible. It simply organizes the other containers. As I said earlier, its primary responsibility is to manage the appearance of its container, which is what the user sees. The menu bar is visible, of course; and the root pane must ensure that the other containers don't occlude it. This keeps the root pane container busy.

Lest you forget the original purpose for this new containment model, I will restate it here: It enhances the AWT model by abstracting a hierarchy of special purpose containers. Using AWT containers, you simply add a component to the container. You saw some code examples of this in Listings 4.1, 4.2, and 4.3. The AWT container class to which you add children itself implements all the functions to meet its role as a container; and it also defines the containment abstraction.

But you can no longer simply add components to your Swing containers. You must now add all child components to your container's content pane, not to the enclosing container itself.

Listing 6.1 shows one of your previous simple applications rewritten to use a Swing container.

LISTING 6.1   Using the Content Pane to Add Components to a Swing Heavyweight Container

```java
import java.awt.Container;
import java.awt.Dimension;
import java.awt.FlowLayout;
import java.awt.Font;
import java.awt.Window;

import java.awt.event.WindowAdapter;
import java.awt.event.WindowEvent;
import java.awt.event.WindowListener;

import javax.swing.JButton;
import javax.swing.JFrame;
import javax.swing.JLabel;
import javax.swing.JList;
import javax.swing.JPanel;
```

Swing Concepts and Architecture

CHAPTER 6

155

6

SWING CONCEPTS
AND
ARCHITECTURE

```
import javax.swing.JRootPane;
import javax.swing.JTextField;

/**
   A class that demonstrates adding some components to a Swing
   container.  This class defines a container that is a subclass of
   java.awt.Frame.
*/
class FrameWithComponents extends JFrame
{
  /**
     No-arg constructor.
  */
  public FrameWithComponents()
  {
    super("A Swing frame with some components");

    // The root pane holds a reference to the content pane of the
    // Swing heavyweight containers. You can also get the content
    // pane directly by calling the convenience method
    // getContentPane().
    //
    JRootPane rootPane = getRootPane();
    Container contentPane = rootPane.getContentPane();

    // Must set the layout manager on the container's
    // content pane, not the container itself.
    //
    contentPane.setLayout(new FlowLayout());

    Font font14 = new Font("SansSerif", Font.PLAIN, 14);
    Font font18 = new Font("SansSerif", Font.PLAIN, 18);

    label = new JLabel("A simple label in a frame");
    label.setFont(font18);

    // Add the label to the content pane of the JFrame, not to the
    // JFrame directly.
    //
    contentPane.add(label);

    button = new JButton("Push me");
    button.setFont(font14);

    textField = new JTextField("A text field");
    textField.setFont(font14);
```

continues

LISTING 6.1   Continued

```java
    String [] strings =
    { "Button", "Canvas", "Checkbox", "Label",
      "List", "Scrollbar", "ScrollPane",
      "TextField", "TextArea"
    };
    list = new JList(strings);
    list.setVisibleRowCount(7);
    list.setFont(font14);

    // Also add these three components to the frame's content
    // pane.
    //
    contentPane.add(button);
    contentPane.add(textField);
    contentPane.add(list);
  }

  public Dimension getPreferredSize()
  {
    return new Dimension(300, 300);
  }

  public static void main(String [] args)
  {
    FrameWithComponents f = new FrameWithComponents();
    WindowListener wL = new WindowAdapter()
      {
        public void windowClosing(WindowEvent e)
          {
            ((Window) e.getSource()).dispose();
            System.exit(0);
          }
      };
    f.addWindowListener(wL);

    f.pack();
    f.setVisible(true);
  }

  JButton button;
  JTextField textField;
  JLabel label;
  JList list;

}
```

Swing Concepts and Architecture

CHAPTER 6

157

6

SWING CONCEPTS
AND
ARCHITECTURE

If you run this program, you see a screen that looks like that shown in Figure 6.3. You're now using Swing components, so the members that you add to your frame have a slightly different look than the ones in previous examples.

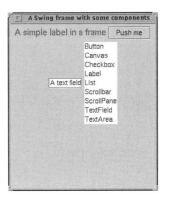

FIGURE 6.3

A simple frame with components rewritten to use Swing components instead of AWT components. You add the components to the frame's content pane instead of to the frame itself.

Note how you add the child components to the content pane of the primary container, not to the primary container. Attempting to add components to one of the standard Swing containers directly will yield a runtime exception. If you see some output on your console that looks like Listing 6.2, you definitely forgot to add your components to the content pane! You probably added them directly to the primary container.

LISTING 6.2   Runtime Errors That Result from Attempting to Add Components to a Heavyweight Swing Container Directly Instead of to Its Content Pane

```
$ java FrameWithComponents
Warning: Cannot allocate colormap entry for default background
java.lang.Error: Do not use FrameWithComponents.add() use
 FrameWithComponents.getContentPane().add() instead
        at com.sun.java.swing.JFrame.createRootPaneException(JFrame.java:323)
        at com.sun.java.swing.JFrame.addImpl(JFrame.java:345)
        at java.awt.Container.add(Container.java:179)
        at FrameWithComponents.<init>(FrameWithComponents.java:29)
        at FrameWithComponents.main(FrameWithComponents.java:57)
```

In order to add components to the content pane, you must first acquire a reference to your primary Swing container's content pane. Notice that you used the `getContentPane()` method to access the content pane. This might seem strange because I said earlier that the Swing containers use a root pane, which in turn uses a content pane.

In fact, the `getContentPane()` method is just syntactic sugar. Underneath the covers, it really accesses the root pane, which acquires and returns a handle to the content. You might also write your code to look like the following. This grabs the root pane explicitly, and then gets the content pane from it.

Listing 6.3 shows you how to acquire the content pane directly using the `getContentPane()` method. This code can replace the first two lines of the constructor in Listing 6.1 so I don't repeat the whole example here.

LISTING 6.3   How to Acquire the Content Pane of a Swing Heavyweight Container

```
public FrameWithComponents()
{
  super("A Swing frame with some components");

  JRootPane rootPane = getRootPane();
  Container contentPane = rootPane.getContentPane();

  contentPane.add(label);

  // The rest of the constructor is unchanged.
  //

}
```

Looking at the relationship between these different panes, you can get a better feeling for what is happening with the acquisitions of different panes. Figure 6.4 shows a UML diagram of the relationship between the root pane and all its constituent panes.

It's generally considered good design to implement a class that does one job well, and that is exactly how these different containers collaborate to produce the Swing containment model.

The root pane seems to have its hands full managing the layout of the menu bar, the glass pane, and the other containers. This is its primary purpose—to manage the layout of these other elements.

Similarly, the content pane has one primary responsibility—to manage the actual child components of the primary container. You add the children to the content pane.

There's one more major part to Swing's containment abstraction. Earlier I mentioned that one new abstraction is the capability of Swing's containers to simulate a front-to-back layering of components. Your last container, the `JLayeredPane`, is the one responsible for creating this abstraction. I'll discuss it now.

Swing Concepts and Architecture

CHAPTER 6

159

6

SWING CONCEPTS
AND
ARCHITECTURE

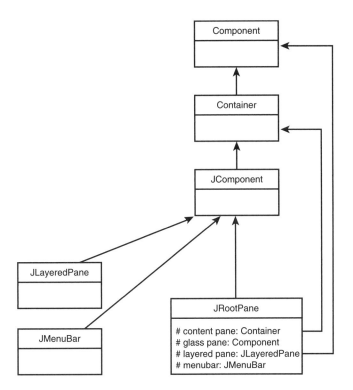

FIGURE 6.4

The four JFC heavyweight containers all contain a `javax.swing.JRootPane` *instance that manages the other panes. This diagram shows the relationship of the panes using UML notation.*

The JLayeredPane Class

The layered pane is a member of the `JRootPane` container hierarchy. It helps the root pane manage the organization and layout of the container's actual children. The layered pane is not visible, but its contents are. Its contents are the actual children of the primary container that is utilizing the root pane—one of the five container types listed in Table 6.4 that you use in your program.

The layered pane serves one primary purpose: it implements a layering abstraction. It stores the actual child components on behalf of the other containers. You can specify in which layer to place a component. The `JLayeredPane` class offers five predefined layers to you, any of which you can specify as one into which you would like to place components when you add them to the container.

The motivation for this class is to enable you to specify a z-order for the container's components. This abstraction is quite useful in a GUI toolkit. It enables you to provide a behavioral abstraction that is friendly and easy to use. For instance, it allows the programmer to ensure that dialog boxes appear above all other components in the container, or to ensure that a pop-up menu—perhaps belonging to a modal dialog box—appears above all components, including the dialog box that owns it.

Figure 6.5 shows a schematic representation of the five layers defined by the JLayeredPane class.

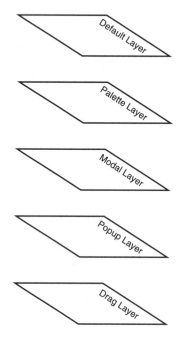

FIGURE 6.5

The five layers enable the JLayeredPane *class to maintain the abstraction of front-to-back layering of its contained components.*

Table 6.7 shows the five predefined layers of the JLayeredPane class.

TABLE 6.7   JLayeredPane's Z-Order Layers

Layer name	Predefined constant	Purpose of layer
Default layer	DEFAULT_LAYER	Contains most of the components contained by this container

Swing Concepts and Architecture

CHAPTER 6

161

6

SWING CONCEPTS
AND
ARCHITECTURE

Layer name	Predefined constant	Purpose of layer
Palette layer	PALETTE_LAYER	Allows floating tool bars and palettes to be displayed over the normal contained components
Modal layer	MODAL_LAYER	Contains modal dialogs, so that they will not be occluded by the contained components
Popup layer	POPUP_LAYER	Contains all pop ups, including those that are part of a dialog
Drag layer	DRAG_LAYER	Allows drawing over all other layers, transcending component boundaries

You can actually specify to which layer you want to add a child component. Table 6.8 below shows some of the methods of JLayeredPane's public interface that support this layering capability.

TABLE 6.8   JLayeredPane's Methods Let You Add Components to Specific Layers

JLayeredPane *method*	Description
int getComponentCountInLayer(int layer)	Counts the number of components in this layer
Component [] getComponentsInLayer(int layer)	Gets all the components in the specified layer
int getLayer(Component c)	Gets the layer that contains this component
int getPosition(Component c)	Gets the relative position of a component within its layer
int highestLayer()	Gets the highest layer in which there are any children
int lowestLayer()	Gets the lowest layer in which there are any children
void moveToBack(Component c)	Moves this component to the back within its current layer
void moveToFront(Component c)	Moves this component to the back within its current layer
void remove(int index)	Removes the component with this index from this JLayeredPane
void setPosition(Component c, int position)	Moves this component to the specified position in its current layer

Figure 6.6 shows a simple GUI that exhibits components in different layers. The top–level frame contains a panel, which contains an internal frame of type JInternalFrame. The menu is displayed in the pop-up layer, so it sits above everything else.

FIGURE 6.6
Layering enables certain components to be displayed on top of others when they need to be visible.

Lightweight and Heavyweight Containers

You might have noticed that all along I've been careful to distinguish between lightweight and heavyweight when discussing various Swing components or when talking about them in general terms. When I talk about how to use the Swing containment model, the inheritance ancestry of the Swing containers is irrelevant because they delegate the containment function to a JRootPane object. However, when I discuss where and how to use Swing containers, you must be aware of their ancestry and their nature as either heavyweight or lightweight containers.

The first five entries of Table 6.9 highlight the five Swing containers that employ the new containment model. Looking more closely at these, you can see that four of them are heavyweight and one is lightweight.

Table 6.9 shows you which of Swing's containers are lightweight and which are heavyweight.

TABLE 6.9   Swings Containers and Their Types

Swing container	Container type	Superclass
JApplet	Heavyweight	java.awt.Applet
JDialog	Heavyweight	java.awt.Dialog
JFrame	Heavyweight	java.awt.Frame
JWindow	Heavyweight	java.awt.Window
JInternalFrame	Lightweight	javax.swing.JComponent
JLayeredPane	Lightweight	javax.swing.JComponent

Swing container	Container type	Superclass
JRootPane	Lightweight	javax.swing.JComponent
JDesktopPane	Lightweight	javax.swing.JLayeredPane
JPanel	Lightweight	javax.swing.JComponent
JScrollPane	Lightweight	javax.swing.JComponent

The container's nature is actually a separate issue from its containment policy. Most Swing containers adopt the new container policy because it gives uniformity to the way Swing containers work. Nevertheless, just as important as uniformity is the notion that using delegation means that any container can adopt this policy without changing its own implementation and without affecting where and how it can be used.

You know that all Java GUI programs require at least one heavyweight container in order to display on the screen. Swing programs are no different. Even though the majority of components have lightweight implementations, you need the four heavyweight containers, which typically serve as your application's outermost container.

The first five entries are containers that you explicitly use as top-level containers in your program. The first four are heavyweight and can be used as outermost containers that can be managed by the native platform window system. You can use a JApplet, JFrame, or JWindow as the outermost container for your application. You use these in exactly the same manner as you use their AWT counterpart containers. The difference is that you now have access to all the new abstractions supported by the Swing tool set.

The JInternalFrame is useful when you want your application to produce a new frame that appears to be managed separately by the native window system or that appears to contain a major functional area of your application. It appears to be a window that exists independently from the rest of your application, and yet it enjoys the benefits afforded all lightweight components.

Unlike the four heavyweight Swing containers, the JInternalFrame class is lightweight. Although it is lightweight, it acts like a heavyweight frame. The only difference is that, because it is lightweight, you can place it inside other containers. However, you still need one heavyweight container to serve as your application's top-level container; you can't use JInternalFrame for this purpose. Using full-featured containers with lightweight implementations means that you don't have to worry about how the multiple native windows are layered by the native window system. The JInternalFrame, as a component inside your other container, will be properly drawn along with all the other components in your application's outermost heavyweight container. Now you have the best of both worlds. Your application is under control, and you haven't lost any capability. You can use an internal frame to produce a frame with a menu bar, making it appear to be an "application-level" container.

Defining the `JDialogBox` class as a heavyweight container comes in very handy. This feature enables you to place a dialog box outside your application's outermost container. It and the other four heavyweight containers produce native peer windows. This means that the management and layering of these windows is out of the control of the application; it's handled by the native window system.

Because of delegation, lightweight and heavyweight containers can both implement the same containment policy even though they are fundamentally different. Any container, regardless of the other aspects of its features or implementation, can choose to delegate the duties of its containment abstraction to a `JRootPane` container, which manages the whole containment abstraction.

> **NOTE**
>
> The use of the new Swing containment model by both lightweight and heavyweight Swing containers is a prime example of *policy versus mechanism* in computer science.
>
> Although the nature of the various containers can be quite different because of their different derivations and implementations, they adhere to the same interface.
>
> The implementation reflects the mechanism used to create the container definition. Support for the API publicizes the implementation's adherence to the containment policy.

From Figure 6.7 you can see that Swing's heavyweight and lightweight components derive from different parents. They are truly different in their nature. The heavyweight containers derive from AWT heavyweight containers, whereas the lightweight containers and components derive from the abstract `JComponent` class.

Here's a perfect example of how delegation enables the different containers to retain their primary nature. Swing needs some heavyweight containers to act as the outermost application container, which can ensure that a native window peer is created to display your application. Without these, all Swing programs would still have to use an AWT container. But the other Swing containers can be used as internal containers and don't need to have native peers. Remember, creating a tool set of lightweight component implementations was one of the primary goals of the Swing architecture in the first place.

Because the `JRootPane` and `JLayeredPane` classes are lightweight, they can be used in either lightweight or heavyweight contexts, without having to create a native window that might interfere with your container's native window.

Swing Concepts and Architecture
CHAPTER 6
165

6

SWING CONCEPTS
AND
ARCHITECTURE

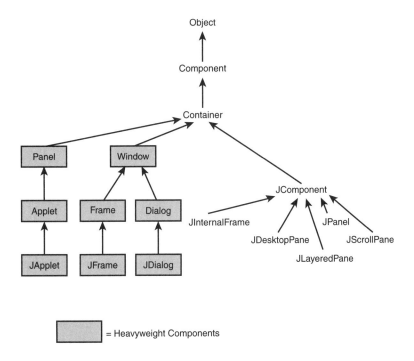

FIGURE 6.7
Swing's heavyweight containers derive from the AWT containers, whereas Swing's lightweight containers are truly lightweight.

Lightweight containers make Swing programs generally more lightweight; they use fewer resources. However, at least one container in every program must still be heavyweight to be able to create the native peer window object that contains the application context. This hasn't changed from the AWT. This means Swing must still define four heavyweight containers, even though the rest of the Swing component set is lightweight.

Now you can see why the delegation model is so powerful. It doesn't matter if your containers are lightweight or heavyweight. They delegate the job of creating the containment abstraction to another dedicated `JRootPane` container class. This approach also allows both container types to present the same containment abstraction, giving the Swing toolkit more consistency.

Heavyweight containers can take on the roles of outermost application containers, whereas lightweights can be used internally. Yet both can still be used where a container is needed.

Configuring Look-and-Feel

By now you're probably getting the idea that `JComponent` is responsible for laying the foundation for many of the features of the Swing components. Swing's customizable look-and-feel, often called Pluggable Look-and-Feel, is also supported by `JComponent`.

Because the AWT components were all heavyweight, each concrete class had to specify the creation of a native peer window that rendered the component appropriately. Buttons looked like buttons; text fields looked like text fields, and so on. Of course, each component looked like a native component for its platform. For example, a Java GUI running on UNIX displayed a button that looked like a Motif button, whereas the components in the same program ended up having a Windows look-and-feel when run on Windows 95 or Windows NT.

The real world is never perfect, and the peer class approach in the JDK inevitably ran into compatibility problems. It was difficult to completely separate the implementation of components' look-and-feel from platform-dependent constraints. The platform-independent AWT code became speckled with platform-dependent references to make things work consistently. This made maintenance and scalability of the AWT difficult.

The solution is to move away from relying on the peer model. Swing introduces a complete set of lightweight component implementations that does just that. The visual appearance of a lightweight component is actually rendered in the context of its enclosing heavyweight container. The heavyweight container is responsible for drawing it along with all the rest of its lightweight children. So, a heavyweight container that contains all lightweight component instances will cause only one native window peer to be instantiated. There is no coupling of lightweight component instances to native peer instances.

This means that there is no native peer doing the rendering. Instead, the Swing components enlist the help of a user interface delegate object. Lightweight components delegate the responsibility of producing their own representations. Whatever object is doing the job can apply a policy that renders the visual appearance of the component according to any style.

Again, you see the power of the delegation model. A Swing component can substitute one of many delegates that all advertise the same policy, but have different implementations that produce different renderings. Each rendering represents a different look-and-feel. In this manner, each component can plug in the delegate that yields the desired look-and-feel.

This is much more flexible than the peer approach. Using peers, the component determines on which platform it is running, and requests the peer to render a representation for the component. The component is at the mercy of the native window system's implementation of that kind of component.

Swing Concepts and Architecture

CHAPTER 6

167

6

SWING CONCEPTS
AND
ARCHITECTURE

With the pluggable look-and-feel approach, a component can use any look-and-feel, regardless of which platform lies underneath. So, for instance, a Java GUI running on a UNIX machine can still look exactly like a Windows application. The application simply plugs in the Windows look-and-feel.

Applications will start with the look-and-feel of the underlying runtime platform. However, this can be changed dynamically.

Listing 6.4 shows an application that will be the starting point for evolving into a program that sets its look-and-feel at runtime. It uses the program that displayed Figure 6.6.

LISTING 6.4   An Application That Uses the Java Look-and-Feel

```java
import java.awt.*;
import javax.swing.*;

public class Layer extends JPanel
{

  public Layer()
  {
    JMenuBar menuBar = new JMenuBar();
    JMenu file = new JMenu("File");

    JMenu edit = new JMenu("Edit");
    JMenuItem item1 = new JMenuItem("Undo");
    JMenuItem item2 = new JMenuItem("Cut");
    item2.setEnabled(false);
    JMenuItem item3 = new JMenuItem("Copy");
    item3.setEnabled(false);
    JMenuItem item4 = new JMenuItem("Paste");
    item4.setEnabled(false);
    JMenuItem item5 = new JMenuItem("Clear");
    item5.setEnabled(false);

    edit.add(item1);
    edit.add(item2);
    edit.add(item3);
    edit.add(item4);
    edit.add(item5);

    JMenu apps = new JMenu("Apps");
    JMenu options = new JMenu("Options");
    JMenu buffers = new JMenu("Buffers");
    JMenu tools = new JMenu("Tools");
```

continues

LISTING 6.4   Continued

```
    menuBar.add(file);
    menuBar.add(edit);
    menuBar.add(apps);
    menuBar.add(options);
    menuBar.add(buffers);
    menuBar.add(tools);

    add(menuBar);

    JInternalFrame iFrame = new JInternalFrame("An internal frame");
    iFrame.setPreferredSize(new Dimension(300, 300));
    iFrame.setJMenuBar(menuBar);
    add(iFrame);

    setVisible(true);
  }

  public static void main(String [] args)
  {
    Layer app = new Layer();

    JFrame f = new JFrame("Example showing component layering");
    Container contentPane = f.getContentPane();
    contentPane.add(app);
    f.pack();
    f.setVisible(true);
  }
}
```

In this code, you see no mention of look-and-feel attributes. This code, run as is, will display its components with Java's own look-and-feel. This is sometimes referred to as the Metal look-and-feel. It's a unique look to Java.

However, with just the addition of a few lines of code, you can make this same program take on the look-and-feel of a Motif, Windows, or Mac program.

First, let's see how to make the program utilize the look-and-feel of the native platform on which it's executing. This is something practical in the real world.

Listing 6.5 shows how the main() method has changed. I don't list the rest of the program, which is unchanged from Listing 6.4. I catch Exception only to avoid distracting you with a large try-catch block. Actually, the two lines of code in the try-catch block could possibly result in any of the following four exceptions being thrown:

Swing Concepts and Architecture

CHAPTER 6

169

6

SWING CONCEPTS
AND
ARCHITECTURE

`java.lang.ClassNotFoundException, javax.swing.UnsupportedLookAndFeelException,`
`java.lang.IllegalAccessException,` or `java.lang.InstantiationException.`

LISTING 6.5   An Application That Uses Its Platform's Default Look-and-Feel

```
public static void main(String [] args)
  {
    Layer app = new Layer();

    try
      {
        String lookAndFeel = UIManager.getSystemLookAndFeelClassName();
        UIManager.setLookAndFeel(lookAndFeel);
      }
    catch (Exception e)
      {

      }

    JFrame f = new JFrame("Example showing component layering");
    Container contentPane = f.getContentPane();
    contentPane.add(app);
    f.pack();
    f.setVisible(true);
  }
```

This version of the program uses the look-and-feel that is native to the platform on which the program is running. On UNIX, it will set the Motif look-and-feel, on Windows it will set the Windows look-and-feel, and so forth.

Now, suppose that you want your program to adopt the same look-and-feel regardless of the platform on which it is running. You first need to determine which looks-and-feels are available to you and then choose one of them. You can only use those supported by the Java runtime environment (JRE) that you are using.

To demonstrate the discover of the looks-and-feels supported by your environment, you can print out their names using the `main()` method in Listing 6.6.

LISTING 6.6   Printing the Names of the Looks-and-Feels Available to Your Program

```
public static void main(String [] args)
  {
    Layer app = new Layer();

    try
```

continues

LISTING 6.6   Continued

```
      {
        UIManager.LookAndFeelInfo [] looks =
          UIManager.getInstalledLookAndFeels();

        for (int i = 0; i < looks.length; i++)
          {
            System.out.println(looks[i].getName());
          }
      }
    catch (Exception e)
      {
        System.out.println(e.getMessage());
      }

    JFrame f = new JFrame("Changing the GUI's Look-and-Feel");
    Container contentPane = f.getContentPane();
    contentPane.add(app);
    f.pack();
    f.setVisible(true);
  }
}
```

This will print the look-and-feel names in a form that is suitable for human consumption; the above code will actually print

```
Metal
CDE/Motif
Windows
```

However, if you want to determine which looks-and-feels are available so that you may choose one to set for your program, you must retrieve the look-and-feel's fully-qualified class name.

Listing 6.7 shows you how to do this. It prints the fully-qualified names of the installed looks-and-feels. The term *installed* refers to the availability of a look-and-feel in the runtime environment, not whether it is set for use by the program. Once again, Listing 6.7 shows only the modified `main()` method.

LISTING 6.7   Obtaining the Fully-Qualified Look-and-Feel Class Names Installed

```
public static void main(String [] args)
  {
    Layer app = new Layer();

    try
      {
```

Swing Concepts and Architecture

CHAPTER 6

171

6

SWING CONCEPTS
AND
ARCHITECTURE

```
        UIManager.LookAndFeelInfo [] looks =
          UIManager.getInstalledLookAndFeels();

        for (int i = 0; i < looks.length; i++)
          {
            System.out.println(looks[i].getClassName());
          }
      }
    catch (Exception e)
      {
        System.out.println(e.getMessage());
      }

    JFrame f = new JFrame("Changing the GUI's Look-and-Feel");
    Container contentPane = f.getContentPane();
    contentPane.add(app);
    f.pack();
    f.setVisible(true);
  }
}
```

This code will produce output as follows:

```
javax.swing.plaf.metal.MetalLookAndFeel

com.sun.java.swing.plaf.motif.MotifLookAndFeel

com.sun.java.swing.plaf.windows.WindowsLookAndFeel
```

These strings can be passed to the setLookAndFeel() method to actually set the look-and-feel of your program. For instance, your program could check for the availability of a particular look-and-feel, and use it to set the program's look-and-feel.

Listing 6.8 shows the new main() method that checks for the presence of the Motif look-and-feel and sets it if available.

LISTING 6.8 Dynamically Discovering and Setting an Application's Look-and-Feel

```
public static void main(String [] args)
  {
    Layer app = new Layer();

    // Set the l&f of the application.  The println() statements are
    // for demonstration.  You shouldn't put these in a real
    // application unless you are debugging.
    //
    try
      {
```

continues

LISTING 6.8   Continued

```
    UIManager.LookAndFeelInfo [] looks =
      UIManager.getInstalledLookAndFeels();

    for (int i = 0; i < looks.length; i++)
      {
        String className = looks[i].getClassName();
        if (className.indexOf("Motif") != -1)
          {
            // Set the specified look-and-feel.
            //
            UIManager.setLookAndFeel(className);
          }
        else
          // Choose an alternate look-and-feel?
      }
  }
catch (Exception e)
  {
    System.out.println(e.getMessage());
  }

JFrame f = new JFrame("Changing the GUI's Look and Feel");
Container contentPane = f.getContentPane();
contentPane.add(app);
f.pack();
f.setVisible(true);
}
```

The program in Listing 6.8 produces the GUI shown in Figure 6.8.

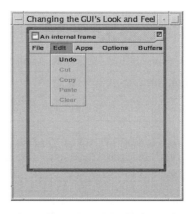

FIGURE 6.8
You can change an application's look-and-feel dynamically.

Table 6.10 lists the classes that are designed to be used by applications to do look-and-feel related tasks.

TABLE 6.10   Look-and-Feel Related Classes

Class	*Description*
`javax.swing.UIDefaults`	A hash table of UI default values available when a program starts
`javax.swing.UIMananger`	Keeps track of the user defaults, current look-and-feel defaults, and system defaults
`javax.swing.UIManager.LookAndFeelInfo`	Inner class of `UIManager` that provides information about an installed look-and-feel

The `UIDefaults` class is really a hash table of UI-related items. You can retrieve the specific instances of these UI elements, which are used to render components in your program.

The `UIManager` class manages three categories of UI-related values. The user defaults are specified by an instance of `UIDefaults` and can be retrieved with a call to `UIManager.getDefaults()`.

You can also retrieve a list of all possible looks-and-feels by calling `getInstalledLookAndFeels()`. The term *installed* refers to those managed by the system, not the ones currently in use. You can create and install a new look-and-feel by calling `installLookAndFeel(String name, String className)` or `installLookAndFeel((UIManager.LookAndFeelInfo info)`.

One other interesting method is the `UIManager.getUI(JComponent target)`, which retrieves a `javax.swing.plafComponentUI` object that is the look-and-feel object that renders the specified component onscreen.

This is an abstract class that defines the nature of all component UI types. Concrete subclasses implement a particular way of rendering a particular component type. Each Swing component has a corresponding concrete `ComponentUI` subclass that can render its appropriate visual representation.

The following list shows the `ComponentUI` subclasses in the `javax.swing.plaf` package.

ButtonUI	MenuBarUI	SplitPaneUI
ColorChooserUI	OptionPaneUI	TabbedPaneUI
ComboBoxUI	PanelUI	TableHeaderUI
DesktopIconUI	PopupMenuUI	TableUI
DesktopPaneUI	ProgressBarUI	TextUI
FileChooserUI	ScrollBarUI	ToolBarUI
InternalFrameUI	ScrollPaneUI	ToolTipUI
LabelUI	SeparatorUI	TreeUI
ListUI	SliderUI	ViewportUI

Notice that the ComponentUI class and its subclasses are defined in the javax.swing.plaf package. The classes in this package implement Swing's pluggable look-and-feel architecture. This replaces the peer approach of the AWT. Instead of each component instantiating a native peer object, Swing components now enlist the help of their associated ComponentUI delegate to render their visual appearance.

The actual object that does the rendering can be any one of several implementations that obey the specified behavior of a component UI object. In fact, when you switch looks-and-feels, each component uses a different component UI object, one that knows how to create a visual representation in the style defined by the current look-and-feel.

Instead of creating their own native peer and drawing into it, lightweight components—or their UI delegate to be precise—draw in the graphics context of their nearest heavyweight container that has a corresponding native window peer. This is how Swing avoids having to create a native window for each component in your program.

Summary

In this chapter I've discussed the Swing concepts and architecture. The most important concepts and abstractions are a new containment model, pluggable look-and-feel, and lightweight components. The lightweight component abstraction provides for the definition of a set of concrete lightweight component implementations.

The JComponent class is the cornerstone of the Swing tool set. It is the root of all Swing's lightweight component and container classes. Additionally, most of the new abstractions and features implemented in Swing are either defined or specified in JComponent.

Creating a set of lightweight components yields significant benefits. First of all, these components use fewer system resources. A program that uses lightweight components will use significantly less memory than an equivalent AWT program. No memory is used to create native peers, and no time is needed to create the native peer for heavyweight components.

Lightweight components don't rely on the native peer model. All lightweight Swing components derive from `JComponent` and inherit its lightweight nature. `JComponent`'s lineage as a descendant of both the AWT `Component` and `Container` classes enables Swing to define lightweight components and containers.

Swing components use a new containment model, supported by `JComponent`, which enables any potential Swing container to take advantage of the new model. Swing containers delegate their containment responsibilities to a root pane object, which uses a proprietary policy for managing elements like menu bars that commonly appear as part of an "application-level" container.

The root pane object in turn enlists the help of a layered pane object that implements yet another abstraction that empowers containers to simulate a z-ordering of their child components.

A container's root pane, content pane, and layered pane can never be null. Attempting to set these to null will generate a runtime exception. Menu bars are optional in a root pane and can be set to null for any container.

Swing components also support a pluggable look-and-feel architecture. Lightweight components no longer rely on the peer model. They are not constrained to use native peer implementations that render components that look like the native look-and-feel. Components can dynamically plug in, or specify, a UI delegate object that implements one of many looks-and-feels. Applications running on one platform can display a looks-and-feel of another native platform.

The `JComponent` class specifies and defines other properties such as support for action objects and internationalization. Action objects depend on an understanding of event handling, so I will cover that subject in Chapter 9.

Now that you have a conceptual understanding of Swing's features and abstractions, it's time to see how the Swing component implementations apply these abstractions to offer you a complete, full-featured, powerful set of concrete components. The next chapter gives you some experience with the pragmatics of using Swing components.

The Swing Components

IN THIS CHAPTER

- The Swing Lightweight Component Tool
  Set   178

In previous chapters, you have essentially looked at the AWT and Swing tool sets from a conceptual perspective. You learned all the major capabilities that are at your fingertips. You were also introduced to the standard AWT components and became familiar with their features and how to use them.

In Chapter 6, "Swing Components and Architecture," you learned how to bring up a simple application on the screen using Swing. You also discovered some important differences between AWT and Swing. The most significant differences are Swing's containment hierarchy and the requirement to use the content pane of Swing containers.

The next step is to take a practical look at how you continue creating applications. It's now time to become familiar with the Swing components, just as you did with the AWT components in Chapter 5, "The AWT Components." I'll introduce the basic Swing lightweight components and help you gain some facility with the mechanics for creating and configuring them.

The Swing Lightweight Component Tool Set

The Swing tool set, which is part of the JFC in JDK Release 2, contains a set of lightweight component implementations. These classes, which comprise the Swing tool set, have two major identifying features:

- New abstractions not in the AWT classes
- Lightweight implementation

In Chapter 6, I introduced the new abstractions supported by the Swing components. Their new features and abstractions define a new interface for Swing components above and beyond what the base AWT classes provide. Most of these abstractions are defined in the JComponent class.

The public interface of the Swing components defines a new policy for behavior. Their lightweight implementation, on the other hand, defines a new implementation mechanism.

I mentioned previously that one of the major enhancements to Release 1.1 of the JDK was support for lightweight components. This support enables the definition of components with lightweight implementations.

The components in the Swing tool set, the JFC components, all have lightweight implementations. There is no rule saying that the Swing components must have lightweight implementations. However, the whole purpose of implementing a new architecture in Release 1.1 of the AWT is to provide the capability to support a more advanced and efficient architecture. Lightweight components are a major part of the enhancements.

It would seem pointless to build the architecture and not take advantage of it. The JFC provides a set of these components to enable you to reap the benefits of the new architecture without having to build a whole lightweight component set yourself. Of course, you are welcome to subclass the standard definitions to suit your specific needs for customization.

Table 7.1 shows the Swing lightweight components and their equivalent AWT classes. Notice that all Swing's lightweight component class names begin with J. This is simply a convention to make it easy for you to identify the classes with a lightweight implementation.

TABLE 7.1   AWT Components and Their Equivalent Swing Components

AWT component class	*Equivalent Swing component class*
java.awt.Applet	javax.swing.JApplet
java.awt.Button	javax.swing.JButton
java.awt.Checkbox	javax.swing.JCheckBox
java.awt.CheckboxMenuItem	javax.swing.JCheckBoxMenuItem
java.awt.Component	javax.swing.JComponent
java.awt.Dialog	javax.swing.JDialog
java.awt.FileDialog	javax.swing.JFileChooser
java.awt.Frame	javax.swing.JFrame
java.awt.Label	javax.swing.JLabel
java.awt.Menu	javax.swing.JMenu
java.awt.MenuBar	javax.swing.JMenuBar
java.awt.MenuItem	javax.swing.JMenuItem
java.awt.Panel	javax.swing.JPanel
java.awt.PopupMenu	javax.swing.JPopupMenu
java.awt.Scrollbar	javax.swing.JScrollBar
java.awt.ScrollPane	javax.swing.JScrollPane
java.awt.TextArea	javax.swing.JTextArea
java.awt.TextField	javax.swing.JTextField
java.awt.Window	javax.swing.JWindow

7

THE SWING COMPONENTS

These Swing versions add to the capabilities of their AWT cousins because of the additional abstractions built into the Swing components, primarily via the auspices of the JComponent class.

In addition to these lightweight implementations, Swing defines some new components not found in the standard AWT. These components round out the tool set, making it much more complete and significantly enhancing its position as a viable platform for serious commercial software development.

Table 7.2 lists some of the new components in the Swing tool set.

TABLE 7.2   New Swing Components in JFC Release 2

Swing component class	Description
JColorChooser	A component that defines color values and allows the selection of colors.
JComboBox	A drop-down list from which items can be selected.
JEditorPane	A text pane that knows how to edit various types of textual content including HTML, RTF, and plain text.
JLayeredPane	A pane that visually simulates several layers of containment into which components can be placed. The simulated layers define a z-order container abstraction to the viewer.
JList	A list of elements that supports various selection policies for the list elements.
JOptionPane	A class that supports several varieties of pop-up dialogs for standard user interactions.
JPasswordField	A text field that doesn't echo characters typed by the user.
JProgressBar	A bar graph that is designed to graphically show progress of a task.
JRadioButton	A standard radio button.
JScrollPane	A pane that can scroll the view of its contents, which are typically other Swing components that adhere to a well-defined interface. The implementation of the Scrollable interface by a component indicates its capability to scroll its contents.
JSlider	A standard slider bar.
JSplitPane	A pane that displays only two views, split horizontally or split vertically.
JTabbedPane	A pane with tabs like a file folder; each folder is a container.
JToggleButton	A button with two states that can be toggled.
JToolBar	A toolbar that can hold components that are tied to application-specific functions.
JToolTip	Fly-over text that can be displayed as part of a component's documentation when the mouse is placed over the component.
JTree	An expandable tree view of hierarchical elements that represents a logical tree organization, that is, a directed, acyclic element hierarchy.
JViewport	A "window" that displays and manages a view of the contents of some other component. Typically the viewport enables scrolling the partial view of the contents of the component whose view it manages.

For the remainder of this chapter, I present the Swing components more or less in alphabetical order. In cases where several components are closely related, such as all the text-related components, I present them together so you can benefit by seeing how they are related and what properties and behavior they share.

Buttons

The Swing component set defines a rich complement of various types of buttons. Swing buttons include the types shown in Table 7.3.

TABLE 7.3   The Swing Button Types

Swing button type	Description
AbstractButton	An abstract class that defines the behavior that is common to all Swing buttons.
JButton	A "standard" button.
JMenuItem	A menu item that can be selected like a button. Menu items also encompass the definition of menus.
JCheckBoxMenuItem	A menu item that can be placed in a menu. It maintains and displays a toggled state like a check box. This class is a subclass of JMenuItem.
JMenu	A menu, which can be selected like a button. It displays a pop up that drops down to display its member menu items. This class is a subclass of JMenuItem.
JRadioButtonMenuItem	A menu item that can be selected like a radio button. It follows the state model of standard radio buttons. This class is a subclass of JMenuItem.
JToggleButton	A button whose state can be toggled.
JCheckBox	A standard check box. This class is a subclass of JToggleButton.
JRadioButton	A standard radio button. This class is a subclass of JToggleButton.

The various button types are arranged in a hierarchy that supports their purpose and function. You can see the organization of the class hierarchy for all the types of buttons in Figure 7.1.

7

THE SWING COMPONENTS

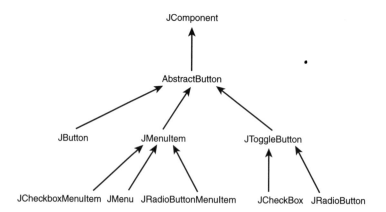

FIGURE 7.1

All types of buttons are rooted at the AbstractButton *class.*

All these button types are extensions of the abstract AbstractButton class, which defines common behavior for all buttons.

Table 7.4 lists the methods and constructors of the AbstractButton class.

NOTE

The table of methods in Table 7.4 is a partial list. Throughout this chapter many of the class descriptions leave out methods that address specific topics covered in subsequent chapters.

Methods that deal with event handling and models, for example, are discussed in their respective chapters.

TABLE 7.4   AbstractButton Class Constructors and Methods

AbstractButton *constructor or method*	*Description*
AbstractButton()	No-arg constructor.
void doClick()	Programmatically simulate the user activating, or clicking, the button. Typically, this method is not called by applications.
Icon getDisabledIcon()	Returns the icon that represents the disabled state of the button.

AbstractButton *constructor or method*	Description
Icon getDisabledSelectedIcon()	Returns the icon used to represent the disabled and selected state of the button.
int getHorizontalAlignment()	Gets the button's policy for aligning its text and icon within its display area. The valid values are AbstractButton.LEFT, AbstractButton.CENTER, or AbstractButton.RIGHT.
int getHorizontalTextPosition()	Gets the position in which the button text label is drawn relative to its icon.
int getIcon()	Gets the default icon used when one is not specified.
Insets getMargin()	Gets the insets object that defines the margin between the button's border and label.
int getMnemonic()	Gets the mnemonic key that activates this button.
Icon getPressedIcon()	Returns the icon that represents the state when the button is pressed.
Icon getRolloverIcon()	Gets the icon displayed when the button is in the rollover state, that is, when the mouse is placed over the button.
Icon getRolloverSelectedIcon()	Gets the icon used to display the button face when the button is selected while in the rollover state.
Icon getSelectedIcon()	Gets the icon displayed on the button face when the button is selected.
Object [] getSelectedObjects()	Returns an array of one element that contains the button's label if selected.
String getText()	Returns the text used as the button label.
int getVerticalAlignment()	Returns the button's vertical alignment, either SwingConstants.TOP, SwingConstants.CENTER, or SwingConstants.BOTTOM.
int getVerticalTextPosition()	Gets the vertical position in which the button label is drawn, relative to its icon.
boolean isRolloverEnabled()	Indicates whether the rollover state is currently set for this button.
boolean isSelected()	Returns the disposition of the selected state of the button.
void setDisabledIcon (Icon disabled)	Sets the icon used to display the disabled state for this button.

continues

7

THE SWING
COMPONENTS

TABLE 7.4 Continued

AbstractButton *constructor or method*	*Description*
`void setDisabledSelectedIcon (Icon disSelIc)`	Sets the icon used to represent the selected disabled state.
`void setEnabled(boolean b)`	Sets the enabled disposition of the button to either enable or disable it.
`void setHorizontalAlignment (int align)`	Sets the horizontal alignment of this button's text and icon within the its display area. Valid values are `SwingConstants.CENTER`, `SwingConstants.LEFT`, or `SwingConstants.RIGHT`.
`void setHorizontalTextPosition(int align)`	Sets the horizontal position of the button's text relative to the placement of its icon. Valid values are `SwingConstants.CENTER`, `SwingConstants.LEFT`, `SwingConstants.RIGHT`, `SwingConstants.LEADING`, or `SwingConstants.TRAILING`.
`void setIcon(Icon defaultIcon)`	Sets the default icon used by this button when no other is specified.
`void setMargin(Insets insets)`	Sets the insets object used by the button.
`void setMnemonic(int mnemonic)`	Sets the mnemonic key represented by the numeric code that represents the keyboard key that activates this button.
`void setMnemonic(char mnemonic)`	Sets the mnemonic key represented by the specified character.
`void setPressedIcon (Icon pressedIcon)`	Sets the icon that is displayed to indicate the button is in the pressed state.
`void setRolloverEnabled (boolean b)`	Sets the button to the rollover state.
`void setRolloverIcon (Icon rolloverIcon)`	Sets the icon displayed when the button is in the rollover state, that is, when the mouse is over the button.
`void setRolloverSelectedIcon(Icon rolloverSelectedIcon)`	Sets the icon displayed when the button is selected while in the rollover state.
`void setSelected(boolean b)`	Sets the disposition of the selected state to the value specified. A value of `True` means the button is selected.

`AbstractButton` *constructor or method*	*Description*
`void setSelectedIcon` `(Icon selectedIcon)`	Sets the icon displayed when the button is selected.
`void setText(String text)`	Sets the text used for the button's label.
`void setVerticalAlignment (int alignment)`	Sets the vertical alignment of this button's text and icon within the button's display area. Valid values are `SwingConstants.CENTER`, `SwingConstants.TOP`, and `SwingConstants.BOTTOM`.
`void setVerticalTextPosition` `(int textPosition)`	Sets the vertical position of this button's text label relative to the placement of its icon. Valid values are `SwingConstants.CENTER`, `SwingConstants.TOP`, and `SwingConstants.BOTTOM`.

As you can see, buttons have quite a rich set of features. They can include an icon as part of their display; in fact, they can display several icons, one for each possible button state.

The `Icon` type is an interface that specifies the operations that are meaningful for images. The `ImageIcon` class is one implementation of the `Icon` interface that you can use to load and manipulate images.

Another feature of Swing buttons is their multistate nature; buttons can have several states, such as enabled/disabled, selected, and rollover. The policy of the rollover state is to display the button's icon only when the mouse is placed over the button.

A button's text and icon can be aligned horizontally and vertically, relative to the button's display area. The positions of the text and icon can also be arranged relative to each other. Horizontally, the text can be to the left or right of the icon, and, vertically, above or beneath the icon.

Buttons also support mnemonic keys. A mnemonic key is a key that can activate the button, in the same manner as a button click. The mnemonic is an integer that represents the key stroke of a particular key, such as a letter. When a mnemonic key is set on the button, the `AbstractButton` class takes care of displaying the appropriate letter with an underline as part of the button's text label.

LISTING 7.1 How to Use Swing Buttons

```
import java.awt.*;
import java.awt.event.*;
import javax.swing.*;
```

continues

LISTING 7.1 Continued

```java
/**
   This class demonstrates the use of Swing buttons.
*/
public class Buttons extends JPanel
{
  /**
     No-arg constructor.
  */
  public Buttons()
  {
    // A normal button with mnemonic key "N".
    //
    JButton b0 = new JButton("Button With No Icon");
    b0.setMnemonic('N');

    // A button with an icon placed to the right of the button text.
    //
    JButton b1 = new JButton("Button With Icon");
    b1.setHorizontalTextPosition(AbstractButton.LEFT);

    // Set the button's icon.
    //
    Icon alarm = new ImageIcon("/home/vartan/dev/book/ch7/alrm_critic.gif");
    b1.setIcon(alarm);
    b1.setMnemonic('I');
    b1.setFocusPainted(true);

    // A disabled button with an icon placed above the button text.
    //
    JButton b2 = new JButton("Disabled Button");
    b2.setVerticalTextPosition(AbstractButton.BOTTOM);
    b2.setHorizontalTextPosition(AbstractButton.CENTER);

    // Set the icon normally displayed.
    //
    b2.setIcon(new ImageIcon("/home/vartan/dev/book/ch7/alrm_minor.gif"));

    // Set the icon displayed when the button is in the disabled state.
    //
    b2.setDisabledIcon(new
        ImageIcon("/home/vartan/dev/book/ch7/alrm_warn.gif"));

    // Set the icon displayed when the button is in the disabled
    // selected state.
    //
    b2.setDisabledSelectedIcon(new
    ImageIcon("/home/vartan/dev/book/ch7/alrm_warn_norm.gif"));
```

```
b2.setMnemonic('D');
b2.setEnabled(false);

// A rollover button. This button has two images. The first is
// usually displayed; the second is displayed when the mouse is
// rolled over the button.
//
JButton b3 = new JButton("Rollover Button");

// Set the normal icon.
//
b3.setIcon(new ImageIcon("/home/vartan/dev/book/ch7/alrm_warn.gif"));
b3.setRolloverEnabled(true);
b3.setVerticalTextPosition(AbstractButton.BOTTOM);

// Set the rollover icon.
//
b3.setRolloverIcon(new
ImageIcon("/home/vartan/dev/book/ch7/alrm_warn_norm.gif"));
b3.setMnemonic('R');

add(b0);
add(b1);
add(b2);
add(b3);
}

public static void main(String [] args)
{
  Buttons app = new Buttons();

  JFrame f = new JFrame("JButton Demo");
  WindowListener wL = new WindowAdapter()
    {
      public void windowClosing(WindowEvent e)
      {
        ((Window) e.getSource()).dispose();
        System.exit(0);
      }
    };
  f.addWindowListener(wL);

  f.getContentPane().add(app);
  f.pack();
  f.setVisible(true);
}

}
```

Listing 7.1 shows how to use the basic features of buttons. Notice the placement of the images relative to the button label text. Relative placement between text and icons is specified with the

```
void setHorizontalTextPosition(int textPos)
void setVerticalTextPosition(int textPos)
```

methods. You specify the desired position of the text relative to the icon. The button object takes care of placing the icon based on your text placement directive.

Also notice the underscore characters beneath the character marked as the button's mnemonic. All types of buttons support the registration of mnemonic keys like this. If you specify a character that is not part of the button's label, no underscore character will appear. In Chapter 9, "Events and Event Handling," I will discuss how to respond to mnemonic key events.

The source code in Listing 7.1 displays the row of buttons shown in Figure 7.2.

FIGURE 7.2

Buttons support a variety of features such as text and icon placement, mnemonic keys, and an enabled or disabled state.

If you disable the third button from the left, it would appear as shown in Figure 7.3. Notice that you are able to display a separate icon for the disabled state of the button. To do this you simply add the following lines of code to your example.

```
b2.setEnabled(false);
b2.setDisabledIcon(new
    ImageIcon("/home/vartan/dev/book/ch7/alrm_warn.gif"));
```

You disable the button and also specify which image to display when the button is disabled.

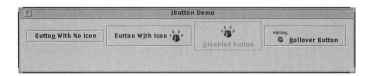

FIGURE 7.3

Buttons can be disabled. When they are, they can display icons showing their disabled state. Additional icons can reveal when buttons are both disabled and selected.

Buttons also support a rollover state, which is characterized by the cursor being placed on top of the button. In Figure 7.3, the cursor is over the right-most button, although it does not appear in the figure because of limitations of the screen capture software. The button displays a different icon than in Figure 7.2 when the cursor is elsewhere. This feature is supported by the following methods.

```
void setRolloverSelected(boolean b)
void setRolloverIcon(Icon rolloverIcon)
void setRolloverSelectedIcon(Icon rolloverSelectedIcon)
```

Check Boxes

Check boxes are defined by the JCheckBox class. Check boxes display a square check box next to their label. Figure 7.4 shows a display that uses some check boxes.

Figure 7.4

Check boxes can have labels and icons, as well as other features defined for all types of buttons.

The label can be placed either to the left or right of the check box, as shown in Figure 7.4. If you try to specify the horizontal text position as CENTER, you will not see the actual box because the label will occlude it.

Listing 7.2 shows the source code that creates the check box display.

Listing 7.2   How to Use Swing Check Boxes

```
import java.awt.*;
import java.awt.event.*;
import javax.swing.*;

/**
  This class demonstrates the use of Swing check boxes.
*/
public class CheckBoxes extends JPanel
{
  /**
    No-arg constructor.
  */
  public CheckBoxes()
  {
```

continues

LISTING 7.2   Continued

```
// A disabled check box.
//
JCheckBox cb1 = new JCheckBox("Carbohydrate");
cb1.setMnemonic('C');
cb1.setEnabled(false);

// An enabled check box. The text for these first four check boxes
// is placed to the right of the actual square check box.
//
JCheckBox cb2 = new JCheckBox("Fat");
cb2.setMnemonic('F');
cb2.setRolloverEnabled(true);

JCheckBox cb3 = new JCheckBox("Protein");
cb3.setMnemonic('P');
cb3.setFocusPainted(true);

JCheckBox cb4 = new JCheckBox("Starch");
cb4.setVerticalTextPosition(AbstractButton.TOP);
cb4.setMnemonic('S');

// Create the panel for the above check boxes. This is the
// left-hand column of check boxes.
//
JPanel chem = new JPanel();
chem.setLayout(new GridLayout(0, 1));
chem.add(cb1);
chem.add(cb2);
chem.add(cb3);
chem.add(cb4);

// A check box with the text to the left of the square check box.
//
JCheckBox cb5 = new JCheckBox("Dairy");
cb5.setHorizontalTextPosition(AbstractButton.LEFT);
cb5.setMnemonic('D');

// Notice the mnemonic keys are the same as one letter in the
// check box text.
//
JCheckBox cb6 = new JCheckBox("Poultry");
cb6.setMnemonic('l');

JCheckBox cb7 = new JCheckBox("Meat");
```

```
    cb7.setMnemonic('M');

    JCheckBox cb8 = new JCheckBox("Vegetables");
    cb8.setMnemonic('V');

    // Create the panel for the second column of check boxes. These
    // appear to the right of the first column.
    //
    JPanel foodGroups = new JPanel();
    foodGroups.setLayout(new GridLayout(0, 1));
    foodGroups.add(cb5);
    foodGroups.add(cb6);
    foodGroups.add(cb7);
    foodGroups.add(cb8);

    add(chem);
    add(foodGroups);
  }

  public static void main(String [] args)
  {
    CheckBoxes app = new CheckBoxes();

    JFrame f = new JFrame("JCheckBox Demo");
    WindowListener wL = new WindowAdapter()
      {
        public void windowClosing(WindowEvent e)
        {
          ((Window) e.getSource()).dispose();
          System.exit(0);
        }
      };
    f.addWindowListener(wL);

    f.getContentPane().add(app);
    f.pack();
    f.setVisible(true);
  }
}
```

Notice that attempting to set the vertical text position makes no sense on check boxes. You can see from the example source that such a request is ignored on the check box labeled Starch.

Because check boxes are types of buttons, they, too, can have a mnemonic key or any other feature defined in the AbstractButton class, such as images.

Radio Buttons

Radio buttons inherit all the same capabilities as other buttons from the `AbstractButton` class. As in the `JButton` and `JCheckBox` classes, radio buttons don't really add many additional methods to those supplied by the `AbstractButton` class.

The `JCheckBox` and `JRadioButton` classes are subclasses of the `JToggleButton` class. Consequently, the states of both of these types of buttons can be toggled simply by clicking the button twice.

Table 7.5 shows the different ways you can construct `JRadioButton` objects.

TABLE 7.5   `JRadioButton` Constructors and Methods

JRadioButton *constructors*	*Description*
JRadioButton()	No-arg constructor, which constructs a radio button that has an empty label
JRadioButton(Icon icon)	Constructs a radio button that displays the specified icon
JRadioButton(Icon icon, boolean selected)	Constructs a radio button that displays the specified icon, and that is initially in the indicated selection state
JRadioButton(String text)	Constructs a radio button that displays the specified string as its text label
JRadioButton(String text, boolean selected)	Constructs a radio button with the specified string as its text label, and that is initially in the indicated selected state
JRadioButton(String text, Icon icon)	Constructs a radio button that displays the specified label and icon
JRadioButton(String text, Icon icon, boolean selected)	Constructs a radio button that displays the specified icon and label and that is initially in the selected state

In fact, radio buttons are very similar in characteristics and implementation to check boxes. The most notable visual difference is that radio buttons present a circle instead of a square in which a solid dot is drawn to indicate their selected state.

However, by convention and not implementation, radio buttons are used differently than check boxes. A group of check boxes places no restriction on how many can be selected. Radio buttons, on the other hand, are normally configured so that only one radio button in a group is selected at a time.

The `JRadioButton` class does not enforce this policy. It is only by convention that programmers use radio buttons in this way. To enforce single selection only, you can use a `ButtonGroup` to group the radio buttons that are to be mutually exclusive in their selection.

Figure 7.5 shows the previous example using radio buttons instead of check boxes. The vertical group on the left does not use a `ButtonGroup`, while the radio buttons in the vertical group on the right-hand side are grouped together with a `ButtonGroup`.

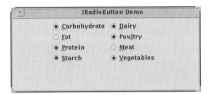

FIGURE 7.5

Radio buttons are displayed with a slightly different look than check boxes. Also, by convention, they are intended to be organized in button groups where only one radio button in a group is selected.

Note that the button group object does not actually physically group the buttons. It only logically enforces the mutual exclusion of selection. The actual radio button objects must still be organized by putting them in a separate panel that lays them out in the desired arrangement.

Table 7.6 shows the constructor and methods of the `ButtonGroup` class.

TABLE 7.6   `ButtonGroup` Constructor and Methods

ButtonGroup *constructor or method*	*Description*
`ButtonGroup()`	No-arg constructor, which constructs a new button group object
`void add(AbstractButton b)`	Adds the specified button to the button group
`Enumeration getElements()`	Returns all buttons that are currently members of this button group
`ButtonModel getSelection()`	Returns the currently selected button
`boolean isSelected (ButtonModel m)`	Indicates if the specified button is selected
`void remove(AbstractButton b)`	Removes the specified button from the button group
`void setSelected(ButtonModel m, boolean b)`	Sets the specified button to the state represented by the specified button model object

Notice that several of the methods in Table 7.6 refer to a new type `ButtonModel`, which is an interface. I will cover models in great detail in Chapter 10, "Models." For now, you can think of a `ButtonModel` as a type that can refer to any button object whose class implements this interface.

7

THE SWING
COMPONENTS

To enforce exclusion of multiple selection among a group of buttons, place the buttons in a button group. Listing 7.3 shows the code that creates Figure 7.6. The radio buttons on the right side belong to a button group.

LISTING 7.3   How to Use Swing Radio Buttons

```
import java.awt.*;
import java.awt.event.*;
import javax.swing.*;

/**
   This class demonstrates use of Swing radio buttons. Radio buttons
   by convention are used where only one radio button out of a set
   should be selected. The JRadioButton class doesn't enforce this
   policy however.
*/
public class RadioButtons extends JPanel
{
  /**
    No-arg constructor.
  */
  public RadioButtons()
  {
    // Construct some radio buttons with mnemonic keys. These first
    // four buttons do not enforce mutual selection exclusion.
    //
    JRadioButton rb1 = new JRadioButton("Carbohydrate");
    rb1.setMnemonic('C');

    JRadioButton rb2 = new JRadioButton("Fat");
    rb2.setMnemonic('F');
    rb2.setRolloverEnabled(true);

    JRadioButton rb3 = new JRadioButton("Protein");
    rb3.setMnemonic('P');
    rb3.setFocusPainted(true);

    JRadioButton rb4 = new JRadioButton("Starch");
    rb4.setVerticalTextPosition(AbstractButton.TOP);
    rb4.setMnemonic('S');

    // Create a panel to hold this first group of radio buttons. This
    // column appears to the left of the GUI.
    //
    JPanel chem = new JPanel();
    chem.setLayout(new GridLayout(0, 1));
```

```
    chem.add(rb1);
    chem.add(rb2);
    chem.add(rb3);
    chem.add(rb4);

    // Create a second set of radio buttons.
    //
    JRadioButton rb5 = new JRadioButton("Dairy");
    rb5.setMnemonic('D');

    JRadioButton rb6 = new JRadioButton("Poultry");
    rb6.setMnemonic('l');

    JRadioButton rb7 = new JRadioButton("Meat");
    rb7.setMnemonic('M');

    JRadioButton rb8 = new JRadioButton("Vegetables");
    rb8.setMnemonic('V');

    // Create a button group, which does enforce mutual exclusion
    // of selection.
    ButtonGroup bg = new ButtonGroup();

    // Place the second set of buttons in this button group.
    //
    bg.add(rb5);
    bg.add(rb6);
    bg.add(rb7);
    bg.add(rb8);

    // Create the panel to hold the second group of buttons. This
    // panel appears as the right-hand column of buttons on the GUI.
    //
    JPanel foodGroups = new JPanel();
    foodGroups.setLayout(new GridLayout(0, 1));
    foodGroups.add(rb5);
    foodGroups.add(rb6);
    foodGroups.add(rb7);
    foodGroups.add(rb8);

    add(chem);
    add(foodGroups);
}

public static void main(String [] args)
{
```

continues

LISTING 7.3   Continued

```
    RadioButtons app = new RadioButtons();

    JFrame f = new JFrame("JRadioButton Demo");
    WindowListener wL = new WindowAdapter()
      {
        public void windowClosing(WindowEvent e)
        {
          ((Window) e.getSource()).dispose();
          System.exit(0);
        }
      };
    f.addWindowListener(wL);

    f.getContentPane().add(app);
    f.pack();
    f.setVisible(true);
  }
}
```

The code is much the same as that in Listing 7.2 with the exception of the ButtonGroup instance that manages the buttons in the right column. It is this button group object that enforces the multiple selection exclusion, not the radio buttons themselves.

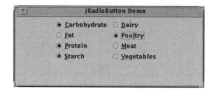

FIGURE 7.6

Radio buttons can be placed in a button group that enforces exclusion of multiple selection. The buttons in the right column comprise a button group.

Combo Boxes

Combo boxes are components that provide the user with a pull-down list of choices. The pull-down list is called the *pop up* of the combo box. The pop up is either shown or hidden (toggled) when the user clicks the combo box's arrow.

Swing combo boxes come in two varieties, editable and noneditable. Editable combo boxes enable you to edit the text in the combo box's selection field, which always displays the currently selected item.

Figure 7.7 shows a combo box with the pop-up window hidden. When you click the button, the pop up is shown. Now the combo box looks like Figure 7.8.

FIGURE 7.7

A combo box that is not displaying its pop-up menu.

In Figures 7.7 and 7.8, the text field of the combo box is gray, signifying that this is an uneditable combo box. The item Java displays initially is the one that you set to be the selected item of this combo box. After the pop up is shown, you can, of course, change the current selection.

FIGURE 7.8

A combo box with its pop-up window shown. This displays all the items that are included in this combo box.

Listing 7.4 shows the source code that produces the combo box shown in Figures 7.7 and 7.8.

LISTING 7.4   How to Use Swing Combo Boxes

```java
import java.awt.*;
import java.awt.event.*;
import javax.swing.*;

/**
   This class demonstrates the use of Swing combo boxes.
*/
public class Combo extends JPanel
{
  /**
    No-arg constructor.
  */
  public Combo()
  {
    // The strings that are used as elements of the combo box.
    //
    String [] progLangs = {"Ada", "Algol", "APL", "C", "C++", "Eiffel",
                            "Forth", "Fortran", "Java", "Lisp", "Modula-3",
                            "Pascal", "PL-1", "Prolog", "Scheme", "Self",
                            "Smalltalk"};

    // Create the combo box with the set of elements.
    //
    JComboBox cb = new JComboBox(progLangs);

    // Make this combo box editable. The window shows with a white
    // background by default.
    //
    cb.setEditable(true);
    cb.setAlignmentX(Component.LEFT_ALIGNMENT);

    // Set the maximum number of rows of display (not the number of
    // elements that the combo box can hold).
    //
    cb.setMaximumRowCount(20);
    cb.setSelectedIndex(8);

    // Not part of the combo box. This label appears above the
    // combo box.
    //
```

```
    JLabel label = new JLabel("Programming languages");

    Box box = Box.createVerticalBox();

    box.add(label);
    box.add(Box.createRigidArea(new Dimension(0, 10)));
    box.add(cb);

    add(box);
  }

  public static void main(String [] args)
  {
    Combo app = new Combo();

    JFrame f = new JFrame("JComboBox Demo");
    WindowListener wL = new WindowAdapter()
      {
        public void windowClosing(WindowEvent e)
        {
          ((Window) e.getSource()).dispose();
          System.exit(0);
        }
      };
    f.addWindowListener(wL);

    f.getContentPane().add(app);
    f.pack();
    f.setVisible(true);
  }
}
```

Figure 7.9 shows an editable combo box. Notice that the text field now has white background, indicating that its contents can be edited. The snapshot shows the state of the combo box and its text field after you selected the item Eiffel and edited it.

The only statement you added to make the combo box editable is the following.

```
    cb.setEditable(true);
```

FIGURE 7.9

You can edit the text field of an editable combo box. The white background tells you that the field is editable. The field Eiffel was selected and then edited to add the word Tower.

Table 7.7 shows the constructors and primary methods of the JComboBox class.

TABLE 7.7   JComboBox Constructors and Methods

JComboBox *constructor or method*	*Description*
JComboBox()	No-arg constructor that constructs a new combo box
JComboBox(ComboBoxModel model)	Constructs a new combo box that uses the specified model to store its elements
JComboBox(Object [] items)	Constructs a new combo box that stores the items in the specified array
JComboBox(Vector items)	Constructs a new combo box that stores the items in the specified vector
void addItem(Object anItem)	Adds the specified item to this combo box
Object getItemAt(int index)	Gets the item located in the specified index in this combo box
int getItemCount()	Gets the number of items currently stored by combo box
int getMaximumRowCount()	Gets the maximum number of items that can be displayed without using a scroll bar
int getSelectedIndex()	Returns the index of the selected item
Object getSelectedItem()	Gets the item that is currently marked as selected

JComboBox *constructor* *or method*	*Description*
Object [] getSelectedObjects()	Returns an array whose element is the single selected item of this combo box
void hidePopup()	Closes the pop-up window used by the combo box to display its elements
void insertItemAt(Object item, int index)	Inserts the specified item at the specified index
boolean isEditable()	Indicates whether the combo box items can be edited
boolean isPopupVisible()	Indicates if the pop up that displays the combo box items is visible
void removeAllItems()	Removes all items from this combo box
void removeItem(Object item)	Removes the specified item from this combo box
void removeItemAt(int index)	Removes the item at the index indicated from the combo box
void setEditable(boolean flag)	Sets the editing policy for this combo box and indicates if items can be edited
void setEnabled(boolean enabled)	Sets the enabled state of this combo box to either enabled or disabled
void setMaximumRowCount (int count)	Sets the maximum number of rows that this combo box can store
void setPopupVisible(boolean v)	Sets whether or not this combo box makes its pop-up window visible
void setSelectedIndex (int anIndex)	Sets the item represented by the specified index to the selected state
void setSelectedItem (Object anObject)	Sets the state of the specified object to selected
void showPopup()	Displays the pop-up window of this combo box

7

THE SWING COMPONENTS

File Choosers

The JFileChooser class defines a handy component for doing file selection. File choosers are used most commonly to select or save a file. However, they cannot do the actual file i/o operation; they simply handle the file specification-related tasks. They enable you to navigate directories.

Figure 7.10 shows a file dialog that can be used for selecting a file to open.

FIGURE 7.10

A file chooser behaves like a dialog, enabling you to select one or more files.

Figure 7.10 shows only one file selected, but you can just as easily select multiple files from the file list.

Listing 7.5 shows the code that produces this dialog. Notice how simple it is to bring up a file chooser.

LISTING 7.5 How to Use a Swing File Chooser

```java
import java.awt.*;
import java.awt.event.*;
import java.io.*;
import javax.swing.*;

/**
  This class demonstrates the use of the Swing file chooser.
*/
public class FileChoose extends JPanel
{
  public FileChoose()
  {
    // Create a file chooser. Specify the directory whose contents
    // should be displayed by the file chooser.
    //
    JFileChooser fc = new JFileChooser(new File("/usr/local"));

    // Set the font for displaying the file names.
    //
    fc.setFont(new Font("SansSerif", Font.PLAIN, 14));
```

```
    Box box = Box.createVerticalBox();

    box.add(Box.createRigidArea(new Dimension(0, 10)));
    box.add(fc);

    add(box);
  }

  public static void main(String [] args)
  {
    FileChoose app = new FileChoose();

    JFrame f = new JFrame("JFileChooser Demo");
    WindowListener wL = new WindowAdapter()
    {
      public void windowClosing(WindowEvent e)
      {
        ((Window) e.getSource()).dispose();
        System.exit(0);
      }
    };
    f.addWindowListener(wL);

    f.getContentPane().add(app);
    f.pack();
    f.setVisible(true);
  }
}
```

You essentially create the file chooser, and it provides a wealth of capabilities by default. After the file chooser is instantiated, the object is capable of navigating directories, filtering, and going directly to the user's home directory.

> **NOTE**
>
> The term *look-and-feel* is often abbreviated to L&F or l&f in Java parlance. A related term, *pluggable look-and-feel*, is often abbreviated by the acronym PLAF, as in a PLAF module.
>
> The `javax.swing.plaf` package contains the implementations of the various pluggable looks-and-feels supplied by the standard JDK.

TABLE 7.8   JFileChooser **CONSTRUCTORS AND METHODS**

JFileChooser *constructor or method*	*Description*
JFileChooser()	No-arg constructor. It creates a JFileChooser that displays the contents of the user's home directory.
JFileChooser (File currentDirectory)	Creates a JFileChooser that displays the contents of the directory specified by the path argument.
JFileChooser (File currentDirectory, FileSystemView fsv)	Creates a JFileChooser that specifies file system view to use to display the contents of the specified directory.
JFileChooser(FileSystemView fsv)	Creates a JFileChooser that uses the specified FileSystemView to access the underlying file system.
JFileChooser (String currentDirectoryPath)	Creates a JFileChooser that displays the contents of the directory represented by the specified string.
JFileChooser (String currentDirectoryPath, FileSystemView fsv)	Creates a JFileChooser that uses the specified file system view to display the contents of the directory represented by the specified string.
boolean accept(File f)	Indicates if the specified file should be displayed— True if yes; False otherwise.
void addActionListener (ActionListener l)	Adds an ActionListener to the button.
void addChoosableFileFilter (FileFilter filter)	Adds a filter to the list of filters that appear in the Files of Type combo box.
void approveSelection()	Changes the object's state in response to being called by the UI when the user hits the Approve button, also known as the Open or Save button.
void cancelSelection()	Changes the object's state in response to being called by the UI when the user hits the cancel button.
void changeToParentDirectory()	Sets the directory viewed by the file chooser to be the parent of the currently viewed directory.
void ensureFileIsVisible(File f)	Scrolls the display to make the specified file visible.
FileFilter getAcceptAllFileFilter()	Returns the file filter that accepts all matches.
AccessibleContext getAccessibleContext()	Gets the AccessibleContext associated with this JFileChooser.
JComponent getAccessory()	Returns the accessory component.
int getApproveButtonMnemonic()	Returns the mnemonic for the Approve button. The Approve button is the Open or Save button by which the user approves the operation.

JFileChooser *constructor or method*	*Description*
String getApproveButtonText()	Returns the text used in the ApproveButton in the FileChooserUI.
String getApproveButtonToolTipText()	Returns the Approve button's ToolTip text.
FileFilter[] getChoosableFileFilters()	Retrieves an array of all the file filters that the user can select.
File getCurrentDirectory()	Returns a file object that represents the current directory.
String getDescription(File f)	Returns a string that describes the specified file.
String getDialogTitle()	Retrieves the string displayed in the file chooser's title bar.
int getDialogType()	Returns the type of the file chooser dialog.
FileFilter getFileFilter()	Returns the file filter that is currently selected.
int getFileSelectionMode()	Returns the mode currently used for file selection.
FileSystemView getFileSystemView()	Returns the file system view object currently used.
FileView getFileView()	Returns the file view currently used. The file view provides a platform-independent view of a file.
Icon getIcon(File f)	Returns the icon for the specified file or file category to which the file belongs. The icon used is governed by the underlying file system.
String getName(File f)	Returns the string name of the specified file.
File getSelectedFile()	Returns the file object that represents the currently selected file.
File[] getSelectedFiles()	Returns an array of file objects that represents all files currently selected.
String getTypeDescription(File f)	Returns the type of the file represented by the specified file argument.
FileChooserUI getUI()	Gets the UI object that implements the L&F (look-and-feel) for this component.
String getUIClassID()	Returns a string that specifies the name of the L&F class that renders this component.
boolean isDirectorySelectionEnabled()	Indicates whether or not directories can be selected, based on the current file selection mode.
boolean isFileHidingEnabled()	Indicates the file chooser's policy for displaying hidden files, that is, those that are not shown by default.

7

continues

TABLE 7.8   JFileChooser **CONSTRUCTORS AND METHODS**

JFileChooser *constructor or method*	*Description*
`boolean isFileSelectionEnabled()`	Indicates if files can be selected, based on the current file selection mode.
`boolean isMultiSelectionEnabled()`	Indicates whether multiple file selection is allowed.
`boolean isTraversable(File f)`	Indicates whether the specified directory can be viewed.
`protected String paramString()`	Returns a string representation of this `JFileChooser`.
`void removeActionListener (ActionListener l)`	Removes an `ActionListener` from the button.
`boolean removeChoosableFileFilter (FileFilter f)`	Removes the specified filter from the set of file display filters.
`void rescanCurrentDirectory()`	Causes the UI to rescan its list of files in the currently viewed directory.
`void resetChoosableFileFilters()`	Resets the set of file display filters to its initial state.
`void setAccessory(JComponent newAccessory)`	Sets the accessory component.
`void setApproveButtonMnemonic (char mnemonic)`	Sets the approve button's mnemonic key using the specified character.
`void setApproveButtonMnemonic (int mnemonic)`	Sets the mnemonic for the Approve Button to the key represented by the specified numeric key code.
`void setApproveButtonText (String approveButtonText)`	Sets the text used in the Approve button in the `FileChooserUI`.
`void setApproveButtonToolTipText (String toolTipText)`	Sets the ToolTip text for the Approve Button.
`void setCurrentDirectory (File dir)`	Sets the current directory to that represented by the specified file object.
`void setDialogTitle (String dialogTitle)`	Sets the file chooser's string title, displayed in the title bar of its window.
`void setDialogType (int dialogType)`	Sets the type of this dialog; valid values are `JFileChooser.OPEN_DIALOG`, `JFileChooser.SAVE_DIALOG`, or `JFileChooser.CUSTOM_DIALOG`.
`void setFileFilter (FileFilter filter)`	Sets the current filter used to filter files displayed in the view.

JFileChooser *constructor* *or method*	*Description*
void setFileHidingEnabled (boolean b)	Sets the policy for hiding files.
void setFileSelectionMode (int mode)	Sets the file chooser's behavior for selecting file system elements to display; valid values are JFileChooser.FILES_ONLY, JFileChooser.DIRECTORIES_ONLY, or JFileChooser.FILES_AND_DIRECTORIES.
void setFileSystemView (FileSystemView fsv)	Sets the file system view used by the file chooser to discern and represent platform-specific file system information in a platform-independent manner.
void setFileView (FileView fileView)	Sets the file view used by the file chooser to retrieve UI information.
void setMultiSelectionEnabled (boolean b)	Sets the selection policy of the file chooser to that represented by the argument. A value of true allows multiple selections; false allows single selections.
void setSelectedFile (File selectedFile)	Sets the specified file to the selected state.
void setSelectedFiles(File[] selectedFiles)	Sets each of the files in the specified array to the selected state, if the file chooser currently allows multiple selections.
protected void setup (FileSystemView view)	Set the configuration of the file chooser to use the specified file system view.
int showDialog(Component parent, String approveButtonText)	Displays a custom dialog with the specified text as the Approve button text. The specified parent is this file chooser.
int showOpenDialog(Component parent)	Pops up a file chooser with an Open File Approve button. The L&F determines the Approve button text.
int showSaveDialog(Component parent)	Pops up a file chooser with a Save File Approve button. The L&F determines the Approve button text.

7

THE SWING COMPONENTS

Table 7.8 shows the constructors and methods of the JFileChooser class. This class defines a wealth of information and capabilities.

As a convenience for programmers, the showOpenDialog() and showSaveDialog() methods present a file chooser dialog with appropriately labeled buttons.

Labels

Swing labels are similar to AWT labels. Swing labels are defined by the `JLabel` class. Labels represent, or display, unselectable text in a container.

Labels are usually used to label some other component in a container, or to give some kind of prompt indication, text, or feedback to the user. A nice feature is that they display an image along with the label text (or alone if no text is desired).

Like buttons, you can specify the relative placement of a label's text and image, horizontally and vertically. You can also position the text and image relative to the label's display area, enabling different alignment locations.

Figure 7.11 shows some labels in a container.

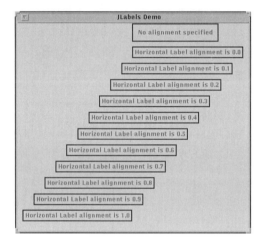

FIGURE 7.11
Labels can be aligned horizontally and vertically.

One of the features available to Swing components like buttons and labels is that they specify their horizontal and vertical alignment within the screen area allocated for their display. Alignment is a very useful feature that gives you more flexibility in choosing a layout for the components in a container.

In Figure 7.11, I intentionally placed a black border around each label so you can see the area allocated for each component's rendering. Listing 7.6 shows the source code for Figure 7.11. By comparing the visual appearance of each label with its corresponding source code, you can see how specifying the alignment changes the position of the label's text within its allotted area.

LISTING 7.6   How to Specify Alignment of Swing Labels

```java
import java.awt.*;
import java.awt.event.*;
import java.io.*;
import javax.swing.*;
import javax.swing.border.*;

/**
   This class demonstrates use of Swing labels. The program paints a
   black border around each label to demonstrate label alignment.

   <p>You must distinguish between the area taken by a label's text
   and the area occupied by the whole label component. The black
   borders outline the component area. This enables you to see the
   alignment of the label's text within its display area.
*/
public class Labels extends JPanel
{
  /**
     No-arg constructor.
  */
  public Labels()
  {
    setLayout(new BoxLayout(this, BoxLayout.Y_AXIS));

    // No alignment specified. The default is 0.0.
    //
    JLabel label4 = new JLabel("No alignment specified");
    label4.setBorder(BorderFactory.createCompoundBorder(
    BorderFactory.createLineBorder(Color.black, 2),
    BorderFactory.createEmptyBorder(10, 10, 10, 10)));

    // Create a label.
    //
    JLabel zero = new JLabel("Horizontal Label alignment is 0.0");

    // Set the alignment to 0.0.
    //
    zero.setAlignmentX(0f);

    // Place a border around the label.
    //
    zero.setBorder(BorderFactory.createCompoundBorder(
    BorderFactory.createLineBorder(Color.black, 2),
    BorderFactory.createEmptyBorder(3, 3, 3, 3)));
```

continues

LISTING 7.6   Continued

```
// Repeat the above steps for all labels, increasing the shift
// in alignment by 10%. Each subsequent label will have 10%
// more of its width aligned to the left of the CENTER of its
// display area.
//
JLabel point1 = new JLabel("Horizontal Label alignment is 0.1");
point1.setAlignmentX(0.1f);
point1.setBorder(BorderFactory.createCompoundBorder(
BorderFactory.createLineBorder(Color.black, 2),
BorderFactory.createEmptyBorder(3, 3, 3, 3)));

// 20% of the label's width will appear to the left of the center
// of the component's display area.
//
JLabel point2 = new JLabel("Horizontal Label alignment is 0.2");
point2.setAlignmentX(0.2f);
point2.setBorder(BorderFactory.createCompoundBorder(
BorderFactory.createLineBorder(Color.black, 2),
BorderFactory.createEmptyBorder(3, 3, 3, 3)));

// 30% of the label's width will appear to the left of the center
// of the component's display area.
//
JLabel point3 = new JLabel("Horizontal Label alignment is 0.3");
point3.setAlignmentX(0.3f);
point3.setBorder(BorderFactory.createCompoundBorder(
BorderFactory.createLineBorder(Color.black, 2),
BorderFactory.createEmptyBorder(3, 3, 3, 3)));

// 40% of the label's width will appear to the left of the center
// of the component's display area.
//
JLabel point4 = new JLabel("Horizontal Label alignment is 0.4");
point4.setAlignmentX(0.4f);
point4.setBorder(BorderFactory.createCompoundBorder(
BorderFactory.createLineBorder(Color.black, 2),
BorderFactory.createEmptyBorder(3, 3, 3, 3)));

// And so forth...
//
JLabel point5 = new JLabel("Horizontal Label alignment is 0.5");
point5.setAlignmentX(0.5f);
point5.setBorder(BorderFactory.createCompoundBorder(
BorderFactory.createLineBorder(Color.black, 2),
BorderFactory.createEmptyBorder(3, 3, 3, 3)));
```

```java
JLabel point6 = new JLabel("Horizontal Label alignment is 0.6");
point6.setAlignmentX(0.6f);
point6.setBorder(BorderFactory.createCompoundBorder(
BorderFactory.createLineBorder(Color.black, 2),
BorderFactory.createEmptyBorder(3, 3, 3, 3)));

JLabel point7 = new JLabel("Horizontal Label alignment is 0.7");
point7.setAlignmentX(0.7f);
point7.setBorder(BorderFactory.createCompoundBorder(
BorderFactory.createLineBorder(Color.black, 2),
BorderFactory.createEmptyBorder(3, 3, 3, 3)));

JLabel point8 = new JLabel("Horizontal Label alignment is 0.8");
point8.setAlignmentX(0.8f);
point8.setBorder(BorderFactory.createCompoundBorder(
BorderFactory.createLineBorder(Color.black, 2),
BorderFactory.createEmptyBorder(3, 3, 3, 3)));

JLabel point9 = new JLabel("Horizontal Label alignment is 0.9");
point9.setAlignmentX(0.9f);
point9.setBorder(BorderFactory.createCompoundBorder(
BorderFactory.createLineBorder(Color.black, 2),
BorderFactory.createEmptyBorder(3, 3, 3, 3)));

JLabel one = new JLabel("Horizontal Label alignment is 1.0");
one.setAlignmentX(1f);
one.setBorder(BorderFactory.createCompoundBorder(
BorderFactory.createLineBorder(Color.black, 2),
BorderFactory.createEmptyBorder(3, 3, 3, 3)));

// Layout management stuff to make it display properly.
//
Box box = Box.createVerticalBox();

Dimension dim = new Dimension(0, 10);

box.add(label4);
box.add(Box.createRigidArea(dim));

box.add(zero);
box.add(Box.createRigidArea(dim));

box.add(point1);
box.add(Box.createRigidArea(dim));

box.add(point2);
```

continues

LISTING 7.6 Continued

```
  box.add(Box.createRigidArea(dim));

  box.add(point3);
  box.add(Box.createRigidArea(dim));

  box.add(point4);
  box.add(Box.createRigidArea(dim));

  box.add(point5);
  box.add(Box.createRigidArea(dim));

  box.add(point6);
  box.add(Box.createRigidArea(dim));

  box.add(point7);
  box.add(Box.createRigidArea(dim));

  box.add(point8);
  box.add(Box.createRigidArea(dim));

  box.add(point9);
  box.add(Box.createRigidArea(dim));

  box.add(one);

  add(box);
}

public static void main(String [] args)
{
  Labels app = new Labels();

  JFrame f = new JFrame("JLabels Demo");
  WindowListener wL = new WindowAdapter()
  {
    public void windowClosing(WindowEvent e)
    {
      ((Window) e.getSource()).dispose();\
      System.exit(0);
    }
  };
  f.addWindowListener(wL);

  f.getContentPane().add(app);
```

```
      f.pack();
      f.setVisible(true);
   }
}
```

In Figure 7.11, each label has a specified horizontal alignment value. The first label uses the default alignment, which means that it is aligned along its left edge. When you align a component along the horizontal axis—the x-axis—you specify how much of the component should lie to the left of the center of the area given for that label.

Alignment values range from 0 to 1. The value 0 means all the label should be to the right of the label's screen area. Another way to think of this is that none of it should be to the left.

Each of the subsequent labels changes its alignment by 0.1, which means each one moves its left edge another 10 percent to the left. You can think of this to mean that you align the left edge of a label to a position such that x percent of the horizontal length of the label is to the left of the center of its allotted area. Thus, a value of 1 would mean align the label along its right edge.

The Component class defines the following useful constants, shown in Table 7.9, which are defined to be used for specifying horizontal and vertical alignment. These can be used instead of specifying a float value. Usually, these constants will be sufficient, unless you are doing a very complex layout.

TABLE 7.9   Component Class Alignment Constants

Component *class constant*	*Description*
static float BOTTOM_ALIGNMENT	A constant that represents a possible value for vertical alignment
static float CENTER_ALIGNMENT	A constant that represents a possible value for horizontal or vertical alignment
static float LEFT_ALIGNMENT	A constant that represents a possible value for horizontal alignment
static float RIGHT_ALIGNMENT	A constant that represents a possible value for horizontal alignment
static float TOP_ALIGNMENT	A constant that represents a possible value for vertical alignment

Table 7.10 lists the JLabel class constructors and methods.

7

THE SWING
COMPONENTS

TABLE 7.10   JLabel Class Constructors and Methods

JLabel constructor or method name	Description
JLabel()	No-arg constructor that creates a Jlabel instance with no display string or image
JLabel(Icon image)	Creates a JLabel instance that displays the specified image
JLabel(Icon image, int horizontalAlignment)	Creates a JLabel instance with the specified image, horizontally aligned within its display area using the specified alignment
JLabel(String text)	Creates a JLabel instance that displays the specified text
JLabel(String text, Icon icon, int horizontalAlignment)	Creates a JLabel instance that displays the specified text and image, aligned as indicated by the horizontal alignment argument
JLabel(String text, int horizontalAlignment)	Creates a JLabel instance that uses the specified text and horizontal alignment
Icon getDisabledIcon()	Returns the icon used to represent the disabled state of the label
int getDisplayedMnemonic()	Returns the keycode that represents the label's mnemonic key
int getHorizontalAlignment()	Returns the label's horizontal alignment within its display area
int getHorizontalTextPosition()	Returns the horizontal position of the label's text, relative to its image
Icon getIcon()	Returns the graphic icon image that the label displays
int getIconTextGap() and its icon	Returns the amount of space between the label's text
Component getLabelFor()	Gets the component labeled by this label
String getText()	Returns the label's text string
int getVerticalAlignment() area	Returns the label's vertical alignment within its display
int getVerticalTextPosition() to its image	Returns the vertical position of the label's text, relative
void setDisabledIcon(Icon disabledIcon)	Sets the icon that represents the disabled state of the label
void setDisplayedMnemonic (char aChar)	Sets the list's mnemonic character represented by the specified char value

`void setDisplayedMnemonic` `(int key)`	Sets the list's mnemonic character represented by the specified integer key code
`void setHorizontalAlignment` `(int alignment)`	Sets the label's horizontal alignment
`void setHorizontalTextPosition` `(int textPosition)`	Sets the label text's horizontal position relative to its image
`void setIcon(Icon icon)`	Sets the icon this component will display
`void setIconTextGap(int` `iconTextGap)`	Sets the space between the label's text and icon
`void setLabelFor(Component c)`	Sets the component labeled by this label
`void setText(String text)`	Sets the text (a single line only) displayed as part of this label
`void setVerticalAlignment` `(int alignment)`	Sets the vertical alignment of the label's display attributes, namely, text and icon
`void setVerticalTextPosition` `(int textPosition)`	Sets the vertical position of the label's text, relative to its icon image

Lists

Swing lists are defined by the `JList` class. Conceptually, they are similar to AWT `List` objects, but much more fully featured. Figure 7.12 shows three `JList` objects.

FIGURE 7.12

`JList` objects can support different selection models, which specify a policy for the number and range of the items that can be selected at the same time.

Lists provide the user with a way to make selections from its set of stored items. When I discussed AWT lists in Chapter 5, "The AWT Components," I showed text strings as the items contained by the list. Of course `JList` objects can also contain text string items, but they can contain much more. In fact, they can contain any `Object`. For example, you can put an image, or a table or a button in a list.

JList objects enable you to select one or more of the items that they contain. When you click on one of the items, it changes its visual appearance to indicate its selected state.

Listing 7.7 shows the code that produces Figure 7.12.

LISTING 7.7   How to Use Swing Lists

```java
import java.awt.*;
import java.awt.event.*;
import javax.swing.*;

/**
   This class demonstrates the use of JList objects, and, indirectly,
   JScrollPanes.
   */
public class Lists extends JPanel
{
  /**
     No-arg constructor.
     */
  public Lists()
  {
    Font f14 = new Font("SansSerif", Font.PLAIN, 14);
    Dimension dim = new Dimension(0, 10);

    // The elements of the left-most list.
    //
    String [] philosophers = {"Aristotle", "Confucius", "Laotze",
                              "Pascal", "Plato", "Rousseau",
                              "Socrates", ""};

    // The elements of the center list.
    //
    String [] painters = {"Michelangelo", "Rembrandt", "Renoir",
                          "da Vinci", "van Gogh", "Monet", "Manet",
                          "Picasso"};

    // The elements of the right-most list.
    //
    String [] mathematicians = {"Abel", "Chebyshev", "Dirichlet",
                                "Fourier", "Lagrange", "Galois",
                                "Gauss", "Laplace", "Landau"};

    // The left-most list supports single selection.
    //
    JList singleSelectionList = new JList();
    singleSelectionList.setVisibleRowCount(7);
```

```java
singleSelectionList.setFont(f14);
singleSelectionList.setAlignmentX(Component.LEFT_ALIGNMENT);
singleSelectionList.setListData(philosophers);
singleSelectionList.setSelectionMode(
    ListSelectionModel.SINGLE_SELECTION);

// Place the JList in a scroll pane so that its contents can be
// scrolled.
//
JScrollPane ssPane = new JScrollPane(singleSelectionList);
ssPane.setVerticalScrollBarPolicy(
    JScrollPane.VERTICAL_SCROLLBAR_ALWAYS);

Box singleSelectionBox = Box.createVerticalBox();

// This label identified the single selection list.
//
JLabel singleSelectionLabel = new JLabel("Single Selection List");
singleSelectionLabel.setAlignmentX(Component.LEFT_ALIGNMENT);

singleSelectionBox.add(singleSelectionLabel);
singleSelectionBox.add(Box.createRigidArea(dim));
singleSelectionBox.add(ssPane);

// This list supports the selection of a single contiguous range
// of list elements.
//
JList singleIntervalList = new JList();
singleIntervalList.setVisibleRowCount(7);
singleIntervalList.setAlignmentX(Component.LEFT_ALIGNMENT);
singleIntervalList.setFont(f14);
singleIntervalList.setListData(painters);
singleIntervalList.setSelectionMode(
    ListSelectionModel.SINGLE_INTERVAL_SELECTION);

Box singleIntervalBox = Box.createVerticalBox();

// This label identifies the single interval list on the GUI.
//
JLabel singleIntervalLabel = new JLabel("Single Interval List");
singleIntervalLabel.setAlignmentX(Component.LEFT_ALIGNMENT);

singleIntervalBox.add(singleIntervalLabel);
singleIntervalBox.add(Box.createRigidArea(dim));
singleIntervalBox.add(new JScrollPane(singleIntervalList));
```

7

THE SWING COMPONENTS

continues

LISTING 7.7   Continued

```java
// This list supports the selection of multiple contiguous ranges
// of list elements.
//
JList multipleIntervalList = new JList();
multipleIntervalList.setVisibleRowCount(7);
multipleIntervalList.setAlignmentX(Component.LEFT_ALIGNMENT);
multipleIntervalList.setFont(f14);
multipleIntervalList.setListData(mathematicians);
multipleIntervalList.addSelectionInterval(0, 2);
multipleIntervalList.addSelectionInterval(4, 5);

Box multipleIntervalBox =  Box.createVerticalBox();

// This label identifies the multiple selection list on the GUI.
//
JLabel multipleIntervalLabel = new JLabel("Multiple Interval List");
multipleIntervalLabel.setAlignmentX(Component.LEFT_ALIGNMENT);

multipleIntervalBox.add(multipleIntervalLabel);
multipleIntervalBox.add(Box.createRigidArea(dim));
multipleIntervalBox.add(new JScrollPane(multipleIntervalList));

Box mainBox = Box.createHorizontalBox();

mainBox.add(singleSelectionBox);
mainBox.add(Box.createHorizontalStrut(20));
mainBox.add(singleIntervalBox);
mainBox.add(Box.createHorizontalStrut(20));
mainBox.add(multipleIntervalBox);

add(mainBox);
}

public static void main(String [] args)
{
  Lists app = new Lists();

  JFrame f = new JFrame("JList Demo");
  WindowListener wL = new WindowAdapter()
    {
      public void windowClosing(WindowEvent e)
        {
          ((Window) e.getSource()).dispose();
          System.exit(0);
```

```
        }
    };
    f.addWindowListener(wL);
    f.getContentPane().add(app);
    f.pack();
    f.setVisible(true);
  }

}
```

Swing lists support different *selection models*. A selection model specifies a policy for determining the number and range of items that can be selected at once. The JList class can support three different selection models.

- Single selection model—Supports at most one selected item at a time.

- Single interval model—Supports at most one contiguous interval of selected items at a time. For example, in a list of ten items, the contiguous range of items between indices two and five might all be selected together as one interval.

- Multiple interval model—Supports multiple contiguous intervals of selected items at the same time. For example, the items with indices two through five *and* those with indices seven through nine could all be in the selected state at once.

The JList class supports this capability by using a model that handles the details of implementing one of the policies. When you instantiate the JList class, you specify which selection model you desire. The constructor then creates the model object that knows how to adhere to the policy you specified.

This is an example of the Model-View-Controller architecture that I introduced conceptually in Chapter 2, "Introducing the Java Foundation Classes." All Swing components are designed to support the MVC paradigm.

Swing components use the type of model that is appropriate for the kind of data abstraction that the component presents to the user. The model itself is the Model component of the MVC triad, although the Swing component is the View component that gives you a visual representation of the data managed by the model.

In the JList example, you can see that regardless of the exact details of the selection model's policy, all three of the models are of the same general type.

Models are an involved topic, and I devote Chapter 10, "Models," to them. It is important for you to understand conceptually what models are and how they work within the Swing component framework before you can use them effectively. I gently introduce this concept here, with your first concrete look at how Swing uses models. Repetition is the key to learning, and you will have seen models a few times by the time you dive headlong into the topic in Chapter 10.

Table 7.11 lists the constructors and methods of the JList class. Notice that the second constructor takes an argument of type ListModel. This is an interface that specifies the API that *all* types of list models must support. The idea is that it captures the nature of any specific implementation of a data structure whose contents can be viewed as a list of items.

A specific implementation of this interface can specify its own policy. In fact, this is exactly the difference between the three types of list models that the JList class can use.

The

```
ListModel getModel()
void setModel(ListModel model)
```

methods support changing a list's model.

TABLE 7.11   JList Constructors and Methods

JList *constructor or method name*	*Description*
JList()	No-arg constructor. It constructs a JList with an empty data model.
JList(ListModel dataModel)	Creates a JList populated with elements contained in the specified model.
JList(Object[] listData)	Creates a JList populated with the elements in the specified array.
JList(Vector listData)	Creates a JList populated with the elements in the specified Vector.
void addSelectionInterval(int anchor, int lead)	Sets the list's selection to be the union of the specified interval and the list's current selection.
void clearSelection()	Clears the list's selection.
protected ListSelectionModel createSelectionModel()	Returns an instance of DefaultListSelectionModel.
void ensureIndexIsVisible(int index)	Scrolls the view port, if any, to make the element represented by the specified index completely visible.
protected void fireSelectionValueChanged (int firstIndex, int lastIndex, boolean isAdjusting)	Notifies registered listeners of a change in the list's selection model.
int getAnchorSelectionIndex()	Returns the value that represents the low index that marks the current selection from the most recent addSelectionInterval or setSelectionInterval call.

JList *constructor or* *method name*	*Description*
Rectangle getCellBounds(int index1, int index2)	Returns the bounds of the items contained in the range specified by the two index arguments.
ListCellRenderer getCellRenderer()	Returns the object that renders the list items.
int getFirstVisibleIndex()	Returns the index of the first visible cell, that is, the cell in the upper-left corner of the JList. It returns -1 if nothing is visible or if the list is empty.
int getFixedCellHeight()	Returns the value of the fixedCellHeight variable.
int getFixedCellWidth()	Returns the value of the fixedCellWidth property.
int getLastVisibleIndex()	Returns the index of the last visible cell, that is, the cell in the lower right corner of the JList. It returns -1 if nothing is visible or if the list is empty.
int getLeadSelectionIndex()	Returns the value of the index that marks the "lead" item of the set of selected items.
int getMaxSelectionIndex()	Returns the largest selected cell index.
int getMinSelectionIndex()	Returns the smallest selected cell index.
ListModel getModel()	Returns the data model used by this JList to store its elements.
Dimension getPreferredScrollable ViewportSize()	Computes the size of the view port needed to display the number of rows represented by the visibleRowCount variable.
Object getPrototypeCellValue()	Returns the cell width used to represent the width of the cells for all the list's elements.
int getScrollableBlockIncrement (Rectangle visibleRect, int orientation, int direction)	Returns the value of the block increment, which is used to scroll the list by one block.
boolean getScrollableTracksViewport Height()	Indicates if the height of this JList changes when the height of its JViewport, if any, changes.
boolean getScrollableTracks ViewportWidth()	Indicates if the width of this JList changes when the width of its JViewport, if any, changes.
int getScrollableUnitIncrement (Rectangle visibleRect, int orientation, int direction)	Returns the amount by which the list is scrolled during a unit scroll event.
int getSelectedIndex()	Returns the index of the first selected item.

7

THE SWING COMPONENTS

continues

TABLE 7.11   Continued

JList *constructor or method name*	*Description*
int[] getSelectedIndices()	Returns an array of the indices of all the selected items.
Object getSelectedValue()	Returns the value of the first selected item, or null if nothing is selected.
Object[] getSelectedValues()	Returns an array of the values of the selected elements.
Color getSelectionBackground()	Returns the background color used to paint the selected cells.
Color getSelectionForeground()	Returns the color used to paint the foreground of the selected cells.
int getSelectionMode()	Indicates whether the selection policy is single-item or multiple-item.
ListSelectionModel getSelectionModel()	Returns the selection model object.
boolean getValueIsAdjusting()	Indicates the adjustment state of the data model, that is, the value of the model's isAdjusting property.
int getVisibleRowCount()	Returns the preferred number of visible rows.
Point indexToLocation(int index)	Returns the point that represents the origin of the list item specified by the index argument.
boolean isSelectedIndex(int index)	Indicates if the element at the specified index is selected.
boolean isSelectionEmpty()	Indicates if there are any list elements currently selected.
int locationToIndex(Point location)	Converts a point relative to the JList component's upper left corner to the index of the cell at that location.
void removeSelectionInterval (int index0, int index1)	Sets the list's selection to be the difference between the specified interval and the current selection.
void setFixedCellHeight(int height)	Defines the height of every cell in the list.
void setFixedCellWidth(int width)	Defines the width of every cell in the list.
void setListData(Object[] listData)	Constructs a ListModel object from the specified array of Objects and sets it to be the list's model object.

JList *constructor or method name*	*Description*
void setListData(Vector listData)	Constructs a ListModel object from the specified Vector and sets it to be the list's model object.
void setPrototypeCellValue (Object prototypeCellValue)	Sets the value of the list's fixedCellWidth and fixedCellHeight variables.
void setSelectedIndex(int index)	Sets the list's selection to be the specified single cell.
void setSelectedIndices(int[] indices)	Sets the list's selection to be the cells represented by the array of indices.
void setSelectedValue(Object anObject, boolean shouldScroll)	Sets the specified object to be the selected element of this list.
void setSelectionBackground (Color selectionBackground)	Sets the color used to paint the background of selected cells.
void setSelectionForeground (Color selectionForeground)	Sets the color used to paint the foreground of selected cells.
void setSelectionInterval(int anchor, int lead)	Sets the list's selection to be the cells contained in the specified interval.
void setSelectionMode(int selectionMode)	Sets the selection policy for the list, either single-item or multiple-item selections.
void setValueIsAdjusting (boolean b)	Sets the adjustment state of the data model. If this is True, only one selection event is fired when all the selections have stabilized, for example, when the user stops dragging the mouse.
void setVisibleRowCount(int visibleRowCount)	Sets the preferred number of list rows to be displayed without using a scrollbar.

Menus and Menu Bars

Menus provide a convenient place to store selectable components. Menus are placed on a menu bar. In the Swing tool set, only top-level containers like JFrame and JInternalFrame have menu bars.

Some aspects of Swing's menu-related components are similar in organization to their AWT counterparts, but there are also some differences in their organizational hierarchy.

Figure 7.13 shows the part of the Swing class hierarchy that contains Swing's menu-related components.

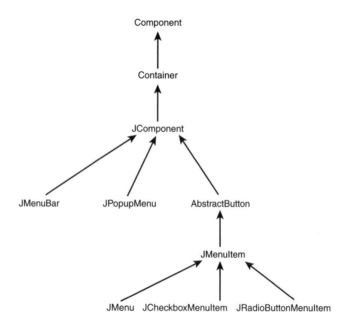

FIGURE 7.13

The Swing component hierarchy defines menu-related classes differently than the AWT. In Swing, menus and menu items are types of buttons.

Swing menus are defined by the JMenu class. All menus are a type of JMenuItem. This relationship is a manifestation of the Composite design pattern that I mentioned in Chapter 4, "AWT Concepts and Architecture."

If you compare Figure 7.13 with Figure 4.1 you will notice that Swing menus and menu items are types of buttons, but AWT menus and menu items are types of menu components. This is one outstanding difference between Swing and AWT menus.

Swing does not have the equivalent of the AWT MenuComponent class; the JMenuItem and JMenu classes directly subclass AbstractButton. In the chapter on event handling, you will see that this abstraction of making menu items buttons enables menu items to perform event handling just as buttons do.

The JMenuBar class defines a menu bar, which can contain multiple menus. The Swing components that know how to manage a menu bar place their menu bars at the top of their containers. Notice that the JMenuBar class is a subclass of JComponent. Its lightweight nature makes it rather easy for any component to contain it. For example, the JInternalFrame class, which is itself lightweight, contains a menu bar. Top-level, heavyweight containers are not the only components that can manage menu bars.

The JPopupMenu class defines pop-up menus. It, too, directly subclasses JComponent. This means that any container can contain a pop-up menu, which supports a very flexible and powerful model for enabling pop ups to be used by almost any component.

Figure 7.14 shows a menu bar and some menus in a container. After the leftmost menu is dropped down, you can see that it contains a nested menu, sometimes called a walking menu.

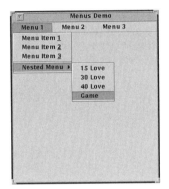

FIGURE 7.14

Menus are components managed by containers. Menus contain menu items that can include other menus, giving a cascading menu organization.

Because menus and menu items are types of buttons, they inherit all the definitions of AbstractButton. For example, you can see in Figure 7.14 that the first three menu items in the first menu each have a mnemonic key set. This is an example of the power of defining menu components to be types of buttons; they can act like buttons.

Listing 7.8 shows the source code for Figure 7.14.

LISTING 7.8   How to Use Swing Menus

```
import java.awt.*;
import java.awt.event.*;
import java.io.*;
import javax.swing.*;

/**
  This class demonstrates use of Swing menus. Menus in Swing are
  organized differently than AWT menus in the component hierarchy.
*/
public class Menus extends JFrame
{
  /**
```

continues

LISTING 7.8   Continued

```
    No-arg constructor.
*/
public Menus()
{
  super("Menus Demo");

  Container contentPane = getContentPane();

  Font f14 = new Font("SansSerif", Font.PLAIN, 14);
  Dimension dim = new Dimension(0, 10);

  // Create the menu "Menu 1", which is the leftmost menu on the
  // menu bar.
  //
  JMenu menu1 = new JMenu("Menu 1");

  // Create the menu items that are part of "Menu 1".
  //
  JMenuItem mi1 = new JMenuItem("Menu Item 1");
  mi1.setMnemonic('1');
  JMenuItem mi2 = new JMenuItem("Menu Item 2");
  mi2.setMnemonic('2');
  JMenuItem mi3 = new JMenuItem("Menu Item 3");
  mi3.setMnemonic('3');

  // Create the sub-menu "Nested Menu" that is the last item of
  // the "Menu 1" menu.
  //
  JMenu menu1_1 = new JMenu("Nested Menu");

  // Create the menu items for the "Nested Menu" menu.
  //
  JMenuItem mi1_1 = new JMenuItem("15 Love");
  mi1_1.setHorizontalAlignment(SwingConstants.LEFT);
  JMenuItem mi1_2 = new JMenuItem("30 Love");
  JMenuItem mi1_3 = new JMenuItem("40 Love");
  JMenuItem mi1_4 = new JMenuItem("Game");

  // Add the "Nested Menu" menu items to the "Nested Menu".
  //
  menu1_1.add(mi1_1);
  menu1_1.add(mi1_2);
  menu1_1.add(mi1_3);
  menu1_1.add(mi1_4);
```

```
// Add the first three menu items to the "Menu 1" menu. Then add
// a separator to separate the nested menu. Finally, add the
// "Nested Menu" last.
//
menu1.add(mi1);
menu1.add(mi2);
menu1.add(mi3);
menu1.addSeparator();
menu1.add(menu1_1);

// Create the second and third menus, "Menu 2" and "Menu 3", which
// are placed to the right of "Menu 1" on the menu bar.
//
JMenu menu2 = new JMenu("Menu 2");
JMenu menu3 = new JMenu("Menu 3");

// --------

// Insert code for Listing 7.9 and Figure 7.15 here.

// --------

// Create the menu bar; don't forget this step!
//
JMenuBar menuBar = new JMenuBar();

// Add the three top-level menus, "Menu 1", "Menu 2", and "Menu 3"
// to the menu bar.
//
menuBar.add(menu1);
menuBar.add(menu2);
menuBar.add(menu3);

  setJMenuBar(menuBar);
}

public Dimension getPreferredSize()
{
  return new Dimension(300, 400);
}

public static void main(String [] args)
{
  Menus app = new Menus();
  WindowListener wL = new WindowAdapter()
    {
```

continues

LISTING 7.8   Continued

```
      public void windowClosing(WindowEvent e)
      {
        ((Window) e.getSource()).dispose();
        System.exit(0);
      }
    };
    app.addWindowListener(wL);

    app.pack();
    app.setVisible(true);
  }
}
```

You can also add check boxes and radio buttons to menus by using the JCheckboxMenuItem
and JRadioButtonMenuItem classes. Their names reflect their intended use, which is to act as
check boxes and menu items that can be placed in a menu.

Figure 7.15 shows the menus after adding some check boxes and radio buttons.

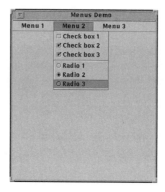

FIGURE 7.15
Swing defines two classes that make it easy for you to add check boxes and radio buttons to a menu.

Like other radio buttons defined by the JRadioButton class, the JRadioButtonMenuItem itself
does not enforce multiple selection exclusion. You must do that by using a ButtonGroup object
as you did earlier.

Listing 7.9 shows the code you add to Listing 7.8 to create your second menu of check boxes
and radio buttons. The code in Listing 7.9 can be added to the constructor in Listing 7.8 in
place of the comment "Insert code for Listing 7.9 and Figure 7.15 here."

LISTING 7.9 How to Use Swing Check Box Menu Items and Radio Button Menu Items

```
...

JCheckBoxMenuItem cbmi1 = new JCheckBoxMenuItem("Check box 1");
JCheckBoxMenuItem cbmi2 = new JCheckBoxMenuItem("Check box 2");
JCheckBoxMenuItem cbmi3 = new JCheckBoxMenuItem("Check box 3");

menu2.add(cbmi1);
menu2.add(cbmi2);
menu2.add(cbmi3);
menu2.addSeparator();

JRadioButtonMenuItem rbmi1 = new JRadioButtonMenuItem("Radio 1");
JRadioButtonMenuItem rbmi2 = new JRadioButtonMenuItem("Radio 2");
JRadioButtonMenuItem rbmi3 = new JRadioButtonMenuItem("Radio 3");

ButtonGroup bg = new ButtonGroup();
bg.add(rbmi1);
bg.add(rbmi2);
bg.add(rbmi3);

menu2.add(rbmi1);
menu2.add(rbmi2);
menu2.add(rbmi3);

...
```

Let's take a look at the methods of the menu related classes. Table 7.12 shows the constructors and methods of the JMenu class.

TABLE 7.12 JMenu Class Constructors and Methods

JMenu *constructor or method name*	*Description*
JMenu()	No-arg constructor. It creates a new JMenu with no text label.
JMenu(String s)	Creates a new JMenu with the specified string as its text label.
JMenu(String s, boolean b)	Creates a new JMenu with the specified string as its text label. The boolean argument specifies whether or not the menu is a tear-off menu. A tear-off menu can exist in its own window even after the pop-up window of its parent menu is closed.

continues

TABLE 7.12   Continued

JMenu *constructor or method name*	*Description*
`Component add(Component c)`	Appends the specified component to the end of the menu.
`JMenuItem add(JMenuItem menuItem)`	Appends the specified menu item to the end of the menu.
`JMenuItem add(String s)`	Creates a new menu item with the specified text. The menu item is appended to the end of the menu.
`void addMenuListener (MenuListener l)`	Adds the specified listener for menu events on this menu.
`void addSeparator()`	Appends a new separator to the end of the menu. Separators are rendered as raised horizontal lines.
`void doClick(int pressTime)`	Programmatically perform a selection of the menu that simulates the user clicking on the menu.
`Component getComponent()`	Returns the component that paints this menu.
`int getDelay()`	Returns the value of the time delay that transpires before the menu's pop-up menu is popped up or down.
`JMenuItem getItem(int pos)`	Returns the JMenuItem located at the specified position.
`int getItemCount()`	Returns the number of items on the menu, including separators.
`Component getMenuComponent(int n)`	Returns the component at the specified position.
`int getMenuComponentCount()`	Returns the number of components in the menu.
`Component[] getMenuComponents()`	Returns an array of the menu's subcomponents.
`JPopupMenu getPopupMenu()`	Returns this menu's pop-up menu.
`MenuElement[] getSubElements()`	Returns an array of the submenu components for this menu.
`String getUIClassID()`	Returns the name of the L&F class that renders this component.
`JMenuItem insert (Action a, int pos)`	Inserts a new menu item at the specified position in the menu. The specified Action object is registered as an action listener on the new menu item.
`JMenuItem insert (JMenuItem mi, int pos)`	Inserts the specified JMenuitem at the specified position.
`void insert(String s, int pos)`	Constructs a new menu item with the specified text and inserts it at the specified position.

`JMenu` *constructor or method name*	*Description*
`void insert(String s, int pos)`	Constructs a new menu item with the specified text and inserts it at the specified position.
`void insertSeparator(int index)`	Inserts a separator at the specified position.
`boolean isMenuComponent (Component c)`	Returns True if the specified component is a submenu of this menu.
`boolean isPopupMenuVisible()`	Indicates if the menu's pop-up window is visible.
`boolean isSelected()`	Indicates if the menu is currently selected (popped up).
`boolean isTearOff()`	Indicates if the menu is a tear-off menu—that is, if it can be torn from its containing menu or menu bar.
`boolean isTopLevelMenu()`	Indicates if the menu is a top-level menu, that is, if it is the direct child of a menu bar.
`void menuSelectionChanged (boolean isIncluded)`	Changes the selection state of this menu.
`void remove(Component c)`	Removes the specified component from this menu.
`void remove(int pos)`	Removes the menu item located at the specified index from this menu.
`void remove(JMenuItem item)`	Removes the specified menu item from this menu.
`void removeAll()`	Removes all this menu's items.
`void setAccelerator (KeyStroke keyStroke)`	Does nothing for the `JMenu` class.
`void setDelay(int d)`	Sets the delay time that transpires before the menu's pop-up menu is popped up or down.
`void setMenuLocation (int x, int y)`	Sets the location of the pop-up menu component.
`void setModel (ButtonModel newModel)`	Sets the data model for the menu item.
`void setPopupMenuVisible (boolean b)`	Sets the visibility of the menu's pop-up portion.
`void setSelected(boolean b)`	Sets the selection status of the menu.

Table 7.13 lists the `JMenuItem` class constructors and methods. Notice that most of the capabilities of menus are defined in the `JMenu` class. Although menus are menu items, the `JMenuItem` class cannot define the behavior that is special for menus, that is, the way menus manage their member items.

This situation is somewhat different than the earlier one in which the `AbstractButton` class could define most of the capabilities for all types of buttons.

TABLE 7.13 `JMenuItem` Constructors and Methods

`JMenuItem` constructor or method name	Description
`JMenuItem()`	No-arg constructor. It creates a menu item with no defined text or icon.
`JMenuItem(Icon icon)`	Creates a menu item that displays the specified icon.
`JMenuItem(String text)`	Creates a menu item that displays the specified text.
`JMenuItem(String text, Icon icon)`	Creates a menu item that displays both the specified text and icon.
`JMenuItem(String text, int mnemonic)`	Creates a menu item that displays the specified text and keyboard mnemonic, represented by an underline beneath the mnemonic character in the menu item's text.
`KeyStroke getAccelerator()`	Returns the `KeyStroke` object that is the accelerator for the menu item.
`AccessibleContext getAccessibleContext()`	Gets the `AccessibleContext` associated with this menu item.
`Component getComponent()`	Returns the component used to paint the menu item.
`MenuElement[] getSubElements()`	Returns an array of the submenu components of this menu item. This menu item must be a menu to contain submenus.
`String getUIClassID()`	Returns the name of the L&F class that renders this component.
`protected void init (String text, Icon icon)`	Initializes the string and icon displayed for the menu item with the specified quantities.
`boolean isArmed()`	Indicates whether the menu item is Armed. An armed button is one that has been pressed but not released.
`void menuSelectionChanged (boolean isIncluded)`	Sets the menu item's state when it is selected or deselected. It is called by the `MenuSelectionManager`, not applications.
`void setAccelerator (KeyStroke keyStroke)`	Set the `KeyStroke` object that represents the key combination which selects the menu item. This is equivalent to the user selecting the menu item.
`void setArmed(boolean b)`	Sets the state of the menu item to Armed or Not Armed.
`void setEnabled(boolean b)`	Sets the enabled or disabled state of the menu item.

For completeness, I've also included the JMenuBar class description in Table 7.14.

TABLE 7.14   JMenuBar Constructors and Methods

JMenuBar *constructor or method name*	*Description*
JMenuBar()	No-arg constructor. It creates a new menu bar.
JMenu add(JMenu c)	Appends the specified menu to the end of the menu bar.
AccessibleContext getAccessibleContext()	Gets the AccessibleContext associated with this menu bar.
Component getComponent()	Returns the component that is used to paint the menu bar. The component determines if event occurs inside the menu bar.
Component getComponentAtIndex (int i)	Returns the component at the specified index.
int getComponentIndex (Component c)	Returns the index of the specified component.
JMenu getHelpMenu()	Gets the Help menu for the menu bar. The Help menu is the far right menu.
Insets getMargin()	Returns the insets object that defines the margin between the menu bar's border and its menus.
JMenu getMenu(int index)	Returns the menu located at the specified position in the menu bar.
int getMenuCount()	Returns the number of menu elements in the menu bar.
SingleSelectionModel getSelectionModel()	Returns the model object used by the menu bar.
MenuElement[] getSubElements()	Returns an array of all the menus contained in this menu bar.
boolean isBorderPainted()	Indicates if the menu bar's policy is to paint its border.
boolean isManagingFocus()	Indicates if the menu bar manages focus events internally.
boolean isSelected()	Indicates if one of the menu bar's menu elements is currently selected.
void menuSelectionChanged (boolean isIncluded)	Currently does nothing, but must be implemented to fulfill the requirement to implement the MenuElement interface.
void setBorderPainted(boolean s)	Sets the menu bar's policy for painting its border.

continues

7

THE SWING COMPONENTS

TABLE 7.14   Continued

JMenuBar *constructor or method name*	*Description*
void setHelpMenu(JMenu menu)	Sets the help menu for this menu bar, which appears when the user selects the Help menu. The Help menu is always placed to the far right of the bar.
void setMargin(Insets margin)	Sets the insets object that defines the margin between the menu bar's border and its menus.
void setSelected(Component sel)	Sets the currently selected component; results in a change to the state of the menu bar's selection model.
void setSelectionModel (SingleSelectionModel model)	Set the model object used by the menu bar.
void setUI(MenuBarUI ui)	Sets the L&F object that renders this component.

Progress Indicators

The JFC contains two classes to help you do progress reporting or progress monitoring. The first class is JProgressBar, which displays a bar that indicates the amount of progress towards finishing a certain task. Your program monitors the amount of progress towards finishing a certain task and updates the progress bar to reflect the status.

Figure 7.16 shows a snapshot of a running progress bar.

FIGURE 7.16
Progress bars can be oriented horizontally or vertically and show a string that represents the percentage of completion of the task.

Progress bars are just that—bars. They are not dialogs. Figure 7.16 shows not only the progress bar but the dialog that contains it. You might have to build a dialog around a progress bar for your applications. Progress bars have some useful features. You can choose to have a progress bar display a string that indicates the percentage of completion of the task as shown in Figure 7.16.

Progress bars can be set to have either a vertical or horizontal orientation. The one in Figure 7.16 has a horizontal orientation.

Listing 7.10 shows a simple scenario that uses a progress bar. In this example, you just repeatedly update the value of the progress bar, and the progress bar object repaints its visual state to reflect the value you set.

LISTING 7.10   How to Use Swing Progress Bars

```java
import java.awt.*;
import java.awt.event.*;
import java.io.*;
import javax.swing.*;

public class Progress extends JFrame
{
  public Progress()
  {
    super("Progress Demo");

    Box box = Box.createVerticalBox();
    Dimension dim = new Dimension(0, 10);

    Container contentPane = getContentPane();

    message = new JLabel("This label is not part of the progress bar.");

    pb = new JProgressBar(0, 100);
    pb.setMaximum(100);
    pb.setValue(0);
    pb.setStringPainted(true);

    box.add(message);
    box.add(Box.createRigidArea(dim));
    box.add(pb);

    contentPane.add(Box.createVerticalStrut(30), BorderLayout.NORTH);
    contentPane.add(Box.createHorizontalStrut(30), BorderLayout.WEST);
    contentPane.add(box, BorderLayout.CENTER);
    contentPane.add(Box.createVerticalStrut(30), BorderLayout.SOUTH);
    contentPane.add(Box.createHorizontalStrut(30), BorderLayout.EAST);
  }

  private void updateBar()
  {
    for (int i = 0; i <= 100; i++)
```

continues

LISTING 7.10   Continued

```
      {
        pb.setValue(i);
        try
          {
            Thread.sleep(50);
          }
        catch(InterruptedException e)
          {

          }
      }
  }

  public static void main(String [] args)
  {
    Progress app = new Progress();
    WindowListener wL = new WindowAdapter()
      {
        public void windowClosing(WindowEvent e)
        {
          ((Window) e.getSource()).dispose();
          System.exit(0);
        }
      };
    app.addWindowListener(wL);

    app.pack();
    app.setVisible(true);

    app.updateBar();
  }

  JLabel message;
  JProgressBar pb;
}
```

When you use a progress bar you are typically monitoring the progress of some task that affects the state of some data model. You can see from Table 7.15 that progress bars have an associated data model of type BoundedRangeModel. In the usual scenario, the program changes the state of the data model, and then it changes the state of the progress bar to reflect the state of the data model.

TABLE 7.15 JProgressBar Constructors and Methods

JProgressBar *constructor or method name*	*Description*
`JProgressBar()`	No-arg constructor that creates a horizontally oriented progress bar
`JProgressBar (BoundedRangeModel newModel)`	Creates a horizontal progress bar that uses the specified model
`JProgressBar(int orient)`	Creates a progress bar with the specified orientation, either `JProgressBar.VERTICAL` or `JProgressBar.HORIZONTAL`
`JProgressBar(int min, int max)`	Creates a horizontal progress bar with the specified minimum and maximum values
`JProgressBar(int orient, int min, int max)`	Creates a progress bar using the specified orientation and minimum and maximum values
`AccessibleContext getAccessibleContext()`	Get the `AccessibleContext` associated with this progress bar
`int getMaximum()`	Returns the maximum value of the progress bar's model
`int getMinimum()`	Returns the minimum value of the progress bar's model
`BoundedRangeModel getModel()`	Returns the data model used by the progress bar
`int getOrientation()`	Returns the progress bar's orientation, either `JProgressBar.VERTICAL` or `JProgressBar.HORIZONTAL`
`double getPercentComplete()`	Returns the value that represents the percent complete for the progress bar
`String getString()`	Returns the current value of the progress string, which displays a string representation of the percent complete
`ProgressBarUI getUI()`	Returns the L&F object that renders this component
`String getUIClassID()`	Returns the name of the L&F class that renders this component
`int getValue()`	Returns the current value of the model
`boolean isBorderPainted()`	Indicates if a border is painted around the progress bar
`boolean isStringPainted()`	Indicates if the progress bar will paint a progress string onto the progress bar
`protected void paintBorder (Graphics g)`	Paints the progress bar's border, if the `BorderPainted` property is True
`protected String paramString()`	Returns a string representation of the `JProgressBar`
`void setBorderPainted(boolean b)`	Sets the progress bar's policy for painting its border

continues

TABLE 7.15   Continued

JProgressBar *constructor or method name*	*Description*
void setMaximum(int n)	Sets the model's maximum value to x
void setMinimum(int n)	Sets the model's minimum value to x
void setModel (BoundedRangeModel newModel)	Sets the data model used by the JProgressBar
void setOrientation (int newOrientation)	Sets the progress bar's orientation to the specified value, which must be either JProgressBar.VERTICAL or JProgressBar.HORIZONTAL
void setString(String s)	Sets the value of the progress string
void setStringPainted(boolean b)	Sets the progress bar's policy for painting the progress string
void setUI(ProgressBarUI ui)	Sets the L&F object that renders this component
void setValue(int n)	Sets the model's current value to x
void updateUI()	Notification from the UIFactory that the L&F has changed

Sliders

Sliders are components that let the user move a thumb along a bar that is optionally marked with a scale of ticks. Moving the thumb sets the value of the slider. A slider's thumb is the part that you reposition by clicking or dragging. It indicates the current value of the slider. Besides clicking and dragging on the slider's thumb, the user can click on either side of the thumb, causing the slider's value to increment or decrement.

Swing sliders can be displayed either horizontally or vertically. You have the choice of whether or not to display major or minor tick marks, and it also lets you choose the scale resolution. Figure 7.17 shows two sliders, one oriented horizontally and one oriented vertically. The horizontal slider has its minor tick spacing set to 1; whereas the vertical slider has its minor tick spacing set to 5.

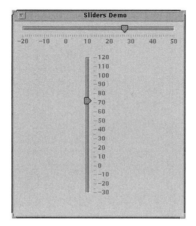

FIGURE 7.17
Sliders can be oriented either horizontally or vertically. You can choose the scale resolution and what combination of major and minor tick marks to display.

Listing 7.10 shows the source code that produces Figure 7.17.

LISTING 7.11   How to Use Swing Sliders

```java
import java.awt.*;
import java.awt.event.*;
import javax.swing.*;

/**
  This class demonstrates use of Swing sliders.
*/
class Sliders extends JPanel
{
  /**
    No-arg constructor.
  */
  public Sliders()
  {
    JLabel msg = new JLabel("Set your ideal temperature (Celsius)");

    // Create a horizontally oriented slider that shows Celsius
    // temperatures.
    //
```

continues

LISTING 7.11   Continued

```java
JSlider horizSlider = new JSlider();

// Set the minimum, maximum scale values displayed, and the initial
// value (my favorite Celsius temperature).
//
horizSlider.setMinimum(-20);
horizSlider.setMaximum(50);
horizSlider.setValue(27);

// Set the resolution of the major and minor tick marks. You also
// have to explicitly request that tick marks be displayed, even
// if you set the resolution for the major and minor tick spacing.
//
horizSlider.setPaintTicks(true);
horizSlider.setPaintLabels(true);
horizSlider.setMajorTickSpacing(10);
horizSlider.setMinorTickSpacing(1);
horizSlider.setPreferredSize(new Dimension(350, 60));

// Create a vertically oriented slider. Do all the same
// intializations. This one shows Fahrenheit temperatures.
//
JSlider vertSlider = new JSlider(JSlider.VERTICAL, -30, 120, 72);
vertSlider.setPaintTicks(true);
vertSlider.setPaintLabels(true);
vertSlider.setMajorTickSpacing(10);
vertSlider.setMinorTickSpacing(5);
vertSlider.setPreferredSize(new Dimension(60, 300));

Box box = Box.createVerticalBox();

box.add(horizSlider);
box.add(vertSlider);

add(box);
}


public static void main(String [] args)
{
  JFrame f = new JFrame("Sliders Demo");
  WindowListener wL = new WindowAdapter()
    {
      public void windowClosing(WindowEvent e)
```

```
    {
      ((Window) e.getSource()).dispose();
      System.exit(0);
    }
  };
  f.addWindowListener(wL);

  Sliders app = new Sliders();

  f.getContentPane().add(app);
  f.pack();
  f.setVisible(true);
  }


}
```

Table 7.16 lists the constructors and methods of the JSlider class. Looking at the second constructor listed reminds you again of the importance of models. Sliders are a visual representation of a data model, just like all other Swing components. The JSlider's model is a BoundedRangeModel. Based on your knowledge of the abstraction presented by a slider, you can guess the nature of this model. This is one of the models I will discuss in the chapter on models.

TABLE 7.16 JSlider Constructors and Methods

JSlider *constructor or method name*	*Description*
JSlider()	No-arg constructor. It creates a horizontal slider with an initial value of 50.
JSlider(BoundedRangeModel brm)	Creates a horizontal slider using the specified model.
JSlider(int orientation)	Creates a slider with the specified orientation and an initial value of 50 by default.
JSlider(int min, int max)	Creates a horizontal slider with the specified minimum and maximum values, and with an initial value of 50 by default.
JSlider(int min, int max, int value)	Creates a horizontal slider with the specified minimum, maximum, and initial values.
JSlider(int orientation, int min, int max, int value)	Creates a slider with the specified orientation, minimum, maximum, and initial values.

continues

TABLE 7.16   Continued

JSlider *constructor or method name*	*Description*
Hashtable createStandardLabels (int increment)	Creates a hashtable that stores the labels for the slider's hash marks. The hash marks appear at each interval specified by the increment argument, from the minimum to maximum values.
Hashtable createStandardLabels (int increment, int start)	Creates a hashtable that stores the labels for the slider's hash marks, which appear at each interval specified by the increment argument, starting at the specified starting value.
protected void fireStateChanged()	Notifies listeners of the occurrence of a ChangeEvent on this slider.
AccessibleContext getAccessibleContext()	Get the AccessibleContext associated with this JComponent.
int getExtent()	Returns the value of the slider's Extent, which is the range of values spanned by the slider's knob.
boolean getInverted()	Returns true if the slider's scale is marked in reverse, that is, descending from left-to-right or top-to-bottom.
Dictionary getLabelTable()	Returns the dictionary object that stores an associative set of labels and values.
int getMajorTickSpacing()	Returns the value of the interval at which major ticks are spaced.
int getMaximum()	Returns the maximum value supported by the slider.
int getMinimum()	Returns the minimum value supported by the slider.
int getMinorTickSpacing()	Returns the value of the interval at which minor ticks are spaced.
BoundedRangeModel getModel()	Returns the data model that defines the slider's minimum, maximum, and current value properties.
int getOrientation()	Returns this slider's orientation, either JSlider.VERTICAL or JSlider.HORIZONTAL.
boolean getPaintLabels()	Indicates if labels are painted.
boolean getPaintTicks()	Indicates if tick marks are painted.
boolean getPaintTrack()	Indicates if the track, the area in which the slider slides, should be painted.

JSlider *constructor or* *method name*	*Description*
`boolean getSnapToTicks()`	Indicates if the knob position and the slider's data value are always set to the value of the tick mark that is closest to the point where the user positioned the knob.
`SliderUI getUI()`	Gets the UI object that implements the L&F for this component.
`String getUIClassID()`	Returns the name of the L&F class that renders this component.
`int getValue()`	Returns the slider's value.
`boolean getValueIsAdjusting()`	Indicates if the slider's knob is currently being dragged.
`protected String paramString()`	Returns a string representation of this `JSlider`.
`void removeChangeListener` `(ChangeListener l)`	Removes a listener previously registered for change event notification.
`void setExtent(int extent)`	Sets the slider's Extent, which is the size of the range spanned by the slider's knob.
`void setInverted(boolean b)`	Sets the policy for marking the slider's tick marks. A value of `true` indicates that the marks should be drawn descending from left-to-right or from top-to-bottom.
`void setLabelTable` `(Dictionary labels)`	Sets the dictionary that stores the association between slider values and their labels.
`void setMajorTickSpacing(int n)`	Sets the major tick spacing interval.
`void setMaximum(int maximum)`	Sets the maximum value of the model.
`void setMinimum(int minimum)`	Sets the minimum value of the model.
`void setMinorTickSpacing(int n)`	Sets the minor tick spacing interval.
`void setModel` `(BoundedRangeModel newModel)`	Sets the slider's model to the specified object.
`void setOrientation` `(int orientation)`	Set the scrollbar's orientation. Valid values are `JSlider.VERTICAL` or `JSlider.HORIZONTAL`.
`void setPaintLabels(boolean b)`	Sets the policy for painting labels on the slider.
`void setPaintTicks(boolean b)`	Sets the policy for painting tick marks on the slider.
`void setPaintTrack(boolean b)`	Sets the policy for painting the track on the slider.

continues

TABLE 7.16 Continued

JSlider *constructor or method name*	*Description*
void setSnapToTicks(boolean b)	Sets the policy for positioning the knob. If true, the knob is always positioned at the tick mark closest to the location where it was last placed by the user.
void setUI(SliderUI ui)	Sets the UI object that implements the L&F for this component.
void setValue(int n)	Sets the slider's current value.
void setValueIsAdjusting (boolean b)	Sets the state to indicate if the model's value is currently adjusting.
protected void updateLabelUIs()	Update the label UIs with the latest versions from the UIFactory. This is called internally when the UIFactory notifies the slider that the L&F has changed.
void updateUI()	Notifies the UIFactory that the L&F has changed.

Split Panes

The JSplitPane component is a special kind of pane that can show a split view—two panes.

Split panes can split their view either horizontally or vertically. Notice the stippled divider that separates the two horizontal views in Figure 7.18. The size and location of this divider can be configured.

In Listing 7.12, I simply reuse two of the lists from a previous example, inserting them into the split pane for display.

FIGURE 7.18

Split panes show either a horizontal or vertical split view of two panes.

LISTING 7.12 How to Use Swing Split Panes

```
import java.awt.*;
import java.awt.event.*;
import javax.swing.*;
import javax.swing.border.*;

/**
  This class demonstrates use of the Swing split pane. This demo
  resuses two of the JList components from a previous example.
*/
class SplitPaneDemo extends JPanel
{
  /**
    No-arg constructor.
  */
  public SplitPaneDemo()
  {
    // Construct a JSplitPane object. Specify a horizontal split.
    //
    JSplitPane splitPane1 = new JSplitPane(JSplitPane.HORIZONTAL_SPLIT);
    splitPane1.setOneTouchExpandable(true);

    // JSplitPanes can take two containers. Create a JPanel to
    // place in the left split. Set a border on it so you can see
    // its bounds more clearly.
    //
    JPanel left1 = new JPanel();
    left1.setBorder(BorderFactory.createEmptyBorder(5, 5, 5, 5));
    left1.add(new JScrollPane(createList1()));
    splitPane1.setLeftComponent(left1);

    // Create a similar panel for the right-hand side of the split
    // pane.
    //
    JPanel right1 = new JPanel();
    right1.add(new JScrollPane(createList2()));
    right1.setBorder(BorderFactory.createEmptyBorder(5, 5, 5, 5));
    splitPane1.setRightComponent(right1);

    add(splitPane1);
  }

  // Create the list components that will be placed in the two halves
  // of the split pane. Just reuse two list components from an
  // earlier example.
```

7

THE SWING
COMPONENTS

continues

LISTING 7.12   Continued

```java
// Create the component for the left-hand side of the split pane.
//
Component createList1()
{
    Font f14 = new Font("SansSerif", Font.PLAIN, 14);

    String [] philosophers = {"Aristotle", "Confucious", "LaoTse",
                              "Pascal", "Plato", "Rousseau",
                              "Socrates", ""};

    String [] mathematicians = {"Abel", "Chebyshev", "Dirichlet",
                                "Fourier", "LaGrange", "Galois",
                                "Gauss", "Laplace", "Landau"};

    JList singleSelectionList = new JList();
    singleSelectionList.setVisibleRowCount(7);
    singleSelectionList.setFont(f14);
    singleSelectionList.setListData(philosophers);

    Box singleSelectionBox = Box.createVerticalBox();

    JLabel singleSelectionLabel = new JLabel("My Favorite Philosophers");
    singleSelectionBox.add(singleSelectionLabel);
    singleSelectionBox.add(Box.createRigidArea(new Dimension(0, 10)));

    JScrollPane scrollPane = new JScrollPane(singleSelectionList);
    scrollPane.setVerticalScrollBarPolicy(
    JScrollPane.VERTICAL_SCROLLBAR_ALWAYS);
    singleSelectionBox.add(scrollPane);

    return singleSelectionBox;
}

// Create the second component for the right-hand side of the split
// pane.
//
public Component createList2()
{
    Font f14 = new Font("SansSerif", Font.PLAIN, 14);

String [] painters = {"Michelangelo", "Rembrandt", "Renoir",
```

```
                                     "deviance", "VanGogh", "Monet", "Manet",
                                     "Picasso"};

    JList singleIntervalList = new JList();
    singleIntervalList.setVisibleRowCount(7);
    singleIntervalList.setFont(f14);
    singleIntervalList.setListData(painters);

    Box singleIntervalBox = Box.createVerticalBox();

    JLabel singleIntervalLabel = new JLabel("My Favorite Artists");
    singleIntervalBox.add(singleIntervalLabel);
    singleIntervalBox.add(Box.createRigidArea(new Dimension(0, 10)));

    JScrollPane scrollPane = new JScrollPane(singleIntervalList);
    singleIntervalBox.add(scrollPane);

    return singleIntervalBox;
  }


  public static void main(String [] args)
  {
    JFrame f = new JFrame("JSplitPane Demo");

    WindowListener wL = new WindowAdapter()
      {
        public void windowClosing(WindowEvent e)
        {
          ((Window) e.getSource()).dispose();
          System.exit(0);
        }
      };
    f.addWindowListener(wL);

    SplitPaneDemo app = new SplitPaneDemo();

    f.getContentPane().add(app);
    f.pack();
    f.setVisible(true);
  }
}
```

Table 7.17 lists the members of the `JSplitPane` class.

TABLE 7.17   JSplitPane **CONSTRUCTORS AND METHODS**

JSplitPane *constructor or method name*	*Description*
JSplitPane()	No-arg constructor. It constructs a new `JSplitPane` that arranges its child components adjacent horizontally.
JSplitPane(int newOrientation)	Constructs a new `JSplitPane` with the specified orientation.
JSplitPane(int newOrientation, boolean newContinuousLayout)	Constructs a new `JSplitPane` with the specified orientation and redrawing behavior. If `true`, the components redraw continuously as the divider is repositioned.
JSplitPane(int newOrientation, boolean newContinuousLayout, Component newLeftComponent, Component newRightComponent)	Constructs a new `JSplitPane` with the specified orientation, redrawing behavior and specified components.
JSplitPane(int newOrientation, Component newLeftComponent, Component newRightComponent)	Constructs a new `JSplitPane` with the specified orientation and with the specified components. This new constructor does not do continuous redrawing.
AccessibleContext getAccessibleContext()	Get the `AccessibleContext` associated with this `JComponent`.
Component getBottomComponent()	Returns the bottom or right component.
int getDividerLocation()	Gets the location of the divider from the L&F implementation.
int getDividerSize()	Gets the size of the divider.
int getLastDividerLocation()	Gets the divider's last location.
Component getLeftComponent()	Returns the top or left component.
int getMaximumDividerLocation()	Returns a UI specific value for the maximum location of the divider.
int getMinimumDividerLocation()	Returns a UI specific minimum location value of the divider.
int getOrientation()	Returns the split pane's orientation.
Component getRightComponent()	Returns the right or bottom component.
Component getTopComponent()	Returns the top or left component.
SplitPaneUI getUI()	Returns the `SplitPaneUI` that is providing the current L&F.

JSplitPane *constructor or method name*	*Description*
`String getUIClassID()`	Returns the name of the L&F class that renders this component.
`boolean isContinuousLayout()`	Indicates the currently set redrawing behavior.
`boolean isOneTouchExpandable()`	Indicates if the pane has a UI widget to collapse or expand the divider.
`void remove(Component component)`	Removes the specified child component from the pane.
`void remove(int index)`	Removes the child component at the specified index.
`void removeAll()`	Removes both child components from the pane.
`void resetToPreferredSizes()`	Recalculates the layout to accommodate the preferred size of the children components.
`void setBottomComponent (Component comp)`	Places the specified component below or to the right of the divider.
`void setContinuousLayout (boolean newContinuousLayout)`	Sets the redraw behavior, either to redraw continuously or not as the divider is repositioned.
`void setDividerLocation (double proportionalLocation)`	Sets the location of the divider to a point that represents a percentage of the JSplitPane's height or width.
`void setDividerLocation (int location)`	Sets the divider's location.
`void setDividerSize (int newSize)`	Sets the divider's size.
`void setLastDividerLocation (int newLastLocation)`	Remembers the specified location as the last location of the divider.
`void setLeftComponent (Component comp)`	Sets the component above or to the left of the divider.
`void setOneTouchExpandable (boolean newValue)`	Sets the policy for the JSplitPane to provide a UI widget on the divider to quickly expand/collapse the divider.
`void setOrientation (int orientation)`	Sets the pane's orientation, which determines if it is split horizontally or vertically.
`void setRightComponent (Component comp)`	Sets the specified component to the bottom or right of the divider.
`void setTopComponent (Component comp)`	Sets the component above or to the left of the divider.
`void setUI(SplitPaneUI ui)`	Sets the L&F object that renders this component.
`void updateUI()`	Notifies the pane that the L&F has changed. Notification originates from the UIManager object.

7

THE SWING COMPONENTS

Tabbed Panes

Tabbed panes are components that manage several subordinate panes, each with a representative tab along the top. All the tabs show, like the tabs in a hanging file folder. Clicking on a tab brings the pane containing the tab to the front, making its contents visible.

Each tab is connected to a container. The container associated with a tab can contain any component. So, for instance, you can create a tabbed pane and place a JPanel in each tab's container, building up a complex hierarchy of components in each pane.

Figure 7.19 shows a tabbed pane with five tabs. Tab 2 is selected, so its pane shows on top of all the other panels. The label "Looking at Panel 2" is a component contained by the container belonging to Tab 2. Figure 7.20 shows how the tabbed pane looks after selecting Tab 4. Notice that a different label now shows. This simple example puts a different label in each pane to illustrate how the pane associated with the selected tab is brought to the front.

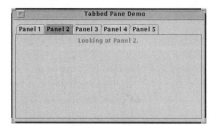

FIGURE 7.19
Tabbed panes are a handy way to organize several panes. Each pane is identified with a tab that can contain a label, icon, or both. Clicking on the tab moves the pane to the front.

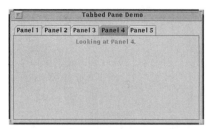

FIGURE 7.20
Clicking on a different tab brings the pane containing that tab to the front. In this Figure, Pane 4 is visible. Notice the label in the pane is different.

Listing 7.13 shows the code that produces Figure 7.19.

LISTING 7.13 How to Use Swing Tabbed Panes

```java
import java.awt.*;
import com.sun.java.swing.*;

class TabbedPaneDemo extends JPanel
{

  public TabbedPaneDemo()
  {
    Box box = Box.createVerticalBox();

    Dimension dim = new Dimension(500, 50);

    JPanel panel1 = new JPanel();
    JLabel label1 = new JLabel("Looking at Panel 1.");
    panel1.add(label1);

    JPanel panel2 = new JPanel();
    JLabel label2 = new JLabel("Looking at Panel 2.");
    panel2.add(label2);

    JPanel panel3 = new JPanel();
    JLabel label3 = new JLabel("Looking at Panel 3.");
    panel3.add(label3);

    JPanel panel4 = new JPanel();
    JLabel label4 = new JLabel("Looking at Panel 4.");
    panel4.add(label4);

    JPanel panel5 = new JPanel();
    JLabel label5 = new JLabel("Looking at Panel 5.");
    panel5.add(label5);

    JTabbedPane tabbedPane1 = new JTabbedPane();
    tabbedPane1.setPreferredSize(new Dimension(400, 200));

    tabbedPane1.add("Panel 1", panel1);
    tabbedPane1.add("Panel 2", panel2);
    tabbedPane1.add("Panel 3", panel3);
    tabbedPane1.add("Panel 4", panel4);
    tabbedPane1.add("Panel 5", panel5);

    box.add(tabbedPane1);

    add(box);
```

7

THE SWING
COMPONENTS

continues

LISTING 7.13   Continued

```
}

public static void main(String [] args)
{
  JFrame f = new JFrame("Text Field Demo");

  TabbedPaneDemo app = new TabbedPaneDemo();

  f.getContentPane().add(app);
  f.pack();
  f.setVisible(true);
}
}
```

Table 7.18 lists the members of the JTabbedPane class.

TABLE 7.18   JTabbedPane Constructors and Methods

JTabbedPane *constructor or method name*	*Description*
JTabbedPane()	No-arg constructor. It creates an empty tabbed pane.
JTabbedPane(int tabPlacement)	Creates a new, empty tabbed pane. Any new tabs will be added to the side specified by the argument, which can be TOP, BOTTOM, LEFT, or RIGHT.
Component add (Component component)	Adds the specified component to the pane with a new tab whose name is taken from the name of the component.
Component add (Component component, int index)	Adds the specified component at the specified tab index. The tab name is taken from the name of the component.
void add(Component component, Object constraints)	Adds a component to the tabbed pane.
void add(Component component, Object constraints, int index)	Adds a component at the specified tab index.
Component add(String title, Component component)	Adds a component whose tab has the name specified.
void addChangeListener (ChangeListener l)	Adds a listener for change events.
void addTab(String title, Component component)	Adds a component whose tab has the specified title.

JTabbedPane *constructor or method name*	*Description*
void addTab(String title, Icon icon, Component component)	Adds a component whose tab has the specified title and icon. Either the string or icon can be null.
void addTab(String title, Icon icon, Component component, String tip)	Adds a component whose tab has the specified string and icon. The specified ToolTip text is set on the tab.
AccessibleContext getAccessibleContext()	Get the AccessibleContext associated with this JComponent.
Color getBackgroundAt(int index)	Returns the background color of the tab at the specified index.
Rectangle getBoundsAt(int index)	Returns the bounds of the tab at the specified index.
Component getComponentAt (int index)	Returns the component whose position is indicated by the index argument.
Icon getDisabledIconAt(int index)	Returns the disabled icon for the tab at the specified index.
Color getForegroundAt(int index)	Returns the foreground color of the tab at the specified index.
Icon getIconAt(int index)	Returns the icon of the tab at the specified index.
SingleSelectionModel getModel()	Returns this tabbed pane's model.
Component getSelectedComponent()	Returns the tabbed pane's currently selected component.
int getSelectedIndex()	Returns the currently selected index.
int getTabCount()	Returns the number of tabs contained in the tabbed pane.
int getTabPlacement()	Returns the side at which the tabs are placed in this tabbed pane.
int getTabRunCount()	Returns the number of rows (for top or bottom placement) or columns (for left or right placement) currently used to display the pane's tabs.
String getTitleAt(int index)	Returns the title of the tab at the specified index.
String getToolTipText (MouseEvent event)	Returns the ToolTip text for the component that is located at the position where the mouse event occurred.
TabbedPaneUI getUI()	Returns the UI object that implements the L&F for this component.
String getUIClassID()	Returns the name of the UI class that implements the L&F for this component.

continues

7

THE SWING COMPONENTS

TABLE 7.18   Continued

JTabbedPane *constructor or method name*	*Description*
`int indexOfComponent (Component component)`	Returns the index of the tab that contains the specified component.
`int indexOfTab(Icon icon)`	Returns the index of the first tab with the specified icon.
`int indexOfTab(String title)`	Returns the index of the first tab with the specified title. Returns -1 if no tab has the specified title.
`void insertTab(String title, Icon icon, Component component, String tip, int index)`	Inserts a component at the specified index. The new tab displays the specified text and icon, if not null.
`boolean isEnabledAt(int index)`	Indicates if the tab located at the specified index is currently enabled.
`void remove(Component component)`	Removes the specified component's tab.
`void removeAll()`	Removes all the pane's tabs.
`void removeChangeListener (ChangeListener l)`	Removes a listener for change events from this tabbed pane.
`void removeTabAt(int index)`	Removes the tab at the specified index.
`void setBackgroundAt (int index, Color background)`	Sets the background color of the tab at the specified index to the specified color.
`void setComponentAt(int index, Component component)`	Sets the specified component to be located at the specified index.
`void setDisabledIconAt (int index, Icon disabledIcon)`	Sets the specified icon to indicate the disabled state for the tab at the specified index.
`void setEnabledAt(int index, boolean enabled)`	Indicates if the tab at the specified index is enabled or not.
`void setForegroundAt (int index, Color foreground)`	Sets the foreground color of the tab at the specified index to the specified color. If the color is null, the tab's foreground color will be set to the foreground color of the tabbed pane.
`void setIconAt (int index, Icon icon)`	Sets the specified icon to be the icon of the tab at the specified index.
`void setModel (SingleSelectionModel model)`	Sets the pane's model to the indicated object.
`void setSelectedComponent (Component c)`	Sets the specified component to the selected state.
`void setSelectedIndex(int index)`	Sets the tab at the specified index to the selected state.

JTabbedPane *constructor or method name*	*Description*
void setTabPlacement (int tabPlacement)	Specifies that the tabs should be placed on the side specified for this pane—TOP, LEFT, RIGHT, or BOTTOM.
void setTitleAt (int index, String title)	Sets the title of the tab at the specified index to the specified string.
void setUI(TabbedPaneUI ui)	Sets the UI object that implements the L&F for this component.
void updateUI()	Notifies the pane that the L&F has changed.

Text Components

The Swing tool set defines several components that operate on text, as shown in Table 7.19. The five that I will present here are JTextField, JPasswordField, JTextArea, JEditorPane, and JTextPane.

All text components are related through a common ancestor called JTextComponent. Figure 7.21 shows the inheritance hierarchy that relates all text components. The JTextComponent class is abstract, yet it defines most of the implementation for all the text component classes. It is quite large in fact. Table 7.20 lists its constructors and methods.

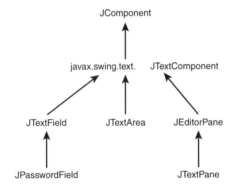

FIGURE 7.21

The JTextComponent class is the ancestor of all Swing text components, and it contains all the implementation that is applicable to all text components.

Swing text components are quite sophisticated, and I won't discuss all their features here. However, I will revisit these components in subsequent chapters that discuss topics that include some of the features found in text components. For example, the model of all text components is called a document model, and it is quite complicated. I'll discuss this in Chapter 10.

Just to put things in perspective, the following table lists the various Swing text components and their basic functions.

TABLE 7.19   Swing Text Components and Their Basic Functions

Text component	Description
JTextField	Allows display and editing of a single line of text.
JPasswordField	Allows display and editing of a single line of text. A special Echo character visually replaces typed characters, hiding them.
JTextArea	Allows display and editing of multiple lines of text. Text areas can only display plain text. Text areas can handle scrolling.
JEditorPane	Editor panes are multiline text areas. Editor panes edit specific kinds of content such as text/plain, text/HTML, and text/RTF.
JTextPane	Text panes are multiline text areas that can edit mixed content. Each element can have attributes such as font and size and can be handled individually.

TABLE 7.20   JTextComponent Constructors and Methods

JTextComponent *constructor or method name*	Description
JTextComponent()	No-arg constructor. It creates a new JTextComponent.
static Keymap addKeymap (String nm, Keymap parent)	Adds a new keymap to the set of keymaps available to all text components.
void copy()	Copies the currently selected text to the system clipboard.
void cut()	Transfers the currently selected text to the system clipboard and deletes the contents from the text component.
AccessibleContext getAccessibleContext()	Gets the AccessibleContext associated with this JComponent.
Action[] getActions()	Retrieves the list of editor commands.
Caret getCaret()	Retrieves the caret object associated with the text component. The caret marks the current position in the document affected by editing actions.
Color getCaretColor()	Indicates the current color used to display the caret.

`JTextComponent` *constructor or method name*	*Description*
`int getCaretPosition()`	Returns the offset within the document from the beginning of the current caret position.
`Color getDisabledTextColor()`	Indicates the color currently used to display disabled text.
`Document getDocument()`	Fetches the document model object associated with this component's text editor.
`char getFocusAccelerator()`	Returns the key accelerator character that results in the target text component acquiring the keyboard focus.
`Highlighter getHighlighter()`	Retrieves the highlighter object that does highlighting.
`InputMethodRequests getInputMethodRequests() request`	Returns an input method handler. This object handles input method requests for the text component.
`Keymap getKeymap()`	Retrieves this text component's currently active keymap.
`static Keymap getKeymap (String nm)`	Retrieves the keymap with the specified name, which was previously added to the document used by this text component.
`Insets getMargin()`	Returns the insets object that represents the space between the text component's border and its text.
`Dimension getPreferredScrollable ViewportSize()`	Returns the preferred size of the text component.
`int getScrollableBlockIncrement (Rectangle visibleRect, int orientation, int direction)`	Returns the scroll block increment amount that will expose one complete block of rows or columns as a result of a scroll operation.
`boolean getScrollableTracksViewport Height()`	Indicates if this text component's height should match the height of any view port that presents a view of its content.
`boolean getScrollableTracks ViewportWidth()`	Indicates if this text component's width should match the height of any view port that presents a view of its content.
`int getScrollableUnitIncrement (Rectangle visibleRect, int orientation, int direction)`	Returns the scroll unit increment amount that will expose one complete row or column as a result of a scroll operation.
`String getSelectedText()`	Returns this component's currently selected text.
`Color getSelectedTextColor()`	Retrieves the color currently used to display text that is selected.

7

THE SWING COMPONENTS

continues

TABLE 7.20   Continued

JTextComponent *constructor or method name*	*Description*
`Color getSelectionColor()`	Retrieves the color currently used to indicate selected text.
`int getSelectionEnd()`	Returns the end position of the selected text.
`int getSelectionStart()`	Returns the start position of the selected text.
`String getText()`	Returns the text component's text content.
`String getText(int offs, int len)`	Retrieves the subset of the text component's text delineated by the two offsets, which represent caret positions.
`TextUI getUI()`	Fetches the user-interface factory for this text-oriented editor.
`boolean isEditable()`	Indicates whether or not the content of this component can be edited.
`boolean isFocusTraversable()`	Returns `true` if this component can acquire the keyboard focus.
`boolean isOpaque()`	Indicates if this component is completely opaque.
`static void loadKeymap(Keymap map, JTextComponent. KeyBinding[] bindings, Action[] actions)`	Loads an existing keymap with a set of key bindings.
`Rectangle modelToView(int pos)`	Converts the given position in the text component's document to a location in the component's view.
`void moveCaretPosition(int pos)`	Repositions the caret. It sets a mark where the caret was located the last time `setCaretPosition` was called.
`protected String paramString()`	Returns a string representation of this `JTextComponent`.
`void paste()`	Copies the contents of the system clipboard into this component's text model.
`void read(Reader in, Object desc)`	Initializes this component's text content from a stream.
`void removeCaretListener (CaretListener listener)`	Removes a previously registered listener for caret events.
`static Keymap removeKeymap (String nm)`	Removes the specified keymap, which was previously added to the document, from the set of available keymaps.
`void removeNotify()`	Notifies this component that it has been removed from the container in which it existed.

JTextComponent *constructor or method name*	*Description*
void replaceSelection (String content)	Replaces the currently selected text with the specified string.
void select(int selectionStart, int selectionEnd)	Marks as selected the text delineated by the specified start and end positions.
void selectAll()	Selects all the text in the text component.
void setCaret(Caret c)	Sets the caret to be used by this text component.
void setCaretColor(Color c)	Sets the color used to render the caret.
void setCaretPosition (int position)	Sets the position of the caret for text insertion operations.
void setDisabledTextColor (Color c)	Sets the color used to display text that is marked disabled.
void setDocument(Document doc)	Sets the document object used by this text component.
void setEditable(boolean b)	Specifies whether or not this text component is editable.
void setEnabled(boolean b)	Sets the enabled state of the component.
void setFocusAccelerator (char aKey)	Sets the key accelerator whose activation will cause the receiving text component to get the focus.
void setHighlighter (Highlighter h)	Sets the highlighter used by the component.
void setKeymap(Keymap map)	Sets the keymap used by the component. A keymap binds keys to actions.
void setMargin(Insets m)	Sets the text component's insets object, which specifies the amount of space between the component border and its container.
void setOpaque(boolean o)	Sets whether or not the UI should be opaque.
void setSelectedTextColor (Color c)	Sets the color used to display text marked selected.
void setSelectionColor(Color c)	Sets the color used to highlight selected text.
void setSelectionEnd (int selectionEnd)	Sets the selection end to the specified offset position within the document.
void setSelectionStart (int selectionStart)	Sets the selection start to the specified offset position within the document.
void setText(String t)	Sets the text component's contained text to the specified text.
void setUI(TextUI ui)	Sets the user-interface factory for this text-oriented editor.

7

THE SWING COMPONENTS

continues

TABLE 7.20 Continued

JTextComponent *constructor* *or method name*	*Description*
void updateUI()	Reloads the pluggable UI.
int viewToModel(Point pt)	Produces the character position offset from the beginning of the document, which represents the character closest to the specified point.
void write(Writer out)	Loads the text component's content by reading the specified stream.

Text Fields

Text fields are the first of five text components that I will present here. In some sense, text fields are the simplest text component. They display and allow editing of a single line of text.

Figure 7.22 shows the use of the JTextField class. Listing 7.14 shows the program that creates Figure 7.22.

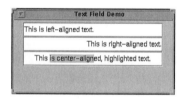

FIGURE 7.22
Text fields display a single line of text. You can specify the alignment of the text within the text field's display area.

LISTING 7.14 How to Use Swing Text Fields

```
import java.awt.*;
import com.sun.java.swing.*;

class TextFieldDemo extends JPanel
{

  public TextFieldDemo()
  {
    Box box = Box.createVerticalBox();
```

```
Font f14 = new Font("SansSerif", Font.PLAIN, 14);
Dimension dim = new Dimension(300, 30);

JTextField text1 = new JTextField("This is left-aligned text.");
text1.setFont(f14);
text1.setPreferredSize(dim);
text1.setScrollOffset(10);

JTextField text2 = new JTextField("");
text2.setFont(f14);
text2.setText("This is right-aligned text.");
text2.setHorizontalAlignment(JTextField.RIGHT);
text2.setPreferredSize(dim);

JTextField text3 = new
  JTextField("This is center-aligned, highlighted text.");
text3.setFont(f14);
text3.setHorizontalAlignment(JTextField.CENTER);
text3.setPreferredSize(dim);
text3.setSelectionStart(5);
text3.setSelectionEnd(20);

box.add(text1);
box.add(text2);
box.add(text3);

add(box, BorderLayout.CENTER);
}

public static void main(String [] args)
{
  JFrame f = new JFrame("Text Field Demo");

  TextFieldDemo app = new TextFieldDemo();

  f.getContentPane().add(app);
  f.pack();
  f.setVisible(true);
}
}
```

Table 7.21 lists the members of the JTextField class.

TABLE 7.21   `JTextField` Constructors and Methods

`JTextField` *constructor or method name*	*Description*
`JTextField()`	No-arg constructor, which constructs a new text field
`JTextField(Document doc, String text, int columns)`	Constructs a new `JTextField` that stores the specified text using the given text storage model and the given number of columns
`JTextField(int columns)`	Constructs a new text field with the specified number of columns and no initial content
`JTextField(String text)`	Constructs a new text field that initially contains the specified text
`JTextField(String text, int columns)`	Constructs a new text field with the specified text and number of columns
`AccessibleContext getAccessibleContext()`	Get the `AccessibleContext` associated with this `JTextField`
`Action[] getActions()`	Returns the list of editor commands
`int getColumns()`	Returns the number of columns in this text field
`int getHorizontalAlignment()`	Returns the horizontal alignment of the text
`BoundedRangeModel getHorizontalVisibility()`	Returns the range of text that is currently visible
`Dimension getPreferredSize()`	Returns the preferred size of this text field
`int getScrollOffset()`	Gets the scroll offset
`String getUIClassID()`	Gets the class ID for a UI
`boolean isValidateRoot()`	Indicates whether or not calls to revalidate this component will be processed by validating this component itself
`void postActionEvent()`	Dispatches action events to registered listeners
`void removeActionListener (ActionListener l)`	Removes the specified action listener from the notification list
`void scrollRectToVisible (Rectangle r)`	Scrolls the field left or right
`void setActionCommand (String command)`	Sets the name of the string that represents the name of the action command
`void setColumns(int columns)`	Sets the number of columns and invalidates the layout so the component will be redrawn with the new number of columns
`void setFont(Font f)`	Sets the font used to display the content

JTextField *constructor or method name*	*Description*
void setHorizontalAlignment (int alignment)	Sets the horizontal alignment of the text
void setScrollOffset (int scrollOffset)	Sets the scroll offset

Password Fields

7

Password fields are a special kind of text field. They enable you to enter and edit a single line of text. Unlike text fields, however, they mask the actual characters typed and replace them with a special echo character. This makes password fields suitable for entering login pass codes with a form of visual security. You can set the echo character to the character of your choice.

Figure 7.23 shows a panel with two password fields. The first uses a pound sign as its echo character, and the second uses the default echo character, an asterisk. Listing 7.15 shows the program that creates Figure 7.23.

FIGURE 7.23

Password fields mask user key strokes by displaying an echo character for each character typed by the user. The echo character can be specified by the program.

LISTING 7.15   How to Use Swing Password Fields

```
import java.awt.*;
import com.sun.java.swing.*;

class PasswordDemo extends JPanel
{

  public PasswordDemo()
  {
    Box box = Box.createVerticalBox();

    Font f14 = new Font("SansSerif", Font.PLAIN, 14);
```

continues

LISTING 7.15   Continued

```java
    Dimension dim = new Dimension(300, 30);

    JPasswordField pw1 = new JPasswordField();
    pw1.setPreferredSize(dim);
    pw1.setEchoChar('#');

    JPasswordField pw2 = new JPasswordField();
    pw2.setText("This is right-aligned text.");
    pw2.setPreferredSize(dim);

    JPasswordField pw3 = new JPasswordField();

    box.add(pw1);
    box.add(pw2);

    add(box);

  }


  public static void main(String [] args)
  {
    JFrame f = new JFrame("Text Field Demo");

    PasswordDemo app = new PasswordDemo();

    f.getContentPane().add(app);
    f.pack();
    f.setVisible(true);
  }
}
```

Table 7.22 lists the members of the `JPasswordField` class.

TABLE 7.22   `JPasswordField` Constructors and Methods

`JPasswordField` *constructor or method name*	*Description*
`JPasswordField()`	No-arg constructor that constructs a new `JPasswordField`
`JPasswordField(Document doc, String txt, int columns)`	Constructs a new `JPasswordField` with the specified number of columns and that uses the specified document storage model

JPasswordField *constructor or method name*	*Description*
JPasswordField(int columns)	Constructs a new JPasswordField with the specified number of columns and no content
JPasswordField(String text)	Constructs a new JPasswordField initialized with the specified text
JPasswordField(String text, int columns)	Constructs a new JPasswordField with the specified number of columns, initialized with the specified text
void copy()	Transfers the currently selected text range to the system clipboard
void cut()	Transfers the currently selected text to the system clipboard, removing the contents from the model
boolean echoCharIsSet()	Returns true if this JPasswordField echoes characters typed by the user
AccessibleContext getAccessibleContext()	Gets the AccessibleContext associated with this JPasswordField
char getEchoChar()	Returns the echo character
char[] getPassword()	Returns the text component's currently contained text
String getUIClassID()	Returns the name of the L&F class that renders this component
protected String paramString()	Returns a string representation of this JPasswordField
void setEchoChar(char c)	Sets the character used to echo user typing

Text Area

Text areas are panes that can display multiple lines of text. You can specify the number of rows and columns when you create a text area.

The characters in a text area can be displayed in any font, but all the text must be handled with only one font. You cannot mix text styles in a text area.

Figure 7.24 shows two text areas that have been placed in scroll panes. Each uses a different font, but you can see that all the text uses the same font in each component. Listing 7.16 shows the program that creates Figure 7.24.

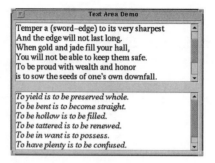

FIGURE 7.24
Text areas are multiline areas that can display text that is all in one style.

LISTING 7.16   How to Use Swing Text Areas

```
import java.awt.*;
import com.sun.java.swing.*;

class TextAreaDemo extends JPanel
{

  public TextAreaDemo()
  {
    Box box = Box.createVerticalBox();

    Dimension dim = new Dimension(100, 60);

    StringBuffer str = new StringBuffer();
    str.append("Stretch (a bow) to the very full, \n");
    str.append("And you will wish you had stopped in time.  \n");
    str.append("Temper a (sword-edge) to its very sharpest \n");
    str.append("And the edge will not last long.  \n");
    str.append("When gold and and jade fill your hall, \n");
    str.append("You will not be able to keep them safe.  \n");
    str.append("To be proud with wealth and honor \n");
    str.append("is to sow the seeds of one's own downfall.  \n");
    str.append("Retire when your work is done, \n");
    str.append("Such is Heaven's way.  \n");

    JTextArea textArea1 = new JTextArea(str.toString(), 6, 25);
    textArea1.setLineWrap(true);
    textArea1.setWrapStyleWord(true);
    textArea1.setFont(new Font("Serif", Font.PLAIN, 18));

    str = new StringBuffer();
```

```
str.append("To yield is to be preserved whole.  \n");
str.append("To be bent is to become straight.  \n");
str.append("To be hollow is to be filled.  \n");
str.append("To be tattered is to be renewed.  \n");
str.append("To be in want is to possess.  \n");
str.append("To have plenty is to be confused.  \n");

JTextArea textArea2 = new JTextArea(str.toString(), 6, 25);
textArea2.setLineWrap(true);
textArea2.setWrapStyleWord(true);
textArea2.setFont(new Font("Serif", Font.ITALIC, 18));

JScrollPane sp1 = new JScrollPane(textArea1);
JScrollPane sp2 = new JScrollPane(textArea2);

box.add(sp1);
box.add(Box.createVerticalStrut(20));
box.add(new JScrollPane(textArea2));

add(box);
}

public static void main(String [] args)
{
  JFrame f = new JFrame("Text Field Demo");

  TextAreaDemo app = new TextAreaDemo();

  f.getContentPane().add(app);
  f.pack();
  f.setVisible(true);
}
}
```

Table 7.23 lists the members of the JTextArea class.

TABLE 7.23   JTextArea Constructors and Methods

JTextArea *constructor or method name*	*Description*
JTextArea()	No-arg constructor that constructs a new JTextArea
JTextArea(Document doc)	Constructs a new JTextArea whose content is initialized to display the text in the specified document

continues

TABLE 7.23   Continued

JTextArea *constructor or method name*	*Description*
JTextArea(Document doc, String text, int rows, int columns)	Constructs a new JTextArea with the specified number of rows and columns, initialized to the contents of the specified document
JTextArea(int rows, int columns)	Constructs a new JTextArea with the specified number of rows and columns, but initialized with no content
JTextArea(String text)	Constructs a new JTextArea that displays the specified text
JTextArea(String text, int rows, int columns)	Constructs a new JTextArea with the specified number of rows and columns, initialized to contain the specified text
void append(String str)	Appends the specified text to the end of the document
protected Document createDefaultModel()	Creates the document implementation that is used by default if none is specified in a constructor
AccessibleContext getAccessibleContext()	Get the AccessibleContext associated with this JTextArea
int getColumns()	Returns the number of columns that this text area displays
protected int getColumnWidth()	Gets the width in pixels of a display column
int getLineCount()	Returns the number of lines of content contained in the text area component
int getLineEndOffset(int line)	Determines the offset of the character at the end of the specified line, relative to the beginning of the document
int getLineOfOffset(int offset)	Translates the specified character offset, relative to the beginning of the document, into a line number
int getLineStartOffset(int line)	Returns the offset of the first character of the specified line, relative to the beginning of the document
boolean getLineWrap()	Indicates the line-wrapping policy of the text area
Dimension getPreferredScrollable ViewportSize()	Returns the preferred size of the viewport that contains this component
Dimension getPreferredSize()	Returns the preferred size of the text area
protected int getRowHeight()	Indicates the height of a row
int getRows()	Returns the number of rows in the text area
boolean getScrollableTracks ViewportWidth()	Indicates if the text area's view port forces the text area to have the view port's width

JTextArea *constructor or method name*	*Description*
int getScrollableUnitIncrement (Rectangle visibleRect, int orientation, int direction)	Returns the unit increment that enables one whole row to be scrolled up or down
int getTabSize()	Gets the number of characters equivalent to a tab
String getUIClassID()	Returns the class ID for the UI
boolean getWrapStyleWord()	Gets the wrap style used when wrapping is enabled
void insert(String str, int pos)	Inserts the specified text at the specified position
boolean isManagingFocus()	Disables the traversal effect of tabs
protected String paramString()	Returns a string representation of the text area instance
protected void processComponentKeyEvent (KeyEvent e)	Consumes TAB and Shift-TAB events
void replaceRange(String str, int start, int end)	Replaces the text delineated by the specified start and end position with the new text specified
void setColumns(int columns)	Sets this text area's number of columns
void setFont(Font f)	Sets the current font used to display the text area's content
void setLineWrap(boolean wrap)	Sets the line-wrapping policy of the text area
void setRows(int rows)	Sets the number of rows for this text area
void setTabSize(int size)	Sets the number of characters to be equivalent to a tab
void setWrapStyleWord (boolean word)	Sets the wrap style used when line wrapping is enabled

7

THE SWING
COMPONENTS

Editor Panes

Editor panes basically enable you to display different kinds of formatted text in their pane. The caveat is that an editor pane instance can only display one type of format. The Swing implementation supports HTML, ASCII, and Microsoft Rich Text Format (RTF).

When you construct the editor pane instance, you specify either a java.io.URL of the HTML page to load, a string that specifies a URL to load, or a Java String object that contains the contents you wish to display. The second form takes a second argument, which should be a MIME type that represents the type of content contained in the URL.

Figure 7.25 shows a JEditorPane that has been initialized from a string that represents a URL. In this case, the editor pane constructor constructs an object that knows how to render and manage HTML specifically. This same instance, as is, would not be able to handle another format—RTF, for example.

You can see from Listing 7.17 how the editor pane is initialized. You could have alternatively called the setPage method to set the contents of the page you wish to display. Table 7.24 lists all the JEditorPane methods.

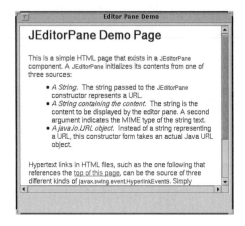

FIGURE 7.25

Editor panes basically have the capability to contain different kinds of content, albeit only one kind for each object instance.

LISTING 7.17   How to Use Swing Editor Panes

```java
import java.awt.*;
import java.io.*;
import java.net.URL;

import com.sun.java.swing.*;

class EditorPaneDemo extends JPanel
{

  public EditorPaneDemo()
  {
    JEditorPane editorPane = new JEditorPane();
    JScrollPane scrollPane = new JScrollPane(editorPane);
    scrollPane.setPreferredSize(new Dimension(450, 250));
```

```
    scrollPane.setVerticalScrollBarPolicy(JScrollPane.VERTICAL_
    [ccc]SCROLLBAR_ALWAYS);
    scrollPane.setHorizontalScrollBarPolicy(JScrollPane.HORIZONTAL_
    [ccc]SCROLLBAR_ALWAYS);
editorPane.setEditable(false);

    try
      {
    URL url = new
      URL("file:/home/vartan/dev/book/ch7//editor-pane-demo.html");
    editorPane.setPage(url);
      }
    catch (Exception e)
      {

      }

    Box box = Box.createVerticalBox();
    box.add(scrollPane);
    add(box);
  }

  public static void main(String [] args)
  {
    JFrame f = new JFrame("Text Field Demo");

    EditorPaneDemo app = new EditorPaneDemo();
    f.getContentPane().add(app);
    f.pack();
    f.setVisible(true);
  }
}
```

TABLE 7.24   JEditorPane Constructors and Methods

JEditorPane *constructor or method name*	*Description*
JEditorPane()	No-arg constructor that constructs a new JEditorPane
JEditorPane(String url)	Creates a new JEditorPane that contains the contents of a file indicated by the specified string, which represents a URL specification
JEditorPane(String type, String text)	Creates a new JEditorPane whose content is initialized to the given text string

continues

7

THE SWING
COMPONENTS

TABLE 7.24   Continued

JEditorPane *constructor or method name*	*Description*
JEditorPane(URL initialPage)	Creates a new JEditorPane whose input is taken from the specified URL
void addHyperlinkListener (HyperlinkListener listener)	Adds a listener for events that represent hyperlink activations, that is, anoccurrence of a link selection
protected EditorKit createDefaultEditorKit()	Creates the default editor kit (PlainEditorKit) that is used by the component when it is first created
static EditorKit createEditorKitForContentType (String type)	Create an editor that is appropriate for the editor pane's content, which is indicated by the argument
void fireHyperlinkUpdate (HyperlinkEvent e)	Notifies all registered listeners of the occurrence of a hyperlink event on this editor pane
AccessibleContext getAccessibleContext()	Gets the AccessibleContext associated with this JEditorPane object
String getContentType()	Retrieves the type of content that this editor currently manipulates
EditorKit getEditorKit()	Retrieves the editor kit currently installed for this editor pane
EditorKit getEditorKitForContentType (String type)	Returns an editor kit of the type appropriate for use with the type of content specified
URL getPage()	Gets the URL that is currently being displayed
Dimension getPreferredSize()	Gets the preferred size of the editor pane
boolean getScrollableTracks ViewportHeight()	Indicates if this editor pane's view port forces it to be the same height as the view port
boolean getScrollableTracks ViewportWidth()	Indicates if this editor pane's view port forces it to be the same width as the view port
String getText()	Returns the text manipulated by this editor pane
String getUIClassID()	Gets the class ID for the UI
boolean isManagingFocus()	Disables tab traversal in the component after the focus is gained
void read(InputStream in, Object desc)	Initializes the editor's content from the specified input stream
static void registerEditorKitForContentType (String type, String classname)	Associates the type of the editor kit's content to the specified name

JEditorPane *constructor or method name*	*Description*
static void registerEditorKit ForContentType(String type, String classname, ClassLoader loader)	Associates the type of the editor kit's content to the specified name
void removeHyperlinkListener (HyperlinkListener listener)	Removes a listener for hyperlink events
void replaceSelection(String content)	Replaces the currently selected content with the specified content
void setContentType(String type)	Sets the type of content that this editor manipulates
void setEditorKit(EditorKit kit)	Sets the editor kit to use to edit this component's content
void setEditorKitForContentType (String type, EditorKit k)	Sets the editor kit to use for the type of content specified
void setPage(String url)	Sets the content displayed to that contained by the URL represented by the specified string
void setPage(URL page)	Sets the content displayed to that contained by the specified URL

7

Text Panes

The JEditorPane is quite useful because it can display documents that are formatted with well-known formatting languages like HTML.

The JTextPane class is an even more powerful text component. In fact, it is Swing's most powerful text component. If you refer again to Figure 7.21, you will see that the JTextPane class is a special kind of editor pane.

Like the JEditorPane class, the JTextPane class supports displaying, managing, and rendering styled text. Unlike editor panes, however, text panes need not get their contents from a particular document type such as HTML or RTF.

The text read and managed by text panes can be any stream of text. In contrast, the editor panes I discussed earlier only know how to initialize themselves by reading a document that has an overall structure.

Text panes enable you to format the text they hold by specifying one or more text styles and then associating a style with some subset of the pane's text. Each textual element in the pane can be assigned a style, and it will be rendered with that style. An element can be anything from the whole text to a paragraph down to an individual character. This is indeed a powerful and flexible text container that is designed to support creating sophisticated text editors. You can also insert images as elements in your pane.

Figure 7.26 shows a text pane with text that is formatted in several different styles. Listing 7.18 shows the source code that produces this text pane. You can easily see that nothing comes for free! It takes a good deal more code to produce multistyled text.

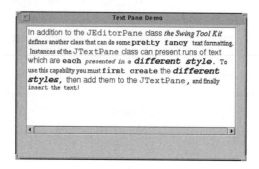

FIGURE 7.26

Text panes enable you to assign complex formatting styles to text elements down to the character. Unlike an editor pane, your text does not have to belong to a certain document style like HTML.

In order to create a document that contains multiple runs of text in multiple styles, you must do three things.

1. Create the different text styles. Text styles are objects.
2. Associate, or add, the text styles to the JTextPane instance you are building.
3. Insert each run of text into the JTextPane, along with the style object with which the run of text should be rendered.

The JTextPane class actually collaborates with several other types to bring you its full set of features. In Listing 7.18 I use the Style interface and the StyleContext and StyleConstants classes.

Style is an interface that extends another interface, MutableAttributeSet, which in turn extends the AttributeSet interface. Figure 7.27 shows the inheritance hierarchy that contains these types.

As you can see from Figure 7.27, a Style is a set of attributes. The Style interface captures the notion of a set of characteristics—or attributes—that represent a certain style of text.

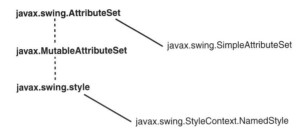

FIGURE 7.27
A `Style` *is a set of attributes that represent the different characteristics of a style of text.*

When you create a text style, you are specifying a set of attributes and their values. The attributes have standard names, such as font family, font size, etc. These attributes are easily recognizable, and predefining them gives consistency to any style; you know what attribute key to use to retrieve a value from a style object.

You create a style by doing the following:

1. Get the default `StyleContext` object.
2. From this object, get the default style for all text panes.
3. Customize the default style by setting the well-known attributes to the values you desire. This creates an aggregate of values that represent the style you are building.

After you create a style, you add it to the text pane component. Then you associate a run of text with a certain style and add it to the text pane.

The first step is accomplished by these two statements:

```
StyleContext context = StyleContext.getDefaultStyleContext();
Style defaultStyle = context.getStyle(StyleContext.DEFAULT_STYLE);
```

The `StyleContext` class defines a group of styles. One of those is a default style, which has some set of default values assigned to all its attributes. You obtain this object by using the `StyleContext.getStyle()` method.

After you have this default style, you can use it as a launching point to customize the values of certain attributes, thereby defining a new style. This is exactly what I do in the following three statements.

```
Style newStyle = pane.addStyle("normal", defaultStyle);
StyleConstants.setFontFamily(newStyle, "SansSerif");
StyleConstants.setFontSize(newStyle, 16);
```

It is not at all obvious by looking at the examples, and the Java documentation does not explain it, but the `JTextPane.addStyle()` method actually creates a new style object.

You assign a new name to your style when you create it. This gives you a way to refer to it later. Then, you set the values for the attributes you wish to change. In this example, you change the font family and the font size. Notice that you are changing the value of the attributes in the new style object you created, not in the default style object.

Now you've created a style and added it to your text pane. You continue this process for as many styles as you wish to define. For instance, the following four lines of code create yet another style.

```
newStyle = pane.addStyle("italic-16", defaultStyle);
StyleConstants.setItalic(newStyle, true);
StyleConstants.setFontFamily(newStyle, "Serif");
StyleConstants.setFontSize(newStyle, 16);
```

It's a good idea to choose a name that conceptually represents the style, so you know what you are doing when you refer to the style later. Here you set the font family and size and make the font italic.

After you've created all your styles, you need to associate certain runs of text—elements in your text pane's document—with one of the styles and insert it into the text pane. The following snippet of code associates the string with the Normal style you defined and adds it to the text pane object's document. This is the object that actually does the work of managing the text for the text pane.

```
StringBuffer str = new StringBuffer("In addition to the ");
document.insertString(document.getLength(),
                      str.toString(),
                      pane.getStyle("normal"));
```

You repeatedly add text with the desired style until you've populated your text pane with all the text you wish to display.

The `JTextPane` class is much more powerful than what I've just described. You can do sophisticated editing of the text. However, I'll save this topic for Chapter 10 because I have to explain the complex document model first. By now you're probably realizing that this concept of models plays a central role in the design of Swing.

LISTING 7.18 How to Use Swing Text Panes

```
import java.awt.*;

import com.sun.java.swing.*;
import com.sun.java.swing.text.*;
```

```java
class TextPaneDemo extends JPanel
{

  public TextPaneDemo()
  {
    Font f14 = new Font("SansSerif", Font.PLAIN, 14);
    Font if14 = new Font("SansSerif", Font.ITALIC, 14);

    Dimension dim = new Dimension(300, 30);

    String newline = System.getProperty("line.separator");

    JTextPane textPane1 = new JTextPane();
    initializeStyles(textPane1);
    setPaneText(textPane1);

    JScrollPane scrollPane1 = new JScrollPane(textPane1);
    scrollPane1.setVerticalScrollBarPolicy(JScrollPane.VERTICAL_
    [ccc]SCROLLBAR_ALWAYS);
    scrollPane1.setHorizontalScrollBarPolicy(JScrollPane.HORIZONTAL_
    [ccc]SCROLLBAR_ALWAYS);
scrollPane1.setPreferredSize(new Dimension(450, 225));

    Box box = Box.createVerticalBox();
    box.add(scrollPane1);
    add(box);
  }


  public void initializeStyles(JTextPane pane)
  {
    StyleContext context = StyleContext.getDefaultStyleContext();
    Style defaultStyle = context.getStyle(StyleContext.DEFAULT_STYLE);

    // addStyle() actually creates a new style.  Then we have to set
    // the attribute values to match its name and intended use.
    // Styles are associated in a hierarchy.  If an attribute can't
    // be found in a style, its parent is searched.  The second
    // argument is the parent.
    //
    Style newStyle = pane.addStyle("normal", defaultStyle);
    StyleConstants.setFontFamily(newStyle, "SansSerif");
    StyleConstants.setFontSize(newStyle, 16);

    // Create another new style.
    newStyle = pane.addStyle("italic-14", defaultStyle);
```

continues

LISTING 7.18   Continued

```java
StyleConstants.setItalic(newStyle, true);

newStyle = pane.addStyle("italic-16", defaultStyle);
StyleConstants.setItalic(newStyle, true);
StyleConstants.setFontFamily(newStyle, "Serif");
StyleConstants.setFontSize(newStyle, 16);

newStyle = pane.addStyle("monospaced", defaultStyle);
StyleConstants.setFontFamily(newStyle, "Monospaced");
StyleConstants.setFontSize(newStyle, 18);

newStyle = pane.addStyle("bold", defaultStyle);
StyleConstants.setBold(newStyle, true);
StyleConstants.setFontSize(newStyle, 16);

newStyle = pane.addStyle("serif-14", defaultStyle);
StyleConstants.setFontFamily(newStyle, "Serif");
StyleConstants.setFontSize(newStyle, 14);

newStyle = pane.addStyle("serif-16", defaultStyle);
StyleConstants.setBold(newStyle, false);
StyleConstants.setFontFamily(newStyle, "Serif");
StyleConstants.setFontSize(newStyle, 16);

newStyle = pane.addStyle("bold-italic-18", defaultStyle);
StyleConstants.setBold(newStyle, true);
StyleConstants.setItalic(newStyle, true);
StyleConstants.setFontSize(newStyle, 18);

}

public void setPaneText(JTextPane pane)
{
  Document document = pane.getDocument();

  try
    {
  StringBuffer str = new StringBuffer("In addition to the ");
  document.insertString(document.getLength(), str.toString(),
               pane.getStyle("normal"));

  str = new StringBuffer("JEditorPane");
  document.insertString(document.getLength(), str.toString(),
               pane.getStyle("monospaced"));

  str = new StringBuffer(" class ");
```

```
document.insertString(document.getLength(), str.toString(),
          pane.getStyle("normal"));

str = new StringBuffer("the Swing Tool Kit ");
document.insertString(document.getLength(), str.toString(),
          pane.getStyle("italic-16"));

str = new StringBuffer("defines another class that can do some ");
document.insertString(document.getLength(), str.toString(),
          pane.getStyle("serif-14"));

str = new StringBuffer("pretty fancy ");
document.insertString(document.getLength(), str.toString(),
          pane.getStyle("bold"));

str = new StringBuffer("text formatting.  ");
document.insertString(document.getLength(), str.toString(),
          pane.getStyle("serif-14"));

str = new StringBuffer("Instances of the ");
document.insertString(document.getLength(), str.toString(),
          pane.getStyle("serif-14"));

str = new StringBuffer("JTextPane");
document.insertString(document.getLength(), str.toString(),
          pane.getStyle("monospaced"));

str = new StringBuffer(" class can present runs of text which are ");
document.insertString(document.getLength(), str.toString(),
          pane.getStyle("normal"));

str = new StringBuffer("each ");
document.insertString(document.getLength(), str.toString(),
          pane.getStyle("bold"));

str = new StringBuffer("presented in a ");
document.insertString(document.getLength(), str.toString(),
          pane.getStyle("italic-14"));

str = new StringBuffer("different style.");
document.insertString(document.getLength(), str.toString(),
          pane.getStyle("bold-italic-18"));

str = new StringBuffer("  To use this capability you must ");
document.insertString(document.getLength(), str.toString(),
          pane.getStyle("serif-14"));
```

continues

LISTING 7.18   Continued

```java
        str = new StringBuffer("first create");
        document.insertString(document.getLength(), str.toString(),
                    pane.getStyle("bold"));

        str = new StringBuffer(" the ");
        document.insertString(document.getLength(), str.toString(),
                    pane.getStyle("normal"));

        str = new StringBuffer("different styles,");
        document.insertString(document.getLength(), str.toString(),
                    pane.getStyle("bold-italic-18"));

        str = new StringBuffer(" then add them to the ");
        document.insertString(document.getLength(), str.toString(),
                    pane.getStyle("normal"));

        str = new StringBuffer("JTextPane,");
        document.insertString(document.getLength(), str.toString(),
                    pane.getStyle("monospaced"));

        str = new StringBuffer(" and finally ");
        document.insertString(document.getLength(), str.toString(),
                    pane.getStyle("serif-14"));

        str = new StringBuffer("insert the text!   ");
        document.insertString(document.getLength(), str.toString(),
                    pane.getStyle("italic"));
      }
    catch (BadLocationException e)
      {

      }
  }

  public static void main(String [] args)
  {
    JFrame f = new JFrame("Text Pane Demo");

    TextPaneDemo app = new TextPaneDemo();

    f.getContentPane().add(app);
    f.pack();
    f.setVisible(true);
  }
}
```

Table 7.25 lists the members of the JTextPane class.

TABLE 7.25 JTextPane Constructors and Methods

JTextPane *constructor or method name*	*Description*
JTextPane()	No-arg constructor. It constructs a new JTextPane.
JTextPane(StyledDocument doc)	Constructs a new JTextPane, which uses the specified document object.
Style addStyle(String nm, Style parent)	Adds a new document style into the hierarchy of document styles.
AttributeSet getCharacterAttributes()	Retrieves the attributes in effect for the character located at the position indicated by the caret. It can possibly return null.
MutableAttributeSet getInputAttributes()	Gets the input attributes for the pane.
Style getLogicalStyle()	Returns the logical style associated with the paragraph that contains the character at the position represented by the caret. It can possibly return null.
AttributeSet getParagraphAttributes()	Returns the set of paragraph attributes currently in effect for the paragraph that contains the character at the position represented by the caret. It can possibly return null.
boolean getScrollableTracks ViewportWidth()	Indicates if the text pane should always be sized to match the size of its view port.
Style getStyle(String nm)	Retrieves the document style previously added with the specified name to the set of available document styles.
StyledDocument getStyledDocument()	Retrieves this object's model.
protected StyledEditorKit getStyledEditorKit()	Retrieves the editor kit.
String getUIClassID()	Returns the class ID for the UI.
void insertComponent (Component c)	Inserts a component into the document that replaces the currently selected document content.
void insertIcon(Icon g)	Inserts an icon into the document that replaces the currently selected content.
protected String paramString()	Returns a string representation of this JTextPane.
void removeStyle(String nm)	Removes the document style with the specified name that was previously added to the set.

7

THE SWING COMPONENTS

continues

TABLE 7.25 Continued

JTextPane *constructor or method name*	*Description*
void replaceSelection (String content)	Substitutes the specified string for the currently selected content.
void setCharacterAttributes (AttributeSet attr, boolean replace)	Sets the specified set of attributes to apply to the text pane's character content.
void setDocument(Document doc)	Associates the text pane's editor with a text document.
void setEditorKit(EditorKit kit)	Sets the specified editor kit as the text pane's editor.
void setLogicalStyle(Style s)	Sets the logical style for the paragraph that contains the character located at the current caret position.
void setParagraphAttributes (AttributeSet attr, boolean replace)	Sets the specified attributes to apply to the text pane's paragraphs.
void setStyledDocument (StyledDocument doc)	Associates the text pane's editor with a text document.

ToolTips

ToolTips are small banners of text that can be registered with components. The ToolTip pops up when you move the mouse over the component.

Figure 7.28 shows a ToolTip displayed for the button over which the mouse is located. The screen capture software does not show that the mouse is actually over the right button.

ToolTips are probably the simplest Swing component to use. Support for ToolTips is actually a part of the JComponent class. Normally, you don't have to create and manipulate JToolTip objects directly. Listing 7.19 shows how to add ToolTip text to two buttons.

FIGURE 7.28
ToolTips pop up under components with which they are registered. They are typically used as a quick reference or Help text.

Listing 7.19 How to Use Swing Tool Tips

```
import java.awt.*;
import com.sun.java.swing.*;

class ToolTips extends JPanel
{
  public ToolTips()
  {
    JButton button1 = new JButton("Do Something");
    button1.setToolTipText("Describes what it means to 'do something'");

    JButton button2 = new JButton("Do Nothing");
    button2.setToolTipText("I think this is pretty self-explanatory");

    add(button1);
    add(button2);
  }

  public static void main(String [] args)
  {
    JFrame f = new JFrame("Tool Tips Demo");

    ToolTips app = new ToolTips();

    f.getContentPane().add(app);
    f.pack();
    f.setVisible(true);
  }
}
```

In this example, you didn't actually create any JToolTip objects. The JComponent objects (buttons in your case) create the ToolTip as a result of your calls to setToolTipText.

Table 7.26 lists the members of the JToolTip class.

Table 7.26 JToolTip Constructor and Methods

JToolTip *constructor or method name*	*Description*
JToolTip()	No-arg constructor that creates a ToolTip
AccessibleContext getAccessibleContext()	Gets the AccessibleContext associated with this component
JComponent getComponent()	Returns the component that the ToolTip represents

continues

TABLE 7.26   Continued

JToolTip *constructor or method name*	*Description*
`String getTipText()`	Returns the text that is displayed when the ToolTip is activated
`ToolTipUI getUI()`	Returns the L&F object that renders this component
`String getUIClassID()`	Returns the name of the L&F class that renders this component
`protected String paramString()`	Returns a string representation of this `JToolTip`
`void setComponent(JComponent c)`	Sets the component that the ToolTip will represent
`void setTipText(String tipText)`	Sets the text that is displayed when the ToolTip is activated
`void updateUI()`	Indicates that the L&F has changed

Trees

Trees are one of the cornerstone data structures in computer science. The `JTree` component class is essentially a view onto a tree data structure. A `JTree` visually represents the internal nodes and leaf objects in a tree in a vertical display.

The tree data displayed by a `JTree` component is represented by the `javax.swing.tree.TreeModel` interface. Like all other Swing components that use the MVC architecture, a `JTree` maintains a reference to a model that contains the data it represents. `JTrees` reference `TreeModel` objects.

By its name, you can guess that this is another interface that serves the function of capturing the nature of a tree data structure, and indeed it is. The `javax.swing.tree` package also defines a `TreeNode` interface that captures the nature of a tree node. A tree node is a nonleaf component in a tree hierarchy. `JTree` components also know how to work with tree nodes.

Figure 7.29 shows what a tree looks like visually, when it is collapsed. Figure 7.30 shows the same tree in an expanded form. Listing 7.20 shows the source code that produces such a `JTree`.

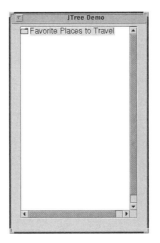

FIGURE 7.29

Trees are built from the Swing JTree *class that provides, among other things, the capability to expand and contract the tree's nodes. This tree shows all its nodes in their collapsed state.*

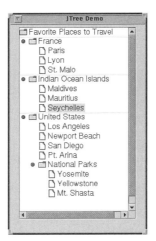

FIGURE 7.30

The same tree from Figure 7.29, when expanded, looks like this. This tree shows all its nodes in the expanded state.

LISTING 7.20   How to Use Swing Trees

```
import java.awt.*;
import java.util.*;
import com.sun.java.swing.*;
```

continues

LISTING 7.20   Continued

```java
import com.sun.java.swing.tree.*;

class TreeDemo extends JPanel
{

  public TreeDemo()
  {
    DefaultMutableTreeNode travelPlaces = new
      DefaultMutableTreeNode("Favorite Places to Travel");

    DefaultMutableTreeNode france = new
      DefaultMutableTreeNode("France");

    DefaultMutableTreeNode paris = new
      DefaultMutableTreeNode("Paris");

    DefaultMutableTreeNode lyon = new
      DefaultMutableTreeNode("Lyon");

    DefaultMutableTreeNode stMalo= new
      DefaultMutableTreeNode("St. Malo");

    france.add(paris);
    france.add(lyon);
    france.add(stMalo);

    travelPlaces.add(france);

    DefaultMutableTreeNode indianOcean = new
      DefaultMutableTreeNode("Indian Ocean Islands");

    DefaultMutableTreeNode maldives = new
      DefaultMutableTreeNode("Maldives");

    DefaultMutableTreeNode mauritius = new
      DefaultMutableTreeNode("Mauritius");

    DefaultMutableTreeNode seychelles = new
      DefaultMutableTreeNode("Seychelles");

    indianOcean.add(maldives);
    indianOcean.add(mauritius);
    indianOcean.add(seychelles);

    travelPlaces.add(indianOcean);
```

```
DefaultMutableTreeNode us = new
  DefaultMutableTreeNode("United States");

DefaultMutableTreeNode la = new
  DefaultMutableTreeNode("Los Angeles");

DefaultMutableTreeNode nb = new
  DefaultMutableTreeNode("Newport Beach");

DefaultMutableTreeNode sd = new
  DefaultMutableTreeNode("San Diego");

DefaultMutableTreeNode boston = new
  DefaultMutableTreeNode("Pt. Arina");

us.add(la);
us.add(nb);
us.add(sd);
us.add(boston);

DefaultMutableTreeNode parks = new
  DefaultMutableTreeNode("National Parks");

DefaultMutableTreeNode yosemite = new
  DefaultMutableTreeNode("Yosemite");

DefaultMutableTreeNode yellowstone = new
  DefaultMutableTreeNode("Yellowstone");

DefaultMutableTreeNode shasta = new
  DefaultMutableTreeNode("Mt. Shasta");

parks.add(yosemite);
parks.add(yellowstone);
parks.add(shasta);

us.add(parks);
travelPlaces.add(us);

JTree tree = new JTree(travelPlaces);
tree.setPreferredSize(new Dimension(250, 400));
tree.setFont(new Font("SansSerif", Font.PLAIN, 16));
JScrollPane treePane = new JScrollPane(tree);
treePane.setHorizontalScrollBarPolicy(JScrollPane.HORIZONTAL_
➥SCROLLBAR_ALWAYS);
treePane.setVerticalScrollBarPolicy(JScrollPane.VERTICAL_SCROLLBAR_ALWAYS);
```

continues

LISTING 7.20   Continued

```
    treePane.setPreferredSize(new Dimension(250, 400));

    add(treePane);
  }


  public static void main(String [] args)
  {
    JFrame f = new JFrame("JTree Demo");

    TreeDemo app = new TreeDemo();

    f.getContentPane().add(app);
    f.pack();
    f.setVisible(true);
  }
}
```

As you can see from the example, or by looking at the constructors in Table 7.27, you can construct a JTree object by passing it several different types of data structures, including a TreeModel or a TreeNode, which is treated as the root of the tree represented by the JTree object.

Fortunately, you don't have to implement these interfaces. As with most models, Swing provides a default implementation of its interfaces for you. You can instantiate the DefaultMutableTreeNode class to build a node and then initialize your JTree with it.

TABLE 7.27   JTree Constructors and Methods

JTree *constructor or method name*	*Description*
JTree()	No-arg constructor.
JTree(Hashtable value)	Creates a JTree populated with the values in the specified hash table.
JTree(Object[] value)	Creates a JTree populated with the elements of the specified array. The elements become immediate children of the tree's root node, which is not displayed.
JTree(TreeModel newModel)	Creates a JTree whose elements are taken from the specified tree model object. The tree root is displayed.
JTree(TreeNode root)	Creates a JTree with the specified TreeNode as its root. The new tree retains the structure of the elements in the specified root tree node.

JTree *constructor or method name*	*Description*
JTree(TreeNode root, boolean asksAllowsChildren)	Creates a JTree with the specified TreeNode as its root. It sets the capability for tree nodes to have children based on the value of the second argument.
JTree(Vector value)	Creates a JTree populated with each element of the specified Vector as the direct child of a new tree root. The new root node is not displayed.
void addSelectionInterval (int index0, int index1)	Adds new paths to the tree from the root node to each of the items represented by the specified selection interval, inclusive.
void addSelectionPath (TreePath path)	Adds a new tree path, specified by the path argument, to the end of the currently selected path in the tree.
void addSelectionPaths (TreePath[] paths)	Adds all the paths, specified in the path array argument, to be paths emanating from the node marked by the current selection.
void addSelectionRow(int row)	Adds the path, whose position in the tree is indicated by the row argument, to the current selection.
void addSelectionRows(int[] rows)	Adds the paths, whose positions in the tree are indicated by the specified row argument, to the current selection.
void addTreeExpansionListener (TreeExpansionListener tel)	Adds a listener for TreeExpansion events.
void addTreeSelectionListener (TreeSelectionListener tsl)	Adds a listener for TreeSelection events.
void addTreeWillExpandListener (TreeWillExpandListener tel)	Adds a listener for TreeWillExpand events.
void cancelEditing()	Cancels the current editing session.
void clearSelection()	Clears the current tree selection.
void collapsePath(TreePath path)	Collapses the node identified by the specified path and makes the node viewable.
void collapseRow(int row)	Collapses the node in the row specified by the argument.
String convertValueToText (Object value, boolean selected, boolean expanded, boolean leaf, int row, boolean hasFocus)	Converts the specified value to text that represents the state indicated.
void expandPath(TreePath path)	Expands the node indicated by the tree path argument.

continues

7

TABLE 7.27   Continued

JTree *constructor or method name*	*Description*
void expandRow(int row)	Expands the node whose position in the tree is indicated by the argument.
void fireTreeCollapsed (TreePath path)	Notifies all listeners that the tree rooted at the specified path has been collapsed.
void fireTreeExpanded (TreePath path)	Notifies all listeners that the tree rooted at the specified path has been expanded.
void fireTreeWillCollapse (TreePath path)	Notifies all listeners that the tree rooted at the specified path will collapse.
void fireTreeWillExpand (TreePath path)	Notifies all listeners that the tree rooted at the specified path will expand.
AccessibleContext getAccessibleContext()	Gets this component's AccessibleContext.
TreeCellEditor getCellEditor()	Returns the editor object that is used to edit entries in the tree.
TreeCellRenderer getCellRenderer()	Returns the TreeCellRenderer object that is rendering each cell.
TreePath getClosestPathForLocation (int x, int y)	Returns the path from the tree root to the node that is closest to the x,y coordinate.
int getClosestRowForLocation (int x, int y)	Returns the row to the node that is closest to the x,y coordinate.
TreePath getEditingPath()	Returns the path to the currently edited tree element.
Enumeration getExpandedDescendants (TreePath parent)	Returns an Enumeration of the descendants of the specified tree node that are currently expanded.
Object getLastSelected PathComponent()	Returns the component that is the last selected element in the path starting at the tree root. The path examined is the first node of the current selection.
TreePath getLeadSelectionPath()	Returns the path of the last node, starting from the root, that is part of the selection.
int getLeadSelectionRow()	Returns the row index of the last node added to the selection.
int getMaxSelectionRow()	Gets the last selected row.
int getMinSelectionRow()	Gets the first selected row.
TreeModel getModel()	Returns the TreeModel model object used by this tree.

JTree *constructor or* *method name*	*Description*
`Rectangle getPathBounds` `(TreePath path)`	Returns the `Rectangle` that bounds the specified node when it is drawn.
`TreePath getPathForLocation` `(int x, int y)`	Returns the path that contains the node at the specified location.
`TreePath getPathForRow(int row)`	Returns the path that contains the specified row.
`Dimension getPreferred` `ScrollableViewportSize()`	Returns the tree's preferred display size.
`Rectangle getRowBounds(int row)`	Returns the `Rectangle` that bounds the specified node when drawn.
`int getRowCount()`	Returns the number of rows currently displayed.
`int getRowForLocation` `(int x, int y)`	Returns the row that contains the specified location.
`int getRowForPath(TreePath path)`	Returns the row that displays the node at the end of the specified path.
`int getRowHeight()`	Returns the height of each row. (All rows are made the same height.)

`int getScrollableUnitIncrement`
`(Rectangle visibleRect,`
`int orientation, int direction)`
	Returns the unit amount by which to scroll.

`boolean getScrollsOnExpand()`	Indicates if the tree scrolls to show previously hidden children.
`int getSelectionCount()`	Returns the number of selected nodes.
`TreeSelectionModel` `getSelectionModel()`	Returns the model used to identify tree selections.
`TreePath getSelectionPath()`	Returns the path to the tree's first selected node.
`TreePath[] getSelectionPaths()`	Returns the paths of all selected elements.
`int[] getSelectionRows()`	Returns all the currently selected rows.
`boolean getShowsRootHandles()`	Indicates if root nodes are identified visually when displayed.
`int getVisibleRowCount()`	Indicates the number of rows that are currently displayed in the display area.
`boolean hasBeenExpanded` `(TreePath path)`	Indicates if the node at the end of the specified path has ever been expanded.
`boolean isCollapsed(int row)`	Indicates if the node at the specified display row is collapsed.

continues

TABLE 7.27 Continued

JTree *constructor or method name*	*Description*
`boolean isCollapsed (TreePath path)`	Returns true if the node at the end of the specified path is currently collapsed.
`boolean isEditable()`	Indicates if the tree is editable.
`boolean isEditing()`	Indicates if the tree is being edited.
`boolean isExpanded(int row)`	Returns true if the node located in the specified display row is currently expanded.
`boolean isExpanded(TreePath path)`	Returns true if the node at the end of the specified path is currently expanded.
`boolean isFixedRowHeight()`	Returns true if each display row's height is constant.
`boolean isPathEditable (TreePath path)`	Indicates if the specified path can be edited.
`boolean isPathSelected (TreePath path)`	Indicates if the element at the end of the path is currently selected.
`boolean isRootVisible()`	Returns true if the root node of the tree is currently displayed.
`boolean isRowSelected(int row)`	Indicates if the node identified by the specified row is selected.
`boolean isSelectionEmpty()`	Returns true if there are currently no elements selected.
`boolean isVisible(TreePath path)`	Indicates if the node or leaf at the end of the specified path is currently viewable. A viewable element is either the root or is an inner element whose ancestors are all expanded.
`void makeVisible(TreePath path)`	Makes the node at the end of the specified path currently viewable.
`void removeSelectionInterval (int index0, int index1)`	Removes the indicated nodes, inclusive, from the current selection. index0 and index1 indicate the beginning and end of the selection, respectively.
`void removeSelectionPath (TreePath path)`	Removes the specified node from the current selection.
`void removeSelectionPaths (TreePath[] paths)`	Removes all the nodes represented by the paths in the specified array from the current selection.
`void removeSelectionRow(int row)`	Removes from the current selection the path containing the specified index row.
`void removeSelectionRows (int[] rows)`	Removes from the current selection the paths that contain elements in the specified rows.

JTree *constructor or* *method name*	*Description*
void removeTreeExpansionListener (TreeExpansionListener tel)	Removes the specified event listener.
void removeTreeSelectionListener (TreeSelectionListener tsl)	Removes the specified event listener.
void removeTreeWillExpand Listener(TreeWillExpandListener tel)	Removes the specified event listener.
void scrollPathToVisible (TreePath path)	Scrolls the tree view so that the node identified by the specified path is visible. In order for the node to be visible, all ancestors must be expanded.
void scrollRowToVisible(int row)	Scrolls the tree view so that the item represented by the specified row is visible.
void setCellEditor (TreeCellEditor cellEditor)	Sets the cell editor for the tree.
void setCellRenderer (TreeCellRenderer x)	Sets the TreeCellRenderer for the tree.
void setEditable(boolean flag)	Sets the edit policy for the tree.
void setInvokesStopCellEditing (boolean newValue)	Indicates the tree's behavior when editing is interrupted by one of the following: the selection of another tree node, a change in the tree's data, some other unspecified means.
void setLargeModel (boolean newValue)	Sets the indication that the UI should use a large model to accommodate the tree's content.
void setModel(TreeModel newModel)	Sets the TreeModel object used by the tree.
void setRootVisible (boolean rootVisible)	Sets whether or not the tree's root node is visible.
void setRowHeight(int rowHeight)	Sets the height of each cell.
void setScrollsOnExpand (boolean newValue)	Determines whether or not the tree view is scrolled to display as many descendants as possible when a node is expanded.
void setSelectionInterval (int index0, int index1)	Selects the nodes within the interval specified by the arguments index0 and index1, inclusive.
void setSelectionModel (TreeSelectionModel selectionModel)	Sets the type of the tree's selection model.
void setSelectionPath (TreePath path)	Selects the node at the end of the specified path.

7

THE SWING
COMPONENTS

continues

TABLE 7.27   Continued

JTree *constructor or method name*	*Description*
`void setSelectionPaths (TreePath[] paths)`	Selects the nodes that are found at the end of the paths identified by the specified path array.
`void setSelectionRow(int row)`	Selects the node represented by the specified row.
`void setSelectionRows (int[] rows)`	Selects the nodes represented by the rows indicated in the specified array.
`void setShowsRootHandles (boolean newValue)`	Set the policy for displaying a visual indication of which elements are nodes.
`void setUI(TreeUI ui)`	Sets the L&F object that renders this component.
`void setVisibleRowCount (int newCount)`	Sets the number of rows that should be displayed.
`void startEditingAtPath (TreePath path)`	Selects and starts editing the node identified by the specified path.
`boolean stopEditing()`	Terminates the current editing session.
`void treeDidChange()`	Indicates that the tree structure or its state changed— whether nodes were added, removed, expanded, or contracted. This is called by the UI, not by applications.
`void updateUI()`	Indicates that the L&F has changed. This is called by the UI manager.

Summary

This chapter presented the basic Swing components. It started out with a conceptual overview of the Swing component set. The AWT components have Swing equivalents which are more fully featured. The Swing implementations are also lightweight. In addition to the components that have AWT counterparts, Swing defines new components that have no corresponding AWT version.

The Swing examples highlighted typical scenarios for using each of the Swing components. These components are the basic building blocks of Swing GUI programs.

Keep in mind that these Swing components are the objects that your programs will manipulate.

At this point, you have a grounding in the pragmatic use of the AWT and Swing components. The next step is to learn how to organize and manage the layout of concrete components in a container. Unlike the relatively focused examples in this chapter, your programs will aggregate many components in each container.

Organizing the layout of components in a container is the job of the layout manager. This is the topic that you will learn about next.

Layout Managers

IN THIS CHAPTER

- The Role of the Layout Manager   296
- The FlowLayout Class   303
- The GridLayout Class   308
- The BorderLayout Class   313
- The CardLayout   318
- The BoxLayout Class   322
- The GridBagLayout Class   334
- Collaboration Between Containers and Layout Managers   359

So far, I have discussed many of the conceptual topics that surround the Java GUI platform. Mostly I've focused on taking the broad perspective to help you understand how to structure an application.

However, Chapter 7, "The Swing Components," also focused on some of the pragmatics of Java GUI programming, namely, becoming familiar with Swing's concrete components. The next few chapters present some topics essential to properly understanding and using the JFC platform to create a fully functioning GUI application.

At this point, you know how to display the basic GUI. I've covered the concept of nesting containers to help you organize the components in your containers. Now you can create more meaningful examples using the concrete components of Chapter 7.

Although nesting containers helped somewhat in your attempts to organize components in an outer container, you still need control over how the components in any one of those nested containers are arranged.

You still must know how to add components to containers and organize them so your GUI looks exactly the way you want. To do this, you will use the layout manager whose function it is to arrange, or lay out, the components in a container.

This chapter introduces layout managers conceptually and also discusses each of the standard AWT and Swing layout manager classes in-depth.

The Role of the Layout Manager

Recall the technique of nesting containers to organize all the components on the GUI. In spite of this attempt at organization, it still doesn't seem as if there is any rhyme or reason to the arrangement—or layout—of any of the components in a container.

To achieve a precise layout of the components in any container, you must enlist the help of a *layout manager*. Layout managers are objects that are responsible for two tasks:

- To arrange, or lay out, the components in a container.
- To calculate the preferred size and the minimum size of a container based on the sizes and positions of the components it contains.

To lay out a component involves calculating its size and location within the container.

Layout managers are the workhorses that containers call upon to lay out their child components. In other words, containers delegate the job of maintaining their layout to a layout manager object.

Each container class has a default layout manager type. Each container instance maintains a reference to an instance of a layout manager object. Actually `java.awt.Container` is an exception to this rule. It does not have a default layout manager.

When a container is first created it is *invalid*, which means it does not have a valid layout. Before it is displayed, its layout manager must determine the appropriate size of the container based on the minimum and preferred sizes of its children, or upon its container's own preferred and minimum sizes.

If you recall from Listing 3.1, you had to call a method `pack()` in the `Frame` class before anything showed up on your screen. This method resulted in the frame being laid out. Without this calculation, the frame has no way of knowing how big it needs to be or if it needs to display at all, which is the case if it has no children.

Besides performing initial size calculations, the layout manager must also recalculate the container's layout after any event that may *invalidate* the container's current layout. A container's layout is invalidated after any of the following events:

- The container is hidden and then re-exposed.
- The size of the container changes.
- The bounds of the container change.
- A component is added to the container.
- A component is removed from the container.

Because layout managers have no visual attributes, it's sometimes easy to forget all the work that they are doing to make your GUI look the way you want. Whenever the container is displayed or resized or whenever new children are added to it, the layout manager must recalculate the layout so that the components fit inside the visible bounds of the container.

Invoking any of the methods listed in Table 8.1 causes a container's layout to become invalid and require revalidation.

TABLE 8.1   Methods That Invalidate a Container's Layout

Method name	Class	Description
`void setVisible(boolean b)`	Component	Specifies whether this component (the component on which the method is called) should be displayed on screen
`void setBounds(int x, int y, int w, int h)`	Component	Sets the bounds for this component
`void setSize(int w, int h)`	Component	Sets the component's size

continues

TABLE 8.1   Continued

Method name	Class	Description
`add(Component comp)`	`Container`	Adds the specified component to this container
`void remove(Component comp)`	`Container`	Removes the specified component from this container
`void removeAll()`	`Container`	Removes all this container's children
`void setLayout` `(LayoutManager m)`	`Container`	Sets the specified layout manager to be the object used by this container to lay out its children

You can force a container's layout to become invalid by calling the `Container.invalidate()` method. Afterwards, call the `Container.validate()` method to revalidate the container.

Each type of layout manager implements its own algorithm that dictates *how* it lays out a container's components. Each layout manager class defines a different algorithm, giving you a set of layout managers with different specific behaviors.

Although each layout manager uses a different *algorithm* to do its job, they all have one thing in common. Conceptually, they all do the same thing; that is, they all adhere to the same *policy* that defines the job that layout managers are chartered to do. However, they each use a different implementation to do it.

This standard policy is specified by an interface that all layout managers implement. The `java.awt.LayoutManager` interface is implemented by all layout manager classes. It defines what all layout managers must do.

A layout manager can use whatever mechanism it desires to lay out a container's children, as long as it adheres to the interface that defines the nature of all layout managers, and as long as it doesn't violate any rules regarding the way components or containers work.

Table 8.2 lists the methods in the `LayoutManager` interface. Of particular interest are the methods that take a `Container` as an argument. Earlier I said that each container has a layout manager to which it delegates its layout duties. However, more than one container can use the same layout manager object. Thus, all the methods that require referencing the container context must be passed a reference to the container.

TABLE 8.2   The `java.awt.LayoutManager` Interface

Method name	Description
`void addLayoutComponent` `(String name, Component comp)`	Adds the specified component with the specified name to the set of components managed by the container's layout manager

Method name	Description
`void layoutContainer (Container parent)`	Lays out the container's children
`Dimension minimumLayoutSize (Container parent)`	Calculates the dimensions of the minimum area needed to lay out the children of the specified container
`Dimension preferred LayoutSize(Container parent)`	Calculates the preferred dimensions of the specified container based on the preferred sizes of its children
`void removeLayoutComponent (Component comp)`	Removes the specified component from the layout of the implementing container

The `minimumLayoutSize()` and `preferredLayoutSize()` methods calculate the minimum and preferred sizes of the container based on the needs of the components that are children of the container.

Components play an important role in aiding the layout manager to determine how big to make the container so that all its children display properly. The two methods that provide this information are

- public Dimension `getMinimumSize()`
- public Dimension `getPreferredSize()`

These methods, in class `java.awt.Component`, are implemented by all component classes. They indicate their minimum and preferred sizes, respectively. The layout manager calculates the container's size based on the size and position requirements of the children.

There is no requirement that the layout manager honor either of these component requests. In fact, each layout manager adopts different behaviors regarding how its algorithm uses these parameters to calculate the container's size. When I discuss each of the layout managers later, you will see that some layout manager implementations honor a component's height request, although others honor its width request, and still others honor both or neither.

Table 8.3 lists the layout manager classes that extend `LayoutManager` directly.

TABLE 8.3 Layout Managers That Implement the Interface

Layout manager class	Layout policy
`java.awt.GridLayout`	Lays out the container's components in a rectangular grid, one component per grid square. Each grid square has the same dimensions.
`java.awt.FlowLayout`	Lays out components in a left-to-right, top-to-bottom flow, like lines in a paragraph of English or other Western European languages.
`javax.swing.ViewportLayout`	Lays out its view to be the same size as the `JViewport` component that uses this layout manager.

8

LAYOUT MANAGERS

Earlier I said that all the AWT layout manager classes directly or indirectly implement the `java.awt.LayoutManager` interface. I say indirectly because another interface, `java.awt.LayoutManager2`, extends the `java.awt.LayoutManager` interface. Some layout manager classes implement this second interface.

The `LayoutManager2` interface is defined as follows in Table 8.4.

TABLE 8.4   The `LayoutManager2` Interface Methods

Method name	Description
`void addLayoutComponent (Component comp, Object constraints)`	Adds the specified component to the container's layout, using the specified constraint object. The constraints object must be compatible with the layout policy defined by the layout manager implementation.
`float getLayoutAlignmentX (Container target)`	Returns the alignment of the layout of the child components along the x axis of the container.
`float getLayoutAlignmentY (Container target)`	Returns the alignment of the layout of the child components along the y axis of the container.
`void invalidateLayout (Container target)`	Invalidates the layout of the container. This indicates that the layout manager should discard any information stored that pertains to the previously valid component layout.
`Dimension maximumLayoutSize (Container target)`	Returns the maximum size of this component.

The `LayoutManager2` interface represents another category of layout managers, namely, those that know how to lay out components given a set of constraints. Some of the AWT layout managers implement this `LayoutManager2` interface, and all the Swing layout managers implement `LayoutManager2` directly.

Constraints information is encapsulated in the form of a constraints object that is associated with each component when it is added to the container. The constraints object indicates any constraints on how the component is to be laid out inside the container. Different layout managers use different kinds of constraint information.

The semantics of a particular layout manager implementation dictate the kind of constraints information it expects. For example, constraints could represent the restrictions on a component's layout dimensions imposed by the size of the container.

Some layout managers specify constraints objects that represent the way a component should be laid out within the area allotted to it. In this case, the constraints serve more as a directive rather than a constraint.

Table 8.4 lists the methods in the `LayoutManager2` interface. The
`addLayoutComponent(Component comp, Object constraints)` method takes a `constraints`
parameter whose type is `Object`. Defining the interface this way makes it flexible enough to
accommodate any type of constraints object that may be required by a particular layout manager class implementation.

Table 8.5 lists the layout managers that directly implement the `LayoutManager2` interface.

TABLE 8.5   Layout Managers That Implement the `LayoutManager2` Interface

Layout manager class	*Layout policy*
`java.awt.BorderLayout`	Lays out a container's components to fit into one of five regions, `NORTH`, `SOUTH`, `WEST`, `EAST`, `CENTER`. Components can only be added to one of the five regions. It is suitable only to layout a maximum of five components, which are usually other containers.
`java.awt.CardLayout`	Lays out each component as equal sized cards, and stacks the cards back to front, like a deck of cards. Only one card (and therefore one component) is visible at a time.
`java.awt.GridBagLayout`	Produces a uniform grid of cells. It lays out each component in a container within the grid so that component boundaries line up along the grid lines. Each component's display area may take up more than one grid location. Components do not have to be laid out with equal areas. You can specify how each component is laid out within its allotted area with great detail and flexibility. Useful for irregular layouts with unequal sized components.
`javax.swing.BoxLayout`	Lays out its components either horizontally or verti-cally, without wrapping. Components remain the same size when the container is resized.
`javax.swing.OverlayLayout`	Lays out its components over the top of each other.
`javax.swing.JRootPane.RootLayout`	Lays out the layered pane, glass pane and menu bar of a `JRootPane` container. This is a special layout manager not normally used by applications. It is designed specifically to lay out a `JRootPane`.

8

LAYOUT MANAGERS

Of the layout managers listed in Table 8.5, you will use the first four most often.

Most containers have an associated default layout manager. When you instantiate such a container type, there will be an associated layout manager ready to lay out the container's child components. Table 8.6 lists the standard AWT and Swing containers and their default layout manager types.

TABLE 8.6   The Standard AWT and Swing Containers and Their Default Layout Managers

Container class	Default layout manager
java.awt.Frame	java.awt.BorderLayout
java.awt.Panel	java.awt.FlowLayout
java.awt.Window	java.awt.BorderLayout
javax.swing.JFrame	javax.swing.BorderLayout
javax.swing.JLayeredPane	No layout manager; use absolute positioning
javax.swing.JPanel	java.awt.FlowLayout
javax.swing.Box	javax.swing.BoxLayout
javax.swing.JViewport	javax.swing.ViewportLayout
javax.swing.JWindow	java.awt.BorderLayout

You can set a container's layout manager to a different type if you wish. Simply call the `Container.setLayout()` method to set a new layout manager instance for the container.

Back in Chapter 6, "Swing Concepts and Architecture," Table 6.4 listed five containers that use the new Swing container model. Recall that you don't add components to these containers directly, but add them to the container's content pane. These five containers are listed again here.

- JFrame
- JApplet
- JDialog
- JWindow
- JInternalFrame

When dealing with the layout managers of these five containers, you must also remember the content pane. If you want to change the layout manager for one of these containers, remember to change the layout manager of the content pane, not of the primary container itself! Instead of doing

```
container.setLayout(...)
```

you should do

```
container.getContentPane().setLayout(...)
```

to set a new layout manager object for your container.

For much of the remainder of this chapter, you will examine in detail the most commonly used layout managers. You'll look at code examples that show how to choose the appropriate layout manager from the arsenal at your disposal, and how to use it to lay out your GUI exactly as you desire.

For this purpose, I will keep the examples simple so you will not be distracted by fancy usage of components or complex containers. You will simply set the layout manager of a container and add some buttons to the container. You can then see how the container's layout is affected by the various layout managers when you resize the container or specify configuration parameters for the layout manager.

The FlowLayout Class

The FlowLayout class defines one of simplest and easiest-to-understand layout managers. The FlowLayout class lays out components in a left-to-right and top-to-bottom flow, the way words in a paragraph flow in Western European languages.

FlowLayout implements the LayoutManager interface directly, and, therefore, does not use any constraints information.

Figure 8.1 shows a simple JPanel, whose default layout manager is a FlowLayout instance. Simply add some JButton components to your containers to demonstrate the behavior of the layout managers.

FIGURE 8.1
A simple flow layout that is centered horizontally.

Because you did not specify a preferred size for the panel in Figure 8.1, the buttons are all laid out in one row, and the panel is stretched horizontally to accommodate the layout. Notice that the row of buttons is centered horizontally in the panel.

If you add more buttons, the layout manager will determine that it needs to make the panel larger. Figure 8.2 shows a wider panel with more buttons.

8

LAYOUT
MANAGERS

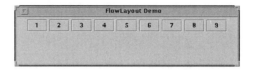

FIGURE 8.2
Components continue to be laid out in a row as long as the container is not constrained in size.

If you manually resize the container (you resize the JFrame that contains the panel) to shrink its horizontal width, the layout manager must recalculate the panel's layout; it revalidates the container. If it cannot fit all the buttons in one row, it places the remainder in a second row, or even a third or additional row as necessary.

This is a good example of why a layout manager must query the container regarding its minimum and preferred sizes. Figure 8.3 shows your container after it has been shrunk horizontally.

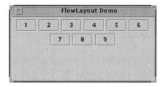

FIGURE 8.3
When the container is resized, the layout manager recalculates the container's layout.

Listing 8.1 shows the source code that produces Figures 1–3.

LISTING 8.1   Demonstration of the FlowLayout Layout Manager Class

```java
import java.awt.*;
import javax.swing.*;

public class FlowLayoutDemo extends JPanel
{
  public FlowLayoutDemo()
  {
    // The default layout manager for JPanel
    // is FlowLayout.
    //

    add(new JButton("1"));
    add(new JButton("2"));
    add(new JButton("3"));
    add(new JButton("4"));
```

```
      add(new JButton("5"));
      add(new JButton("6"));
      add(new JButton("7"));
      add(new JButton("8"));
      add(new JButton("9"));
  }

  public static void main(String [] args)
  {
    FlowLayoutDemo app = new FlowLayoutDemo();

    JFrame f = new JFrame("FlowLayout Demo");
    f.getContentPane().add(app);
    f.pack();
    f.setVisible(true);
  }
}
```

The FlowLayout class lets you specify the justification of components within each row. You have five choices, as shown in Table 8.7.

TABLE 8.7   FlowLayout Component Alignment Options

FlowLayout justification	*Description*
CENTER	Each row is centered in the container.
LEFT	Each row is left-justified.
RIGHT	Each row is right-justified.
LEADING	Each row is aligned with the leading edge of the container encountered. That is, the row is aligned with the container's left edge in left-to-right orientations, and with its right edge in right-to-left orientations.
TRAILING	Each row is aligned to the leading edge of the container encountered, that is, with the right in left-to-right orientations.

The latter two constants, LEADING and TRAILING are pending approval of a change to the API, so they are not available at this time.

As an example, you can specify that you want rows of components to be justified to the right, as shown in Figure 8.4. To realize this configuration, simply add the following two lines to your previous source example before you add the child components:

```
LayoutManager lm = getLayout();
((FlowLayout) lm).setAlignment(FlowLayout.RIGHT);
```

You know that the default layout manager for a JPanel is FlowLayout, so it appears that this use of *downcasting* is safe.

However, technically, this is not the best coding practice. In a more complex real-world application, you may forget that you already changed the layout manager for your container. This would cause the above code to result in a runtime class cast exception. A better approach would be to do the following:

```
FlowLayout fl = new FlowLayout();
fl.setAlignment(FlowLayout.RIGHT);
setLayout(fl);
```

or better yet, to take advantage of the available constructors as follows:

```
FlowLayout fl = new FlowLayout(FlowLayout.RIGHT, 5, 5);
setLayout(fl);
```

Figure 8.4 shows you how a RIGHT alignment affects your layout. If you resize your container so that more than one row is required, the components in rows after the first are aligned on the right-hand side of the container.

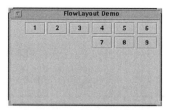

FIGURE 8.4

FlowLayout *lets you set the alignment of components in rows. Here components in each row are aligned to the right-hand side of the container.*

Of course, you can specify left-alignment, giving you components aligned on the left-hand side of the container as shown in Figure 8.5.

FIGURE 8.5

Components can also be aligned with the container's left-hand side.

FlowLayout also lets you set the horizontal and vertical gaps between components. For instance, you can change the vertical gap between rows as follows:

```
FlowLayout fl = new FlowLayout();
fl.setVgap(20);
setLayout(fl);
```

This would change the example to look like Figure 8.6. Comparing this with Figure 8.4, you can see that indeed the space between rows is greater. The description of the FlowLayout class in Table 8.8 indicates all the other capabilities of this layout manager.

FIGURE 8.6

FlowLayout *lets you change the vertical gap between rows of components.*

TABLE 8.8   The `FlowLayout` Class

FlowLayout constructor or method name	*Description*
`FlowLayout()`	No-arg constructor which constructs a new flow layout object with a centered alignment and a 5-pixel horizontal and vertical gap between the edges of the container and the edges of the components
`FlowLayout(int align)`	Constructs a new flow layout object with the specified alignment and a 5–pixel horizontal and vertical gap
`FlowLayout(int align, int hgap, int vgap)`	Creates a new flow layout object with the indicated alignment and the indicated horizontal and vertical gaps
`void addLayoutComponent (String name, Component comp)`	Adds the specified component with the specified name to the set of components laid out by this container
`int getAlignment()`	Gets the alignment used by this layout manager object
`int getHgap()`	Gets the horizontal gap between components
`int getVgap()`	Gets the vertical gap between components
`void layoutContainer (Container target)`	Lays out the children in the specified container
`Dimension minimumLayoutSize (Container target)`	Returns the minimum dimensions needed to lay out the components contained in the specified target container
`Dimension preferredLayoutSize (Container target)`	Returns the preferred dimensions for this layout based on the preferred sizes of the components in the specified target container
`void removeLayoutComponent (Component comp)`	Removes the specified component from the layout
`void setAlignment(int align)`	Sets the alignment used by this layout manager object
`void setHgap(int hgap)`	Sets the horizontal gap between components
`void setVgap(int vgap)`	Sets the vertical gap between components
`String toString()`	Returns a string representation of this `FlowLayout` object and its values

The GridLayout Class

The `GridLayout` class is a layout manager that lays out a container's components in a rectangular grid of equal-sized grid squares. A `GridLayout` instance essentially enlarges the grid squares needed to contain most components so that they are as large as the one required to lay out the largest of the components.

Like `FlowLayout`, `GridLayout` directly implements `LayoutManager` and is a layout manager class that does not work with constraints objects. Also like the `FlowLayout` class, `GridLayout` lets you specify horizontal and vertical gaps between components.

Because `GridLayout` lays out its components in a grid, you must specify the grid dimensions. In Listing 8.2, you create the simplest possible panel and do not specify any grid dimensions in your layout manager; you use the default values.

LISTING 8.2   Demonstration of the `GridLayout` Layout Manager Class

```
import java.awt.*;
import javax.swing.*;

public class GridLayoutDemo extends JPanel
{
  public GridLayoutDemo()
  {
    // The default layout manager for JPanel
    // is GridLayout.  But we specify our own
    // configuration.

    GridLayout fl = new GridLayout(0, 2);
    setLayout(fl);

    add(new JButton("1"));
    add(new JButton("2"));
    add(new JButton("3"));
    add(new JButton("4"));
    add(new JButton("5"));
    add(new JButton("6"));
    add(new JButton("7"));
    add(new JButton("8"));
    add(new JButton("9"));
  }

  public static void main(String [] args)
  {
    GridLayoutDemo app = new GridLayoutDemo();

    JFrame f = new JFrame("GridLayout Demo");
    f.getContentPane().add(app);
    f.pack();
    f.setVisible(true);
  }
}
```

8

Figure 8.7 shows the layout produced by this program. Because you didn't specify any grid dimensions, you acquired the default grid, which has only one row and as many columns as components.

FIGURE 8.7

By default, GridLayout *produces a grid of one row and as many columns as there are components to lay out.*

If you resize your container, the components are resized in width and height to maintain equal-sized grid "squares" for all components. Figure 8.8 shows a wider layout after you stretch the frame horizontally. The buttons are wider but not taller.

FIGURE 8.8

Widening a container results in GridLayout *widening all components equally.*

If you shrink the width of your container too much, the numbers in the buttons disappear. In Figure 8.9, your container is no longer wide enough for your GridLayout to render the components in one row. Unlike FlowLayout, the components that cannot fit into the first row are not placed into a second row by GridLayout.

FIGURE 8.9

If a container's width shrinks too much, the GridLayout *will not wrap the components into an additional row.*

Figure 8.10 proves that increasing the height of the container doesn't help. All components are still laid out in equal-size grid rectangles, but none of them are still wide enough to display the button numbers. You can correct this. Make your container wide enough for the button numbers to display and still choose to stretch it vertically, producing Figure 8.11. All the grid rectangles are still sized equally. This is the behavior of GridLayout.

FIGURE 8.10
If you increase the height of a container, more rows are not added to a container that uses a GridLayout *layout manager instance.*

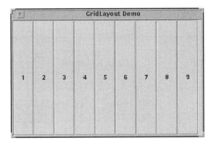

FIGURE 8.11
Any resizing maintains previously configured grid dimensions. The grid rectangles are all resized together to ensure they are of equal dimension.

The preceding examples demonstrate the different algorithms used by the different layout managers. After you understand how each behaves under various circumstances, such as resizing, you can choose the most appropriate one for each the containers in your GUI.

Table 8.9 lists the GridLayout class. You can see that instead of relying on a default grid, you can specify the grid dimensions when you create a GridLayout instance.

After you create a GridLayout instance, you can still change its dimensions. Normally you specify the dimensions initially and then add components to your container.

One of the rows or columns arguments can be 0, but not both. The value zero means "use as many as needed." So, if you specified your grid to have zero rows and two columns, the layout manager would use as many rows as needed to lay out all the components in two columns.

8

LAYOUT
MANAGERS

```
GridLayout fl = new GridLayout(0, 2);
setLayout(fl);
```

Figure 8.12 shows how your buttons are laid out with this configuration.

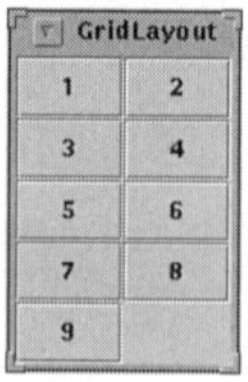

FIGURE 8.12
Either the row or column parameter may be zero when creating a GridLayout *instance.*

TABLE 8.9   The GridLayout Class

GridLayout *constructor* or *method name*	*Description*
GridLayout()	No-arg constructor. It creates a grid layout object which lays out components in a grid of one row and multiple columns, one column per component.
GridLayout(int rows, int cols)	Creates a grid layout object with the specified number of rows and columns.
GridLayout(int rows, int cols, int hgap, int vgap)	Creates a grid layout object with the specified number of rows and columns. Components are separated horizontally and vertically by the specified gap amounts.
void addLayoutComponent (String name, Component comp)	Adds the specified component with the specified name to the layout.
int getColumns()	Returns the number of columns in this layout.
int getHgap()	Returns the horizontal gap between components.
int getRows()	Returns the number of rows in this layout.
int getVgap()	Returns the vertical gap between components.
void layoutContainer (Container parent)	Lays out the specified container using this layout manager object.
Dimension minimumLayoutSize (Container parent)	Determines the minimum size of the specified container when its children are laid out using this grid layout object.
Dimension preferredLayoutSize (Container parent)	Returns the preferred size of the specified container using this grid layout object to lay out its children.

GridLayout *constructor or method name*	*Description*
`void removeLayoutComponent (Component comp)`	Removes the specified component from the layout.
`void setColumns(int cols)`	Configures this layout manager object to lay out a container with the specified number of columns.
`void setHgap(int hgap)`	Configures this layout manager object to maintain the specified horizontal gap between components.
`void setRows(int rows)`	Configures this layout manager object to layout a container using the specified number of rows.
`void setVgap(int vgap)`	Configures this layout manager object to maintain the specified vertical gap between components.
`String toString()`	Returns the string representation of this grid layout's values.

The BorderLayout Class

The `BorderLayout` layout manager class is the first of three classes that use *constraints* to specify how and where the layout manager is supposed to lay out each component in the container.

Don't think of constraints information only as a restriction. Indeed constraints information can be a specification of restriction, but it can also be a directive or specification of where and how a component should be placed in the container.

Constraints are valid values of some domain, which can be thought of as a particular category of directive. Different categories define different kinds of placement and positioning data. Each layout manager that uses constraints defines the semantics of its constraints information. Therefore, it only makes sense to use constraints information with the layout manager that understands these semantics.

For example, the constraints used by the `BorderLayout` class are compass points that identify possible regions in which a component can be placed in a container. The five possible compass points are presented in Table 8.10.

TABLE 8.10 Regions of the `Borderlayout` Class in Which Components Can Be Placed

Compass point	*Region represented*
`NORTH`	The top of the container
`SOUTH`	The bottom of the container

continues

8

LAYOUT MANAGERS

TABLE 8.10 Continued

Compass point	Region represented
WEST	The left side of the container
EAST	The right side of the container
CENTER	The center of the container

Because there are only five regions, containers which use this layout manager cannot really contain more than five children. BorderLayout is the default layout manager for both the AWT and Swing frame classes.

Figure 8.13 shows your—by now—familiar buttons placed in a container that uses a layout manager. All you have to do is set your container's layout manager to a BorderLayout instance as follows:

```
BorderLayout fl = new BorderLayout();
    setLayout(fl);

    add(new JButton("1"), BorderLayout.NORTH);
    add(new JButton("2"), BorderLayout.SOUTH);
    add(new JButton("3"), BorderLayout.WEST);
    add(new JButton("4"), BorderLayout.EAST);
    add(new JButton("5"), BorderLayout.CENTER);
```

You only add five buttons to your container. You must specify a region when you add components to a container that uses a BorderLayout layout manager. If you don't, by default, the component is placed in the CENTER region. Figure 8.13 is shown in its original size. Buttons 3, 4, and 5 appear to be the "normal" size, but buttons 1 and 2 are wider than normal.

The reason for this is that BorderLayout layout managers horizontally stretch the components placed in the NORTH and SOUTH regions to take up the entire width of the container. The width calculated will equal the width required by the three components placed in the WEST, CENTER, and EAST regions.

FIGURE 8.13
BorderLayout *lays out components in regions represented by compass points, which represent positions of the regions relative to one another.*

Of course, you can resize your container to be even wider. The result will be that the northern, center and southern components will have a greater absolute width. Figure 8.14 shows your container after you stretch it horizontally.

This is an example of constraints information at work. The BorderLayout algorithm implements a certain constraints policy that dictates that each component must remain in the compass point region in which it was originally placed. This positioning is relative to the other regions.

When you stretch your container horizontally, the layout manager honors the horizontal size request of the components in the western and eastern regions. However, it does not honor the preferred size of the CENTER component; it stretches the CENTER component to fill any remaining width.

It must then stretch the northern and southern components to make them as wide as the whole container. Buttons 1 and 2 in Figure 8.13 were stretched beyond their preferred sizes to fill the complete width of the container.

The placement of the components is constrained to remain in one of the five regions defined by the BorderLayout class. But it is not a restriction on the size of the component, which is enlarged in some cases to comply with the directive that specifies its relative positioning.

FIGURE 8.14
Stretching the container horizontally increases the area used by the components, but maintains their relative sizes.

Figure 8.15 shows the same container stretched vertically. Now the BorderLayout algorithm honors the preferred height of the components in the NORTH and SOUTH regions, stretching the CENTER component to take up the remaining vertical space. Buttons 3 and 4 are also stretched vertically.

The explanation is that BorderLayout uses the constraints information that you supply, which constrains the layout of the components to remain in the regions that you specify.

There is by definition only one component in each of the northern and southern regions. Therefore, they must be as wide as the width used by the WEST, CENTER, and EAST components.

Similarly, there is only one component in each of the western and eastern regions. Therefore, their heights must match the cumulative heights of the components in the northern, center and southern regions.

FIGURE 8.15

Stretching the container vertically results in the WEST, CENTER, *and* EAST *regions being allocated more height to fill the full height of the container.*

Figure 8.16 shows your panel with only two components, one in the NORTH and one in the SOUTH regions. The layout manager honors the preferred heights of the buttons, but stretches their widths to fill the width of the container.

To create this configuration you simply do the following:

```
BorderLayout fl = new BorderLayout();
setLayout(fl);

add(new JButton("1"), BorderLayout.NORTH);
add(new JButton("2"), BorderLayout.SOUTH);
```

If instead, you add the buttons to the WEST and EAST regions, you get a different layout:

```
add(new JButton("3"), BorderLayout.WEST);
add(new JButton("4"), BorderLayout.EAST);
```

Now the layout manager honors the preferred width of the components in the WEST and EAST regions, stretching their heights to fill the full height of the container. In all these cases, the layout manager constrains the position of components in certain regions. When you specify a region in which to place a component, you give constraints information to the layout manager.

The layout manager uses these directives to restrict the placement and size of components. But it only does so in order to honor your directive, which indicates where within the container you wish to place the component relative to others.

FIGURE 8.16
BorderLayout *honors the preferred height of components added to the container's* NORTH *and* SOUTH *regions.*

Figure 8.17 demonstrates what happens when you place the two buttons in the WEST and EAST regions. The layout manager now honors the width requests of the components but stretches them vertically.

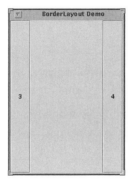

FIGURE 8.17
BorderLayout *honors the preferred width of components added to the container's* WEST *and* EAST *regions.*

You don't have to place five components in a container that uses a BorderLayout layout manager. Figure 8.18 shows your container with only one component added to the center. However you resize the container, this one component will be laid out so that it covers the whole area of the container. By design, BorderLayout always fills the entire area of the container with the components.

FIGURE 8.18

A single component must be sized to fill the container's entire area.

Earlier I said that you can't effectively add more than five components in a container whose layout is managed by a BorderLayout. Only one component can display in each of the regions. If you add a second component in the same region, only the last one added will display.

The CardLayout

The CardLayout class is another of the layout managers that implement the LayoutManager2 interface, making it a constraints-based layout manager.

CardLayout objects layout their containers to look like a stack of cards. Each component added to the container is treated as a card. Only one card can be visible at a time, namely, the one on top of the stack.

When adding components to a container, the first one added is the one initially displayed. Thereafter, your application can programmatically specify which card is to appear on top. The layout manager uses the container's own ordering of its children to determine the stacking order, which means that the order in which you call the Container.add method is the same order that the card layout uses.

Table 8.11 lists the methods in the CardLayout class that are specific to the CardLayout implementation. Those that are defined in the LayoutManager and LayoutManager2 interfaces are the same for all the layout manager implementations.

TABLE 8.11   The CardLayout Class

CardLayout *constructor or method name*	*Description*
CardLayout()	No-arg constructor. It creates a new card layout object with gaps of size zero pixels between components.

CardLayout *constructor or method name*	*Description*
CardLayout(int hgap, int vgap)	Creates a new card layout object with the specified horizontal and vertical gaps between components.
void first(Container parent)	Displays the first card of the container.
int getHgap()	Returns the horizontal gap maintained between components.
float getLayoutAlignmentX (Container parent)	Returns the alignment along the x axis with which components are laid out within their container.
float getLayoutAlignmentY (Container parent)	Returns the alignment along the y axis with which components are laid out within their container.
int getVgap()	Gets the vertical gap maintained between components by this layout manager.
void last(Container parent)	Displays the last card of the container.
void next(Container parent)	Displays the next card of the specified container, that is, the one "below" the one currently displayed in z-order.
void previous(Container parent)	Displays the previous card of the specified container, that is, the one "above" the currently displayed one in z-order.
void setHgap(int hgap)	Sets the horizontal gap between components maintained by the layout manager.
void setVgap(int vgap)	Sets the vertical gap between components maintained by the layout manager.
void show (Container parent, String name)	Displays the component that was added to this layout with the specified name. It calls the addLayoutComponent method to do the work.

Listing 8.3 creates a simple panel which uses a CardLayout layout manager. You simply add three buttons to your container. All the buttons have an image icon. This is the simplest way to load an image using Swing. Figure 8.19 shows the panel and an image of a sand dune, which is the image icon of the first button you added to your panel.

A CardLayout object will resize the component that is showing to fill the entire viewable area of the container. The size of the container dictates the size of the components.

8

LAYOUT MANAGERS

In Figure 8.20, you resize your container. The layout manager does indeed resize the bounds of your button to fill the entire visible area of your panel. Although the image size remains the same, the button really has been enlarged.

LISTING 8.3   Demonstration of the CardLayout Layout Manager Class

```java
import java.awt.*;
import javax.swing.*;

public class CardLayoutDemo extends JPanel
{
  public CardLayoutDemo()
  {
    setPreferredSize(new Dimension(350, 300));

    CardLayout layout = new CardLayout();
    setLayout(layout);

    ImageIcon image1 = new ImageIcon("../images/sanddune.gif");
    ImageIcon image2 = new ImageIcon("../images/snowy-peaks.gif");
    ImageIcon image3 = new ImageIcon("../images/surf-rock.gif");

    add(new JButton(image1), "sanddune", 0);
    add(new JButton(image2), "snowy-peaks", 1);
    add(new JButton(image3), "surf-rock", 2);

    layout.show(this, "snowy-peaks");
  }

  public static void main(String [] args)
  {
    CardLayoutDemo app = new CardLayoutDemo();

    JFrame f = new JFrame("CardLayout Demo");
    f.getContentPane().add(app);
    f.pack();
    f.setVisible(true);
  }
}
```

FIGURE 8.19

The CardLayout *layout manager initially displays the first component added to the container on top.*

FIGURE 8.20

Resizing a container that uses a CardLayout *layout manager will result in the component on top being resized to occupy the full visible area of the container.*

You know that CardLayout objects implement a constraint policy, but the ordering of components in a container is not it. The constraints object associated with a CardLayout is a string that identifies a card in the layout.

Such strings serve as a *tag*, that is, the key in a key-value pair that defines an association between the tag and a particular component. The tag is the key and the component is the value. The layout manager uses these key-value pairs to be able to identify and access an arbitrary component managed by the layout.

You can programmatically specify which card to display in the panel. For example, to display the image that I tagged "snowy-peaks", simply execute the following statement

```
layout.show(this, "snowy-peaks");
```

from anywhere in your CardLayoutDemo class. Figure 8.21 shows the resulting display. You must specify the container in the first argument because, like all other layout managers, instances of CardLayout can manage the layout for multiple containers simultaneously.

The CardLayout class's string constraints object is a good example of constraints information that is not defined or used to restrict the component in any way. Rather, it is simply identification information. You could think of this name-value pair as a constraint on the method of identification for a component, but this is really an abuse of the term *constraints*.

The point here is that constraints objects mean different things to different layout manager implementations. It is the particular layout manager type that defines the notion and semantics of how it uses constraints information. This is a good thing to keep in mind if you define your own constraints-based layout manager class, which you can do by implementing the LayoutManager2 interface. The term *constraints* can be misleading at times.

FIGURE 8.21
You can programmatically select which one of a container's components are displayed in a CardLayout.

The BoxLayout Class

The BoxLayout class defines a layout manager that lays out components in a box. A box represents a rectangular area that must have either a horizontal or vertical orientation. This means that components are added to the container either along the X-axis or Y-axis, respectively.

When you create an instance of BoxLayout, you must specify its orientation. Those with horizontal orientations lay out their components from left-to-right, whereas those with vertical orientations lay out their components from top-to-bottom.

This layout manager first attempts to arrange components to have their preferred width for horizontal orientations or their preferred height for vertical orientations. For horizontal layouts, the layout manager attempts to make all its components the same height as the tallest component.

For vertical layouts, the layout manager attempts to make all components as wide as the widest component.

Table 8.12 lists the new elements of the BoxLayout class. That is, it only lists new constants and constructors. All other members are defined by the LayoutManager2 interface implemented by BoxLayout.

TABLE 8.12   The BoxLayout Class Members

BoxLayout *member*	*Description*
static int X_AXIS	Specifies that components should be laid out left-to-right
static int Y_AXIS	Specifies that components should be laid out top-to-bottom
BoxLayout(Container target, int axis)	Creates a layout manager that will lay out components either left-to-right or top-to-bottom, as specified in the axis parameter

The first example of BoxLayout in Listing 8.4 looks similar to previous examples that used other layout managers. You simply create an instance and set it to be the layout manager for your container. This lets you use BoxLayout with any container. Notice that you have to specify the container's orientation in the constructor. If you run this program, you will see the layout of Figure 8.22.

LISTING 8.4   Demonstration of the BoxLayout Layout Manager Class

```
import java.awt.*;
import javax.swing.*;

public class BoxLayoutDemo extends JPanel
{
  public BoxLayoutDemo()
  {
    BoxLayout boxLayout = new BoxLayout(this, BoxLayout.X_AXIS);
    setLayout(boxLayout);

    add(new JButton("1"));
    add(new JButton("2"));
    add(new JButton("3"));
    add(new JButton("4"));
    add(new JButton("5"));
    add(new JButton("6"));
    add(new JButton("7"));
```

continues

LISTING 8.4   Continued

```
    add(new JButton("8"));
    add(new JButton("9"));
  }

  public static void main(String [] args)
  {
    BoxLayoutDemo app = new BoxLayoutDemo();

    JFrame f = new JFrame("BoxLayout Demo");
    f.getContentPane().add(app);
    f.pack();
    f.setVisible(true);
    }
}
```

FIGURE 8.22

The BoxLayout *class only lays out components in a single row or column depending on the layout manager's orientation.*

Because you specified that you wanted your layout manager to use a horizontal orientation to lay out the components, your buttons are placed left-to-right inside the box. BoxLayout objects create and maintain only a single row or column, depending on the chosen orientation.

Figure 8.22 is shown in its original size; you didn't resize the container. Figure 8.23 shows how the layout is affected after you increase the width and height of the container. The components are not resized to fill the container's entire area. This is different than, say, BorderLayout.

FIGURE 8.23

Stretching the dimensions of a container with a BoxLayout *layout manager does not resize the components.*

If you shrink the width of your container, you see another example that shows BoxLayout doesn't resize its components. In Figure 8.24, buttons 8 and 9 are only partially or no longer visible. In particular, you can see that these last two buttons are not moved to a second row. BoxLayout maintains a constant-sized box based on the preferred sizes of the components it lays out.

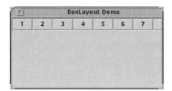

FIGURE 8.24

Shrinking a container does not induce wrapping by a BoxLayout *layout manager. Components are simply not visible if they can't fit into the visible bounds of a container.*

Vertical layouts work the same way. Figure 8.25 shows your buttons laid out with a layout manager instance that uses a vertical layout strategy. You simply change your previous program source to specify the vertical orientation for the layout manager. Again you can see in Figure 8.25 that the components are neither widened nor lengthened to occupy the full area of their container.

FIGURE 8.25

Complex arrangements can be constructed using only BoxLayout *layout managers. Containers are nested, each with its own layout manager instance that lays out its components in either an X-axis or Y-axis orientation, whichever is appropriate.*

It may not seem that the BoxLayout is a very interesting class; its layout may look rather boring and simplistic. On the contrary, though, this layout manager provides a very useful function, namely, to give you a way to ensure that components are not resized in a layout. This is the BoxLayout class's primary purpose, and it can be quite useful at times.

And, actually, the BoxLayout class's characteristic single-row or column layout is not really limiting. You can still use it to create complex layouts. The trick is to use your old friend, the nested container.

You can create multiple-row and column layouts by nesting containers which each use a BoxLayout layout manager. Each nested container's layout manager uses either a horizontal or vertical layout policy, and you achieve the overall desired arrangement of components.

For example, you can rearrange the nine buttons of your previous example in three rows of three buttons each. Schematically, it looks like Figure 8.26. The rectangular boxes represent containers.

Listing 8.5 shows how you change your program to achieve this layout by using nested containers with different layout managers.

LISTING 8.5   Using Nested Containers with BoxLayout Layout Managers

```java
import java.awt.*;
import javax.swing.*;

public class BoxLayoutDemo extends JPanel
{
  public BoxLayoutDemo()
  {
    setLayout(new BorderLayout());

    // Create the panel that holds buttons 1, 2, and 3.
    // This container will have a horizontal layout.
    //
    JPanel oneToThree = new JPanel();
    BoxLayout box_1_3_Layout = new BoxLayout(oneToThree, BoxLayout.X_AXIS);
    oneToThree.setLayout(box_1_3_Layout);

    // Add the buttons to the container.
    //
    oneToThree.add(new JButton("1"));
    oneToThree.add(new JButton("2"));
    oneToThree.add(new JButton("3"));

    // Create the panel that holds buttons 4, 5, and 6.
    // This container will have horizontal layout too.
    //
    JPanel fourToSix = new JPanel();
    BoxLayout box_4_6_Layout = new BoxLayout(fourToSix, BoxLayout.X_AXIS);
    fourToSix.setLayout(box_4_6_Layout);

    // Add the buttons to the container.
    //
    fourToSix.add(new JButton("4"));
```

```
      fourToSix.add(new JButton("5"));
      fourToSix.add(new JButton("6"));

      // Create the panel that holds the buttons 7, 8, and 9.
      // It also has a horizontal layout.
      //
      JPanel sevenToNine = new JPanel();
      BoxLayout box_7_9_Layout = new BoxLayout(sevenToNine, BoxLayout.X_AXIS);
      sevenToNine.setLayout(box_7_9_Layout);

      // Add the buttons to the container.
      //
      sevenToNine.add(new JButton("7"));
      sevenToNine.add(new JButton("8"));
      sevenToNine.add(new JButton("9"));

      // Create the panel that will hold the first three panels.
      // We are nesting panels here.
      // Notice that this panel uses a vertical layout (Y_AXIS).
      // It places the other three panels in one vertical column.
      //
      JPanel intermediatePanel = new JPanel();
      BoxLayout intermediateLayout = new BoxLayout(intermediatePanel,
      BoxLayout.Y_AXIS);

      intermediatePanel.setLayout(intermediateLayout);

      // Add the nested panels to the intermediate panel.
      //
      intermediatePanel.add(oneToThree);
      intermediatePanel.add(fourToSix);
      intermediatePanel.add(sevenToNine);

      // Added to the CENTER of our BorderLayout by default.
      //
      add(intermediatePanel);
   }

   public static void main(String [] args)
   {
      BoxLayoutDemo app = new BoxLayoutDemo();

      JFrame f = new JFrame("BoxLayout Demo");
      f.getContentPane().add(app);
      f.pack();
      f.setVisible(true);
   }
}
```

Figure 8.26 shows the layout of an outermost `JPanel` (which uses a `BoxLayout.Y_AXIS` layout strategy) which has one column of three components. The three components are themselves containers. Each container is a `JPanel` (which uses a `BoxLayout.X_AXIS` layout strategy). Each of these innermost `JPanel` instances contains one row of three buttons.

The `JPanel` that contains the three nested containers itself sits inside the `BorderLayout.CENTER` region of the GUI's outermost `JPanel`, which uses a `BorderLayout`. This whole structure is contained by the application's `JFrame`.

Figure 8.26 shows your nine buttons in this new arrangement.

FIGURE 8.26

You can achieve complex layouts using BoxLayout *layout managers by nesting various containers that mix the* BoxLayout *class's horizontal and vertical layout strategies.*

The skeptical reader can verify that indeed this example uses a series of `BoxLayout` layout manager instances. Enlarging the container, as in Figure 8.27, reveals that the panels are not enlarged to fill the outermost panel's display area. None of the box layout instances resizes its respective container because this layout manager's policy is to maintain a fixed layout size after it is calculated.

Figures 8.26 and 8.27 each use five panels. Four of them use `BoxLayout` layout managers and none of those panels is resized. Thus, even when the outermost `JPanel` is resized, its single component still resides in the center region of its `BorderLayout`. The area used by the component in the center region is not enlarged because the component uses a `BoxLayout`.

FIGURE 8.27

After the required area is calculated for a container using a BoxLayout, *it is never changed.*

It's difficult to see the boundaries of the various panels because the strategy of the `BoxLayout` class is to place components almost flush against each other. This layout manager doesn't give you a way to set any horizontal or vertical gaps between components as do the other layout manager classes you examined previously.

If there were only a way to introduce some component that takes a fixed amount of vertical or horizontal space, you could insert it between the components in your containers.

You can think of such an *invisible* component as a fixed-sized strut. A *strut* is a component that can be added to the layout like any other. This flexibility enables a container's `BoxLayout` layout manager to lay out components flush against each other and still give the appearance that there are gaps between the components. You don't see the invisible struts.

It probably comes as no surprise that Swing does have a mechanism for achieving this effect; it is the `javax.swing.Box` class, which is a lightweight container that extends `java.awt.Container` directly.

Table 8.13 lists the members of the `Box` class.

TABLE 8.13   The Box Class

`Box` *constructor or method name*	*Description*
`Box(int axis)`	Creates a `Box` container that displays its components along the specified axis.
`static Component createGlue()`	Creates an invisible "glue" component that can be useful in a `Box` whose visible components have a maximum width (for a horizontal box) or height (for a vertical box). The size of a glue component can expand to fill the empty space between components.
`static Box createHorizontalBox()`	Creates a `Box` container that arranges its components from left-to-right. Components have a fixed width.
`static Component createHorizontalGlue()`	Creates a horizontal glue component.
`static Component createHorizontalStrut(int width)`	Creates an invisible component that's always the same width, even if the container is widened.
`static Component createRigidArea(Dimension d)`	Creates an invisible component that always has the same specified area, even if the container is resized.
`static Box createVerticalBox()`	Creates a `Box` container that arranges its components from top-to-bottom. Components have a fixed height.

continues

TABLE 8.13   Continued

Box *constructor or method name*	*Description*
`static Component createVerticalGlue()`	Creates a vertical glue component.
`static Component createVerticalStrut(int height)`	Creates an invisible component that's always the same height, even if the container is lengthened.
`AccessibleContext getAccessibleContext()`	Gets the `AccessibleContext` associated with this `JComponent`.
`void setLayout(LayoutManager l)`	Throws an `AWTError`, because a Box container can only use a `BoxLayout` layout manager.

The `Box` class has several static methods that produce various types of "glue" components, which have a fixed size but are invisible. You can insert these invisible components into your container, and they will be laid out like all the other components. The result will be a container that still uses a `BoxLayout` and has the desired amount of spacing between components.

The `Box` class's term for a fixed amount of space is *strut*. You want to create horizontal and vertical struts to separate your components. You arbitrarily decide to use a space of ten pixels between horizontally adjacent components, and twenty-five pixels between vertically adjacent pixels. Listing 8.6 is the source code.

LISTING 8.6   Demonstration of the Use of Struts to Specify Spacing in a Layout

```
import java.awt.*;
import javax.swing.*;

/**
   This program demonstrates how to use invisible "glue" to give
   spacing between components managed by BoxLayout layout manager.
   The container used is a Box container, which always uses a
   BoxLayout layout manager.
   */
public class GlueDemo extends JPanel
{
   public GlueDemo()
   {
     // "this" container is a JPanel so we can use any layout manager
     // we want.
     setLayout(new BorderLayout());

     // Create the Box container that holds buttons 1, 2, and 3. The
     // Box containers must use a BoxLayout. We can only specify the
     // orientation.
     //
```

```
Box oneToThree = Box.createHorizontalBox();
BoxLayout box_1_3_Layout = new BoxLayout(oneToThree, BoxLayout.X_AXIS);

oneToThree.add(new JButton("1"));

// Within this Box container that holds buttons 1, 2, and 3, add
// horizontal struts between the buttons.
//
oneToThree.add(Box.createHorizontalStrut(15));
oneToThree.add(new JButton("2"));
oneToThree.add(Box.createHorizontalStrut(15));
oneToThree.add(new JButton("3"));

// Create the Box container that holds buttons 4, 5, and 6.
//
Box fourToSix = Box.createHorizontalBox();
BoxLayout box_4_6_Layout = new BoxLayout(fourToSix, BoxLayout.X_AXIS);

// Also add horizontal struts between the buttons 4, 5, and 6 of
// this second Box container.
//
fourToSix.add(new JButton("4"));
fourToSix.add(Box.createHorizontalStrut(15));
fourToSix.add(new JButton("5"));
fourToSix.add(Box.createHorizontalStrut(15));
fourToSix.add(new JButton("6"));

// Create the Box container that holds buttons 7, 8, and 9.
//
Box sevenToNine = Box.createHorizontalBox();
BoxLayout box_7_9_Layout = new BoxLayout(sevenToNine, BoxLayout.X_AXIS);

// And, finally, add horizontal struts between these buttons too.
//
sevenToNine.add(new JButton("7"));
sevenToNine.add(Box.createHorizontalStrut(15));
sevenToNine.add(new JButton("8"));
sevenToNine.add(Box.createHorizontalStrut(15));
sevenToNine.add(new JButton("9"));

// Create the intermediate container that holds the three
// containers with the buttons. Notice that this container uses a
// vertical layout. Vertical space (struts) will be added between
// each row of buttons.
//
Box intermediatePanel = Box.createVerticalBox();
```

8

**LAYOUT
MANAGERS**

continues

LISTING 8.6   Continued

```
    BoxLayout intermediateLayout = new BoxLayout(intermediatePanel,
    BoxLayout.Y_AXIS);

    intermediatePanel.add(oneToThree);

    // Add a vertical strut between the first and second rows of
    // buttons, that is, between the first and second Box container.
    //
    intermediatePanel.add(Box.createVerticalStrut(25));
    intermediatePanel.add(fourToSix);


    // Add another vertical strut between the second and third rows of
    // buttons, that is, between the second and third Box containers.
    //
    intermediatePanel.add(Box.createVerticalStrut(25));
    intermediatePanel.add(sevenToNine);

    // Added to the CENTER of our BorderLayout by default.
    //
    add(intermediatePanel);
  }

  public static void main(String [] args)
  {
    GlueDemo app = new GlueDemo();

    JFrame f = new JFrame("Glue and Strut Demo");
    f.getContentPane().add(app);
    f.pack();
    f.setVisible(true);
  }
}
```

Figure 8.28 verifies that you have indeed put invisible glue between your components. Struts can be used to ensure that a container has at least a certain horizontal or vertical size.

The three buttons in each row have horizontal struts between them. Additionally, there are vertical struts between the three rows of buttons.

The Box class also defines two static methods. Box.createRigidArea(Dimension d) can be used to create an invisible area that has both a fixed width and height. Like struts, such a component can also be added to a container.

FIGURE 8.28
Struts can be used to force a minimum amount of spacing between components in a container managed by a BoxLayout *layout manager.*

Although struts have a fixed amount of one-dimensional space, rigid areas have a fixed amount of area specified by an x and y dimension. Use rigid areas when you need a fixed amount of *area* in a layout instead of just a fixed amount of spacing between components.

The Box class defines a container that is useful in its own right. You can create Box containers and use them in your GUIs. Typically, this is what Swing developers do when they want a container which uses a BoxLayout layout manager.

One reason for using Box containers is that you can easily create a ready-made container that already has an installed BoxLayout layout manager by using one of the following two methods that are defined in the Box class:

```
static Box createHorizontalBox()
static Box createVerticalBox()
```

You can modify the last example to use these factory methods as shown in Listing 8.7. The new Box containers take the place of the JPanels you used earlier. The only difference between Listings 8.7 and 8.6 occur in the constructor. Therefore, I only show the code that is different in Listing 8.7. The changes are confined to the constructor code shown.

LISTING 8.7   Demonstration of the Use of the Box Container

```
public BoxDemo()
{
  setLayout(new BorderLayout());

  // Instead of a JPanel, we now use a new Box container to contain
  // the three intermediate Box containers that each hold one of
  // the three rows of buttons.
  //
  Box oneToThree = Box.createHorizontalBox();
  BoxLayout box_1_3_Layout = new BoxLayout(oneToThree, BoxLayout.X_AXIS);

  oneToThree.add(new JButton("1"));
  oneToThree.add(Box.createHorizontalStrut(15));
  oneToThree.add(new JButton("2"));
```

continues

LISTING 8.7   Continued

```
    oneToThree.add(Box.createHorizontalStrut(15));
    oneToThree.add(new JButton("3"));

    Box fourToSix = Box.createHorizontalBox();
    BoxLayout box_4_6_Layout = new BoxLayout(fourToSix, BoxLayout.X_AXIS);

    fourToSix.add(new JButton("4"));
    fourToSix.add(Box.createHorizontalStrut(15));
    fourToSix.add(new JButton("5"));
    fourToSix.add(Box.createHorizontalStrut(15));
    fourToSix.add(new JButton("6"));

    Box sevenToNine = Box.createHorizontalBox();
    BoxLayout box_7_9_Layout = new BoxLayout(sevenToNine, BoxLayout.X_AXIS);

    sevenToNine.add(new JButton("7"));
    sevenToNine.add(Box.createHorizontalStrut(15));
    sevenToNine.add(new JButton("8"));
    sevenToNine.add(Box.createHorizontalStrut(15));
    sevenToNine.add(new JButton("9"));

    Box intermediatePanel = Box.createVerticalBox();
    BoxLayout intermediateLayout = new BoxLayout(intermediatePanel,
                     BoxLayout.Y_AXIS);

    intermediatePanel.add(oneToThree);
    intermediatePanel.add(Box.createVerticalStrut(25));
    intermediatePanel.add(fourToSix);
    intermediatePanel.add(Box.createVerticalStrut(25));
    intermediatePanel.add(sevenToNine);

    // Added to the CENTER of our BorderLayout by default.
    //
    add(intermediatePanel);
  }
```

You changed two things in this version. First, you changed your JPanel objects to Box objects. Secondly, you removed the setLayout calls, because the layout manager is set by the createVerticalBox and createHorizontalBox methods. Moreover, calling setLayout on such a box would result in a runtime exception because it is prohibited to set the layout of a box; the Box class is implemented so that it only knows how to use a BoxLayout layout manager.

The GridBagLayout Class

In the last section you saw that the BoxLayout class arranges components in fixed relative sizes within fixed sized areas.

This type of layout manager is extremely useful for certain jobs. However, `BoxLayout` does not always give you the flexibility you need because it tries to make all components the same size. Furthermore, it only lays out one row or column of components.

Another layout manager, the `GridLayout` class discussed earlier, uses an x–y grid of cells, but each grid cell is the same size. The components are stretched to fill the size of the grid cell. This restriction limits control in certain cases. You need something a bit more flexible, a layout manager which doesn't require all components to be the same size, and one which allows more freedom in specifying how components are aligned.

The `GridBagLayout` class is designed exactly for this purpose. It is the most powerful and flexible layout manager in the JDK. It implements a very powerful layout strategy that gives you fine-grained control over the exact size and positioning of components in a container.

This flexibility doesn't come for free, however. `GridBagLayout` is the most complicated of all the JDK layout manager classes. It can be quite daunting and has exasperated many developers. But with a structured, methodical approach to its features, it's not so overwhelming at all. It's well worth some investment of time to learn to master it.

The `GridBagLayout` class lays out components in an x–y grid of squares. These squares are called *grid cells*.

Each component can occupy one or more grid cells, which collectively define the component's *display area*. As you have seen many times before, a component's display area need not be square. It can be rectangular.

When using `GridBagLayout`, component display areas do not all have to be the same width or height. This means that the layout manager does not resize components. It honors the preferred width and height requests of each component; components are not stretched to conform to the sizes of other components.

Notwithstanding these characteristics of the layout algorithm, the top and leading edges of the component display areas are still aligned along the imaginary grid lines that run parallel to the x and y axes of the container. Figure 8.29 shows a container superimposed with a grid of dashed grid lines. The solid rectangles delineate the display areas occupied by the components.

You can see that although grid lines appear regularly spaced, the cells occupied by the components are not. The grid lines are only shown for illustration and never appear in a container. They delineate grid cells. The layout manager models such a grid for calculation and positioning purposes only. These squares, however, do not represent the actual areas to which a component is restricted.

The grid lines define grid cells of equal size that are spaced in rows and columns along the x-axis and y-axis. Their width and height are equal to the smallest width or height, respectively, of the smallest component being laid out. This is how `GridBagLayout` can align the

8

LAYOUT
MANAGERS

component edges along grid lines. Components can take up several grid cells along either axis, essentially defining their rectangular area within their layout. Nevertheless, the layout manager still aligns the component's display area along the grid lines.

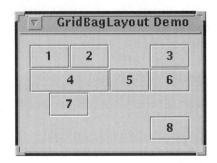

FIGURE 8.29

The GridBagLayout *layout manager uses a grid, represented by the dashed lines, to align component display areas horizontally and vertically. Button 4 is filled to use the complete width of its display area. Button 7 is centered in a display area that is two grid cells wide.*

GridBagLayout is a constraints-based layout manager class, and, therefore, must use a constraints object to specify how each component should be laid out in a container. The constraints object used by GridBagLayout is itself a substantial object defined by the java.awt.GridBagConstraints class.

Most of the effort required to understand how to use the GridBagLayout class really involves learning the quantities defined by the GridBagConstraints class and what they represent. These quantities come in the form of instance variables defined in the GridBagConstraints class. You set the value of these variables to customize the constraints object for each component you wish to add to your container.

By setting the variable values in the constraints object you customize it to represent the specific layout characteristics for a particular component. Each quantity—variable—represents a specific type of layout attribute. In order to use the GridBagLayout layout manager effectively, you must understand what each of these quantities in the GridBagConstraints class represents and the valid values for each.

The key to understanding GridBagConstraints is to understand what constraint each of its variables define semantically and how to use them. You should learn the acceptable values for each field and then study when to use a particular value to obtain a particular layout effect. This insight will come partly from experience.

The quantities in Table 8.14 represent the variables in the GridBagConstraints class. You set their values to stipulate the constraints for a particular component.

TABLE 8.14 The Configurable Quantities of the `GridBagConstraints` Class

`GridBagConstraints` *variable*	*Description*
`gridx`	Specifies the column in which to place the left edge of the component's display area. The leftmost column is `gridx 0`.
`gridy`	Specifies the row in which to place the top edge of the components display area. The topmost row is `gridy = 0`.
`gridwidth`	Specifies the width in grid cells taken up by the component.
`gridheight`	Specifies the height in grid cells taken up by the component.
`fill`	Specifies the preferred policy for enlarging the component when its display area is greater than it's preferred size.
`ipadx`	Specifies the component's internal spacing, which is the minimum amount of space in pixels to add to the component's minimum width.
`ipady`	Specifies the component's internal spacing, which is the minimum amount of space in pixels to add to the component's minimum height.
`insets`	Specifies the component's external padding, which is the minimum amount of space between the component and the edges of its display area. (Insets defines the space located between the component's padding and the edges of its display area.)
`anchor`	Specifies the location within the component's display area to place (to anchor) the component when it is smaller than its display area. The component will always be anchored in this part of its display area, even when you enlarge the display area.
`weightx`	Specifies how much extra space to distribute to this component, relative to others in the same row, when the container is larger than the requested widths of all components.
`weighty`	Specifies how much extra space to distribute to this component, relative to others in the same column, when the container is larger than the requested heights of all components.

8

**LAYOUT
MANAGERS**

There are essentially two general categories of constraints quantities defined by the `GridBagConstraints` class. Some of the quantities belong to one or the other, and some belong to both categories. The distinction between the two delineates the difference between a component and its display area; the bounds of a component can be less than the bounds of its display area.

The first category defines the location of the component's display area within the grid. The `GridBagConstraints` variables in this category apply to the display area's placement, not to the placement of the component itself.

The `gridx`, `gridy` quantities specify a grid position relative to a reference grid cell, which is the upper-leftmost grid square in the layout. These two quantities, as well as the `gridwidth` and `gridheight` variables, all belong to the first category of constraints because their values affect the size and position of a component's display area.

The second category defines information about a component itself, namely, its size and position within its display area.

The `anchor` and `fill` variables belong to the second category because they specify how a component is positioned and sized within its display area.

The `insets`, `ipadx`, and `ipady` parameters apply to both categories because they affect the size of both the component and its display area. The values of these parameters affect the size of the component, which indirectly affects the size of the display area, and, consequently, the overall layout.

Each constraint parameter has a default value. Table 8.15 indicates the valid values for each constraint and its default value.

TABLE 8.15   Allowed Values of the `GridBagConstraints` Parameters and Their Default Values

GridBagConstraints *parameter*	*Valid values*	*Default value*
`gridx`, `gridy`	Integer parameter; GridBagConstraints class> 0, `RELATIVE`.	`RELATIVE`
`gridwidth`, `gridheight`	An Integer parameter; GridBagConstraints class> 0, `REMAINDER`, `RELATIVE`.	1
`fill`	`NONE, HORIZONTAL, VERTICAL, BOTH.`	`NONE`
`ipadx`, `ipady`	An Integer parameter; GridBagConstraints class> 0.	0
`insets`	A `java.awt.Insets` object.	`new Insets(0, 0, 0, 0)`
`anchor`	`CENTER, NORTH, NORTHEAST, EAST, SOUTHEAST, SOUTH, SOUTHWEST, WEST, NORTHWEST.`	`CENTER`
`weightx`, `weighty`	A Double value> 0.	0

Rather than trying to grasp abstractly what these parameters are and how they affect a component's layout, it's better to see some examples. First, however, look at how the `GridBagLayout` object and the `GridBagConstraints` collaborate.

Conceptually, the standard scenario that your program should implement for containers that use a `GridBagLayout` layout manager is as follows:

1. Instantiate the `GridBagConstraints` class to produce a constraints object.
2. Set the values of each quantity in the constraints object to represent the desired constraints for a particular component.
3. Associate the constraints object with the component.
4. Add the component to the container. When the component is added to your container, the layout manager reads the values of the fields in the constraints object you associated with your component. It saves these values and uses them subsequently whenever it lays out that component.
5. Repeat steps 2–4 for each component you wish to add to your container.

Step 1 is self-explanatory; you need a `GridBagConstraints` object. In step 2, you configure the constraints object so that its variable values reflect the specific layout attributes for a component.

In step 3, you tie together the settings in the constraints object with a component. By doing this, you tell the layout manager instance to extract the configuration from the constraints object, that was set in step 2, and associate it with the object. Each time the layout manager lays out this particular component, it uses these settings.

Step 4 is also self-explanatory. You simply add the component to the container's family of children.

For each component you wish to add to your container, you must indicate the constraints values that should always be applied when laying out that component. The layout manager must keep a record of these settings. It references the correct constraints for each object it lays out.

The first example shows the simplest and, decidedly, the most uninteresting layout; nevertheless, it demonstrates the steps outlined previously. Listing 8.8 shows the source code that produces Figure 8.30.

LISTING 8.8   Setting Component Constraints for Use in a `GridBagLayout` Controlled Container

```
import java.awt.*;
import javax.swing.*;

public class GridBagLayoutDemo extends JPanel
```

continues

8

LAYOUT
MANAGERS

LISTING 8.8   Continued

```java
{
  public GridBagLayoutDemo()
  {
    GridBagLayout gbl = new GridBagLayout();
    GridBagConstraints constraints = new GridBagConstraints();

    setLayout(gbl);

    JButton one = new JButton("1");
    gbl.setConstraints(one, constraints);

    JButton two = new JButton("2");
    gbl.setConstraints(two, constraints);

    JButton three = new JButton("3");
    gbl.setConstraints(three, constraints);

    JButton four = new JButton("4");
    gbl.setConstraints(four, constraints);

    JButton five = new JButton("5");
    gbl.setConstraints(five, constraints);

    JButton six = new JButton("6");
    gbl.setConstraints(six, constraints);

    JButton seven = new JButton("7");
    gbl.setConstraints(seven, constraints);

    JButton eight = new JButton("8");
    gbl.setConstraints(eight, constraints);

    JButton nine = new JButton("9");
    gbl.setConstraints(nine, constraints);

    add(one);
    add(two);
    add(three);
    add(four);
    add(five);
    add(six);
    add(seven);
    add(eight);
    add(nine);
```

```
    }

    public static void main(String [] args)
    {
        GridBagLayoutDemo app = new GridBagLayoutDemo();

        JFrame f = new JFrame("GridBagLayout Demo");
        f.getContentPane().add(app);
        f.pack();
        f.setVisible(true);
    }
}
```

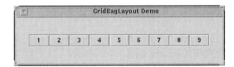

FIGURE 8.30

The layout manager associates a component with the values of a constraints object. This step indicates the component's constraints to the layout manager, which the layout manager uses whenever it lays out the component.

In this example, you only create one instance of `GridBagConstraints`. You can create one for each component, but this is neither necessary nor recommended because doing so uses extra objects superfluously. After you set a component's constraints, you no longer need to keep that constraints object intact. It can be reused on another component.

gridx and gridy

In Listing 8.8, you don't set the values of the constraints variables before associating the constraints object with the components. You do this so the default values will be used for every component placement. The result is the layout in Figure 8.30.

You do, however, associate the constraints object with each component by calling the `setConstraints()` method on the layout manager, not on the constraints object.

Basic grid cell layout is determined by the value of the `gridx` and `gridy` variables. These can be assigned either an integer value greater than or equal to zero, or the defined constant `GridBagConstraints.RELATIVE`.

The nine buttons are laid out in a row because the default setting for the `gridx` field is `GridBagConstraints.RELATIVE`.

A value of RELATIVE for the gridx field means that a component should be laid out along the x-axis at a position to the right of the last component added in that row. A value of RELATIVE for the gridy field means that the component should be added to the row below that of the last component added in the same column.

To specify a particular position in the grid, you can explicitly set either of the gridx or gridy values.

Figure 8.31 shows three rows of three buttons. Each time you start a new row, you must change the value of gridx to zero

```
constraints.gridx = 0;
```

and increment the value of gridy.

FIGURE 8.31

Manually setting the grid cell in which to place a component enables you to lay out your components in exactly the position desired.

Notice that you have to change the value of gridx back to RELATIVE after you add the first component of each row.

```
constraints.gridx = GridBagConstraints.RELATIVE;
```

If you increment gridx and gridy after you add each component, you get the layout in Figure 8.32.

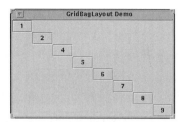

FIGURE 8.32

Incrementing gridx *and* gridy *before adding each component gives this diagonal pattern.*

gridwidth and gridheight

Constraints parameters like `gridx` and `gridy` specify the position of a components display area within the overall layout. They do not affect the size of either the component or its display area.

The next few sections introduce constraints quantities that affect the positioning and sizing of a component within its display area, and also the sizing of the display area itself.

Let's next look at how you can vary the width or height of a component's display area. Doing so will allocate more than one grid cell to the component's display area in the x or y dimension, respectively.

```
constraints.gridwidth = 2;
```

Figure 8.33 shows your layout after assigning button 5 a `gridwidth` value of 2.

8

LAYOUT
MANAGERS

FIGURE 8.33

Increasing the width of a component's display area repositions other components in the same row. The component gets positioned in the center of its display area by default.

In Figure 8.33, button 5 is positioned in the center of a display area that is twice as wide as the others. Button 6 must be shoved to the right by an amount equal to the width of one whole grid cell.

You can also give button 5 twice the height of the other buttons by specifying a value of 2 for its `gridheight` parameter. Figure 8.34 shows the effect on the overall layout.

```
constraints.gridwidth = 2;
constraints.gridheight = 2;
```

FIGURE 8.34

Increasing a component's height repositions the other components in the same column.

It seems that something is not quite right here; button 5 overlaps the buttons in the third row. But upon closer examination, you can see that the GridBagLayout layout manager did exactly what you asked; it allocated a display area two grid cells wide and high for button 5, and positioned button 5 in the center of this area.

However, you continue to place buttons 7 through 9 in row 2, so you get a resulting overlap. If this is the effect you want then all is well. But if not, then you must reposition your components in row 2 so they fall below the reach of button 5's extent.

Incidentally, when components overlap, their *z-order* in the container determines which is visible. Z-order is the front-to-back stacking of components in a container. The component with the highest z-order appears on top of the others. Because you added button 5 to the container first, it is first in the container's z-order, and, therefore, appears in front of the others.

But let's say that you really want to remove any overlap. In that case you really want to put the third row components in row 3, not row 2 in order to avoid this overlap.

Nevertheless, you must still put something in row 3 or the layout manager will move everything below row 3 up one row. It thinks there is no need to reserve space in row 2 when no components are added to that row. Remember that grid row and column numbers are zero-based, so row 2 is the third row.

Figure 8.35 shows the result with this correction.

FIGURE 8.35

Button 5 now has a width and height of two grid cells and is again positioned in the center of its double-wide display area.

Listing 8.9 shows the source code that produces Figure 8.35. Notice where the gridwidth and gridheight variables are set to obtain the desired layout.

LISTING 8.9   Customizing Component Layout by Specifying Constraints Parameter Values

```java
import java.awt.*;
import javax.swing.*;

public class GridBagLayoutDemo
{
  public GridBagLayoutDemo()
```

```
{
  GridBagLayout gbl = new GridBagLayout();
  GridBagConstraints constraints = new GridBagConstraints();

  setLayout(gbl);

  JButton one = new JButton("1");
  gbl.setConstraints(one, constraints);

  JButton two = new JButton("2");
  gbl.setConstraints(two, constraints);

  // Configure the constraints object before associating
  // the component with it.
  //
  constraints.gridwidth = 1;
  JButton three = new JButton("3");
  gbl.setConstraints(three, constraints);

  // Do the same for every component.  You must set the
  // values of any constraints object parameters that
  // you want to use to define the component's layout
  // information.
  //
  constraints.gridx = 0;
  constraints.gridy = 1;
  JButton four = new JButton("4");
  gbl.setConstraints(four, constraints);

  // Button 5 is still in column 2 because gridy
  // still equals 1.  It will be placed in the
  // same row as Button 4.
  //
  constraints.gridx = GridBagConstraints.RELATIVE;
  constraints.gridwidth = 2;
  constraints.gridheight = 2;
  JButton five = new JButton("5");
  gbl.setConstraints(five, constraints);

  // gridx = RELATIVE and gridy = 1 still.
  //
  constraints.gridwidth = 1;
  constraints.gridheight = 1;
  JButton six = new JButton("6");
  gbl.setConstraints(six, constraints);

  constraints.gridx = 0;
```

8

LAYOUT
MANAGERS

continues

LISTING 8.9 Continued

```java
        constraints.gridy = 2;
        JButton seven = new JButton("7");
        gbl.setConstraints(seven, constraints);

        constraints.gridx = 3;
        JButton eight = new JButton("8");
        gbl.setConstraints(eight, constraints);

        constraints.gridx = 2;
        constraints.gridy = 3;
        JButton nine = new JButton("9");
        gbl.setConstraints(nine, constraints);

        add(one);
        add(two);
        add(three);
        add(four);
        add(five);
        add(six);
        add(seven);
        add(eight);
        add(nine);

    }

    public static void main(String [] args)
    {
        GridBagLayoutDemo app = new GridBagLayoutDemo();

        JFrame f = new JFrame("GridBagLayout Demo");
        f.getContentPane().add(app);
        f.pack();
        f.setVisible(true);
    }
}
```

Each time you specify size or position for a component, you must be careful to reset the width and height back to the "normal" values before adding subsequent components. Remember that when you bind a constraints object to a component with the setConstraints() method, the layout manager uses whatever constraints values are set at that time to lay out the component.

fill

You might have noticed that increasing a component's display area does not increase the size of the component itself. In Figures 8.34 and 8.35, button 5 remains the same size even though its display area increases.

By default, GridBagLayout places a component in the center of its display area when there is more room than the component needs. But GridBagLayout also gives you a way to increase the size of a component itself.

You can stretch a component horizontally or vertically within its display area by specifying a fill strategy. The GridBagConstraints.fill constraints variable can take one of three values, GridBagConstraints.HORIZONTAL, GridBagConstraints.VERTICAL GridBagConstraints.BOTH or GridBagConstraints.NONE—the latter being the default value.

To stretch your button 5 from the last example so that it fills its display area horizontally, simply add the statement

```
constraints.fill = GridBagConstraints.HORIZONTAL;
```

before calling setConstraints() on the component. Figure 8.36 shows the result.

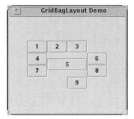

FIGURE 8.36
Filling a component horizontally stretches the component's width to fill the width of its display area.

If you fill vertically instead, your layout will look like that shown in Figure 8.37.

FIGURE 8.37
Filling vertically increases the component's height to fill the full space of the display area's height.

If you fill both horizontally and vertically, you fill the complete display area of the component, as shown in Figure 8.38.

FIGURE 8.38
Filling both horizontally and vertically increases the component's width and height to use the component's full display area.

anchor

Filling is one technique to get a desired effect when your component's spatial requirements are less than the display area provides.

Another technique available to you when a display area is larger than its component is to anchor the component in a certain part of the display area. You already saw that GridBagLayout centers components in the display area by default. But you have no fewer than nine choices for positioning components within a display area that is larger than the component needs.

The valid values for the anchor quantity in GridBagConstraints are listed in Table 8.15. These are compass points that specify where the component should be anchored, regardless of how the container is resized.

Let's start with the layout shown in Figure 8.35. Button 5 has more room in its display area than it needs for its size. By default, the component is positioned in the center of the display area. Using the anchor parameter, you can anchor it in no fewer than eight other positions.

Figures 8.39 through 8.46 show how the layout changes when you specify different anchor directive values for button 5.

FIGURE 8.39

Changing the anchor constraints value anchors a component at a particular compass point within its display area. This parameter is useful when the display area is larger than the component.

FIGURE 8.40

NORTH *anchor position.*

FIGURE 8.41

NORTHEAST *anchor position.*

8

LAYOUT
MANAGERS

FIGURE 8.42

WEST *anchor position.*

FIGURE 8.43

EAST *anchor position.*

FIGURE 8.44

SOUTHWEST *anchor position.*

FIGURE 8.45
SOUTH *anchor position.*

FIGURE 8.46
SOUTHEAST *anchor position.*

insets

Sometimes it's useful to be able to increase the size of a component's display area without specifying that it take up more than one unit of width or height. The GridBagConstraints class defines the insets variable exactly for this purpose.

Officially, this parameter defines a component's external padding, which is not a very descriptive term. *External padding* refers to the space between the component's bounds and the edges of its display area.

Insets are defined by the java.awt.Insets class. To set a value for GridBagConstraints.insets, you must instantiate the Insets class and set the insets variable equal to the new object.

Insets define the amount of space, in pixels, that surround the component on all four sides. The four parameters of the Insets constructor specify, respectively, the spacing at the top, left, bottom, and right edges of the component.

For example, to add some spacing to the left and right sides of button 2 in this example, simply do the following:

```
constraints.insets = new Insets(0, 30, 0, 30);
```

This produces the layout in Figure 8.47. Now the display area for button 2 is wider than the space required to render the button. To align columns of components that appear in subsequent rows, the layout manager must also widen the display areas of the components in column 1 for all rows. This action, of course, also pushes column 2 further to the right.

Note that insets do not increase the size of the component itself, but only the size of its display area.

FIGURE 8.47

Using insets is another way to increase the size of a component's display area. This figure shows extra space added to the left and right sides of components in column 1.

Each of the four fields of the Insets class can also take a negative value. A negative setting causes the component's layout to cross over the boundaries of its display area.

Figure 8.48 shows the previous layout with negative insets of 10 pixels specified for each side of button 5. Actually, to get this exact layout, you must change the order in which you add the buttons to the container. Because you want button 5 on top, you must add it first. If you maintain your usual sequence of adding buttons to the container in numerical order, the top and left sides of button 5 will be occluded by buttons 1, 2, 3, and 4 because those components were added before button 5.

You can combine insets and anchor settings to achieve even more flexible layouts. By simply adding the line

```
constraints.anchor = GridBagConstraints.WEST;
```

to the constraints configuration for button 5, you achieve the layout depicted in Figure 8.49.

FIGURE 8.48
A negative value for a component's insets makes the component larger than its display area.

FIGURE 8.49
Button 5 is anchored to the WEST, and its left edge is up against the left edge of its display area. The space between buttons 4 and 5 is the extra insets space you added to button 4.

ipadx and ipady

There is another kind of spacing recognized by GridBagLayout in addition to insets. The GridBagConstraints.ipadx and GridBagConstraints.ipady variables define *internal padding*, which is the amount of extra space added to the component's size, not to the size of the display area.

The ipadx and ipady quantities are specified in pixels. They cause the layout manager to add at least twice the specified amount of space to the width or height of the component, respectively.

Twice the specified amount is added because the same padding gets added to the left and right sides, or to the top and bottom of the component. Adding padding to the component results in the component being rendered with a larger size.

Now add 10 pixels of padding to your overworked button 5 in both the x and y dimensions. Figure 8.50 shows the result.

FIGURE 8.50

The extra padding increases the size of the component itself, but not its display area. The edges of button 5's display area are flush against its neighbors, but there now appears to be extra space between the other components.

weightx and weighty

You may have noticed in the previous examples in this section that the components clump together in the center of the container. If you enlarge the size of the container, the layout of your components retains its size, thereby occupying an even smaller percentage of the total space for the container. By default, GridBagLayout distributes extra space in the container around the four edges of the grid.

By *extra space,* I mean that the container's size is larger than the combined preferred sizes of all the components in the container. For instance, in the previous examples in this section, you set the preferred size of the container to be larger than required by the components.

It shouldn't really surprise you that GridBagLayout doesn't resize components to fill extra space, because I said at the beginning of the discussion of GridBagLayout that this layout manager honors the size requests of its components. It only resizes components at your request. Automatic resizing is the whole purpose of the GridBagConstraints.fill quantity.

Yet even though GridBagLayout honors the size request of components, there is a way to distribute extra container space among the display areas of all the components.

The weightx and weighty variables enable you to specify a weighting for each component's display area that specifies how much of the container's extra space should be distributed to it.

A component's weightx value specifies how much of the container's extra width should be added to the width of the component's display area. Likewise, the weighty value specifies how much of the container's extra height should be added to the height of the component's display area.

The `weightx` and `weighty` values are both specified relative to those of the other components in the same row or column, respectively.

Both `weightx` and `weighty` are defined as `double` values. The values you set must be positive. The larger the value, the greater the percentage of space is allocated to all the display areas in that column or row, respectively.

The default value for both quantities is zero. The default behavior, as stated earlier, is the insertion of extra space between the grid and the edges of the container by the layout manager. Therefore, to avoid this bunching in the center, you must specify a weight for at least one component in a row and column.

Typically, programmers use values between 0 and 1.0 for these quantities. Although this is not a requirement, it makes it easier for you to calculate the relative weighting assigned to different components. For example, if you think of the values as some percentage between 0 and 100, you can easily picture the layout.

To see exactly how weighting works, apply a `weightx` value, and then a `weighty` value, in turn, so you can see the precise effect each has on the layout.

Taking the previous source example, assign a weighting of `1.0` to the first column, which contains button 1. Of course, you set the weighting back to zero before setting the constraints for subsequent components. You've also removed any statements that set the preferred size for any components or the container.

```
constraints.weightx = 1;
JButton one = new JButton("1");
gbl.setConstraints(one, constraints);

constraints.weightx = 0;
constraints.weighty = 0;
JButton two = new JButton("2");
gbl.setConstraints(two, constraints);
```

A weighting of 1.0 should allocate all extra space to the display areas of the components in column 1. You can see this layout in Figure 8.51.

FIGURE 8.51

Applying weighting values does not affect the initial layout, only the layout that results from resizing the container.

This looks familiar, and there is no indication of weighting. Remember, weighting applies only to redistribution of extra space upon resizing a container.

If you widen the container, you get the layout shown in Figure 8.52. It appears that all extra space in the container has been allocated to the display areas of each component in the first column.

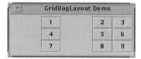

FIGURE 8.52

Giving all the weighting to the first column results in all extra horizontal space being distributed to the display areas in that column.

To be sure, you can turn on Filling and see the exact boundaries of the display areas. Figure 8.53 indeed confirms that extra space was allocated to column 1.

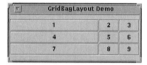

FIGURE 8.53

By specifying filling, you can verify that the display areas have been allocated extra space upon resizing.

Notice that all the display areas of column one get extra space, not just the display area for button 1 in row 1. This is necessary for GridBagLayout to maintain a grid. Figure 8.29 illustrated the idea that there is a hidden grid that GridBagLayout uses to align the edges of the display areas.

With the weighting of the last example, lengthening your container has no effect on the height of the display areas. The grid is still centered vertically upon resizing.

Next, you assign a weighty value to one component in your container, which gives a weighting to each display area in the row that contains the component.

```
constraints.weighty = 1;
JButton one = new JButton("1");
gbl.setConstraints(one, constraints);
```

```
constraints.weightx = 0;
constraints.weighty = 0;
JButton two = new JButton("2");
gbl.setConstraints(two, constraints);
```

Figure 8.54 shows the layout after you lengthen the container. You can see that the first row, which contains button 1, gets all the extra space.

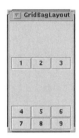

FIGURE 8.54
Assigning a value for the weighty *parameter distributes extra vertical space to each display area in the row.*

So far you've only assigned weightings to one row or column. Each row or column can have a relative weighting value. In the next example, you assign 50% of the extra horizontal space to the first column, 37.5% to the second column, and the remaining 12.5% to the third column. Figure 8.55 shows the resulting layout.

FIGURE 8.55
Specifying multiple weightx *weightings allocates extra space in proportion to the different columns.*

For one final example, assign weightx and weighty values simultaneously. This distributes extra space to rows and columns together.

Figure 8.56 uses 50%, 37.5%, and 12.5% for the three columns and rows of your running example. When you increase both the width and height of your container, you can see how the extra space is distributed according to the proportions specified.

FIGURE 8.56

Extra space in a container can be distributed among rows and columns.

Now is a good time to summarize the GridBagConstraints parameters, while their definitions are still fresh. Figure 8.57 shows a schematic diagram of all the GridBagConstraints parameters except gridx and gridy. This is a handy figure to help you distinguish the different parameters and to see how they complement each other.

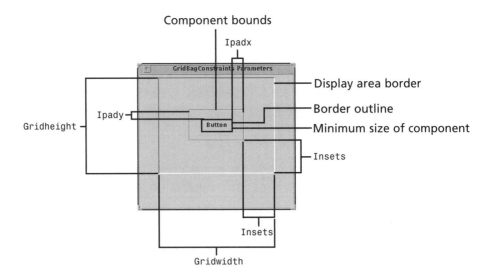

FIGURE 8.57

GridBagConstraints *parameters that affect a component's size and positioning within its display area, and parameters that affect the size of the display area itself.*

Collaboration Between Containers and Layout Managers

Perusing the online AWT and Swing class documentation will reveal that all the add() methods by which you add components to containers are defined in the java.awt.Container class. All container subclasses use these methods that they inherit from java.awt.Container. I say "all the add() methods" because Container defines several overloaded versions.

CAUTION

You must use the correct overloaded form of Container.add() to add components to your containers. You must use the form that reflects the layout manager object used by the container. Using the wrong version will result in a runtime exception, and your program will fail when it encounters code that tries to add a component to a container.

This requirement is necessary in order to support the different constraints policies of the different layout managers.

The layout manager must know how to lay out each component based on the component's constraints information, and it needs this information at the time the component is added to the container. In other words. the add() method is the vehicle by which you pass the constraints information to the layout manager; the container helps you do this.

Table 8.16 lists the overloaded add methods in the Container class. Based on previous discussions of the different layout managers, you should now be able to see more clearly how the different versions of add() support the requirements of their corresponding layout manager classes. Table 8.16 also portrays the differences in the types of constraints information used by the different constraints-based layout managers.

Looking at containers and layout managers from this perspective should help you remember the different layout managers and their constraints policies. You will probably also glean a better intuitive feeling for what is going on underneath the APIs that you are using.

TABLE 8.16   Layout Manangers and Their Corresponding `Container.add()` Methods

Overloaded `Container.add` *method*	*Used by this layout manager*
`Component add(Component comp)`	`FlowLayout, GridLayout, BoxLayout`
`Component add(Component comp, int index)`	`FlowLayout`
`void add(Component comp, Object constraints)`	`BorderLayout, CardLayout`
`void add(Component comp, Object constraints, int index)`	`CardLayout`
`Component add(String name, Component comp)`	Arcane; do not use. Use `add(Component, Object)` instead of this method.

Summary

All containers have a reference to a layout manager. Layout managers are the objects to which containers delegate the responsibility of arranging, or laying out, the container's child components.

The `LayoutManager` and `LayoutManager2` interfaces capture the nature of the work required by layout manager implementations. Each specific implementation implements its own layout strategy or algorithm.

Although containers have a default layout manager, you can set the container's layout manager to be any type that meets your needs. The requirements of your GUI's layout will determine which type of layout manager is most suited for the job.

Previously, you used nested containers to help you organize your GUI layout. Layout managers are the second tool that you use regularly to refine your GUI layout to look exactly as you want. At this point, you have the knowledge to create and display a complex arrangement of GUI components.

Events and Event Handling

IN THIS CHAPTER

- Events 362
- Event Type Hierarchy 362
- Event Types 363
- Handling Events 371
- Adapters 386
- Inner Classes 388
- Combining Event Sources and Listeners 401
- Notifying Multiple Listeners 402
- Using AWT Events 402
- Using Swing Events 433
- Swing Action Objects 488

If you've been reading the chapters of this book in order, at this point you know how to construct a visible GUI with components arranged just the way you want. But your GUI still doesn't really do anything. Your application doesn't as yet respond to external actions.

In order for an application to do anything meaningful, it must be able to respond to events. This process is called *event handling*. This chapter discusses events and event handling. In it, you will learn exactly how to make your program capable of performing event handling for the various types of events defined and supported by the Java GUI programming environment.

Events

Conceptually, in the context of GUI program environments, an event is an occurrence that affects the GUI. Events represent some physical action that can be interpreted by the application.

Usually events represent external actions initiated by the user which target the GUI. Examples of events are button clicks, mouse movements, mouse drags, mouse clicks, keys typed, and so forth.

In Java, events are represented by object instances, which, of course, have an associated type and class definition. Event types represent the different possible events and the sources of the events. An event object represents the occurrence of a specific physical event of a certain type.

Often, what appears to the user as a single action can result in the creation of multiple events in a program. For example, wheeling the mouse into the bounds of a component may cause a mouse motion event and also a focus event as the mouse rolls into the bounds of a component.

Events are the result of actions that occur on components. When a component detects that an action has occurred on it, the component *generates* an event. Generating an event results in the creation of an event object, which is passed to any objects that are interested in being notified of the occurrence of that event type on that source.

After I define more precisely the nature of events and the different types of events, I will examine in detail the whole process of identifying event sources, events, and how to handle them.

Event Type Hierarchy

The different GUI event types are organized in a type hierarchy that is rooted in the `java.util.EventObject` class.

The `java.awt.AWTEvent` class is a direct subclass of `java.util.EventObject` and is the ancestor of all AWT event types. All the AWT events are located in the `java.awt.event` package.

The AWT event types define events that can occur on both AWT and Swing GUI components. Figure 9.1 shows a hierarchy of all the AWT event types.

Swing defines some additional events that do not exist in the regular AWT. Although four of the Swing event types derive from AWT events, the vast majority of Swing events derive from `java.util.EventObject` directly. The Swing events are all located in the `javax.swing.event` package.

It's worthwhile to remark that the `EventObject` class is not defined in the `java.awt` package. It is not an AWT event. This organization makes possible the creation of event types that are not AWT events. Most of the Swing events fall into this category. Although AWT events define basic component events, Swing events define actions that have special significance to particular types of components. They define a higher-level type event with different semantics from the basic AWT component events. It would be misleading, if not incorrect, to organize Swing event types as subtypes of the AWT event types. Conceptually, they are somewhat different.

The existence of the `EventObject` type also gives you the flexibility to define events that, conceptually, do not directly identify actions on GUI components. In fact, such event types exist throughout the `javax.swing.event` package. Many of the Swing event types define actions that result in a change, not to GUI components, but to their model objects.

Models are the subject of Chapter 10, " Models," and I don't want to put the cart before the horse by discussing them now. Nevertheless, just reflect upon one idea that was mentioned previously. Models are objects whose type encapsulates a data abstraction; they store data that represents a particular instance of the abstraction created by the model's class definition.

Whereas GUI component events define actions that change the state of a component with a visual representation, model event types represent an action that changes the state of a model object. Often, programs are interested in knowing when and how data has changed in a model. Swing defines many change event types for this purpose, and you will see their importance and power in Chapter 10.

Event Types

Because all events must derive from `java.util.EventObject`, the information defined by `EventObject` should be useful to all event types. Let's start your study of event objects by examining this class. Table 9.1 lists the methods and constructors of the `EventObject` class.

TABLE 9.1 `java.util.EventObject` Constructors and Methods

Constructor or method name	Description
`EventObject(Object source)`	Constructs a generic event object with an event source. It is usually invoked by the AWT.
`Object getSource()`	Returns the object on which the event initially occurred.
`String toString()`	Returns a String representation of this `EventObject`.

As you can see it's a relatively small class. The `EventObject` class has a `source` field (not shown in Table 9.1) which references the object that is the source of an event. The value of this field can be retrieved using the `getSource` method.

An *event source* is the object, or component, on which the event initially occurred. This is the object passed to the `EventObject` constructor. All events must have a source. For example, a button pressed by the user is an example of the source of an event.

AWT events are special types of events and are defined by classes that extend `java.awt.AWTEvent`. This class adds an `id` field to the information defined by the `EventObject` class.

The `id` field identifies the event type. In some cases, this information is necessary to identify the specific nature of an event. For example, mouse events are defined by the `MouseEvent` class, but there are several specific types of mouse events—such as mouse entered, mouse exited, mouse clicked, mouse pressed, and so forth. To define a separate class for each would result in too many event classes. Instead, the value of the `id` field delineates several related events that are defined by a single event-type definition.

Table 9.2 lists the important members of the `java.awt.AWTEvent` class.

TABLE 9.2   `java.awt.AWTEvent` Constructors and Methods

Constructor or method name	Description
`AWTEvent(Event event)`	Constructs an AWT 1.1 style `AWTEvent` object by converting an AWT 1.0 Event object. Typically, it is not called by application programs. This method enables platforms to provide backward compatibility with the old AWT 1.0 event mechanism. You should design your applications to use the new AWT 1.1 event mechanism described in this chapter.
`AWTEvent(Object source, int id)`	Constructs an `AWTEvent` object with the specified source object and specified type.
`protected void consume()`	Consumes this event. The event is not passed to the source object's native peer. Valid for input events only.
`protected void finalize()`	Finalizes this object.
`int getID()`	Returns the event type of this event.
`protected boolean isConsumed()`	Indicates if this event has been consumed.
`String paramString()`	Returns a String representation of this event object's state.
`String toString()`	Returns a String representation of this event.

The getID() method retrieves the integer value that identifies the particular type of event.

AWT Event Types

I've been discussing event types somewhat abstractly up until now. It's time to take a high-level look at the different concrete event types.

I've said before that event types exist in a hierarchy, like all other types in Java. Figure 9.1 shows the hierarchy of the AWT event types, which extend AWTEvent. From this picture, you can get a conceptual understanding of what events can occur in a running Java program. You can also see how the different events relate to each other.

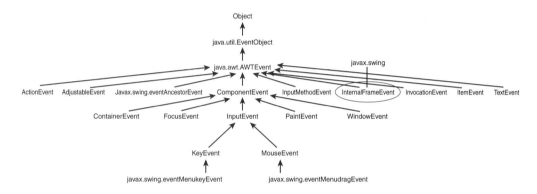

FIGURE 9.1

The AWT event types all extend java.util.AWTEvent. *Unless otherwise noted, these events are all defined in the* java.awt.event *package. These events are also used by Swing programs.*

As might be expected, each AWT event type enhances the generic definition of AWTEvent by adding fields and methods appropriate to its nature. Certain events can only occur on certain types of components. So, the event source will be different for different event types. Naturally, each event type will define constants and fields that represent the actions and the components on which those actions can occur.

AWT events are actually divided into two categories, *component events* and *semantic events*. Figure 9.1 shows the delineation of the two types clearly. All component event types are descendents of java.awt.ComponentEvent.

Component events are also called *low-level* events. They have a single, concrete interpretation, regardless of the type of component on which they occur. The meaning of a component event is always clear.

For example, the meaning of an input event, such as a KeyEvent, is always the same, regardless of whether the event source is a TextField or a TextArea. Likewise, the semantics of a MouseEvent is always the same, regardless of whether the event source is a button or a panel.

Although the information in a component event should always be interpreted consistently, it can be used for different purposes as the application sees fit.

Table 9.3 lists the different AWT component event types and the type of action that each represents.

TABLE 9.3   The AWT Component Event Types

AWT event class	Description
ComponentEvent	Indicates that a component was moved, resized, or changed visibility.
ContainerEvent	Indicates that a container's contents changed because a component was added or removed.
FocusEvent	Indicates that a component gained or lost the keyboard focus.
InputEvent	Indicates that some keyboard input occurred. This is the root class of all types of input events.
KeyEvent	Indicates that a keystroke occurred.
MouseEvent	Indicates that a mouse action occurred. These include mouse click, enter, exit, move, and drag events.
PaintEvent	A special event used by the AWT to indicate that a request to paint a component has been scheduled. Applications should not use this event explicitly.
WindowEvent	Indicates that a window has been opened, closed, iconified, or deiconified.

Any AWT component can dispatch any of the AWT component events in Table 9.3. Additionally, some components can fire semantic events.

In contrast to component events, semantic events are events whose semantics are defined by the type of the event source. Components which fire semantic events define the semantics when that event is fired from that component source.

Each such component class typically defines different semantics for a given semantic event type. Therefore, it is the responsibility of the object receiving notification of the event to understand its intended meaning based upon the event source.

Table 9.4 lists the AWT semantic events and the components that fire them.

TABLE 9.4   The AWT Semantic Event Types

AWT event type	Fired by	Description
ActionEvent	AWTEventMulticaster Button,	Indicates that a component-defined action has occurred

AWT event type	Fired by	Description
	ButtonModel,	
	List,	
	MenuItem,	
	TextField,	
	AbstractButton,	
	ComboBoxEditor,	
	DefaultButtonModel,	
	JButton,	
	JCheckBox,	
	JColorChooser,	
	JComboBox,	
	JComponent,	
	JFileChooser,	
	JMenuItem,	
	JRadioButton,	
	JTextField,	
	JToggleButton,	
	Timer	
Adjustment Event	Scrollbar, JScrollBar, AWTEvent Multicaster	Indicates that the adjustment value has changed for an adjustable component
InputMethod Event	AWTEventMulticaster, Component	Indicates that text has been composed using an input method editor for multilingual input
Invocation Event	None at this time.	Indicates that the event object did or will execute the run method on a Runnable
ItemEvent	Checkbox, Choice, CheckboxMenuItem, List, ItemSelectable, AWTEventMulticaster, AbstractButton, ButtonModel, JComboBox, DefaultButtonModel	Indicates that an item was selected or deselected
TextEvent	TextComponent, AWTEventMulticaster	Indicates that an object's text has changed

By examining the names of the event types in Table 9.4, you can see that they represent conceptual actions that could have meaning for more than one component type. This conceptual interpretation is the whole motivation for defining semantic events.

For example, an `ActionEvent` conceptually represents an action that occurs on a component. Each component can independently define what physical event should correspond to an action.

For example, buttons define the occurrence of an `ActionEvent` to mean that the user clicked on the button. On the other hand, `TextField` defines an `ActionEvent` that means the user typed the carriage return key in the text field.

Similarly, any component that is adjustable, such as a scrollbar, can meaningfully fire an `AdjustmentEvent`. In fact, the `java.awt.Adjustable` interface defines the behavior that all adjustable components must support!

Swing Event Types

Swing defines additional events, not in the AWT, that are fired only by Swing components. Because they are events, the Swing event types are also part of a `java.util.EventObject` hierarchy. Figure 9.2 shows the hierarchy that contains most of the Swing event types. In Figure 9.1, you saw that four Swing event types derive from the `java.awt.AWTEvent` class directly instead of from `java.util.EventObject`.

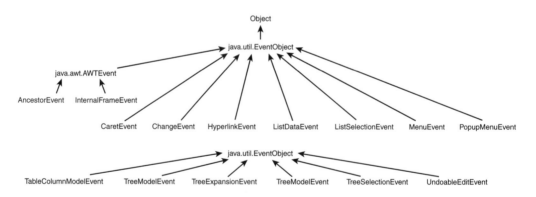

FIGURE 9.2

Most Swing event types extend `java.util.EventObject`, *although a few extend* `java.awt.AWTEvent`.

Table 9.5 lists the Swing event types and the actions that they define.

TABLE 9.5 The Swing Event Types

Swing event type	Fired by	Description
AncestorEvent	JComponent	Indicates an event that originated in the ancestor of the component receiving the event notification.
CaretEvent	JTextComponent	Indicates that the text caret position changed in the event source.
ChangeEvent	JSlider, BoundedRangeModel, MenuSelectionManager, AbstractButton, DefaultSingleSelectionModel, ButtonModel, JProgressBar, JViewport, DefaultBoundeRangeModel, DefaultButtonModel, JTabbedPane, SingleSelectionModel	Indicates that the source's state has changed.
DocumentEvent	AbstractDocument, DefaultStyledDocument, Document	Indicates that a change has occurred to the document that is the event source.
HyperlinkEvent	JEditorPane	Indicates some kind of activation has happened to a hypertext link.
InternalFrame Event	JinternalFrame	Indicates some state change has occurred on a JInternalFrame object.
ListDataEvent	AbstractListModel, ListModel	Indicates a change has occurred in a component that supports changes to a list of data.
ListSelectionEvent	DefaultListSelectionModel, ListSelectionModel, JList	Indicates a change has occurred in a component that supports changing its current selection.
MenuDragMouse Event	JmenuItem	Indicates that a menu element has received a MouseEvent passed to it during a drag operation.
MenuKeyEvent	JMenuItem	Indicates that a key has been typed that activates a menu item.

continues

9

EVENTS AND EVENT HANDLING

TABLE 9.5   Continued

Swing event type	Fired by	Description
MenuEvent	JMenu	Indicates that the menu source has been posted, selected, or canceled.
PopupMenuEvent	JPopupMenu	Indicates that the source, a JPopupMenu, has been popped up.
TableColumn ModelEvent	DefaultTableColumnModel TableColumnModel	Indicates that the state of a table column model has changed by either adding, removing, or moving a table column.
TableModelEvent	AbstractTableModel TableModel	Indicates that a table model has changed.
TreeExpansion Event	JTree	Indicates that a particular path in a tree has changed state.
TreeModelEvent	AbstractTableModel TableModel	Indicates that a tree model has changed.
TreeSelection Event	JTree	Indicates that the selection of a tree has changed.
UndoableEdit Event	AbstractDocument Document	Indicates that a reversible edit operation has occurred.

Contrasting the EventObject and AWTEvent classes, you see that the id field, defined in the AWTEvent class, is not available to Swing events.

Swing event types do not have an id field because they directly extend java.util.EventObject instead of java.awt.AWTEvent. Swing events do not need this information because they do not define so-called component events.

Recall that the purpose of the id field is to consolidate information about various types of related events, without defining a separate event class for each. MouseEvents are a good example of this consolidation.

Examining the names of the Swing event types gives us insight as to their true nature. Unlike the AWT low-level component events, the events fired by Swing components only make sense with a particular component or type of component.

In fact, most of the Swing events are semantic events for Swing components. For instance, the ChangeEvent type signifies that a change has occurred on the event source. What is this change? Well, like AWT semantic events, its semantics must be defined by the particular component that fires it.

Besides defining new semantic events, Swing also enhances the event architecture by defining events that signify changes to a Swing component's model object. Such events indicate that the component's model has changed, not the visual component itself.

Swing events enhance and complement the AWT events; they do not supersede AWT events. Remember that all Swing components are true AWT components because they extend `java.awt.Component` or `java.awt.Container`. It would seem, then, that the Swing components should still have the capability to generate AWT component events. Indeed, they can. There is no need to replicate component event definitions in the Swing APIs.

Handling Events

At this point you should have a solid conceptual understanding of the nature of events; events are actions in which one or more parts of your program may be interested.

Now that you understand events, you can turn your attention to event handling. Events exist in order to identify what actions take place during the course of a program's execution and to enable the program to respond appropriately, based on the type of event and the job slated for the application.

In the previous discussion of events, I kept referring to the notion of components "firing" events. Before you tackle event handling proper, it's helpful to understand just how events are created and dispatched.

Delivering Events

Recall that all heavyweight components have a native platform peer object that is managed by the system's window manager. When the user performs some action "outside" the program, such as clicking the mouse or typing a key, the native system's window manager isolates the native peer involved. The AWT then determines the target AWT component, and delivers the event to that component, which becomes the event source.

Regardless of whether the source is an AWT or Swing component, the peer delivers the event by invoking the `Component.dispatchEvent(AWTEvent)` method on the component. Remember Swing components are `Components` and can generate AWT component events.

The `dispatchEvent()` method is declared `final`. It is fundamental to the Java component architecture, and programmers cannot and should not change what it does or how it does it.

The `dispatchEvent()` method, in turn, calls the `processEvent(AWTEvent)` method, which determines the exact type of the event, and then calls one of several `Component.process`*XXX*`Event(`*XXX*`Event)` methods. There is one such method for each component event type.

Below are listed all these event dispatch methods. Notice that the dispatchEvent() method is public, whereas the others are all protected. Only dispatchEvent() should invoke these other methods.

```
public final void dispatchEvents(AWTEvent)

protected void processComponentEvent(ComponentEvent)

protected void processEvent(AWTEvent)

protected void processFocusEvent(FocusEvent)

protected void processInputMethodEvent(InputMethodEvent)

protected void processKeyEvent(KeyEvent)

protected void processMouseEvent(MouseEvent)

protected void processMouseMotionEvent(MouseEvent)
```

The process*XXX*Event() method simply notifies each object on the component's lists of objects that are interested in being notified of that type of event on *this* component.

The Component class defines one such list of interested parties for each type of component event. Each object instance of Component maintains its own set of lists.

If any objects are registered to receive events of a specific type, they are notified. Thereafter, they can respond meaningfully.

From the earlier discussions, you know that certain components only fire semantic events and not component events. Notification of semantic events works the same way with one additional step.

Take the example of a button which fires action events. When a button fires an action event, that means the button was pressed. Buttons are components and, therefore, are still subject to receiving component events such as mouse events.

The AWT still creates the component event object and dispatches it to the button. Additionally, the AWT dispatches an ActionEvent to the button. The processEvent() method in the Button class overrides the default version in Component. It checks to see if the event is an ActionEvent, and if so, calls its processActionEvent(ActionEvent) method, which notifies its list of all objects interested in notification of action events.

You can see how the occurrence of one component event from the user's mouse click resulted in the creation of an additional ActionEvent. This is a typical scenario for semantic events.

Event Listeners

If you read the previous section carefully, you probably noticed that I skipped over some important details of the event notification process. I said that objects can register to be notified of certain event occurrences on components.

Objects that are interested in being *notified* of events are called *event listeners*, or simply *listeners*, because they are "listening" for event notification. These objects can be any valid Java language object.

Listeners register their interest in being notified of the occurrence of certain events generated by specific event sources. By doing so, the listener is requesting to be notified when the event occurs on that particular component.

A listener can register its interest in a particular event type only if the source can generate that type of event. Every component that can generate a particular type of event has a method of the form

```
public void addXXXListener(XXXListener)
```

where *XXX* is the name of an event type. The following is a list of the methods of this form in the `Component` class.

```
public void addComponentListener(ComponentListener)
public void addFocusListener(FocusListener)
public void addInputMethodListener(InputMethodListener)
public void addKeyListener(KeyListener)
public void add(MouseListener(MouseListener)
public void addMouseMotionListener(MouseMotionListener)
```

The preceding list supports the previous statement that the `Component` class defines the capability for all components to generate component events. Component subclasses may be defined to fire additional events.

You already know that the `Button` class fires the semantic `ActionEvent`. Looking at the `Button` class's API, you indeed find a

```
public void addActionListener(ActionListener)
```

method, by which listeners can register their interest in being notified when a particular button is pressed.

Incidentally, you also find a

```
public void removeActionListener(ActionListener)
```

method that allows you to remove a previously added listener. All event sources define pairs of methods of the form

```
public void addXXXListener(XXXListener)
public void removeXXXListener(XXXListener)
```

The latter enables you to remove a previously registered listener.

In order to understand how this notification process works, look at the argument in any of the add*XXX*Listener methods. For a listener add method of the form add*XXX*Listener, the argument is a type whose name has the form *XXX*Listener.

These types are Java interfaces which define the methods which must be implemented by any class whose object instances want to register as listeners for events of the corresponding event type.

Each event listener interface type specifies methods that define what a listener for that type must be able to do to handle events. An important part of these interfaces is the set of methods that enable the event source to deliver information about the occurrence of an event to the listener.

Because the add methods for each component take an argument whose type is one of these listener interfaces, the component can be confident that the listener implements the methods that the source needs to call to notify it that the action has taken place.

For example, the Button class defines the addActionListener(ActionListener) method. The ActionListener interface specifies one method, public void actionPerformed(ActionEvent).

When an action event occurs, the source can invoke the actionPerformed method on each registered listener. The button "knows" the listener implements this method because it implements the ActionListener interface. If it didn't, it could not have been passed as an argument to the addActionListener method in the first place.

This is the pattern for all event sources and listeners:

1. The listener registers for notification with the component.
2. When an event occurs on that component, the AWT creates and delivers the event to the component.
3. The component dispatches the event to listeners interested in events of that type.
4. The listener responds in some manner.

The event source invokes a method on each registered listener. The name of the method is defined by the listener interface that corresponds to that event type; its argument is an event type that conveys the details of the event.

Table 9.6 lists the different listener interfaces and their corresponding event types. All the AWT listener interfaces are defined in the java.awt.event package along with the AWT event types.

TABLE 9.6   AWT Event Listener Interfaces and Their Corresponding Event Types

Listener interface	Interface methods
ActionListener	actionPerformed(ActionEvent)
AdjustmentListener	adjustmentValueChange(AdjustmentEvent)
AWTEventListener	eventDispatched(AWTEvent)
ComponentListener	componentHidden(ComponentEvent)
	componentMoved(ComponentEvent)
	componentResized(ComponentEvent)
	componentShown(ComponentEvent)
ContainerListener	componentAdded(ContainerEvent)
	componentRemoved(ContainerEvent)
FocusListener	focusGained(FocusEvent)
	focusLost(FocusEvent)
InputMethodListener	caretPositionChanged(InputMethodEvent)
	inputMethodTextChanged(InputMethodEvent)
ItemListener	itemStateChanged(ItemEvent)
KeyListener	keyPressed(KeyEvent)
	keyReleased(KeyEvent)
	keyTyped(KeyEvent)
MouseListener	mouseClicked(MouseEvent)
	mouseEntered(MouseEvent)
	mouseExited(MouseEvent)
	mousePressed(MouseEvent)
	mouseReleased(MouseEvent)
MouseMotionListener	mouseDragged(MouseEvent)
	mouseMoved(MouseEvent)
TextListener	textValueChanged(TextEvent)
	WindowListener
	windowActivated(WindowEvent)
	windowClosed(WindowEvent)
	windowClosing(WindowEvent)
	windowDeactivated(WindowEvent)
	windowDeiconified(WindowEvent)
	windowIconified(WindowEvent)
	windowOpened(WindowEvent)

9

EVENTS AND
EVENT HANDLING

Event listener registration and notification works exactly the same way in Swing. The Swing listener interfaces and their event counterparts are listed in Table 9.7.

TABLE 9.7   Swing Event Listener Interfaces and Their Corresponding Event Types

Listener interface	Interface method
AncestorListener	ancestorAdded(AncestorEvent)
	ancestorMoved(AncestorEvent)
	ancestorRemoved(AncestorEvent)
CaretListener	caretUpdate(CaretEvent)
CellEditorListener	editingCanceled(CellEvent)
	editingStopped(CellEvent)
ChangeListener	stateChanged(ChangeEvent)
DocumentListener	changeUpdate(DocumentEvent)
	insertUpdate(DocumentEvent)
	removeUpdate(DocumentEvent)
HyperlinkListener	hyperlinkUpdate(HyperlinkEvent)
InternalFrameListener	internalFrameActivated(InternalFrameEvent)
	internalFrameClosed(InternalFrameEvent)
	internalFrameClosing(InternalFrameEvent)
	internalFrameDeactivated(InternalFrameEvent)
	internalFrameDeiconified(InternalFrameEvent)
	internalFrameIconified(InternalFrameEvent)
	internalFrameOpened(InternalFrameEvent)
ListDataListener	contentsChanged(ListDataEvent)
	intervalAddeed(ListDataEvent)
	intervalRemoved(ListDataEvent)
ListSelectionListener	valueChanged(ListSelectionEvent)
MenuDragMouseListener	menuDragMouseDragged(MenuDragMouseEvent)
	menuDragMouseEntered(MenuDragMouseEvent)
	menuDragMouseExited(MenuDragMouseEvent)
	menuDragMouseReleased(MenuDragMouseEvent)
MenuKeyListener	menuKeyPressed(MenuKeyEvent)
	menuKeyReleased(MenuKeyEvent)
	menuKeyTyped(MenuKeyEvent)
MenuListener	menuCanceled(MenuEvent)
	menuDeselected(MenuEvent)
	menuSelected(MenuEvent)
MouseInputListener	mouseClicked(MouseEvent)
	mouseDragged(MouseEvent)
	mouseEntered(MouseEvent)
	mouseExited(MouseEvent)
	mouseMoved(MouseEvent)
	mousePressed(MouseEvent)
	mouseReleased(MouseEvent)

Listener interface	Interface method
PopupMenuListener	popupMenuCanceled(PopupMenuEvent)
	popupMenuWillBecomeInVisible(PopupMenuEvent)
	popupMenuWillBecomeVisible(PopupMenuEvent)
TableColumnModelListener	columnAdded(TableColumnModelEvent)
	columnmMarginChanged(TableColumnModelEvent)
	columnMoved(TableColumnModelEvent)
	columnRemoved(TableColumnModelEvent)
	columnSelectionChanged(TableColumnModelEvent)
TableModelListener	tableChanged(TableModelEvent)
TreeExpansionListener	treeCollapsed(TreeExpansionEvent)
	treeExpanded(TreeExpansionEvent)
TreeModelListener	treeNodesChanged(TreeModelEvent)
	treeNodesInserted(TreeModelEvent)
	treeNodesRemoved(TreeModelEvent)
	treeStructureChanged(TreeModelEvent)
TreeSelectionListener	valueChanged(TreeSelectionEvent)
TreeWillExpandListener	treeWillCollapse(TreeExpansionEvent)
	treeWillExpand(TreeExpansionEvent)
UndoableEditListener	undoableEditHappened(UndoableEditEvent)

Event listener types all derive from the `java.util.EventListener` interface. This is an empty interface; it specifies no methods. It is a *tagging* interface which "tags" other interfaces as event listener interfaces.

All sub-interfaces of `EventListener` are defined in the `java.awt.event` and `javax.swing.event` packages.

AWT and Swing Events Are Complementary

Swing components *require* the AWT component events. They do not supersede nor obsolete the AWT events in any way. As we stated earlier, Swing components are valid components because they extend the `java.awt.Component` class.

The AWT component events can all be generated by any Swing component that derives from `Component`. Removing this capability would have widespread and profound impact on the whole JDK component architecture.

Swing semantic events are also compatible with the AWT event model. The Swing semantic events do not supersede the AWT semantic events, but rather, complement them. They do not clash in any way.

An example that shows this complementary behavior is the AWT `List` class. It can fire both `java.awt.ActionEvents` and `java.awt.ItemEvents`. So, different listeners—or the same listener for that matter—can listen for these events.

The `JList` component class also fires `ActionEvents`. However, instead of firing `ItemEvents`, it fires `javax.swing.event.ListSelectionEvents`. The `ListSelectionEvent` does not supersede the `ItemEvent`; it is a different semantic event altogether. The `JList` designers simply used the new Swing `ListSelectionEvent` because they thought it more accurately conveyed the nature of the action.

A Sample Event Handler

Lest you get lost in conceptual abstraction, you will now follow through a complete example to show how an application uses events and event handling to make itself a functional, meaningful program.

Figure 9.3 shows this simple application just after startup. This application displays a set of images, one at a time. At start up, the image displayed is the first in the set. Clicking any of the four buttons will display a different image according to the button's function, which is indicated by its name.

FIGURE 9.3

Example of an application that uses ActionListeners *to respond to user actions. The application performs some action in response to clicks of each of its four buttons in a manner. The actions correspond to the advertised function of each button.*

The event processing scenario is always the same in Java programs. The following list describes the sequence of steps that occur during event processing in the context of the application represented in Figure 9.3.

1. The user clicks the mouse on a button.

2. The AWT creates an event object.

3. The AWT delivers the event object to the source component.

4. The `Button` event source calls `actionPerformed(ActionEvent)` on each of its registered listener.

5. Each listener handles the event according to its definition; it modifies the state of the application in some way.

Listing 9.1 shows the complete source code for this application.

LISTING 9.1   Adding Event Handling to an Application

```
import java.awt.BorderLayout;
import java.awt.CardLayout;
import java.awt.Color;
import java.awt.Dimension;
import java.awt.Image;

import java.awt.event.ActionEvent;
import java.awt.event.ActionListener;
import java.awt.event.WindowAdapter;
import java.awt.event.WindowEvent;
import java.awt.event.WindowListener;

import javax.swing.BorderFactory;
import javax.swing.ImageIcon;
import javax.swing.JButton;
import javax.swing.JFrame;
import javax.swing.JPanel;

import javax.swing.border.BevelBorder;

public class ImageGallery extends JPanel
{
  public ImageGallery()
  {
    super();
    create();
    loadImages();
  }

  protected void create()
  {
```

continues

LISTING 9.1   Continued

```java
    first = new JButton("First");
    previous = new JButton("Previous");
    next = new JButton("Next");
    last = new JButton("Last");

    buttonPanel = new JPanel();

    buttonPanel.add(first);
    buttonPanel.add(previous);
    buttonPanel.add(next);
    buttonPanel.add(last);

    imagePanel = new JPanel();
    imagePanel.setBorder(BorderFactory.createBevelBorder(BevelBorder.LOWERED));
    imagePanel.setLayout(new CardLayout());

    setLayout(new BorderLayout());
    add(buttonPanel, BorderLayout.NORTH);
    add(imagePanel, BorderLayout.CENTER);

    ButtonHandler handler = new ButtonHandler(this);

    first.addActionListener(handler);
    previous.addActionListener(handler);
    next.addActionListener(handler);
    last.addActionListener(handler);
}

protected void loadImages()
{
    images = new Image [NUM_IMAGES];

    imagePanel.add(new JButton(new ImageIcon("../images/alpine-lake.gif")),
                "alpine-lake");
    imagePanel.add(new JButton(new ImageIcon("../images/beach1.gif")),
                "beach1");
    imagePanel.add(new JButton(new ImageIcon("../images/buds.gif")),
                "buds");
    imagePanel.add(new JButton(new ImageIcon("../images/golden-fish.gif")),
                "golden-fish");
    imagePanel.add(new JButton(new ImageIcon("../images/morning-walk.gif")),
                "morning-walk");
    imagePanel.add(new JButton(new ImageIcon("../images/observatory.gif")),
                "observatory");
```

```
        imagePanel.add(new JButton(new ImageIcon("../images/open-gate.gif")),
                    "open-gate");
        imagePanel.add(new JButton(new ImageIcon("../images/pebble-beach.gif")),
                    "pebble-beach");
        imagePanel.add(new JButton(new ImageIcon("../images/tree-lined-path.gif")),
                    "tree-lined-path");
        imagePanel.add(new JButton(new ImageIcon("../images/stormy-pier.gif")),
                    "stormy-pier");
    }

    public Dimension getPreferredSize()
    {
      return new Dimension(350, 400);
    }

    public Dimension getMinimumSize()
    {
      return getPreferredSize();
    }

    public static void main(String [] args)
    {
      ImageGallery app = new ImageGallery();

      JFrame f = new JFrame("Image Selector Demo");
      f.getContentPane().add(app);
      f.pack();
      f.setVisible(true);
    }

    static final int NUM_IMAGES = 10;

    public JButton first, next, previous, last;
    private JPanel buttonPanel;
    JPanel imagePanel;

    ButtonHandler handler;

    Image [] images;
}


class ButtonHandler implements ActionListener
{
  public ButtonHandler(ImageGallery application)
```

continues

LISTING 9.1   Continued

```
{
  super();
  app = application;
}

public void actionPerformed(ActionEvent e)
{
  CardLayout layout = (CardLayout) app.imagePanel.getLayout();

  if (e.getSource() == app.first)
    {
      layout.first(app.imagePanel);
    }
  else if (e.getSource() == app.next)
    {
      layout.next(app.imagePanel);
    }
  else if (e.getSource() == app.previous)
    {
      layout.previous(app.imagePanel);
    }
  else if (e.getSource() == app.last)
    {
      layout.last(app.imagePanel);
    }

  app.imagePanel.invalidate();
  app.imagePanel.validate();
}

ImageGallery app;
}
```

A few things are new in this application. Instead of just one class you now have two class definitions. In real life, it is often useful to place class definitions in their own files.

The ButtonHandler class defines the event handler for action events that occur on application buttons. You can construct an instance of the ButtonHandler class.

```
ButtonHandler handler = new ButtonHandler(this);
```

This is your action event listener. At the end of the create() method, register this object as an action listener for all four buttons. There is nothing wrong with using the same listener to listen for events from different sources.

```
first.addActionListener(handler);
previous.addActionListener(handler);
next.addActionListener(handler);
last.addActionListener(handler);
```

You are able to register your `ButtonHandler` instance on your buttons by calling the `addActionListener(ActionListener)` method because the `ButtonHandler` class implements the `ActionListener` interface.

The `ButtonHandler` constructor must take a parameter that gives it a reference to the application. This is what really ties this class to the main application class. Event handlers must have an object context that represents the application containing the event source if they are to modify the application state in some way.

After the application starts, click the Last button, and a new image displays, as shown in Figure 9.4.

FIGURE 9.4

The ImageGallery application after the Last button is pressed.

The button that was clicked is the source of the action event that it fires. In this case, there is only one listener to notify, and the button invokes the `actionPerformed()` method on your listener.

The listener determines the exact source by using the `getSource()` method and checking its reference value. Your listener changes the image displayed according to which button was pressed.

Let's enhance your application by adding a different listener that listens for mouse events on your buttons. For purposes of illustration, you just want to be notified when a mouse click occurs on a button, and then you want to print out some information to the console.

In Listing 9.2, we add the definition of your new MouseMonitor class to your ImageGallery.java file. This is your second event handling class, and it knows only how to respond to mouse events.

In real life, of course, it might be best to place these event-handling classes in their own files.

LISTING 9.2   An Implementation of a MouseListener Class

```
import java.awt.event.MouseEvent;
import java.awt.event.MouseListener;

class MouseMonitor implements MouseListener
{
  public MouseMonitor(ImageGallery application)
  {
    app = application;
  }

  public void mouseClicked(MouseEvent e)
  {
    System.out.println(e.getSource().toString());
  }

  ImageGallery app;
}
```

This event listener implements the java.awt.event.MouseListener interface because you want it to respond to mouse events. Because you only care about mouse clicks, and not the other mouse events (like mouse motions), you only implement the mouseClicked() method.

You modify the create method in your ImageGallery application to instantiate your new mouse event-handler class and register the instance with each of your buttons.

```
MouseMonitor mm = new MouseMonitor(this);

first.addMouseListener(mm);
previous.addMouseListener(mm);
next.addMouseListener(mm);
last.addMouseListener(mm);
```

Note that now your buttons have two registered listeners each, an ActionListener and a MouseListener.

When you recompile, you might be shocked to see the following errors!

```
ImageGallery.java:103: class MouseMonitor is an abstract class. It can't be
instantiated.
    MouseMonitor mm = new MouseMonitor(this);
                      ^

ImageGallery.java:216: class MouseMonitor must be declared abstract. It does
not define void mousePressed(java.awt.event.MouseEvent) from interface
java.awt.event.MouseListener.
class MouseMonitor implements MouseListener
      ^

ImageGallery.java:216: class MouseMonitor must be declared abstract. It does
not define void mouseReleased(java.awt.event.MouseEvent) from interface
java.awt.event.MouseListener.
class MouseMonitor implements MouseListener
      ^

ImageGallery.java:216: class MouseMonitor must be declared abstract. It does
not define void mouseEntered(java.awt.event.MouseEvent) from interface
java.awt.event.MouseListener.
class MouseMonitor implements MouseListener
      ^

ImageGallery.java:216: class MouseMonitor must be declared abstract. It does
not define void mouseExited(java.awt.event.MouseEvent) from interface
java.awt.event.MouseListener.
```

Suddenly you remember that the `MouseListener` type is an interface, which requires implementing classes to implement all its methods.

But you aren't planning on using the other four methods in the `MouseListener` class because you aren't interested in receiving anything but mouse click events.

Nevertheless, you must provide a full implementation. One way to do this is to provide empty method bodies as shown in Listing 9.3.

LISTING 9.3   Providing Empty Methods to Fully Implement a Listener Interface

```
public void mouseEntered(MouseEvent e)
  {

  }

  public void mouseExited(MouseEvent e)
  {

  }

  public void mousePressed(MouseEvent e)
```

continues

9

EVENTS AND
EVENT HANDLING

LISTING 9.3   Continued

```
    {

    }

    public void mouseReleased(MouseEvent e)
    {

    }
```

Now the compiler is happy, but you're not. You suddenly realize that each event handling class that you define must do this for every listener interface that it implements. This could amount to much more work than you want to do, not to mention cluttering your code.

It's worth stating that the listener interface architecture is not at fault. Defining a set of listener interfaces is a powerful mechanism. It allows any class that implements a listener interface to take on the role of a listener for the events defined by the listener.

Such a listener class may already extend another class. But implementing an interface gives it the capability to adopt the behavior necessary to act like an event listener.

Without the listener interfaces, classes would be required to subclass another class that defines the listener, prohibiting your class from subclassing another class in your application. This use of interfaces to define listeners is a wonderful example of the power of interfaces in Java.

But getting back to your problem, thankfully, there is another solution, which is the subject of the next section.

Adapters

The `java.awt.event` and `javax.swing.event` packages define an adapter for many of its event listener interfaces.

An *adapter* is a class that implements its corresponding listener interface. The implementations are empty. However, your listener class can now simply override the correct subset of methods needed in order to define meaningful event handling for your purposes.

Tables 9.8 and 9.9 list the event listeners and their corresponding adapter classes. All adapters are defined in the same package as their related interface, and their names reflect their functions.

TABLE 9.8   AWT Listeners and Their Corresponding Adapter Classes

Event listener type	*Adapter class*
ComponentListener	ComponentAdapter
ContainerListener	ContainerAdapter
FocusListener	FocusAdapter
KeyListener	KeyAdapter
MouseListener	MouseAdapter
MouseMotionListener	MouseMotionAdapter
WindowListener	WindowAdapter

TABLE 9.9   Swing Listeners and Their Corresponding Adapter Classes

Event listener type	*Adapter class*
InternalFrameListener	InternalFrameAdapter
MouseInputListener	MouseInputAdapter

You can rewrite your MouseMonitor class to extend the java.awt.event.MouseAdapter class instead of implementing the MouseListener interface, as shown in Listing 9.4. To compile the code in Listing 9.4 you must add the following import statements to your code.

LISTING 9.4   Implementing a Listener Class to Extend an Adapter Class

```
import java.awt.event.MouseAdapter;
import java.awt.event.MouseEvent;

class MouseMonitor extends MouseAdapter
{
  public MouseMonitor(ImageGallery application)
  {
    app = application;
  }

  public void mouseClicked(MouseEvent e)
  {
    System.out.println(e.getSource().toString());
  }

  ImageGallery app;
}
```

You still instantiate your class and add the instance as a listener to your buttons in exactly the same way. Recompiling and running your application now prints a line for each button click on one of your four buttons:

```
javax.swing.JButton[,263,5,63x25,layout=javax.swing.OverlayLayout
javax.swing.JButton[,193,5,65x25,layout=javax.swing.OverlayLayout
javax.swing.JButton[,193,5,65x25,layout=javax.swing.OverlayLayout
javax.swing.JButton[,93,5,95x25,layout=javax.swing.OverlayLayout]
```

Inner Classes

The use of adapters greatly simplifies your work when you are implementing a listener interface with more than just one or two methods.

Notwithstanding the benefits of using adapters, you still have some challenges to writing real world applications. Let's reexamine the first version of your ImageGallery application.

One problem with your first version is that you must expose the members of your ImageGallery class. At the very least, the four buttons and the image panel must be package protected, assuming any listener class is defined in the same package. In the worst case, you might have to make them public.

```
JButton first, next, previous, last;
JPanel imagePanel;
```

Exposing fields in this way is not really good class design. You could provide accessor methods to your application members, but this solution could get complicated very quickly, clutter or obfuscate your code, and be very cumbersome to use.

Another problem with the original example is that your ButtonHandler class has to define a parameter of type ImageGallery in its constructor so listener objects have a reference to the correct context in order to be able to manipulate the application instance.

This definition restricts us to using this handler with this application. Perhaps this restriction is a good safety mechanism because, otherwise, the logic of your event handling class would have to change for each new application.

On the other hand, it means you have to write separate event handler classes for each application, even if each application does almost the same thing. To reuse your event handler, it seems you must take one of two approaches:

- Write a different handler class for each application.
- Build in some logic in the event listener interface methods to distinguish the application type—definitely the wrong approach from the object-oriented programming perspective!

Fortunately, you can take advantage of the Java language's support for *inner classes* to take still another approach.

> **NOTE**
>
> Inner classes are a rich and complex feature of the Java programming language. A full treatment of this topic is beyond the scope of this book. For a wonderfully written, clear and concise treatment of inner classes, refer to
>
> `http://java.sun.com/products/jdk/1.1/docs/guide/innerclasses/index.html`
>
> Here I discuss the characteristics and capabilities of inner classes that relate most pragmatically to event handling.

Named Inner Classes

Inner classes are nested classes, that is, classes that are defined within the scope of another class. Like fields and methods, inner classes are members of their enclosing class. And, like other members, they have access to even the `private` members of the class in which they're defined.

You can redefine your `ButtonHandler` as a named inner class of `ImageGallery`. This inner class now becomes a new member of your application. You also now make the fields of `ImageGallery` `private`. Only your event handler needs to access these, and it's now a member of your class—so it has access to private members.

Listing 9.5 shows the new definitions. The definition of the `ImageGallery` class is the same as in Listing 9.1, except that its fields are now declared `private`. Therefore, I won't list the whole class definition again. Only the `ButtonHandler` class definition has changed, and is now an inner class of the `ImageGallery` class.

LISTING 9.5   Defining a Named Inner Class

```
public class ImageGallery extends JPanel
{
  ...
  class ButtonHandler implements ActionListener
  {
    public ButtonHandler()
    {
      super();
    }
```

9

EVENTS AND
EVENT HANDLING

continues

LISTING 9.5   Continued

```java
public void actionPerformed(ActionEvent e)
{
  CardLayout layout = (CardLayout) imagePanel.getLayout();

  if (e.getSource() == first)
    {
      layout.first(imagePanel);
    }
  else if (e.getSource() == next)
    {
      layout.next(imagePanel);
    }
  else if (e.getSource() == previous)
    {
      layout.previous(imagePanel);
    }
  else if (e.getSource() == last)
    {
      layout.last(imagePanel);
    }

  imagePanel.invalidate();
  imagePanel.validate();
}
}
...
```

Defining `ButtonHandler` as an inner class enables you to simplify its definition.

You no longer have to pass a reference to your `ImageGallery` instance to the constructor because the enclosing scope created by the `ImageGallery` class defines the context of the application instance.

The code in the `ButtonHandler.actionPerformed()` method has direct access to the fields of your application. Your event listener instance creation now looks like

```java
ButtonHandler handler = new ButtonHandler();
```

Moreover, you can simplify the code in your `actionPerformed()` method. It no longer needs to reference the `ImageGallery` fields through the app variable that `ButtonHandler` defined previously.

Besides the benefits of cleaner code, defining `ButtonHandler` as a named inner class unmistakably advertises your intent to use it as an event listener for this particular application. There is no mistake about where it should or can be used. In effect, its presence in its enclosing scope self-documents its intended use.

This is not a compromise in flexibility because you have to recode the logic in the listener methods anyway, if you want to reuse your event handler implementation with another application. No two applications have the same fields, structure, or semantics.

You also simplify your application by eliminating one `.java` file for each inner class that you define. But make no mistake, there are still two class definitions. You've only changed the relationship between the classes. If you list the `.class` files in the directory where you compiled your program, you see the following:

```
-rw-r--r--  1 vartan   users    1309 Mar 21 19:48
ImageGallery$ButtonHandler.class
-rw-r--r--  1 vartan   users    4020 Mar 21 19:48 ImageGallery.class
```

The compiler keeps track of named inner class definitions by creating names which separate the names of enclosing classes with a `$`.

Keep in mind that there are also still two object instances created—there must be. You must still have an application instance, as well as an event handler.

One fundamentally important point is that instantiating an inner class creates a relationship between an *inner object*, your handler, and the *enclosing object*, your application instance. When your instance of `ButtonHandler` makes references to members defined in the `ImageGallery` class, it must do so using the context of the application object instance that you created.

Anonymous Inner Classes

In your original implementation, you had only one event listener definition for all four of your application buttons. This design required your event handler's `actionPerformed()` method to check the source of the event with a series of `if` statements before responding with the correct action.

Because you defined only one event handler class, `ButtonHandler`, any object instances you created were destined to perform in exactly the same manner. The same `actionPerformed()` method was called—there was only one. In order to accommodate multiple event sources, it had to check the source of the event.

In more complex cases, this approach quickly becomes untenable. In addition to being inefficient, the presence of code that checks for the type or instance of each possible event source quickly obscures the true task being done.

Furthermore, each time you add a new button—or other possible `ActionEvent` source—you will need to go back and update the definition of your event handler method to ensure it checks for the new event source. This affects maintainability and program correctness.

What you really need is the flexibility to have *different* implementations of the methods specified in the event listener interface so that each can be used for a unique event source. Each method could then do one task well—respond to an event generated by a specific button.

Well, you certainly cannot overload your `actionPerformed()` method without changing its formal parameter list. But to change it, you must circumvent the event notification architecture. Components only know how to call one `actionPerformed()` method to notify action listeners. They would know nothing of overloaded versions. The same problem exists for all event listener interface definitions.

The solution is that you must define four separate versions of your `ButtonHandler` class, and simply change the definition of the `actionPerformed()` method in each. Then you must register a unique instance of the correct definition with the correct button.

However, you are not required to implement four complete versions of your class for such a small change.

Instead, you can employ an *anonymous inner class* definition. An anonymous inner class is different from a named inner class. An anonymous inner class definition combines the type definition expression with its instance creation expression.

Using anonymous inner classes, you can recode your application as shown in Listing 9.6.

LISTING 9.6   Recoding Your Application with Anonymous Inner Classes

```java
import java.awt.BorderLayout;
import java.awt.CardLayout;
import java.awt.Color;
import java.awt.Dimension;
import java.awt.Image;
import java.awt.Window;

import java.awt.event.ActionEvent;
import java.awt.event.ActionListener;
import java.awt.event.MouseAdapter;
import java.awt.event.MouseEvent;
import java.awt.event.MouseListener;
import java.awt.event.WindowAdapter;
import java.awt.event.WindowEvent;
import java.awt.event.WindowListener;
```

```java
import javax.swing.BorderFactory;
import javax.swing.ImageIcon;
import javax.swing.JButton;
import javax.swing.JFrame;
import javax.swing.JPanel;

import javax.swing.border.BevelBorder;

public class ImageGallery extends JPanel
{
  public ImageGallery()
  {
    super();
    create();
    loadImages();
  }


  protected void create()
  {
    first = new JButton("First");
    previous = new JButton("Previous");
    next = new JButton("Next");
    last = new JButton("Last");

    buttonPanel = new JPanel();

    buttonPanel.add(first);
    buttonPanel.add(previous);
    buttonPanel.add(next);
    buttonPanel.add(last);

    imagePanel = new JPanel();
    imagePanel.setBorder(BorderFactory.createBevelBorder(BevelBorder.LOWERED));
    imagePanel.setLayout(new CardLayout());

    setLayout(new BorderLayout());
    add(buttonPanel, BorderLayout.NORTH);
    add(imagePanel, BorderLayout.CENTER);

    ActionListener firstListener = new ActionListener()
      {
        public void actionPerformed(ActionEvent e)
          {
            CardLayout layout = (CardLayout) imagePanel.getLayout();
```

continues

LISTING 9.6 Continued

```
            layout.first(imagePanel);
        }
    };
    first.addActionListener(firstListener);


    ActionListener previousListener = new ActionListener()
      {
        public void actionPerformed(ActionEvent e)
          {
            CardLayout layout = (CardLayout) imagePanel.getLayout();
            layout.previous(imagePanel);
          }
      };
    previous.addActionListener(previousListener);

    ActionListener nextListener = new ActionListener()
      {
        public void actionPerformed(ActionEvent e)
          {
            CardLayout layout = (CardLayout) imagePanel.getLayout();
            layout.next(imagePanel);
          }
      };
    next.addActionListener(nextListener);

    ActionListener lastListener = new ActionListener()
      {
        public void actionPerformed(ActionEvent e)
          {
            CardLayout layout = (CardLayout) imagePanel.getLayout();
            layout.last(imagePanel);
          }
      };
    last.addActionListener(lastListener);

    first.addActionListener(firstListener);
    previous.addActionListener(previousListener);
    next.addActionListener(nextListener);
    last.addActionListener(lastListener);

    MouseListener mm = new MouseAdapter()
      {
        public void mouseClicked(MouseEvent e)
          {
```

```
            System.out.println(e.getSource().toString());
        }
    };

  first.addMouseListener(mm);
  previous.addMouseListener(mm);
  next.addMouseListener(mm);
  last.addMouseListener(mm);
}


protected void loadImages()
{
  images = new Image [NUM_IMAGES];

  imagePanel.add(new JButton(new ImageIcon("../images/alpine-lake.gif")),
                 "alpine-lake");
  imagePanel.add(new JButton(new ImageIcon("../images/beach1.gif")),
                 "beach1");
  imagePanel.add(new JButton(new ImageIcon("../images/buds.gif")),
                 "buds");
  imagePanel.add(new JButton(new ImageIcon("../images/golden-fish.gif")),
                 "golden-fish");
  imagePanel.add(new JButton(new ImageIcon("../images/morning-walk.gif")),
                 "morning-walk");
  imagePanel.add(new JButton(new ImageIcon("../images/observatory.gif")),
                 "observatory");
  imagePanel.add(new JButton(new ImageIcon("../images/open-gate.gif")),
                 "open-gate");
  imagePanel.add(new JButton(new ImageIcon("../images/pebble-beach.gif")),
                 "pebble-beach");
  imagePanel.add(new JButton(new ImageIcon("../images/tree-lined-path.gif")),
                 "tree-lined-path");
  imagePanel.add(new JButton(new ImageIcon("../images/stormy-pier.gif")),
                 "stormy-pier");
}


public void actionPerformed(ActionEvent e)
{

}


public Dimension getPreferredSize()
```

continues

LISTING 9.6   Continued

```
  {
    return new Dimension(350, 400);
  }


  public Dimension getMinimumSize()
  {
    return getPreferredSize();
  }


  public static void main(String [] args)
  {
    ImageGallery app = new ImageGallery();

    JFrame f = new JFrame("Image Selector Demo");
    WindowListener wl = new WindowAdapter()
      {
        public void windowClosing(WindowEvent e)
        {
          ((Window) e.getSource()).dispose();
          System.exit(0);
        }
      };
    f.addWindowListener(wl);
    f.getContentPane().add(app);
    f.pack();
    f.setVisible(true);
  }

  static final int NUM_IMAGES = 10;

  private JButton first, next, previous, last;
  private JPanel buttonPanel;
  private JPanel imagePanel;

  Image [] images;
}
```

The first and most obvious change is the absence of your ButtonHandler class. What class defines your event listeners? You must still have *objects* that act as action listeners (because your program still works), and these objects must have a class definition.

Their class definitions are now anonymous inner class definitions in the `create()` method.

You create four definitions similar to the following:

```
ActionListener firstListener = new ActionListener()
  {
    public void actionPerformed(ActionEvent e)
      {
        CardLayout layout = (CardLayout) imagePanel.getLayout();
        layout.first(imagePanel);
      }
  };
first.addActionListener(firstListener);
```

This expression creates a new class definition and an *object instance*. The new class implements `ActionListener`. Because it implements `ActionListener`, it must provide a concrete definition of the `actionPerformed()` method, which it does.

In general, the anonymous inner class expression syntax calls for the `new` operator to be applied to the name of the interface being implemented.

The new class does not have a name; it is *anonymous*. You simultaneously define the new class, create an instance of your new class, and assign it to the variable `firstListener`. You then register this listener on the button labeled First in your application.

The latest version of your program creates four such anonymous inner class definitions and corresponding object instances, and registers each one on its own button.

The advantage of this approach is that you can now remove any logic that you previously needed to determine the event source. Now each listener object receives event notifications from only one button.

Your new anonymous types are indeed inner classes of your `ImageGallery` class. But now they are anonymous. Looking at your directory after compiling this new version reveals no less than four new `.class` files.

```
-rw-r--r--   1 vartan    users        861 Mar 21 20:14 ImageGallery$1.class
-rw-r--r--   1 vartan    users        864 Mar 21 20:14 ImageGallery$2.class
-rw-r--r--   1 vartan    users        860 Mar 21 20:14 ImageGallery$3.class
-rw-r--r--   1 vartan    users        860 Mar 21 20:14 ImageGallery$4.class
-rw-r--r--   1 vartan    users       3899 Mar 21 20:14 ImageGallery.class
-rw-r--r--   1 vartan    users        820 Mar 21 20:14 MouseMonitor.class
```

Because you created classes with no name, you really can't refer to them again. The purpose of anonymous inner class definitions is to provide an actual new class—an implementation of a type—to be used for a very specific purpose which requires only a small, concise change in the definition of its super type. Event handling is one of the primary uses of event handling in Java programming.

You can create the same metamorphosis for your MouseMonitor class. Now try to create yet another anonymous inner class definition.

This time your new class will simultaneously implement the MouseListener interface and create an object instance. Again you change the code in your create() method. You simply replace your existing code with the code in Listing 9.7.

Again, I only show the new definition of the class that previously was called MouseMonitor. The rest of the application code is unchanged.

LISTING 9.7   Redefining the MouseListener Class as an Anonymous Inner Class

```
...
    MouseListener mm = new MouseListener()
      {
        public void mouseClicked(MouseEvent e)
          {
            System.out.println(e.getSource().toString());
          }
      };
    ...
```

But you are not done yet. The compiler has the audacity to spit out an invective of error messages, suggesting that you did something terrible! The abbreviated compiler errors that follow look familiar, don't they?

```
ImageGallery.java:102: interface java.awt.event.MouseListener is an abstract
class. It can't be instantiated.
    MouseListener mm = new MouseListener()
                       ^

ImageGallery.java:102: local class ImageGallery. 5 must be declared abstract
and not final. It does not define void mousePressed(java.awt.event.MouseEvent)
from interface java.awt.event.MouseListener.
    MouseListener mm = new MouseListener()
...
```

Your code in Listing 9.7 creates an anonymous inner class definition that *implements* the java.awt.event.MouseListener interface. Therefore, it must provide concrete implementations for all its methods, which you didn't do.

Are you on the right track? Certainly providing five such methods does not qualify as a concise modification to a super type. If you did provide a large number of method implementations in an anonymous inner class expression, it would create an unmanageable, difficult-to-read monster.

This anonymous inner class idiom was not intended to be used in such a fashion. The solution is to call upon your old friend the adapter class. Adapters are classes, not interfaces. Instead of implementing the MouseListener interface, you subclass the MouseAdapter *class*, which already provides a full implementation of the interface.

You simply change your anonymous inner class definition to that shown in Listing 9.8.

LISTING 9.8 Extending an Adapter Class to Implement an Anonymous Inner Class

```
...
MouseListener mm = new MouseAdapter()
  {
    public void mouseClicked(MouseEvent e)
      {
        System.out.println(e.getSource().toString());
      }
  };
...
```

This is the other form of anonymous inner class definition, which combines the creation of a subclass of the named class with the creation of an object instance of the new class. This expression creates an anonymous subclass of the MouseAdapter class and also creates an object instance of your new subclass. The expression syntax requires that you apply the new operator to the superclass.

To define the subclass you need, you simply override the definitions of the methods of interest. For your example, you only need to override the mouseClicked() method.

Anonymous inner class expressions combine the creation of either an *implementation* of an interface or the *subclass* of a class with the object creation expression of the newly created class.

Listing 9.8 offers a more poignant lesson when used with a listener interface such as MouseListener which defines five methods. It is clear that defining anonymous inner classes is not such a friendly undertaking when trying to implement large interfaces.

You probably noticed in Tables 9.8 and 9.9 that you could not find adapter classes for all the listener interfaces. Many of the listener interfaces that define only one or two methods do not need adapter classes because it is easy to implement the interface with an anonymous inner class. Your anonymous inner class expressions should subtype the appropriate type for maximum effectiveness.

Let's make one more enhancement to your application, which involves creating a window listener. If you've recreated and run any of the programs encountered thus far in the book, you noticed that you cannot exit the application by using the Close button on your frame. You had to hit Ctrl+C to exit the program.

Let's add a `WindowListener` to your frame. You do this in your main function, as shown in Listing 9.9.

The code in Listing 9.9 only shows the new `main()` method for the complete `ImageGallery` program. The rest of the program is unchanged. In order to compile the code in Listing 9.9 you need to add the following import statements to the file.

```
import java.awt.event.WindowAdapter;
import java.awt.event.WindowEvent;
import java.awt.event.WindowListener;
```

LISTING 9.9   Adding a `WindowListener` to Your Frame

```
...
public static void main(String [] args)
{
  ImageGallery app = new ImageGallery();

  JFrame f = new JFrame("Image Selector Demo");
  WindowListener wl = new WindowAdapter()
    {
      public void windowClosing(WindowEvent e)
      {
        ((Window) e.getSource()).dispose();
        System.exit(0);
      }
    };
  f.addWindowListener(wl);
  f.getContentPane().add(app);
  f.pack();
  f.setVisible(true);
}
...
```

Referring back to Table 9.6, you see that the `WindowListener` interface specifies no less than seven methods. It seems prudent to use `WindowAdapter` instead in your anonymous inner class creation expression of a window listener.

You are only interested in listening for events that indicate the user attempted to close the window. You then dispose of the window. Calling the `Window.dispose()` method releases all native screen resources used for this window. It doesn't exit your application, however. So you need the call to `System.exit(0)`.

Frequently, you will find a very simple event handler like this to terminate an application. More robust applications often handle other window events to do things like suspend background processing if the user iconifies a window.

Combining Event Sources and Listeners

It's possible to have the same object take on the role of event source and event listener. This is useful when you have a small application, such as your ImageGallery. It saves you the work of defining and maintaining additional classes.

In your initial version, you were interested only in action events generated by the application's four buttons. Instead of defining your ButtonHandler class, you could simply define an actionPerformed() method in your application, and modify your ImageGallery class definition to implement the ActionListener interface.

Then, your application instance becomes its own listener as shown in Listing 9.10.

LISTING 9.10 Making an Application Its Own Listener

```
public class ImageGallery extends JPanel implements ActionListener
{
  ...
  public void actionPerformed(ActionEvent e)
  {
    ...
  }
  ...
}
```

Now, you can simply register the application as its own listener by adding the following statements in your create() method.

```
first.addActionListener(this);
previous.addActionListener(this);
next.addActionListener(this);
last.addActionListener(this);
```

Here, this refers to your instance of ImageGallery. This certainly saves the trouble of creating and maintaining a separate listener class. However, you reintroduce a previous malady. The new actionPerformed() method must again resort to identifying the button source so it knows what to do.

This actually may be an acceptable trade-off between the amount of work required to define a second class and the amount of work anticipated to keep the actionPerformed() method updated to handle changes to the application.

9

EVENTS AND
EVENT HANDLING

It is advisable to use this technique only for programs of small scope which handle a very small subset of event types. You can imagine how quickly your class would add methods to be able to act as a proper listener for a variety of event types.

For example, to be a valid `MouseListener` your `ImageGallery` class would have to also implement the `MouseListener` interface and provide the five methods in this interface.

Your simple application would quickly become cluttered. Good object-oriented design stipulates that classes should generally do one thing well. You should avoid defining a class that tries to serve too many purposes so that the true purpose of your class and what it does remains clear.

Notifying Multiple Listeners

In the previous example, you added your `ImageGallery` application as a listener for action events. You didn't mention anything about removing the other listeners you added. You still have the following four lines of code in your program.

```
first.addActionListener(firstListener);
previous.addActionListener(previousListener);
next.addActionListener(nextListener);
last.addActionListener(lastListener);
```

These statements add instances of your anonymous class definitions as listeners. Now, each of your buttons has two listeners. When an action event occurs on any of them, they will deliver the event to *all* listeners.

Only one instance of the event object is created, and it is passed to each listener. This is not a problem, because event objects have read-only fields that simply convey information about the event.

An important point is that the order of event notification is undefined. You cannot be certain that the listeners you add first will be notified first.

If such timing issues are critical to your application, you need to determine an alternate mechanism to do this. Generally, applications should not rely on timing issues. It might be wise to consider an alternate design in which such timing issues are not critical.

Using AWT Events

Now that you've addressed the conceptual issues related to events and event handling, let's visit some examples that illustrate the use of the different event types. Throughout this section, you might find Table 9.6 a useful reference. The names of the methods in the different listener interfaces are the best way to understand what kind of event information is available to listeners.

Component and Container Events

Because component and container events are somewhat related in nature, you'll see them both demonstrated here. You already have a conceptual understanding of the event handling process, so let's jump right in and look at some code.

Listing 9.11 lists a small program that handles component events on a label and container events on the main application container.

LISTING 9.11   Handling Component and Container Events

```java
import java.awt.*;
import java.awt.event.*;
import javax.swing.*;

public class ComponentEventDemo extends JPanel
{
  public ComponentEventDemo()
  {
    label = new JLabel("This label is an event source");

    // Listen for events on our label.
    ComponentMonitor compL = new ComponentMonitor();
    label.addComponentListener(compL);

    // Listen for events on the application panel.
    ContainerMonitor contL = new ContainerMonitor();

    // Listen for mouse clicks on the panel, and
    // toggle the presence of the label in the panel.
    MouseAdapter mL = new MouseAdapter()
      {
        public void mouseClicked(MouseEvent e)
          {
            Container cont = (Container) e.getSource();
            if (cont.getComponentCount() == 0)
              cont.add(label);
            else
              cont.remove(label);
            repaint();
          }
      };

    this.addMouseListener(mL);
    this.addContainerListener(contL);
```

continues

404   *Java GUI Development*

LISTING 9.11   Continued

```java
    add(label, BorderLayout.SOUTH);
  }


  public Dimension getPreferredSize()
  {
    return new Dimension(300, 80);
  }

  public static void main(String [] args)
  {
    ComponentEventDemo app = new ComponentEventDemo();

    JFrame f = new JFrame("Component Event Demo");
    WindowListener wl = new WindowAdapter()
      {
        public void windowClosing(WindowEvent e)
          {
            ((Window) e.getSource()).dispose();
            System.exit(0);
          }
      };
    f.addWindowListener(wl);
    f.getContentPane().add(app);
    f.pack();
    f.setVisible(true);
  }


  JLabel label;
}


class ComponentMonitor implements ComponentListener
{

  public void componentHidden(ComponentEvent e)
  {
    System.out.println("Component hidden.");
  }

  public void componentMoved(ComponentEvent e)
  {
    System.out.println("Component moved.");
  }
  public void componentResized(ComponentEvent e)
```

```
  {
    Component c = (Component) e.getSource();
    System.out.println("Component resized: " + c.getSize());
    System.out.println("\tBounds = " + c.getBounds());
    System.out.println("\tLocation = " + c.getLocation());
  }

  public void componentShown(ComponentEvent e)
  {
    System.out.println("Component shown.");
  }
}


class ContainerMonitor implements ContainerListener
{
  public void componentAdded(ContainerEvent e)
  {
    System.out.println("Component added.");
  }

  public void componentRemoved(ContainerEvent e)
  {
    System.out.println("Component removed");
  }
}
```

You register a ComponentListener on the label, and a ContainerListener on the container.
When the program starts up, you see the display in Figure 9.5.

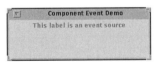

FIGURE 9.5

A small program to demonstrate component and container events. The label can be added or removed from the container by clicking within the container bounds. This action also generates component move and resize events.

Immediately upon startup you see the following console output.

```
Component added.
Component resized: java.awt.Dimension[width=200,height=14]
        Bounds = java.awt.Rectangle[x=50,y=5,width=200,height=14]
        Location = java.awt.Point[x=50,y=5]
Component moved.
```

The `ContainerListener` produces the first line of output when you add the label to the container. The latter two lines are produced by the `ComponentListener` methods. The label is resized and moved by the layout manager during construction and layout of the container.

You also added a `MouseListener` to your panel so you could respond to mouse clicks on the container by toggling the presence of the label in the container. The first time you click in the container you see the label disappear and the following additional line of console output appears.

```
Component removed
```

Clicking again adds the label to the container, and the container listener indicates the action.

```
Component added.
```

It's worth making a few points about this example. First, it is a good example of how Swing lightweight components still use the AWT event definitions and listener interface definitions. Your example uses only Swing components. All AWT component events apply to Swing components.

Another point of interest is the `MouseListener` you added to your panel. You needed a way to obtain information about mouse clicks in your panel so you could add and remove the label.

Why didn't you simply use an `ActionListener` and define one `actionPerformed()` method to do this relatively simple chore? It would have been simple to have your class implement the `ActionListener` interface and define the `actionPerformed()` method:

```java
public class ComponentEventDemo extends JPanel implements ActionListener
{
    ...
    public ComponentEventDemo()
    {
        ...
        this.addActionListener(this);
        ...
    }

    public void actionPerformed(ActionEvent e)
    {
        ...
    }
    ...
}
```

If you try this, you get the following compilation error.

```
ComponentEventDemo.java:36: Method addActionListener(ComponentEventDemo) not
found in class ComponentEventDemo.
    this.addActionListener(this);
                          ^
```

1 error

Your `ComponentEventDemo` is a subclass of `javax.swing.JPanel`. It's a true component, so what's the problem? The problem is that `ActionPerformed` is a semantic event and is not generated by all components. It is only generated by certain components, and, therefore, support for adding listeners is not—and should not be—in the `Component` class.

The `JPanel` class doesn't fire `ActionEvents` either, so there is no `addActionListener()` method anywhere to be found.

Often, knowing what components generate which events is a crucial part of application design. Familiarity with the relationship between components and events can help you anticipate these types of problems.

Focus Events

Focus events are another of the AWT component events. Even though they are component events, some components do not generate them. For instance, neither AWT nor Swing labels generate focus events.

Focus events indicate a change in the keyboard focus. The term *keyboard focus* refers to the capability of a component to accept input from the keyboard. Only one component can have the focus at any particular time. This restriction is usually enforced by the underlying native platform window system (such as the X-Window system window manager for Unix systems).

The keyboard focus can be changed by clicking on a component, such as a button, moving the mouse to a different window, or hitting the TAB key when the mouse in inside a container. The latter action traverses the container's list of components, giving the focus to the next one.

Your demo uses a panel that contains two buttons. You transfer the focus between the two. Figure 9.6 shows the application upon startup.

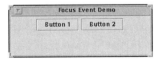

FIGURE 9.6

Components such as buttons can acquire the keyboard focus.

Often, the visual appearance of the component changes slightly to indicate it has the focus. Swing buttons draw a light purple border around their text when they gain the keyboard focus.

The FocusEvent class defines a method, isTemporary(), that indicates if a focus event represents a temporary acquisition of the focus by the event source.

Temporary transfers of the focus occur in certain cases, such as when the cursor moves out of your application window and into another window. Whichever of your two buttons has the focus temporarily loses the focus to the other window. However, when the cursor is moved back, the same button has the focus.

If you deliberately transfer the focus by hitting TAB or clicking on the other button in your application, you call the focus transfer *permanent*, for lack of a better term. You already know it's not really permanent, but the term is meant to convey a meaning relative to *temporary*. Probably they should be called *explicit* and *implicit*, or *explicit* and *automatic*.

Listing 9.12 shows a FocusEvent demo.

LISTING 9.12 The FocusEvent Demo

```
import java.awt.*;
import java.awt.event.*;
import javax.swing.*;

public class FocusEventDemo extends JPanel
{
  public FocusEventDemo()
  {
    JButton b1 = new JButton("Button 1");
    JButton b2 = new JButton("Button 2");

    FocusMonitor fL = new FocusMonitor();
    b1.addFocusListener(fL);
    b2.addFocusListener(fL);

    add(b1);
    add(b2);
  }

  public Dimension getPreferredSize()
  {
    return new Dimension(300, 80);
  }

  public static void main(String [] args)
```

```
   {
      FocusEventDemo app = new FocusEventDemo();

      JFrame f = new JFrame("Focus Event Demo");
      WindowListener wl = new WindowAdapter()
        {
           public void windowClosing(WindowEvent e)
             {
                ((Window) e.getSource()).dispose();
                System.exit(0);
             }
        };
      f.addWindowListener(wl);
      f.getContentPane().add(app);
      f.pack();
      f.setVisible(true);
   }
}


class FocusMonitor implements FocusListener
{
   public void focusGained(FocusEvent e)
   {
      Component c = (Component) e.getSource();
      System.out.print("Focus gained.  " + ((JButton) c).getText());

      if (e.isTemporary())
         System.out.print("  temporarily");
      System.out.println();
   }

   public void focusLost(FocusEvent e)
   {
      Component c = (Component) e.getSource();
      System.out.print("Focus lost.  " + ((JButton) c).getText());

      if (e.isTemporary())
         System.out.print("  temporarily");
      System.out.println();
   }
}
```

After placing the cursor in your window, hitting the TAB key causes the first button to be rendered with a light purple rectangle, shown in Figure 9.7 as a light gray color.

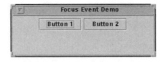

FIGURE 9.7
When the keyboard focus is transferred to a button, a visual change indicates the focus event.

You also see the following console output.

```
Focus gained.  Button 1
```

The next four TAB keys produce

```
Focus lost.  Button 1
Focus gained.  Button 2
Focus lost.  Button 2
Focus gained.  Button 1
Focus lost.  Button 1
Focus gained.  Button 2
Focus lost.  Button 2
Focus gained.  Button 1
```

However, if you move the mouse out of the window, you see an indication of a temporary loss of focus.

```
Focus lost.  Button 1  temporarily
```

It's temporary, because moving the mouse back into the window shows that the same button regains the focus.

```
Focus gained.  Button 1
Focus lost.  Button 1  temporarily
Focus gained.  Button 1
Focus lost.  Button 1  temporarily
```

Key Events

The InputEvent class is an abstract class that defines all common attributes of *input events*. All keyboard and mouse events are input events. They are defined by the KeyEvent and MouseEvent classes, respectively.

A KeyEvent indicates that a keystroke occurred in a component. The methods in the KeyListener interface suggest that there are three types of key events: key press events, key typed events, and key released events.

Key press events represent a key being pressed down but not released, whereas a key typed event indicates a key was pressed and released.

It is preferable to trap `KeyTyped` events in order to determine information about typed characters. These events are higher level and do not depend on any specific platform configurations.

Sometimes, however, you need to trap key pressed and key released events; information about keys that do not generate any character input cannot be obtained from key typed events. Examples of such keys are the Ctrl, Alt, Shift, and other modifier keys.

Methods in the `KeyEvent` class enable you to get the information from a key event shown in Table 9.10.

TABLE 9.10 `KeyEvent` Information

Method	*Event information*
`char getKeyChar()`	Unicode char of character key
`int getKeyCode()`	An integer key code representing the virtual key
`String getKeyModifiersText(int mods)`	String representation of modifier keys held down during key event
`String getKeyText(int keycode)`	The text of the key—obtained from the keycode

Listing 9.13 shows your `KeyEvent` demo program.

LISTING 9.13 The `KeyEvent` Demo Program

```
import java.awt.*;
import java.awt.event.*;
import javax.swing.*;

public class KeyEventDemo extends JPanel
{
  public KeyEventDemo()
  {
    JTextField textField = new JTextField(25);
    textField.setFont(new Font("SansSerif", Font.PLAIN, 14));

    KeyMonitor tL = new KeyMonitor();
    textField.addKeyListener(tL);

    add(textField);
  }

  public Dimension getPreferredSize()
```

continues

LISTING 9.13   Continued

```java
  {
    return new Dimension(300, 80);
  }

  public static void main(String [] args)
  {
    KeyEventDemo app = new KeyEventDemo();

    JFrame f = new JFrame("Key Event Demo");
    WindowListener wl = new WindowAdapter()
      {
        public void windowClosing(WindowEvent e)
          {
            ((Window) e.getSource()).dispose();
            System.exit(0);
          }
      };
    f.addWindowListener(wl);
    f.getContentPane().add(app);
    f.pack();
    f.setVisible(true);
  }
}


class KeyMonitor implements KeyListener
{
  public void keyPressed(KeyEvent e)
  {
    System.out.println("Key pressed...");
    printKeyEventInfo(e);
  }

  public void keyReleased(KeyEvent e)
  {
    System.out.println("Key released...");
    printKeyEventInfo(e);
  }

  public void keyTyped(KeyEvent e)
  {
    System.out.println("Key typed...");
    printKeyEventInfo(e);
  }
```

```
private void printKeyEventInfo(KeyEvent e)
{
  int keyCode = e.getKeyCode();

  // Defined in InputEvent class.
  int modifiers = e.getModifiers();

  System.out.println("Key char = " + e.getKeyChar());

  System.out.println("Key code = " + keyCode);
  System.out.println("Key text = " + e.getKeyText(keyCode));

  System.out.println(e.getKeyModifiersText(modifiers));
  System.out.println();
}
}
```

Figure 9.8 shows the initial state of the GUI.

FIGURE 9.8
The TextField is initially displayed with no contained text. Typing keys in the TextField will generate instances of KeyEvents.

If you type a key that has no printable character representation, such as a Ctrl key, you see the following output:

```
Key pressed...
Key char =
Key code = 17
Key text = Ctrl


Key released...
Key char =
Key code = 17
Key text = Ctrl
Ctrl
```

Keys with no printable character representation only generate `key pressed` and `key released` events. They can never generate `key typed` events.

Typing a key with a character representation, on the other hand, also produces a key typed event. For instance, typing a key such as v produces the following output:

```
Key pressed...
Key char = v
Key code = 86
Key text = V


Key typed...
Key char = v
Key code = 0
Key text = Unknown keyCode: 0x0


Key released...
Key char = v
Key code = 86
Key text = V
```

You can see from the output that you are trapping all three types of key events, so you get output for each. The Unknown keyCode corresponds to the v key. In fact, all keys with character representations always have an undefined key code, represented by the KeyEvent.VK_UNDEFINED constant.

Capital letters are typed by holding down the shift key and a key simultaneously. If you type a capital letter, such as A, you get the following output which represents both keys:

```
Key pressed...
Key char = A
Key code = 65
Key text = A
Shift

Key typed...
Key char = A
Key code = 0
Key text = Unknown keyCode: 0x0


Key released...
Key char = A
Key code = 65
Key text = A
Shift
```

```
Key released...
Key char =
Key code = 16
Key text = Shift
Shift
```

Mouse Events

You are already somewhat familiar with mouse events because of your earlier exposure. Now I'll cover all the mouse events in detail.

Table 9.6 and Table 9.8 list only one event type related to mouse events, namely, `MouseEvent`. Yet Table 9.8 lists two related listeners, `MouseListener` and `MouseMotionListener`. As its name and member methods suggest, the `MouseMotionListener` enables delivery of information related to mouse motions instead of just mouse actions. Nevertheless, all the pertinent information is encapsulated in the `MouseEvent` type, therefore, an additional event type is not necessary.

The `javax.swing.event` package defines yet another mouse listener, `MouseInputListener`, which is an interface that extends both `MouseListener` and `MouseMotionListener`. This is convenient for listeners which want to listen for both types of events. But, alas, there is no `addMouseInputListener` method in any of the component classes, so you must add your listener once as a `MouseListener` and once as a `MouseMotionListener` using the `addMouseListener` and `addMouseMotionListener` methods, respectively.

`MouseEvent` is one of the event classes that service multiple related events. One of the seven methods in `MouseListener` and `MouseMotionListener` gets called in response to a mouse event, depending on the exact variation of the mouse action.

Sometimes, you may process the event in such a way that you want to check the id field of the event. The `MouseEvent` class defines constants whose value matches the possible event id values for each of the different mouse events. Table 9.11 lists these constants.

TABLE 9.11 Constant Defined by the `MouseEvent` Class

MouseEvent *constant*	*Description*
MOUSE_CLICKED	The mouse was clicked (button down and up).
MOUSE_DRAGGED	The mouse was pressed and dragged before release.
MOUSE_ENTERED	The mouse entered the bounds of a component.
MOUSE_EXITED	The mouse exited the component bounds.
MOUSE_FIRST	The value corresponds to the smallest id value out of all mouse ids.

continues

9

EVENTS AND
EVENT HANDLING

TABLE 9.11   Continued

MouseEvent *constant*	*Description*
MOUSE_LAST	The value corresponds to the largest id value out of all mouse ids.
MOUSE_MOVED	The mouse was moved (no buttons pressed).
MOUSE_PRESSED	The mouse was pressed down (not released).
MOUSE_RELEASED	The mouse was released after a press.

Listing 9.14 creates a container with two panels, shown in Figure 9.9. By moving, clicking, and dragging the mouse you can produce volumes of console output, mainly as a result of the mouse motion events. Each time the native platform window manager detects a mouse motion, it creates a mouse motion event. This could potentially result in one event for each displacement of one pixel!

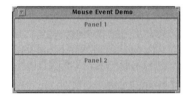

FIGURE 9.9
Both panels have registered mouse input listeners and generate events that represent detection of mouse clicks, motion, and entrance into and exit from the panels.

LISTING 9.14   Registering Listeners for MouseEvents

```
import java.awt.*;
import java.awt.event.*;
import javax.swing.*;
import javax.swing.event.*;

public class MouseEventDemo extends JPanel
{
  public MouseEventDemo()
  {
    setLayout(new GridLayout(2, 0));

    JPanel one = new JPanel();
    one.setBorder(BorderFactory.createLineBorder(Color.red, 1));

    MouseMonitor mL = new MouseMonitor();
```

```
    one.addMouseListener(mL);
    one.addMouseMotionListener(mL);

    JLabel l1 = new JLabel("Panel 1");
    one.add(l1);

    JPanel two = new JPanel();
    two.setBorder(BorderFactory.createLineBorder(Color.red, 1));
    two.addMouseListener(mL);
    two.addMouseMotionListener(mL);

    JLabel l2 = new JLabel("Panel 2");
    two.add(l2);

    add(one);
    add(two);
  }

  public Dimension getPreferredSize()
  {
    return new Dimension(350, 150);
  }

  public static void main(String [] args)
  {
    MouseEventDemo app = new MouseEventDemo();

    JFrame f = new JFrame("Mouse Event Demo");
    WindowListener wl = new WindowAdapter()
      {
        public void windowClosing(WindowEvent e)
          {
            ((Window) e.getSource()).dispose();
            System.exit(0);
          }
      };
    f.addWindowListener(wl);
    f.getContentPane().add(app);
    f.pack();
    f.setVisible(true);
  }
}


class MouseMonitor implements MouseInputListener
```

continues

LISTING 9.14   Registering Listeners for MouseEvents

```
{
  // The first five methods are defined in the
  // java.awt.event.MouseListener interface.
  //
  public void mouseClicked(MouseEvent e)
  {
    System.out.println("Mouse clicked: num clicks = " + e.getClickCount());
    System.out.println("                    location = " + e.getPoint());
  }

  public void mouseEntered(MouseEvent e)
  {
    System.out.println("Mouse entered.");
  }

  public void mouseExited(MouseEvent e)
  {
    System.out.println("Mouse exited.");
  }

  public void mousePressed(MouseEvent e)
  {
    System.out.println("Mouse pressed: location = ");
    System.out.println("                    x = " + e.getX());
    System.out.println("                    x = " + e.getY());
  }

  public void mouseReleased(MouseEvent e)
  {
    System.out.println("Mouse released: location = " + e.getPoint());
  }


  // These two methods are defined in the
  // java.awt.event.MouseMotionListener interface.
  //
  public void mouseDragged(MouseEvent e)
  {
    System.out.println("Mouse clicked: num clicks = " + e.getClickCount());
  }

  public void mouseMoved(MouseEvent e)
  {
    System.out.println("Mouse moved: location = " + e.getPoint());
  }
}
```

For example, if you just barely move the mouse into one of the panels, you produce the following output:

```
Mouse entered.
Mouse moved: location = java.awt.Point[x=334,y=67]
Mouse moved: location = java.awt.Point[x=348,y=67]
Mouse exited.
```

Then you move outward to exit the panel. You must enter a component to click in it, and this sequence of actions generates the following output:

```
Mouse entered.
Mouse moved: location = java.awt.Point[x=348,y=82]
Mouse pressed: location = java.awt.Point[x=348,y=82]
Mouse released: location = java.awt.Point[x=348,y=82]
Mouse clicked: num clicks = 1
               location = java.awt.Point[x=348,y=82]
Mouse moved: location = java.awt.Point[x=349,y=82]
Mouse exited.
```

You get the idea. You might want to track every pixel of motion or drag if you are writing an application that does drawing on a canvas or panel. Tracking mouse events is the way to figure out when the drag occurs and where the cursor is.

Consuming Input Events

Input events are all subclasses of `java.awt.InputEvent`. These include all key and mouse events, namely, `java.awt.KeyEvent`, `java.awt.MouseEvent` and all their subclasses. Figure 9.1 includes input events in the type hierarchy.

Only input events have the special characteristic that allows them to be *consumed*, which means the event is not passed to the native peer object of the event source. This might be useful, for example, if you don't want to echo the characters typed in a text field.

Normally, input events are passed to a component's native peer object. However, the event is first passed to all listeners, giving them a chance to consume the event if need be. The event handler has the option to do as it pleases with the event.

To consume an event and block its delivery to the event source's native peer, call the `InputEvent.consume()` method on the input event instance.

You can add some code to your earlier key event demo in Listing 9.13. Recall that you had the following method, shown in Listing 9.15.

LISTING 9.15   Logging KeyEvent Information

```
private void printKeyEventInfo(KeyEvent e)
{
  int keyCode = e.getKeyCode();

  // Defined in InputEvent class.
  int modifiers = e.getModifiers();

  System.out.println("Key char = " + e.getKeyChar());

  System.out.println("Key code = " + keyCode);
  System.out.println("Key text = " + e.getKeyText(keyCode));

  System.out.println(e.getKeyModifiersText(modifiers));
  System.out.println();
}
```

You can add a few lines of code that filter, say, the character A. You do this by checking the key code of every character typed. If it matches VK_A, the defined constant that represents the A key, then you call InputEvent.consume().

Listing 9.16 shows the slightly modified method.

LISTING 9.16   Consuming InputEvents to Prevent Delivery to Native Peers

```
private void printKeyEventInfo(KeyEvent e)
{
  int keyCode = e.getKeyCode();

  // Defined in InputEvent class.
  int modifiers = e.getModifiers();

  if (keyCode == KeyEvent.VK_A)
    {
      System.out.println("Consuming key...");
      e.consume();
       return;
    }

  System.out.println("Key char = " + e.getKeyChar());

  System.out.println("Key code = " + keyCode);
  System.out.println("Key text = " + e.getKeyText(keyCode));

  System.out.println(e.getKeyModifiersText(modifiers));
  System.out.println();
}
```

If you run the earlier key event demo with this minor modification, you still see key strokes echoed to the text field. Perhaps you are puzzled, because the console output indicates that indeed the consume method is called.

Figure 9.10 shows the a or A key you typed is echoed, but the console output shows that it has been consumed.

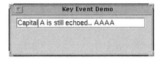

FIGURE 9.10

This figure shows that the a *key has been echoed, even though it was consumed by the event handler.*

```
Key pressed...
Consuming key...
Key typed...
Key char = a
Key code = 0
Key text = Unknown keyCode: 0x0


Key released...
Consuming key...
```

If you look carefully at the application, notice that you used a JTextField instead of a TextField. The JTextField class is lightweight and, therefore, has no native peer.

Yes, there must be at least one heavyweight container—and there is; your JFrame. But arbitrary components are not interested in key strokes and do not process them. As a result of this policy, the AWT doesn't deliver keystrokes to most components.

Therefore, the keystroke ends up being rendered on the output of the JTextField. If you simply substitute a regular AWT TextField for your JTextField, indeed all consumed keystrokes will not be delivered to the TextField's peer, and you will not see them on screen.

Incidentally, if you want to distinguish between upper and lower case characters, you can use the InputEvent.isShiftDown() method to determine if the shift key is down when a character is typed. The InputEvent class also defines several other methods for determining the state of the so-called modifier keys.

9

EVENTS AND
EVENT HANDLING

Paint Events

Paint events are special events. What makes them special is that the AWT handles these events internally, instead of dispatching them to components in your program. Because these events are handled internally, you don't have to handle them.

Paint events are created whenever any part of a component is exposed after being occluded by another component or window. A paint event eventually results in a sequence of calls to a component's repaint(), update(), and paint() methods. I will discuss this more in Chapter 11, "Graphics."

Window Events

Window events are another one of the AWT component events to which you've already had some exposure. A window event is generated whenever a window operation is performed. Table 9.12 lists the constants in the WindowEvent class that define these different window events.

TABLE 9.12   Constants in the WindowEvent Class

Window event type	Description
WINDOW_ACTIVATED	A new window has been activated.
WINDOW_CLOSED	A window has been closed. The request to close the window has been delivered in the form of a window event of this type.
WINDOW_CLOSING	The window closing event is pending. The window may not yet have received the event from the AWT.
WINDOW_DEACTIVATED	A window has lost focus.
WINDOW_DEICONIFIED	A window has been reopened from its iconified form.
WINDOW_FIRST	A value that indicates the smallest integer constant of all the window event type constants.
WINDOW_ICONIFIED	A window has been iconified.
WINDOW_LAST	A value that indicates the largest integer constant of all the window event type constants.
WINDOW_OPENED	A window has been opened.

Listing 9.17 builds a simple window that you can manipulate to generate window events. Figure 9.11 shows your little application window.

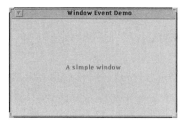

FIGURE 9.11

Moving, resizing, iconifying, or closing a window generates WindowEvents, *which can be handled by a* WindowListener.

LISTING 9.17 Registering a Listener for WindowEvents

```
import java.awt.*;
import java.awt.event.*;
import javax.swing.*;
import javax.swing.event.*;

public class WindowEventDemo extends JPanel
{
  public WindowEventDemo()
  {
    setLayout(new BorderLayout());
    JLabel label = new JLabel("A simple window");
    label.setHorizontalAlignment(SwingConstants.CENTER);

    add(label, BorderLayout.CENTER);
  }

  public Dimension getPreferredSize()
  {
    return new Dimension(350, 200);
  }

  public static void main(String [] args)
  {
    WindowEventDemo app = new WindowEventDemo();

    JFrame f = new JFrame("Window Event Demo");

    WindowListener wl = new WindowMonitor() ;
    f.addWindowListener(wl);
```

9

EVENTS AND EVENT HANDLING

continues

LISTING 9.17   Continued

```java
    f.getContentPane().add(app);
    f.pack();
    f.setVisible(true);
  }

  JLabel label;
}


class WindowMonitor implements WindowListener
{
  public void windowActivated(WindowEvent e)
  {
    System.out.println("Window activated.");
  }

  public void windowClosed(WindowEvent e)
  {
    System.out.println("Window closed.");
    ((Window) e.getSource()).dispose();
    System.exit(0);
  }

  public void windowClosing(WindowEvent e)
  {
    System.out.println("Window closing.");
    ((Window) e.getSource()).dispose();
  }

  public void windowDeactivated(WindowEvent e)
  {
    System.out.println("Window deactivated.");

  }

  public void windowDeiconified(WindowEvent e)
  {
    System.out.println("Window deiconified.");

  }

  public void windowIconified(WindowEvent e)
  {
    System.out.println("Window iconified.");
```

```
    }

    public void windowOpened(WindowEvent e)
    {
      System.out.println("Window opened.");
    }
}
```

Item Events

Item events are semantic events. They indicate that an item has been selected. In the spirit of the meaning and purpose of semantic events, a component which generates an item event must define the semantics of the event.

Items that can be selected are defined by the `java.awt.ItemSelectable` interface. Actually, the details of this interface are not intimately related to handling events of this type, but its methods are listed in Table 9.13 anyway, as extra exposure to the design philosophy of the JFC.

TABLE 9.13   Items Defined by the `java.awt.ItemSelectable` Interface

ItemSelectable method name	Description
void addItemListener (ItemListener l)	Adds a listener for item events on this object when its state changes.
Object[] getSelectedObjects()	Returns a data structure of all the component's selected items. It returns null if no items are selected.
void removeItemListener (ItemListener l)	Removes an item listener from this event source.

The four AWT components that are item-selectable objects are `Checkbox`, `CheckboxMenuItem`, `Choice`, and `List`. All these components generate `ItemEvents`.

Additionally, several Swing components implement the `ItemSelectable` interface and also generate `ItemEvents`.

Choose a `JComboBox` for your demonstration. Looking up the `javadoc` documentation page confirms that `JComboBox` implements the `ItemSelectable` interface.

Your program in Listing 9.18 creates an `ItemListener` and registers it with the combo box.

9

EVENTS AND
EVENT HANDLING

LISTING 9.18   Creating an `ItemListener` and Registering It with the Combo Box

```java
import java.awt.*;
import java.awt.event.*;
import javax.swing.*;
import javax.swing.event.*;

public class ItemEventDemo extends JPanel
{
  public ItemEventDemo()
  {
    String [] grocery = {"Eggs", "Milk", "Chicken", "Endive lettuce",
                "Vegetables", "Peanut butter", "Orange juice",
                "Apples", "Bananas", "Yogurt", "Cottage cheese",
                "Bread", "Tuna fish", "Spices"};

    JComboBox cb = new JComboBox(grocery);
    cb.setEditable(true);
    cb.setAlignmentX(Component.LEFT_ALIGNMENT);
    cb.setMaximumRowCount(20);
    cb.setSelectedIndex(8);

    ItemMonitor iL = new ItemMonitor();
    cb.addItemListener(iL);

    add(cb);
  }

  public Dimension getPreferredSize()
  {
    return new Dimension(200, 250);
  }

  public static void main(String [] args)
  {
    ItemEventDemo app = new ItemEventDemo();

    JFrame f = new JFrame("Item Event Demo");

    f.getContentPane().add(app);
    f.pack();
    f.setVisible(true);
  }
}
```

```
class ItemMonitor implements ItemListener
{
  public void itemStateChanged(ItemEvent e)
  {
    // Gets the source, just like EventObject.getSource.
    JComboBox c = (JComboBox) e.getItemSelectable();

    if (e.getStateChange() == ItemEvent.SELECTED)
      System.out.println("Selection now = " + c.getSelectedItem().toString());
  }
}
```

Figure 9.12 shows what the application looks like upon startup.

FIGURE 9.12

If a selection or deselection occurs in an item selectable component, the event source will fire an item event.

Figure 9.12 shows your application just before you select the item Eggs in your combo box. After the selection, two item events are fired, one to indicate the current item has been deselected, and one to indicate the new selection. You choose to print only the newly selected item information.

```
Selection now = Eggs
```

Text Events

Text events are generated by AWT text components to indicate a change to their textual content. The TextEvent object doesn't give details about the changed text other than the fact that the text component's text has changed.

Swing text components do not use this event. Swing defines a rather complex text package, javax.swing.text, that defines a completely different model and architecture for manipulating text.

The `TextListener` interface defines only one method, `textValueValueChanged(TextEvent)`.

Each character typed in an AWT `TextField` or `TextArea` generates a `TextEvent`. Running the program in Listing 9.19 results in the string `TEXT_VALUE_CHANGED` printing for each character typed.

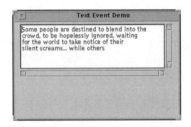

FIGURE 9.13
Each character typed in a text component generates a `TextEvent`.

LISTING 9.19   Registering a `TextListener` with a `TextArea` Component

```java
import java.awt.*;
import java.awt.event.*;
import javax.swing.*;

public class TextEventDemo extends JPanel
{
  public TextEventDemo()
  {
    StringBuffer buf = new StringBuffer();
    buf.append("Some people are destined to blend into ");
    buf.append("the\n crowd, to be hopelessly ignored, ");
    buf.append("waiting\n for the world to take notice of ");
    buf.append("their\n silent screams... while others ");

    TextArea t = new TextArea(7, 50);
    t.setText(buf.toString());

    TextMonitor tL = new TextMonitor();
    t.addTextListener(tL);

    add(t);
  }
```

```
  public Dimension getPreferredSize()
  {
    return new Dimension(350, 200);
  }

  public static void main(String [] args)
  {
    TextEventDemo app = new TextEventDemo();

    JFrame f = new JFrame("Text Event Demo");

    f.getContentPane().add(app);
    f.pack();
    f.setVisible(true);
  }
}


class TextMonitor implements TextListener
{
  public void textValueChanged(TextEvent e)
  {
    String param = e.paramString();

    // Indicates the type of change, not the
    // updated component text.
    System.out.println(param);
  }
}
```

Adjustment Events

Adjustment events are semantic events that are generated by adjustable components, that is, components which visually represent a value that can lie within a bounded range. You probably won't be surprised to learn of the existence of the java.awt.Adjustable interface that defines the nature of items that can be adjusted. Only AWT and Swing scrollbars fire AdjustmentEvents.

The full details of the use of the Adjustable interface are beyond the scope of your present discussion on event handling. Nevertheless, Table 9.14 lists the methods in the interface to give you more exposure to this data abstraction.

TABLE 9.14   Methods in the `Adjustable` Interface

Adjustable interface method name	*Description*
`void addAdjustmentListener (AdjustmentListener l)`	Adds a listener for adjustment events from the adjustable object event source. This method fires when the source's adjustment value changes.
`int getBlockIncrement()`	Gets the value that defines the block increment for the adjustable object.
`int getMaximum()`	Gets the maximum value of the adjustable event source.
`int getMinimum()`	Gets the minimum value of the adjustable event source.
`int getOrientation()`	Gets the adjustable object's orientation.
`int getUnitIncrement()`	Gets the value that defines the amount of unit increments for the adjustable object.
`int getValue()`	Gets the adjustable object's current value.
`int getVisibleAmount()`	Gets the value that indicates the amount of the adjustable range of values that is visible at any given time.
`void removeAdjustmentListener (AdjustmentListener l)`	Removes the specified adjustment listener.
`void setBlockIncrement(int b)`	Sets the value of the block increment amount.
`void setMaximum(int max)`	Sets the value that represents the maximum adjustable value of the adjustable object.
`void setMinimum(int min)`	Sets the value that represents the minimum adjustable value of the adjustable object.
`void setUnitIncrement(int u)`	Sets the value that represents the unit increment amount for the adjustable object.
`void setValue(int v)`	Sets the current value of the adjustable object.
`void setVisibleAmount(int v)`	Sets the value that indicates the amount of the adjustable range of values that is visible at any given time.

For the purposes of this discussion, the most important members of this interface are the two methods `addAdjustmentListener()` and `removeAdjustmentListener()`. You can be sure that any component that advertises its capability to be adjustable will implement these two methods, giving listeners the chance to register their interest in receiving adjustment events.

Figure 9.14 shows the simplest possible demo of an adjustable component. The Swing scrollbar has value 0 when it initially displays. You can click on the arrows, click within the scrollbar area, or drag the scrollbar's thumb. Each of these actions generates a different type of adjustment event. Table 9.15 lists the constants defined by the AdjustmentEvent interface that indicate the different types of adjustment events.

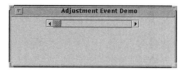

FIGURE 9.14
Scrollbars generate six different types of adjustment events depending on the type of adjustment made to the adjustable component.

TABLE 9.15 The Different Types of AdjustmentEvent

AdjustmentEvent *type*	*Description*
ADJUSTMENT_VALUE_CHANGED	Indicates that some change occurred to the value that indicates the position of the scrollbar's thumb
BLOCK_DECREMENT	Indicates that the value decreased by the block decrement value
BLOCK_INCREMENT	Indicates that the value increased by the block increment value
TRACK	Indicates that the adjustable value is currently continuously changing because the thumb is being dragged
UNIT_DECREMENT	Indicates that the left or up arrow was clicked (for horizontal or vertical scrollbars, respectively) to change the value by the decrement unit
UNIT_INCREMENT	Indicates that the right or down arrow was clicked (for horizontal or vertical scrollbars, respectively) to change the value by the decrement unit

AdjustmentEvent objects store the adjustment type and the value. The AdjustmentEvent.getAdjustable() method gives you an alternate way to get the event source, in addition to the getSource() method inherited from the EventObject type.

Listing 9.20 shows the source for your demo. When the GUI appears, if you move the scrollbar thumb in the ways described previously, you see the new scrollbar position value print on the console.

LISTING 9.20   Registering an AdjustmentListener with a JScrollBar

```
import java.awt.*;
import java.awt.event.*;
import javax.swing.*;
```

9

EVENTS AND
EVENT HANDLING

continues

LISTING 9.20   Continued

```java
public class AdjustmentEventDemo extends JPanel
{
  public AdjustmentEventDemo()
  {
    JScrollBar sb = new JScrollBar(JScrollBar.HORIZONTAL);
    sb.setPreferredSize(new Dimension(200, 17));

    AdjustmentListener aL = new AdjustmentMonitor();
    sb.addAdjustmentListener(aL);

    add(sb);
  }

  public Dimension getPreferredSize()
  {
    return new Dimension(350, 100);
  }

  public static void main(String [] args)
  {
    AdjustmentEventDemo app = new AdjustmentEventDemo();

    JFrame f = new JFrame("Adjustment Event Demo");

    f.getContentPane().add(app);
    f.pack();
    f.setVisible(true);
  }
}


class AdjustmentMonitor implements AdjustmentListener
{
  public void adjustmentValueChanged(AdjustmentEvent e)
    {
      System.out.println("Value = " + e.getValue());
    }
}
```

The scrollbar is really a visual representation of a piece of data whose value must be within certain bounds. The position of the scrollbar's thumb reflects the current value within the range of possible values. Essentially, the scrollbar presents a visual abstraction of a bounded set of values, and it enables a human to interpret the value in a natural way.

The `Adjustable` interface captures the notion of how the data and its visual graphic—the scrollbar—communicate.

Using Swing Events

The Swing event types are all defined in the `javax.swing.event` package. Other than a few exceptions, all Swing event types directly extend `java.util.EventObject`.

Two of the four renegade Swing types descend from `java.awt.ComponentEvent`, making them component events just like other AWT component events. The first of these, `javax.swing.event.MenuKeyEvent`, directly extends `java.awt.event.KeyEvent`; and the second, `javax.swing.event.MenuDragMouseEvent`, directly extends the `java.awt.event.MenuEvent` type.

Two other Swing event types, `javax.swing.event.AncestorEvent` and `javax.swing.event.InternalFrameEvent`, directly extend `java.util.AWTEvent`. Although these two Swing events directly extend `AWTEvent`, they are semantic events. The rest of the Swing event types extend `EventObject` directly and are also semantic events.

In this section you will learn most of the Swing event types, their basic purpose, and their use. Graphics are a wonderful learning tool, and I again refer you to Figure 9.1, to help you remember the organization of all the JFC event types. Figure 9.1 clearly shows that both the AWT and Swing component event types are part of the `ComponentEvent` hierarchy. All other Swing event types essentially define semantic events.

Semantic events, you recall, define events whose semantics make sense for a variety of components that can be quite different in nature. The component firing the event defines the exact semantics. Component events, on the other hand, only make sense for specific types of components.

I have chosen to introduce all the AWT event types together, followed by the Swing event types. I might have chosen a different presentation approach, completely separating component and semantic events, regardless of their AWT or Swing packaging.

However, that organization might be potentially confusing because the derivation of an event type does not indicate which components generate it. For example, although four of the Swing event types derive from AWT events, they are still only generated by Swing components.

Pragmatically, you need to understand what events can be generated by the components you use in your applications. Because, realistically, you will create Java programs that use either AWT or Swing components, I have chosen to group the presentation of event type according to the components that fire them.

9

EVENTS AND
EVENT HANDLING

Ancestor Events

Ancestor events are described by the `javax.swing.event.AncestorEvent` class. An `AncestorListener` can register to receive these events. Table 9.16 lists the methods of the `AncestorListener` interface.

TABLE 9.16 `AncestorListener` Methods

AncestorListener *method*	*Description*
void ancestorAdded (AncestorEvent event)	Indicates to the listener that the source component or one of its ancestors is made visible either by a call to `setVisible(true)` or by its being added to the component hierarchy.
void ancestorMoved (AncestorEvent event)	Indicates to the listener that the source or one of its ancestors is moved.
void ancestorRemoved (AncestorEvent event)	Indicates to the listener that the source or one of its ancestors is made invisible either by a call to the `setVisible(false)` method or by its being removed from the component hierarchy.

An `AncestorEvent` indicates that a change has occurred to a `JComponent` or one of its ancestors. For instance, the program in Listing 9.21 toggles the visibility of a panel in a container.

When the panel is hidden, the `ancestorRemoved()` method is called on the event listener. When it's made visible again, the `ancestorAdded()` is called. Granted, these method names are misleading because you are only changing the visibility, not actually adding and removing the component from its container.

If you move the native frame that holds your application, you see evidence of `ancestorMoved()` method invocations on the console.

Your application initially looks like Figure 9.15. A black border surrounds the disappearing panel. After clicking the button, your panel is hidden—evidenced by the disappearance of the black border. Clicking a second time brings back the panel.

FIGURE 9.15
Ancestor events refer to the source component or its ancestors.

The AncestorEvent class defines three methods that enable you to discern details about the affected component. The getComponent method returns a JComponent, confirming my previous statement that only Swing components generate these events. Table 9.17 lists the methods of the AncestorEvent class.

TABLE 9.17 AncestorEvent Methods

AncestorEvent *method*	*Description*
Container getAncestor()	Returns the ancestor that is the actual event source
Container getAncestorParent()	Returns the parent of the ancestor that is the actual event source
JComponent getComponent()	Returns the component to which the listener was added

Caret Events

A *caret* indicates the position within a text document between two textual elements. It indicates where the next input event will occur—for instance, where the next key stroke character will be inserted or deleted.

A CaretEvent is the occurrence of a change to the position of the caret in a text document. It makes sense that only text components generate these events; and, consequently, only JTextComponent subclasses can be the source of CaretEvents.

The CaretEvent class defines two pieces of information related to caret positioning, a *dot* and a *mark*. The two methods defined by the CaretEvent class, getDot() and getMark() return the values of these two quantities, respectively.

The dot represents the current position of the caret itself. The mark represents another logical position in the text document. It anchors a *logical selection* called a *region*, which contains the characters between the dot and mark (included).

In Swing text components, you can select a region by dragging the mouse. The position of the mark will be at the beginning of the drag, and the dot will be at the position where the drag ends.

Figure 9.16 shows the initial state of a simple text field. Listing 9.21 shows the source code. The event listener prints the position of the dot and mark in response to each caret event. If you simply click the mouse within the text field, the dot and mark are at the same position.

```
The mark is at position 2
The dot is at position 2

The mark is at position 20
The dot is at position 20
```

9

EVENTS AND
EVENT HANDLING

However, if you drag the mouse, the text component highlights the region you've selected, as shown in Figure 9.17, and you see the output from your listener showing that the dot and mark are at different positions.

```
The mark is at position 6
The dot is at position 24
```

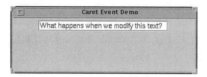

FIGURE 9.16
Swing text components generate CaretEvents.

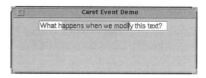

FIGURE 9.17
Dragging the mouse selects a region, which results in a CaretEvent *that has different values for its dot and mark.*

LISTING 9.21 Registering a CaretListener with a JTextField

```java
import java.awt.*;
import java.awt.event.*;

import javax.swing.*;
import javax.swing.event.*;


public class CaretEventDemo extends JPanel
{
  public CaretEventDemo()
  {
    String str = "What happens when we modify this text?";
    JTextField textField = new JTextField(str, 25);
    textField.setFont(new Font("SansSerif", Font.PLAIN, 14));

    CaretListener cL = new CaretMonitor();

    // Add a listener for CaretEvents.
    textField.addCaretListener(cL);
```

```
      add(textField);
    }

    public Dimension getPreferredSize()
    {
      return new Dimension(390, 110);
    }

    public static void main(String [] args)
    {
      CaretEventDemo app = new CaretEventDemo();

      JFrame f = new JFrame("Caret Event Demo");
      WindowListener wL = new WindowAdapter()
        {
          public void windowClosing(WindowEvent e)
            {
              e.getWindow().dispose();
              System.exit(0);
            }
        };
      f.addWindowListener(wL);

      f.getContentPane().add(app);
      f.pack();
      f.setVisible(true);
    }
}


class CaretMonitor implements CaretListener
{
  public void caretUpdate(CaretEvent e)
  {
    System.out.println("The mark is at position " + e.getMark());
    System.out.println("The dot is at position " + e.getDot());
    System.out.println();
  }
}
```

Change Events

A ChangeEvent represents a change to the state of a Swing component. Believe it or not, this is the only information provided by a ChangeEvent. The ChangeListener interface defines a single method, stateChanged(ChangeEvent) that is called on each ChangeListener object in response to a change on the source component.

Change events are arguably the most generic of all semantic events. Potentially, any component that has state can be defined to fire change events when its state changes. This contrasts with the definition of other semantic events.

For example, item events (which were introduced earlier) indicate a change to the item selected in components that present a visual representation of a collection, such as the AWT `Checkbox`, `CheckboxMenuItem`, or `List` components. It only makes sense to fire item events from components that aggregate various items, whereas change events simply define the notion of state.

Figure 9.18 shows a slider used to fire change events when the position of its thumb is moved. The thumb position defines the state of the slider at any given moment.

When a change event fires, it only tells listeners the event source. Listeners must query the source directly to obtain precise state information.

The `ChangeMonitor` class in Listing 9.22 does just that. Clicking on various parts of the slider's scale repositions the thumb, generating events. The listener prints the current position of the scrollbar after it has stopped adjusting:

```
Slider value is now 32
Slider value is now 33
Slider value is now 56
Slider value is now 7
Slider value is now 8
Slider value is now 9
Slider value is now 10
```

FIGURE 9.18

Change events are perhaps the most generic semantic event. They simply indicate that a change has occurred to the component which generated the event. No further specific information is available.

LISTING 9.22   Registering a `ChangeListener` with a `JSlider`

```
import java.awt.*;
import java.awt.event.*;

import javax.swing.*;
import javax.swing.event.*;


public class ChangeEventDemo extends JPanel
{
```

```
public ChangeEventDemo()
{
  JSlider slider = new JSlider(JSlider.HORIZONTAL, 0, 100, 50);
  slider.setPreferredSize(new Dimension(350, 50));
  slider.setSnapToTicks(true);
  slider.setMajorTickSpacing(10);
  slider.setMinorTickSpacing(5);
  slider.setPaintTicks(true);
  slider.setPaintLabels(true);

  ChangeListener cL = new ChangeMonitor();

  // Add a listener for ChangeEvents.
  slider.addChangeListener(cL);

  add(slider);
}

public Dimension getPreferredSize()
{
  return new Dimension(390, 110);
}

public static void main(String [] args)
{
  ChangeEventDemo app = new ChangeEventDemo();

  JFrame f = new JFrame("Change Event Demo");
  WindowListener wL = new WindowAdapter()
    {
      public void windowClosing(WindowEvent e)
        {
          e.getWindow().dispose();
          System.exit(0);
        }
    };
  f.addWindowListener(wL);

  f.getContentPane().add(app);
  f.pack();
  f.setVisible(true);
}
}


class ChangeMonitor implements ChangeListener
{
```

continues

LISTING 9.22   Continued

```
public void stateChanged(ChangeEvent e)
{
  JSlider source = (JSlider) e.getSource();

  if (source.getValueIsAdjusting())
    return;

  System.out.println("Slider value is now " + source.getValue());
  }
}
```

Hyperlink Events

Hyperlink events are generated when an HTTP hypertext link is updated. *Updated* is a somewhat confusing term. Actually, hyperlink events are generated when links are entered, exited, or activated.

The JEditorPane component is the only one that currently fires the HyperlinkEvent. If you recall from Chapter 7, "The Swing Components," JEditorPanes can display an HTML page. Figure 9.19 shows a JEditorPane that displays an HTML page with a hypertext link. This is almost the same example used in Chapter 7, but it has a HyperlinkListener added to the editor pane. Listing 9.23 shows the source code. Listing 9.24 shows the HTML file that generates HyperlinkEvents in a JEditorPane.

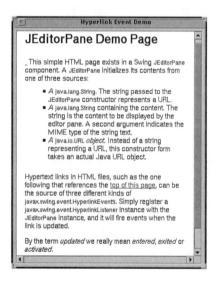

FIGURE 9.19

The JEditorPane class fires hyperlink events to registered listeners when a hypertext link in its displayed page is updated.

LISTING 9.23 Registering a `HyperlinkListener` with a `JEditorPane`

```java
import java.awt.*;
import java.awt.event.*;
import java.io.*;
import java.net.URL;

import javax.swing.*;
import javax.swing.event.*;

class HyperlinkEventDemo extends JPanel
{

  public HyperlinkEventDemo()
  {
    JEditorPane editorPane = new JEditorPane();
    JScrollPane scrollPane = new JScrollPane(editorPane);
    scrollPane.setPreferredSize(new Dimension(400, 485));
    scrollPane.setVerticalScrollBarPolicy(
                JScrollPane.VERTICAL_SCROLLBAR_ALWAYS);
    scrollPane.setHorizontalScrollBarPolicy(
                JScrollPane.HORIZONTAL_SCROLLBAR_ALWAYS);
    editorPane.setEditable(false);

    // Add a HyperlinkListener to the JEditorPane.
    //
    HyperlinkListener hyperlinkEventMonitor = new
      HyperlinkEventMonitor();

    // Add the hyperlink listener to our editor pane.
    //
    editorPane.addHyperlinkListener(hyperlinkEventMonitor);

    try
      {
        // To run this application you will need to point
        // this url to a location on your system.  Place
        // the "editor-pane-demo.html" file in a
        // location on your local file system.
        URL url = new
          URL("file:/home/vartan/dev/book/ch7/editor-pane-demo.html");
        editorPane.setPage(url);
      }
    catch (Exception e)
      {

      }
```

9

EVENTS AND
EVENT HANDLING

continues

LISTING 9.23   Continued

```java
      Box box = Box.createVerticalBox();
      box.add(scrollPane);
      add(box);
  }

  public static void main(String [] args)
  {
    JFrame f = new JFrame("Hyperlink Event Demo");
    WindowListener wL = new WindowAdapter()
      {
        public void windowClosing(WindowEvent e)
          {
            e.getWindow().dispose();
            System.exit(0);
          }
      };
    f.addWindowListener(wL);

    HyperlinkEventDemo app = new HyperlinkEventDemo();
    f.getContentPane().add(app);
    f.pack();
    f.setVisible(true);
  }
}


class HyperlinkEventMonitor implements HyperlinkListener
{
  public void hyperlinkUpdate(HyperlinkEvent e)
  {
    System.out.println("HyperlinkEvent: ");
    System.out.println("Link description: " + e.getDescription());
    System.out.println("Event type: " + e.getEventType());
    System.out.println("URL: " + e.getDescription());
    System.out.println();
  }
}
```

LISTING 9.24 An HTML File with a HyperLink That Generates HyperlinkEvents in a
JEditorPane

```
<!DOCTYPE HTML PUBLIC "-//IETF//DTD HTML//EN">
<html>
<head>
<title>JEditorPane Demo Page</title>
</head>

<body>
<h1>JEditorPane Demo Page</h1>

<a name=top></a>

This simple HTML page exists in a Swing <code>JEditorPane</code>
component.  A <code>JEditorPane</code> initializes its contents from
one of three sources:

<ul>

<li><em>A</em> <code>java.lang.String</code>. The string passed to the
<code>JEditorPane</code> constructor represents a URL.</li>

<li><em>A</em> <code>java.lang.String</code> containing the
content</em>.  The string is the content to be displayed by the editor
pane.  A second argument indicates the MIME type of the string
text.</li>

<li><em>A</em> <code>java.io.URL</code> <em>object</em>.  Instead of a
string representing a URL, this constructor form takes an actual Java
URL object.</li>

</ul>

<p>
Hypertext links in HTML files, such as the one following that
references the <a href=#top>top of this page</a>, can be the source of
three different kinds of
<code>javax.swing.event.HyperlinkEvent</code>s.  Simply register a
<code>javax.swing.event.HyperlinkListener</code> instance with the
<code>JEditorPane</code> instance, and it will fire events when the
link is updated.
```

continues

9

EVENTS AND
EVENT HANDLING

LISTING 9.24 Continued

```
<p>
By the term <em>updated</em> we really mean <em>entered</em>,
<em>exited</em> or <em>activated</em>.

<br>
<br>

<hr>
</body>
</html>
```

The `HyperlinkListener` interface defines only one method,
`hyperlinkUpdate(HyperlinkEvent)`. The `HyperlinkEvent` class defines three methods, shown
in Table 9.18.

TABLE 9.18 The `HyperlinkEvent` Class

HyperlinkEvent *method name*	*Description*
`String getDescription()`	Gets a string description of the link
`HyperlinkEvent.EventType getEventType()`	Gets the type of the hyperlink event, namely ACTIVATED, ENTERED, or EXITED
`URL getURL()`	Gets the URL referred to by the activated link

Incidentally, the `HyperlinkEvent.EventType` type specification is an example of an inner class
definition. The `EventType` class is an inner class of `HyperlinkEvent`. The `javadoc` utility generates a qualified name in order to unambiguously refer to the `EventType` in `HyperlinkEvent`.
There might very well be another class named `EventType` defined elsewhere.

When you click on the hypertext link in your editor pane, your listener prints out

```
HyperlinkEvent:
Link description: #top
Event type: ACTIVATED
URL: #top
```

indicating that the editor pane fired the event. It also prints out some additional information for
the purposes of illustration.

Internal Frame Events

The `InternalFrameEvent` event defines changes to an internal frame. Based on its name, it
probably doesn't surprise you that the only Swing component that fires the
`InternalFrameEvent` is `JInternalFrame`.

Table 9.19 lists the different types of changes that are accounted for by the `InternalFrameEvent` class. These constants correspond to the methods in the `InternalFrameListener` interface, which is listed in Table 9.20.

TABLE 9.19 The `InternalFrameEvent` Class

`InternalFrameEvent` *constants and methods*	*Description*
`int INTERNAL_FRAME_ACTIVATED`	The window activated event type
`int INTERNAL_FRAME_CLOSED`	The window closed event
`int INTERNAL_FRAME_CLOSING`	The "window is closing" event
`int INTERNAL_FRAME_DEACTIVATED`	The window deactivated event type
`int INTERNAL_FRAME_DEICONIFIED`	The window deiconified event type
`int INTERNAL_FRAME_FIRST`	The first number in the range of IDs used for window events
`int INTERNAL_FRAME_ICONIFIED`	The window iconified event
`int INTERNAL_FRAME_LAST`	The last number in the range of IDs used for window events
`int INTERNAL_FRAME_OPENED`	The window opened event
`String paramString()`	Returns a parameter string identifying this event

TABLE 9.20 The `InternalFrameListener` Interface

`InternalFrameListener` *method name*	*Description*
`void internalFrameActivated (InternalFrameEvent e)`	Invoked on listeners when an internal frame is activated
`void internalFrameClosed (InternalFrameEvent e)`	Invoked on listeners in response to an internal frame being closed
`void internalFrameClosing (InternalFrameEvent e)`	Invoked on listeners in response to an internal frame being closed
`void internalFrameDeactivated (InternalFrameEvent e)`	Invoked on listeners when an internal frame is deactivated
`void internalFrameDeiconified (InternalFrameEvent e)`	Invoked on listeners in response to an internal frame being deiconified
`void internalFrameIconified (InternalFrameEvent e)`	Invoked on listeners as a result of an internal frame being iconified
`void internalFrameOpened (InternalFrameEvent e)`	Invoked on listeners when an internal frame has been opened

9

EVENTS AND
EVENT HANDLING

Figure 9.20 shows three internal frames in a JPanel. You register the same listener to listen for InternalFrameEvents on all three internal frames. Initially, all the frames are inactive. You can reposition, resize, or activate, any of the frames and generate InternalFrameEvents.

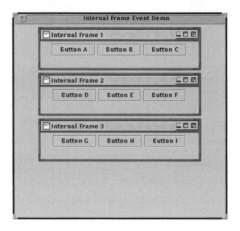

FIGURE 9.20

The three internal frames all have a registered InternalFrameListener. *Any manipulation of the frame causes this event to fire.*

Listing 9.25 lists the demo program.

LISTING 9.25 Registering an InternalFrameListener with a JInternalFrame

```java
import java.awt.*;
import java.awt.event.*;

import javax.swing.*;
import javax.swing.event.*;


public class InternalFrameEventDemo extends JPanel
{
  public InternalFrameEventDemo()
  {
    JInternalFrame iF1 = new JInternalFrame("Internal Frame 1", true, true,
                                            true, true);
    iF1.setPreferredSize(new Dimension(350, 90));
    Container contentPane = iF1.getContentPane();
    contentPane.setLayout(new FlowLayout());
    contentPane.add(new JButton("Button A"));
    contentPane.add(new JButton("Button B"));
    contentPane.add(new JButton("Button C"));
```

```
    JInternalFrame iF2 = new JInternalFrame("Internal Frame 2", true, true,
                                            true, true);
    iF2.setPreferredSize(new Dimension(350, 90));
    contentPane = iF2.getContentPane();
    contentPane.setLayout(new FlowLayout());
    contentPane.add(new JButton("Button D"));
    contentPane.add(new JButton("Button E"));
    contentPane.add(new JButton("Button F"));

    JInternalFrame iF3 = new JInternalFrame("Internal Frame 3", true, true,
                                            true, true);
    iF3.setPreferredSize(new Dimension(350, 90));
    contentPane = iF3.getContentPane();
    contentPane.setLayout(new FlowLayout());
    contentPane.add(new JButton("Button G"));
    contentPane.add(new JButton("Button H"));
    contentPane.add(new JButton("Button I"));

    // Create an internal frame event listener.
    InternalFrameListener fL = new InternalFrameMonitor();

    // Add this same listener as a listener on all three of
    // our internal frames.
    //
    iF1.addInternalFrameListener(fL);
    iF2.addInternalFrameListener(fL);
    iF3.addInternalFrameListener(fL);

    add(iF1);
    add(iF2);
    add(iF3);
  }

  public Dimension getPreferredSize()
  {
    return new Dimension(450, 400);
  }

  public static void main(String [] args)
  {
    InternalFrameEventDemo app = new InternalFrameEventDemo();

    JFrame f = new JFrame("Internal Frame Event Demo");
    WindowListener wL = new WindowAdapter()
      {
        public void windowClosing(WindowEvent e)
```

9

EVENTS AND
EVENT HANDLING

continues

LISTING 9.25   Continued

```java
        {
          e.getWindow().dispose();
          System.exit(0);
        }
      };
    f.addWindowListener(wL);

    f.getContentPane().add(app);
    f.pack();
    f.setVisible(true);
  }


}


class InternalFrameMonitor implements InternalFrameListener
{
  public void internalFrameActivated(InternalFrameEvent e)
  {
    JInternalFrame f = (JInternalFrame) e.getSource();
    System.out.println(e.paramString());
  }

  public void internalFrameClosed(InternalFrameEvent e)
  {
    JInternalFrame f = (JInternalFrame) e.getSource();
    System.out.println("Frame \"" + f.getTitle() + "\" closed.");
    System.out.println();
  }

  public void internalFrameClosing(InternalFrameEvent e)
  {
    JInternalFrame f = (JInternalFrame) e.getSource();
    System.out.println("Frame \"" + f.getTitle() + "\" closing.");
    System.out.println();
  }

  public void internalFrameDeactivated(InternalFrameEvent e)
  {
    JInternalFrame f = (JInternalFrame) e.getSource();
    System.out.println("Frame \"" + f.getTitle() + "\" deactivated.");
    System.out.println();
  }
```

```
  public void internalFrameDeiconified(InternalFrameEvent e)
  {
    JInternalFrame f = (JInternalFrame) e.getSource();
    System.out.println("Frame '" + f.getTitle() + "' de-iconified.");
    System.out.println();
  }

  public void internalFrameIconified(InternalFrameEvent e)
  {
    JInternalFrame f = (JInternalFrame) e.getSource();
    System.out.println("Frame '" + f.getTitle() + "' iconified.");
    System.out.println();
  }

  public void internalFrameOpened(InternalFrameEvent e)
  {
    JInternalFrame f = (JInternalFrame) e.getSource();
    System.out.println("Frame '" + f.getTitle() + "' opened.");
    System.out.println();
  }
}
```

You might recall from Table 6.4 in Chapter 6, "Swing Concepts and Architecture," that the JInternalFrame class was one of the five Swing containers that use a JRootPane container. Looking at the constructor in Listing 9.25, you see the following code:

```
JInternalFrame iF1 = new JInternalFrame("Internal Frame 1", true, true,
                                        true, true);
    iF1.setPreferredSize(new Dimension(350, 90));
    Container contentPane = iF1.getContentPane();
    contentPane.setLayout(new FlowLayout());
    contentPane.add(new JButton("Button A"));
    contentPane.add(new JButton("Button B"));
    contentPane.add(new JButton("Button C"));
```

As a point of review, notice that the layout manager is set on the content pane of the JInternalFrame before you add the buttons to it. You do not set the layout manager of the JInternalFrame itself, because doing that would get rid of the JRootPane instance. Do the same for all three of your JInternalFrame instances.

List Data Events

Earlier in the introductory section on Swing event types I stated that the Swing tool set introduces the concept of events that can be fired by models. By contrast, AWT events—and most of the Swing events—are fired only by components.

I briefly mentioned the notion that models are objects that represent a particular data abstraction, often a data structure that is well-known to computer science and frequently used in programming.

The `ListDataEvent` is the first of these new Swing events that are fired not by Swing components, but by Swing models. The `ListDataListener` interface must be implemented by any objects that wish to listen for `ListDataEvents`. This interface defines three methods, shown in Table 9.21.

TABLE 9.21   `ListDataListener` **Methods**

`ListDataListener` method name	Description
`void contentsChanged` `(ListDataEvent e)`	Invoked on listeners when the content of the list changes in a complex way that can't be more precisely characterized by the other methods in this interface.
`void intervalAdded` `(ListDataEvent e)`	Invoked in response to a change in the indices index0 and index1. These indices indicate the beginning and end of the interval that was added.
`void intervalRemoved` `(ListDataEvent e)`	Invoked in response to a removal of an interval. The index0 and index1 indices represent the beginning and end of the interval that was removed from the data model.

The `ListDataEvent` class represents the different possible types of changes to a list model. Essentially, one can add or remove members from a list. If either of these two actions occurs in a way that is too complex to be characterized by the interface, the list object can call the `contentsChanged` method.

Table 9.22 lists the members of the `ListDataEvent` class.

TABLE 9.22   The `ListDataEvent` **Class**

`ListDataEvent` *constants and methods*	Description
`int getIndex0()`	Returns the lower index of the interval involved in the event
`int getIndex1()`	Returns the upper index of the interval involved in the event
`int getType()`	Returns the type of the event, either `CONTENTS_CHANGED`, `INTERVAL_ADDED`, or `INTERVAL_REMOVED`

Table 9.22 indicates that the `ListDataEvent` is only fired by the `AbstractListModel` and the `DefaultListModel` types.

The DefaultListModel is a concrete implementation that defines objects that store a list of items. When an item is added or removed from the list object, it fires a ListDataEvent to all registered ListDataListeners.

Unfortunately, a DefaultListModel is a model, not a GUI component; it has no visual representation. To make a meaningful demo you have to take one or two extra steps.

Figure 9.21 shows your demo program upon startup. You include two buttons in your demo that add or remove, respectively, items from a DefaultListModel object. The buttons each have a registered ActionListener that responds by adding or removing, respectively, an item from the list. Listing 9.26 shows the demo program source code.

The two action listeners do different things; one adds and one removes elements from the list object. Instead of defining two separate classes that implement ActionListener, you use two anonymous inner class definitions to easily accomplish the same thing with less coding.

FIGURE 9.21

The add and remove buttons add or remove an item from the combo box. This lets you visually represent the changes occurring to your DefaultListModel object.

The list in turn fires a ListDataEvent to its listeners. In your demo, the listener simply prints some information to the console about the list data event.

To make it easier to see what's happening, make your buttons' ActionListeners pop up the JComboBox's pop-up window after each addition or removal.

After a few additions, your GUI looks like Figure 9.22.

Your ListDataListener prints information about each ListDataEvent as follows:

```
Adding interval:    Index0 = 10
                    Index1 = 10

Adding interval:    Index0 = 11
                    Index1 = 11
```

```
Removing interval: Index0 = 11
                   Index1 = 11

Removing interval: Index0 = 10
                   Index1 = 10
```

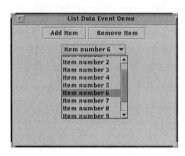

FIGURE 9.22

The combo box pops up after each insertion or deletion to show the user the results of each button click.

LISTING 9.26   Registering a `ListDataListener` with a `ListModel`

```java
import java.awt.*;
import java.awt.event.*;

import javax.swing.*;
import javax.swing.event.*;


public class ListDataEventDemo extends JPanel
{
  public ListDataEventDemo()
  {
    JPanel compPanel = createCompPanel();
    JPanel buttonPanel = createButtonPanel();

    ListDataListener ldl = new ListDataMonitor();

    defaultListModel = new DefaultListModel();
    defaultListModel.addListDataListener(ldl);

    setLayout(new BorderLayout());
    add(buttonPanel, BorderLayout.NORTH);
    add(compPanel, BorderLayout.CENTER);
  }
```

```
JPanel createCompPanel()
{
  comboBox = new JComboBox();

  JPanel p = new JPanel();
  p.add(comboBox);

  return p;
}


JPanel createButtonPanel()
{
  JButton addItem = createAddButton();
  JButton removeItem = createRemoveButton();

  JPanel p = new JPanel();
  p.add(addItem);
  p.add(removeItem);

  return p;
}


JButton createAddButton()
{
  JButton b = new JButton("Add Item");

  ActionListener aL = new ActionListener()
    {
      public void actionPerformed(ActionEvent e)
        {
          String str = "Item number " + Integer.toString(lastValue++, 10);
          defaultListModel.addElement(str);
          comboBox.addItem(str);
          comboBox.showPopup();
        }
    };
  b.addActionListener(aL);

  return b;
}


JButton createRemoveButton()
```

9

EVENTS AND
EVENT HANDLING

continues

LISTING 9.26   Continued

```java
{
  JButton b = new JButton("Remove Item");

  ActionListener aL = new ActionListener()
    {
      public void actionPerformed(ActionEvent e)
        {
          defaultListModel.removeElementAt(--lastValue);
          comboBox.removeItemAt(lastValue);
          comboBox.showPopup();
        }
    };
  b.addActionListener(aL);

  return b;
}


public Dimension getPreferredSize()
{
  return new Dimension(350, 250);
}


public static void main(String [] args)
{
  ListDataEventDemo app = new ListDataEventDemo();

  JFrame f = new JFrame("List Data Event Demo");
  WindowListener wL = new WindowAdapter()
    {
      public void windowClosing(WindowEvent e)
        {
          e.getWindow().dispose();
          System.exit(0);
        }
    };
  f.addWindowListener(wL);

  f.getContentPane().add(app);
  f.pack();
  f.setVisible(true);
}
```

```
  DefaultListModel defaultListModel;

  int lastValue;

  JComboBox comboBox;
}


class ListDataMonitor implements ListDataListener
{
  public void contentsChanged(ListDataEvent e)
  {
    System.out.println("Contents changed.");
    System.out.println("Index0 = " + e.getIndex0());
    System.out.println("Index1 = " + e.getIndex1());
    System.out.println();
  }

  public void intervalAdded(ListDataEvent e)
  {
    System.out.println("Adding interval:   Index0 = " + e.getIndex0());
    System.out.println("                   Index1 = " + e.getIndex1());
    System.out.println();
  }

  public void intervalRemoved(ListDataEvent e)
  {
    System.out.println("Removing interval: Index0 = " + e.getIndex0());
    System.out.println("                   Index1 = " + e.getIndex1());
    System.out.println();
  }
}
```

List Selection Events

Like the ListDataEvent class, the ListSelectionEvent class represents changes to lists.
However, there are two important differences.

First of all, unlike the ListDataListener, the ListSelectionListener interface is implemented by at least one GUI component, JList, in addition to any non-GUI classes, such as the
DefaultListSelectionModel class.

Second, in contrast to the ListDataEvent, the ListSelectionEvent describes a change to the
list's selection. Table 9.23 lists the members of the ListSelectionEvent class.

TABLE 9.23 The ListSelectionEvent Class

ListSelectionEvent *methods*	*Description*
int getFirstIndex()	Returns the smallest value of any index that represents the position of an element that might have changed in the selection event
int getLastIndex()	Returns the greatest value of any index that represents the position of an element that might have changed in the selection event
boolean getValueIsAdjusting()	Returns true if the selection is currently changing, that is, if the component is generating a series of change events
String toString()	Returns a string that displays and identifies this object's properties

Figure 9.23 shows your list selection demo. You make selections to the list component by clicking one of its items. If you drag the mouse over several items, the list component generates a series of events and tags them as Adjusting, meaning it detects that the mouse is down and more selection events can be anticipated.

FIGURE 9.23

List *components can fire list selection events that notify listeners of a change in the component's selection.*

In your demo you don't want to print information about adjusting events, so you print only when the event is singular. Listing 9.27 shows the source code for your list selection demo.

LISTING 9.27 Registering a ListSelectionListener with a JList

```
import java.awt.*;
import java.awt.event.*;

import javax.swing.*;

import javax.swing.event.*;
```

```
public class ListSelectionEventDemo extends JPanel
{
  public ListSelectionEventDemo()
  {
    String [] listElements = {"Archery", "Badminton", "Cross-Country Skiing",
                              "Diving", "Golf", "Ice Hockey", "Lacrosse",
                              "Skiing", "Swimming", "Soccer", "Surfing",
                              "Tennis", "Water polo",
                              "Yoga"};

    JList list = new JList(listElements);
    list.setFont(new Font("sansserif", Font.PLAIN, 14));
    JScrollPane sp = new JScrollPane(list);

    ListSelectionListener lSL = new ListSelectionMonitor();

    // Add a list selection listener to the list, not to the
    // scroll pane.
    //
    list.addListSelectionListener(lSL);

    add(sp);
  }


  public Dimension getPreferredSize()
  {
    return new Dimension(280, 180);
  }


  public static void main(String [] args)
  {
    ListSelectionEventDemo app = new ListSelectionEventDemo();

    JFrame f = new JFrame("List Selection Event Demo");
    WindowListener wL = new WindowAdapter()
      {
        public void windowClosing(WindowEvent e)
          {
            e.getWindow().dispose();
            System.exit(0);
          }
      };
    f.addWindowListener(wL);
```

9

continues

LISTING 9.27 Continued

```
      f.getContentPane().add(app);
      f.pack();
      f.setVisible(true);
   }
}


class ListSelectionMonitor implements ListSelectionListener
{
  public void valueChanged(ListSelectionEvent e)
  {
    if (e.getValueIsAdjusting())
      return;

    System.out.println("First index = " + e.getFirstIndex());
    System.out.println("Last index  = " + e.getLastIndex());
    System.out.println();
  }

}
```

Menu Events

The `MenuEvent` class defines events that occur only on menus, which, of course, includes nested menus. Only the `JMenu` component class defines the `addMenuListener(MenuListener)` and `removeMenuListener(MenuListener)` methods. This precludes menu items that are not menus, such as simple strings, from registering event listeners.

The `MenuEvent` class doesn't define any methods or fields in addition to those defined in its direct superclass, `EventObject`.

Objects interested in listening for menu events from a menu must implement the `MenuListener` interface and register with a menu. The `MenuListener` interface, shown in Table 9.24, neatly captures the different actions that can occur on a menu. A menu can be selected, deselected, or canceled.

The only real information about menu events available to listeners is the particular variety of the event, which is conveyed by the specific method invoked on the listener.

TABLE 9.24   The MenuListener Interface

MenuListener *methods*	*Description*
void menuCanceled(MenuEvent e)	Invoked when the menu selection is canceled or deactivated
void menuDeselected(MenuEvent e)	Invoked when a menu item is deselected
void menuSelected(MenuEvent e)	Invoked in response to a menu item selection

Figure 9.24 shows an application that has three menus on its menu bar. It registers the same listener on all three of the top-level menus. The source code in Listing 9.28 comments the lines that add the listener to the different menus.

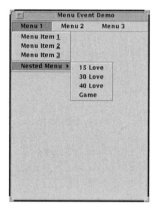

FIGURE 9.24

MenuListener *instances must register as menu listeners with menus.*

When a menu is activated the listener prints the name of the affected menu and the type of the event.

```
Menu "Menu 1" deselected
Menu "Menu 3" selected
Menu "Menu 3" deselected
Menu "Menu 2" selected
```

LISTING 9.28   Registering a MenuListener with a JMenu

```
import java.awt.*;
import java.awt.event.*;

import javax.swing.*;
import javax.swing.event.*;
```

continues

LISTING 9.28 Continued

```java
public class MenuKeyEventDemo extends JFrame
{
  public MenuKeyEventDemo()
  {
    super("Menu Event Demo");

    Container contentPane = getContentPane();

    Font f14 = new Font("SansSerif", Font.PLAIN, 14);
    Dimension dim = new Dimension(0, 10);

    JMenu menu1 = new JMenu("Menu 1");

    MenuMonitor menuMonitor = new MenuMonitor();

    // Add a listener for menu events to "Menu 1".
    //
    menu1.addMenuListener(menuMonitor);

    JMenuItem mi1 = new JMenuItem("Menu Item 1");
    mi1.setMnemonic('1');
    JMenuItem mi2 = new JMenuItem("Menu Item 2");
    mi2.setMnemonic('2');
    JMenuItem mi3 = new JMenuItem("Menu Item 3");
    mi3.setMnemonic('3');

    JMenu menu1_1 = new JMenu("Nested Menu");

    // Add a listener for menu events to the menu nested
    // under "Menu 1".
    //
    menu1_1.addMenuListener(menuMonitor);

    JMenuItem mi1_1 = new JMenuItem("15 Love");
    mi1_1.setHorizontalAlignment(SwingConstants.LEFT);
    JMenuItem mi1_2 = new JMenuItem("30 Love");
    JMenuItem mi1_3 = new JMenuItem("40 Love");
    JMenuItem mi1_4 = new JMenuItem("Game");

    menu1_1.add(mi1_1);
    menu1_1.add(mi1_2);
    menu1_1.add(mi1_3);
    menu1_1.add(mi1_4);
```

```
menu1.add(mi1);
menu1.add(mi2);
menu1.add(mi3);
menu1.addSeparator();
menu1.add(menu1_1);

JMenu menu2 = new JMenu("Menu 2");

// Add the same menu listener object that listens for
// events on menu "Menu 1" to "Menu 2".
//
menu2.addMenuListener(menuMonitor);

JMenu menu3 = new JMenu("Menu 3");

// Add the same menu listener object that listens for
// events on menu "Menu 1" to "Menu 3".
//
menu3.addMenuListener(menuMonitor);

JCheckBoxMenuItem cbmi1 = new JCheckBoxMenuItem("Check box 1");
JCheckBoxMenuItem cbmi2 = new JCheckBoxMenuItem("Check box 2");
JCheckBoxMenuItem cbmi3 = new JCheckBoxMenuItem("Check box 3");

menu2.add(cbmi1);
menu2.add(cbmi2);
menu2.add(cbmi3);
menu2.addSeparator();

JRadioButtonMenuItem rbmi1 = new JRadioButtonMenuItem("Radio 1");
JRadioButtonMenuItem rbmi2 = new JRadioButtonMenuItem("Radio 2");
JRadioButtonMenuItem rbmi3 = new JRadioButtonMenuItem("Radio 3");

ButtonGroup bg = new ButtonGroup();
bg.add(rbmi1);
bg.add(rbmi2);
bg.add(rbmi3);

menu2.add(rbmi1);
menu2.add(rbmi2);
menu2.add(rbmi3);

JMenuBar menuBar = new JMenuBar();

menuBar.add(menu1);
```

9

EVENTS AND
EVENT HANDLING

continues

LISTING 9.28   Continued

```java
    menuBar.add(menu2);
    menuBar.add(menu3);

    setJMenuBar(menuBar);
  }


  public Dimension getPreferredSize()
  {
    return new Dimension(300, 400);
  }


  public static void main(String [] args)
  {
    MenuKeyEventDemo app = new MenuKeyEventDemo();
    WindowListener wL = new WindowAdapter()
      {
        public void windowClosing(WindowEvent e)
          {
            e.getWindow().dispose();
            System.exit(0);
          }
      };
    app.addWindowListener(wL);

    app.pack();
    app.setVisible(true);
  }
}

class MenuMonitor implements MenuListener
{
  public void menuCanceled(MenuEvent e)
  {
    System.out.println("Menu \"" + ((JMenu) e.getSource()).getText() +
                      "\" canceled");
  }


  public void menuDeselected(MenuEvent e)
  {
    System.out.println("Menu \"" + ((JMenu) e.getSource()).getText() +
                      "\" deselected");
  }
```

```
  public void menuSelected(MenuEvent e)
  {
    System.out.println("Menu \"" + ((JMenu) e.getSource()).getText() +
                        "\" selected");
  }
}


class MenuKeyMonitor implements MenuKeyListener
{
  public void menuKeyPressed(MenuKeyEvent e)
  {
    System.out.println("MenuKeyEvent: Menu key pressed.");
    System.out.println("Menu item path: " + e.getPath().toString());
    System.out.println();
  }


  public void menuKeyReleased(MenuKeyEvent e)
  {
    System.out.println("MenuKeyEvent: Menu key released.");
    System.out.println("Menu item path: " + e.getPath().toString());
    System.out.println();
  }


  public void menuKeyTyped(MenuKeyEvent e)
  {
    System.out.println("MenuKeyEvent: Menu key typed.");
    System.out.println("Menu item path: " + e.getPath().toString());
    System.out.println();
  }
}


class MenuDragMouseEventMonitor implements MenuDragMouseListener
{
  public void menuDragMouseDragged(MenuDragMouseEvent e)
  {
    System.out.println("MenuDragMouseEvent: Menu drag mouse dragged.");
    System.out.println("Menu item path: " + e.getPath().toString());
    System.out.println();
  }


  public void menuDragMouseEntered(MenuDragMouseEvent e)
```

continues

LISTING 9.28 Continued

```
{
  System.out.println("MenuDragMouseEvent: Menu drag mouse entered.");
  System.out.println("Menu item path: " + e.getPath().toString());
  System.out.println();
}


public void menuDragMouseExited(MenuDragMouseEvent e)
{
  System.out.println("MenuDragMouseEvent: Menu drag mouse exited.");
  System.out.println("Menu item path: " + e.getPath().toString());
  System.out.println();
}


public void menuDragMouseReleased(MenuDragMouseEvent e)
{
  System.out.println("MenuDragMouseEvent: Menu drag mouse released.");
  System.out.println("Menu item path: " + e.getPath().toString());
  System.out.println();
}
}
```

Pop-up Menu Events

The PopupMenuEvent is used to convey information about the occurrence of a JPopupMenu being popped up. Listeners that wish to register to receive pop-up event notifications must implement the PopupMenuListener interface, the members of which are listed in Table 9.25.

TABLE 9.25 The PopupMenuListener Interface

PopupMenuListener *method name*	*Description*
void popupMenuCanceled (PopupMenuEvent e)	Invoked on listeners when the pop-up menu source is canceled
void popupMenuWillBecome Invisible(PopupMenuEvent e)	Invoked on listeners before the pop-up menu becomes invisible
void popupMenuWillBecome Visible(PopupMenuEvent e)	Called before the pop-up menu becomes visible

The `PopupMenuEvent` class doesn't define any methods or fields in addition to those of its `EventObject` superclass. The only information available, other than the source of the event, indicates the exact nature of the event. This is evident by the particular event listener method called.

To make a meaningful illustration, the demo in Listing 9.29 listens for button clicks to indicate when the display of the pop-up menu should be toggled. You use the technique introduced earlier. Listing 9.29 registers an `ActionListener` for button clicks on the main application container so that the user can control the appearance of the pop-up menu.

If the pop-up menu is visible, the action listener closes it; if it is closed, the action listener makes it visible. Another listener, the `PopupMenuListener`, listens for all events on the pop-up menu and prints some information to the console.

LISTING 9.29   Registering a `PopupMenuListener` with a `JPopupMenu`

```
import java.awt.*;
import java.awt.event.*;

import javax.swing.*;
import javax.swing.event.*;


public class PopupMenuEventDemo extends JPanel
{
  public PopupMenuEventDemo()
  {
    final JPopupMenu popup = new JPopupMenu("Popup Menu");
    popup.setLabel("Popup Menu");
    popup.add(new JMenuItem("Menu item 1"));
    popup.add(new JMenuItem("Menu item 2"));
    popup.add(new JMenuItem("Menu item 3"));
    popup.addSeparator();
    popup.add(new JMenuItem("Menu item 4"));
    popup.add(new JMenuItem("Menu item 5"));
    popup.add(new JMenuItem("Menu item 6"));

    popup.setInvoker(this);

    PopupMenuListener pL = new PopupMenuMonitor();
    popup.addPopupMenuListener(pL);

    MouseListener mL = new MouseAdapter()
      {
        public void mouseClicked(MouseEvent e)
```

9

**EVENTS AND
EVENT HANDLING**

continues

LISTING 9.29   Continued

```
        {
          if (visible)
            {
              visible = false;
              popup.setVisible(false);
            }
          else
            {
              visible = true;
              popup.show(PopupMenuEventDemo.this, 60, 25);
            }
        }
    };
  addMouseListener(mL);

  add(popup);
}


public Dimension getPreferredSize()
{
  return new Dimension(282, 180);
}


public static void main(String [] args)
{
  PopupMenuEventDemo app = new PopupMenuEventDemo();

  JFrame f = new JFrame("Popup Event Demo");
  WindowListener wL = new WindowAdapter()
    {
      public void windowClosing(WindowEvent e)
        {
          e.getWindow().dispose();
          System.exit(0);
        }
    };
  f.addWindowListener(wL);

  f.getContentPane().add(app);
  f.pack();
  f.setVisible(true);
}

  boolean visible;
}
```

```
class PopupMenuMonitor implements PopupMenuListener
{
  public void popupMenuCanceled(PopupMenuEvent e)
  {
    System.out.println("Popup menu canceled.");
  }


  public void popupMenuWillBecomeInvisible(PopupMenuEvent e)
  {
    System.out.println("Popup menu will become invisible.");
  }


  public void popupMenuWillBecomeVisible(PopupMenuEvent e)
  {
    System.out.println("Popup menu will become visible.");
  }
}
```

Figure 9.25 shows the application container after startup. After clicking in the container, the pop-up menu appears as in Figure 9.26. The JPopupMenu fires the events before the menu changes visibility, hence the names of the methods in the PopupMenuListener interface.

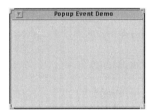

FIGURE 9.25
The application listens for mouse clicks as an indication to change the disposition of the pop-up menu. A separate listener handles the PopupMenuEvent*s.*

FIGURE 9.26
The application makes the pop-up menu visible after the first mouse click.

9

EVENTS AND
EVENT HANDLING

Tree Expansion Events

The TreeExpansionEvent is the first of three tree-related event types. Occurrences of TreeExpansionEvents cause two kinds of listeners to be notified by the event source—namely, listeners that implement either the TreeExpansionListener or TreeWillExpandListener interfaces.

The javax.swing.JTree component is the only component that supports listeners of either type to register for the TreeExpansionEvent.

From Tables 9.26 and 9.27 you can see that these listeners are closely related. One enables a tree component to notify listeners before a tree node is expanded or collapsed, whereas the other notifies listeners after the fact.

TABLE 9.26   The TreeExpansionListener Interface

TreeExpansionListener method name	Description
void treeCollapsed (TreeExpansionEvent event)	Invoked in response to the collapse of an item in the tree
void treeExpanded (TreeExpansionEvent event)	Invoked in response to the expansion of an item in the tree

TABLE 9.27   The TreeWillExpandListener Interface

TreeWillExpandListener method name	Description
void treeWillCollapse (TreeExpansionEvent event)	Invoked before a tree node is actually collapsed
void treeWillExpand (TreeExpansionEvent event)	Invoked before a tree node is expanded

The TreeExpansionEvent has a single method, TreePath getPath, which returns the path from the root of the tree to the node that is affected.

Listing 9.30 shows how to use both the TreeExpansionListener and TreeWillExpandListener interfaces to listen for and handle TreeExpansionEvents.

LISTING 9.30 Registering Listeners for Tree-Related Events with a `JTree`

```java
import java.awt.*;
import java.awt.event.*;
import java.util.*;
import javax.swing.*;
import javax.swing.tree.*;
import javax.swing.event.*;

class TreeEventDemo extends JPanel
{

  public TreeEventDemo()
  {
    TreeExpansionEventMonitor expansionMonitor = new
      TreeExpansionEventMonitor();

    TreeModelListener treeModelEventMonitor = new
      TreeModelEventMonitor();

    DefaultMutableTreeNode travelPlaces = new
      DefaultMutableTreeNode("Favorite Places to Travel");

    JTree tree = new JTree(travelPlaces);

    // Add a TreeExpansionEvent listener.
    //
    tree.addTreeExpansionListener(expansionMonitor);

    // Create sub-menu "France"
    //
    DefaultMutableTreeNode france = new
      DefaultMutableTreeNode("France");

    DefaultMutableTreeNode paris = new
      DefaultMutableTreeNode("Paris");

    DefaultMutableTreeNode lyon = new
      DefaultMutableTreeNode("Lyon");

    DefaultMutableTreeNode stMalo = new
      DefaultMutableTreeNode("St. Malo");

    france.add(paris);
```

continues

LISTING 9.30   Continued

```java
france.add(lyon);
france.add(stMalo);

travelPlaces.add(france);

// Create sub-menu "Indian Ocean"
//
DefaultMutableTreeNode indianOcean = new
  DefaultMutableTreeNode("Indian Ocean Islands");

DefaultMutableTreeNode maldives = new
  DefaultMutableTreeNode("Maldives");

DefaultMutableTreeNode mauritius = new
  DefaultMutableTreeNode("Mauritius");

DefaultMutableTreeNode seychelles = new
  DefaultMutableTreeNode("Seychelles");

indianOcean.add(maldives);
indianOcean.add(mauritius);
indianOcean.add(seychelles);

travelPlaces.add(indianOcean);

// Create sub-menu U.S.
//
DefaultMutableTreeNode us = new
  DefaultMutableTreeNode("United States");

travelPlaces.add(us);

DefaultMutableTreeNode la = new
  DefaultMutableTreeNode("Los Angeles");

DefaultMutableTreeNode nb = new
  DefaultMutableTreeNode("Newport Beach");

DefaultMutableTreeNode sd = new
  DefaultMutableTreeNode("San Diego");

DefaultMutableTreeNode boston = new
  DefaultMutableTreeNode("Pt. Arina");
```

```
    us.add(la);
    us.add(nb);
    us.add(sd);
    us.add(boston);

    // Create sub-menu U.S. -> National Parks
    //
    DefaultMutableTreeNode parks = new
      DefaultMutableTreeNode("National Parks");

    DefaultMutableTreeNode yosemite = new
      DefaultMutableTreeNode("Yosemite");

    DefaultMutableTreeNode yellowstone = new
      DefaultMutableTreeNode("Yellowstone");

    DefaultMutableTreeNode shasta = new
      DefaultMutableTreeNode("Mt. Shasta");

    parks.add(yosemite);
    parks.add(yellowstone);
    parks.add(shasta);

    us.add(parks);

    // Add a TreeWillExpandListener.
    //
    //
    TreeWillExpandListener treeWillExpandMonitor = new
      TreeWillExpandEventMonitor();
    tree.addTreeWillExpandListener(treeWillExpandMonitor);

    tree.setPreferredSize(new Dimension(250, 360));
    tree.setFont(new Font("SansSerif", Font.PLAIN, 16));

    JScrollPane treePane = new JScrollPane(tree);
    treePane.setHorizontalScrollBarPolicy(
            JScrollPane.HORIZONTAL_SCROLLBAR_ALWAYS);
    treePane.setVerticalScrollBarPolicy(JScrollPane.VERTICAL_SCROLLBAR_ALWAYS);
//      treePane.setPreferredSize(new Dimension(300, 420));

    add(treePane);
  }
```

9

EVENTS AND
EVENT HANDLING

continues

LISTING 9.30   Continued

```java
public static void main(String [] args)
{
  TreeEventDemo app = new TreeEventDemo();

  JFrame f = new JFrame("Tree Event Demo");
  WindowListener wL = new WindowAdapter()
    {
      public void windowClosing(WindowEvent e)
        {
          e.getWindow().dispose();
          System.exit(0);
        }
    };
  f.addWindowListener(wL);

  f.getContentPane().add(app);
  f.pack();
  f.setVisible(true);
  }
}


class TreeExpansionEventMonitor implements TreeExpansionListener
{
  public void treeCollapsed(TreeExpansionEvent e)
  {
    TreePath path = e.getPath();

    System.out.println("TreeExpansionEvent: Tree collapsed.");
    System.out.println("---> " + path.toString());
    System.out.println();
  }

  public void treeExpanded(TreeExpansionEvent e)
  {
    TreePath path = e.getPath();

    System.out.println("TreeExpansionEvent: Tree expanded.");
    System.out.println("Number of path elements = " + path.getPathCount());
    System.out.println("---> " + path.toString());
    System.out.println();
  }
}
```

```
class TreeSelectionEventMonitor implements TreeSelectionListener
{
  public void valueChanged(TreeSelectionEvent e)
  {
    System.out.println("TreeSelectionEvent:");
    System.out.println("---> " + e.getPath().toString());
    System.out.println();
  }
}


class TreeWillExpandEventMonitor implements TreeWillExpandListener
{
  public void treeWillCollapse(TreeExpansionEvent e)
  {
    System.out.println("TreeExpansionEvent: Tree will collapse.");
    System.out.println("---> " + e.getPath().toString());
    System.out.println();
  }


  public void treeWillExpand(TreeExpansionEvent e)
  {
    System.out.println("TreeExpansionEvent: Tree will expand.");
    System.out.println("---> " + e.getPath().toString());
    System.out.println();
  }
}


class TreeModelEventMonitor implements TreeModelListener
{
  public void treeNodesChanged(TreeModelEvent e)
  {
    TreePath path = e.getTreePath();

    System.out.println("TreeModelEvent: Tree nodes changed");
    printTreePathInfo(path);
  }


  public void treeNodesInserted(TreeModelEvent e)
  {
    TreePath path = e.getTreePath();
    System.out.println("TreeModelEvent: Tree nodes inserted.");
```

continues

LISTING 9.30   Continued

```
    printTreePathInfo(path);
  }


  public void treeNodesRemoved(TreeModelEvent e)
  {
    TreePath path = e.getTreePath();

    System.out.println("TreeModelEvent: Tree nodes removed.");
    printTreePathInfo(path);
  }


  public void treeStructureChanged(TreeModelEvent e)
  {
    TreePath path = e.getTreePath();

    System.out.println("TreeModelEvent; Tree structure changed.");
    printTreePathInfo(path);
  }


  void printTreePathInfo(TreePath path)
  {
    System.out.println("Number of path elements = " + path.getPathCount());
    System.out.println("---> " + path.toString());
    System.out.println();
  }
}
```

Your demo program builds one tree. The following excerpt instantiates and registers two listeners on that tree, one of each type.

```
TreeExpansionEventMonitor expansionMonitor = new
    TreeExpansionEventMonitor();
  ...

  // Add a TreeExpansionEvent listener.
  //
  tree.addTreeExpansionListener(expansionMonitor);


  ...

  // Add a TreeWillExpandListener.
  //
```

```
//
TreeWillExpandListener treeWillExpandMonitor = new
  TreeWillExpandEventMonitor();

tree.addTreeWillExpandListener(treeWillExpandMonitor);
```

You choose to register your listeners with the topmost root of the tree displayed by your application, shown in Figure 9.27, instead of with some internal node of the tree. This way, any subtree that is expanded or collapsed will generate events for you to catch because it is part of tree with which you registered your listeners.

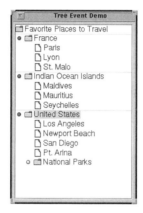

FIGURE 9.27
Double clicking any of the tree nodes (not the leaves) generates TreeExpansionEvents *and* TreeWillExpandEvents.

Double clicking on a leaf doesn't generate any events. However, double clicking on any nodes (subtrees) generates two TreeExpansionEvents. If the node is collapsing, then the two events are will collapse and has collapsed events. If it is expanding, you see will expand and has expanded events.

```
TreeExpansionEvent: Tree will collapse.
---> [Favorite Places to Travel, Indian Ocean Islands]

TreeExpansionEvent: Tree collapsed.
---> [Favorite Places to Travel, Indian Ocean Islands]

TreeExpansionEvent: Tree will expand.
---> [Favorite Places to Travel, United States, National Parks]

TreeExpansionEvent: Tree expanded.
Number of path elements = 3
---> [Favorite Places to Travel, United States, National Parks]
```

The `TreeExpansionEvent.getPath()` method returns the tree path to the affected node. You use the `toString()` method to print this path, which is a comma-separated list of the nodes that form the root to the affected node.

Tree Selection Events

The next type of tree event is the `TreeSelectionEvent`. From its name you can correctly surmise that this event type indicates changes to the selection of a tree.

The `TreeSelectionListener` interface that all `TreeSelectionEvent` listeners must implement defines only one method, `void valueChanged(TreeSelectionEvent)`.

The `TreeSelectionEvent` class contains several methods, shown in Table 9.28. The reason this event type is more complicated than the `TreeExpansionEvent` type is that the `JTree` component supports a range of selections to its elements.

Unlike expansion events, selection events can occur on nodes or leaves. You can select a range of tree elements by clicking on one and then another. The event object will store the new selection and the previous selection. The paths leading to these elements are retrieved by calling the `getNewLeadSelection()` and `getOldLeadSelection()` methods, respectively.

TABLE 9.28   The `TreeSelectionEvent` Class

TreeSelectionEvent *method name*	*Description*
`Object cloneWithSource (Object newSource)`	Creates a clone of the listener, registered as a listener on the new event source specified by newSource.
`TreePath getNewLeadSelectionPath()`	Returns the path which currently marks the beginning or lead of a selection range in the tree.
`TreePath getOldLeadSelectionPath()`	Returns the previous path which marked the beginning or lead of the selection range in the tree.
`TreePath getPath()`	Returns the first element in the path down to the currently affected tree element.
`TreePath[] getPaths()`	Returns all elements in the path down to the tree element affected in the tree selection event.
`boolean isAddedPath()`	Returns `true` if the first path element has been added to the selection, `false` if it has been removed. The first path element is the one furthest down the path to the current selection.
`boolean isAddedPath (TreePath path)`	Returns `true` if the specified path was added to the selection.

You can reuse your previous demo to experiment with TreeSelectionEvents. You first add a new class that implements TreeSelectionListener, shown in Listing 9.31. You can add the new class in Listing 9.31 to the file that contains Listing 9.30.

LISTING 9.31   A `TreeSelectionEventListener` Class

```
class TreeSelectionEventMonitor implements TreeSelectionListener
{
  public void valueChanged(TreeSelectionEvent e)
  {
    System.out.println("TreeSelectionEvent:");
    System.out.println("New lead selection path = ");
    System.out.println("---> " + e.getNewLeadSelectionPath().toString());
    System.out.println();

    TreePath path = e.getOldLeadSelectionPath();
    if (path != null)
      {
        System.out.println("Old lead selection path = ");
        System.out.println("---> " + path.toString());
        System.out.println();
      }
  }
}
```

Now you must add a listener for TreeSelectionEvents to your tree, which you do in your constructor.

```
    // Add a TreeSelectionListener that listens for changes in the
    // selection of tree nodes or leaves.  We can add this last
    // because this listener only listens for user selections.
    //
    TreeSelectionListener treeSelectionEventMonitor = new
      TreeSelectionEventMonitor();
    tree.addTreeSelectionListener(treeSelectionEventMonitor);
```

When you run your program, the event generated by the first button click has no information about the old selection path because there is no previous selection.

```
TreeExpansionEvent: Tree will expand.
---> [Favorite Places to Travel]

TreeExpansionEvent: Tree expanded.
Number of path elements = 1
---> [Favorite Places to Travel]
```

```
TreeSelectionEvent:
New lead selection path =
---> [Favorite Places to Travel, United States]
```

However, subsequent clicking does result in reporting of both a new selection and an old selection.

```
TreeSelectionEvent:
New lead selection path =
---> [Favorite Places to Travel, United States, National Parks, Mt. Shasta]

Old lead selection path =
---> [Favorite Places to Travel, United States]
```

Tree Model Events

The last of your tree related events is the TreeModelEvent. Its name makes you highly suspicious that this event is generated by a tree model and not by a tree component. Swing defines the DefaultTreeModel class, which is a concrete implementation of the TreeModel interface.

Tree models create and maintain a data abstraction that stores tree data. Tree components delegate the job of storing data to such an object. The TreeModelEvent enables you to register objects to listen for changes to this data structure instead of the visual representation of the tree itself.

The TreeModelListener interface defines the four methods shown in Table 9.29.

TABLE 9.29   The TreeModelListener Class

TreeModelListener method name	Description
void treeNodesChanged (TreeModelEvent e)	Invoked in response to some kind of change to a node (or a set of siblings)
void treeNodesInserted (TreeModelEvent e)	Invoked in response to an insertion of nodes into the tree
void treeNodesRemoved (TreeModelEvent e)	Invoked in response to removal of nodes from the tree
void treeStructureChanged (TreeModelEvent e)	Invoked in response to a change in the tree that cannot be characterized by the other methods in this interface

All these method invocations pass an instance of a TreeModelEvent object to the listener. This event type defines several methods that enable you to extract information about the state of the tree data. Table 9.30 lists the methods of the TreeModelEvent class.

TABLE 9.30   The `TreeModelEvent` Class

TreeModelEvent *method name*	*Description*
`int[] getChildIndices()`	Returns the values of the indices that indicate where there are currently children of the source tree
`Object[] getChildren()`	Returns the valid children of the tree event source, that is, those which are located in tree positions represented by the indices returned by `getChildIndices()`
`Object[] getPath()`	Retrieves an array of objects that are the elements contained in the `TreePath` instance returned by the `getTreePath()` method
`TreePath getTreePath()`	Returns the `TreePath` object that contains the elements that comprise the path from the root of the tree event source down to the changed node
`String toString()`	Returns a string representing the object that is the event source

Let's enhance your tree model demo program one more time to handle `TreeModelEvents`. As usual when handling a new event type, you first define a class that implements the appropriate interface, this time `TreeModelListener`, shown in Listing 9.32.

LISTING 9.32   A `TreeModelEventListener` Class

```
class TreeModelEventMonitor implements TreeModelListener
{
  public void treeNodesChanged(TreeModelEvent e)
  {
    TreePath path = e.getTreePath();

    System.out.println("TreeModelEvent: Tree nodes changed");
    printTreePathInfo(path);
  }


  public void treeNodesInserted(TreeModelEvent e)
  {
    TreePath path = e.getTreePath();
    System.out.println("TreeModelEvent: Tree nodes inserted.");
    printTreePathInfo(path);
  }


  public void treeNodesRemoved(TreeModelEvent e)
```

9

EVENTS AND
EVENT HANDLING

LISTING 9.32   Continued

```
{
  TreePath path = e.getTreePath();

  System.out.println("TreeModelEvent: Tree nodes removed.");
  printTreePathInfo(path);
}


public void treeStructureChanged(TreeModelEvent e)
{
  TreePath path = e.getTreePath();

  System.out.println("TreeModelEvent; Tree structure changed.");
  printTreePathInfo(path);
}


void printTreePathInfo(TreePath path)
{
  System.out.println("Number of path elements = " + path.getPathCount());
  System.out.println("---> " + path.toString());
  System.out.println();
}
}
```

You then instantiate your class to create a listener. You want to add your listener to a tree model. You don't have to create a `DefaultTreeModel` object because each `JTree` creates one as its default object to which it delegates the job of storing the tree data.

You simply need a reference to it so you can register your listener. You obtain the reference and add your listener as shown:

```
DefaultTreeModel treeModel = (DefaultTreeModel) tree.getModel();

treeModel.addTreeModelListener(treeModelEventMonitor);
```

You're not quite done yet. Models often use a policy that is somewhat different from that used by components for dictating when to fire events. A component almost always fires an event when any part of its visual state changes. This is not always the case with models.

In your case, you must force the `DefaultTreeModel` object to fire the `TreeModelEvent`. Fortunately, the `DefaultTreeModel` class defines a `reload` method that causes all listeners to be notified that a change to the tree data has occurred.

You can take advantage of this method to make a `TreeModelEvent` fire when you add nodes to your tree. You add your listener to your tree's `DefaultTreeModel` object before you add any nodes to your tree. Thereafter, each time you add a node to your tree, the tree updates the state of the model to reflect the newly added data.

The following snippet of code, taken from your program's constructor, shows how you force the events to occur.

```
france.add(paris);
treeModel.reload();

// Force a TreeModel event to occur.
//
france.add(lyon);
treeModel.reload();

// Force a TreeModel event to occur.
//
france.add(stMalo);
treeModel.reload();
```

It might be helpful to refer to Figure 9.27, which shows your tree fully expanded, to correlate this code with the visual tree elements.

You should see output on the console that indicates the firing of the `TreeModelEvents` even before the GUI appears on screen. Indeed, you do.

```
TreeModelEvent; Tree structure changed.
Number of path elements = 1
---> [Favorite Places to Travel]

TreeModelEvent; Tree structure changed.
Number of path elements = 1
---> [Favorite Places to Travel]

TreeModelEvent; Tree structure changed.
Number of path elements = 1
---> [Favorite Places to Travel]

TreeModelEvent; Tree structure changed.
Number of path elements = 1
---> [Favorite Places to Travel]
```

As you finish your presentation of these semantic events, it may be worthwhile to quickly reflect on why these Swing events are semantic events and not component events. For example, it may seem that tree events should be component events, for they only make sense when fired by tree components.

The distinction is that semantic events address an abstraction that is independent of any particular implementation.

For example, tree events capture the notion of changes to the state of a tree, which is an abstract type. Tree events can be fired by any component that implements a tree view or tree abstraction and are not restricted to being fired by just the JTree class. These events do not depend on the details of the component's implementation, nor do they reflect a physical event or change of state. They reflect a logical change to the component (which may coincide with a physical change to a view).

In contrast, component events are related to implementation issues. A FocusEvent, for example, describes a particular physical event, obtaining the keyboard focus. A WindowEvent represents a change to the physical state of the window, such as its iconification.

Menu Key Events

It's now time to discuss the two Swing component events. The javax.swing.event.MenuKeyEvent defines the first of two Swing component events. The MenuKeyEvent class is a special type of java.awt.event.*KeyEvent, that is, a subclass of KeyEvent, which is a subclass of java.awt.InputEvent.

MenuKeyEvents are only fired by menu elements, the nature of which is aptly captured by the javax.swing.MenuElement interface. As shown by the hierarchy in Figure 9.28, the JMenuItem class implements the javax.swing.MenuElement interface. Because all types of menu elements extend JMenuItem, they inherit JMenuItem's implementation of this interface.

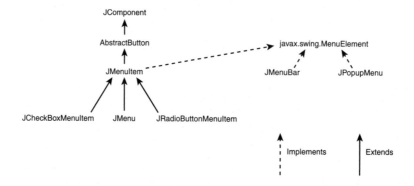

FIGURE 9.28

Swing's menu element types all descend from JMenuItem, *enabling them to share behavior common to all menu elements, including event generation.*

The javax.swing.JMenuItem class also conveniently defines the addMenuKeyListener and removeMenuKeyListener methods. Naturally, all other menu element types inherit these definitions too.

These methods associate JMenuItems with the MenuKeyListener interface. The MenuKeyListener methods are listed in Table 9.31. This listener enables menu items to handle occurrences of MenuKeyEvents.

Menu key events are events that indicate a key event received by a menu element, as opposed to some other type of component like a text field. The event object has information about the event source. Additionally, the MenuKeyEvent class defines a getPath() method that returns a path to the actual menu element that received the event.

TABLE 9.31 The MenuKeyListener Interface

MenuKeyListener *methods*	*Description*
void menuKeyPressed (MenuKeyEvent e)	Invoked in response to a key being pressed
void menuKeyRelease (MenuKeyEvent e)	Invoked in response to the release of a key
void menuKeyTyped (MenuKeyEvent e)	Invoked as a result of a key being typed

Listing 9.33 shows one new listener class that you can add to your earlier Menu Demo program in Listing 9.26.

LISTING 9.33 Defining a Listener for MenuKeyEvents

9

```
class MenuKeyMonitor implements MenuKeyListener
{
  public void menuKeyPressed(MenuKeyEvent e)
  {
    System.out.println("MenuKeyEvent: Menu key pressed.");
    System.out.println("Menu item path: ");
    printPath(e.getPath());
    System.out.println();
  }

  public void menuKeyReleased(MenuKeyEvent e)
  {
    System.out.println("MenuKeyEvent: Menu key released.");
```

continues

LISTING 9.33   Continued

```
      System.out.println("Menu item path: ");
      printPath(e.getPath());
      System.out.println();
    }

    public void menuKeyTyped(MenuKeyEvent e)
    {
      System.out.println("MenuKeyEvent: Menu key typed.");
      System.out.print("Menu item path: ");
      printPath(e.getPath());
      System.out.println();
    }

    private void printPath(MenuElement [] path)
    {
      for (int i = 0; i < path.length; i++)
        {
          System.out.print(((Component) path[i]).toString() + ", ");
        }
      System.out.println();
    }
}
```

You now add a listener for MenuKeyEvents (as opposed to MenuEvents) to your top level menu
Menu 1 as follows:

```
    JMenu menu1 = new JMenu("Menu 1");

    // Add a listener for menu key events.  These are different
    // than menu events.
    //
    menu1.addMenuKeyListener(new MenuKeyMonitor());
```

Figure 9.29 shows Menu 1 expanded. Notice that you have assigned keys to each of the first
three menu elements.

Typing either 1, 2, or 3 when Menu 1 is active will result in several events, evidenced by the
following output:

```
Menu "Menu 1" selected
MenuKeyEvent: Menu key pressed.
Menu item path:
javax.swing.JMenuBar[,0,0,290x21,
layout=javax.swing.BoxLayout],
```

```
javax.swing.JMenu[,0,1,87x19,
layout=javax.swing.OverlayLayout, JMenu],

Menu "Menu 1" deselected
MenuKeyEvent: Menu key typed.
Menu item path: javax.swing.JMenuBar[,0,0,290x21,
layout=javax.swing.BoxLayout],
javax.swing.JMenu[,0,1,87x19,
layout=javax.swing.OverlayLayout, JMenu],
```

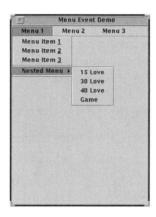

FIGURE 9.29

Menu key events are generated when a key event occurs whose key code represents a key assigned to a menu item in the selected menu.

First, you see the menu selection variety of a MenuEvent. Following that is the MenuKeyEvent that indicates that you typed one of the defined menu keys.

After a menu element selection, menus are deactivated. Thus, you see a menu deselection MenuEvent. Finally, you see a menu key typed variety of a MenuKeyEvent.

What happens if you activate a menu but press a key that is *not* a defined menu key? What if for example, you press the 9 key. You see the following output:

```
MenuKeyEvent: Menu key pressed.
Menu item path:
javax.swing.JMenuBar[,0,0,290x21,
layout=javax.swing.BoxLayout],
javax.swing.JMenu[,0,1,87x19,
layout=javax.swing.OverlayLayout, JMenu],

MenuKeyEvent: Menu key typed.
Menu item path: javax.swing.JMenuBar[,0,0,290x21,
```

```
layout=javax.swing.BoxLayout],
javax.swing.JMenu[,0,1,87x19,
layout=javax.swing.OverlayLayout, JMenu],

MenuKeyEvent: Menu key released.
Menu item path:
javax.swing.JMenuBar[,0,0,290x21,
layout=javax.swing.BoxLayout],
javax.swing.JMenu[,0,1,87x19,
layout=javax.swing.OverlayLayout, JMenu],
```

Now you see a different set of events. You see evidence of key events, but you don't see any evidence of menu selection or deselection events. The key you typed does not correspond to the selection of any menu element in any of your three menus. In addition to the key typed and key pressed events, you now see a key released event.

Menu Drag Mouse Events

The MenuDragMouseEvent is the second of the Swing component events. It differs from the MenuKeyEvent in that it indicates that the mouse was dragged on the menu element which is the event source.

The MenuDragMouseEvent is a special kind of MouseEvent, which, as you already know from Figure 9.1, is a kind of InputEvent.

The MenuDragMouseEvent class defines the same two methods, shown in Table 9.32, defined by the MenuKeyEvent class.

TABLE 9.32 The MenuDragMouseEvent Class

MenuDragMouseEvent method name	Description
MenuSelectionManager getMenuSelectionManager()	Returns the current menu selection manager
MenuElement[] getPath()	Returns the path to the selected menu item

Objects can listen for these events by implementing the MenuDragMouseListener interface, whose methods are listed in Table 9.33.

TABLE 9.33   The `MenuDragMouseListener` Interface

`MenuDragMouseListener` *method name*	*Description*
void menuDragMouseDragged (MenuDragMouseEvent e)	Invoked in response to the mouse being clicked and dragged in a menu component's display area
void menuDragMouseEntered (MenuDragMouseEvent e)	Invoked in response to the dragged mouse entering a menu component's display area
void menuDragMouseExited (MenuDragMouseEvent e)	Invoked in response to the dragged mouse exiting a menu component's display area
void menuDragMouseReleased (MenuDragMouseEvent e)	Invoked in response to a dragged mouse released in a menu component's display area

Let's add one final class to your menu event demo program. The `MenuDragMouseEventMonitor` class (shown in Listing 9.34) implements the `MenuDragMouseListener`.

LISTING 9.34   A Listener for `MenuDragMouseEvents`

```
class MenuDragMouseEventMonitor implements MenuDragMouseListener
{
  public void menuDragMouseDragged(MenuDragMouseEvent e)
  {
    System.out.println("MenuDragMouseEvent: Menu drag mouse dragged.");
    System.out.println("Menu item path: " + e.getPath().toString());
    System.out.println();
  }

  public void menuDragMouseEntered(MenuDragMouseEvent e)
  {
    System.out.println("MenuDragMouseEvent: Menu drag mouse entered.");
    System.out.println("Menu item path: " + e.getPath().toString());
    System.out.println();
  }

  public void menuDragMouseExited(MenuDragMouseEvent e)
  {
    System.out.println("MenuDragMouseEvent: Menu drag mouse exited.");
    System.out.println("Menu item path: " + e.getPath().toString());
    System.out.println();
  }
```

continues

9

EVENTS AND
EVENT HANDLING

LISTING 9.34   Continued

```
public void menuDragMouseReleased(MenuDragMouseEvent e)
{
  System.out.println("MenuDragMouseEvent: Menu drag mouse released.");
  System.out.println("Menu item path: " + e.getPath().toString());
  System.out.println();
}
}
```

Incidentally, any `JMenuItem` can register menu drag mouse listeners. In your demo program, you add such a listener to the menu labeled `Menu 2` on the menu bar.

```
// Add a menu drag mouse event listener to "Menu 2".
  //
  MenuDragMouseListener menuDragMouseEventMonitor = new
    MenuDragMouseEventMonitor();
  menu2.addMenuDragMouseListener(menuDragMouseEventMonitor);
```

Now, when you drag the mouse on this menu element while it is active, you should see a stream of events:

```
MenuDragMouseEvent: Menu drag mouse dragged.
Menu item path: [Ljavax.swing.MenuElement;@80fee22

MenuDragMouseEvent: Menu drag mouse dragged.
Menu item path: [Ljavax.swing.MenuElement;@80feda4

MenuDragMouseEvent: Menu drag mouse dragged.
Menu item path: [Ljavax.swing.MenuElement;@80fed75

MenuDragMouseEvent: Menu drag mouse dragged.
Menu item path: [Ljavax.swing.MenuElement;@80fed49
...
```

If you then release the mouse, and then drag it again, you see no events, because the click associated with the second drag deactivates the menu item.

Swing Action Objects

The first event type described in this chapter was the `java.awt.ActionEvent` class. Objects that wish to register as an action listener and be notified of occurrences of this semantic event type must implement the `ActionListener` interface.

Various AWT and Swing components, listed in Table 9.4, fire action events. Earlier you learned that each of these components defines the semantics for the action event it fires. That is, the conditions under which the component fires the event imply how the event should be interpreted. For example, buttons define `ActionEvent` to mean that the button was clicked, whereas text fields define it to mean that the carriage return was entered in the text field.

These events are called action events because listeners respond by executing some pertinent action in response to the user's action. Without some agreement between the component that fires the action event and the action executed by its action listeners, the `ActionListener` interface is no more than a vehicle that enables delivery of events to listeners.

An `ActionListener` implementation must respond—perform some action—in a manner that is congruent with the semantic meaning that the component imparts on the action event. You can think of an implementation of `ActionListener` as an action that is performed in response to events with a particular meaning.

An action listener can only perform one task—one action—that adheres to the semantics of the event source. Therefore, an application must provide a different `ActionListener` implementation for each semantic action in an application. For instance, an application may contain six buttons which all represent different tasks or actions. The associated listener for each button must implement the appropriate logic to execute in response to action events.

It would be nice to have a way to identify an action, to encapsulate the conceptual nature of an action—in essence to document it—so that its attributes and the conditions under which it can be used are easily understood.

If you had a uniform way to do this, you could be assured that you would always encounter a consistent, familiar interface whenever you examined a specific action implementation.

Actually, perhaps what you really want to do is capture the conceptual nature of any action. Specific implementations could then advertise details of the conditions and situations in which it is intended to be used.

Interfaces are the perfect vehicle for encapsulating the nature of a type without requiring a specific implementation. Essentially, you would like such a type to define the nature of any action, that is, the attributes and behavior that are common to all such `ActionListener` implementations—all *actions*.

The Swing `javax.swing.Action` interface is intended for just this purpose. It presents an interface that provides for the description of any action, that is, any `ActionListener` implementation. It accommodates the implementation of behavior that all action listeners must have, and it also neatly encapsulates the definition of attributes generally useful to actions. You can say that the `Action` interface defines a framework for capturing the nature, specific behavior, and attributes of actions. In essence, it enables an `ActionListener` implementation to document what action it performs.

NOTE

Actions are *not* GUI components; nor are they event types. They are
`ActionListeners`. They differ from plain `ActionListeners` by subclassing the `Action`
interface, which enables all action implementations to present a consistent interface
that enables programs to extract information about their attributes.

Table 9.34 lists the complete `javax.swing.Action` interface. The `Action` interface is a
subinterface of `java.awt.event.ActionListener`. First and foremost, it is a type of
`ActionListener` and defines the `addActionListener(ActionListener)` and
`removeActionListener(ActionListener)` interfaces.

Second, it accommodates the definition of attributes that are common to actions. The values
of these attributes in specific implementations offer details of a particular action. The
`getValue(String key)` and `putValue(String key, Object value)` methods that support
attribute definitions suggest a hash table model.

The `Action` constants are predefined attribute keys that define a convention for naming attributes and for storing and retrieving their values. Essentially, they define a predictable and consistent interface for retrieving attributes about any action object.

The same is true for the methods in the `Action` interface. This is the whole purpose of defining
this interface. It defines a consistent nature for all action objects. Applications know exactly
how to go about retrieving information about an action.

TABLE 9.34   The `javax.swing.Action` Interface

Action field or method name	*Description*
`static String DEFAULT`	A constant that can be used as a default key to retrieve some property value.
`static String LONG_DESCRIPTION`	The key used for storing a string value of a "long" descrip- tion of this action's function. This could be used, for exam- ple, as tool tip text.
`static String NAME`	The key used for storing a string value for the name of this action. This could be used, for instance, as the text of a but- ton or menu item that invokes this action.
`static String SHORT_DESCRIPTION`	The key used for storing and retrieving a short description of the action's function. The exact usage is defined by the implementing class.

Action field or method name	Description
`static String SMALL_ICON`	The key used for storing and retrieving a small icon, which could be used as a button's icon.
`void addPropertyChangeListener` `(PropertyChangeListener listener)`	Adds a `PropertyChange` listener.
`Object getValue(String key)`	Retrieves the value of the action's property indexed by the specified key.
`boolean isEnabled()`	Returns `true` if the action is currently enabled, `false` otherwise.
`void putValue(String key,` `Object value)`	Sets the specified value for the object's attribute indicated by the key specified in the first argument.

`void removeProperty`
`ChangeListener`
`(PropertyChangeListener`
`listener)`
	Removes a `PropertyChange` listener.

`void setEnabled(boolean b)`	Sets the state of the action to be enabled or disabled, with a value of true or false, respectively.

Another important feature represented by the `Action` interface is the support for enabling or disabling an action. This allows an application to disable the function that normally gets executed in response to an action event. An action object registered to receive action events from some source can be disabled so that it does nothing in response to receiving the event notification. The action can be disabled instead of the source component (such as a button).

Listings 9.35 and 9.36 each show the implementation of a simple action. These examples are obviously simplistic and contrived. The purpose is to show the implementation of an action object and its relationship to one or more event sources.

The `ConcreteAction` class extends the `javax.swing.AbstractAction` class, which implements the `Action` interface. Primarily, it provides a convenient implementation of a mechanism that supports storage and retrieval of properties.

Figure 9.30 shows the hierarchical relationship between the `ActionListener`, `Action`, and `AbstractAction` types.

Your `ConcreteAction` class sets some attributes that describe its name, text that can be used for fly-over text, and an icon that can be placed on a button that might fire this event. Of course, the `ConcreteAction` class also implements the `actionPerformed()` method to do whatever function is prescribed by the intended use of this action. The `AbstractAction` superclass does not implement this method, forcing concrete subclasses to provide an appropriate definition.

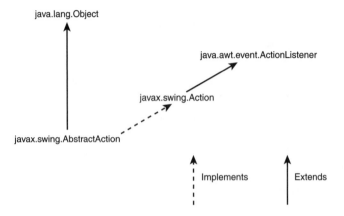

FIGURE 9.30

The Action *interface adds the ability to specify attributes to an action. All* Actions *are* ActionListeners, *and, therefore, extend the* ActionListener *interface. The* AbstractAction *class provides a convenient implementation of the framework that enables specification of attributes.*

LISTING 9.35   A Concrete Implementation of an Action

```java
import java.awt.event.*;
import javax.swing.ImageIcon;
import javax.swing.Action;
import javax.swing.AbstractAction;


class ConcreteAction extends AbstractAction
{
  public ConcreteAction()
  {
    putValue(Action.NAME, "ConcreteAction");
    putValue(Action.SHORT_DESCRIPTION, shortDesc);
    putValue(Action.LONG_DESCRIPTION, longDesc);
    putValue(Action.SMALL_ICON, new ImageIcon(""));
  }

  public void actionPerformed(ActionEvent e)
  {
    // Do some "action" in response to the activation of
    // the event source, which fires the ActionEvent
    // event.
    System.out.println("ConcreteAction did its action.");
  }
```

```
  static String shortDesc = "Example action";

  static String longDesc =
    "Demonstrates implementation of the Action interface.";
}
```

LISTING 9.36   An Action That Exits an Application

```
import java.awt.event.*;
import javax.swing.ImageIcon;
import javax.swing.Action;
import javax.swing.AbstractAction;


class ExitAction extends AbstractAction
{
  public ExitAction()
  {
    putValue(Action.NAME, "Exit");
    putValue(Action.SHORT_DESCRIPTION, shortDesc);
    putValue(Action.LONG_DESCRIPTION, longDesc);
    putValue(Action.SMALL_ICON, new ImageIcon("../images/alrm_critic.gif"));
  }

  public void actionPerformed(ActionEvent e)
  {
    // Do some "action" in response to the activation of
    // the event source, which fires the ActionEvent
    // event.
    System.exit(0);
  }

  static String shortDesc = "Exits the application";

  static String longDesc =
  "Activating this action exits the application.";

}
```

Listing 9.36 shows a class that represents an application that uses your two defined action types. Figure 9.31 shows a picture of the application, which will be useful in order to understand what actions the action objects represent.

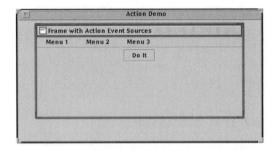

FIGURE 9.31

The internal frame has three event sources: The Exit menu item in Menu 1, the Concrete Action menu item in Menu 2, and the Do It button in the internal frame. The ConcreteAction menu item and the Do It button are tied to the same action object, which will execute the same function in response to either source being activated.

The source code in Listing 9.37 implements the application represented by Figure 9.31. This trivial application requires the definition of your two action classes. The Exit action is executed in response to the selection of the Exit menu item of Menu 1. So, you must register an instance of your Exit action as an action listener on the menu item.

The first thing to notice about the application, however, is that you do not explicitly create the menu item, add it to your menu, and then register the action with it. Instead, you simply add the action to the menu. This seems strange, for menus contain menu items. What does it mean to add an action to a menu?

Three Swing components, `JToolBar`, `JPopupMenu`, and `JMenu`, provide an overloaded `add(Action)` method. In the case of the `JMenu` class, this method creates a menu item with the action's name, adds the new menu item to the menu, and registers the action as an action listener on the new menu item.

You can see the power and convenience of having an `Action` interface that presents a uniform representation of action objects. The `JMenu.add()` method can query the action object for its name attribute, using the `Action.NAME` key, and use it to construct a new menu item with that name. The same code can be used to register any action object on a menu item.

The `Action.LONG_DESCRIPTION` key can be used to define tool tip text for actions. In fact, you use this key to store tool tip text for your actions and retrieve it to set the tool tip text with one method call.

```
menuItem.setToolTipText((String)
                    concreteAction.getValue(Action.LONG_DESCRIPTION));
```

If you activate your Exit menu item, as shown in Figure 9.32, you can see that there is an image icon associated with the button. You certainly didn't put it there! How did it get there? Actually, the `JMenu.add()` method did this too, by querying the action and getting the value of its `Action.SMALL_ICON` property to use as the menu item's icon.

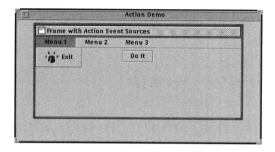

FIGURE 9.32

The uniform interface of Action *objects enables a program to extract and use information for tasks like the automatic configuration of menu item icons.*

LISTING 9.37   An Application That Uses Action Objects

```java
import java.awt.*;
import javax.swing.*;

class ActionDemo extends JPanel
{
  public ActionDemo()
  {
    // Create an instance of our action.
    //
    Action concreteAction = new ConcreteAction();

    // Create an internal frame to place in our main panel.
    //
    JInternalFrame intFrame = new
      JInternalFrame("Frame with Action Event Sources",
                     true);
    intFrame.setPreferredSize(new Dimension(450, 200));
    intFrame.getContentPane().setLayout(new BorderLayout());

    // Create a menu bar and add some menus to it.
    //
    JMenuBar menuBar = new JMenuBar();

    JMenu menu1 = new JMenu("Menu 1");
    JMenu menu2 = new JMenu("Menu 2");
    JMenu menu3 = new JMenu("Menu 3");

    menuBar.add(menu1);
    menuBar.add(menu2);
```

9

continues

LISTING 9.37   Continued

```java
menuBar.add(menu3);

// Add an action to "Menu 2".  This form of "add" creates a
// menu item and adds it to the menu.  It also registers the
// action object as an action listener on the menu item.
//
JMenuItem menuItem = menu2.add(concreteAction);

// However, we must set the tool tip text ourselves....
//
menuItem.setToolTipText((String)
                        concreteAction.getValue(Action.LONG_DESCRIPTION));

// Create another action.  The "action" that this object does is to
// exit the application when any of its event sources fire the
// action event.
//
Action exit = new ExitAction();
menu1.add(exit);



// Add the tool bar to the JInternalFrame.
//
intFrame.setJMenuBar(menuBar);

// Create the button that will be added to our application.
//
JButton doIt = new JButton("Do It");

// Use the action object's long description as our tool tip text.
//
String toolTipText = (String)
  concreteAction.getValue(Action.LONG_DESCRIPTION);
doIt.setToolTipText(toolTipText);



// Add our action object as an action listener on our
// stand-alone button.  Notice that this button is the second
// event source to which we add the same action object.
//
doIt.addActionListener(concreteAction);

// Add our stand-alone button to the internal frame.
//
```

```
    JPanel buttonPanel = new JPanel();
    buttonPanel.add(doIt);

    intFrame.getContentPane().add(buttonPanel, BorderLayout.NORTH);

    add(intFrame, BorderLayout.NORTH);

  }

  public Dimension getPreferredSize()
  {
    return new Dimension(610, 250);
  }


  public static void main(String [] args)
  {
    ActionDemo app = new ActionDemo();

    JFrame f = new JFrame("Action Demo");
    f.getContentPane().add(app);
    f.pack();
    f.setVisible(true);
  }

}
```

Your application also registers an action listener on two more event sources. In fact, you use a single instance of your ConcreteAction action class to listen for action events on both of these sources. The ConcreteAction class defines a name and some descriptive text that is used as tool tip text.

One of the event sources to which your action object is tied is another menu item, this time on Menu 2. The other is the Do It button in the application's internal frame. Figure 9.33 shows the menu item created from your action object.Notice that, again, the JMenu.add() method extracted the action's name and the tool tip text, and it has used this information to construct the menu item.

You've already added your concrete action on your new menu item. Now you also register this same action object on your Do It button, albeit manually this time. You also manually set the tool tip text, but you still extract it from the action object. Again, you can see how convenient it is to have this Action mechanism that stores all the attributes of an action object in one convenient place.

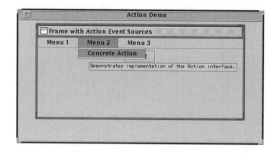

FIGURE 9.33

Your second menu uses an action object that will also be tied to a button in the internal frame. Actions provides a convenient way to access functionality with a simple reference to an object that can be reused.

Figures 9.33 and 9.34 show that the tool tip is the same text for both your menu item and button. You used the same action object for both sources because, semantically, in the context of your application, you want the same action to occur as a result of activating either. Having a definition of an Action object saved the trouble of having to define two separate ActionListeners that perform the exact same function.

Of course, in this silly example, your action simply prints out a message on the console. But you get the idea.

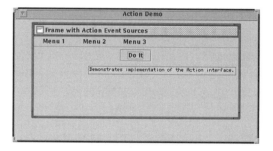

FIGURE 9.34

The same action object is registered on your plain button and the menu item, as evidenced by the tool tip text.

Actions represent semantic events. Define your Actions to implement the logic that represents the work that supports the high-level semantic tasks defined by your application.

Typically, Actions can be best used for toolbar buttons and menu items that are part of an application's common functions, such as those on the outermost application menubar.

> The Action interface is designed to enhance the ActionListener interface by providing a uniform interface for objects that are canonical in their nature. This interface allows programs to manipulate similar objects in the same way.

Summary

Event handling is the process that gives life to a GUI application and makes it truly interactive. Event handling enables you to define how your program responds to external events, and it enables users to interact meaningfully with your program.

All events have a type and are defined in a type hierarchy. The two major categories of events are component events and semantic events. Both the AWT and Swing packages define event types. The Swing event types do not supersede the AWT events. In fact, the AWT events are a fundamental part of any JFC program.

The type of an event determines the external or semantic action that it represents. Different components fire different types of events. Knowing what events a component fires allows event listeners to register for notification of particular events on particular components and to be notified of the occurrence of those events.

Event listeners are defined by interfaces which provide a medium for event sources to notify objects that are interested in particular events. Event listener interfaces are associated with particular event types. This connects event listeners to the types of events in which they are interested. An application must provide an implementation of the logic that defines how it wishes to handle each type of event in which it is interested.

Programmers have several options for defining and organizing the classes that represent an application's event handling code. Inner classes are particularly useful for architecting event handling in a program. Anonymous inner classes provide a means to quickly and concisely create event handlers that are small and simple in scope, without increasing a program's complexity.

At this point, you have all the basic skills needed to create fully-functional, meaningful Java GUI programs. By "basic" I certainly don't mean "beginning" or "trivial." I mean that every Java GUI program, regardless of complexity, must address the issues that these chapters have covered, namely, containers, components, layout managers, and particularly event handling.

I have stressed an understanding of concepts, and these concepts apply even to the most complex aspects of the GUI tool kit and APIs.

Models

IN THIS CHAPTER

- Identifying and Targeting
  Abstractions   502

- Utilizing the MVC Paradigm   503

- The Swing Model Architecture   504

- Swing Model Anatomy   506

- Swing Models and Their Related
  Types   521

- Swing Models   525

- Defining Your Own Models   534

Now that you have a command of the pragmatics needed to write GUI programs using the JFC, this chapter will examine one particularly ubiquitous and fundamental feature of the Swing architecture and APIs, namely, the Swing model architecture.

You already know the importance of understanding the paradigms of any programming environment; it's important to use tools in accordance with their design. The Swing model architecture is one such paradigm. Understanding how to use it properly will help you understand the JFC toolkit better and also help you write better JFC programs.

This chapter gives a thorough conceptual overview of models and the JFC model architecture. Following the overview is an examination of how the Swing components support this architecture. Finally, I explain the most frequently encountered models defined and implemented by the Swing package.

In this chapter, I depart from using code samples and, instead, use schematic diagrams as the primary presentation mechanism to conceptually represent the abstractions being discussed. Now that you have a solid foundation in events and event handling, using models in your programs becomes rather straightforward because you understand the abstractions they capture.

Identifying and Targeting Abstractions

In Chapter 1, "UI Programming Concepts," I talked about the importance of designing a user interface that communicates with the user on his or her own terms. In other words, the GUI should represent the application conceptually in a way that makes it easy for the user to understand its purpose and function.

For the GUI designer, this means using visual components that conceptually represent the application's purpose, data, and functions. The abstractions presented by the GUI must be familiar—or at least comprehensible—to the user.

Programs use visual components, such as the Swing components discussed in Chapter 7, "The Swing Components," to abstract the logical entities they represent. These logical entities are program data. Individual data items are grouped to represent real-life objects that are familiar to humans. After all, computer programs are meant to simulate our interaction with real-world entities.

In object-oriented programming languages, logically related data are aggregated into objects. An object represents an instance of an abstract data type. By abstract, I mean two things. First, it is not a built-in type such as int or float. Second, you can abstract the characteristics and attributes shared by all instances of that type, despite the details of any particular concrete implementation. In Java, an object's class defines a concrete implementation of its abstract type.

The engineer chooses an implementation that addresses engineering constraints while faithfully adhering to the characteristics and attributes of the abstraction.

The user focuses on identifying the abstractions presented by the application's visual components. If they are familiar, the user will be able to interact with the GUI effectively. The user is not interested in the abstractions used to implement internal application logic.

Consequently, the GUI components should present abstractions that are appropriate for the people who will interact with them.

For example, the Swing toolkit provides a JList component that represents a conceptual list of elements. Figure 7.12 displays an example of such a list. By looking at this visual representation, the user is not aware of how lists are implemented internally. They could be implemented internally as an array, a linked data structure, or by some other means.

It's clear that these abstractions belong to two very different abstraction domains. The GUI engineer must, therefore, address two fairly orthogonal design efforts. The first is to create abstractions that enable easy implementation of application logic. The second is to create or use abstractions that are meaningful to users.

The point is that an abstraction must target a specific kind of user, and it must be meaningful to those who use it.

Utilizing the MVC Paradigm

I first introduced the Model-View-Controller paradigm in Chapter 1. The MVC paradigm defines three related elements. The model and view elements provide different implementations of the same abstraction. That is, they represent the same data.

The power of the MVC paradigm is that it defines a way to bridge different implementations of the same abstraction. It stipulates that the model and view maintain synchronized states, and it provides a controller as the medium by which the model and view communicate. Figure 2.8 shows a schematic diagram of the interaction between the three objects in an MVC relationship.

Bridging disparate implementations of the same abstraction is exactly the purpose of the Model-View-Controller paradigm. A view object, for instance a GUI component, presents a visual representation of some abstraction, whereas another object, a model, provides a different implementation of the same abstraction to be used by the application logic.

The two implementations are fundamentally related because both represent the same data. Nevertheless, each implementation serves the needs of their respective users. Following the object-oriented design principle that a class should do one thing well, each class provides its own clean, focused implementation of its abstraction.

For example, the JList GUI component maintains a visual representation—a view—of the state of some list data object. Another class, a model, logically defines a list. Both the internal object and the visual component represent the same program data. Therefore, the state of the visual component should accurately reflect the state of the internal object at all times.

Conceptually, the controller can interpret events that cause the state of either the model or view to change and update the other view or model accordingly so that their states remain synchronized.

The Swing Model Architecture

The Swing model architecture is essentially a framework, supported by the Swing components, that manifests the MVC paradigm. The visual Swing components each abstract a certain type of data with which users are familiar—lists, tables, trees, and so forth. A new set of types defined in Swing, called models, capture the nature of the logical abstractions presented by the Swing components.

Swing models are interfaces. As you've seen many times before, Java interfaces are an excellent mechanism for capturing the nature of a data type without enforcing an implementation.

A Swing model defines an interface that captures the nature of the characteristics and behavior that relate to a data abstraction. A model can be implemented by any class while preserving the nature of the abstraction.

Swing GUI component classes use an implementation of an appropriate model to delegate the job of maintaining the data that they visually represent to the user. This is the MVC paradigm at work.

Each of the Swing components reference an instance of a model to which they delegate the task of storing the state of the data represented by the component. The component's visual state is a reflection of the logical state of the data maintained by the underlying model.

The power of this abstraction is twofold:

- It reduces the complexity of your classes.

  It allows each class to focus on doing one thing well, in accordance with good object-oriented design. The Swing component classes can focus on presenting an effective visual representation and user interface for a particular abstraction. The model can focus on providing a lucid, efficient implementation of the data abstraction.

- Using Java interfaces to define data abstractions gives you the flexibility to define any implementation that is faithful to the nature of the abstraction.

  The interface that defines the model captures the nature of the abstraction for you. You are free to implement it any way you like. As long as the code in a component class accesses the data abstraction through the methods in the model's interface, it doesn't need to know any details of the model's logical implementation.

Moreover, the MVC paradigm is flexible. Changes to either the component or model implementations can be done independently as long as the model's interface doesn't change.

Integrating the View and Controller

In a pure MVC architecture, the controller object is responsible for ensuring that the states of both the view and model are updated in response to events that affect these two objects.

In practice, it is difficult to implement such an architecture without giving the controller specific knowledge of the implementation of the view class. However, integrating the view and controller increases coupling between them, which reduces the flexibility to change one without affecting the other.

Moreover, this approach makes it difficult to define a generalized controller class that doesn't define or use implementation details about any specific view implementation.

In reality, the Swing designers created a modified MVC architecture in which the Swing component classes define both the view and controller. Whenever a change occurs to the view, the view object itself acts as the controller that updates its visual appearance. It also directly invokes methods on its associated model object to update its state.

Figure 10.1 shows a schematic that conveys the integrated view and controller design used by Swing component implementations.

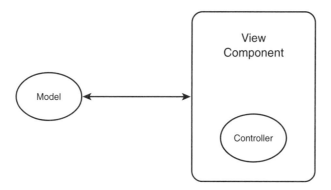

FIGURE 10.1

Swing components implement a modified MVC design in which the view and controller objects are integrated into a single Swing component.

Swing Model Anatomy

Naturally, models must be designed in conjunction with the components that use them in order to be able to work together. Conceptually, the visual component must represent the same data abstraction as the model; the MVC paradigm stipulates this condition.

For example, the JList component class delegates the job of maintaining a list of elements to a javax.swing.ListModel object. Each JList instance maintains a reference to a ListModel object.

The ListModel type is an abstraction that simply defines the nature of a list—any list—which is an ordered collection of elements. The interface says nothing about the implementation.

Figure 10.2 shows how a model and view address the same abstraction. Any one of several internal model implementations can be used in the application logic and still support the view. As long as the interface remains unchanged, the model and view implementations remain decoupled.

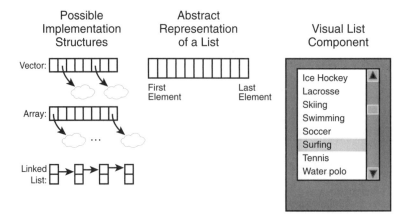

FIGURE 10.2

The ListModel interface defines a type that abstracts an ordered list of elements. It separates the abstraction from the implementation, leaving the choice of data structures used to store actual list contents to implementing classes.

Looking at the definition of the ListModel interface in Table 10.1 should convince you that indeed it does capture the nature of this data abstraction. You can count the number of elements in a list, and retrieve any element by specifying the position of the element in which you are interested.

TABLE 10.1   The `ListModel` Interface

`ListModel` *method name*	*Description*

`void`
`addListDataListener`
`(ListDataListener l)`
	Adds a listener to this model's list of listeners that are notified each time there is a change to the state of the model

`Object getElementAt` `(int index)`	Returns the value of the element at the specified index
`int getSize()`	Returns the length of the list

`void`
`removeListDataListener`
`(ListDataListener l)`
	Removes a listener from the model's list of listeners that are notified each time there is a change to the state of the model

Swing Component Support for MVC

All Swing components manifest support for the MVC paradigm. This feature was one of the primary design goals of Swing. Essentially, Swing components support MVC by using one or more instances of a model to store and manipulate the information that they represent visually. The component classes must also provide ways in which a program can access the model and the information it contains.

Swing components usually provide at least one constructor that takes an argument whose type is that of the model used by the component. For example, the `JList` class defines a constructor

```
public JList(ListModel dataModel)
```

that installs the specified model object as the one used by the newly constructed `JList` object.

Remember, models are interfaces, so this form of the constructor enables an instance of any concrete class that implements `ListModel` to be passed to the constructor. Figure 10.3 shows a hierarchy of types derived from the `ListModel` interface.

The `javax.swing.AbstractListModel` type is an abstract class that implements some of the basic capabilities, leaving the rest for concrete subclasses to implement. The most generic of these concrete classes is `DefaultListModel`.

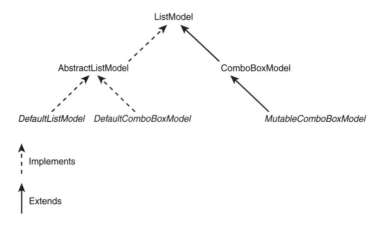

FIGURE 10.3

The javax.swing package defines several types related to the list abstraction. The naming convention used for these types follows the one used to name the abstract and concrete Swing component classes.

Besides passing model instances to constructors, alternatively, you can set the model object after the component is constructed. Swing components have a set of methods

```
public <model type>Model getModel()
public void setModel(<model type>Model)
```

that accommodate the types of models they use. The type <model type>Model specifies the type of model used by the component. For example, JList defines the two methods

```
public ListModel getModel()
public void setModel(ListModel model)
```

which allow you to specify and retrieve the model object used by a JList component. You can then use the reference to the model to extract information about its state.

Supporting Events and Event Handling

I have said that the states of both the view and model elements of a data abstraction must remain synchronized so that the view accurately reflects the contents of the model. This requirement suggests that the Swing components must be notified of changes to the state of their model in order to update their visual representation accordingly. Alternatively, some other object can be notified of model changes so it can update the state of the corresponding component.

Models support this notification process by providing for the registration of event listeners as follows.

```
public void add<model type>Listener(<model type>Listener)
public void remove<model type>Listener(<model type>Listener)
```

The argument types constrain the model to register only listeners that are able to handle event notifications of the correct type. You can surmise that there must be a listener interface that corresponds to each type of model.

Reviewing Table 10.1 reveals that the listener registration methods in the `ListModel` interface are of the type `javax.swing.event.ListDataListener`. Table 10.2 lists the methods of the `ListDataListener` interface.

TABLE 10.2   `ListDataListener` Methods

`ListDataListener` *method name*	*Description*
`void contentsChanged` `(ListDataEvent e)`	Indicates that the contents of the list firing the event has changed. The change is too complex to characterize with the other methods.
`void intervalAdded` `(ListDataEvent e)`	Indicates that a new interval of elements has been added to the list.
`void intervalRemoved` `(ListDataEvent e)`	Indicates that an interval of elements has been removed from the list.

There are no new event or listener types being introduced here. You saw these same types in Chapter 9, "Events and Event Handling." Now you are simply viewing the same functionality from the perspective of the MVC paradigm.

Instances of any class that implement the `ListDataListener` interface can register as listeners with a `ListModel`. Table 10.2 tells you that registered listeners will be notified of events of the type `javax.swing.event.ListDataEvent` that occur on the list with which they registered.

For instance, Listing 9.24 from Chapter 9 created a `DefaultListModel` instance and registered an instance of a `ListDataListener`, which was actually an instance of the `ListDataListener` subclass `ListDataMonitor`.

Whenever the program adds or removes an element from the list model, all registered listeners are notified. In response to the event, the listener updates the contents of the `JComboBox`.

This is the pattern that you must use to make your application execute some logic in response to a change in a model's state. You must create an appropriate listener and add it to your model. Because the component does not support adding the listener directly, you must first acquire a reference to the model and then add the listener explicitly.

```
JComboBox comboBox = new JComboBox();
ListModel model = comboBox.getModel();

// Create the listener.
```

```
ListDataListener ldl = new ListDataMonitor();

// Add the listener to the model.
model.addListDataListener(ldl);
```

Notice that the listener is registered with the model (the list object) and not the JComboBox instance that uses the model. In fact, you cannot register a ListDataListener with a JComboBox component because the JComboBox class does not provide the appropriate methods.

Actually, this arrangement makes sense because the bulk of a program's application logic usually manipulates data, typically when adding and removing elements to a list. The visual representation of the list is the responsibility of another object, the Swing component. The representation can be done independently of changes to the list. This is the MVC paradigm in action. It separates the two abstractions and creates a clean, easily comprehensible division of labor.

Notice that in the previous example, the end result of the action initiated by the user was a change to the state of the JComboBox. Nevertheless, the program first changes the state of the model and then changes the state of the component to reflect the model's state.

This is the preferred pattern that you should follow to design your own applications. It is much better to center your application design around your data than around the UI. The UI reflects the state of the application data, not the other way around.

This is often a subtle and confusing point. Chapter 1 proselytized about designing a UI from the point of view of the user. The previous statement seems to contradict that notion, but actually it does not.

Here I am talking about the design of the application logic and the implementation of an MVC architecture in particular. I am not discussing the UI design, but how the UI interacts with the application logic. This doesn't affect the organization or metaphors presented by the UI itself.

NOTE

It is much better to focus your design effort on creating the abstractions and implementation of the application logic rather than on creating the abstractions suitable for the UI. This is particularly true when designing models for an MVC architecture.

You should place secondary importance to designing the UI. Designing the UI and specifying the UI are two different tasks. Chapter 1 discussed the importance of specifying a UI that is meaningful and comprehensible to the target audience.

Although creating a useful UI is important, from the perspective of the software engineer, the real challenge is creating powerful logical abstractions.

Before moving on, you need to become familiar with the `ListDataEvent` class in order to understand how it conveys information about changes to a list object's state. Table 10.3 lists the members of the `ListDataEvent` class.

Table 10.3   The Members of the `ListDataEvent` Class

`ListDataEvent` *member name*	*Description*
`static int` `CONTENTS_CHANGED`	A constant that represents an event in which one or more changes occurred in the list contents.
`static int` `INTERVAL_ADDED`	A constant that represents an event in which an interval of contiguous items were added to the list.
`static int` `INTERVAL_REMOVED`	A constant that represents an event in which a contiguous interval of items was removed from the list.

`ListDataEvent(Object`
`source, int type, int`
`index0, int index1)`
	Constructs a `ListDataEvent` object.

`int getIndex0()`	Returns the lower index of the range of elements affected in the event.
`int getIndex1()`	Returns the upper index of the range of elements affected in the event.
`int getType()`	Returns the type of the event, one of `CONTENTS_CHANGED`, `INTERVAL_ADDED`, or `INTERVAL_REMOVED`.

The `ListDataEvent` class defines two quantities, `index0` and `index1`, which represent the upper and lower indices that delineate the range of list elements affected by the event. The names of these variables is sometimes confusing. They do not represent the zero or first element of the list.

Figure 10.4 gives a schematic example of the meaning of these two indices.

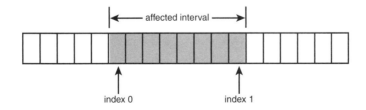

Figure 10.4
The `index0` *and* `index1` *quantities mark the range of the interval of items affected in a* `ListDataEvent`.

One final word on event handling and models. For every model, there is a corresponding listener interface that defines the pertinent methods for notifying listeners of that type of changes to the model. There is also a corresponding event type that the model uses to communicate changes in its state information.

Our first example highlighted a `ListModel`, `ListDataListener`, and a `ListDataEvent`. It's easy to keep track of the related types because they use a canonical naming convention.

The name of the model has the form `<abstraction>Model`; in this first example `<abstraction>` would be `List`. The name of the listener is `<abstraction>DataListener`, in this case, `ListDataListener`. Finally, the event name is `<data type>Event`, which in our case is `ListDataEvent`.

Two Kinds of Models

By now you know that a model represents a particular abstraction. Different abstractions should be represented by different models. The usefulness of any type definition is measured in part by how well it conveys meaning to the programmer; and models are no different. The clarity with which the details of a model suggest its intended use is very important.

The Swing package defines two general categories of models: GUI-state and application-data models. The model definitions in the GUI-state category define abstractions that capture information about the state of GUI components. Application-data models, on the other hand, capture state relating to data abstractions used by application logic.

There is absolutely no difference in the way these two types of models are defined. Both types are simply interface definitions. The difference between the two types is inherently captured by the way you, the programmer, interpret their applicability. A little later in this chapter, I will highlight some of the Swing model definitions and place them in their appropriate category. First, however, let's look at why a model might belong to one category or the other. Understanding their taxonomy will help you understand what the various models do and why certain components use them.

Distinguishing Between Types of Models

In the previous section, the running example demonstrates how a `ListModel` notifies interested listeners of changes to the structure of the data it stores. It supports the detection of changes to the selection represented by the visual `JList` component.

One of the things users can do with a `JList` or `JComboBox` instance is select some subset of the elements that they display. But the `ListModel` interface doesn't seem to support any notion of selection.

Intuitively, this situation seems incomplete. We know that the user can specify a selection of the items represented by a JList. Furthermore, the state of the view and model objects must remain synchronized. Therefore, you expect the ListModel to represent the notion of selection in some way so it can be updated to reflect the selection state of the component's elements.

Perhaps the ListModel interface is not missing anything. The notion of selection really involves new and different information beyond that presented by simple lists. It is a different abstraction. Furthermore, its very name suggests that it represents not a list but a selection of the elements of a list. That is, it represents only the elements of a list that are marked as selected, not all the elements of a list as does the ListModel.

We really have the basis of a new model here. Therefore, it makes sense to define a new interface that captures the abstraction of a selection on a list of elements. That is, such an interface should provide a means to convey information pertaining to the state of a selection of some subset of the elements of the list.

A second interface, javax.swing.ListSelectionModel, defines the abstraction of a selection of some subset of the members of a list. The JList class uses a second model to track its selection state. The following JList methods support the use of a second model for this job.

```
public void setSelectionModel(ListSelectionModel selectionModel)
public ListSelectionModel getSelectionModel()
```

In addition to using a ListModel instance, each JList instance employs an instance of a ListSelectionModel to track its selection state. You can get and set this model using these two JList methods.

Each JList instance must be able to track changes to selections on the elements it presents visually. The component itself doesn't maintain information about its selection state; it delegates this job to the list selection model. This means that the JList component must also support the registration of listeners for selection events, which it does with the following two methods.

```
public void addListSelectionListener(ListSelectionListener listener)
public void removeListSelectionListener(ListSelectionListener listener)
```

You invoke these methods on the JList component, which registers the listener with the ListSelectionModel.

Listeners can respond to selection events by updating the component's ListSelectionModel accordingly. The events that are generated are of the type ListSelectionEvent. Here is another example of a triad of types that collaborate to support the MVC paradigm, namely, ListSelectionModel, ListSelectionListener, and ListSelectionEvent.

Conceptually, one of the most important attributes of the `ListSelectionModel` abstraction is that it supports multiple selection intervals. Different contiguous sets of elements can be marked as selected simultaneously.

Figure 10.5 shows a schematic representation of the information defined by the `ListSelectionModel` interface.

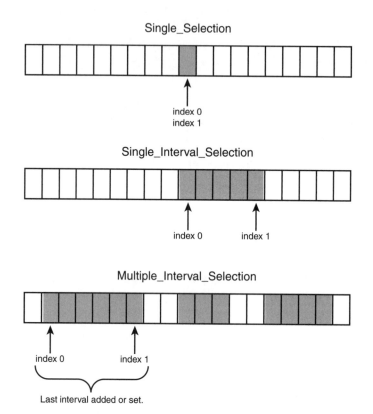

FIGURE 10.5

The `ListSelectionModel` abstracts different kinds of selections. A single element or a single interval can be selected, or multiple intervals can be selected simultaneously. The `index0` and `index1` quantities only identify the contiguous range of elements last added or set.

The `ListSelectionModel` defines two quantities, `index0` and `index1`, which identify the anchor and lead selection indices, respectively. The anchor index marks the *stationary* index, that is, the first index set when defining a contiguous range of indices. The *lead* index is the one whose value is changing during the process of identifying a selection range.

Although the `ListSelectionModel` supports multiple selection intervals, there is only one pair of `index0`, `index1` indices. Their values only represent the last contiguous interval of list elements specified in an operation that either added or selected the interval. Other intervals are still valid, but they are just not represented with these indices.

Table 10.4 lists the members of the `ListSelectionModel` interface.

TABLE 10.4   The `ListSelectionModel` Interface Members

ListSelectionModel member name	Description
`static int MULTIPLE_INTERVAL_SELECTION`	A constant that represents one of the supported selection modes, in which one or more ranges of contiguous elements can be marked as selected simultaneously.
`static int SINGLE_INTERVAL_SELECTION`	A constant that represents one of the supported selection modes, in which only one range of contiguous elements can be marked as selected at any given time.
`static int SINGLE_SELECTION`	A constant that represents one of the supported selection modes, in which only one single element can be marked as selected at any one time.
`void addListSelectionListener (ListSelectionListener x)`	Adds a listener to the list of objects to be notified of the occurrence of changes to the selection.
`void addSelectionInterval (int index0, int index1)`	Adds the specified contiguous interval to the set of selected elements. The resulting selection is the union of the current selection and the elements represented by the indices between `index0` and `index1` inclusive.
`void clearSelection()`	Removes all selections.
`int getAnchorSelectionIndex()`	Returns the first index argument, which represents the anchor or stationary selection of the last active selection interval. An active interval is the one affected by the most recent call to `setSelectionInterval()` or `addSelectionInterval()`.
`int getLeadSelectionIndex()`	Returns the second index argument, or lead index, of the last active selection interval, affected by the most recent call to `setSelectionInterval()` or `addSelectionInterval()`.
`int getMaxSelectionIndex()`	Returns the index that marks the highest indexed element in any selection interval, or -1 if the selection is empty.

continues

10

MODELS

TABLE 10.4 Continued

ListSelectionModel *member name*	*Description*
int getMinSelectionIndex()	Returns the index that marks the lowest indexed element in any selection interval, or -1 if the selection is empty.
int getSelectionMode()	Returns the current selection mode.
boolean getValueIsAdjusting()	Returns true if the selection value is currently being adjusted.
void insertIndexInterval (int index, int length, boolean before)	Inserts the specified number of indices, either before or after the specified index position.
boolean isSelectedIndex (int index)	Indicates whether the specified index is selected. A value of true means it's selected.
boolean isSelectionEmpty()	Returns true if no indices are selected.
void removeIndexInterval (int index0, int index1)	Removes from the selected set all the indices in the interval, bounded by the specified indices index0 to index1 from the selection model.
void removeListSelectionListener (ListSelectionListener x)	Removes a listener from the list of listeners that are notified of the occurrence of list selection events.
void removeSelectionInterval (int index0, int index1)	Removes the set of contiguous indices in the interval represented by the specified indices from the set of selected indices.
void setAnchorSelectionIndex (int index)	Sets the anchor index of the selection.
void setLeadSelectionIndex (int index)	Sets the lead index of the selection.
void setSelectionInterval (int index0, int index1)	Sets the current selection to be the contiguous interval whose indices are bounded by the specified indices index0 to index1, inclusive.
void setSelectionMode (int selectionMode)	Sets the selection mode.
void setValueIsAdjusting (boolean valueIsAdjusting)	Indicates whether subsequent changes to the model should be considered part of the same event (such as the user dragging the mouse on a list component).

Why do we need two models? The most compelling reason is that we are really addressing two different abstractions. Looking carefully at the methods in `ListModel` and `ListSelectionModel` should convince you that they really do abstract different information. For instance, there is no `getElementAt(int index)` or `getSize()` methods in the `ListSelectionModel` interface.

The selection model gives you information about the selection of a list, not about the whole list. It tells you which subset of the elements of a list are marked Selected. This explains why `ListSelectionModel` is not a subinterface of `ListModel`. It simply defines different information.

Users make the selection on a `JList`, not on the underlying model. The underlying model represents the selection state of the component, and the model instance maintains this selection information. The model's state is set in response to the user's selection of the component's elements.

You can see that the `ListSelectionModel` abstraction conceptually addresses the notion of state changes to a GUI component caused by user actions; a selection is something that a user specifies. This qualifies it as a GUI-state model.

In contrast, the information maintained by the `ListModel` interface in no way implies the presence of a GUI component. Although it can be used to represent the elements of a component, this use is not implied by the abstraction. Therefore, it is an application—data model.

> **NOTE**
>
> Use different models for different abstractions. Think about what abstraction is addressed by a particular event or piece of data. Don't try to force the use of a model where its abstraction doesn't fit.

Dual Context Models

There is nothing special about either the GUI-state or application-data categories that dictates which models can be included in them. The way in which a model is intended to be used determines whether it is interpreted as a GUI-state model or an application-data model. The definition of the model itself in no way suggests the inherent nature of the model. It is the nature of the abstraction captured by the model that suggests its intended use and the category to which it belongs.

In fact, a single interface may capture the characteristics of a GUI-state and an application-data model. This would make it suitable for use in both contexts. A model can be used for any interpretation supported by its characteristics and attributes.

For example, the `javax.swing.BoundedRangeModel` interface defines an abstraction that represents a monotonically increasing set of values that have an upper and lower bound (a maximum and minimum value for the range). It also addresses the notion of a current value within the range. This interface characterizes both the GUI state of components like `JProgressBar`, `JSlider`, and `JScrollbar`, and the state of an application-data object.

The model's value attribute can represent, for instance, the amount of progress accomplished so far toward completing some task. This same value can be used by a `JProgressBar` to determine how much of the progress bar to fill in to represent the percentage of work completed.

Figure 10.6 shows a schematic representation of the data abstracted by the `BoundedRangeModel`. The *extent* is a quantity that defines a span of values between the current value and the maximum value. This quantity can be used, for example, to determine how long to make the thumb of a `JScrollBar`. This is a useful abstraction for GUI components that wish to use this model. Application logic may not need to exploit the extent quantity, but it is there, nevertheless, to be used if appropriate.

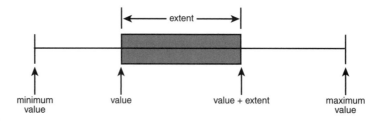

FIGURE 10.6

The `BoundedRangeModel` interface defines four quantities that make it suitable for use as both a GUI-state model and an application-data model.

Table 10.5 lists the methods defined by the `BoundedRangeModel` interface.

TABLE 10.5   The `BoundedRangeModel` Methods

Method name	Description
`void addChangeListener (ChangeListener x)`	Adds a listener for occurrences of `ChangeEvents`
`int getExtent()`	Returns the value of the model's extent
`int getMaximum()`	Returns the maximum value supported by the model
`int getMinimum()`	Returns the minimum value supported by the model
`int getValue()`	Returns the current value of the model
`boolean getValueIsAdjusting()`	Indicates if the current value is temporary, that is, one of a sequence of adjustments

Method name	*Description*
`void removeChangeListener` `(ChangeListener x)`	Removes the specified listener from the model's list of `ChangEvent` listeners
`void setExtent(int newExtent)`	Sets the value of the model's extent quantity
`void setMaximum(int newMaximum)`	Sets the maximum value supported by the model
`void setMinimum(int newMinimum)`	Sets the minimum value supported by the model
`void setRangeProperties` `(int value, int extent,` `int min, int max, boolean` `adjusting)`	Sets the four quantities defined by the model to the respective values specified
`void setValue(int newValue)`	Sets the model's current value to the specified value
`void setValueIsAdjusting` `(boolean b)`	Specifies that the current value of the model should be considered temporary, that is, it is part of a sequence of settings of the value

At first glance, the `BoundedRangeModel` interface seems to be similar in nature to the `ListModel`, with some added features. Both represent an ordered set of values.

But really their purpose is quite different. Don't focus on the concrete attributes of the interface, but rather think about the abstraction being captured. The abstractions are different. This is why the Swing models are not arranged in a hierarchy; mostly the interfaces do not extend each other. This gives designers—and users—the flexibility to use the model where it fits, without being encumbered by having to force an implementation to conform to an abstraction that's inappropriate.

Where and When To Use Models

Swing models are intended to reduce the complexity of your programs by giving you a built-in MVC implementation. They help to simplify the management of potentially complex data by defining useful abstractions.

However, you are not required to use these models. Most of the Swing components define convenience methods that directly return a value normally derived from the information in the component's model. For example, the `JList` class defines the methods

```
public int getSelectedIndex()
public void setSelectedIndex(int index)
```

which you call on your `JList` instance. The presence of these methods lets you retrieve information stored by the `JList`'s `ListSelectionModel` object. Instead of writing

10

```
JList list = new JList();
...
ListSelectionModel selModel = list.getSelectionModel();
selModel.setSelectionMode(ListSelectionModel.SINGLE_INTERVAL_SELECTION);
```

you can write

```
JList list = new JList();
list.setSelectionMode(ListSelectionModel.SINGLE_INTERVAL_SELECTION);
```

Of course, you are not changing the behavior of the component. It still interacts with its model(s) accordingly.

The JList.getSelectedIndex() method simply queries its model to get the information and pass it to the program. The JList.setSelectedIndex() method sets its model instance for subsequent use. Invoking methods on the component is often just a convenience.

Sometimes the component can actually do some extra work for you, saving you some programming. Consider the following JList methods.

```
public Object getSelectedValue()
public void setSelectedValue(Object obj)

public int [] getSelectedIndices()
public void setSelectedIndices(int[] indices)

public Object [] getSelectedValues()
```

If you look back at Table 10.4, you will see that no such methods exist in the ListSelectionModel interface. Here, the JList methods save you some work, so you might want to call them directly instead of obtaining a reference to the model and working with it.

For example, to determine the currently selected element using the ListSelectionModel directly, you have to get the selected index from the ListSelectionModel, and then get the value represented by that index from the ListModel by calling ListModel.getElementAt(). This is more work than simply calling JList.getSelectedValue().

However, this convenience doesn't come free. The JList.getSelectedValue() method always returns the element represented by the lowest valued index marked Selected in the ListSelectionModel. If this policy suits your purpose, use the available method rather than coding more logic.

However, this policy may not suit your needs. If not, then your logic needs to specify a policy for defining which single element is considered the selected value. But which index, out of all the model's indices marked Selected, should be considered the true selected value?

Your application logic needs to specify a policy that determines the selected index, and to use it for manipulating the model directly to extract the corresponding value. You can also create your own concrete implementation of `ListSelectionModel` and implement policies exactly suited to your needs. In either case, you manipulate the model directly instead of relying on the `JList.getSelectedValue()` method.

Let's look at one more example. You may need to get all the selected indices in a list. Unlike the previous example, the semantics of this operation are well-defined, It makes sense to use the `JList.getSelectedIndices()` method in this case.

Extracting this information from the model directly requires calling both `getMinSelectionIndex()` and `getMaxSelectionIndex()`, and then calling the `isSelected()` method on every index. There seems to be no benefit in doing all this extra work.

The point is that you have the flexibility to either use the model directly or access its information by simply invoking the component's supporting methods. You should evaluate each situation individually and choose the appropriate course of action.

All components don't provide the same level of convenient methods to help you extract information from their models. When you choose a GUI component, consider how you plan to use it and the information you need from its model. Compare the capabilities of the model and the component to decide which approach will work best.

It may be that you need to create a subclass of one of the concrete model implementations to get the behavior you need. The component class may not always provide the level of detail needed to access the information in the model.

Swing Models and Their Related Types

As stated earlier, the purpose of this chapter is to give you a conceptual understanding of models, to introduce you to the different available models, and to help you understand the abstractions they represent and how to apply them. This chapter is not a compendium that presents every facet of each model.

The concepts in this chapter have been presented by calling upon the three most prevalent Swing models as a presentation medium. Now that you understand the nature of models and how they manifest an MVC architecture along with the Swing components, you will be able to examine any of the remaining model definitions and recognize the abstractions they represent and how to use them effectively. The main idea is to understand the abstraction presented by a model and how the corresponding component uses that type of model to present data to the users.

This section will give a broad overview of the rest of the Swing models, focusing on just their conceptual organization, their interrelation, and the components that use them. Table 10.6 lists all the models defined in Swing.

TABLE 10.6   The Swing Models

Swing model interface name	Description
`javax.swing.BoundedRangeModel`	Defines the characteristics of a range of values that have an upper and lower bound
`javax.swing.ButtonModel`	Creates an abstraction that defines state for all kinds of buttons including check boxes, radio buttons, and normal buttons
`javax.swing.ComboBoxModel`	Subinterface of `ListModel`, which adds the capability to specify one of the items as Selected
`javax.swing.ListModel`	Defines an ordered list of elements
`javax.swing.ListSelectionModel`	Defines the abstraction of a selection on a list and creates the capability to specify those elements that are selected
`javax.swing.MutableComboBoxModel`	Defines an abstraction that represents a combo box that can be edited
`javax.swing.SingleSelectionModel`	Defines an abstraction that supports the specification of a single list element to be selected
`javax.swing.table.TableModel`	Defines a two-dimensional table of objects
`javax.swing.table.TableColumnModel`	Defines a column in a two-dimensional table of objects
`javax.swing.tree.TreeModel`	Defines a directed, acyclic graph, also called a tree data abstraction
`javax.swing.tree.TreeSelectionModel`	Defines the characteristics of a selection of some subset of the elements in a tree
`javax.swing.text.Document`	Defines the characteristics of a generalized document that contains various kinds of text

Table 10.7 associates each of the models with the classes that provide partial or full implementations of their abstraction. As a convenience, the Swing package defines these implementations for you. The naming convention is uniform. Abstract classes have the name `Abstract<model name>`, for example, `AbstractListModel`. The names of the default implementations follow the pattern `Default<model name>`.

Abstract classes implement the behavior that can reasonably be considered common to all concrete implementations. For example, the `AbstractListModel` implements the mechanics of the `ListModel` interface, leaving details that differentiate specific concrete implementations to the concrete subclasses, such as `DefaultListModel` and `DefaultComboBoxModel`.

TABLE 10.7 Swing Models Implementations

Model name	Partial or full implementing class
BoundedRangeModel	DefaultBoundedRangeModel
ButtonModel	DefaultButtonModel
ComboBoxModel	MetalFileChooserUI. DirectoryComboBoxModel, MetalFileChooserUI. FilterComboBoxModel
ListModel	AbstractListModel
ListSelectionModel	DefaultListSelectionModel
MutableComboBoxModel	DefaultComboBoxModel
SingleSelectionModel	DefaultSingleSelectionModel
TableModel	AbstractTableModel
TableColumnModel	DefaultTableColumnModel
TreeModel	DefaultTreeModel
TreeSelectionModel	DefaultTreeSelectionModel
Document	AbstractDocument, DefaultStyledDocument, PlainDocument

One principle of GUI design says that you should focus more heavily on the abstractions created and used by your application logic. This suggests that you need to be aware of and examine the models used by your GUI components and understand how you plan to manipulate them in your application logic. Table 10.8 associates the Swing models with the Swing components that use them.

TABLE 10.8 Swing Components and Related Models

Model name	Used by these components
BoundedRangeModel	JSlider, JScrollBar, JProgressBar
ButtonModel	AbstractButton, JMenu, ButtonGroup
ComboBoxModel	JComboBox
ListModel	JList

10

MODELS

continues

TABLE 10.8   Continued

Model name	Used by these components
ListSelectionModel	JList, JTable
MutableComboBoxModel	None
SingleSelectionModel	JTabbedPane, JMenuBar, JPopupMenu
TableModel	JTable
TableColumnModel	JTable, JTableHeader
TreeModel	JTree
TreeSelectionModel	JTree
Document	JTextField, JTextArea, JPasswordField, JTextPane

Events can change the state of either a component or its model. The two states must remain synchronized, which means that the component and model must be notified of the occurrence of events. This implies that listeners must register for notification on event sources, a process that involves event listener interfaces.

Earlier I discussed the triad of model, event listener, and event type that collaborate to provide this capability. Table 10.9 associates each model with its related event listener interface and event type.

TABLE 10.9   Swing Models and Associated Listener and Event Types

Model name	Associated event listener	Event type
BoundedRangeModel	ChangeListener	ChangeEvent
ButtonModel	ActionListener, ChangeListener, ItemListener	ActionEvent, ChangeEvent, ItemEvent
ComboBoxModel	ListDataListener	ListDataEvent
ListModel	ListDataListener	ListDataEvent
ListSelectionModel	ListSelectionListener	ListSelection Event
MutableComboBoxModel	ListDataListener	ListDataEvent
SingleSelectionModel	ChangeListener	ChangeEvent
TableModel	TableModelListener	TableModelEvent
TableColumnModel	TableColumnModel TableColumnModel Listener	Event

Model name	Associated event listener	Event type
TreeModel	TreeModelListener	TreeModelEvent
TreeSelectionModel	TreeSelectionListener	TreeSelection Event
Document	DocumentListener	DocumentEvent

When designing your application, you need to anticipate what events to handle to provide model-component state synchronization. If you go back to Chapter 9, you will see that the event types listed in Table 10.9 are already familiar to you.

The only new concept is that we are now associating the occurrence of a particular event type with a model, as well as with a component. Now you need to think about what your application might want to do differently to manipulate or query the model associated with the component on which the user initiated some action.

The model is the object that stores the information in a manner suitable for interaction with your application logic. This is the point of using models.

Swing Models

At this point, you understand all the conceptual and architectural underpinnings of the Swing model architecture. At this time, a quick introduction to the abstractions defined by the Swing models is in order.

Now that you understand the model architecture, event handling, and event objects, you have all the background you need to use models effectively. The only task left is for you to visualize the logical abstraction captured by each model.

ButtonModel

The ButtonModel model is the first model discussed in this chapter that actually extends another interface; it is a subinterface of java.awt.ItemSelectable.

The ItemSelectable interface defines an abstraction that represents a group of items from which zero or more can be selected. Buttons can be selected, so, by the ButtonModel name, you can guess that this model abstracts the characteristic states of buttons.

The ButtonModel interface defines several states applicable to buttons. Table 10.10 lists the different button states.

TABLE 10.10   States Defined by the `ButtonModel` Interface

State	Description
Enabled	The state in which the button can be selected or pressed
Rollover	The state in which the mouse is positioned over the button
Selected	The state in which the button has been activated
Armed	The state in which the button has been pressed, but not activated
Pressed	The state in which the user has pressed the mouse down on the button, but not released it

The hierarchy in Figure 10.7 shows the organization of the `ButtonModel` interface among related classes. The `ButtonModel` interface defines a more sophisticated or complete model than `ItemSelectable`. You can see that it is applicable to the classes that implement `ItemSelectable`.

Of course, only the `javax.swing.AbstractButton` class uses `ButtonModel` because it is a Swing class. The other classes are AWT classes. Changing them to use the Swing model would disrupt backward compatibility. This arrangement emphasizes that Swing models are only used by Swing components.

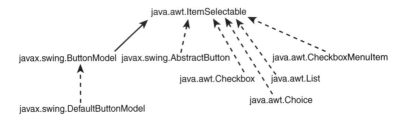

FIGURE 10.7

Swing models can extend AWT interfaces, but are not employed by AWT components. Only the Swing components use a model architecture.

ComboBoxModel and MutableComboBoxModel

A combo box is a list of elements, one of which can be selected. It shouldn't surprise you that `ComboBoxModel` extends `ListModel`. You can also infer that `MutableComboBoxModel` adds the notion of modifying the elements of a combo box. Figure 10.8 shows the relationship between these types.

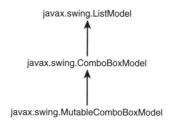

FIGURE 10.8
Combo boxes are essentially lists that can indicate a selected state for one of their items.

This hierarchy lets the combo box models take advantage of the abstraction already defined by
`ListModel`. Tables 10.11 and 10.12 list the methods of `ComboBoxModel` and
`MutableComboBoxModel`, respectively. You can see how little needs to be added to accommodate the behavior related to the additional abstractions.

TABLE 10.11   The `ComboBoxModel` Interface

Method name	Description
`Object getSelectedItem()`	Returns the item currently marked selected
`void setSelectedItem` `(Object anItem)`	Sets the specified item to be selected

TABLE 10.12   The `MutableComboBoxModel` Interface

Method name	Description
`void addElement(Object obj)`	Adds an element to the end of the model
`void insertElementAt` `(Object obj, int index)`	Inserts an element at a specific index in the model
`void removeElement(Object obj)`	Removes the specified element from the list represented by the model
`void removeElementAt(int index)`	Removes the element located at a specific index in the model

These two models are examples of extensions of the capabilities of an abstraction that is
already defined. As Figure 10.2 illustrates, these two models represent an ordered collection of
elements—a list—with some additional behavior.

The lesson here is that existing model definitions can be reused, if they create a suitable
abstraction for the data you are manipulating.

10

MODELS

SingleSelectionModel

At first glance, the SingleSelectionModel may seem superfluous because there is already a ListSelectionModel available for you to use. Upon closer consideration of its name and behavior, the abstraction it supports does look different.

First of all, its name implies that it characterizes only a single selection. Secondly, its name doesn't imply that it is specifically intended to model lists.

The SingleSelectionModel represents any collection of elements, one of which can be selected at a time. Knowing that the JMenu, JPopupMenu, and JTabbedPane components all use this model should help you visualize its intent. Table 10.13 lists the SingleSelectionModel methods.

TABLE **10.13**   The SingleSelectionModel Interface

Method name	Description
void addChangeListener (ChangeListener listener)	Adds a listener to be notified of change events on this model
void clearSelection()	Clears the selection so no elements are selected
int getSelectedIndex()	Returns the currently selected element
boolean isSelected()	Indicates (returns true) if the model currently has an element marked selected
void removeChangeListener (ChangeListener listener)	Removes the specified listener from the list of listeners forchange events
void setSelectedIndex (int index)	Sets the specified index to represent the selected index of this model

One other difference is that a SingleSelectionModel fires ChangeEvents instead of the ListSelectionEvent fired by ListSelectionModel. Recall from our discussion of these events in Chapter 9 that the ChangeEvent class only indicates the object that was changed. The ListSelectionEvent indicates a lot of information about a range of selections.

This is another example of how being familiar with the listener and event types related to a model can help you determine if it's suitable for your use. Make sure that the model you use supports all the information you need. If not, use another model, or define one that does.

TableModel and TableColumnModel

The TableModel interface abstracts a two-dimensional table of objects. This model is used by the JTable component, which is a fairly complex component. Much of the complexity, however, arises from implementation constraints relating to efficiency.

In terms of the table model, you should focus on its abstraction. Table 10.14 lists the methods in the `TableModel` interface. You can see that it provides the means to determine the dimensions of the table data and to set or retrieve the contents of a particular table cell.

TABLE 10.14   Methods of the `TableModel` Interface

Method name	Description
`void addTableModelListener` `(TableModelListener l)`	Adds the specified listener to be notified of the occurrence of the `TableModelEvent`
`Class getColumnClass` `(int columnIndex)`	Returns the class that accommodates the inclusion of all desired types into the table
`int getColumnCount()`	Returns the number of columns of table data presently in the table model
`String getColumnName` `(int columnIndex)`	Returns the name of the column represented by the speci fied column index
`int getRowCount()`	Returns the number of rows of table data presently in the table model
`Object getValueAt` `(int rowIndex, int columnIndex)`	Returns the object stored in the specified row and column of the object that stores the table data
`boolean isCellEditable` `(int rowIndex, int columnIndex)`	Indicates (returns `true`) if the cell at the specified row and column can be edited
`void removeTableModelListener` `(TableModelListener l)`	Removes the specified listener from the list of listeners that are notified of changes to the data in this model
`void setValueAt` `(Object aValue, int rowIndex, int columnIndex)`	Inserts the specified object as the element that is stored in the specified row and column of the table model

TreeModel and TreeSelectionModel

The `TreeModel` interface abstracts a standard directed acyclic graph, commonly called a tree. Intermediate nodes can have zero or more child elements, which may either be nodes or leaves if they have no children. Figure 10.9 shows a logical representation of a tree.

10

MODELS

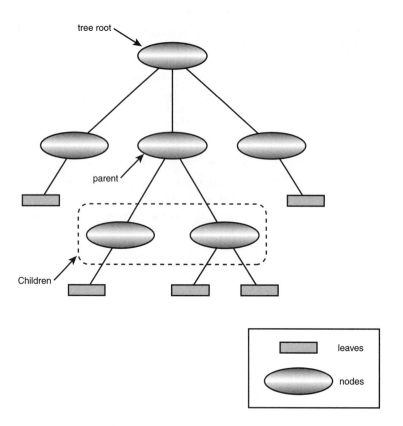

FIGURE 10.9

The TreeModel *interface represents a logical tree data structure.*

Table 10.15 lists the members of the TreeModel interface.

TABLE 10.15   Methods of the TreeModel Interface

Method name	*Description*
void addTreeModelListener (TreeModelListener l)	Adds a listener to be notified of the occurrence of TreeModelEvents
Object getChild(Object parent, int index)	Returns the tree element that is the child of the specified parent node, represented by the index in the array of children of this parent
int getChildCount(Object parent)	Returns the number of child elements of the specified parent node

Method name	*Description*
`int getIndexOfChild(Object parent, Object child)`	Returns the index of the specified child in the array of children of the specified parent
`Object getRoot()`	Returns the root node of this tree
`boolean isLeaf(Object node)`	Returns `true` if the specified node is a leaf
`void removeTreeModelListener (TreeModelListener l)`	Removes the specified listener from the list of previ ously added listeners interested in event notification
`void valueForPathChanged (TreePath path, Object newValue)`	Indicates a change to the specified tree path, invoked when the user has altered the specified value

The `TreeSelectionModel` interface complements the `TreeModel` interface. It abstracts a selection of one or more tree elements. If you recall from Chapter 9, a `JTree` component lets you select one or more of its nodes or leaves. Dragging the mouse selects several elements.

A selection is represented by the path that leads from the root of the tree to the node. Figure 10.10 shows a schematic representation of a logical path to one of the tree's elements.

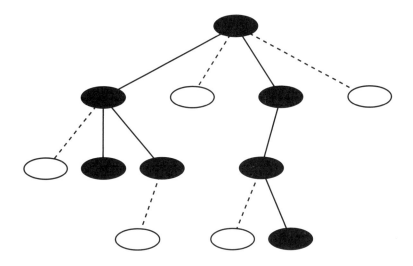

FIGURE 10.10

A path is defined by specifying every element from the tree root to the selected element, inclusive. The tree in this fig-ure shows three paths, indicated by the darkened links. The darkened nodes are part of the path. The root node will always be part of every path.

Table 10.16 describes the `TreeSelectionModel` interface. Clearly this model captures a different abstraction than the `TreeModel` interface. Nevertheless, they are closely related by a third abstraction that they use.

Both models rely on the `TreePath` abstraction, which models a path. Paths are the entities that `TreeModel` uses to describe the location of a node or leaf in a tree. Paths are also used by `TreeSelectionPath` to describe a selection, which is simply the identification of a leaf or node that is marked as selected.

It is wise to separate the two abstractions for clarity and simplification. By now you are well aware of the advantages of defining types that focus on one abstraction.

TABLE 10.16 Methods of the `TreeSelectionModel` Interface

Method name	Description
void addPropertyChangeListener (PropertyChangeListener listener)	Adds the specified listener to the list of listeners to be notified of property change events
void addSelectionPath (TreePath path)	Adds the specified path as an element of the current selection
void addSelectionPaths (TreePath[] paths)	Adds each path specified in the array to the current selection
void addTreeSelectionListener (TreeSelectionListener x)	Adds the specified listener to the list of listeners that are notified of selection events
void clearSelection()	Clears the current selection
TreePath getLeadSelectionPath()	Returns the last path that was added to the model's current selection
int getLeadSelectionRow()	Returns the index that represents the lead selection, which represents the path last added to the selection
int getMaxSelectionRow()	Gets the number of the row that represents the path last added to the selection
int getMinSelectionRow()	Gets the number of the row that represents the first path added to the selection
RowMapper getRowMapper()	Returns the `RowMapper` instance that is able to map a path to a row
int getSelectionCount()	Returns the number of paths that are currently selected
int getSelectionMode()	Returns the selection mode, one of `TreeSelectionModel.SINGLE_TREE_SELECTION`, `TreeSelectionModel.CONTIGUOUS_TREE_SELECTION`, `TreeSelectionModel.DISCONTIGUOUS_TREE_SELECTION`

Method name	Description
`TreePath getSelectionPath()`	Returns the path that was the first added to the current selection
`TreePath[] getSelectionPaths()`	Returns all the paths that comprise the current selection
`int[] getSelectionRows()`	Returns all the rows that represent the currently selected paths
`boolean isPathSelected (TreePath path)`	Returns `true` if the indicated path is part of the current selection
`boolean isRowSelected(int row)`	Indicates whether the specified row is selected
`boolean isSelectionEmpty()`	Indicates if the selection is currently empty
`void removePropertyChangeListener (PropertyChangeListener listener)`	Removes the specified listener from the list of listeners for property change events
`void removeSelectionPath (TreePath path)`	Removes the specified path from the selection
`void removeSelectionPaths (TreePath[] paths)`	Removes all the paths specified in the array from the selection
`void removeTreeSelectionListener (TreeSelectionListener x)`	Removes the specified listener from the list of listeners that are notified of the occurrence of changes to the model's selection
`void resetRowSelection()`	Updates the model's record of what rows are selected
`void setRowMapper(RowMapper newMapper)`	Sets the `RowMapper` instance used by this tree selection model
`void setSelectionMode(int mode)`	Sets the selection mode, which is one of `TreeSelectionModel.SINGLE_TREE_SELECTION`, `TreeSelectionModel.CONTIGUOUS_TREE_SELECTION`, or `TreeSelectionModel.DISCONTIGUOUS_TREE_SELECTION`
`void setSelectionPath (TreePath path)`	Sets the specified path to be the current selection
`void setSelectionPaths (TreePath[] paths)`	Sets the selection to be the paths specified in the array

10

MODELS

Defining Your Own Models

What is the difference between an arbitrary interface and a model? A model is intended to play the role of an abstraction that coincides with a visual view of the same abstraction. In the context of GUI programming and MVC architectures, the term model implies the existence of a related view component that uses the model.

You may find that none of the predefined Swing models suit your needs. Even if an existing model addresses the right abstraction, you might need a different concrete implementation.

If you define a new model and use it with an existing Swing component, you must define it to extend an existing model of the appropriate type. It must be compatible with the

```
public void setModel(<model type>Model model)
```

methods defined by the Swing components. Remember that each Swing component defines this method to restrict you from using an inappropriate type of model.

If you define a new model and a new component to use it, you need to consider what kind of support your component will provide for the model. At the very least, you should provide methods like

```
public <model type>Model getModel()
public void setModel(<model type>Model model)
```

Depending on the nature and complexity of the model, you may also want to define some convenient methods on the component that manipulate its underlying model.

The main idea is to try to follow the paradigm built into the JFC. This will bring uniformity and predictability to your applications. Others will recognize the paradigm and immediately understand your abstractions and how to use your new definitions.

Summary

Models are interface definitions. A model defines an abstraction that represents the characteristics and behavior of some type of data.

The Swing package contains some predefined model definitions that collaborate with the Swing visual components. An instance of a Swing model implementation is an MVC model object, whereas a Swing component is an instance of an MVC view. The model abstracts the data for which the component provides a view. By definition, models differ from ordinary abstract types because they play the role of the model object in the MVC paradigm.

The relationship between models and components in Swing creates an implementation of a modified MVC paradigm architecture. Swing's model architecture collapses the MVC view and controller into a single component definition.

The presence of an MVC architecture in Swing saves you a lot of design and implementation work. It enables you to take advantage of an existing MVC architecture without having to design an MVC relationship each time you need to use a Swing component.

Furthermore, it supports a clean separation of abstractions. Those abstractions that are suitable for implementing application logic are isolated from the abstractions suitable for implementing visual components. The capability to independently change the abstraction or implementation of either a model or its view gives you great flexibility when engineering GUI programs.

Graphics

IN THIS CHAPTER

- **The AWT Graphics Model** 538
- **The Graphics Class** 549
- **Using Graphics for Basic Drawing** 551
- **Clipping** 562
- **Translating the Graphics Origin** 569
- **Graphics Modes** 574
- **How Components Are Painted** 581

The AWT and Swing toolkits support a mechanism for drawing two-dimensional graphical shapes within the bounds of any component. The Java 2D API, which is part of the JFC, defines a much more sophisticated graphics model for performing sophisticated two-dimensional graphics operations. The Java 2D API is not discussed here. This chapter only describes the basic graphics model available to AWT and Swing components.

Part of drawing graphics involves learning the JFC model for painting components. The AWT and Swing have different models for painting. The AWT model lays the foundation for the Swing model. The Swing model adds some enhancements that offer greater efficiency and accommodates the Swing lightweight component architecture. The Swing lightweight component architecture is discussed in Chapter 6, "Swing Concepts and Architecture."

In this chapter, you will learn how to use the graphics model to draw graphics, and also how to use the JFC paint model correctly to ensure that your components are drawn properly.

The AWT Graphics Model

The Java graphics model enables a component to draw basic two-dimensional geometric shapes within its bounds. Components use a graphics object to define the context in which they do all drawing. The task of drawing is called painting in Java.

Every component—lightweight or heavyweight—has access to a graphics object, or graphics context. This graphics context is an instance of the class `java.awt.Graphics`. It is the heart of the graphics drawing system.

Through the manipulation of its graphics object, a component can paint various kinds of graphics within its bounds. The `Graphics` class defines several quantities that support the drawing capabilities available to components:

- A current color that is used as the color of the graphics pen
- A current font for drawing text
- A clipping region, which defines a subset of a component's area in which to draw
- A current mode, either XOR or paint
- A translation origin that supports translating the position of rendered graphical data

The values of these properties affect the drawing operations. For example, the color property indicates the color of the pen used to draw the geometric shapes or the text characters; characters will be drawn in the font specified by the font property, and so forth.

The `Graphics` class also defines many methods that enable you to draw a variety of geometric shapes. You will learn about the details of these `Graphics` objects in the section in this chapter titled "The Graphics Class."

Obtaining Graphics Objects for Drawing

Just as every component must have an associated heavyweight container somewhere in its containment hierarchy, so must every `Graphics` object correspond to a native platform graphics context defined by the native windowing system. These graphics contexts are native window system resources and are finite in number.

To perform drawing, a component must manipulate its associated native graphics object at some level. The components in your program are insulated from their native graphics, and, instead they manipulate copies of their native graphics object.

Copies of the native graphics objects are instances of the `java.awt.Graphics` class. Components invoke methods defined by the `Graphics` class on their `Graphics` instance to perform various drawing functions.

Listing 11.1 shows an application that draws a string on its panel. Incidentally, notice that the string is not a `Label` component. Rather, the graphics rendering routine `drawString()` draws the representation of the text into the graphics context. Figure 11.1 shows you the GUI produced by this program.

The `paint()` method is the center of all graphics drawing activity. It is always passed a `Graphics` reference on which it invokes all the methods that produce rendering operations.

When the program in Listing 11.1 executes, the AWT identifies the component's existing native graphics, creates a copy of it that is an instance of `Graphics`, and passes it to the component's `paint()` method.

This all happens in response to certain events that dictate that the component should be painted. You will learn about these events later in the section titled "How Components Are Painted."

LISTING 11.1 Drawing the Graphics Representation of a String

```
import java.awt.*;
import java.awt.event.*;
import javax.swing.*;

/**
   Creates a simple demonstration of drawing custom graphics
   on a component.
*/
class GraphicsDemo extends Panel
{
  /**
     Paints (renders) a string on the component.
```

continues

LISTING 11.1   Continued

```java
   @param g the Graphics context in which the painting
   is done.
*/
public void paint(Graphics g)
{
  g.setFont(new Font("sansserif", Font.PLAIN, 16));
  g.drawString("Our first attempt at drawing Graphics",
            20, 150);
}


/**
   Specifies the preferred size of this component.

   @return the component's preferred screen size.
*/
public Dimension getPreferredSize()
{
  return new Dimension(300, 300);
}


public static void main(String [] args)
{
  GraphicsDemo app = new GraphicsDemo();
  JFrame f = new JFrame("Graphics Demo");
  WindowListener wl = new WindowAdapter()
    {
      public void windowClosing(WindowEvent e)
        {
          e.getWindow().dispose();
          System.exit(0);
        }
    };
  f.addWindowListener(wl);

  f.getContentPane().add(app);
  f.pack();
  f.setVisible(true);
}
}
```

FIGURE 11.1
Java Graphics enable you to draw the graphical representation of strings.

Several methods defined in the AWT and Swing component classes take a parameter of type `Graphics`. These methods are listed in Table 11.1. Methods defined in any of the peer classes or classes found in any of the `javax.swing.plaf` packages are not listed. Like the `paint()` method, these methods are called in response to events that obviate the need for painting a component.

TABLE 11.1   JFC Methods That Are Passed a Graphics Reference

Package	Class name	Method name
java.awt	Component	paint(Graphics g)
	Component	update(Graphics g)
	Component	paintAll(Graphics g)
	Component	print(Graphics g)
	Component	printAll(Graphics g)
	Container	paint(Graphics g)
	Container	update(Graphics g)
	Container	print(Graphics g)
	Container	paintComponents(Graphics g)
	Container	printComponents(Graphics g)
java.beans	PropertyEditor Support	paintValue(Graphics g, Rectangle r)
	PropertyEditor	paintValue(Graphics g, Rectangle r)

continues

TABLE 11.1   Continued

Package	Class name	Method name
javax.swing	JComponent	getComponentGraphics(Graphics g)
	JComponent	paintComponent(Graphics g)
	JComponent	paintChildren(Graphics g)
	JComponent	paintBorder(Graphics g)
	JComponent	update(Graphics g)
	JComponent	paint(Graphics g)
	JLayeredPane	paint(Graphics g)
	JApplet	update(Graphics g)
	JToolBar	paintBorder(Graphics g)
	JSplitPane	paintChildren(Graphics g)
	AbstractButton	paintBorder(Graphics g)
	ImageIcon	paintIcon(Component c, Graphics g, int x, int y)
	JProgressBar	paintBorder(Graphics g)
	JViewport	paint(Graphics g)
	Icon	paintIcon(Graphics g)
	JMenuBar	paintBorder(Graphics g)
	SwingUtilities	paintComponent(Graphics g, Component c, Container cont, int x, int y, int w, int h)
	SwingUtilities	paintComponent(Graphics g, Component c, Container p, Rectangle r)
	JPopupMenu	paintBorder(Graphics g)
	JDialog	update(Graphics g)
	CellRenderPane	paint(Graphics g)
	CellRenderPane	update(Graphics g)
	CellRenderPane	paintComponent(Graphics g, Component c, Container p, int x, int y, int w, int h)
	CellRenderPane	paintComponent(Graphics g, Component c, Container p, Rectangle r)
	JFrame	update(Graphics g)

When any of these methods are called, the AWT creates a *copy* of the component's native window graphics context and passes a reference of the copy to the method being called. It is important to emphasize that the reference passed to the various paint-related methods of your class refers to a copy of the native window graphics object associated with the component.

Before the AWT passes the `Graphics` object to your method, however, it initializes it with relevant information about the graphics-related state information of its corresponding component. The AWT uses the following component-specific information to initialize the `Graphics` object:

- Graphics color is set to the component's foreground color.
- Graphics font is set to the component's current font.
- Graphics translation origin is set to represent the object's upper-left corner.
- Graphics clip rectangle is set to the rectangle that represents the subset of the component's area that needs repainting.

Because this initialization is done before the copy of the graphics is passed to your method, any changes you make to the component's state within the scope of the `paint()` method (that is, after the `Graphics` object is created) will not affect the screen rendering performed on the `Graphics` object.

Listing 11.2 shows a modified. version of the program in Listing 11.1.

LISTING 11.2   Changing the Component's State after Obtaining a Copy of Its Graphics

```
import java.awt.*;
import java.awt.event.*;
import javax.swing.*;

/**
   Creates a simple demonstration of drawing custom graphics
   on a component.  This class demonstrates the
   synchronization problems that occur if you change the
   state of the component's graphics-related
   parameters after obtaining a graphics object in which to
   draw.
*/
class GraphicsSyncDemo extends Panel
{
  /**
     Paints (renders) a string on the component.

     @param g the Graphics context in which the painting is done.
  */
  public void paint(Graphics g)
  {
    // Change the state of the component.  This will not
    // affect the graphics object passed in to this method,
```

continues

LISTING 11.2   Continued

```
        // which was configured with information from the
        // component BEFORE the call.
        //
        setFont(new Font("sansserif", Font.ITALIC, 12));

        g.drawString("Our first attempt at drawing Graphics",
                        20, 150);
    }


    /**
        Specifies the preferred size of this component.

        @return the component's preferred screen size.
    */
    public Dimension getPreferredSize()
    {
        return new Dimension(300, 300);
    }


    public static void main(String [] args)
    {
        GraphicsSyncDemo app = new GraphicsSyncDemo();
        JFrame f = new JFrame("Graphics Synchronization Demo");
        WindowListener wl = new WindowAdapter()
            {
                public void windowClosing(WindowEvent e)
                    {
                        e.getWindow().dispose();
                        System.exit(0);
                    }
            };
        f.addWindowListener(wl);

        f.getContentPane().add(app);
        f.pack();
        f.setVisible(true);
    }
}
```

This program changes the component's font. Nevertheless, this change does not affect the graphics object that has already been initialized and passed to the component's `paint()` method. The difference between this example and the previous one is that the program in Listing 11.1 set the font for the graphics object, not for the component.

The next time the `paint()` method is called, the changes that the program makes to the component's state will take effect, because a new copy of the native graphics is created and initialized with state information from the component. Try running this program, hiding the window, and then re-exposing it. You should see the text rendered in the font specified in the `setFont()` call.

Figure 11.2 shows the state of the GUI in Listing 11.2 when it first displays. Figure 11.3 shows how the font changes after you hide and then re-expose the window.

Before the second call to the paint method, the AWT creates and initializes a new `Graphics` object based on the component's current state, and it passes the new object to the component's `paint()` method.

FIGURE 11.2
Each time a `Graphics` *is constructed, it is initialized from the component's state.*

FIGURE 11.3
Setting the component's graphics parameters does not affect `Graphics` *objects that have already been constructed.*

In the previous two examples, the AWT created the graphics objects for you and passed it to your paint method. This is always the case whenever any of the methods in Table 11.1 execute.

Within the scope of any method call, however, you can obtain references to additional `Graphics` objects. To do this, you must make explicit calls to methods defined in the AWT that return references to new `Graphics` objects. Each new `Graphics` object will be a unique copy of the native platform graphics of the component that creates the copy.

Table 11.2 lists the methods that you can call to obtain a graphics reference from within the scope of any of the methods in Table 11.1. Only the methods in the `java.awt`, `java.beans`, and `javax.swing` packages are listed. Methods in AWT peer classes or any Swing pluggable look-and-feel class are not listed.

TABLE 11.2   Methods that Return a Copy of a Component's Graphics Instance

Package name	Class name	Method name
java.awt	Component	getGraphics()
	PrintJob	getGraphics()
	Graphics	create() create(int x, int y, int width, int height)
	Image	getGraphics()
javax.swing	JComponent	getComponentGraphics (Graphics g)
	JComponent	getGraphics()
	DebugGraphics	create()
	DebugGraphics	create(int x, int y, int width, int height)

After you have any graphics object, you can use it to execute drawing functions on a component.

Listing 11.3 shows the previous example rewritten to ignore the graphics object passed to the `paint()` method. Instead, the program creates a new `Graphics` object and draws into it. Just for variety, this program is written as an applet instead of an application.

LISTING 11.3   Using an Explicitly Created Graphics for Drawing

```
import java.applet.*;
import java.awt.*;
import javax.swing.*;

/**
   A class that demonstrates use of graphics in an Applet.
*/
public class GraphicsDemoApplet extends JApplet
```

```
{
  /**
     Draws the custom graphics in the Applet container.

     @param g the graphics context in which the drawing
     directives take place.
  */
  public void paint(Graphics g)
  {
    Graphics newG = getGraphics();

    // Use the newly created graphics and ignore the one
    // passed to this method.
    //
    if (newG == null)
      return;

    newG.drawString("Our first attempt at drawing Graphics",
                20, 150);

    // Must destroy any graphics that we create.
    //
    newG.dispose();
  }


  // The Applet execution is stopped when the user leaves the
  // page containing the Applet. We don't need any event handlers
  // to dispose of the frame; the browser handles this.

}
```

Listing 11.4 lists the HTML file that goes along with the applet in Listing 11.3.

LISTING 11.4   An HTML File for the `GraphicsDemoApplet` Program

```html
<!DOCTYPE HTML PUBLIC "-//IETF//DTD HTML//EN">
<html>
  <head>
    <title>Graphics Demo</title>
  </head>

  <body>
    <h1>Graphics Demo</h1>
```

continues

LISTING 11.4   Continued

```
<applet code=GraphicsDemoApplet.class
  width=300 height=300>
</applet>

<hr>
</body>
</html>
```

> **NOTE**
>
> The program in Listing 11.3 is an applet. If you execute this program using the `appletviewer` program that comes with the JDK, you will see a menu bar with a menu called "Applet" that contains several menu items.
>
> This menu is created by the `appletviewer` program and not the applet itself. If you run the applet in a browser, this menu would not appear.

Disposing of Graphics Instances

When the AWT creates .graphics instances for you, it takes care of destroying the `Graphics` object after the `paint()` call is done.

However, when you create new graphics resources, you are responsible for their destruction when you are finished using them. The last example explicitly creates a new `Graphics` object as a result of the `getGraphics()` call.

The `paint()` method calls `dispose()` on the graphics object that it created before returning. This ensures that the native window system will not deplete its graphics resources. Also notice that the `paint()` method checks for a null pointer after requesting new graphics. This is defensive programming in case the system has no more graphics contexts to create, which could happen if programmers who are less responsible than you don't release the graphics contexts they create.

> **CAUTION**
>
> It is the AWT that does the job of actually creating the `Graphics` objects passed to the methods in Table 11.1. Each `Graphics` object corresponds to a unique native platform graphics.
>
> The AWT handles the proper disposal of all `Graphics` objects that it creates. This occurs after the call to your `paint()` method returns.

When you create Graphics objects, however, you are responsible for disposing of them. The AWT cannot dispose of Graphics objects created by your program code.

If your program fails to dispose of Graphics objects that it creates, it's possible to exhaust the system's supply of native graphics resources. This is especially true of commercial applications, which typically run for days without being terminated and restarted.

The Graphics Class

The Graphics class defines a graphics context into which a component performs all graphics drawing operations. In addition to providing all the methods that enable you to draw various geometric shapes, it defines certain state information that affects how drawing operations are rendered.

The state defined by the Graphics class includes the following quantities:

- The current color of the graphics pen
- The current font for drawing characters
- The current clip region
- The current logical pixel operation (either paint or XOR)
- The current XOR alternation color
- The current origin to be used for translation operations

The Graphics class supports drawing with a graphics pen. The pen can only draw lines one pixel wide. If you want to make lines thicker than one pixel, you must do additional drawing operations that render adjacent pixels to give the effect of drawing thicker lines. The Java 2D API supports a much more sophisticated model in which the pen can have varying widths.

When you draw, you must specify a position or coordinate point for the graphics pen. The Graphics class defines an x, y plane of coordinate points that represent a grid of pixels into which you can draw.

Coordinates lie between pixels much the same way that the cursor in a text editor is positioned between characters. For example, even if your text editor's cursor appears to be positioned on top of a character, as is the case with many editors, it is really between that character and the previous one (to the left for languages that read left to right). The next character typed will be inserted before the character underneath the cursor.

Similarly, graphics pen coordinates lie between pixels. The Graphics class documentation says that the graphics pen "hangs down and to the right from the path it traverses." This means that the pen will draw on the pixel that is below and to the right of its coordinate position. You can think of coordinates as being infinitely thin because pixels appear to be flush against each other.

Figure 11.4 shows a schematic diagram that represents the relationship between pixels and coordinates. The pixels are represented by the squares, and the coordinates are represented by dots.

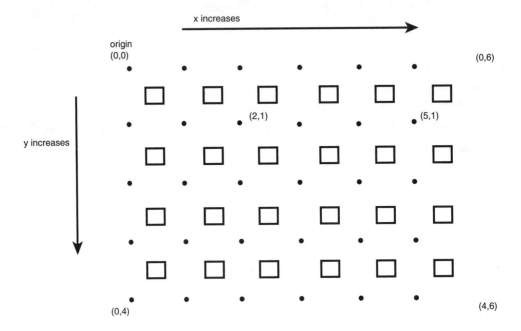

FIGURE 11.4

The Graphics class represents the display as an array of pixels addressed by coordinate points.

Notice that the origin (0, 0) is above and to the left of the pixel in the top-left corner. If you want to draw a vertical line starting from the origin and extending downward for three pixels, you draw a line from point (0, 0) to (0, 3). This line is shown darkened on the diagram. In reality, pixels really are flush against each other, but the diagram must show space between them so you can see the presence of the coordinates.

Coordinates are infinitely thin; however, the graphics pen always has width and height both equal to one. The vertical line in Figure 11.4 indicates this because it covers the whole width of the pixels. To create the appearance of a vertical line two pixels wide, you could draw another line adjacent to the first from point (0, 1) to point (3, 1), as shown in the Figure 11.4. Without the artificial space between rows and columns of pixels, these two vertical lines would appear as one line, two pixels wide.

Notice in both cases that the coordinates you specify should be above and to the left of the pixels you wish to render. To draw the horizontal line between points (2, 1) and (5, 1) you would locate the coordinates relative to the pixels in the same way.

Some of the routines in the Graphics class support drawing lines by specifying two coordinates, (x, y), (x1, y1). As you will see in the next section, you can also draw rectangles by specifying a starting point and a width and height. In these cases remember that the width will be (x2 - x1 - 1), and the height will be (y2 - y1 - 1).

> **NOTE**
>
> The routines in the Graphics class that do drawing and filling take arguments that specify the location of the drawing anchor, the point that specifies the offset from the top-left corner of the Graphics region.
>
> For geometric shapes, this (x, y) coordinate specifies the top-left corner of the area that bounds the geometric shape being drawn.
>
> The drawString() method also takes an anchor location. However, the anchor position is the bottom-left corner of the rectangle that bounds the characters of the string.

Using Graphics for Basic Drawing

The methods in the Graphics class support drawing rectangles, circles, arcs, 3D rectangles, ovals, polygons, polylines, and filled versions of these shapes. I won't list the methods in tabular form, but instead, simply jump in and show a few examples of what you can do with graphics rendering.

The main point to remember when using any of the methods in the Graphics class is that they all use the graphics coordinate plane described in the preceding section.

Listing 11.5 shows an applet that demonstrates the use of the drawing methods in the Graphics class.

LISTING 11.5   Using the Graphics Class Drawing Routines

```
import java.applet.Applet;

import java.awt.Choice;
import java.awt.Color;
import java.awt.Graphics;
import java.awt.Rectangle;
```

continues

LISTING 11.5   Continued

```java
import java.awt.event.ItemEvent;
import java.awt.event.ItemListener;

/**
   This class demonstrates some of the geometric figures you
   can draw with a Graphics object.  Egregious use of colors
   is avoided.
*/
public class DrawingDemoApplet extends Applet
{
  /**
     Called by the browser.  Initializes the GUI.
  */
  public void init()
  {
    // Add a Choice component.  Selecting one of the
    // categories of geometric figures will draw some
    // examples from that set.
    //
    Choice choice = new Choice();
    choice.add("Lines");
    choice.add("Ovals");
    choice.add("Polygons");
    choice.add("Rectangles");
    choice.add("Round Rectangles");
    choice.add("Arcs");
    choice.add("Clear");

    add(choice);

    // Create and add a listener for the Choice selection.
    // Set the selection in the instance field.  The paint()
    // method reads the field and calls a helper method to
    // paint the correct geometric figures.
    //
    ItemListener iL = new ItemListener()
      {
        public void itemStateChanged(ItemEvent e)
          {
            selection = ((String) e.getItem());
            repaint();
          }
      };
    choice.addItemListener(iL);
```

```
    }
/**
    Paints the applet accordingly.  This method overrides
    the paint method in Applet.  We don't need to dispose
    of the graphics object; the caller will do it.

    <p>Checks the selection made last and calls the
    appropriate method to paint the correct geometric
    shapes.

    @param g the graphics context in which to draw.
 */
public void paint(Graphics g)
{
  Rectangle r = g.getClipBounds();
  System.out.println("Clip Rectangle: x = " + r.x +
                     "; y = " + r.y +
                     "; width  = " + r.width +
                     "; height = " + r.height);

  g.setClip(0, 0, getSize().width, getSize().height);
  g.clearRect(0, 0, getSize().width, getSize().height);

  if (selection == "Lines")
    drawLines(g);
  else if(selection == "Ovals")
    drawOvals(g);
  else if(selection == "Polygons")
    drawPolygons(g);
  else if(selection == "Rectangles")
    drawRectangles(g);
  else if(selection == "Round Rectangles")
    drawRoundRectangles(g);
  else if (selection == "Arcs")
    drawArcs(g);
  else if (selection == "Clear")
    g.clearRect(0, 0, getSize().width, getSize().height);

  g.setClip(r);
  g.drawRect(r.x, r.y, r.width - 2, r.height - 2);
  g.drawRect(r.x + 1, r.y + 1, r.width - 4, r.height - 4);
}

/**
```

continues

LISTING 11.5   Continued

```
        Draw some sample lines.  For all the drawing routines
        the Graphics passed is the same graphics passed to the
        paint() method.  A new one is not created.

        @param g a reference to the graphics in which to draw.
      */
      private void drawLines(Graphics g)
      {
        // You can effectively create lines thicker than one pixel
        // by drawing adjacent pixels.  The following six calls
        // draw in adjacent rows of pixels.
        //
        g.drawLine(50, 50, 280, 280);
        g.drawLine(50, 51, 280, 281);
        g.drawLine(50, 52, 280, 282);
        g.drawLine(50, 53, 280, 283);
        g.drawLine(50, 54, 280, 284);
        g.drawLine(50, 55, 280, 285);

        // The following three calls creates a line of thickness
        // 3 pixels.
        //
        g.drawLine(50, 75, 280, 305);
        g.drawLine(50, 76, 280, 306);
        g.drawLine(50, 77, 280, 307);

        g.drawLine(50, 100, 280, 330);
      }

    private void drawOvals(Graphics g)
      {
        g.drawOval(75, 100, 200, 125);
        g.drawOval(100, 125, 150, 100);
        g.fillOval(125, 150, 100, 75);
      }

    private void drawPolygons(Graphics g)
      {
        // A set of (x, y) points that are connected with straight
        // lines to form the polygon.  The polygon is automatically
        // closed if the start and end points are not the same.
        //
```

```
    int [] xPoints = {75, 150, 175, 200, 275, 210, 240, 175,
                      115, 140};
    int [] yPoints = {150, 150, 75, 150, 150, 185, 260, 210,
                      260, 185};

    g.drawPolygon(xPoints, yPoints, 10);
  }

private void drawRectangles(Graphics g)
  {
    g.drawRect(50, 100, 250, 150);
    g.draw3DRect(75, 125, 200, 100, true);
    g.fill3DRect(125, 160, 100, 25, true);
  }

private void drawRoundRectangles(Graphics g)
  {
    // The arc width and height is the same as the width and
    // height of the bounding rectangle.  The sides of the
    // oval look smooth.
    //
    g.drawRoundRect(20, 50, 50, 125, 50, 125);

    // The bounding rectangle is a square, so this draws a
    // circle.
    //
    g.setColor(Color.magenta);
    g.fillRoundRect(100, 50, 50, 50, 50, 50);

    g.setColor(Color.black);

    // The arc width and height are less than the width and
    // height of the bounding rectangle.  The sides of the
    // oval will be compressed.
    //
    g.drawRoundRect(100, 125, 200, 90, 150, 75);

    // No compression of the arcs will be done here.
    //
    g.drawRoundRect(50, 250, 250, 75, 250, 75);
  }

private void drawArcs(Graphics g)
```

continues

LISTING 11.5   Continued

```
{
  g.drawArc(100, 75, 150, 100, 160, 300);
  g.fillArc(100, 200, 150, 100, 0, 250);
}


/**
    Store the last selection so the paint routine can
    dispatch a call to the appropriate helper routine for
    drawing the right shape examples.
*/
String selection;
}
```

Listing 11.6 shows the HTML file for Listing 11.5

LISTING 11.6   The HTML File for the `DrawingDemoApplet` Program

```
<!DOCTYPE HTML PUBLIC "-//IETF//DTD HTML//EN">
<html>
  <head>
    <title>Graphics Drawing Demo</title>
  </head>

  <body>
    <h1>Graphics Drawing Demo</h1>

    <applet code=DrawingDemoApplet.class width=350 height=350> </applet>

    <hr>
  </body>
</html>
```

The `Choice` component in the applet contains a list of items that represent different categories of geometric shapes. Upon startup, the applet panel shown in Figure 11.5 is blank. Selecting one of the items in the choice box will draw some geometric shapes that belong to the category represented by the choice item.

A call to `paint()` results from each selection. The `paint()` method determines the selection and calls another method to help it render the pertinent geometric shapes. This is an example of using methods called within the scope of the `paint()` method to do all graphics drawing.

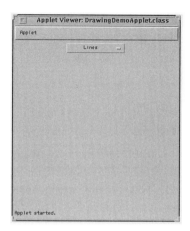

FIGURE 11.5
The applet draws various families of geometric shapes based on the selected item in the Choice *component.*

Each of the methods called from paint() are passed a Graphics reference. This reference refers to the same graphics object; no new graphics objects are created.

Drawing Lines

The first selection draws three lines on the applet panel. The Graphics.drawLine() method defines four parameters. The first two give the x and y coordinates of the start point, and the second two give the coordinates of the end point.

Figure 11.6 shows the lines drawn by the applet's drawLines() method.

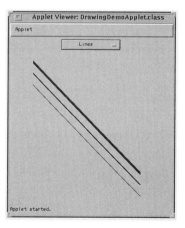

FIGURE 11.6
Lines can only be drawn with a thickness of one pixel, but drawing adjacent lines gives the appearance of thicker lines.

The AWT `Graphics` class only supports drawing lines with a thickness of one pixel. You can create the appearance of thicker lines by drawing adjacent lines as demonstrated by the top and middle lines of Figure 11.6.

Drawing Ovals

The next item in the applet's `Choice` component draws and fills some ovals using the `drawOval()` and `fillOval()` methods.

The first two parameters of these methods indicate the coordinate of the top-left corner of the box that bounds the oval. The last two parameters specify the width and height of the bounding box. This combination of parameters is commonly used by many of the `Graphics` methods. Figure 11.7 shows the ovals drawn by the applet.

The smallest oval is filled by calling the `fillOval()` method. In all the methods that fill the geometric shapes they draw, the inside of the shape is filled with the current color of the `Graphics` object.

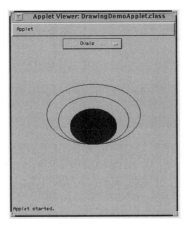

FIGURE 11.7
Ovals are created by specifying their bounding box. The oval is drawn to be as big as possible and still fit within the bounding box.

Drawing Polygons

Polygons are drawn with the overloaded `drawPolygon()` methods. One form takes a `Polygon` object as an argument that specifies the points of the polygon. The second form takes two `int` arrays that specify the x and y coordinates of the points that are connected by the polygon.

Figure 11.8 shows the polygon drawn by the applet in Listing 11.5.

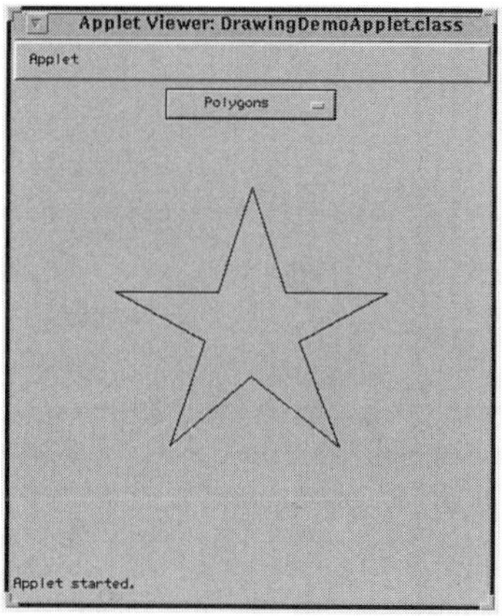

FIGURE 11.8
You can draw arbitrarily complex polygons with the `drawPolygon()` *methods.*

The difference between polygons and polylines is that polygons are closed. The `drawPolygon()` methods will close the polygon by drawing a line between its first and last points, if they are not the same.

The `drawPolyline()` method, on the other hand, will not close the figure by drawing a line between the first and last points specified in the `Polygon` or `int` array arguments.

Drawing Rectangles

Rectangles are specified in a manner similar to ovals. The `drawRect()` method takes four parameters, an `x` and `y` coordinate that indicate the top-left corner of the rectangle, and the width and height of the rectangle. All such parameters are always specified in pixels.

Rectangles can also be filled by calling the `fillRect()` method. Two additional methods, `draw3DRect()` and `fill3DRect()`, enable you to draw rectangles with raised borders, which gives a 3D effect. Figure 11.9 shows some rectangles drawn by the applet.

Another kind of rectangle is a rounded rectangle. Rounded rectangles look like ovals at first sight because they are rectangles with rounded corners. They are bounded by a rectangle in the same way as ovals or regular rectangles. The difference, however, is that you can specify some degree of compression of the width or height of the actual outline of the rectangle. You specify a compression factor as a number of pixels.

With no compression, the point of greatest width or height of the rectangle will match the width or height of its bounding box. If you specify a compression of the width or height, the rectangle's outline at its left and right or top and bottom, respectively, is compressed.

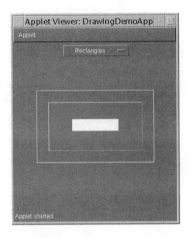

FIGURE 11.9

Rectangles can be raised to give a three-dimensional effect.

Figure 11.10 shows some rounded rectangles. The rectangle to the far left and the one at the bottom are not rounded. Examining the source code in the `drawRoundRectangles()` method of Listing 11.5 shows you why.

The last two parameters of the `drawRoundRect()` and `fillRoundRect()` methods indicate the arc width and arc height, respectively. If these values are less than the width and height of the rectangle, the outline of the rounded rectangle at the widest or tallest points is compressed.

Incidentally, you can draw circles by specifying equal widths and heights. This example fills the circle, located immediately below the `Choice` component, just to demonstrate how to set the graphics color.

Drawing Arcs

Arcs are the next category of geometric shapes you can draw. Arcs are also created by specifying the coordinate of the top-left corner of its bounding box and a width and height. Additionally, you must specify two angles. The first is the start angle in degrees. Zero degrees is the three o'clock position, just as in classical geometry. The second angle indicates the angle subtended by the arc that is drawn. Either angle can have a value between 0 and 360. Figure 11.11 shows two arcs, one outlined and one filled in.

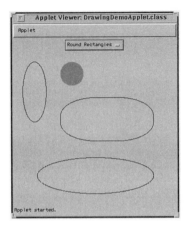

FIGURE 11.10

Rounded rectangles have rounded corners instead of right angles. The sides can also be compressed to be less than the width or height of the bounding box.

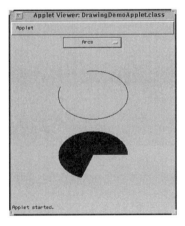

FIGURE 11.11

The start angle and arc angle required to specify an arc can be any value between 0 and 360.

Drawing Text

Earlier in this chapter, Listing 11.1 displayed some text drawn into the applet created by the program. The text was not a `Label` or `JLabel` component, but the rendering of graphics that represented text.

The following three methods in the `Graphics` class support drawing text.

```
void drawBytes(byte[] data, int offset, int length,
               int x, int y)

void drawChars(char[] data, int offset, int length,
               int x, int y)

abstract void drawString(String str, int x, int y)
```

Listing 11.1 uses the `drawString()` method. The other two methods are provided so that you don't have to convert byte or character arrays to `String` objects.

Drawing text is similar to specifying other drawing operations, except that the x and y coordinates specify the lower—left corner of the rectangle that bounds the rendered graphics representing the string.

Figure 11.1 shows the GUI displayed by the program in Listing 11.1. The following statement from Listing 11.1 specifies that the string text should be rendered so that the bottom-left corner of the rectangle that encloses the text is located at point (20, 150).

```
g.drawString("Our first attempt at drawing Graphics", 20, 150);
```

Clipping

At the beginning of this chapter you were introduced to the attributes that every `Graphics` object contains. One of those attributes is a clip region. A `Graphics` object's clip region is the region to which graphics rendering operations are constrained.

In the AWT, the clip region is called the clip rectangle because it is represented by a `java.awt.Rectangle` object. However, in the Java 2D API, clip regions can be any arbitrary `Shape` object. The `Shape` class is abstract, but supports the definition of concrete subclasses that represent arbitrary geometric shapes.

Whenever a component in your program is displayed, its `paint()` method is called by the AWT. The `Graphics` object passed in is clipped. That is, its clip rectangle is set so that the point (0, 0) refers to the upper-left corner of the component.

The AWT sets this clip rectangle before calling a component's `paint()` method. It must, because the `Graphics` object corresponds to a physical native window graphics context which addresses the whole physical area allocated to that component. Your components should not be able to render outside of their bounds—and indeed they can't.

Your program's components can still address graphics coordinates that lie outside of the range of coordinates encapsulated by their clip rectangle, but the corresponding pixels will not be rendered on screen. For instance, you could invoke the following method

```
g.fillRect(-50, -50, 100, 75)
```

which requests the Graphics object to render a filled rectangle beyond the upper-left bounds of your component. And, in fact, the drawing operations will take place as you requested. However, you will only see the pixels that draw the part of the rectangle that is contained within the component's clip rectangle.

When your program GUI is first rendered on screen, the AWT sets the clip rectangle for every component on which it calls paint() to include the whole component's display area. After the GUI is initially displayed, however, the AWT, in response to certain events, will pass your paint() method a Graphics context whose clip rectangle is set to some subset of the total area taken by the component.

For example, whenever your application—or applet—is partially occluded by another window and subsequently raised, one or more of the GUI components can be damaged and might need to be redrawn. For each damaged component, the AWT will set the component's clip rectangle to represent only the area that is to be redrawn.

Figure 11.12 shows the drawing program in Listing 11.5 after it has been occluded by another window, but just before it executes its paint() method to repair the damage. Of course, normally you cannot see your GUI in this state because the repaint operation takes place too quickly.

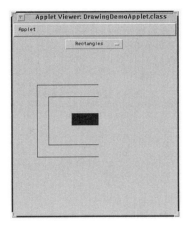

FIGURE 11.12
This figure shows the state of the applet just before its paint() *method is called to repair the damage created by an occluding window. The AWT sets the clip rectangle of the graphics to the damaged region.*

You may wonder why the whole drawing still appears—why the full rectangles are drawn. After all, you know that any rendering of coordinates outside of the damaged area will be clipped, because the clip rectangle is set to represent only the damaged area of the just raised applet window. The answer is that the original pixels that were not occluded by the other window were not damaged and, therefore, still exist intact in the native graphics context.

To prove that (regardless of the drawing method calls you make) the rendering is clipped to the area represented by the clip rectangle, you can modify the `paint()` method in Listing 11.5 and perform a little experiment. Listing 11.7 shows a slightly modified version of the `paint()` method. The rest of the applet code is unchanged, so I won't list it again.

LISTING 11.7   A Program That Shows Only the Drawing of Repaired Pixels

```java
public void paint(Graphics g)
  {
    // Grab and keep the current clip rectangle.
    //
    Rectangle r = g.getClipBounds();
    System.out.println("Clip Rectangle: x = " + r.x +
                       "; y = " + r.y +
                       "; width  = " + r.width +
                       "; height = " + r.height);

    // Clear the whole applet.
    //
    g.setClip(0, 0, getSize().width, getSize().height);
    g.clearRect(0, 0, getSize().width, getSize().height);

    // Reset the clip rectangle to that passed into paint().
    //
    g.setClip(r);

    // Draw as usual.  Nothing changes here.
    //
    if (selection == "Lines")
      drawLines(g);
    else if(selection == "Ovals")
      drawOvals(g);
    else if(selection == "Polygons")
      drawPolygons(g);
    else if(selection == "Rectangles")
      drawRectangles(g);
    else if(selection == "Round Rectangles")
      drawRoundRectangles(g);
    else if (selection == "Arcs")
      drawArcs(g);
    else if (selection == "Clear")
      g.clearRect(0, 0, getSize().width, getSize().height);
  }
```

11

This new version clears the applet before redrawing the damaged area so that you can see only the pixels that are redrawn. You wouldn't normally do this, but this illustrates the point of the example.

Executing the applet with this new version of `paint()` first clears the window of all rendered pixels and then only paints the pixels that are contained in the clip rectangle passed to `paint()`.

Figure 11.13 shows the applet partially hidden by an `xterm` terminal window. If you click on the frame to raise the applet window to the front, you now see that only the portion of the rectangles that are in the damaged area are repainted.

Figure 11.14 shows the repainted applet window.

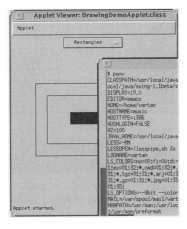

FIGURE 11.13

The applet is partially occluded. When the window is raised, only the pixels contained in the area damaged by the other window will be rendered.

Now you can see what part of your geometric figures were damaged and subsequently repaired. However, you still can't see the extent of the whole clip rectangle. Figure 11.14 only shows you the part of your drawing that is inside the clip rectangle, not the clip rectangle itself.

In order to see the clip rectangle itself, you can modify the `paint()` method of Listing 11.7 one more time. Listing 11.8 shows the latest modified `paint()` method. This time it will draw a box around the clip rectangle.

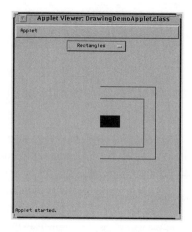

FIGURE 11.14

The applet drawing methods still draw the full geometric shape in the Graphics *context, but the rendering is clipped to the area represented by the clip rectangle.*

LISTING 11.8   Showing the Clip Rectangle Passed to a Component's Graphics

```java
public void paint(Graphics g)
  {
    Rectangle r = g.getClipBounds();
    System.out.println("Clip Rectangle: x = " + r.x +
                       "; y = " + r.y +
                       "; width  = " + r.width +
                       "; height = " + r.height);

    g.setClip(0, 0, getSize().width, getSize().height);
    g.clearRect(0, 0, getSize().width, getSize().height);

    if (selection == "Lines")
      drawLines(g);
    else if(selection == "Ovals")
      drawOvals(g);
    else if(selection == "Polygons")
      drawPolygons(g);
    else if(selection == "Rectangles")
      drawRectangles(g);
    else if(selection == "Round Rectangles")
      drawRoundRectangles(g);
    else if (selection == "Arcs")
      drawArcs(g);
    else if (selection == "Clear")
```

```
        g.clearRect(0, 0, getSize().width, getSize().height);

    // Draw a visible rectangle around the clip rectangle.
    //
    g.setClip(r);
    g.drawRect(r.x, r.y, r.width - 2, r.height - 2);
    g.drawRect(r.x + 1, r.y + 1, r.width - 4, r.height - 4);
}
```

Partially hiding the applet window will again cause a repainting of the damaged area when the window is raised. Figure 11.15 shows the repaired applet. You can see that the applet now also draws a box around the clip rectangle that represents the damaged area just repaired. Remember, it is the AWT that calculates where the damaged area is and sets the clip rectangle accordingly. The Graphics class knows how to clip your drawing operations to render pixels that fall inside the clip rectangle. You don't have to calculate either of these quantities.

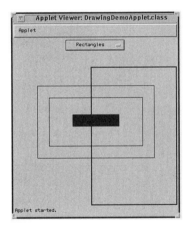

FIGURE 11.15
The damaged area is bordered by the two-pixel–wide rectangle.

NOTE

It's important to distinguish between *drawing* and *rendering* of graphics operations. Drawing refers to the execution of Graphics methods that perform calculations that represent two-dimensional figures. Rendering refers to the display of the associated bits in the physical graphics context.

A Graphics clip rectangle does not restrict your drawing; it only restricts the rendering of pixels to those contained in the current clip rectangle.

continues

You can still specify the drawing of graphics operations that address the area outside the current clip rectangle—even beyond the bounds of your GUI's outermost window. However, you can never render outside the bounds of your component's outermost container.

The full range of rendering allowed for a component is represented by the rectangle whose top-left corner is (0, 0) and whose width and height are given by the component's quantities `getSize().width` and `getSize().height`, respectively.

In the last two listings, you may have noticed the presence of two new method calls. The `Graphics.getClipBounds()` method gives you the clip rectangle as a `Rectangle` object. Another method not used in these examples is the `Graphics.getClip()` method, which returns the clip region as a `Shape` object.

```
abstract Shape getClip()
abstract Rectangle getClipBounds()
```

The capability to discern the clip regions is important for programs that perform complex drawing operations, which can use a lot of system resources. In such cases, the `paint()` method can restrict its drawing to only those pixels that fall in the clip rectangle, vastly improving performance. For simple drawing operations, such as those in our examples, the calculation to restrict the drawing is not worth the small performance gain that might be realized.

Another important function is the capability to set the clip rectangle. Two overloaded versions of `Graphics.setClip()` methods give you this capability.

```
abstract void setClip(int x, int y, int width, int height)
abstract void setClip(Shape clip)
```

The last two versions of `paint()` in Listings 11.7 and 11.8 use the `setClip()` method to set the clip rectangle to the whole applet bounds in order to ensure that all pixels are cleared. You can set the clip to any region in which you want to restrict rendering.

NOTE

It is important to understand that clipping a `Graphics` object does not change its coordinate system. That is, the point (0, 0) still refers to the top-left corner of a component's area, which is its origin. The bottom-right corner of the `Graphics` is still referenced by the point whose x and y coordinates are given by `getSize().width` - 1 and `getSize().height` - 1, respectively.

The position of a pixel contained in a `Graphics` object's clip region is still specified relative to the coordinate system of the `Graphics` object, not relative to the clip region.

Translating the Graphics Origin

It is possible to translate the origin of a `Graphics`. After translation, the origin coincides with some point other than the original (`0, 0`) of the component's display area.

The `Graphics.translate()` method translates the origin of its `Graphics` object. Its two integer arguments are the x and y coordinates of the point that is to be the new origin. This new origin is thereafter represented by the point (`0, 0`).

Listing 11.9 shows a program that translates its `Graphics` object before painting. This program paints an image so that the upper-left corner is located at the point where the user clicks the mouse in the application window.

LISTING **11.9**   Translating a Graphics Origin

```
import java.awt.*;
import java.awt.event.*;
import javax.swing.*;

/**
   A class that demonstrates use of Graphics translation.
   This program draws an image whose top left corner is
   located at the position where the user clicks the mouse
   button.
*/
class TranslationDemo extends JPanel
{
  /**
     No-arg constructor.  Creates the listener for the mouse
     clicks, and initially loads the image.
  */
  public TranslationDemo()
  {
    createListeners();
    loadImage("../images/tree-lined-path.gif");
  }


  /**
     Creates the mouse listener that handles the user mouse
     clicks.  Upon a user click, the listener determines the
     location of the click and translates the graphics
     origin to that point.
  */
  private void createListeners()
```

continues

LISTING 11.9   Continued

```
{
    // An anonymous inner class that handles the mouse clicks.
    //
    MouseListener mL = new MouseAdapter()
      {
        public void mouseClicked(MouseEvent e)
          {
            // Determine where the user clicked the mouse.
            Point click = e.getPoint();

            Point lastPosition = origin;

            // Save the click location.  The paint method uses
            // this location to redraw the image in the last
            // location specified by a mouse click in response
            // to the window being hidden and then raised.
            //
            origin = click;

            // Get a new graphics; we don't have one yet.
            Graphics g = getGraphics();

            g.drawImage(image, lastPosition.x, lastPosition.y,
                        TranslationDemo.this);

            // Clear the whole applet so we don't have residue
            // from previous images drawn in other positions.
             g.clearRect(0, 0, getWidth(), getHeight());

            // Translate the origin of the Graphics to the point
            // clicked by the user in the applet's window.
            g.translate(click.x, click.y);

            // The image will now be drawn from the new origin,
            // which is still referred to as the point (0, 0).
            //
            g.drawImage(image, 0, 0, TranslationDemo.this);

            // Dispose of the graphics that we created.
            //
            g.dispose();
          }
      };
    addMouseListener(mL);
```

```
    }

    private void loadImage(String path)
    {
      image = Toolkit.getDefaultToolkit().getImage(path);
    }

    public Dimension getPreferredSize()
    {
      return new Dimension(400, 300);
    }

/**
    Paints the image.  This call displays the image the
    first time the applet is started.  Also, if the applet
    window is hidden and then raised, this method will
    redraw the applet at the location it was last drawn in
    response to last user mouse click.

    @param g the graphics created by the AWT and passed in.
  */
  public void paint(Graphics g)
  {
    g.clearRect(0, 0, getWidth(), getHeight());
    g.drawImage(image, origin.x, origin.y, this);
  }

public static void main(String [] args)
  {
    TranslationDemo app = new TranslationDemo();
    JFrame f = new JFrame("Translation Demo");
    WindowListener wl = new WindowAdapter()
      {
        public void windowClosing(WindowEvent e)
          {
            e.getWindow().dispose();
            System.exit(0);
          }
      };
    f.addWindowListener(wl);
    f.getContentPane().add(app);
    f.pack();
    f.setVisible(true);
  }
```

continues

LISTING 11.9   Continued

```
// The image to display.
Image image;

// Initializes a new Point which specifies the location of
// the top left corner where the image should first be
// drawn.
Point origin = new Point(30, 20);
}
```

Figure 11.16 shows the application upon startup. Initially, the point (0, 0) refers to the top-left corner of the frame.

After clicking within the frame, the image is redrawn at the new location. Note that the following two statements translate the graphics and then draw the image.

```
g.translate(click.x, click.y);

// The image will now be drawn from the new origin,
// which is still referred to as the point (0, 0).
//
g.drawImage(image, 0, 0, TranslationDemo.this);
```

The drawImage() method still specifies the point (0, 0) as the top-left corner of the image it draws. But (0, 0) now refers to the new origin, which corresponds to the point where the mouse was clicked. If the translation had not been done, (0, 0) would still refer to the application's original upper-left corner.

FIGURE 11.16

The application initially centers the image in its frame. Clicking the mouse redraws the upper-left corner of the image at the point of the mouse click.

Figure 11.17 shows how the image is translated after the mouse click. The original location of the image is drawn as a white rectangle for comparison.

FIGURE 11.17
Translating the Graphics *origin enables the program to still refer to the image's top-left corner as* (0, 0) *but draw it in a different location.*

After translating a Graphics, all point specifications are relative to the point specified in the translation. However, it's still entirely possible to access any of the points on the application's frame. However, you must now access the absolute location of points relative to the translated origin of your Graphics.

For instance, given the translation represented in Figure 11.17, you would have to reference points above and to the left of the new origin with negative coordinate values.

This is possible because translation only changes the relative coordinate system of the Graphics object on which the translation occurs. Remember, any Graphics object you have is a copy of the component's native platform graphics context. The native graphics context is unaltered because it must always represent the absolute screen area allocated to the component it represents.

> **NOTE**
>
> Translating a Graphics means translating its coordinate system.
>
> Performing a translation only translates the origin of the copy of the Graphics context on which the translation is performed. It never translates the corresponding native window graphics context.

Graphics Modes

The `Graphics` class supports two graphics *modes*. You have already used one of them; all the previous examples in this chapter use the *paint* mode.

The paint mode is the default mode. However, the `Graphics` class defines the `setPaintMode()` method to enable you to set this mode explicitly.

The second mode is called *XOR mode* because `Graphics` objects perform an XOR operation on pixels drawn by any of the drawing methods while in this mode.

The XOR mode enables you to draw over previously rendered pixels without disturbing the original drawing. Performing a second XOR drawing operation on the same pixels reverts them back to their original state.

The XOR mode is set with the following method:

```
public void setXORMode(Color c)
```

The `Color` argument specifies an XOR mode alternation color. In XOR mode, graphics operations that draw onto pixels whose color is the current color of the `Graphics` object will be changed to the specified XOR mode alternation color. The colors of all other pixels drawn will be changed randomly.

However, performing the same drawing operations again on the same pixels will revert the state of all pixels to their original colors. That is, pixels that were painted in the alternation color will once again be painted in the current color of the `Graphics` object. Pixels that were originally in any color other than the current color of the `Graphics` will be reverted to their original color.

This feature is useful for a number of standard graphics functions such as rubber-banding. For instance, a very common function is to outline a rectangle in response to the user's mouse drag. The top-left corner of the rectangle is the point where the user performed the mouse down action, and its lower-right corner is the extent of the drag.

To support this feature, it is necessary to draw a rectangle in a color that shows over the image or graphics on top of which it is being drawn. Moreover, each mouse drag event must erase the rectangle drawn by the previous drag.

You can draw the rectangles in XOR mode. You then erase the previous rectangle by redrawing the same rectangle again in XOR mode. All pixels are reverted to their original color.

Listing 11.10 shows an application that adds this feature to the previous translation demo in Listing 11.9.

LISTING 11.10   Using XOR Mode for Rubber-Band–Like Drawing

```java
import java.awt.*;
import java.awt.event.*;
import javax.swing.*;

/**
   A class that demonstrates use of Graphics translation.
   This program draws an image whose top left corner is
   located at the position where the user clicks the mouse
   button.
*/
class GraphicsModesDemo extends JPanel
{
  /**
     No-arg constructor.  Creates the listener for the mouse
     clicks, and initially loads the image.
  */
  public GraphicsModesDemo()
  {
    String path = "../images/snowy-peaks.gif";
    image = Toolkit.getDefaultToolkit().getImage(path);

    try
      {
        MediaTracker tracker = new MediaTracker(this);
        tracker.addImage(image, 0);
        tracker.waitForID(0);
      }
    catch (InterruptedException e)
      {

      }
    createListeners();
  }


  /**
     Creates the mouse listener that handles the user mouse
     clicks.  Upon a user click, the listener determines the
     location of the click and translates the graphics
     origin to that point.
  */
  private void createListeners()
  {
    MouseListener mL = new MouseHandler();
```

continues

LISTING 11.10   Continued

```java
    MouseMotionListener mmL = new MouseMotionHandler();

    addMouseListener(mL);
    addMouseMotionListener(mmL);
}


public Dimension getPreferredSize()
{
    return new Dimension(400, 300);
}


/**
    Paints the image.  This call displays the image the
    first time the applet is started.  Also, if the applet
    window is hidden and then raised, this method will
    redraw the applet at the location it was last drawn in
    response to last user mouse click.

    @param g the graphics created by the AWT and passed in.
*/
public void paint(Graphics g)
{
    g.clearRect(0, 0, getWidth(), getHeight());
    g.drawImage(image, origin.x, origin.y, this);
}


public static void main(String [] args)
{
    GraphicsModesDemo app = new GraphicsModesDemo();
    JFrame f = new JFrame("Graphics Modes Demo");
    WindowListener wl = new WindowAdapter()
        {
            public void windowClosing(WindowEvent e)
                {
                    e.getWindow().dispose();
                    System.exit(0);
                }
        };
    f.addWindowListener(wl);
    f.getContentPane().add(app);
    f.pack();
```

Graphics

CHAPTER 11 577

```
    f.setVisible(true);
}

// The image to display.
//
Image image;

// Initializes a new Point which specifies the location of
// the top left corner where the image should first be
// drawn.
//
Point origin = new Point(30, 20);


// Indicates if the user has dragged the mouse yet.  If
// so, the mouse motion listener needs to erase the
// previously drawn rectangle in XOR mode, which will
// revert the colors to their original state.
//
boolean firstDrag = true;


// The point where the user pressed the mouse.  This marks
// the top left corner of the rectangle drawn by the
// MouseMotionHandler.
//
Point topLeft;


// The bottom right corner of the rectangle drawn by the
// the last drag event.
Point lastDrag;


// The XOR mode alternation color used.
//
Color xorColor = Color.white;


/**
    A class to handle the mouse events.  A mouse click
    redraws the image so that its top left corner is at the
    position of the click.  A mouse drag draws a rectangle
    around the area whose upper left corner is at the point
    where the mouse was pressed and whose lower right
    corner is at the point where the mouse was released.
```

continues

LISTING 11.10   Continued

```java
*/
public class MouseHandler extends MouseAdapter
{
  /**
     Draws the image with its upper left corner at the
     point where the mouse was clicked.
  */
  public void mouseClicked(MouseEvent e)
  {
    // Determine where the user clicked the mouse.
    Point click = e.getPoint();

    Point lastPosition = origin;

    // Save the click location.  The paint method uses
    // this location to redraw the image in the last
    // location specified by a mouse click in response to
    // the window being hidden and then raised.
    //
    origin = click;

    // Get a new graphics; we don't have one yet.
    Graphics g = getGraphics();

    g.drawImage(image, lastPosition.x, lastPosition.y,
               GraphicsModesDemo.this);

    // Clear the whole applet so we don't have residue
    // from previous images drawn in other positions.
    g.clearRect(0, 0, getWidth(), getHeight());

    // Translate the origin of the Graphics to the point
    // clicked by the user in the applet's window.
    g.translate(click.x, click.y);

    // The image will now be drawn from the new origin.
    // Notice the new origin is referred to as the point
    // (0, 0).
    //
    g.drawImage(image, 0, 0, GraphicsModesDemo.this);

    // Dispose of the graphics that we created.
    //
    g.dispose();
```

```
    }

/**
    Stores the point at which the mouse was pressed.
    This is used by the mouseDragged() method of the
    MouseMotionHandler to know the top left corner of the
    rectangle is drawn.
*/
public void mousePressed(MouseEvent e)
{
  Graphics g = getGraphics();
  g.setXORMode(xorColor);

  // Erase the last rectangle from the previous drag if
  // there was one.
  //

  // Set up the data for this drag.
  //
  topLeft = e.getPoint();
  firstDrag = true;

  // Dispose of the graphics created here.
  g.dispose();
}

/**
   Erases the last rectangle drawn when the user releases
   the mouse.
 */
public void mouseReleased(MouseEvent e)
{
  Graphics g = getGraphics();

  g.setXORMode(xorColor);
  g.drawRect(topLeft.x, topLeft.y,
           lastDrag.x - topLeft.x,
           lastDrag.y - topLeft.y);
  g.drawRect(topLeft.x + 1, topLeft.y + 1,
           lastDrag.x + 1 - topLeft.x - 1,
           lastDrag.y + 1 - topLeft.y - 1);
  g.dispose();
}

}
```

continues

LISTING 11.10   Continued

```java
/**
   A class that defines listeners that draw a rectangle in
   XOR mode around a region whose top left and bottom
   right corners are given by the point where the user
   presses the mouse and the point where it is released,
   respectively.
 */
public class MouseMotionHandler extends MouseMotionAdapter
{
  public void mouseDragged(MouseEvent e)
  {
    Graphics g = getGraphics();
    g.setXORMode(xorColor);

    if (firstDrag)
      {
        // There's no rectangle to erase.
        firstDrag = false;
      }
    else
      {
        // Must erase a previously drawn rectangle.  In
        // graphics XOR mode, drawing over a rectangle
        // previously drawn in XOR mode reverts those pixels
        // to their original color.
        //
        g.drawRect(topLeft.x, topLeft.y,
                   lastDrag.x - topLeft.x,
                   lastDrag.y - topLeft.y);
        g.drawRect(topLeft.x + 1, topLeft.y + 1,
                   lastDrag.x + 1 - topLeft.x - 1,
                   lastDrag.y + 1 - topLeft.y - 1);
      }

    // Finally, draw the new rectangle.
    g.drawRect(topLeft.x, topLeft.y,
               e.getPoint().x - topLeft.x,
               e.getPoint().y - topLeft.y);
    g.drawRect(topLeft.x + 1, topLeft.y + 1,
               e.getPoint().x + 1 - topLeft.x - 1,
               e.getPoint().y + 1 - topLeft.y - 1);

    // Store the location of this drag event for the next
    // time around.
```

```
        lastDrag = e.getPoint();

        // Dispose of the graphics.
        g.dispose();
      }
    }
}
```

Figure 11.18 shows the image after clicking and dragging the mouse over a portion of the GUI. Ample comments exist in Listing 11.10 to help you follow each step.

FIGURE 11.18
After dragging the mouse, any image pixels that were in the Graphics *current color are painted white; the colors of all other pixels are altered randomly.*

How Components Are Painted

So far you know that an AWT component's paint() method defines how a component looks. All drawing operations should be defined in your component's paint() method.

Components need repainting at various times, for instance after being damaged, as you learned earlier. The AWT is ultimately responsible for ensuring that your components get painted. The AWT determines what components need repainting and performs a sequence of actions that result in a call to the paint() method of one or more of your GUI's components.

It's important to understand the sequence of events that lead up to a call to a component's paint() method. This section discusses how that happens and how this knowledge helps you write AWT and Swing programs.

Events Trigger Painting

Components perform their graphics drawing operations only at certain times. They perform their painting operations in response to the occurrence of certain types of events such as the following:

- The component first becomes visible on screen.
- The component is resized or moved.
- A portion of the component's visible area is partially damaged. For example, the component becomes exposed after having been completely or partially occluded by another component in your application, or your application's window becomes exposed after being occluded by another window on your desktop.
- The application itself requests to paint the component. That is, some part of the application, possibly the component itself, requests the component to be painted in response to a change of state of the component.

The first three items in the previous list fall under the category of system-triggered painting, whereas the fourth item falls under the category of application-triggered painting.

These four types of stimuli result in the creation of a `PaintEvent`. These events are generated and handled internally by the AWT, which is why you did not learn about them in Chapter 9. Your programs should never handle paint events.

Regardless of whether a paint event results from a system request or an application request to paint, components use the same mechanism to render their visual look. However, there is a slight difference between the AWT and Swing paint models.

This is another case where the Swing model enhances the AWT model; it does not supersede it. Therefore, as is often the case, you must understand the AWT mechanism first.

The AWT Paint Model

The heart of the JFC paint system is in the AWT `Component` class, which defines the paint-related methods listed in Table 11.3.

TABLE 11.3   The AWT Paint-Related Methods

Method name	Function
`public void paint (Graphics g)`	Executes the drawing functions that create the look of the component
`public void paintAll (containe (Graphics g)`	Paints this component and all its children, if it is a containe (Graphics g)

Method name	Function
`public void repaint()`	Schedules a call to repaint this component as soon as possible
`public void repaint(long tm)`	Repaints the component within the specified number of milliseconds
`void repaint(int x, int y, int width, int height)`	Repaints only the specified rectangle of this component
`public void repaint(long tm, int x, int y, int width, int height)`	Repaints the rectangle with the specified dimensions within the specified number of milliseconds
`public void update (Graphics g)`	Clears the component's background and calls the `paint()` method

You're already familiar with the `paint()` method; it executes the drawing operations for its component. The AWT, however, does not call this method directly when it initiates the painting or repainting of a component. Instead it calls the `repaint()` method.

> **NOTE**
>
> To perform custom graphics drawing in components that subclass AWT components, always override your component's `paint()` method. All paint code should be called from inside the scope of `paint()`. The `paint()` method itself can call other methods to help it paint the component, but these methods should only be executed by `paint()`.

The AWT always calls your component's `repaint()` method in response to events that trigger painting. This method schedules your component to be repainted. The implementation of `repaint()` in the Component class calls the `repaint()` method on the component's peer.

The peer `repaint()` method calls your component's `update()` method with a Graphics instance that is a copy of the native graphics context for the component. The `update()` method then clears the component and finally calls your component's `paint()` method.

You can override the `update()` method to call `paint()` directly. This will result in any drawing not being cleared before the `paint()` is called. An application can use this technique to render new pixels on top of—in addition to—the pixels that are currently painted. This layering of drawing is a very specialized technique that you will rarely—if ever—use so I won't discuss it in this chapter.

More common, however, is the case where the application, or one of its components, determines that it should be repainted and initiates the repainting. In this case, the application should call its `repaint()` method. Your programs should never call `paint()` directly.

Notice in Listing 11.5 that the `itemStateChanged()` method in the `ItemListener` calls `repaint()` after storing the selection of the `Choice` component. This sets in motion the AWT processing that eventually results in a call to your `paint()` method.

> **NOTE**
>
> You should never call `paint()` directly because the AWT schedules repaint requests along with all other event processing on a special queue called the AWT Event Dispatch queue. A separate VM thread, the AWT event dispatch thread, monitors this queue and services the requests sequentially. The AWT updates the GUI only through the use of this thread, which guarantees that two threads do not attempt to update the GUI simultaneously. When your paint request is serviced, it is the AWT event dispatch thread, and not your program thread, that calls your component's `paint()` methods.

Table 11.3 indicated that you actually have four options for calling the `repaint()` method. You can specify some delay time in milliseconds after which your repaint request should be serviced.

Another form of the `repaint()` method takes arguments that specify the bounds of the rectangle to repaint. Component's that perform complex paint operations can use this version to narrow the scope of their painting. Doing so can improve paint performance dramatically.

The Swing Paint Model

Like many other elements of Swing, the Swing paint model extends the related AWT model. Swing defines enhancements to the AWT paint model in order to increase flexibility and improve performance. The Swing paint model enhancements are also necessary to work with the new lightweight component architecture and pluggable L&F framework. In this section, you'll learn what things you must do differently to make Swing components paint properly.

Remember that Swing components are still instances of `java.awt.Component`. Based on the discussion in the previous section, you might expect the AWT to still use its `repaint()`, `update()`, `paint()` calling sequence to repaint a lightweight component.

In fact, this is exactly what happens. However, the `JComponent` class overrides the definitions of these three methods to create paint behavior that is congruent with Swing's lightweight component architecture.

Remember that Swing components are lightweight, and they borrow part of the screen area from their closest heavyweight ancestor in order to render their appearance. Unlike heavyweight AWT components, several Swing components can share one native graphics context.

Back in Chapter 4, "AWT Concepts and Architecture," you learned that the AWT `Component` and `Container` classes were the foundation of the Swing architecture. One of the ways these classes support Swing's lightweight component implementations is that they create the abstraction of allocating individual native windows for each Swing component.

Actually, a lightweight component's `Graphics` object is translated relative to the origin of its closest heavyweight parent, based on calculations of its position by the layout manager. Its characteristic graphics are then drawn in some portion of the heavyweight parent's graphics context.

Because of this abstraction, the `update()` method in `Component` is overridden in `JComponent` so that it does not clear any rendered graphics. Doing so would also clear the rendering of the associated native graphics context of the heavyweight parent. This action essentially erases all the rendered pixels that represent the appearance of all other lightweight children in the heavyweight container.

Therefore, `JComponent.update()` simply calls the `JComponent.paint()` method. `JComponent` also overrides the `paint()` method to support the whole Swing pluggable look-and-feel model. A discussion of Swing's UI delegate architecture is beyond the scope of this chapter. One of the reasons why `JComponent` overrides `paint()`, however, is central to this discussion. The `JComponent.paint()` method calls three other methods defined in `JComponent`, namely `paintComponent()`, `paintBorder()`, and `paintChildren()`, in that order.

The Swing paint model is designed so that lightweight component implementations will put custom rendering graphics operations in their `paintComponent()` method and not in the `paint()` method. If you extend a Swing component, you must put all graphics drawing calls in your class's `paintComponent()` method. Failing to do so will result in a malfunctioning program.

Listing 11.11 illustrates a naive implementation of a lightweight application. It is very similar to Listing 11.1, which just created a panel and drew a string in its center.

LISTING 11.11   An Incorrect Approach to Painting a Lightweight Component

```
import java.awt.*;
import java.awt.event.*;
import javax.swing.*;

/**
   Creates a simple demonstration of drawing custom graphics
```

continues

LISTING 11.11   Continued

```java
   on a component.
*/
class SwingPaintDemo extends JPanel
{
  /**
     Paints (renders) a string on the component.

     @param g the Graphics context in which the painting
     is done.
  */
  public void paint(Graphics g)
  {
    g.setFont(new Font("sansserif", Font.PLAIN, 16));
    g.drawString("A simple string of text",
                 60, 145);
  }


  /**
     Specifies the preferred size of this component.

     @return the component's preferred screen size.
  */
  public Dimension getPreferredSize()
  {
    return new Dimension(300, 300);
  }


  public static void main(String [] args)
  {
    SwingPaintDemo app = new SwingPaintDemo();
    JFrame f = new JFrame("Swing Graphics Demo");
    WindowListener wl = new WindowAdapter()
      {
        public void windowClosing(WindowEvent e)
          {
            e.getWindow().dispose();
            System.exit(0);
          }
      };
    f.addWindowListener(wl);
```

```
        f.getContentPane().add(app);
        f.pack();
        f.setVisible(true);
    }
}
```

Notice that this application differs from Listing 11.1 in that it extends the lightweight `JPanel` instead of the heavyweight AWT `Panel` class.

After you hide all or part of the application's frame and then raise it to the front, the AWT then calls the `repaint()` method which, in turn, calls `update()` and eventually `paint()`.

However, because you have now subclassed a lightweight component, the `update()` method in `JComponent` is the method called. It does not first erase the existing graphics. Figure 11.19 shows the garbage that results.

Furthermore, when `update()` eventually calls `paint()`, it calls your `paint()` method, which overrides the one in `JComponent`. Of course, your version doesn't do any of the complex processing that `JComponent` does—such as translating graphics so that your component draws its graphics in the correct portion of its heavyweight ancestor's graphics context. The result is a program that doesn't perform correctly. The string doesn't always appear in the right place relative to its component context.

FIGURE 11.19

When creating subclasses of Swing lightweight component, failing to place graphics drawing statements in `paintComponent()` *instead of* `paint()` *will display garbage when the component is repainted.*

The solution is to get rid of the `paint()` method and instead place its code in a method called `paintComponent()`. Listing 11.12 shows the corrected version.

LISTING 11.12   A Lightweight Component That Paints Correctly

```java
import java.awt.*;
import java.awt.event.*;
import javax.swing.*;

/**
   Creates a simple demonstration of drawing custom graphics
   on a component.
*/
class SwingPaintDemo2 extends JPanel
{
  /**
     Paints (renders) a string on the component.

     @param g the Graphics context in which the painting
     is done.
  */
  public void paintComponent(Graphics g)
  {
    super.paintComponent(g);
g.setFont(new Font("sansserif", Font.PLAIN, 16));
    g.drawString("A simple string of text",
                 60, 145);
  }


  /**
     Specifies the preferred size of this component.

     @return the component's preferred screen size.
  */
  public Dimension getPreferredSize()
  {
    return new Dimension(300, 300);
  }


  public static void main(String [] args)
  {
    SwingPaintDemo2 app = new SwingPaintDemo2();
    JFrame f = new JFrame("Swing Graphics Demo");
    WindowListener wl = new WindowAdapter()
      {
        public void windowClosing(WindowEvent e)
          {
```

```
            e.getWindow().dispose();
            System.exit(0);
        }
    };
    f.addWindowListener(wl);

    f.getContentPane().add(app);
    f.pack();
    f.setVisible(true);
    }
}
```

Notice that the `paintComponent()` method contains all the drawing code. Also notice that `paintComponent()` calls `super.paintComponent()` before drawing in order to clear the remnants of any previous drawing operations. This solves the problem of screen garbage you saw in the previous version.

Figure 11.20 shows the results of running the corrected version of the program. No matter how you resize, move, or occlude the window, the string will appear centered as it should. The `JComponent.paint()` is called, and it calculates the correct translation of your lightweight graphics relative to its heavyweight ancestor.

FIGURE 11.20
A correct lightweight component implementation erases residue graphics before drawing anew.

NOTE

When defining lightweight components that directly subclass AWT components or directly subclass `java.awt.Component`, you must place all custom drawing code in the `paint()` method.

continues

When creating a lightweight container class that directly subclasses `java.awt.Container`, you must still place all custom drawing code in your class's `paint()` method. Moreover, you must ensure that your `paint()` method calls `super.paint()` after performing its drawing operations.

When you define a class that directly subclasses `javax.swing.JComponent`, you must place all custom drawing code in your class's `paintComponent()` method. Subclasses of Swing components should never override the `paint()` method.

Additionally, if your new class subclasses a Swing container, you must ensure that your class's `paintComponent()` method calls `super.paintComponent()` before performing any drawing operations.

Summary

The AWT defines a mechanism for performing basic graphical rendering operations within a component's display area. The `Graphics` class supports drawing basic geometric shapes and also performing shape filling and rendering of three-dimensional looking figures.

The AWT `Graphics` class also supports common graphics features such as clipping, two rendering modes, and coordinate translation.

Programs perform drawing of graphics by manipulating a `Graphics` object, which is a copy of a native platform graphics context. Native graphics contexts are finite resources. Java programs, therefore, must take care to dispose of these resources when they are finished using them. Although the AWT takes care of this task in many cases, programmers are responsible for disposing of graphics contexts after specifically requesting their creation.

The AWT and Swing toolkits define a mechanism for determining when and how components paint their graphics. Programmers must provide the interface expected by the JFC infrastructure classes in order to ensure that their components appear as expected.

Java GUI programmers can create quite complex applications and rarely have to perform the drawing operations described in this chapter. However, these features can add life to an application when needed. Similarly, the next chapter covers colors and fonts, which are two topics that, strictly speaking, are not required to make a real application completely functional. However, learning to manipulate colors and fonts can make your programs much more presentable.

Fonts and Colors

IN THIS CHAPTER

- **Organization of Color Support Classes   592**

- **Color Models   593**

- **Using Colors   597**

- **Fonts   602**

Judicious use of colors and fonts can make your application more appealing and also improve the clarity of its user interface. This chapter describes the support for colors and fonts in the AWT and Swing toolkits. Please keep in mind that this chapter does not cover the advanced features defined by the Java 2D API.

Organization of Color Support Classes

The classes that support colors in Swing are spread throughout several JFC packages, namely the `java.awt`, `java.awt.color`, and `java.awt.image`. The `java.awt.image` package defines classes that support creating and modifying images.

The `java.awt.color` package defines classes that support color spaces. Color spaces are a new feature in Java 2D. They define an implementation of a proposed industry standard mechanism to standardize the way color models are translated to formats suitable for output devices. This chapter does not discuss color spaces.

Our treatment of colors will only focus on the subset of these color-related classes with which you must be familiar in order to use colors practically.

Table 12.1 lists the color-related classes and their packages you will encounter most frequently. Of these, you will most often use only the `Color` and `SystemColor` classes.

TABLE 12.1 The Main Color-Related Classes

Package	Class	Description
java.awt.image	ColorModel	The abstract base class of all classes that define color models.
java.awt	Color	A class that defines color values and supports construction of color instances using information from various color models.
java.awt	SystemColor	A class that defines system properties and their default color values.
java.awt.color	ColorSpace	An abstract class that defines the nature of color spaces. A color space is a standard mechanism for defining a mapping from a program to the output device that displays colors.

If you define your own color models, become familiar with the `ColorModel` class. Even though you can program effectively without ever defining a color model, you should understand what they are and the different types supported by the AWT and Swing.

Color Models

All color processing involves translating a pixel's color specification into a set of values that represent values of its red, green, and blue components. These are used to display the pixel properly on an output device such as a color monitor. Splitting the color specification in this way reflects the design of modern monitors and other output devices. Monitors, for instance, have cathode emitters for producing the red, green, and blue colors.

In addition to these colors, a pixel's value consists of an *alpha value*, which specifies the degree of opaqueness of the pixel. The values range from completely transparent, represented by the value `0.0`, to completely opaque, represented by the value `1.0`.

Pixel color values can be represented using different schemes. For each scheme a transformation must be defined to map each possible pixel value to a set of representative color values. The definition of this transformation is called a color model.

The `ColorModel` class in the `java.awt.image` package is the foundation of the support for defining color models in the AWT and Swing. Figure 12.1 shows the hierarchy of the core color-model–related classes.

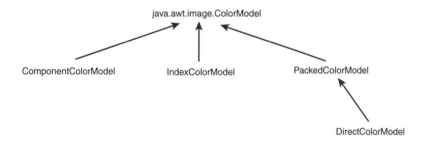

FIGURE 12.1

The `java.awt.image` *package defines three concrete classes that present models for mapping pixel color values to their principal-color constituent values. The* `ColorModel` *and* `PackedColorModel` *classes are abstract.*

The various classes related to color models allow you to define your own color models. However, because the default color model available to you is almost always used by most programmers, this discussion will not present examples of creating your own color models. Rather, this section focuses on conceptually understanding the models.

The Index Color Model

The index color model is so named because color values represent indices into an array of colors. This array is commonly referred to as a *color map*.

The `java.awt.image.IndexColorModel` class defines a concrete index color model implementation. Figure 12.2 shows a logical representation of an index color map.

The `IndexColorModel` defines an array of colors. An index into the color array represents a color value for a pixel. The number of bits, n, that constitute a color value determine the number of indices in the array, and, therefore, the number of possible colors. First and foremost, then, to instantiate the `IndexColorModel` class requires specifying the number of bits per pixel.

The color index value is really comprised of four other indices into arrays that store the range of possible values of the color's constituent red, green, blue, and alpha components. These sub-indices represent the particular RGB and alpha-component values. In fact, the color map of an `IndexColorModel` is defined by specifying separate arrays for the full range of values for each of the red, green, blue, and alpha constituents.

This organization demands that the size of each of the principal-color and alpha-component arrays be specified. This is the second parameter needed to instantiate the `IndexColorModel` class. The size represents the number of bits used to index values in each component array.

For instance, in Figure 12.2, the size of the color value, n, is 32 bits. The indices into the constituent component arrays are each 8 bits. The division of the color value into four 8-bit quantities yields the indices into the separate RGB and alpha arrays. The RGB and alpha arrays each store 8-bit values.

The final required elements are the actual RGB and alpha arrays that store the actual values. These arrays comprise the actual color map for the model. Together these quantities define an index color model.

The following list gives you the constructors of the `IndexColorModel` class. These items give you a more concrete idea of the quantities being discussed.

Constructors of the `IndexColorModel` *Class*

```
IndexColorModel(int bits, int size, byte[] r, byte[] g, byte[] b)
IndexColorModel(int bits, int size, byte[] r, byte[] g, byte[] b,
byte[] a)
IndexColorModel(int bits, int size, byte[] r, byte[] g, byte[] b, int
trans)
IndexColorModel(int bits, int size, byte[] cmap, int start, boolean
hasalpha)
IndexColorModel(int bits, int size, byte[] cmap, int start, boolean
hasalpha, int trans)
IndexColorModel(int bits, int size, int[] cmap, int start, boolean
hasalpha, int trans, int transferType)
```

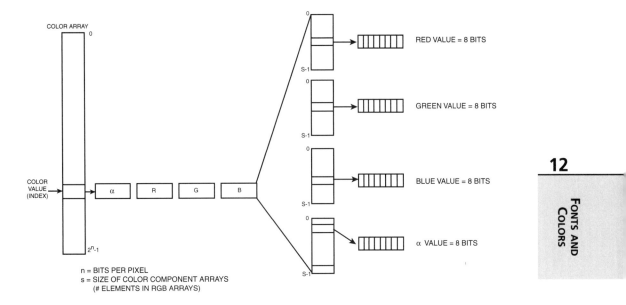

COLOR ARRAY

RED VALUE = 8 BITS

GREEN VALUE = 8 BITS

BLUE VALUE = 8 BITS

α VALUE = 8 BITS

COLOR VALUE (INDEX)

α R G B

n = BITS PER PIXEL
s = SIZE OF COLOR COMPONENT ARRAYS
(# ELEMENTS IN RGB ARRAYS)

Figure 12.2

The index color model defines a color value to be an index into a color array table. The value of the table at the index position can be broken down into four equal-sized quantities that represent indices into four separate tables. These tables store the actual values of the constituent RGB and alpha values that correspond to the original color value.

After an IndexColorModel object is created, you can retrieve the separate RGB values for a pixel using methods getBlue(), getRed(), or getGreen(). You can also get the complete set of values in a component array, for instance, the complete array of red values, using getReds().

A color model provides means for transforming quantities of one domain to the other. For instance, all models must provide a means to transform color values to equivalent RGB values. Therefore, most of the methods defined by the concrete color model classes are specified in the abstract ColorModel superclass. Some of these are listed in Table 12.2.

Table 12.2 Some of the ColorModel Class Methods

Constructor or method name	Description
int getAlpha(int pixel)	Gets the alpha value for the specified pixel value.
void getAlphas(byte[] a)	Gets the array of all valid alpha values.
int getBlue(int pixel)	Gets the blue value for the specified pixel value.
void getBlues(byte[] b)	Gets the array of all valid blue values.

continues

TABLE 12.2   Continued

Constructor or method name	Description
`int[] getComponentSize()`	Gets the size of each of the component arrays that comprise the color map, returned in an array of `int`s.
`int getComponentSize (int componentIdx)`	Gets the number of bits for the specified color component.
`int getGreen(int pixel)`	Gets the green value for the specified pixel value.
`int getMapSize()`	Gets the size of the whole color map.
`int getRed(int pixel)`	Gets the red value for the specified pixel value.
`void getReds(byte[] r)`	Gets the array of all valid red values.
`int getRGB(int pixel)`	Gets the standard RGB value of the specified color value.
`int getTransparency()`	Gets the alpha value used for all pixels. If no alpha array is specified when the color model is created, a default alpha value applies to all pixel values.

The Direct Color Model

The `DirectColorModel` class defines a concrete implementation of the second type of color model available in the AWT and Swing. The `DirectColorModel` extends the abstract `PackedColorModel` class.

The `DirectColorModel` class defines color values to consist of the actual RGB and alpha values. Figure 12.3 shows a logical view of a color specification. The `DirectColorModel` class defines an alpha value of `0.0` to mean complete transparency and `1.0` to mean complete opaqueness. For RGB values, larger values mean greater intensity.

The `DirectColorModel` class is the default RGB color model used in the AWT. The `ColorModel.getRGBdefault()` method returns an instance of `DirectColorModel`. Because the AWT uses a default model for colors, you only manipulate color models when you want to define your own models.

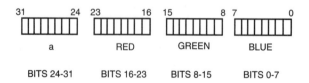

FIGURE 12.3
The direct color model simply defines a color value to be the actual RGB and alpha values for the color.

Using Colors

Throughout this book you have undoubtedly noticed the use of colors in some of the code examples (even though this book's figures are rendered in gray tones). And, as you are about to see, you can use colors effectively for a wide variety of GUI applications without knowing much about color models or color maps. Nevertheless, having a conceptual understanding is important, which is the purpose of including the previous section.

For most of your needs, it's more important to understand how you can use colors to spruce up your GUI. For this purpose, let's go back to the `Component` class. This mainstay of GUI programming defines several methods that address the use of colors; they are listed in Table 12.3.

12

TABLE 12.3   Color Support Methods in `java.awt.Component`

Method name	Description
`ColorModel getColorModel()`	Retrieves this component's color model
`Color getBackground()`	Gets the color used to paint this component's background
`Color getForeground()`	Gets the color used to paint this component's foreground
`void setBackground(Color c)`	Sets the color used to paint this component's background
`void setForeground(Color c)`	Sets the color used to paint this component's foreground

You can specify each component to use a separate background and foreground color with which to be painted. In fact, Figure 2.2 in Chapter 2, "Introducing the Java Foundation Classes," shows two text fields, each with a different specification for foreground and background colors.

Colors are specified to be instances of the `java.awt.Color` class. You need to be familiar with this class in order to specify colors for your components, so this is the next topic presented.

Using the java.awt.Color Class

The most immediately useful feature of the `Color` class is its set of constants that define colors that you can use. These color constants are shown in the following list.

Color Class Constant Color Definitions

`static Color black`
`static Color blue`
`static Color cyan`
`static Color darkGray`
`static Color gray`

continues

Color Class Constant Color Definitions

```
static Color green
static Color lightGray
static Color magenta
static Color orange
static Color pink
static Color red
static Color white
static Color yellow
```

These constants are themselves all instances of the `Color` class. You can also define your own color objects using any of the `Color` class constructors listed in Table 12.4.

TABLE 12.4   Color Class Constructors

Constructor name	Description
`Color(ColorSpace cspace, float[] components, float alpha)`	Creates a color in the specified color space using the array of components and the specified alpha value.
`Color(float r, float g, float b)`	Creates an opaque sRGB color with the specified RGB values, which must be in the range (0.0–1.0).
`Color(float r, float g, float b, float a)`	Creates an sRGB color with the specified RGB and alpha. All values must be in the range (0.0–1.0).
`Color(int rgb)`	Creates an opaque sRGB color with the specified value, which consists of the RGB component values as follows: red component in bits 16–23, green component in bits 8–15, and blue component in bits 0–7.
`Color(int rgba, boolean hasalpha)`	Creates an sRGB color with the specified value that comprises the RGB and alpha values as follows: red component in bits 16–23, green component in bits 8–15, blue component in bits 0–7, alpha component in bits 24–31.
`Color(int r, int g, int b)`	Creates an sRGB color that is opaque. The specified red, green, and blue values must be in the range (0–255).
`Color(int r, int g, int b, int a)`	Creates an sRGB color with the specified component values. All values must be in the range (0–255).

These constructors enable you to define almost any color and use it in your programs. However, as you will see in the next section, you should use this capability judiciously.

The Color class also defines many methods for doing various tasks such as getting a color's individual RGB or alpha component values. These methods are listed in Table 12.5.

TABLE 12.5   The Color Class Methods

Method name	*Description*
Color brighter()	Creates a brighter version of this color.
PaintContext createContext(ColorModel cm, Rectangle r, Rectangle2D r2d, AffineTransform xform, RenderingHints hints)	Creates and returns a PaintContext for generating a new color.
Color darker()	Creates a darker version of this color.
static Color decode (String nm)	Converts the specified string to a Color. The color will be opaque.
boolean equals(Object obj)	Indicates if the specified object is a color equal to this color.
int getAlpha()	Returns the alpha component.
int getBlue()	Returns the blue component.
static Color getColor (String nm)	Retrieves the color with the specified string name from the system properties.
static Color getColor (String nm, Color v)	Finds the color with the specified name in the system proper ties. If none can be found, it returns the specified color.
static Color getColor (String nm, int v)	Finds the color with the specified name in the system properties. If none can be found, it returns the color with the specified int value.
float[] getColorComponents (ColorSpace cspace, float[] compArray)	Returns a float array containing only the RGB color components, in the specified ColorSpace object.
float[] getColorComponents (float[] compArray)	Returns a float array containing the RGB color components of the Color.
ColorSpace getColorSpace()	Returns the ColorSpace of this Color.
float[] getComponents (ColorSpace cspace, float[] compArray)	Returns a float array containing the color and alpha components of this Color.
float[] getComponents (float[] compArray)	Returns a float array containing the color and alpha components of the Color.
int getGreen()	Returns the green component.

continues

TABLE 12.5   Continued

Method name	Description
`static Color getHSBColor (float h, float s, float b)`	Creates a `Color` object from the specified hue, saturation, and brightness values.
`int getRed()`	Returns the red component.
`int getRGB()`	Returns the RGB value representing the specified color in the default sRGB `ColorModel`.
`float[] getRGBColorComponents (float[] compArray)`	Returns an array that contains the RGB color components of this `Color`.
`float[] getRGBComponents (float[] compArray)`	Returns an array containing the RGB and alpha components of this `Color`, defined in the default sRGB color space.
`int getTransparency()`	Returns the transparency mode for this `Color`.
`static int HSBtoRGB(float hue, float saturation, float brightness)`	Converts the HSB (hue, saturation, brightness) components of a color to an equivalent set of values for the default RGB model.
`static float[] RGBtoHSB (int r, int g, int b, float[] hsbvals)`	Converts the components of a color from the default RGB model to an equivalent set of HSB values.

Using System Colors

The `java.awt.SystemColor` class is a direct subclass of `Color`. Its purpose is to define a standard configuration used by a native platform for the colors of specific GUI quantities.

These system quantities are represented by static fields. You can determine the value of any of the quantities for your specific system simply by accessing the static variable. Table 12.6 lists the static fields of the `SystemColor` class.

The fields are all defined as `static SystemColor` although the types are not shown. Some of the default values have no standard name. These colors are represented by the RGB triplet that is passed to the `Color` class constructor to construct the color object.

TABLE 12.6   Static Fields of the `SystemColor` Class

System property name	Default value
`activeCaption`	`Color(0, 0, 128)`
`activeCaptionBorder`	`Color.lightGray`
`activeCaptionText`	`Color.white`

System property name	Default value
control	Color.lightGray
controlDkShadow	Color.black
controlHighlight	Color.white
controlLtHighlight	Color(224,224,224)
controlShadow	Color.gray
controlText	Color.black
desktop	Color(0, 92, 92)
inactiveCaption	Color.gray
inactiveCaptionBorder	Color.lightGray
inactiveCaptionText	Color.lightGray
info	Color(224, 224, 0)
infoText	Color.black
menu	Color.lightGray
menuText	Color.black
scrollbar	Color(224,224,224)
text	Color.lightGray
textHighlight	Color(0,0,128)
textHighlightText	Color.white
textInactiveText	Color.gray
textText	Color.black
window	Color.white
windowBorder	Color.black
windowText	Color.black

The SystemColor class also defines static int values that have capitalized versions of the same names as the variables in Table 12.6. You should not use these. These constants are used internally by the SystemColor class to index the color objects that define the colors represented by the constant.

Normally you don't have to explicitly use these values. If you instantiate AWT or Swing components, they already use the system default values for their various visible elements. For example, the default windowBorder color is black; all window classes set this value for their border color. If you are defining a custom component, you should use the appropriate default system colors for the various attributes of your component so that it maintains a consistent look and feel with the AWT or Swing components used by your program.

Fonts

In Java, a *font* is an object that represents a collection of glyphs. Font support is provided in Java by the `java.awt.Font` class.

The `Font` class defines the nature and attributes of fonts. Instantiating this class to identify a particular font requires specifying values for the font's three major characteristics, namely, its logical font name, style, and point size.

A *glyph* is a symbol rendered on an output device that represents a particular character in a font. The mapping between characters and glyphs is not always one-to-one; sometimes it is one-to-many or many-to-one. Two or more glyphs may be needed to render a particular character, for example, characters with accents in European languages. A French acute *e* uses two glyphs: the letter *e* and the acute accent. Ligatures, on the other hand, are single glyphs that represent two characters. For example the two letters *f* followed by *i* are usually typeset using a single glyph.

The `Font` class supports the logical font names indicated in the following list. When creating a font instance, one of these names is specified as a text string in the `Font` constructor.

Font Names Supported by the Font Class
`Dialog`
`DialogInput`
`Monospaced`
`Serif`
`SansSerif`
`Symbol`
`TimesRoman`

The font style is the second parameter needed to instantiate the `Font` class. The valid styles are listed in the following list.

Valid Font Styles
`Font.BOLD`
`Font.ITALIC`
`Font.PLAIN`

A font style can be specified by combining any of the above to yield a font with combined style attributes. For example, you can specify a bold italic font with the expression `Font.BOLD & Font.ITALIC`.

Finally, a point size is required to specify a font. Point sizes are positive integers. By convention, one point represents 1/72 of an inch on the output device.

I won't list all the methods of the Font class in tabular form here. However, you should be aware that the Font class provides many methods for discerning information about a font object. The following list shows some of the accessor methods that enable you to get the values of the various attributes.

If you look at the complete list of methods in the Font class, you will see that there are no methods to set any of these attributes. After a font object is created, its attributes cannot be changed because doing so would change the definition of the font to a different font.

Some Useful Methods of the Font Class

```
String getFamily()
String getFontName()
int getSize()
int getStyle()
```

Because Java is platform-independent, a Java font used by your program must be mapped to a native system font. Lack of support for a particular font by the native system might sometimes result in different mappings from one platform to the next. The native font will not always support the specified characteristics of the Font object with complete fidelity because not all platforms support the same fonts.

For instance, if a platform does not support a dialog font, Java dialog fonts must be mapped to another system font. The same holds true for point sizes. In order for the size of the glyphs to be rendered accurately, the native system must provide a font with the point size specified by the Font object. If one does not exist, the system must map the requested size to the nearest available point size.

The java.awt.Component class contains the following methods that enable you to set and get the font for any component.

```
public void setFont(Font f)
public Font getFont()
```

The JComponent class also contains a setFont(Font f) method. Any text displayed as part of that component's visual appearance will be rendered using glyphs that match the specified font.

Listing 12.1 shows a program that displays several labels, all in a different font. This program demonstrates some of the different logical font families, styles, and point sizes.

LISTING 12.1   A Program that Demonstrates the Use of Multiple Fonts

```java
import java.awt.Font;

import java.awt.event.WindowAdapter;
import java.awt.event.WindowEvent;
import java.awt.event.WindowListener;

import com.sun.java.swing.Box;
import com.sun.java.swing.JFrame;
import com.sun.java.swing.JLabel;
import com.sun.java.swing.JPanel;

class FontDemo extends JPanel
{
  public FontDemo()
  {
    Box box = Box.createVerticalBox();
    add(box);

    JLabel l1 = new JLabel("Times Roman Plain 36");
    l1.setFont(new Font("TimesRoman", Font.PLAIN, 36));

    JLabel l2 = new JLabel("Times Roman Bold Italic 20");
    l2.setFont(new Font("TimesRoman",
                        Font.BOLD & Font.ITALIC, 20));

    JLabel l3 = new JLabel("Helvetica Plain 20");
    l3.setFont(new Font("Helvetica", Font.PLAIN, 20));

    JLabel l4 = new JLabel("Helvetica Italic 18");
    l4.setFont(new Font("Helvetica", Font.ITALIC, 18));

    JLabel l5 = new JLabel("Sans Serif Plain 16");
    l5.setFont(new Font("SansSerif", Font.PLAIN, 16));

    JLabel l6 = new JLabel("Sans Serif Bold Italic 14");
    l6.setFont(new Font("TimesRoman",
                        Font.PLAIN & Font.BOLD, 14));

    JLabel l7 = new JLabel("Monospaced Plain 14");
    l7.setFont(new Font("Monospaced", Font.PLAIN, 12));
```

```
    JLabel 18 = new JLabel("Dialog Bold 18");
    l8.setFont(new Font("Dialog", Font.BOLD, 12));

    box.add(l1);
    box.add(Box.createVerticalStrut(15));
    box.add(l2);
    box.add(Box.createVerticalStrut(15));
    box.add(l3);
    box.add(Box.createVerticalStrut(15));
    box.add(l4);
    box.add(Box.createVerticalStrut(15));
    box.add(l5);
    box.add(Box.createVerticalStrut(15));
    box.add(l6);
    box.add(Box.createVerticalStrut(15));
    box.add(l8);
    box.add(Box.createVerticalStrut(15));
    box.add(l7);
  }


  public static void main(String [] args)
  {
    FontDemo app = new FontDemo();
    JFrame f = new JFrame("Font Demo");
    WindowListener wL = new WindowAdapter()
      {
        public void windowClosing(WindowEvent e)
          {
            e.getWindow().dispose();
            System.exit(0);
          }
      };
    f.addWindowListener(wL);
    f.getContentPane().add(app);
    f.pack();
    f.show();
  }
}
```

Figure 12.4 shows the GUI produced by this program. You can see the effects of creating different combinations of logical font family, style, and point size. Simply call setFont() with a valid Font object on the component whose font you wish to set.

Figure 12.4
Examples of various fonts that belong to different font families and use different styles and point sizes.

Font Metrics

Sometimes you need to know detailed information about the dimensions of the glyphs used to render the characters in a font. The `java.awt.FontMetrics` class defines a set of metrics that characterize the glyphs in a font.

Font metrics are a measure of typesetting dimensions for a particular font. An instance of `FontMetrics` corresponds to a specific font, that is, an instance of the `Font` class.

The attributes of the `FontMetrics` class represent these typesetting dimensions. Their values represent the various physical dimensions of the glyphs used to render characters in the related font. The dimensions defined by the `FontMetrics` class are listed in Table 12.7.

Table 12.7 Typesetting Quantities Defined in the `FontMetrics` Class

Dimension	Description
Ascent	The amount by which a character ascends above the baseline.
Baseline	The horizontal line that represents the reference line for aligning characters vertically.
Descent	The amount by which a character descends below the baseline.
Leading	The space between a line of text's lowest descent and the following line's highest ascent.
AdvanceWidth	The position at which to place the next character. Effectively, this is a function of the width of the current glyph.

Figure 12.5 shows three lines of text. The various font metrics quantities are indicated on the figure text.

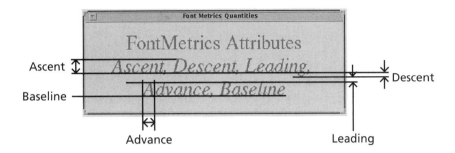

Figure 12.5

The FontMetrics *class defines the typesetting quantities that are needed to render glyphs in the correct relative positions.*

FontMetrics can be useful to determine sizing information about the glyphs being rendered in a component. For example, consider the following program in Listing 12.2, which draws a string in a container.

Listing 12.2   Drawing the Graphics Representing a String

```
import java.awt.*;
import java.awt.event.*;
import com.sun.java.swing.*;

/**
   A class that demonstrates a naive way to center a graphic
   string in a container.  If the container is resized by the
   user, or if the container must accommodate different
   strings of varying length or fonts, the string will no
   longer be centered.
*/
class CenterTextDemo extends JPanel
{
  public CenterTextDemo()
  {
    // Don't need to do anything here.
  }

  /**
     Paints this component.  Notice that this class overrides
     <code>paintComponent()</code> and <em>not</em>
     <code>paint()</code>!!  This is because it is a
     subclass of a Swing component.
  */
  public void paintComponent(Graphics g)
  {
```

continues

LISTING 12.2   Continued

```
    super.paintComponent(g);

    String message = new
      String("How much space does this text use?");

    // Center the message in the container, based on the
    // hard-coded preferred size of this container.
    //
    g.setFont(new Font("SansSerif", Font.PLAIN, 14));
    g.drawString(message, 50, 80);
}


/**
    Return the preferred size of this component suitable for
    one particular string.

    @return the preferred size needed to center the string
    text.
*/
public Dimension getPreferredSize()
{
    return new Dimension(350, 150);
}


public static void main(String [] args)
{
    CenterTextDemo app = new CenterTextDemo();
    JFrame f = new JFrame("Graphics Positioning Demo ");
    WindowListener wL = new WindowAdapter()
      {
        public void windowClosing(WindowEvent e)
          {
            e.getWindow().dispose();
            System.exit(0);
          }
      };
    f.addWindowListener(wL);
    f.getContentPane().add(app);
    f.pack();
    f.show();
}
}
```

This program centers its graphically drawn string. The GUI produced is shown in Figure 12.6. Note that the string is represented by string graphics drawn in the container; it is not part of a label component. The program seems to work correctly; the string is nicely centered in the panel.

But this program doesn't work properly if you specify a different string to be displayed in the panel, perhaps a string with a different number of characters, or a string drawn in a different font. In either case, the space required will undoubtedly be different from the size of the panel that you hard-coded in the program. Undoubtedly, your new string will no longer be centered.

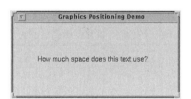

FIGURE 12.6
The position of the string is hard-coded. This approach is inflexible and doesn't adapt to resizing or drawing different strings.

To accommodate strings of different lengths and different fonts, the `paintComponent()` method must know how much space is required by the particular string being displayed. In the initial version of the program in Listing 12.2, the programmer probably determined the correct (x, y) coordinate at which to draw the string in the chosen font by trial and error. Different sizes were tried until the string appeared centered in the panel.

To ensure that other strings, possibly rendered in different fonts, are centered, the program must calculate the amount of space required by the particular string being displayed. The component's `getPreferredSize()` method needs to be able to calculate the dimensions of the glyphs drawn, that is, the values of the font metrics for the font you are using. Otherwise, a longer string might not fit into the container, or a shorter string would not be centered.

For example, Figure 12.7 shows a shorter string displayed in the panel. Obviously it is not centered. The string was drawn starting at the same position relative to the top-left corner of the pane, without considering its size.

Listing 12.3 shows an improved version of the program that will always center the string it draws and size the container appropriately. Its `getPreferredSize()` now calculates the component's preferred size instead of always returning a fixed size.

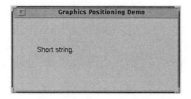

FIGURE 12.7

Because the string position is hard-coded, a string that has a different display width will no longer be centered in a container that always specifies a fixed size.

LISTING 12.3   Calculating FontMetrics to Properly Display String Graphics

```java
import java.awt.*;
import java.awt.event.*;
import com.sun.java.swing.*;

/**
    A class that demonstrates a correct way to center a
    graphic string in a container.  The container calculates
    its size based on the length of the string text and the
    font metrics of the font used to display the text.

    <p>Arbitrarily, the program decides to size the container
    so that there are 50 pixels to the left and right of the
    ends of the string, and 70 pixels above and below the
    string.
*/
class FontMetricsDemo extends JPanel
{
  /**
      No-arg constructor.  Chooses an arbitrary font and
      string to demonstrate the dynamic calculation of the
      container.
  */
  public FontMetricsDemo()
  {
    // Use this font to draw the string text.
    //
    f = new Font("Dialog", Font.PLAIN, 18);

    // Draw the graphics representing this string.
    //
    message = new String("How much space does this text use?");
  }
```

```
/**
    Paints this component.  Notice that this class
    overrides <code>paintComponent()</code> and
    <em>not</em> <code>paint()</code> because it is a
    subclass of a Swing component.
  */
  public void paintComponent(Graphics g)
  {
    super.paintComponent(g);

    // Center the message in the container with padding on
    // each side as follows: 50 pixels from the left and
    // right sides, and 70 pixels from the top and bottom.
    // See the getPreferredSize() method.
    //
    g.setFont(f);
    g.drawString(message, 50, 70);
  }

/**
    Return the preferred size of this component suitable
    for one particular string.

    @return the preferred size needed to center the string text.
  */
  public Dimension getPreferredSize()
  {
    // Get the font metrics for the font we want to use.
    //
    FontMetrics fm = getFontMetrics(f);

    // Determine the total advance width for the whole
    // string.  The container must be this width plus the
    // padding between the ends of the string and the left
    // and right edges of the container.
    //
    int width = fm.stringWidth(message) + 2 * 50;

    int height = fm.getMaxAscent() + 2 * 70;

    return new Dimension(width, height);
  }

Font f;

  String message;
```

continues

LISTING 12.3   Continued

```java
public static void main(String [] args)
{
  FontMetricsDemo app = new FontMetricsDemo();
  JFrame f = new JFrame("Graphics Positioning Demo ");
  WindowListener wL = new WindowAdapter()
    {
      public void windowClosing(WindowEvent e)
        {
          e.getWindow().dispose();
          System.exit(0);
        }
    };
  f.addWindowListener(wL);
  f.getContentPane().add(app);
  f.pack();
  f.show();
}
}
```

This version of the program calculates the total advance width of the string, which is the sum of the advance widths of all the characters in the string. The advance width of a character is essentially the width of the glyph that represents the character.

The getPreferredSize() method calculates the preferred width of the container to be the sum of the width of the rendered string plus the 50 pixels of horizontal space desired between the ends of the string and the container. The container's height is twice seventy pixels, plus the height of the tallest possible glyph of any character in the font being used. The values 50 and 70 are chosen arbitrarily.

Figure 12.8 shows the result of executing the latest version of the program shown in Listing 12.3. The font used is definitely different from the one in Listing 12.2, yet the string is still centered in the container.

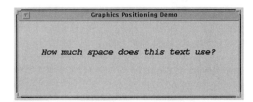

FIGURE 12.8
Any graphics string can be centered in the container because the program can now dynamically calculate the dimensions of the rendered string from the FontMetrics of the font used.

The `FontMetrics` class provides a wealth of methods that give you a way to calculate any of the typesetting quantities in Table 12.7. Table 12.8 lists some of the methods in the `FontMetrics` class that pertain to the discussion in this section.

TABLE 12.8   Useful Methods in the `FontMetrics` Class

Method name	Description
`int bytesWidth(byte[] data, int off, int len)`	Returns the total advance width for rendering the specified portion of the `byte` array
`int charsWidth(char[] data, int off, int len)`	Returns the total advance width for rendering the specified portion of the `char` array
`int charWidth(char ch)`	Returns the advance width of the specified character in Font associated with this font metrics
`int charWidth(int ch)`	Returns the advance width of the specified character in Font associated with this font metrics
`int getAscent()`	Determines the ascent of the Font described by this FontMetrics object
`int getDescent()`	Determines the font descent of the Font described by this FontMetrics object
`Font getFont()`	Gets the Font described by this FontMetrics object
`int getHeight()`	Gets the height above the baseline of a line of text in the associated font
`int getLeading()`	Determines the leading of the Font described by this FontMetrics object
`int getMaxAdvance()`	Gets the advance width that is the maximum for any character in this Font
`int getMaxAscent()`	Determines the ascent that is the maximum for any glyph that represents a character in the Font described by this FontMetrics object
`int getMaxDescent()`	Determines the maximum descent of the Font described by this FontMetrics object
`int stringWidth(String str)`	Returns the total advance width required to render the specified String in the Font described by this FontMetrics

To experiment more with this latest version of the program, you can modify it to let the user enter a string into a `TextField` or `JTextField`, for instance, and select the font in which to display the string. Make the program dynamically calculate the size of the container each time. The examples shown don't do this (to avoid cluttering the code and distracting you from the main point being presented).

Incidentally, as a point of review, notice that the class in Listing 12.3 defines a `paintComponent()` method and not a `paint()` method. You learned in Chapter 11, "Graphics," that all painting must go in the `paintComponent()` method for subclasses of Swing components. Also notice that it calls `super.paintComponent()`. Lightweight containers must all call their superclass paint method so that the `Container.paint()` method can call `paint()` on all the container's children.

The `Component` class defines the `getFontMetrics()` method. A call to this method results in some low-level call to an AWT method that returns an instance of the `FontMetrics` class.

The `FontMetrics` class is abstract. The native platform toolkit must supply an implementation that reflects the metrics of the native system fonts to which Java program `Font` instances are mapped. Because this mapping is different on every system, the system vendor must supply the information as part of its Java runtime environment in the way of concrete `FontMetrics` implementations.

This last example is contrived in order to illustrate the use of `FontMetrics` class. If you really wanted to center text in a container, a simpler and more appealing approach would be to use a label component instead of drawing graphics. You would then choose a layout manager that centers the text in its container.

Summary

This chapter has presented a pragmatic approach to using colors and fonts. Support for colors is provided by classes that support color models. The two kinds of color models supported in the AWT and Swing are the index color model and the direct color model.

Color models provide a mechanism for mapping internal color representations to native platform color support. The Java 2D API defines color spaces, which implement a proposed standard way of mapping a color model to the output format accepted by a variety of output devices such as monitors, printers, and digital cameras. As with colors, support for fonts also requires a mapping between classes that define fonts internally and native platform fonts. Two or more internal program fonts may map to the same native platform font.

Font metrics define information about the actual dimensions of the glyphs that render representations of elements of the native font to which a program font is mapped. This information helps applications do size calculations and so forth.

Judicious use of colors and fonts can improve the clarity and usability of a program's GUI.

INDEX

SYMBOLS

2D (two dimensional) graphics, 538
AWT models, 538
native graphics, 539-541
Paint model, 582-584
clipping, 562-566, 568
component states, 543-546
deleting instances, 548-549
Graphics class, 549-551
arcs, 560-561
lines, 557-558
ovals, 558
polygons, 558-559
rectangles, 559, 561
shapes, 551-557
text, 561-562
graphics origins, translating, 569-573
methods, 541-543, 546
modes, 574, 576-581
painting causing events, 582
strings, 539-541
Swing Paint model, 584-590
3D (three dimensional) graphics, 559

A

Abstract Windowing Toolkit, see AWT
AbstractButton class, 181-182
constructors, 182-185
methods, 182-185
AbstractButton( ) constructor (AbstractButton class), 182
abstraction, 8, 502-503
BoundedRangeModel interface, 518-519
classes, 10
creating, 9-10
event listeners, 508-510
ListSelectionModel, 514-517

models, 512
MVC (Model-View-Controller), 503-504
naming conventions, 522
selection, 513-517
Swing containers, 149-151
Swing model architecture, 504-507
Swing tool set, 141-142
   JComponent class, 146-148
   layered, 159
   lightweight components, 145-146
synchronization, 508-509
AbstractListModel interface, 450, 522
accept(File f) method (JFileChooser class), 204
Accessibility API, 24
Accessible content property (JComponent class), 148
AccessibleContext getAccessibleContext( ) method, 330
   JEditorPane class, 272
   JFileChooser class, 204
   JMenuBar class, 233
   JMenuItem class, 232
   JPasswordField class, 265
   JProgressBar class, 237
   JSlider class, 242
   JSplitPane class, 248
   JTabbedPane class, 253
   JTextArea class, 268
   JTextComponent class, 256
   JTextField class, 262
   JTree class, 290
accessor method, 388
Acquiring the Content Pane of a Swing Heavyweight Container (listing 6.3), 158
action events, 489-499
Action interface, 490-499
Action object property (JComponent class), 147
Action That Exits an Application (listing 9.36), 493
ActionEvent event, 366, 368
ActionListener interface, 375, 383-384, 406, 451, 488-499
actionPerformed method, 374, 383, 390-392, 406, 491
Action[] getActions( ) method
   JTextComponent class, 256
   JTextField class, 262

ACTIVATED constant (WindowEvent class), 422
Adapter Class to Implement an Anonymous Inner Class (listing 9.8), 399
adapters, 386-388
add method, 318
   JTabbedPane class, 252
   listeners, 374
add( ) method, 58, 62, 84, 359-360, 494, 497
add(AbstractButton b) method (ButtonGroup class), 193
add(Component c) method (JMenu class), 230
add(Component comp) method, 298
add(JMenu c) method (JMenuBar class), 233
add(JMenuItem menuItem) method (JMenu class), 230
add(String s) method (JMenu class), 230
addActionListener method, 204, 374, 383
addAdjustmentListener( ) method, 430
addChangeListener method
   BoundedRangeModel interface, 518
   JTabbedPane class, 252
   SingleSelectionModel interface, 528
addChoosableFileFilter method (JFileChooser class), 204
addElement(Object obj) method (MutableComboBoxModel interface), 527
addHyperlinkListener method (JEditorPane class), 272
Adding Components to a Container by Using add( ) Methods (listing 4.1), 85-86
addItem(Object anItem) method (JComboBox class), 200
addLayoutComponent method, 301
addListDataListener method, 507
addListSelectionListener method (ListSelectionModel), 515
addMenuKeyListener method, 483
addMenuListener method (JMenu class), 230
addMenuListener (MenuListener) method, 458
addMouseMotionListener method, 415
addPropertyChangeListener method (TreeSelectionModel interface), 532
addSelectionInterval method
   JLabel class, 220
   JTree class, 289
   ListSelectionModel, 515

addSelectionPath method
JTree class, 289
TreeSelectionModel interface, 532
addSelectionPaths method
JTree class, 289
TreeSelectionModel interface, 532
addSelectionRow(int row) method (JTree class), 289
addSelectionRows(int[] rows) method (JTree class), 289
addSeparator( ) method (JMenu class), 230
addStyle method (JTextPane class), 281
addTab method (JTabbedPane class), 252-253
addTableModelListener method (TableModel interface), 529
addTreeExpansionListener method (JTree class), 289
addTreeModelListener method (TreeModel interface), 530
addTreeSelectionListener method
JTree class, 289
TreeSelectionModel interface, 532
addTreeWillExpandListener method (JTree class), 289
Adjustable interface, 429-430, 433
adjustment events (AWT), 367, 429, 431-433
AdjustmentEvent class, 429, 431
AdjustmentEvent interface, 431
AdjustmentEvent object, 431
AdjustmentListener interface, 375, 431-432
ADJUSTMENT_VALUE_CHANGED object (AdjustmentEvent class), 431
AdvanceWidth (FontMetrics class), 606
algorithms
BorderLayout, 315
layout managers, 298
alignment
AWT labels, 114-117
BorderLayout class, 313-317
FlowLayout, 305-307
Swing labels, 208, 210-213
alpha value
DirectColorModel class, 596
index color models, 594-595
pixels, 593
ancestor events (Swing), 434-435
ancestorAdded( ) method, 434
AncestorEvent class, 369, 434-435

AncestorListener interface, 376, 434
ancestorMoved( ) method, 434
ancestorRemoved( ) method, 434
anchor parameter (GridBagConstraints class), 338
anchor variable (GridBagConstraints class), 337, 348-351
anonymous inner classes, 391-401
Anonymous Inner Classes (listing 9.6), 392-394, 396
APIs (application programming interfaces)
graphics, 538
JFC, see JFC
see also Swing tool set
append(String str) method (JTextArea class), 268
Applet class, 49
appletviewer application, 548
AWT Container classes, 22
Swing containers, 151
Applet container, 54
applet package (AWT), 17
applets
container class, 34, 54
creating, 64-71
methods, 65-66
Swing tool set, 27
appletviewer application, 548
application logic, 10
MVC (Model-View-Controller), 510
selected index policies, 520-521
application model, 11
Application That Uses Action Objects (listing 9.37), 495-497
application-data models, 512, 517-519
applications
creating, 51-54, 67-71
Frame container, 54-55, 57, 59
Panel container, 60-62
ImageGallery, 383-384
starting, 63
stopping, 63
approveSelection( ) method (JFileChooser class), 204
architecture (JFC), 41-46
arcs (Graphics class), drawing, 560-561
areas (text), 131-136
Armed state (ButtonModel interface), 526
arrays (color maps), 593

Ascent (FontMetrics class), 606
AttributeSet getCharacterAttributes( )
  method (JTextPane class), 281
AttributeSet getParagraphAttributes( )
  method (JTextPane class), 281
AttributeSet interface, 274
AWT (Abstract Windowing Toolkit), 16-17, 74,
  102
  buttons, 102-104
  check boxes, 105-107
  Choice class, 108, 110
  classes, 20-21, 49
    Component, 21
    Container, 21-22
    JFC equivalents, 28
    layout managers, 23
    Swing components, 179
    Swing toolkit/JFC comparisons, 40-41
  clip rectangle, see clipping
  color package, 592
  ColorModel class, 593
  Component class, 75-76
    color, 78
    cursors, 80
    events, 79
    locations, 78
    methods, 76-77
    properties, 76
    rendering methods, 81-82
    sizes, 78-79
    visibility, 79
  components, 19, 74-75
  Container class, 82-84
  containers, 33, 74
    adding components, 85-92
    children, 97-98
    limitations, 149
    nested, 92-97
    order of, 98-99
    Swing containers, 154
  dialog boxes, 110-114
  events, 362, 365-366
    adapters, 387
    adjustment events, 429, 431-433
    AWTEvent class, 364-365
    component events, 365-366, 403-407
    container events, 403-407
    focus events, 407-410
    input events, 419-421
    item events, 425-427
    key events, 410-415
    listeners, 375
    mouse events, 415, 417-419
    paint events, 422
    semantic, 365-368
    Swing complements, 377-378
    text events, 427, 429
    window events, 422-425
  graphics
    component states, 543-546
    deleting instances, 548-549
    methods, 541-543, 546
  Graphics class, see Graphics class
  image package (ColorModel class), 592
  labels, 114-117
  lightweight components, see lightweight
    components
  lists, 117-121
  menus, 121-130
  native peers, 74
  packages, 17, 74, 85
  Paint model, 582-584
  platform-independence, 18-20
  Swing tool set, 145-146
    abstractions, 142
    combinations, 141
    comparison, 24
  text areas, 131-136
  text fields, 131-136
AWT Window Classes (listing 3.1), 55-57
AWTEvent class, 362, 364-365
AWTEvent method, 364
AWTEventListener interface, 375

B

background colors (Component class), 76-78
bar graphs (JProgressBar class), 180
Baseline (FontMetrics class), 606
basic look-and-feel package (JFC), 25, 30, 32
beancontext package (AWT), 17
beans package (AWT), 17
bidirectional communication, 12
bits (IndexColorModel class), 594
BLOCK_DECREMENT (AdjustmentEvent class),
  431
BLOCK_INCREMENT (AdjustmentEvent class),
  431

boolean accept(File f) method (JFileChooser class), 204

boolean echoCharIsSet( ) method
JPasswordField class, 265
TextField class, 136

boolean equals(Object obj) method, 599

boolean getInverted( ) method (JSlider class), 242

boolean getLineWrap( ) method (JTextArea class), 268

boolean getPaintLabels( ) method (JSlider class), 242

boolean getPaintTicks( ) method (JSlider class), 242

boolean getPaintTrack( ) method (JSlider class), 242

boolean getScrollableTracks ViewportWidth( ) method
JEditorPane class, 272
JLabel class, 221
JTextArea class, 268
JTextComponent class, 257
JTextPane class, 281

boolean getScrollableTracksViewport Height( ) method
JEditorPane class, 272
JLabel class, 221
JTextComponent class, 257

boolean getScrollsOnExpand( ) method (JTree class), 291

boolean getShowsRootHandles( ) method (JTree class), 291

boolean getSnapToTicks( ) method (JSlider class), 243

boolean getState( ) method (check boxes), 107

boolean getValueIsAdjusting( ) method, 456
BoundedRangeModel interface, 518
JLabel class, 222
JSlider class, 243
ListSelectionModel, 516

boolean getWrapStyleWord( ) method (JTextArea class), 269

boolean hasBeenExpanded method (JTree class), 291

boolean isAddedPath method, 476

boolean isAddedPath( ) method, 476

boolean isAncestorOf method, 83-84

boolean isArmed( ) method (JMenuItem class), 232

boolean isBorderPainted( ) method
JMenuBar class, 233
JProgressBar class, 237

boolean isCellEditable method (TableModel interface), 529

boolean isCollapsed method (JTree class), 292

boolean isCollapsed(int row) method (JTree class), 291

boolean isContinuousLayout( ) method (JSplitPane class), 249

boolean isDirectorySelectionEnabled( ) method (JFileChooser class), 205

boolean isEditable( ) method
JComboBox class, 201
JTextComponent class, 258
JTree class, 292
TextComponent class, 134

boolean isEditing( ) method (JTree class), 292

boolean isEnabled( ) method, 129, 491

boolean isExpanded(int row) method, 292

boolean isExpanded(TreePath path) method (JTree class), 292

boolean isFileHidingEnabled( ) method (JFileChooser class), 205

boolean isFileSelectionEnabled( ) method (JFileChooser class), 206

boolean isFixedRowHeight( ) method (JTree class), 292

boolean isFocusTraversable( ) method (JTextComponent class), 258

boolean isIndexSelected (int index) method (lists), 121

boolean isLeaf(Object node) method (TreeModel interface), 531

boolean isManagingFocus( ) method
JEditorPane class, 272
JMenuBar class, 233
JTextArea class, 269

boolean isMenuComponent method (JMenu class), 231

boolean isModal( ) method (dialog boxes), 114

boolean isMultipleMode( ) method (lists), 121

boolean isMultiSelectionEnabled( ) method (JFileChooser class), 206

boolean isOneTouchExpandable( ) method (JSplitPane class), 249

boolean isOpaque( ) method (JTextComponent class), 258

boolean isPathEditable method (JTree class), 292

boolean isPathSelected method
  JTree class, 292
  TreeSelectionModel interface, 533

boolean isPopupMenuVisible( ) method (JMenu class), 231

boolean isPopupVisible( ) method (JComboBox class), 201

boolean isResizable( ) method (dialog boxes), 114

boolean isRolloverEnabled( ) method (AbstractButton class), 183

boolean isRootVisible( ) method (JTree class), 292

boolean isRowSelected(int row) method
  JTree class, 292
  TreeSelectionModel interface, 533

boolean isSelected method (ButtonGroup class), 193

boolean isSelected( ) method
  AbstractButton class, 183
  JMenu class, 231
  JMenuBar class, 233
  SingleSelectionModel interface, 528

boolean isSelectedIndex method
  JLabel class, 222
  ListSelectionModel, 516

boolean isSelectionEmpty( ) method
  JLabel class, 222
  JTree class, 292
  ListSelectionModel, 516
  TreeSelectionModel interface, 533

boolean isStringPainted( ) method (JProgressBar class), 237

boolean isTearOff( ) method
  JMenu class, 231
  menus, 128

boolean isTopLevelMenu( ) method (JMenu class), 231

boolean isTraversable(File f) method (JFileChooser class), 206

boolean isValidateRoot( ) method (JTextField class), 262

boolean isVisible(TreePath path) method (JTree class), 292

boolean removeChoosableFileFilter method (JFileChooser class), 206

boolean stopEditing( ) method (JTree class), 294

border package (JFC), 25

BorderLayout algorithm, 315

BorderLayout class, 301, 313-314, 318
  AWT (Abstract Windowing Toolkit), 23
  regions, 313-317

BorderLayout object, 314

BOTTOM_ALIGNMENT constant, 213

BoundedRangeModel getHorizontalVisibility( ) method (JTextField class), 262

BoundedRangeModel getModel( ) method
  JProgressBar class, 237
  JSlider class, 242

BoundedRangeModel interface, 44, 518-522

bounds (Component class), 76-78

Box class, 329
  containers, 333-334
  JFC (Java Foundation Classes), 29
  methods, 329-330
  struts, 330-333

Box Container (listing 8.7), 333-334

Box(int axis) method, 329

BoxLayout class, 301, 322-334
  objects, 328
  panels, 328-329

BoxLayout Layout Manager Class (listing 8.4), 323-324

BoxLayout method, 323

BoxLayout object, 322

brighter( ) PaintContext method, 599

Button class, 20, 49, 103-104, 373

Button( ) method (Button class), 104

Button(String label) method (Button class), 104

ButtonGroup class, 192
  constructors, 193
  methods, 193

ButtonHandler class, 382-383

ButtonHandler object, 383

ButtonModel getSelection( ) method (ButtonGroup class), 193

ButtonModel interface, 44, 522, 525-526

buttons
  AWT (Abstract Windowing Toolkit), 102-104
  BorderLayout class, 314
  FlowLayout class, 303-304
  GridLayout class, 312
  JToggleButton class, 180
  keyboard focus transfers, 410
  Swing components, 181-189
bytesWidth method (FontMetrics class), 613

C

Calculating FontMetrics (listing 12.3), 610-612
cancelEditing( ) method (JTree class), 289
cancelSelection( ) method (JFileChooser class), 204
Canvas class (AWT), 20
capital letters (key events), 414-415
CardLayout class, 301, 318-320, 322
  AWT (Abstract Windowing Toolkit), 23
  methods, 318-319
  objects, 318
CardLayout Layout Manager Class (listing 8.3), 320
CardLayout object, 319
CardLayout( ) method, 318
caret events (Swing), 435-437
Caret getCaret( ) method
  JTextComponent class, 256
CaretEvent class, 435-437
CaretEvent event, 369
CaretListener interface, 376, 436-437
CellEditorListener interface, 376
cells (GridLayout class), 335-336
CENTER alignment (FlowLayout), 305
CENTER region (BorderLayout class), 314-317
CENTER_ALIGNMENT constant, 213
change events (Swing), 437-440
ChangeEvent class, 437-440
ChangeEvent event, 369-370
ChangeListener interface, 376, 437-440, 442
changeToParentDirectory( ) method (JFileChooser class), 204
char getEchoChar( ) method
  JPasswordField class, 265
  TextField class, 136

char getFocusAccelerator( ) method (JTextComponent class), 257
char getKeyChar( ) method, 411
characters, mapping, 602
charsWidth method (FontMetrics class), 613
char[] getPassword( ) methods (JPasswordField class), 265
check boxes
  AWT (Abstract Windowing Toolkit), 105-107
  JCheckBox class, 181
  Swing components, 189-191
Checkbox class, 20, 49, 107
Checkbox( ) method (check boxes), 107
CheckboxGroup getCheckboxGroup( ) method (check boxes), 107
CheckboxMenuItem class, 49
children containers, 50
  order of, 98-99
  saving, 97-98
Choice class (AWT), 20, 108, 110
Choice component (graphics), 556-557
Choice Component (listing 5.3), 108-109
Choice( ) method (Choice Class), 110
Class getColumnClass method (TableModel interface), 529
classes, 10, 48-49
  AbstractButton, 181-182
    constructors, 182-185
    methods, 182-185
  abstractions, 10
  adapters, 386-388
  AdjustmentEvent, 429, 431
  AncestorEvent, 434-435
  Applet, 49, 151
  AWT (Abstract Windowing Toolkit), 20-21, 49
    BorderLayout, 23
    Button, 20
    Canvas, 20
    CardLayout, 23
    Checkbox, 20
    Choice, 20, 108, 110
    Component, 20-21
    Container, 20-22
    Dialog, 20
    FlowLayout, 23
    GridBagLayout, 23
    GridLayout, 23

JFC (Java Foundation Classes) equivalents, 28
Label, 20
layout managers, 23
List, 20
Menu, 20
MenuBar, 20
MenuItem, 20
Panel, 20
Swing components, 179
Swing toolkit/JFC comparisons, 40-41
TextArea, 20
TextComponent, 20
TextField, 20
AWTEvent, 362, 364-365
BorderLayout, 301, 313-318
Box, 329
   containers, 333-334
   methods, 329-330
   struts, 330-333
BoxLayout, 301, 322-334
   objects, 328
   panels, 328-329
Button, 49, 103-104, 373
ButtonGroup, 192
   constructors, 193
   methods, 193
ButtonHandler, 382-383
CardLayout, 301, 318-320, 322
   methods, 318-319
CaretEvent, 435-437
ChangeEvent, 437-440
Checkbox, 49, 107
CheckboxMenuItem, 49
Color, 592, 597-598
   constructors, 598
   methods, 599-600
ColorModel, 592-596
ColorSpace, 592
Component, 49, 75-76, 85
   alignments, 213
   color, 78, 597
   cursors, 80
   events, 79
   fonts, 603
   locations, 78
   menus, 127
   methods, 76-77
   paint methods, 582-583
   properties, 76
   rendering methods, 81-82
   sizes, 78-79
   Swing tool set, 143, 145
   visibility, 79
ComponentEvent, 366
ComponentUI, 174
ConcreteAction, 491, 497
Container, 49, 82-85
ContainerEvent, 366
Cursor, 80
DefaultListSelectionModel, 455
DefaultMutableTreeNode, 288
DefaultTreeModel, 478
defining, 51-54
Dialog, 49
DirectColorModel, 596
EventObject, 362-363, 433
FileDialog, 49
FlowLayout, 299, 303-308
FocusEvent, 366, 408
Font, 602-606
FontMetrics, 606-614
   methods, 613
   typesetting, 606
Frame, 20, 49, 85, 151
Frame container, 54-55, 57, 59
Graphics, 538, 549-551
   arcs, 560-561
   AWT Paint model, 582-584
   clip region, 562-566, 568
   lines, 557-558
   modes, 574, 576-581
   ovals, 558
   painting causing events, 582
   polygons, 558-559
   rectangles, 559, 561
   shapes, 551-557
   Swing Paint model, 584-590
   text, 561-562
   translating graphics origins, 569-570, 572-573
GridBagConstraints, 336, 341
   anchor variable, 348-349, 351
   fill variable, 347-348
   gridheight variable, 343-346
   gridwidth variable, 343-346
   gridx variable, 341-342
   gridy variable, 341-342
   insets variable, 351-353
   ipadx variable, 353-354

ipady variable, 353-354
parameters, 338-339
variables, 337
weightx variable, 354-358
weighty variable, 354-358
GridBagLayout, 301
GridLayout, 299, 308-313, 334-341; see also
    GridBagConstraints class
HyperlinkEvent, 440-442, 444
ImageIcon, 185
IndexColorModel, 594, 596
inner classes, 388-389
    anonymous, 391-401
    named, 389-391
InputEvent, 366, 410, 419-421
Insets, 351-352
InternalFrameEvent, 444-449
JApplet, 66, 151
JButton, 181
JCheckBox, 181, 189-191
JCheckBoxMenuItem, 181, 228
JColorChooser, 180
JComboBox, 180, 200-201
JComponent, 143, 145, 179
    abstractions, 146-148
    methods, 148
    properties, 147-148
JDialog (Swing containers), 151
JEditorPane, 180, 256, 269, 271-273
    methods, 271-273
    JEditorPane class, 272
JFC, see JFC
JFileChooser
    constructors, 204-207
    methods, 204-207
JFrame (Swing containers), 151
JInternalFrame (Swing containers), 151
JLabel, 208-213
    constructors, 213-215
    methods, 213-215
JLayeredPane, 38, 159-162, 180
JList, 180, 215-220
    constructors, 220-223
    methods, 220-223
    selection states, 513-514
JMenu, 181, 224-225, 228-229
    constructors, 229-231
    methods, 229-231
JMenuBar, 224
    constructors, 233-234
    methods, 233-234

JMenuItem, 181, 224, 231
    constructors, 232
    methods, 232
JOptionPane, 180
JPasswordField, 180, 256, 263-265
    constructors, 264-265
    methods, 264-265
JPopupMenu, 225
JProgressBar, 180, 234-236
    constructors, 237-238
    methods, 237-238
JRadioButton, 180-181, 192
    constructors, 192
    methods, 192
JRadioButtonMenuItem, 181, 228-229
JRootPane, 151
JScrollPane, 180
JSlider, 180
    constructors, 241-244
    methods, 241-244
JSplitPane, 180, 244-247
    constructors, 248-249
    methods, 248-249
JTabbedPane, 180
    constructors, 252-255
    methods, 252-255
JTextArea, 256, 265-269
JTextComponent, 255-260
JTextField, 256, 260-263, 421
JTextPane, 256, 273-282
JToggleButton, 180-181
JToolBar, 180
JToolTip, 180, 282-284
    constructors, 283-284
    methods, 283-284
JTree, 180, 284, 286-294
    constructors, 288-294
    methods, 288-294
JViewport, 180
JWindow (Swing containers), 151
KeyEvent, 366, 410-411
Label, 49
layout managers, 299-301
ListDataEvent, 449-455, 511-512
ListSelectionEvent, 455-458
LookAndFeelInfo, 173
Menu, 49, 121, 126, 128-129
MenuBar, 49, 130
MenuComponent, 127, 129-130
MenuDragMouseEvent, 486-488
MenuEvent, 458-460, 462-464

MenuItem, 49, 121, 126, 129
MenuKeyEvent, 482-486
MouseEvent, 364-366, 410, 415-416
OverlayLayout, 301
PackedColorModel, 593
PaintEvent, 366
Panel, 49, 60-62, 85
PopupMenu, 49
PopupMenuEvent, 464-467
RootLayout, 301
Scrollbar, 20, 49
ScrollPane, 49
Shape (clip regions), 562
StyleConstants, 274
StyleContext, 274-275
SystemColor, 592, 600-601
TextArea, 49, 131, 135-136
TextComponent, 131-135
TextEvent, 427-428
TextField, 49, 131, 136, 421
TreeExpansionEvent, 468-476
TreeModelEvent, 478-482
TreeSelectionEvent, 476-478
UIDefaults, 173
UIManager, 173
UIMananger, 173
ViewportLayout, 299
Window, 49, 85
WindowEvent, 366, 422-425
see also components
CLASSPATH variable, 57
clearSelection( ) method
JLabel class, 220
JTree class, 289
ListSelectionModel, 515
SingleSelectionModel interface, 528
TreeSelectionModel interface, 532
CLICKED constant (MouseEvent class), 415
**Clip Rectangle Passed to a Component's
Graphics (listing 11.8), 566-567**
clipping (graphics), 562-566, 568
CLOSED constant (WindowEvent class), 422
CLOSING constant (WindowEvent class), 422
codebase parameter, 64
**collapsePath(TreePath path) method (JTree
class), 289**
**collapseRow(int row) method (JTree class),
289**
Color brighter( ) PaintContext method, 599

Color class, 592, 597-598
constructors, 598
methods, 599-600
Color darker( ) method, 599
**Color getBackgroundAt(int index) method
(JTabbedPane class), 253**
**Color getCaretColor( ) method
(JTextComponent class), 256**
**Color getDisabledTextColor( ) method
(JTextComponent class), 257**
Color getForeground( ) method, 597
**Color getForegroundAt(int index) method
(JTabbedPane class), 253**
**Color getSelectedTextColor( ) method
(JTextComponent class), 257**
**Color getSelectionBackground( ) method
(JLabel class), 222**
**Color getSelectionColor( ) method
(JTextComponent class), 258**
**Color getSelectionForeground( ) method
(JLabel class), 222**
color maps, 593
color monitors, 593
color package (AWT), 17, 592
ColorChooser class (JFC), 29
colorchooser package (JFC), 25
ColorModel class, 592-597
colors, 592
Color class, 597-598
constructors, 598
methods, 599-600
color models, 593
direct color model, 596
index color model, 593-596
Component class, 76-78, 597
JColorChooser class, 180
packages, 592
pixels, 593
SystemColor class, 600-601
ColorSpace class, 592
ColorSpace getColorSpace( ) method, 599
combo boxes
JComboBox class, 180
layered panes, 39
Swing components, 196-201
ComboBox class (JFC), 29
ComboBoxModel interface, 522, 526-527
ComboBoxModel model, 44

commands (Swing tool set), 142
communication (controllers), 12
compass points (BorderLayout class), 313-317
Component add method, 252, 360
Component add(Component c) method
  (JMenu class), 230
Component and Container Events
  (listing 9.11), 403-405
Component class, 49, 75-76
  alignments (Swing labels), 213
  AWT, 20-21, 85, 582-583
  color, 78, 597
  fonts, 603
  menus, 127
  methods, 76-77
  properties, 76
  Swing tool set, 143, 145
Component Constraints for Use in a
  GridBagLayout Controlled Container
  (listing 8.8), 339-341
component events, 365-366
Component getBottomComponent( ) method
  (JSplitPane class), 248
Component getComponent( ) method
  JMenu class, 230
  JMenuBar class, 233
  JMenuItem class, 232
Component getComponentAt method
  (JTabbedPane class), 253
Component getComponentAtIndex method
  (JMenuBar class), 233
Component getLabelFor( ) method (JLabel
  class), 214
Component getLeftComponent( ) method
  (JSplitPane class), 248
Component getMenuComponent(int n)
  method (JMenu class), 230
Component getRightComponent( ) method
  (JSplitPane class), 248
Component getSelectedComponent( ) method
  (JTabbedPane class), 253
Component getTopComponent( ) method
  (JSplitPane class), 248
component states (graphics), 543-546
Component [] getComponentsInLayer(int
  layer) method, 161
Component's State after Obtaining a Copy of
  Its Graphics (listing 11.2), 543-544
ComponentEvent class, 366

ComponentListener interface, 375
components, 48-49
  adding to containers, 85-92
  AWT (Abstract Windowing Toolkit), 74-75
    buttons, 102-104
    check boxes, 105-107
    Choice class, 108-110
    dialog boxes, 110-114
    heavyweight, 19
    labels, 114-117
    lists, 117-121
    menus, 121-130
    MenuBar class, 130
    text areas, 131-136
    text fields, 131-136
  Choice (graphics), 556-557
  events, 403-407
    adjustment, 429-433
    ancestor, 434-435
    caret, 435-437
    focus, 407-410
    hyperlink, 440-442, 444
    input, 419-421
    internal frame, 444-447, 449
    item, 425-427
    key, 410-413, 415
    menu drag mouse, 486-488
    menu key, 482-486
    mouse, 415, 417-419
    text, 427, 429
    window, 422-425
  graphics, 538
  hierarchies, 50
  lightweight (Swing Paint model), 585-590
  Swing model architecture, 504
  Swing tool set, see Swing tool set
  see also classes
ComponentUI class, 174
Component[] getMenuComponents( ) method
  (JMenu class), 230
Concrete Implementation of an Action
  (listing 9.35), 492-493
ConcreteAction class, 491, 497
constants
  BOTTOM_ALIGNMENT, 213
  CENTER_ALIGNMENT, 213
  Cursor class, 80
  LEFT_ALIGNMENT, 213
  MouseEvent class, 415-416
  RIGHT_ALIGNMENT, 213

RELATIVE, 341
TOP_ALIGNMENT, 213
WindowEvent class, 422
constraints
BorderLayout class, 313
GridBagConstraints class, 337
anchor variable, 348-351
fill variable, 347-348
gridheight variable, 343-346
gridwidth variable, 343-346
gridx variable, 341-342
gridy variable, 341-342
insets variable, 351-353
ipadx variable, 353-354
ipady variable, 353-354
parameters, 338-339
weightx variable, 354-358
weighty variable, 354-358
layout managers, 300
constraints parameter, 301
constructors
AbstractButton class, 182-185
ButtonGroup, 193
Color class, 598
IndexColorModel class, 594
JComboBox, 200-201
JFileChooser class, 204-207
JLabel class, 213-215
JList class, 220-223
JMenu class, 229-231
JMenuBar class, 233-234
JMenuItem class, 232
JPasswordField class, 264-265
JProgressBar class, 237-238
JRadioButton class, 192
JSlider class, 241-244
JSplitPane class, 248-249
JTabbedPane class, 252-255
JToolTip class, 283-284
JTree class, 288-294
see also methods
consume( ) method, 419-421
consumed input events, 419
**Consuming InputEvents To Prevent Delivery
   To Native Peers (listing 9.16), 420**
Container class, 20-22, 49, 82-85
Container container, 54
**Container that Encompasses All of Your GUI
   (listing 3.2), 60-62**

**Container With Multiple Child Components
   (listing 4.2), 88-91**
ContainerEvent class, 366
ContainerListener interface, 375, 406
containers, 48-50, 74
adding components, 85-89, 91-92
Applet, 54
AWT (Abstract Windowing Toolkit), 74, 149
Box class, 333-334
CardLayout layout manager, sizing, 321
children, 97-98
Container, 54
creating applications, 52-53
events (AWT), 403-407
Frame, 54-55, 57, 59
heavyweight, 52-54
JFC (Java Foundation Classes), 33-38
JRootPane, 301
layout managers, 296-297, 303
add( ) methods, 359-360
algorithms, 298
BorderLayout class, 313-314, 318
BoxLayout class, 322-334
CardLayout class, 318-320, 322
classes, 299-301
FlowLayout class, 303-305, 307-308
GridLayout class, 308-313, 334-341
invalid, 297-298
LayoutManager interface, 298-300
LayoutManager2 interface, 300-302
methods, 298-300
policies, 298
size, 296-297
see also GridBagConstraints class
lightweight, 63-64
nested, 92-97
order of, 98-99
Panel, 54, 60-62
Swing, 301-302
Swing tool set, 145, 148-149
abstractions, 149-151
heavyweight, 63-64
heavyweight/lightweight comparison, 162-165
JDialogBox, 164
JInternalFrame, 163
JRootPane, 151-158
look-and-feel configurations, 166-171,
   173-174
Window, 54

containment models (Swing tool set), 141

Content pane (JRootPane Swing container), 152-157

Content Pane to Add Components (listing 6.1), 154-156

Content panes (container classes), 35

contentsChanged method, 450, 509

CONTENTS_CHANGED constant (ListDataEvent class), 511

controllers, 11, 42-43, 505

convertValueToText method (JTree class), 289

coordinates
    graphics, 549-551
        clipping, 568
        translating graphics origins, 569-573
    Graphics class, 549

copy( ) method
    JPasswordField class, 265
    JTextComponent class, 256

create( ) method, 382, 384, 397

createContext method, 599

createDefaultModel( ) method (JTextArea class), 268

createHorizontalBox method, 334

createStandardLabels method (JSlider class), 242

createVerticalBox method, 334

Creating an ItemListener and Registering It with the Combo Box (listing 9.18), 426-427

Cursor class, 80

cursors (Component class), 76-77, 80

Custom Look-and-Feel (Swing tool set), 166-174

Custom UI Look-and-Feel (Swing tool set), 141

Custom UI property (JComponent class), 147

Customizing Component Layout By Specifying Constraints Parameter (listing 8.9), 344-345

cut( ) method
    JPasswordField class, 265
    JTextComponent class, 256

D

darker( ) method, 599

data abstraction models, 44

Data Model property (JComponent class), 147

datatransfer package (AWT), 17

DEACTIVATED constant (WindowEvent class), 422

decode method, 599

Default layer (JLayeredPane class), 38, 160

DefaultListModel, 451

DefaultListSelectionModel class, 455

DefaultMutableTreeNode class, 288

DefaultTreeModel class, 478

Defining a Listener For MenuKeyEvents (listing 9.33), 483-484

defining classes, 51-54

DEICONIFIED constant (WindowEvent class), 422

Delegation Event Model (Swing tool set), 32-33

delivering events, 371-372

Descent (FontMetrics class), 606

DesktopPane class (JFC), 29

destroy( ) method, 65

dialog boxes
    AWT (Abstract Windowing Toolkit), 110-114
    container class, 34
    file, 202
    layered panes, 39
    Swing tool set, 27

Dialog class, 20-22, 49

Dialog From a Parent Frame (listing 5.4), 111-113

Dialog(Dialog owner) method (dialog boxes), 114

Dictionary getLabelTable( ) method (JSlider class), 242

Dimension getMinimumSize( ) method
    TextArea class, 135
    TextField class, 136

Dimension getPreferredScrollable ViewportSize( ) method
    JLabel class, 221
    JTextArea class, 268
    JTextComponent class, 257

Dimension getPreferredSize( ) method
    JEditorPane class, 272
    JTextArea class, 268
    JTextField class, 262

Dimension maximumLayoutSize method, 300

Dimension minimumLayoutSize method, 299, 308, 312

Dimension preferred method, 299

Dimension preferredLayoutSize method, 308, 312

direct color model, 596

DirectColorModel class, 596

disabling Swing buttons, 188

dispatchEvent method, 371-372

display areas (GridLayout class), 335

dispose( ) method, 400, 548

dnd package (AWT), 17

doClick( ) method (AbstractButton class), 182

doClick(int pressTime) method (JMenu class), 230

Document getDocument( ) method (JTextComponent class), 257

Document interface, 522

DocumentEvent event, 369

DocumentListener interface, 376

dots (CaretEvent class), 435

Double buffering property (JComponent class), 148

double getPercentComplete( ) method (JProgressBar class), 237

downcasting (FlowLayout class), 306

Drag layer (JLayeredPane class), 39, 161

Drag-and-Drop API, 24

DRAGGED constant (MouseEvent class), 415

draw3DRect( ) method, 559

drawImage( ) method, 572

drawing graphics
  AWT model, 538-541
  clipping, 562-566, 568
  component states, 543-546
  deleting instances, 548-549
  Graphics class, 549-551
    arcs, 560-561
    lines, 557-558
    ovals, 558
    polygons, 558-559
    rectangles, 559-561
    shapes, 551-557
    text, 561-562
  graphics pen, 549-550
  methods, 541-546
  rendering comparisons, 567-568
  strings, 539-541

Drawing of Repaired Pixels (listing 11.7), 564

Drawing the Graphics Representing a String (listing 12.2), 607-608

drawLine( ) method, 557

drawOval( ) method, 558

drawPolygon( ) method, 558-559

drawPolyline( ) method, 559

drawRect( ) method, 559

drawRoundRect( ) method, 560

drawRoundRectangles( ) method, 560

drawString( ) method, 551, 562

drawString( ) routine, 539

dual context models, 517-519

Dynamically Discovering and Setting an Application's Look-and-Feel (listing 6.8), 171-172

E

EAST region (BorderLayout class), 314-317

echoCharIsSet( ) method (JPasswordField class), 265

editable Swing combo boxes, 196, 199-200

editor panes (Swing components), 269, 271-273

EditorKit getEditorKit( ) method (JEditorPane class), 272

EditorKit getEditorKitForContentType method (JEditorPane class), 272

EditorKit method (JEditorPane class), 272

EditorPane class (JFC), 29

Empty Methods to Fully Implement a Listener Interface (listing 9.3), 385-386

Enabled state (ButtonModel interface), 526

enabling (Component class), 76-77

ensureFileIsVisible(File f) method (JFileChooser class), 204

ensureIndexIsVisible method (JLabel class), 220

ENTERED constant (MouseEvent class), 415

Enumeration getElements( ) method (ButtonGroup class), 193

Enumeration getExpandedDescendants method (JTree class), 290

Enumeration shortcuts( ) method (MenuBar class), 130

environment variables (CLASSPATH), 57

equals(Object obj) method, 599

event handlers, 32-33, 362, 371
  example of, 378-382, 384-386
  inner classes, 388-389
    anonymous, 391-401
    named, 389-391

Event Handling (listing 9.1), 379-382
event listeners, 32-33, 372-377
  event handling example, 383
  event sources combination, 401-402
  models, 508-510
  multiple, 402
event package
  AWT, 17
  JFC (Java Foundation Classes), 25
event targets, 32
EventObject class, 362-363, 433
EventObject method, 363
events, 362
  action events, 489-499
  ActionEvent, 366
  adapters, 386-388
  Adjustment, 367
  AncestorEvent, 369
  AWT, 362, 365-366
    adjustment events, 429, 431-433
    AWTEvent class, 364-365
    component events, 365-366, 403-407
    container events, 403-407
    focus events, 407-410
    input events, 419-421
    item events, 425-427
    key events, 410-413, 415
    mouse events, 415, 417-419
    paint events, 422
    semantic events, 365-368
    Swing complements, 377-378
    text events, 427, 429
    window events, 422-425
  CaretEvent, 369
  ChangeEvent, 369-370
  Component class (AWT), 79
  Delegation Event Model (Swing tool set), 32-33
  delivering, 371-372
  DocumentEvent, 369
  EventObject class, 363-364
  firing, 371-372
  HyperlinkEvent, 369
  InputMethod, 367
  InternalFrame, 369
  Invocation, 367
  ItemEvent, 367
  ListDataEvent, 369
  listeners (selection events), 513-515
  ListSelection, 369

  MenuDragMouse, 369
  MenuEvent, 370
  MenuKeyEvent, 369
  ModelEvent, 370
  painting causes, 582
  PopupMenuEvent, 370
  sources, 364, 401-402
  Swing, 363, 368-371, 433
    ancestor events, 434-435
    AWT complements, 377-378
    caret events, 435-437
    change events, 437-440
    hyperlink events, 440-444
    internal frame events, 444-449
    list data events, 449-453, 455
    list selection events, 455-458
    menu drag mouse events, 486-488
    menu events, 458-460, 462-464
    menu key events, 482-486
    pop-up menu events, 464-467
    tree expansion events, 468-476
    tree model events, 478-482
    tree selection events, 476-478
  Swing tool set (models), 524-525
  TableColumn, 370
  TableModelEvent, 370
  TextEvent, 367
  TreeExpansion, 370
  TreeModelEvent, 370
  UndoableEdit, 370
  see also event handlers
exceptions (Swing tool set), 168-169
EXITED constant (MouseEvent class), 415
expandPath(TreePath path) method (JTree class), 289
expandRow(int row) method (JTree class), 290
Explicitly Created Graphics (listing 11.3), 546-547
external padding (insets variable), 351

F

fields
  AWT (Abstract Windowing Toolkit), 131-136
  id, 370
  read-only (event listeners), 402
  source (EventObject class), 364

file choosers (Swing components), 201-207
file dialog box, 202
File getCurrentDirectory( ) method
    (JFileChooser class), 205
File getSelectedFile( ) method (JFileChooser
    class), 205
FileChooserUI getUI( ) method (JFileChooser
    class), 205
FileDialog class, 22, 49
FileFilter getFileFilter( ) method (JFileChooser
    class), 205
FileFilter[] getChoosableFileFilters( ) method
    (JFileChooser class), 205
FileSystemView getFileSystemView( ) method
    (JFileChooser class), 205
FileView getFileView( ) method (JFileChooser
    class), 205
File[] getSelectedFiles( ) method (JFileChooser
    class), 205
fill variable (GridBagConstraints class),
    337-338, 347-348
fill3DRect( ), method, 559
fillOval( ) method, 558
fillRect( ) method, 559
fillRoundRect( ) method, 560
findComponentAt method, 83-84
fireHyperlinkUpdate method (JEditorPane
    class), 272
fireStateChanged( ) method (JSlider class),
    242
fireTreeCollapsed method (JTree class), 290
fireTreeExpanded method (JTree class), 290
fireTreeWillCollapse method (JTree class), 290
fireTreeWillExpand method (JTree class), 290
firing events, 371-372
FIRST constant
    MouseEvent class, 415
    WindowEvent class, 422
float getLayoutAlignmentX method, 300, 319
float getLayoutAlignmentY method, 300, 319
float[] getColorComponents method, 599
float[] getComponents method, 599
float[] getRGBColorComponents method, 600
FlowLayout class, 299-308
    alignment, 305-307
    AWT, 23
FlowLayout Layout Manager Class
    (listing 8.1), 304-305

FlowLayout( ) method, 308
fly-over text (JToolTip class), 180
focus events (AWT), 407-410
FocusEvent class, 366, 408
FocusEvent Demo (listing 9.12), 408-409
FocusListener interface, 375
font (Component class), 77
Font class, 602-603, 605-606
Font getFont( ) method
    FontMetrics class, 613
    MenuComponent class, 129
font package (AWT), 17
FontMetrics class, 606-614
    methods, 613
    typesetting, 606
fonts, 592, 602-606
    Component class, 76
    metrics, 606-614
        methods, 613
        typesetting, 606
    size, calculating, 609-612
foreground color (Component class), 76-78
Foundation Classes, see JFC
Frame class, 20, 49
    AWT Container classes, 22, 85
    Swing containers, 151
Frame container, 54-55, 57, 59
frames
    components (Swing containers), 157
    container class, 34
    dialog box comparisons, 110
    Swing tool set, 27
front-to-back ordering (containers), 98

G

geom package (AWT), 17
getAccelerator( ) method (JMenuItem class),
    232
getAccessibleContext( ) method
    JEditorPane class, 272
    JFileChooser class, 204
    JMenuBar class, 233
    JMenuItem class, 232
    JPasswordField class, 265
    JProgressBar class, 237
    JSlider class, 242
    JSplitPane class, 248

JTabbedPane class, 253

JTextArea class, 268

JTextComponent class, 256

JTextField class, 262

JToolTip class, 283

JTree class, 290

getAccessory( ) method (JFileChooser class), 204

getActions( ) method

JTextComponent class, 256

JTextField class, 262

getAdjustable( ) method, 431

getAlpha( ) method, 599

getAlpha(int pixel) method, 595

getAlphas(byte[] a) method, 595

getAncestor( ) method, 435

getAncestorParent( ) method, 435

getAnchorSelectionIndex( ) method

JLabel class, 220

ListSelectionModel, 515

getApproveButtonMnemonic( ) method (JFileChooser class), 204

getApproveButtonText( ) method (JFileChooser class), 205

getApproveButtonToolTipText( ) method (JFileChooser class), 205

getAscent( ) method (FontMetrics class), 613

getBackground( ) method, 597

getBackgroundAt(int index) method (JTabbedPane class), 253

getBlue( ) method, 599

getBlue(int pixel) method, 595

getBlues(byte[] b) method, 595

getBottomComponent( ) method (JSplitPane class), 248

getBoundsAt(int index) method (JTabbedPane class), 253

getCaret( ) method (JTextComponent class), 256

getCaretColor( ) method (JTextComponent class), 256

getCaretPosition( ) method (JTextComponent class), 257

getCellBounds method (JLabel class), 221

getCellEditor( ) method (JTree class), 290

getCharacterAttributes( ) method (JTextPane class), 281

getChild method (TreeModel interface), 530

getChildCount method (TreeModel interface), 530

getChildren( ) method, 479

getChoosableFileFilters( ) method (JFileChooser class), 205

getClip( ) method, 568

getClipBounds( ) method, 568

getClosestPathForLocation method (JTree class), 290

getClosestRowForLocation method (JTree class), 290

getColor method, 599

getColorComponents method, 599

getColorModel( ) method, 597

getColorSpace( ) method, 599

getColumnClass method (TableModel interface), 529

getColumnCount( ) method (TableModel interface), 529

getColumnName method (TableModel interface), 529

getColumns( ) method

JTextArea class, 268

JTextField class, 262

getColumnWidth( ) method (JTextArea class), 268

getComponent method, 83-84, 435

JMenu class, 230

JMenuBar class, 233

JMenuItem class, 232

JToolTip class, 283

getComponent(int n) method, 83

getComponentAt method, 83-84, 253

getComponentAtIndex method (JMenuBar class), 233

getComponentCount( ) method, 83

getComponentCountInLayer(int layer) method, 161

getComponentIndex method (JMenuBar class), 233

getComponents method, 83, 599

getComponentSize method, 596

getContentPane( ) method (Swing tool set containers), 157-158

getContentType( ) method (JEditorPane class), 272

getCurrentDirectory( ) method (JFileChooser class), 205

getCursor( ) method, 80

getDelay( ) method (JMenu class), 230

getDescent( ) method (FontMetrics class), 613

getDescription( ) method, 444

getDescription(File f) method (JFileChooser class), 205

getDialogTitle( ) method (JFileChooser class), 205

getDialogType( ) method (JFileChooser class), 205

getDisabledIcon( ) method
  AbstractButton class, 182
  JLabel class, 214

getDisabledIconAt(int index) method (JTabbedPane class), 253

getDisabledSelectedIcon( ) method (AbstractButton class), 183

getDisabledTextColor( ) method (JTextComponent class), 257

getDisplayedMnemonic( ) method (JLabel class), 214

getDividerLocation( ) method (JSplitPane class), 248

getDividerSize( ) method (JSplitPane class), 248

getDocument( ) method (JTextComponent class), 257

getDot( ) method, 435

getEchoChar( ) method (JPasswordField class), 265

getEditingPath( ) method (JTree class), 290

getEditorKit( ) method (JEditorPane class), 272

getEditorKitForContentType method (JEditorPane class), 272

getElementAt method, 507

getElements( ) method (ButtonGroup class), 193

getEventType( ) method, 444

getExpandedDescendants method (JTree class), 290

getExtent( ) method
  BoundedRangeModel interface, 518
  JSlider class, 242

getFileFilter( ) method (JFileChooser class), 205

getFileSelectionMode( ) method (JFileChooser class), 205

getFileSystemView( ) method (JFileChooser class), 205

getFileView( ) method (JFileChooser class), 205

getFirstVisibleIndex( ) method (JLabel class), 221

getFixedCellHeight( ) method (JLabel class), 221

getFixedCellWidth( ) method (JLabel class), 221

getFocusAccelerator( ) method (JTextComponent class), 257

getFont( ) method (FontMetrics class), 613

getFontMetrics( ) method (FontMetrics class), 614

getForeground( ) method, 597

getForegroundAt(int index) method (JTabbedPane class), 253

getGraphics( ) method, 548

getGreen( ) method, 599

getGreen(int pixel) method, 596

getHeight( ) method (FontMetrics class), 613

getHelpMenu( ) method (JMenuBar class), 233

getHighlighter( ) method (JTextComponent class), 257

getHorizontalAlignment( ) method
  AbstractButton class, 183
  JLabel class, 214
  JTextField class, 262

getHorizontalTextPosition( ) method
  AbstractButton class, 183
  JLabel class, 214

getHorizontalVisibility( ) method (JTextField class), 262

getHSBColor method, 600

getIcon( ) method
  AbstractButton class, 183
  JLabel class, 214

getIcon(File f) method (JFileChooser class), 205

getIconAt(int index) method (JTabbedPane class), 253

getIconTextGap( ) method (JLabel class), 214

getID( ) method, 365

getIndex0( ) method (ListDataEvent class), 511

getIndex1( ) method (ListDataEvent class), 511

getIndexOfChild method (TreeModel
interface), 531
getInstalledLookAndFeels( ) method, 173
getInverted( ) method (JSlider class), 242
getItem(int pos) method (JMenu class), 230
getItemAt(int index) method (JComboBox
class), 200
getItemCount( ) method
JComboBox class, 200
JMenu class, 230
getKeymap( ) method (JTextComponent
class), 257
getKeyModifiersText(int mods) method, 411
getKeyText(int keycode) method, 411
getLabel( ) method (Button class), 103
getLabelFor( ) method (JLabel class), 214
getLabelTable( ) method (JSlider class), 242
getLastDividerLocation( ) method (JSplitPane
class), 248
getLastSelected method (JTree class), 290
getLastVisibleIndex( ) method (JLabel class),
221
getLayer(Component c) method, 161
getLeading( ) method (FontMetrics class), 613
getLeadSelectionIndex( ) method
JLabel class, 221
ListSelectionModel, 515
getLeadSelectionPath( ) method
JTree class, 290
TreeSelectionModel interface, 532
getLeadSelectionRow( ) method
JTree class, 290
TreeSelectionModel interface, 532
getLeftComponent( ) method (JSplitPane
class), 248
getLineCount( ) method (JTextArea class), 268
getLineEndOffset(int line) method (JTextArea
class), 268
getLineOfOffset(int offset) method
(JTextArea class), 268
getLineStartOffset(int line) method
(JTextArea class), 268
getLineWrap( ) method (JTextArea class), 268
getLocationOnScreen( ) method, 78
getLogicalStyle( ) method (JTextPane class),
281
getMajorTickSpacing( ) method (JSlider class),
242

getMapSize( ) method, 596
getMargin( ) method
AbstractButton class, 183
JMenuBar class, 233
JTextComponent class, 257
getMark( ) method, 435
getMaxAdvance( ) method (FontMetrics
class), 613
getMaxAscent( ) method (FontMetrics class),
613
getMaxDescent( ) method (FontMetrics class),
613
getMaximum( ) method
BoundedRangeModel interface, 518
JProgressBar class, 237
JSlider class, 242
getMaximumDividerLocation( ) method
(JSplitPane class), 248
getMaximumRowCount( ) method
(JComboBox class), 200
getMaxSelectionIndex( ) method
JLabel class, 221
ListSelectionModel, 515
getMaxSelectionRow( ) method
JTree class, 290
TreeSelectionModel interface, 532
getMenu(int index) method (JMenuBar class),
233
getMenuComponent(int n) method (JMenu
class), 230
getMenuComponentCount( ) method (JMenu
class), 230
getMenuComponents( ) method (JMenu
class), 230
getMenuCount( ) method (JMenuBar class),
233
getMinimum( ) method
BoundedRangeModel interface, 518
JProgressBar class, 237
JSlider class, 242
getMinimumDividerLocation( ) method
(JSplitPane class), 248
getMinimumSize( ) method, 299
getMinorTickSpacing( ) method (JSlider class),
242
getMinSelectionIndex( ) method
JLabel class, 221
ListSelectionModel, 516

getMinSelectionRow( ) method
 JTree class, 290
 TreeSelectionModel interface, 532
getMnemonic( ) method (AbstractButton class), 183
getModel( ) method
 JLabel class, 221
 JProgressBar class, 237
 JSlider class, 242
 JTabbedPane class, 253
 JTree class, 290
getName(File f) method (JFileChooser class), 205
getNewLeadSelectionPath( ) method, 476
getOldLeadSelectionPath( ) method, 476
getOrientation( ) method
 JProgressBar class, 237
 JSlider class, 242
 JSplitPane class, 248
getPage( ) method (JEditorPane class), 272
getPaintLabels( ) method (JSlider class), 242
getPaintTicks( ) method (JSlider class), 242
getPaintTrack( ) method (JSlider class), 242
getParagraphAttributes( ) method (JTextPane class), 281
getPassword( ) method (JPasswordField class), 265
getPath( ) method, 476, 479
getPathBounds method (JTree class), 291
getPathForLocation method (JTree class), 291
getPathForRow(int row) method (JTree class), 291
getPaths( ) method, 476
getPercentComplete( ) method (JProgressBar class), 237
getPopupMenu( ) method (JMenu class), 230
getPosition(Component c) method, 161
getPreferredScrollable ViewportSize( ) method (JTextArea class), 268
getPreferredSize( ) method, 59, 299, 609, 612
 JEditorPane class, 272
 JTextArea class, 268
 JTextField class, 262
getPressedIcon( ) method (AbstractButton class), 183
getPrototypeCellValue( ) method (JLabel class), 221
getRed( ) method, 600

getRed(int pixel) method, 596
getReds(byte[] r) method, 596
getRGB( ) method, 600
getRGB(int pixel) method, 596
getRGBColorComponents method, 600
getRGBdefault( ) method, 596
getRightComponent( ) method (JSplitPane class), 248
getRolloverIcon( ) method (AbstractButton class), 183
getRolloverSelectedIcon( ) method (AbstractButton class), 183
getRoot( ) method (TreeModel interface), 531
getRowBounds(int row) method (JTree class), 291
getRowCount( ) method
 JTree class, 291
 TableModel interface, 529
getRowForLocation method (JTree class), 291
getRowForPath(TreePath path) method (JTree class), 291
getRowHeight( ) method
 JTextArea class, 268
 JTree class, 291
getRowMapper( ) method (TreeSelectionModel interface), 532
getRows( ) method (JTextArea class), 268
getScrollableBlockIncrement method
 JLabel class, 221
 JTextComponent class, 257
getScrollableTracks ViewportWidth( ) method
 JEditorPane class, 272
 JLabel class, 221
 JTextArea class, 268
 JTextComponent class, 257
 JTextPane class, 281
getScrollableTracksViewport Height( ) method
 JEditorPane class, 272
 JLabel class, 221
 JTextComponent class, 257
getScrollableUnitIncrement method
 JLabel class, 221
 JTextArea class, 269
 JTextComponent class, 257
 JTree class, 291
getScrollOffset( ) method (JTextField class), 262
getScrollsOnExpand( ) method (JTree class), 291

getSelectedComponent( ) method
(JTabbedPane class), 253
getSelectedFile( ) method (JFileChooser class),
205
getSelectedFiles( ) method (JFileChooser
class), 205
getSelectedIcon( ) method (AbstractButton
class), 183
getSelectedIndex( ) method, 520
   JComboBox class, 200
   JLabel class, 221
   JTabbedPane class, 253
   SingleSelectionModel interface, 528
getSelectedIndices( ) method (JLabel class),
222
getSelectedItem( ) method
   ComboBoxModel interface, 527
   JComboBox class, 200
getSelectedObjects( ) method, 425
   AbstractButton class, 183
   check boxes, 107
   JComboBox class, 201
getSelectedText( ) method
   JTextComponent class, 257
getSelectedTextColor( ) method
   JTextComponent class, 257
getSelectedValue( ) method, 222, 520
getSelection( ) method (ButtonGroup class),
193
getSelectionBackground( ) method (JLabel
class), 222
getSelectionColor( ) method (JTextComponent
class), 258
getSelectionCount( ) method
   JTree class, 291
   TreeSelectionModel interface, 532
getSelectionEnd( ) method (JTextComponent
class), 258
getSelectionForeground( ) method (JLabel
class), 222
getSelectionMode( ) method
   JLabel class, 222
   ListSelectionModel, 516
   TreeSelectionModel interface, 532
getSelectionModel( ) method
   JLabel class, 222
   JMenuBar class, 233
   JTree class, 291

getSelectionPath( ) method
   JTree class, 291
   TreeSelectionModel interface, 533
getSelectionPaths( ) method
   JTree class, 291
   TreeSelectionModel interface, 533
getSelectionRows( ) method
   JTree class, 291
   TreeSelectionModel interface, 533
getSelectionStart( ) method (JTextComponent
class), 258
getShowsRootHandles( ) method (JTree class),
291
getSize( ) method, 79, 507, 568
getSnapToTicks( ) method (JSlider class), 243
getSource( ) method, 363-364, 383, 431
getString( ) method (JProgressBar class), 237
getStyle( ) method, 275
getStyle(String nm) method (JTextPane class),
281
getStyledEditorKit( ) method (JTextPane
class), 281
getSubElements( ) method
   JMenu class, 230
   JMenuBar class, 233
   JMenuItem class, 232
getTabCount( ) method (JTabbedPane class),
253
getTabPlacement( ) method (JTabbedPane
class), 253
getTabRunCount( ) method (JTabbedPane
class), 253
getTabSize( ) method (JTextArea class), 269
getText( ) method
   AbstractButton class, 183
   JLabel class, 214
   JTextComponent class, 258
getTipText( ) method (JToolTip class), 284
getTitleAt(int index) method (JTabbedPane
class), 253
getToolTipText method (JTabbedPane class),
253
getTopComponent( ) method (JSplitPane
class), 248
getTransparency( ) method, 596, 600
getTreePath( ) method, 479
getType( ) method, 511

getTypeDescription(File f) method (JFileChooser class), 205
getUI( ) method
  JProgressBar class, 237
  JSlider class, 243
  JSplitPane class, 248
  JTabbedPane class, 253
  JTextComponent class, 258
  JToolTip class, 284
getUI(JComponent target) method, 173
getUIClassID( ) method
  JEditorPane class, 272
  JFileChooser class, 205
  JMenu class, 230
  JMenuItem class, 232
  JPasswordField class, 265
  JProgressBar class, 237
  JSlider class, 243
  JSplitPane class, 249
  JTabbedPane class, 253
  JTextArea class, 269
  JTextField class, 262
  JTextPane class, 281
  JToolTip class, 284
getURL( ) method, 444
getValue( ) method
  BoundedRangeModel interface, 518
  JProgressBar class, 237
  JSlider class, 243
getValue(String key) method, 491
getValueAt method (TableModel interface), 529
getValueIsAdjusting( ) method
  BoundedRangeModel interface, 518
  JLabel class, 222
  JSlider class, 243
  ListSelectionModel, 516
getVerticalAlignment( ) method
  AbstractButton class, 183
  JLabel class, 214
getVerticalTextPosition( ) method
  AbstractButton class, 183
  JLabel class, 214
getVisibleRowCount( ) method
  JLabel class, 222
  JTree class, 291
getWrapStyleWord( ) method (JTextArea class), 269

Glass pane (JRootPane Swing container), 152-154
glass panes, 35, 39
glyphs, 602
  check boxes, 106
  Component classes, 80
  sizes, 603, 609-612
Graphical User Interface, see GUI
graphics, 538
  AWT models, 538
    native graphics, 539-541
    Paint model, 582-584
  clipping, 562-566, 568
  component states, 543-546
  deleting instances, 548-549
  Graphics class, 549-551
    arcs, 560-561
    lines, 557-558
    ovals, 558
    polygons, 558-559
    rectangles, 559, 561
    shapes, 551-557
    text, 561-562
  graphics origins, translating, 569-573
  methods, 541-543, 546
  modes, 574-581
  painting causing events, 582
  rendering, drawing comparisons, 567-568
  strings, 539-541
  Swing Paint model, 584-590
Graphics class, 538, 549-551
  arcs, drawing, 560-561
  AWT Paint model, 582-584
  clip region, 562-566, 568
  graphics origins, translating, 569-573
  lines, drawing, 557-558
  modes, 574-581
  ovals, drawing, 558
  painting causing events, 582
  polygons, drawing, 558-559
  rectangles, drawing, 559, 561
  shapes, drawing, 551-557
  Swing Paint model, 584-590
  text, drawing, 561-562
Graphics Class Drawing Routines (listing 11.5), 551-556
Graphics object, 543
graphics pen, 549-550

Graphics Representation of a String
(listing 11.1), 539-540
grid cells (GridLayout class), 335
GridBagConstraints class, 336, 341
parameters, 338-339
variables, 337
anchor, 348-351
fill, 347-348
gridheight, 343-346
gridwidth, 343-346
gridx, 341-342
gridy, 341-342
insets, 351-353
ipadx, 353-354
ipady, 353-354
weightx, 354-358
weighty, 354-358
GridBagConstraints object, 341
GridBagLayout class, 23, 301
gridheight parameter (GridBagConstraints
class), 338
gridheight variable (GridBagConstraints
class), 337, 343-346
GridLayout class, 299, 308-313, 334-341
AWT, 23
see also GridBagConstraints class
GridLayout Layout Manager Class
(listing 8.2), 309
GridLayout object, 311
GridLayout( ) method, 312
gridwidth parameter (GridBagConstraints
class), 338
gridwidth variable (GridBagConstraints class),
337, 343-346
gridx parameter (GridBagConstraints class),
338
gridx variable (GridBagConstraints class), 337,
341-342
gridy parameter (GridBagConstraints class),
338
gridy variable (GridBagConstraints class), 337,
341-342
grouping radio buttons, 192, 196
GUI (Graphical User Interface), 8
application logic, 10
MVC (Model-View-Controller) paradigm, 10-13
state models, 512, 517-519

H

handling events, 32-33, 371
example of, 378-386
inner classes, 388-389
anonymous, 391-401
named, 389-391
hasBeenExpanded method (JTree class), 291
Hashtable createStandardLabels method
(JSlider class), 242
heavyweight components
AWT, 19
rendering, 81
Swing tool set, 27-28
heavyweight containers, 52-54
JFC (Java Foundation Classes), 33-38
Swing tool set, 63-64, 148-149
abstractions, 149-151
heavyweight/lightweight comparison, 162-165
JDialogBox, 164
JRootPane, 151-158
layers, 150
lightweight comparisons, 162-165
see also panes
height (positioning graphics), 568
height parameter, 64
hidePopup( ) method (JComboBox class), 201
hiding windows (graphics), 567
hierarchies
components, 50
Swing components, 143
highestLayer( ) method, 161
Highlighter getHighlighter( ) method
(JTextComponent class), 257
horizontal fill (GridBagConstraints class), 347
horizontal labels, 208, 210, 212-213
horizontal sizing (BorderLayout class), 315
horizontally split view (JSplitPane class), 180
HSBtoRGB method, 600
HTML File for the DrawingDemoApplet
Program (listing 11.6), 556
HTML File for the GraphicsDemoApplet
Program (listing 11.4), 547-548
HTML File With a HyperLink That Generates
HyperlinkEvents in a JEditorPane
(listing 9.24), 443-444
html package (JFC), 26

HTML Page That Contains an Applet Specification (listing 3.3), 65
hyperlink events (Swing), 440-442, 444
HyperlinkEvent class, 369, 440-442, 444
HyperlinkListener interface, 376, 440, 444
hyperlinkUpdate(HyperlinkEvent) method, 444

I

Icon getDisabledIcon( ) method
    AbstractButton class, 182
    JLabel class, 214
Icon getDisabledIconAt(int index) method (JTabbedPane class), 253
Icon getDisabledSelectedIcon( ) method (AbstractButton class), 183
Icon getIcon( ) method (JLabel class), 214
Icon getIcon(File f) method (JFileChooser class), 205
Icon getPressedIcon( ) method (AbstractButton class), 183
Icon getRolloverIcon( ) method (AbstractButton class), 183
Icon getRolloverSelectedIcon( ) method (AbstractButton class), 183
Icon getSelectedIcon( ) method (AbstractButton class), 183
Icon interface, 185
ICONIFIED constant (WindowEvent class), 422
id field, 370
im package (AWT), 17
image package (AWT), 17, 592
ImageGallery application, 383-384
ImageIcon class, 185
index color model, 593, 595-596
IndexColorModel class, 594-596
IndexColorModel object, 595
indexes
    ListDataEvent class, 511
    selected (application logic policies), 520-521
indexOfComponent method (JTabbedPane class), 254
indexOfTab method (JTabbedPane class), 254
indexToLocation(int index) method (JLabel class), 222
inheritance (Swing components), 143

init( ) method, 65
inner classes, 388-389
    anonymous, 391-395, 397-401
    named, 389-391
inner classes Web site, 389
input events (AWT), 419-421
Input Method Framework API, 24
InputEvent class, 366, 410, 419-421
InputMethod event, 367
InputMethodListener interface, 375
insert method
    JMenu class, 230
    JTextArea class, 269
insertComponent method (JTextPane class), 281
insertElementAt method (MutableComboBoxModel interface), 527
insertIcon(Icon g) method (JTextPane class), 281
insertIndexInterval method (ListSelectionModel), 516
insertItemAt method (JComboBox class), 201
insertSeparator(int index) method (JMenu class), 231
insertTab method (JTabbedPane class), 254
Insets class, 351-352
Insets getMargin( ) method
    AbstractButton class, 183
    JMenuBar class, 233
    JTextComponent class, 257
insets parameter (GridBagConstraints class), 338
insets variable (GridBagConstraints class), 337, 351-353
installed looks-and-feels, 170, 173
instances
    creating, 53
    graphics, deleting, 548-549
    JRootPane, 151
    named inner classes, 391
    Swing model architecture, 504
int bytesWidth method (FontMetrics class), 613
int charsWidth method (FontMetrics class), 613
int deleteShortcut method (MenuBar class), 130
int getAlignment( ) method, 117, 308

int getAlpha( ) method, 599
int getAlpha(int pixel) method, 595
int getAnchorSelectionIndex( ) method
    JLabel class, 220
    ListSelectionModel, 515
int getApproveButtonMnemonic( ) method
(JFileChooser class), 204
int getAscent( ) method (FontMetrics class),
613
int getBlockIncrement( ) method, 430
int getBlue( ) method, 599
int getBlue(int pixel) method, 595
int getCaretPosition( ) method
    JTextComponent class, 257
    TextComponent class, 134
int getChildCount method (TreeModel interface), 530
int getClosestRowForLocation method (JTree
class), 290
int getColumnCount( ) method (TableModel
interface), 529
int getColumns( ) method, 312
    JTextArea class, 268
    JTextField class, 262
    TextArea class, 135
    TextField class, 136
int getComponentCountInLayer(int layer)
method, 161
int getComponentIndex method (JMenuBar
class), 233
int getComponentSize method, 596
int getDelay( ) method (JMenu class), 230
int getDescent( ) method (FontMetrics class),
613
int getDialogType( ) method (JFileChooser
class), 205
int getDisplayedMnemonic( ) method (JLabel
class), 214
int getDividerLocation( ) method (JSplitPane
class), 248
int getDividerSize( ) method (JSplitPane
class), 248
int getExtent( ) method
    BoundedRangeModel interface, 518
    JSlider class, 242
int getFileSelectionMode( ) method
(JFileChooser class), 205
int getFirstIndex( ) method, 456

int getFirstVisibleIndex( ) method (JLabel
class), 221
int getFixedCellHeight( ) method (JLabel
class), 221
int getFixedCellWidth( ) method (JLabel
class), 221
int getGreen( ) method, 599
int getGreen(int pixel) method, 596
int getHeight( ) method (FontMetrics class),
613
int getHgap( ) method, 308, 312, 319
int getHorizontalAlignment( ) method
    AbstractButton class, 183
    JLabel class, 214
    JTextField class, 262
int getHorizontalTextPosition( ) method
    AbstractButton class, 183
    JLabel class, 214
int getIcon( ) method (AbstractButton class),
183
int getIconTextGap( ) method (JLabel class),
214
int getID( ) method, 364
int getIndex0( ) method, 450 (ListDataEvent
class), 511
int getIndex1( ) method, 450 (ListDataEvent
class), 511
int getIndexOfChild method (TreeModel
interface), 531
int getItem(int index) method (menus), 128
int getItemCount( ) method
    Choice Class, 110
    JComboBox class, 200
    JMenu class, 230
    lists, 120
    menus, 128
int getKeyCode( ) method, 411
int getLastDividerLocation( ) method
(JSplitPane class), 248
int getLastIndex( ) method, 456
int getLastVisibleIndex( ) method (JLabel
class), 221
int getLayer(Component c) method, 161
int getLeading( ) method (FontMetrics class),
613
int getLeadSelectionIndex( ) method
    JLabel class, 221
    ListSelectionModel, 515

int **getLeadSelectionRow( ) method**
   JTree class, 290
   TreeSelectionModel interface, 532
int **getLineCount( ) method (JTextArea class)**,
   268
int **getLineEndOffset(int line) method**
   (JTextArea class), 268
int **getLineOfOffset(int offset) method**
   (JTextArea class), 268
int **getLineStartOffset(int line) method**
   (JTextArea class), 268
int **getMajorTickSpacing( ) method (JSlider**
   class), 242
int **getMapSize( ) method, 596**
int **getMaxAdvance( ) method (FontMetrics**
   class), 613
int **getMaxAscent( ) method (FontMetrics**
   class), 613
int **getMaxDescent( ) method (FontMetrics**
   class), 613
int **getMaximum( ) method, 430**
   BoundedRangeModel interface, 518
   JProgressBar class, 237
   JSlider class, 242
int **getMaximumDividerLocation( ) method**
   (JSplitPane class), 248
int **getMaximumRowCount( ) method**
   (JComboBox class), 200
int **getMaxSelectionIndex( ) method**
   JLabel class, 221
   ListSelectionModel, 515
int **getMaxSelectionRow( ) method**
   JTree class, 290
   TreeSelectionModel interface, 532
int **getMenuComponentCount( ) method**
   (JMenu class), 230
int **getMenuCount( ) method**
   JMenuBar class, 233
   MenuBar class, 130
int **getMinimum( ) method, 430**
   BoundedRangeModel interface, 518
   JProgressBar class, 237
   JSlider class, 242
int **getMinimumDividerLocation( ) method**
   (JSplitPane class), 248
int **getMinorTickSpacing( ) method (JSlider**
   class), 242

int **getMinSelectionIndex( ) method**
   JLabel class, 221
   ListSelectionModel, 516
int **getMinSelectionRow( ) method**
   JTree class, 290
   TreeSelectionModel interface, 532
int **getMnemonic( ) method (AbstractButton**
   class), 183
int **getOrientation( ) method, 430**
   JProgressBar class, 237
   JSlider class, 242
   JSplitPane class, 248
int **getPosition(Component c) method, 161**
int **getRed( ) method, 600**
int **getRed(int pixel) method, 596**
int **getRGB( ) method, 600**
int **getRGB(int pixel) method, 596**
int **getRowCount( ) method**
   JTree class, 291
   TableModel interface, 529
int **getRowForLocation method (JTree class),**
   291
int **getRowForPath(TreePath path) method**
   (JTree class), 291
int **getRowHeight( ) method (JTree class), 291**
int **getRows( ) method, 312**
   JTextArea class, 268
   lists, 120
   TextArea class, 135
int **getScrollableBlockIncrement method**
   JLabel class, 221
   JTextComponent class, 257
int **getScrollableUnitIncrement method**
   JLabel class, 221
   JTextArea class, 269
   JTextComponent class, 257
   JTree class, 291
int **getScrollOffset( ) method (JTextField**
   class), 262
int **getSelectedEnd( ) method**
   (TextComponent class), 134
int **getSelectedIndex( ) method**
   Choice Class, 110
   JComboBox class, 200
   JLabel class, 221
   JTabbedPane class, 253
   SingleSelectionModel interface, 528

int getSelectedItem( ) method (Choice Class), 110

int getSelectedStart( ) method (TextComponent class), 134

int getSelectionCount( ) method
JTree class, 291
TreeSelectionModel interface, 532

int getSelectionEnd( ) method (JTextComponent class), 258

int getSelectionMode( ) method
JLabel class, 222
ListSelectionModel, 516
TreeSelectionModel interface, 532

int getSelectionStart( ) method (JTextComponent class), 258

int getSize( ) method, 507

int getTabCount( ) method (JTabbedPane class), 253

int getTabPlacement( ) method (JTabbedPane class), 253

int getTabRunCount( ) method (JTabbedPane class), 253

int getTabSize( ) method (JTextArea class), 269

int getTransparency( ) method, 596, 600

int getType( ) method, 450, 511

int getUnitIncrement( ) method, 430

int getValue( ) method, 430
BoundedRangeModel interface, 518
JProgressBar class, 237
JSlider class, 243

int getVerticalAlignment( ) method
AbstractButton class, 183
JLabel class, 214

int getVerticalTextPosition( ) method
AbstractButton class, 183
JLabel class, 214

int getVgap( ) method, 308, 312, 319

int getVisibleAmount( ) method, 430

int getVisibleIndex( ) method (lists), 121

int getVisibleRowCount( ) method
JLabel class, 222
JTree class, 291

int highestLayer( ) method, 161

int indexOfComponent method (JTabbedPane class), 254

int indexOfTab method (JTabbedPane class), 254

int INTERNAL_FRAME_ACTIVATED method, 445

int INTERNAL_FRAME_CLOSED method, 445

int INTERNAL_FRAME_CLOSING method, 445

int INTERNAL_FRAME_DEACTIVATED method, 445

int INTERNAL_FRAME_DEICONIFIED method, 445

int INTERNAL_FRAME_FIRST method, 445

int INTERNAL_FRAME_ICONIFIED method, 445

int INTERNAL_FRAME_LAST method, 445

int INTERNAL_FRAME_OPENED method, 445

int locationToIndex method (JLabel class), 222

int lowestLayer( ) method, 161

int showDialog(Component parent, String approveButtonText) method (JFileChooser class), 207

int showOpenDialog(Component parent) method (JFileChooser class), 207

int showSaveDialog(Component parent) method (JFileChooser class), 207

int stringWidth(String str) method (FontMetrics class), 613

int viewToModel(Point pt) method (JTextComponent class), 260

int [] getSelectedIndexes( ) method (lists), 121

interfaces, 44
AbstractListModel, 522
Action, 490-499
ActionListener, 384, 406, 451, 488-499
Adjustable, 429-430, 433
AdjustmentEvent, 431
AdjustmentListener, 431-432
AncestorListener, 434
AttributeSet, 274
BoundedRangeModel, 518-522
ButtonModel, 522, 525-526
CaretListener, 436-437
ChangeListener, 437-440, 442
ComboBoxModel, 522, 526-527
ContainerListener, 406
Document, 522
GUI, see GUI
HyperlinkListener, 440, 444
Icon, 185
InternalFrameListener, 445-446
methods, 445
registering, 446-449

ItemListener, 425, 427
ItemSelectable, 425, 525-526
KeyListener, 410
LayoutManager, 298-300
LayoutManager2, 300-302
ListDataListener, 450-455, 509
listeners, 375-377
ListModel, 506-507, 512-513, 522
ListModel Interface, 45
ListSelectionListener, 455-458
ListSelectionModel, 513-517, 522
MenuDragMouseListener, 487-488
MenuKeyListener, 483-486
MenuListener, 458
    methods, 459
    objects, 459
    registering, 459-464
model comparisons, 534
MouseInputListener, 415
MouseListener, 384-385, 406, 415
MouseMotionListener, 415
MutableAttributeSet, 274
MutableComboBoxModel, 522, 526-527
PopupMenuListener, 464-467
SingleSelectionModel, 522, 528
Style, 274
TableColumnModel, 522
TableModel, 522, 528-529
TextListener, 428-429
TreeExpansionListener, 468
TreeModel, 284, 288, 522, 529-531
TreeModelListener, 478-482
TreeNode, 284, 288
TreeSelectionListener, 476-478
TreeSelectionModel, 532-533
TreeSelectionModel (TreeSelectionModel
    interface), 533
TreeWillExpandListener, 468
WindowAdapter, 400
WindowListener, 400, 423-425
internal frame events (Swing), 444-449
internal frames (container class), 34
internal padding (ipad variables), 353
InternalFrame class (JFC), 29
InternalFrame event, 369
InternalFrameEvent class, 444-449
InternalFrameListener interface, 376, 445-446
    methods, 445
    registering, 446-449

internationalization (Swing tool set), 142
intervalAdded method, 509
intervalRemoved method, 509
**INTERVAL_ADDED constant (ListDataEvent
    class), 511**
int[] getChildIndices( ) method, 479
int[] getComponentSize( ) method, 596
**int[] getSelectedIndices( ) method (JLabel
    class), 222**
int[] getSelectionRows( ) method
    JTree class, 291
    TreeSelectionModel interface, 533
**invalid components (layout managers),
    297-298**
invalidate( ) method, 298
Invocation event, 367
**ipadx parameter (GridBagConstraints class),
    338**
**ipadx variable (GridBagConstraints class),
    337, 353-354**
**ipady parameter (GridBagConstraints class),
    338**
**ipady variable (GridBagConstraints class),
    337, 353-354**
isArmed( ) method (JMenuItem class), 232
isBorderPainted( ) method
    JMenuBar class, 233
    JProgressBar class, 237
**isCellEditable method (TableModel interface),
    529**
isCollapsed method (JTree class), 291-292
**isContinuousLayout( ) method (JSplitPane
    class), 249**
**isDirectorySelectionEnabled( ) method
    (JFileChooser class), 205**
isEditable( ) method
    JComboBox class, 201
    JTextComponent class, 258
    JTree class, 292
isEditing( ) method (JTree class), 292
**isEnabledAt(int index) method (JTabbedPane
    class), 254**
isExpanded(int row) method (JTree class), 292
**isExpanded(TreePath path) method (JTree
    class), 292**
**isFileHidingEnabled( ) method (JFileChooser
    class), 205**

isFileSelectionEnabled( ) method
(JFileChooser class), 206
isFixedRowHeight( ) method (JTree class), 292
isFocusTraversable( ) method
(JTextComponent class), 258
isLeaf(Object node) method (TreeModel
interface), 531
isManagingFocus( ) method
JEditorPane class, 272
JMenuBar class, 233
JTextArea class, 269
isMenuComponent method (JMenu class), 231
isMultiSelectionEnabled( ) method
(JFileChooser class), 206
isOneTouchExpandable( ) method (JSplitPane
class), 249
isOpaque( ) method (JTextComponent class),
258
isPathEditable method (JTree class), 292
isPathSelected method
JTree class, 292
TreeSelectionModel interface, 533
isPopupMenuVisible( ) method (JMenu class),
231
isPopupVisible( ) method (JComboBox class),
201
isRolloverEnabled( ) method (AbstractButton
class), 183
isRootVisible( ) method (JTree class), 292
isRowSelected(int row) method
JTree class, 292
TreeSelectionModel interface, 533
isSelected( ) method
AbstractButton class, 183
ButtonGroup class, 193
JMenu class, 231
JMenuBar class, 233
SingleSelectionModel interface, 528
isSelectedIndex method
JLabel class, 222
ListSelectionModel, 516
isSelectionEmpty( ) method
JLabel class, 222
JTree class, 292
ListSelectionModel, 516
TreeSelectionModel interface, 533
isShiftDown( ) method, 421
isStringPainted( ) method (JProgressBar class),
237

isTearOff( ) method (JMenu class), 231
isTemporary( ) method, 408
isTopLevelMenu( ) method (JMenu class), 231
isTraversable(File f) method (JFileChooser
class), 206
isValidateRoot( ) method (JTextField class),
262
isVisible(TreePath path) method (JTree class),
292
item events (AWT), 425-427
ItemEvent event, 367
ItemListener interface, 375, 425, 427
ItemSelectable interface, 425, 525-526

J

JApplet class, 66, 151
Java
Foundation Classes, see JFC
graphics, see graphics
Java 2D API, 24
Java Beans (AWT packages), 17
Java Look-and-Feel (listing 6.4), 167-168
Java runtime environment (JRE), 169
java.awt package, 74
java.awt.Component class, see Component
class
java.awt.Container class, see Container class
javax.swing package, 140-141
JButton class, 181, 303-304
JCheckBox class, 181, 189-191
JCheckBoxMenuItem class, 181, 228
JColorChooser class, 29, 180
JComboBox class, 180
constructors, 200-201
JFC (Java Foundation Classes), 29
methods, 200-201
JComboBox object, 510, 512
JComboBox( ) method, 200
JComponent class, 143, 145, 179
abstractions, 146-148
methods, 148
properties, 147-148
JComponent getAccessory( ) method
(JFileChooser class), 204
JDesktopPane class (JFC), 29
JDialog class (Swing containers), 151
JDialogBox container, 164

JEditorPane class, 180, 256, 269, 271-273
   hyperlink events (Swing), 440
   JFC (Java Foundation Classes), 29
   methods, 271-273
JEditorPane( ) method, 271
JFC (Java Foundation Classes), 9, 16, 23
   APIs (application programming interfaces), 24
   architecture, 41-46
   classes, 29
      AWT equivalents, 28
      AWT/Swing tool set comparisons, 40-41
      see also individual classes
   containers, 33-38
   MVC (Model-View-Controller) paradigm, 12-13
   packages, 25-26
   panes, 35-38
      glass, 39
      layered, 38-39
   Swing tool set
      comparisons, 40-41
      Delegation Event Model, 32-33
      heavyweight components, 27-28
      lightweight components, 25-29
      pluggable look-and-feel, 29-32
JFileChooser class, 204-207
JFileChooser( ) method, 204
JFrame class (Swing containers), 151
JInternalFrame class
   InternalFrameEvent, 444
   JFC (Java Foundation Classes), 29
   Swing containers, 151
JInternalFrame container, 163
JLabel class, 208, 210-213
   constructors, 213-215
   methods, 213-215
JLayeredPane class, 29, 38, 159-162, 180
JList class, 180, 215-220
   constructors, 220-223
   methods, 220-223
   selection states, 513-514
JList object, 512
JMenu class, 181, 224-225, 228-229
   constructors, 229-231
   methods, 229-231
JMenu( ) method, 229
JMenuBar class, 224
   constructors, 233-234
   methods, 233-234

JMenuBar( ) method, 233
JMenuItem class, 181, 224, 231
   constructors, 232
   methods, 232
JMenuItem( ) method, 232
JOptionPane class, 180
JPanel (BoxLayout class), 328
JPasswordField class, 180, 256, 263-265
   constructors, 264-265
   methods, 264-265
JPopupMenu class, 225
**JPopupMenu getPopupMenu( ) method
 (JMenu class), 230**
JProgressBar class, 180, 234-236
   constructors, 237-238
   methods, 237-238
JProgressBar( ) method, 237
JRadioButton class, 180-181, 192
   constructors, 192
   JFC (Java Foundation Classes), 29
   methods, 192
JRadioButton( ) method, 192
JRadioButtonMenuItem class, 181, 228-229
JRE (Java runtime environment), 169
JRootPane class, 151
JRootPane container, 301
JRootPane object, 152
JRootPane Swing container, 151-158
   JLayeredPane class, 159-162
JScrollPane class, 180
JSeparator class (JFC), 29
JSlider class, 180
   constructors, 241-244
   JFC (Java Foundation Classes), 29
   methods, 241-244
JSlider( ) method, 241
JSplitPane class, 180, 244-247
   constructors, 248-249
   JFC (Java Foundation Classes), 29
   methods, 248-249
JSplitPane( ) method, 248
JTabbedPane class, 180
   constructors, 252-255
   methods, 252-255
JTabbedPane method, 252
JTable class (JFC), 29
JTextArea class, 256, 265-269
JTextArea( ) method, 267

JTextComponent class, 255-260
JTextComponent( ) method, 256
JTextField class, 256, 260-263, 421
JTextField( ) method, 262
JTextPane class, 256, 273-282
    JFC (Java Foundation Classes), 29
    methods, 281-282
JToggleButton class, 29, 180-181
JToolBar class, 29, 180
JToolTip class, 180, 282-284
    constructors, 283-284
    JFC (Java Foundation Classes), 29
    methods, 283-284
JTree class, 180, 284, 286-294
    constructors, 288-294
    JFC (Java Foundation Classes), 29
    methods, 288-294
JViewport class, 29, 180
JWindow class (Swing containers), 151

K

key events (AWT), 410-415
keyboard focus
    button transfers, 410
    event handling, 407
    temporary transfers, 408, 410
KeyEvent class, 366, 410-411
KeyEvent Demo Program (listing 9.13),
    411-413
KeyListener interface, 375, 410
Keymap getKeymap( ) method
    (JTextComponent class), 257
keys
    LONG_DESCRIPTION, 494
    mnemonic (Swing buttons), 185-188
    NAME, 494
KeyStroke getAccelerator( ) method
    (JMenuItem class), 232

L

Label class, 20, 49
Label( ) method, 117
labels
    AWT (Abstract Windowing Toolkit), 114-117
    Swing components, 208-215

Labels With Different Alignments (listing 5.5),
    115-116
LAST constant
    MouseEvent class, 416
    WindowEvent class, 422
Layered pane (JRootPane Swing container),
    152-153
layered panes
    container classes, 35
    JFC (Java Foundation Classes), 38-39
LayeredPane class (JFC), 29
layers
    JLayeredPane class, 159-162, 180
    Swing heavyweight containers, 150
layout managers, 48, 50-51, 296-297, 303
    add( ) methods, 359-360
    algorithms, 298
    AWT, 23
    BorderLayout class, 313-318
    BoxLayout class, 322-334
        objects, 328
        panels, 328-329
    CardLayout class, 318-322
    classes, 299-301
    constraints object, 300
    FlowLayout class, 303-308
    GridLayout class, 308-313, 334-341; see also
        GridBagConstraints class
    invalid components, 297-298
    JRootPane, 152
    LayoutManager interface, 298-300
    LayoutManager2 interface, 300-302
    methods, 298-300
    policies, 298
    size, 296-297
    Swing, 302
LayoutSize(Container parent) method, 299
Leading
    FlowLayout, 305
    FontMetrics class, 606
LEFT alignment, 213, 305
Lightweight Component That Paints Correctly
    (listing 11.12), 588-589
lightweight components
    AWT, 74, 179, 406
    rendering, 81
·   Swing tool set, 25-29, 141-146, 178-181
        AWT classes, 179
        buttons, 181-186, 188-189
        AbstractButton class, 182

check boxes, *189-191*
combo boxes, *196, 198-201*
editor panes, *269, 271-273*
file choosers, *201, 203-207*
labels, *208-215*
lists, *215-223*
menu bars, *233-234*
menus, *223, 225-233*
Paint model, *585, 587-590*
password fields, *263-265*
progress bars, *234-238*
radio buttons, *192-196*
sliders, *238, 240-244*
split panes, *244-249*
tabbed panes, *250-255*
text areas, *265-269*
text components, *255-260*
text fields, *260-263*
text panes, *273-282*
tooltips, *282-284*
trees, *284-294*

lightweight containers, 63-64, 162-165
lines
    Graphics class, drawing, 557-558
    GridLayout class, 336
List class (AWT), 20
list data events (Swing), 449-455
list selection events (Swing), 455-458
List( ) method, 120
ListCellRenderer getCellRenderer( ) method (JLabel class), 221
ListDataEvent class, 369, 449-455, 511-512
ListDataListener interface, 376, 450-455, 509
Listener Class to Extend An Adapter Class (listing 9.4), 387
Listener Class to Extend An Adapter Class (listing 9.4), 387
Listener For MenuDragMouseEvents (listing 9.34), 487-488
listeners (event), 372-377
    adapters, 386-388
    CaretListener, 436-437
    ChangeListener, 437-440, 442
    event handling example, 383
    events, 32-33
    HyperlinkListener, 440, 444
    InternalFrameListener interface, 445-449
    ListDataEvent interface, 449-455
    ListSelectionListener interface, 455-458

    MenuKeyListener interface, 483-486
    MenuListener interface, 458-464
    models, 508-510
    mouse events, 415-419
    multiple, 402
    PopupMenuListener interface, 464-467
    selection events, 513, 515
    TreeExpansionListener interface, 468
    TreeModelListener interface, 478-482
    TreeSelectionListener interface, 476-478
    TreeWillExpandListener interface, 468
    WindowListener, 423-425
listings
    Acquiring the Content Pane of a Swing Heavyweight Container, 158
    Action That Exits an Application, 493
    Adapter Class To Implement An Anonymous Inner Class, 399
    Adding Components to a Container by Using add( ) Methods, 85-86
    Anonymous Inner Classes, 392-394, 396
    Application That Uses Action Objects, 495-497
    AWT Window Classes, 55-57
    Box Container, 333-334
    BoxLayout Layout Manager Class, 323-324
    Calculating FontMetrics, 610-612
    CardLayout Layout Manager Class, 320
    Choice Component, 108-109
    Clip Rectangle Passed to a component's Graphics, 566-567
    Component and Container Events, 403-405
    Component Constraints For Use In a GridBagLayout Controlled Container, 339-341
    Component's State after Obtaining a Copy of Its Graphics, 543-544
    Concrete Implementation of an Action, 492-493
    Consuming InputEvents To Prevent Delivery To Native Peers, 420
    Container that Encompasses All of Your GUI, 60-62
    Container With Multiple Child Components, 88-91
    Content Pane to Add Components, 154-156
    Creating an ItemListener and Registering It with the Combo Box, 426-427
    Customizing Component Layout By Specifying Constraints Parameter, 344-345
    Defining a Listener For MenuKeyEvents, 483-484
    Dialog From a Parent Frame, 111-113
    Drawing of Repaired Pixels, 564

Drawing the Graphics Representing a String, 607-608

Dynamically Discovering and Setting an Application's Look-and-Feel, 171-172

Empty Methods to Fully Implement a Listener Interface, 385-386

Event Handling, 379-382

Explicitly Created Graphics, 546-547

FlowLayout Layout Manager Class, 304-305

FocusEvent Demo, 408-409

Graphics Class Drawing Routines, 551-556

Graphics Representation of a String, 539-540

GridLayout Layout Manager Class, 309

HTML File for the DrawingDemoApplet Program, 556

HTML File for the GraphicsDemoApplet Program, 547-548

HTML File With a HyperLink That Generates HyperlinkEvents in a JEditorPane, 443-444

HTML Page That Contains an Applet Specification, 65

Java Look-and-Feel, 167-168

KeyEvent Demo Program, 411-413

Labels With Different Alignments, 115-116

Lightweight Component That Paints Correctly, 588-589

Listener Class to Extend an Adapter Class, 387

Listener Class to Extend An Adapter Class, 387

Listener For MenuDragMouseEvents, 487-488

Logging KeyEvent Information, 420

Look-and-Feel Class Names Installed, 170-171

Making an Application Its Own Listener, 401

Menus and Menu Items, 122-125

MouseListener Class, 384

MouseListener Class as an Anonymous Inner Class, 398

Named Inner Class, 389-390

Nested Containers To Organize Child Components, 92-95

Nested Containers with BoxLayout Layout Managers, 326-327

Painting a Lightweight Component Incorrectly, 585-587

Platform's Default Look-and-Feel, 169

Printing the Names of the Looks-and-Feels, 169-170

Program That Can Be Run As an Applet or Application, 68, 70

Program That Demonstrates The Use of Multiple Fonts, 604-605

Registering a CaretListener With a JTextField, 436-437

Registering a ChangeListener With a JSlider, 438-440, 442

Registering a HyperlinkListener With a JEditorPane, 441-442

Registering a ListDataListener With a ListModel, 452-455

Registering a Listener For WindowEvents, 423-425

Registering a ListSelectionListener With a JList, 456, 458

Registering a MenuListener With a JMenu, 459-464

Registering a PopupMenuListener With a JPopupMenu, 465-467

Registering a TextListener With a TextArea Component, 428-429

Registering an AdjustmentListener With a JScrollBar, 431-432

Registering an InternalFrameListener With a JInternalFrame, 446-449

Registering Listeners For MouseEvents, 416-418

Registering Listeners For Tree-Related Events With a JTree, 469-473

Runtime Errors from Adding Components to a Heavyweight Swing Container, 157

Single and Multiple Selection Lists, 118-119

Standalone Check Boxes and Grouped Checkboxes, 105-106

States of a Button, 103-104

Struts to Specify Spacing In a Layout, 330-332

Swing Buttons, 185-187

Swing Check Box Menu Items and Radio Button Menu Items, 229

Swing Check Boxes, 189-191

Swing Combo Boxes, 198-199

Swing Editor Panes, 270-271

Swing File Chooser, 202-203

Swing Labels, 209-213

Swing Lists, 216-219

Swing Menus, 225-226, 228

Swing Password Fields, 263-264

Swing Progress Bars, 235-236

Swing Radio Buttons, 194-196

Swing Sliders, 239-241

Swing Split Panes, 245-247

Swing Tabbed Panes, 251-252

Swing Text Areas, 266-267

Swing Text Fields, 260-261

Swing Text Panes, 276-280
Swing Tool Tips, 283
Swing Trees, 285-288
Text Component Classes, 131-133
Translating a Graphics Origin, 569-572
TreeModelEvent Listener Class, 479-480
TreeSelectionEventListener Class, 477
WindowListener to Your Frame, 400
**ListModel getModel( ) method (JLabel class),
221**
ListModel interface, 45, 506-507, 512-513, 522
ListModel model, 44
ListModel object, 506-507, 513
lists
AWT (Abstract Windowing Toolkit), 117-121
JList class, 180
Swing components, 215-223
ListSelectionEvent class, 369, 455-458
**ListSelectionListener interface, 376, 455-456,
458**
ListSelectionModel (abstractions), 514-517
**ListSelectionModel getSelectionModel( )
method (JLabel class), 222**
ListSelectionModel interface, 513-517, 522
ListSelectionModel object, 519
locale (Component class), 76-78, 147, 296-297
locationToIndex method (JLabel class), 222
**Logging KeyEvent Information (listing 9.15),
420**
logic (application logic), 10
LONG_DESCRIPTION key, 494
Look-and-Feel API, 18
JFC, 25, 30, 32
pluggable look-and-feel, 203
Swing tool set, 29-32, 141, 166-174
**Look-and-Feel Class Names Installed
(listing 6.7), 170-171**
LookAndFeelInfo class, 173
lowestLayer( ) method, 161

M

**makeVisible(TreePath path) method (JTree
class), 292**
**Making an Application Its Own Listener
(listing 9.10), 401**
managers (layout), see layout managers

mapping (glyphs), 602
maps (color maps), 593
marks (CaretEvent class), 435
**Menu add(Menu m) method (MenuBar class),
130**
menu bars
container classes, 35
Swing components, 233-234
JMenuBar class, 233
JRootPane Swing container, 152-153
Menu class, 20, 49, 121, 126, 128-129
menu drag mouse events (Swing), 486-488
menu events (Swing), 458-460, 462-464
**Menu getHelpMenu( ) method (MenuBar
class), 130**
**Menu getMenu(int i) method (MenuBar
class), 130**
menu key events (Swing), 482-486
Menu( ) method, 128
MenuBar class, 20, 49, 130
MenuBar( ) method (MenuBar class), 130
MenuComponent class, 127, 129-130
**MenuComponent( ) method
(MenuComponent class), 129**
MenuDragMouse event, 369
MenuDragMouseEvent class, 486-488
**MenuDragMouseListener interface, 376,
487-488**
MenuElement[] getSubElements( ) method
JMenu class, 230
JMenuBar class, 233
JMenuItem class, 232
MenuEvent class, 458-464
MenuEvent event, 370
MenuItem class, 20, 49, 121, 126, 129
**MenuItem getShortcut MenuItem( )
(MenuShortcut s) method (MenuBar class),
130**
MenuItem( ) method (MenuItem class), 129
MenuKeyEvent class, 369, 482-486
MenuKeyListener interface, 376, 483-486
MenuListener interface, 376, 458
methods, 459
objects, 459
registering, 459-464
menus
AWT (Abstract Windowing Toolkit), 121-130
JCheckBoxMenuItem class, 181

JMenu class, 181
JMenuItem class, 181
Swing components, 223-233
Menus and Menu Items (listing 5.7), 122-125
menuSelectionChanged method
JMenu class, 231
JMenuBar class, 233
JMenuItem class, 232
MenuShortcut getShortcut( ) method
(MenuItem class), 129
metal look-and-feel package (JFC), 25, 30-32,
168
methods
AbstractButton class, 182-185
accept(File f) (JFileChooser class), 204
AccessibleContext getAccessibleContext( ), 330
accessor, 388
actionPerformed( ), 374, 383, 390-392, 406, 491
add( ), 58, 62, 84, 318, 359-360, 494, 497
JTabbedPane class, 252
listeners, 374
add(AbstractButton b), 193
add(Component c), 230
add(Component comp), 298
add(JMenu c), 233
add(JMenuItem menuItem), 230
add(String s), 230
addActionListener, 204, 374, 383
addAdjustmentListener( ), 430
addChangeListener
BoundedRangeModel interface, 518
JTabbedPane class, 252
SingleSelectionModel interface, 528
addChoosableFileFilter, 204
addElement(Object obj), 527
addHyperlinkListener, 272
addItem(Object anItem), 200
addLayoutComponent, 301
addListDataListener, 507
addListSelectionListener, 515
addMenuKeyListener, 483
addMenuListener, 230
addMenuListener(MenuListener), 458
addMouseMotionListener, 415
addPropertyChangeListener, 532
addSelectionInterval
JLabel class, 220
JTree class, 289
ListSelectionModel, 515

addSelectionPath
JTree class, 289
TreeSelectionModel interface, 532
addSelectionPaths
JTree class, 289
TreeSelectionModel interface, 532
addSelectionRow(int row), 289
addSelectionRows(int[] rows), 289
addSeparator( ), 230
addStyle, 281
addTab, 252-253
addTableModelListener, 529
addTreeExpansionListener, 289
addTreeModelListener, 530
addTreeSelectionListener
JTree class, 289
TreeSelectionModel interface, 532
addTreeWillExpandListener, 289
Adjustable interface, 430
ancestorAdded( ), 434
AncestorEvent class, 435
AncestorListener interface, 434
ancestorMoved( ), 434
ancestorRemoved( ), 434
append(String str), 268
approveSelection( ), 204
AWTEvent class, 364
boolean echoCharIsSet( )
JPasswordField class, 265
TextField class, 136
boolean getState( ), 107
boolean getValueIsAdjusting( ), 222, 456
boolean getWrapStyleWord( ), 269
boolean isAddedPath( ), 476
boolean isAncestorOf, 83-84
boolean isEditable( )
JTextComponent class, 258
TextComponent class, 134
boolean isEnabled( ), 129, 491
boolean isIndexSelected (int index), 121
boolean isModal( ), 114
boolean isMultipleMode( ), 121
boolean isResizable( ), 114
boolean isSelected, 193
boolean isTearOff( ), 128
BoundedRangeModel interface, 518-519
Box class, 329-330
Box(int axis), 329
BoxLayout, 323
brighter( ) PaintContext, 599
Button( ), 104

Button(String label), 104
ButtonGroup, 193
bytesWidth, 613
cancelEditing( ), 289
cancelSelection( ), 204
CardLayout class, 318-319
CardLayout( ), 318
changeToParentDirectory( ), 204
char getEchoChar( )
   JPasswordField class, 265
   TextField class, 136
char getKeyChar( ), 411
charsWidth, 613
Checkbox( ), 107
CheckboxGroup getCheckboxGroup( ), 107
Choice( ), 110
clearSelection( )
   JLabel class, 220
   JTree class, 289
   ListSelectionModel, 515
   SingleSelectionModel interface, 528
   TreeSelectionModel interface, 532
collapsePath(TreePath path), 289
collapseRow(int row), 289
Color class, 599-600
ColorModel class, 595-596
Component add, 360
Component class (AWT), 76-77, 81-82
consume( ), 419-421
Container class, 83-84
contentsChanged, 450, 509
convertValueToText, 289
copy( )
   JPasswordField class, 265
   JTextComponent class, 256
create( ), 382-384, 397
createContext, 599
createDefaultModel( ),, 268
createHorizontalBox, 334
createStandardLabels, 242
createVerticalBox, 334
cut( )
   JPasswordField class, 265
   JTextComponent class, 256
darker( ), 599
decode, 599
destroy( ), 65
Dialog(Dialog owner), 114
Dimension getMinimumSize (int columns), 136

Dimension getMinimumSize( )
   TextArea class, 135
   TextField class, 136
Dimension getPreferredScrollable ViewportSize( )
   JLabel class, 221
   JTextComponent class, 257
Dimension maximumLayoutSize, 300
Dimension minimumLayoutSize, 299, 308, 312
Dimension preferred, 299
Dimension preferredLayoutSize, 308, 312
dispatchEvent( ), 371-372
dispose( ), 400, 548
doClick( ), 182
doClick(int pressTime), 230
Document getDocument( ), 257
draw3DRect( ), 559
drawImage( ), 572
drawLine( ), 557
drawOval( ), 558
drawPolygon( ), 558-559
drawPolyline( ), 559
drawRect( ), 559
drawRoundRect( ), 560
drawRoundRectangles( ), 560
drawString( ), 551, 562
echoCharIsSet( ), 265
EditorKit, 272
ensureFileIsVisible(File f), 204
ensureIndexIsVisible, 220
Enumeration shortcuts( ), 130
equals(Object obj), 599
event listeners, 373
EventObject, 363
expandPath(TreePath path), 289
expandRow(int row), 290
FileChooserUI getUI( ), 205
FileView getFileView( ), 205
fill3DRect( ),, 559
fillOval( ), 558
fillRect( ), 559
fillRoundRect( ), 560
findComponentAt, 83-84
fireHyperlinkUpdate, 272
fireStateChanged( ), 242
fireTreeCollapsed, 290
fireTreeExpanded, 290
fireTreeWillCollapse, 290
fireTreeWillExpand, 290
float getLayoutAlignmentX, 300, 319
float getLayoutAlignmentY, 300, 319
float[] getColorComponents, 599

float[] getComponents, 599
float[] getRGBColorComponents, 600
FlowLayout( ), 308
Font class, 603
Font getFont( ), 129
FontMetrics class, 613
getAccelerator( ), 232
getAccessibleContext( )
   JEditorPane class, 272
   JFileChooser class, 204
   JMenuBar class, 233
   JMenuItem class, 232
   JPasswordField class, 265
   JProgressBar class, 237
   JSlider class, 242
   JSplitPane class, 248
   JTabbedPane class, 253
   JTextArea class, 268
   JTextComponent class, 256
   JTextField class, 262
   JToolTip class, 283
   JTree class, 290
getAccessory( ), 204
getActions( )
   JTextComponent class, 256
   JTextField class, 262
getAdjustable( ), 431
getAlpha( ), 599
getAlpha(int pixel), 595
getAlphas(byte[] a), 595
getAncestor( ), 435
getAncestorParent( ), 435
getAnchorSelectionIndex( )
   JLabel class, 220
   ListSelectionModel, 515
getApproveButtonMnemonic( ), 204
getApproveButtonText( ), 205
getApproveButtonToolTipText( ), 205
getAscent( ), 613
getBackground( ), 597
getBackgroundAt(int index), 253
getBlue( ), 599
getBlue(int pixel), 595
getBlues(byte[] b), 595
getBottomComponent( ), 248
getBoundsAt(int index), 253
getCaret( ), 256
getCaretColor( ), 256
getCaretPosition( ), 257
getCellBounds, 221

getCellEditor( ), 290
getCharacterAttributes( ), 281
getChild, 530
getChildCount, 530
getChildren( ), 479
getChoosableFileFilters( ), 205
getClip( ), 568
getClipBounds( ), 568
getClosestPathForLocation, 290
getClosestRowForLocation, 290
getColor, 599
getColorComponents, 599
getColorModel( ), 597
getColorSpace( ), 599
getColumnClass, 529
getColumnCount( ), 529
getColumnName, 529
getColumns( )
   JTextArea class, 268
   JTextField class, 262
getColumnWidth( ), 268
getComponent( ), 83-84, 435
   JMenu class, 230
   JMenuBar class, 233
   JMenuItem class, 232
   JToolTip class, 283
getComponent(int n), 83
getComponentAt( ), 83-84, 253
getComponentAtIndex, 233
getComponentCount( ), 83
getComponentCountInLayer(int layer), 161
getComponentIndex, 233
getComponents( ), 83, 599
getComponentSize( ), 596
getContentPane( ), 157-158
getContentType( ), 272
getCurrentDirectory( ), 205
getCursor( ), 80
getDelay( ), 230
getDescent( ), 613
getDescription( ), 444
getDescription(File f), 205
getDialogTitle( ), 205
getDialogType( ), 205
getDisabledIcon( )
   AbstractButton class, 182
   JLabel class, 214
getDisabledIconAt(int index), 253
getDisabledSelectedIcon( ), 183
getDisabledTextColor( ), 257

getDisplayedMnemonic( ), 214
getDividerLocation( ), 248
getDividerSize( ), 248
getDocument( ), 257
getDot( ), 435
getEchoChar( ), 265
getEditingPath( ), 290
getEditorKit( ), 272
getEditorKitForContentType, 272
getElementAt, 507
getElements( ), 193
getEventType( ), 444
getExpandedDescendants, 290
getExtent( )
    BoundedRangeModel interface, 518
    JSlider class, 242
getFileFilter( ), 205
getFileSelectionMode( ), 205
getFileSystemView( ), 205
getFileView( ), 205
getFirstVisibleIndex( ), 221
getFixedCellHeight( ), 221
getFixedCellWidth( ), 221
getFocusAccelerator( ), 257
getFont( ), 613
getFontMetrics( ), 614
getForeground( ), 597
getForegroundAt(int index), 253
getGraphics( ), 548
getGreen( ), 599
getGreen(int pixel), 596
getHeight( ), 613
getHelpMenu( ), 233
getHighlighter( ), 257
getHorizontalAlignment( )
    AbstractButton class, 183
    JLabel class, 214
    JTextField class, 262
getHorizontalTextPosition( )
    AbstractButton class, 183
    JLabel class, 214
getHorizontalVisibility( ), 262
getHSBColor, 600
getIcon( )
    AbstractButton class, 183
    JLabel class, 214
getIcon(File f), 205
getIconAt(int index), 253
getIconTextGap( ), 214
getID( ), 365

getIndex0( ), 511
getIndex1( ), 511
getIndexOfChild, 531
getInputAttributes( ), 281
getInstalledLookAndFeels( ), 173
getInverted( ), 242
getItem(int pos), 230
getItemAt(int index), 200
getItemCount( )
    JComboBox class, 200
    JMenu class, 230
getKeymap( ), 257
getKeyModifiersText(int mods), 411
getKeyText(int keycode), 411
getLabel( ), 103
getLabelFor( ), 214
getLabelTable( ), 242
getLastDividerLocation( ), 248
getLastSelected PathComponent( ), 290
getLastVisibleIndex( ), 221
getLayer(Component c), 161
getLeading( ), 613
getLeadSelectionIndex( )
    JLabel class, 221
    ListSelectionModel, 515
getLeadSelectionPath( )
    JTree class, 290
    TreeSelectionModel interface, 532
getLeadSelectionRow( )
    JTree class, 290
    TreeSelectionModel interface, 532
getLeftComponent( ), 248
getLineCount( ), 268
getLineEndOffset(int line), 268
getLineOfOffset(int offset), 268
getLineStartOffset(int line), 268
getLineWrap( ), 268
getLocationOnScreen( ), 78
getLogicalStyle( ), 281
getMajorTickSpacing( ), 242
getMapSize( ), 596
getMargin( )
    AbstractButton class, 183
    JMenuBar class, 233
    JTextComponent class, 257
getMark( ), 435
getMaxAdvance( ), 613
getMaxAscent( ), 613
getMaxDescent( ), 613

getMaximum( )
  BoundedRangeModel interface, 518
  JProgressBar class, 237
  JSlider class, 242
getMaximumDividerLocation( ), 248
getMaximumRowCount( ), 200
getMaxSelectionIndex( )
  JLabel class, 221
  ListSelectionModel, 515
getMaxSelectionRow( )
  JTree class, 290
  TreeSelectionModel interface, 532
getMenu(int index), 233
getMenuComponent(int n), 230
getMenuComponentCount( ), 230
getMenuComponents( ), 230
getMenuCount( ), 233
getMinimum( )
  BoundedRangeModel interface, 518
  JProgressBar class, 237
  JSlider class, 242
getMinimumDividerLocation( ), 248
getMinimumSize( ), 299
getMinorTickSpacing( ), 242
getMinSelectionIndex( )
  JLabel class, 221
  ListSelectionModel, 516
getMinSelectionRow( )
  JTree class, 290
  TreeSelectionModel interface, 532
getMnemonic( ), 183
getModel( )
  JLabel class, 221
  JProgressBar class, 237
  JSlider class, 242
  JTabbedPane class, 253
  JTree class, 290
getName(File f), 205
getNewLeadSelectionPath( ), 476
getOldLeadSelectionPath( ), 476
getOrientation( )
  JProgressBar class, 237
  JSlider class, 242
  JSplitPane class, 248
getPage( ), 272
getPaintLabels( ), 242
getPaintTicks( ), 242
getPaintTrack( ), 242
getParagraphAttributes( ), 281
getPassword( ), 265

getPath( ), 476, 479
getPathBounds, 291
getPathForLocation, 291
getPathForRow(int row), 291
getPaths( ), 476
getPercentComplete( ), 237
getPopupMenu( ), 230
getPosition(Component c), 161
getPreferredScrollable ViewportSize( ), 268
getPreferredSize( ), 59, 299, 609, 612
  JEditorPane class, 272
  JTextArea class, 268
  JTextField class, 262
getPressedIcon( ), 183
getPrototypeCellValue( ), 221
getRed( ), 600
getRed(int pixel), 596
getReds(byte[] r), 596
getRGB( ), 600
getRGB(int pixel), 596
getRGBColorComponents, 600
getRGBdefault( ), 596
getRightComponent( ), 248
getRolloverIcon( ), 183
getRolloverSelectedIcon( ), 183
getRoot( ), 531
getRowBounds(int row), 291
getRowCount( )
  JTree class, 291
  TableModel interface, 529
getRowForLocation, 291
getRowForPath(TreePath path), 291
getRowHeight( )
  JTextArea class, 268
  JTree class, 291
getRowMapper( ), 532
getRows( ), 268
getScrollableBlockIncrement
  JLabel class, 221
  JTextComponent class, 257
getScrollableTracks ViewportWidth( )
  JEditorPane class, 272
  JLabel class, 221
  JTextArea class, 268
  JTextComponent class, 257
  JTextPane class, 281
getScrollableTracksViewport Height( )
  JEditorPane class, 272
  JLabel class, 221
  JTextComponent class, 257

getScrollableUnitIncrement
   JLabel class, 221
   JTextArea class, 269
   JTextComponent class, 257
   JTree class, 291
getScrollOffset( ), 262
getScrollsOnExpand( ), 291
getSelectedComponent( ), 253
getSelectedFile( ), 205
getSelectedFiles( ), 205
getSelectedIcon( ), 183
getSelectedIndex( ), 520
   JComboBox class, 200
   JLabel class, 221
   JTabbedPane class, 253
   SingleSelectionModel interface, 528
getSelectedIndices( ), 222
getSelectedItem( )
   ComboBoxModel interface, 527
   JComboBox class, 200
getSelectedObjects( ), 425
   AbstractButton class, 183
   check boxes, 107
   JComboBox class, 201
getSelectedText( ), 257
getSelectedTextColor( ), 257
getSelectedValue( ), 222, 520
getSelectedValues( ), 222
getSelection( ), 193
getSelectionBackground( ), 222
getSelectionColor( ), 258
getSelectionCount( )
   JTree class, 291
   TreeSelectionModel interface, 532
getSelectionEnd( ), 258
getSelectionForeground( ), 222
getSelectionMode( )
   JLabel class, 222
   ListSelectionModel, 516
   TreeSelectionModel interface, 532
getSelectionModel( )
   JLabel class, 222
   JMenuBar class, 233
   JTree class, 291
getSelectionPath( )
   JTree class, 291
   TreeSelectionModel interface, 533
getSelectionPaths( )
   JTree class, 291
   TreeSelectionModel interface, 533

getSelectionRows( )
   JTree class, 291
   TreeSelectionModel interface, 533
getSelectionStart( ), 258
getShowsRootHandles( ), 291
getSize( ), 79, 507, 568
getSnapToTicks( ), 243
getSource, 364
getSource( ), 363, 383, 431
getString( ), 237
getStyle( ), 275
getStyle(String nm), 281
getStyledDocument( ), 281
getStyledEditorKit( ), 281
getSubElements( )
   JMenu class, 230
   JMenuBar class, 233
   JMenuItem class, 232
getTabCount( ), 253
getTabPlacement( ), 253
getTabRunCount( ), 253
getTabSize( ), 269
getText, 258
getText( )
   AbstractButton class, 183
   JEditorPane class, 272
   JLabel class, 214
getTipText( ), 284
getTitleAt(int index)
   JTabbedPane class, 253
getToolTipText, 253
getTopComponent( ), 248
getTransparency( ), 596, 600
getTreePath( ), 479
getType( ), 511
getTypeDescription(File f), 205
getUI( )
   JProgressBar class, 237
   JSlider class, 243
   JSplitPane class, 248
   JTabbedPane class, 253
   JTextComponent class, 258
   JToolTip class, 284
getUI(JComponent target), 173
getUIClassID( )
   JEditorPane class, 272
   JFileChooser class, 205
   JMenu class, 230
   JMenuItem class, 232
   JPasswordField class, 265

JProgressBar class, 237
JSlider class, 243
JSplitPane class, 249
JTabbedPane class, 253
JTextArea class, 269
JTextField class, 262
JTextPane class, 281
JToolTip class, 284
getURL( ), 444
getValue( )
    BoundedRangeModel interface, 518
    JProgressBar class, 237
    JSlider class, 243
getValue(String key), 491
getValueAt, 529
getValueIsAdjusting( )
    BoundedRangeModel interface, 518
    JLabel class, 222
    JSlider class, 243
    ListSelectionModel, 516
getVerticalAlignment( )
    AbstractButton class, 183
    JLabel class, 214
getVerticalTextPosition( )
    AbstractButton class, 183
    JLabel class, 214
getVisibleRowCount( )
    JLabel class, 222
    JTree class, 291
getWrapStyleWord( ), 269
Graphics class, 538
Graphics parameter, 541-543, 546
GridLayout( ), 312
hasBeenExpanded, 291
hidePopup( ), 201
highestLayer( ), 161
HSBtoRGB, 600
hyperlinkUpdate(HyperlinkEvent), 444
Icon getDisabledIcon( ), 214
indexOfComponent, 254
indexOfTab, 254
indexToLocation(int index), 222
init( ), 65
insert
    JMenu class, 230
    JTextArea class, 269
insertComponent, 281
insertElementAt, 527
insertIcon(Icon g), 281
insertIndexInterval, 516

insertItemAt, 201
insertSeparator(int index), 231
insertTab, 254
int deleteShortcut, 130
int getAlignment( ), 117, 308
int getBlockIncrement( ), 430
int getCaretPosition( ), 134
int getColumns( ), 312
    TextArea class, 135
    TextField class, 136
int getFirstIndex( ), 456
int getHgap( ), 308, 312, 319
int getID( ), 364
int getIndex0( ), 450
int getIndex1( ), 450
int getItem(int index), 128
int getItemCount( )
    Choice Class, 110
    lists, 120
    menus, 128
int getKeyCode( ), 411
int getLastIndex( ), 456
int getMaximum( ), 430
int getMenuCount( ), 130
int getMinimum( ), 430
int getOrientation( ), 430
int getRows( ), 312
    lists, 120
    TextArea class, 135
int getSelectedEnd( ), 134
int getSelectedIndex( ), 110
int getSelectedItem( ), 110
int getSelectedStart( ), 134
int getType( ), 450
int getUnitIncrement( ), 430
int getValue( ), 430
int getVgap( ), 308, 312, 319
int getVisibleAmount( ), 430
int getVisibleIndex( ), 121
int INTERNAL_FRAME_ACTIVATED, 445
int INTERNAL_FRAME_CLOSED, 445
int INTERNAL_FRAME_CLOSING, 445
int INTERNAL_FRAME_DEACTIVATED, 445
int INTERNAL_FRAME_DEICONIFIED, 445
int INTERNAL_FRAME_FIRST, 445
int INTERNAL_FRAME_ICONIFIED, 445
int INTERNAL_FRAME_LAST, 445
int INTERNAL_FRAME_OPENED, 445
int [] getSelectedIndexes( ), 121
InternalFrameEvent class, 445

InternalFrameListener, 445
intervalAdded, 509
intervalRemoved, 509
int[] getChildIndices( ), 479
invalidate( ), 298
isArmed( ), 232
isBorderPainted( )
    JMenuBar class, 233
    JProgressBar class, 237
isCellEditable, 529
isCollapsed, 292
isCollapsed(int row), 291
isContinuousLayout( ), 249
isDirectorySelectionEnabled( ), 205
isEditable( )
    JComboBox class, 201
    JTextComponent class, 258
    JTree class, 292
isEditing( ), 292
isEnabledAt(int index), 254
isExpanded(int row), 292
isExpanded(TreePath path), 292
isFileHidingEnabled( ), 205
isFileSelectionEnabled( ), 206
isFixedRowHeight( ), 292
isFocusTraversable( ), 258
isLeaf(Object node), 531
isManagingFocus( )
    JEditorPane class, 272
    JMenuBar class, 233
    JTextArea class, 269
isMenuComponent, 231
isMultiSelectionEnabled( ), 206
isOneTouchExpandable( ), 249
isOpaque( ), 258
isPathEditable, 292
isPathSelected
    JTree class, 292
    TreeSelectionModel interface, 533
isPopupMenuVisible( ), 231
isPopupVisible( ), 201
isRolloverEnabled( ), 183
isRootVisible( ), 292
isRowSelected(int row)
    JTree class, 292
    TreeSelectionModel interface, 533
isSelected( )
    AbstractButton class, 183
    ButtonGroup class, 193
    JMenu class, 231

JMenuBar class, 233
    SingleSelectionModel interface, 528
isSelectedIndex
    JLabel class, 222
    ListSelectionModel, 516
isSelectionEmpty( )
    JLabel class, 222
    JTree class, 292
    ListSelectionModel, 516
    TreeSelectionModel interface, 533
isShiftDown( ), 421
isStringPainted( ), 237
isTearOff( ), 231
isTemporary( ), 408
isTopLevelMenu( ), 231
isTraversable(File f), 206
isValidateRoot( ), 262
isVisible(TreePath path), 292
JComboBox( ), 200-201
JComponent class, 148
JEditorPane class, 271-273
JEditorPane( ), 271
JFileChooser class, 204-207
JFileChooser( ), 204
JLabel class, 213-215
JLayeredPane class, 161
JList class, 220-223
JMenu class, 229-231
JMenu( ), 229
JMenuBar class, 233-234
JMenuBar( ), 233
JMenuItem class, 232
JMenuItem( ), 232
JPasswordField class, 264-265
JProgressBar class, 237-238
JProgressBar( ), 237
JRadioButton class, 192
JRadioButton( ), 192
JSlider class, 241-244
JSlider( ), 241
JSplitPane class, 248-249
JSplitPane( ), 248
JTabbedPane class, 252-255
JTabbedPane( ), 252
JTextArea class, 267-269
JTextArea( ), 267
JTextComponent class, 256-260
JTextComponent( ), 256
JTextField, 262
JTextField( ), 262

JTextPane class, 281-282
JToolTip class, 283-284
JTree class, 288-294
KeyEvent class, 411
Keymap getKeymap( ), 257
Label( ), 117
layout managers, 298-300
LayoutSize(Container parent), 299
List( ), 120
ListCellRenderer getCellRenderer( ), 221
ListDataEvent class, 450
ListDataListener, 450
ListSelectionEvent class, 456
locationToIndex, 222
lowestLayer( ), 161
makeVisible(TreePath path), 292
Menu add(Menu m), 130
Menu getHelpMenu( ), 130
Menu getMenu(int i), 130
Menu( ), 128
MenuBar( ), 130
MenuComponent( ), 129
MenuDragMouseEvent class, 486
MenuDragMouseListener interface, 487
MenuItem getShortcut MenuItem(
)(MenuShortcut s), 130
MenuItem( ), 129
MenuListener interface, 459
menuSelectionChanged
    JMenu class, 231
    JMenuBar class, 233
    JMenuItem class, 232
MenuShortcut getShortcut( ), 129
minimumLayoutSize( ), 299
modelToView(int pos), 258
mouseClicked( ), 384
moveToBack(Component c), 161
moveToFront(Component c), 161
Object cloneWithSource, 476
Object []
    check boxes, 107
    Choice Class, 110
Object [] getSelectedObjects( ), 121
pack( ), 59
paint( ), 82
    FontMetrics class, 614
    Swing Paint model, 585-587
paint( ), 539-543, 583-584
paint(Graphics g), 81
paintAll, 582

paintComponent( ), 585-589, 609, 614
paramString( ), 364, 445
    JSlider class, 243
    JTextArea class, 269
    JTextComponent class, 258
paste( ), 258
PopupMenuListener Interface, 464-465
postActionEvent( ), 262
preferredLayoutSize( ), 299
processComponentKeyEvent, 269
processEvent( ), 371-372
protected EditorKit, 272
protected ListSelectionModel
   createSelectionModel( ), 220
protected String paramString( )
    JFileChooser class, 206
    JPasswordField class, 265
    JProgressBar class, 237
    JSlider class, 243
    JTextArea class, 269
    JTextComponent class, 258
    JTextPane class, 281
    JToolTip class, 284
protected void consume( ), 364
protected void finalize( ), 364
protected void fireSelectionValueChanged, 220
protected void fireStateChanged( ), 242
protected void init, 232
protected void paintBorder, 237
protected void setup (FileSystemView view), 207
public void paint, 582
public void repaint, 583
public void repaint(long tm), 583
public void update, 583
read
    JEditorPane class, 272
    JTextComponent class, 258
registerEditorKitForContentType, 272-273
remove(AbstractButton b), 193
remove(Component c), 231
remove(Component component)
    JSplitPane class, 249
    JTabbedPane class, 254
remove(int index), 161, 249
remove(int pos), 231
remove(JMenuItem item), 231
removeActionListener
    JFileChooser class, 206
    JTextField class, 262

removeAdjustmentListener( ), 430
removeAll( )
   JMenu class, 231
   JSplitPane class, 249
   JTabbedPane class, 254
removeAllItems( ), 201
removeCaretListener, 258
removeChangeListener
   BoundedRangeModel interface, 519
   JSlider class, 243
   JTabbedPane class, 254
   SingleSelectionModel interface, 528
removeChoosableFileFilter, 206
removeElement(Object obj), 527
removeElementAt(int index), 527
removeHyperlinkListener, 273
removeIndexInterval, 516
removeItem(Object item), 201
removeItemAt(int index), 201
removeListDataListener, 507
removeListSelectionListener, 516
removeMenuKeyListener, 483
removeMenuListener(MenuListener), 458
removeNotify( ), 258
removePropertyChangeListener, 533
removeSelectionInterval
   JLabel class, 222
   JTree class, 292
   ListSelectionModel, 516
removeSelectionPath
   JTree class, 292
   TreeSelectionModel interface, 533
removeSelectionPaths
   JTree class, 292
   TreeSelectionModel interface, 533
removeSelectionRow(int row), 292
removeSelectionRows, 292
removeStyle(String nm), 281
removeTabAt(int index), 254
removeTableModelListener, 529
removeTreeExpansionListener, 293
removeTreeModelListener, 531
removeTreeSelectionListener
   JTree class, 293
   TreeSelectionModel interface, 533
removeTreeWillExpand, 293
repaint( ), 81-82, 583-584, 587
replaceRange, 269

replaceSelection
   JEditorPane class, 273
   JTextComponent class, 259
   JTextPane class, 282
rescanCurrentDirectory( ), 206
resetChoosableFileFilters( ), 206
resetRowSelection( ), 533
resetToPreferredSizes( ), 249
RGBtoHSB, 600
scrollPathToVisible, 293
scrollRectToVisible, 262
scrollRowToVisible(int row), 293
select, 259
selectAll( ), 259
setAccelerator
   JMenu class, 231
   JMenuItem class, 232
setAccessory, 206
setActionCommand, 262
setAnchorSelectionIndex, 516
setApproveButtonMnemonic, 206
setApproveButtonText, 206
setApproveButtonToolTipText, 206
setArmed(boolean b), 232
setBackground(Color c), 597
setBackgroundAt, 254
setBorderPainted(boolean b), 237
setBorderPainted(boolean s), 233
setBottomComponent, 249
setCaret(Caret c), 259
setCaretColor(Color c), 259
setCaretPosition, 259
setCellEditor, 293
setCellRenderer, 293
setCharacterAttributes, 282
setClip( ), 568
setColumns, 269
setColumns(int columns), 262
setComponent(JComponent c), 284
setComponentAt, 254
setConstraints( ), 341, 346-347
setContentType, 273
setContinuousLayout, 249
setCurrentDirectory, 206
setCursor(Cursor), 80
setDelay(int d), 231
setDialogTitle, 206
setDialogType, 206
setDisabledIcon
   AbstractButton class, 183
   JLabel class, 214

setDisabledIconAt, 254
setDisabledSelectedIcon, 184
setDisabledTextColor, 259
setDisplayedMnemonic, 214-215
setDividerLocation, 249
setDividerSize, 249
setDocument(Document doc)
    JTextComponent class, 259
    JTextPane class, 282
setEchoChar(char c), 265
setEditable(boolean b), 259
setEditable(boolean flag)
    JComboBox class, 201
    JTree class, 293
setEditorKit, 273
setEditorKit(EditorKit kit), 282
setEditorKitForContentType, 273
setEnabled(boolean b)
    AbstractButton class, 184
    JMenuItem class, 232
    JTextComponent class, 259
setEnabled(boolean enabled), 201
setEnabledAt, 254
setExtent(int extent), 243
setExtent(int newExtent), 519
setFileFilter, 206
setFileHidingEnabled, 207
setFileSelectionMode, 207
setFileSystemView, 207
setFileView, 207
setFixedCellHeight, 222
setFixedCellWidth, 222
setFocusAccelerator, 259
setFont( ), 605
setFont( ), 545
setFont(Font f)
    JTextArea class, 269
    JTextField class, 262
setForeground(Color c), 597
setForegroundAt, 254
setHelpMenu(JMenu menu), 234
setHighlighter, 259
setHorizontalAlignment
    AbstractButton class, 184
    JLabel class, 215
    JTextField class, 263
setHorizontalTextPosition, 215
setHorizontalTextPosition(int align), 184
setIcon(Icon defaultIcon), 184
setIcon(Icon icon), 215

setIconAt, 254
setIconTextGap, 215
setInverted(boolean b), 243
setInvokesStopCellEditing, 293
setKeymap(Keymap map), 259
setLabel( ), 103
setLabelFor(Component c), 215
setLabelTable, 243
setLargeModel, 293
setLastDividerLocation, 249
setLayout( ), 302
setLeadSelectionIndex, 516
setLeftComponent, 249
setLineWrap(boolean wrap), 269
setListData, 222-223
setLogicalStyle(Style s), 282
setLookAndFeel( ), 171
setMajorTickSpacing(int n), 243
setMargin(Insets insets), 184
setMargin(Insets m), 259
setMargin(Insets margin), 234
setMaximum(int maximum), 243
setMaximum(int n), 238
setMaximum(int newMaximum), 519
setMaximumRowCount, 201
setMenuLocation, 231
setMinimum(int minimum), 243
setMinimum(int n), 238
setMinimum(int newMinimum), 519
setMinorTickSpacing(int n), 243
setMnemonic(char mnemonic), 184
setMnemonic(int mnemonic), 184
setModel
    JMenu class, 231
    JProgressBar class, 238
    JSlider class, 243
    JTabbedPane class, 254
setModel(TreeModel newModel), 293
setMultiSelectionEnabled, 207
setOneTouchExpandable, 249
setOpaque(boolean o), 259
setOrientation
    JProgressBar class, 238
    JSlider class, 243
    JSplitPane class, 249
setPage, 273
setPaintLabels(boolean b), 243
setPaintMode( ), 574
setPaintTicks(boolean b), 243
setPaintTrack(boolean b), 243

setParagraphAttributes, 282
setPopupMenuVisible, 231
setPopupVisible(boolean v), 201
setPosition(Component c, int position), 161
setPressedIcon, 184
setPrototypeCellValue, 223
setRangeProperties, 519
setRightComponent, 249
setRolloverEnabled, 184
setRolloverIcon, 184
setRolloverSelectedIcon, 184
setRootVisible, 293
setRowHeight(int rowHeight), 293
setRowMapper, 533
setRows(int rows), 269
setScrollOffset, 263
setScrollsOnExpand, 293
setSelected
    AbstractButton class, 184
    ButtonGroup class, 193
setSelected(boolean b), 231
setSelected(Component sel), 234
setSelectedComponent, 254
setSelectedFiles, 207
setSelectedIcon (Icon selectedIcon), 185
setSelectedIndex
    JLabel class, 223
    SingleSelectionModel interface, 528
setSelectedIndex (int anIndex), 201
setSelectedIndex(int index), 254
setSelectedIndices, 223
setSelectedItem, 527
setSelectedItem (Object anObject), 201
setSelectedTextColor, 259
setSelectedValue, 223
setSelectionBackground, 223
setSelectionColor(Color c), 259
setSelectionEnd, 259
setSelectionForeground, 223
setSelectionInterval
    JLabel class, 223
    JTree class, 293
    ListSelectionModel, 516
setSelectionMode
    JLabel class, 223
    ListSelectionModel, 516
setSelectionMode(int mode), 533
setSelectionModel
    JMenuBar class, 234
    JTree class, 293

setSelectionPath
    JTree class, 293
    TreeSelectionModel interface, 533
setSelectionPaths
    JTree class, 294
    TreeSelectionModel interface, 533
setSelectionRow(int row), 294
setSelectionRows, 294
setSelectionStart, 259
setShowsRootHandles, 294
setSize(Dimension), 79
setSnapToTicks(boolean b), 244
setString(String s), 238
setStringPainted(boolean b), 238
setStyledDocument, 282
setTabPlacement, 255
setTabSize(int size), 269
setText(String t), 259
setText(String text)
    AbstractButton class, 185
    JLabel class, 215
setTipText(String tipText), 284
setTitleAt, 255
setTopComponent, 249
setUI(MenuBarUI ui), 234
setUI(ProgressBarUI ui), 238
setUI(SliderUI ui), 244
setUI(SplitPaneUI ui), 249
setUI(TabbedPaneUI ui), 255
setUI(TextUI ui), 259
setUI(TreeUI ui), 294
setValue(int n)
    JProgressBar class, 238
    JSlider class, 244
setValue(int newValue), 519
setValueAt, 529
setValueIsAdjusting
    BoundedRangeModel interface, 519
    JLabel class, 223
    JSlider class, 244
    ListSelectionModel, 516
setVerticalAlignment, 215
setVerticalAlignment (int alignment), 185
setVerticalTextPosition, 215
setVerticalTextPosition(int textPosition), 185
setVisible(boolean), 79
setVisibleRowCount
    JLabel class, 223
    JTree class, 294

setWrapStyleWord, 269

showDialog(Component parent, String approveButtonText), 207

showOpenDialog(Component parent), 207

showPopup( ), 201

showSaveDialog(Component parent), 207

start, 66

start( ), 65

startEditingAtPath, 294

stateChanged(ChangeEvent), 437

static Box createHorizontalBox( ), 329

static Box createVerticalBox( ), 329

static Component createGlue( ), 329

static Component createHorizontalGlue( ), 329-330

static Component createRigidArea(Dimension d), 329

static Component createVerticalStrut(int height), 330

static EditorKit, 272

static int X_AXIS, 323

static int Y_AXIS, 323

static Keymap addKeymap, 256

static Keymap getKeymap, 257

static Keymap removeKeymap, 258

static String DEFAULT, 490

static String LONG_DESCRIPTION, 490

static String NAME, 490

static String SHORT_DESCRIPTION, 490

static String SMALL_ICON, 491

static void loadKeymap, 258

stop( ), 65

stopEditing( ), 294

String getActionCommand( ), 129

String getItem(int index)
    Choice Class, 110
    lists, 120

String getLabel( )
    Button class, 104
    check boxes, 107
    MenuItem class, 129

String getName( ), 130

String getSelectedItem( ), 121

String getSelectedText( ), 134

String getText( )
    labels, 117
    TextComponent class, 134

String getTitle( ), 114

String getUIClassID( )
    JFileChooser class, 205
    JSplitPane class, 249

String toString( ), 308, 313

String [] getItems( ), 120

String [] getSelectedItems( ), 121

stringWidth(String str), 613

TextArea( ), 135

TextField( ), 136

TextField(String text), 136

toString( ), 363-364, 456, 476, 479

translate( ), 569

TreeCellEditor getCellEditor( ), 290

treeDidChange( ), 294

TreeModelEvent class, 479

TreeModelListener class, 478

TreeSelectionEvent class, 476

update( ), 82
    Swing Paint model, 585
    Swing Paint model, 587

update(Graphics g), 81

updateLabelUIs( ), 244

updateUI( )
    JProgressBar class, 238
    JSlider class, 244
    JSplitPane class, 249
    JTabbedPane class, 255
    JTextComponent class, 260
    JToolTip class, 284
    JTree class, 294

validate( ), 298

valueForPathChanged, 531

viewToModel(Point pt), 260

void add, 83, 252, 360

void add(MenuItem mi), 128

void add(String item)
    Choice Class, 110
    lists, 120

void add(String label), 128

void addAdjustmentListener, 430

void addChangeListener
    BoundedRangeModel interface, 518
    SingleSelectionModel interface, 528

void addHyperlinkListener, 272

void addItem(String item)
    Choice Class, 110
    lists, 120

void addItemListener, 425

void addLayoutComponent, 298, 300, 308, 312

void addListSelectionListener, 515

void addPropertyChangeListener, 491, 532

void addSelectionInterval
    JTree class, 289
    ListSelectionModel, 515

void addSelectionPath
   JTree class, 289
   TreeSelectionModel interface, 532
void addSelectionPaths
   JTree class, 289
   TreeSelectionModel interface, 532
void addSelectionRow(int row), 289
void addSelectionRows(int[] rows), 289
void addSeparator( ), 128
void addTableModelListener, 529
void addTreeExpansionListener, 289
void addTreeModelListener, 530
void addTreeSelectionListener
   JTree class, 289
   TreeSelectionModel interface, 532
void addTreeWillExpandListener, 289
void ancestorAdded, 434
void ancestorMoved, 434
void ancestorRemoved, 434
void append(String str)
   JTextArea class, 268
   TextArea class, 135
void cancelEditing( ), 289
void clearSelection( )
   JTree class, 289
   ListSelectionModel, 515
   SingleSelectionModel interface, 528
   TreeSelectionModel interface, 532
void collapsePath(TreePath path), 289
void collapseRow(int row), 289
void consume( ), 364
void contentsChanged, 450, 509
void copy( )
   JPasswordField class, 265
   JTextComponent class, 256
void cut( )
   JPasswordField class, 265
   JTextComponent class, 256
void deleteShortcut( ), 129
void deselect(int index), 120
void doClick( ), 182
void expandPath(TreePath path), 289
void expandRow(int row), 290
void finalize( ), 364
void fireHyperlinkUpdate, 272
void fireTreeCollapsed, 290
void fireTreeExpanded, 290
void fireTreeWillCollapse, 290
void fireTreeWillExpand, 290
void first(Container parent), 319
void insert, 269

void insert(MenuItem, int index), 128
void insert(String item, int index), 110
void insert(String label, int index), 128
void insert(String str), 136
void insertComponent, 281
void insertElementAt, 527
void insertIcon(Icon g), 281
void insertIndexInterval, 516
void insertSeparator(int index), 128
void internalFrameActivated, 445
void internalFrameClosed, 445
void internalFrameClosing, 445
void internalFrameDeactivated, 445
void internalFrameDeiconified, 445
void internalFrameIconified, 445
void internalFrameOpened, 445
void intervalAdded, 450, 509
void intervalRemoved, 450, 509
void invalidateLayout, 300
void last(Container parent), 319
void layoutContainer, 299, 308, 312
void makeVisible, 292
void makeVisible(int index), 121
void menuCanceled(MenuEvent e), 459
void menuDeselected(MenuEvent e), 459
void menuDragMouseDragged, 487
void menuDragMouseEntered, 487
void menuDragMouseExited, 487
void menuDragMouseReleased, 487
void menuSelected(MenuEvent e), 459
void next(Container parent), 319
void paste( ), 258
void popupMenuCanceled, 464
void popupMenuWillBecome, 464
void postActionEvent( ), 262
void previous(Container parent), 319
void putValue, 491
void read
   JEditorPane class, 272
   JTextComponent class, 258
void remove, 83
void remove (MenuComponent c), 130
void remove (MenuComponent item), 128
void remove( ), 84
void remove(Component comp), 298
void remove(Component component), 249
void remove(int index)
   JSplitPane class, 249
   MenuBar class, 130
   menus, 128

void remove(int position), 121
void remove(String item), 121
void removeActionListener, 262
void removeAdjustmentListener, 430
void removeAll( ), 83, 298
   JSplitPane class, 249
   lists, 121
   menus, 128
void removeCaretListener, 258
void removeChangeListener, 519
void removeElement(Object obj), 527
void removeElementAt(int index), 527
void removeHyperlinkListener, 273
void removeItemListener, 425
void removeLayoutComponent, 299, 313
void removeListSelectionListener, 516
void removeNotify( ), 258
void removeProperty, 491
void removeSelectionInterval
   JTree class, 292
   ListSelectionModel, 516
void removeSelectionPath
   JTree class, 292
   TreeSelectionModel interface, 533
void removeSelectionPaths
   JTree class, 292
   TreeSelectionModel interface, 533
void removeSelectionRow, 292
void removeSelectionRows, 292
void removeStyle(String nm), 281
void removeTreeExpansionListener, 293
void removeTreeSelectionListener
   JTree class, 293
   TreeSelectionModel interface, 533
void removeTreeWillExpand, 293
void repaint, 583
void replaceItem(String newValue, int index), 121
void replaceRange(String str, int start, int end),
   136
void replaceSelection
   JEditorPane class, 273
   JTextComponent class, 259
   JTextPane class, 282
void resetRowSelection( ), 533
void resetToPreferredSizes( ), 249
void scrollPathToVisible, 293
void scrollRectToVisible, 262
void scrollRowToVisible(int row), 293
void select, 259
void select(int), 134

void select(int index), 121
void select(int pos), 110
void select(String str), 110
void selectAll( )
   JTextComponent class, 259
   TextComponent class, 134
void setAccelerator, 232
void setActionCommand, 262
void setActionCommand (String command), 129
void setAlignment, 308
void setAlignment(int alignment), 117
void setAnchorSelectionIndex, 516
void setBackground(Color c), 597
void setBlockIncrement(int b), 430
void setBorderPainted(boolean b), 237
void setBottomComponent, 249
void setBounds, 297
void setCaret(Caret c), 259
void setCaretColor(Color c), 259
void setCaretPosition, 259
void setCaretPosition (int position), 134
void setCellEditor, 293
void setCellRenderer, 293
void setCharacterAttributes, 282
void setCheckboxGroup, 107
void setColumns, 269
void setColumns(int cols), 313
void setColumns(int columns), 262
void setComponent, 284
void setContentType, 273
void setContinuousLayout, 249
void setDisabledTextColor, 259
void setDividerLocation, 249
void setDividerSize, 249
void setDocument(Document doc)
   JTextComponent class, 259
   JTextPane class, 282
void setEchoChar(char c)
   JPasswordField class, 265
   TextField class, 136
void setEditable(boolean b)
   JTextComponent class, 259
   TextComponent class, 134
void setEditable(boolean flag), 293
void setEditorKit, 273
void setEditorKit(EditorKit kit), 282
void setEditorKitForContentType, 273
void setEnabled( ), 129, 491
void setEnabled(boolean b), 259
void setExtent(int newExtent), 519

void setFileFilter, 206
void setFocusAccelerator, 259
void setFont( ), 130
void setFont(Font f)
    JTextArea class, 269
    JTextField class, 262
void setForeground(Color c), 597
void setHelpMenu(Menu m), 130
void setHgap, 308
void setHgap(int hgap), 313, 319
void setHighlighter, 259
void setHorizontalAlignment, 263
void setInvokesStopCellEditing, 293
void setKeymap(Keymap map), 259
void setLabel, 104
void setLabel(String label)
    check boxes, 107
    MenuItem class, 129
void setLargeModel, 293
void setLastDividerLocation, 249
void setLayout, 298
void setLayout(LayoutManager l), 330
void setLeadSelectionIndex, 516
void setLeftComponent, 249
void setLineWrap(boolean wrap), 269
void setListData, 222
void setLogicalStyle(Style s), 282
void setMargin(Insets m), 259
void setMaximum(int max), 430
void setMinimum(int min), 430
void setMinimum(int newMinimum), 519
void setModal(boolean modal), 114
void setModel(TreeModel newModel), 293
void setMultipleMode(boolean b), 121
void setName (String name), 130
void setOneTouchExpandable, 249
void setOpaque(boolean o), 259
void setOrientation, 249
void setPage, 273
void setParagraphAttributes, 282
void setRangeProperties, 519
void setResizable (boolean resizable), 114
void setRightComponent, 249
void setRootVisible, 293
void setRowHeight(int rowHeight), 293
void setRowMapper, 533
void setRows(int rows), 313
    JTextArea class, 269
    TextArea class, 136

void setScrollOffset, 263
void setScrollsOnExpand, 293
void setSelectedEnd (int selectionEnd), 135
void setSelectedIndex, 528
void setSelectedItem, 527
void setSelectedStart (int selectionStart), 135
void setSelectedTextColor, 259
void setSelectionColor(Color c), 259
void setSelectionEnd, 259
void setSelectionInterval
    JTree class, 293
    ListSelectionModel, 516
void setSelectionMode, 516
void setSelectionMode(int mode), 533
void setSelectionModel, 293
void setSelectionPath
    JTree class, 293
    TreeSelectionModel interface, 533
void setSelectionPaths
    JTree class, 294
    TreeSelectionModel interface, 533
void setSelectionRow(int row), 294
void setSelectionRows, 294
void setSelectionStart, 259
void setShortcut (MenuShortcut s), 129
void setShowsRootHandles, 294
void setSize, 297
void setState(boolean state), 107
void setStyledDocument, 282
void setTabSize(int size), 269
void setText(String t)
    JTextComponent class, 259
    TextComponent class, 135
    TextField class, 136
void setText(String text), 117
void setTipText, 284
void setTitle(String title), 114
void setTopComponent, 249
void setUI, 294
void setUI(SplitPaneUI ui), 249
void setUI(TextUI ui), 259
void setUnitIncrement(int u), 430
void setValue(int newValue), 519
void setValue(int v), 430
void setValueIsAdjusting
    BoundedRangeModel interface, 519
    ListSelectionModel, 516
void setVgap, 308
void setVgap(int vgap), 313, 319

void setVisible, 297
void setVisibleAmount(int v), 430
void setVisibleRowCount, 294
void setWrapStyleWord, 269
void show( ), 114, 319
void showPopup( ), 201
void startEditingAtPath, 294
void treeCollapsed, 468
void treeDidChange, 294
void treeExpanded, 468
void treeNodesChanged, 478
void treeNodesInserted, 478
void treeNodesRemoved, 478
void treeStructureChanged, 478
void treeWillCollapse, 468
void treeWillExpand, 468
void updateUI( )
    JSplitPane class, 249
    JTextComponent class, 260
    JToolTip class, 284
    JTree class, 294
void write(Writer out), 260
write(Writer out), 260
metrics (fonts), 606-614
methods, 613
typesetting, 606
minimumLayoutSize( ) method, 299
mnemonic keys (Swing buttons), 185, 188
modal dialog boxes, 110
Modal layer (JLayeredPane class), 39, 161
Model-View-Controller, see MVC
ModelEvent event, 370
models, 11, 41, 43
abstractions, 512
    event listeners, 508-510
    synchronization, 508-509
application-data models, 512
applications, 11
BoundedRangeModel, 44
ButtonModel, 44
color, 593
    direct color model, 596
    index color model, 593-596
ComboBoxModel, 44
creating, 534
dual context, 517-519
events, 363
GUI-state, 512
interface comparisons, 534

JFC (Java Foundation Classes) architecture, 41-46
ListModel, 44
MutableComboBoxModel, 44
MVC (Model-View-Controller)
    abstractions, 503-504
    application logic, 510
    Swing model support, 508
SingleSelectionModel, 44
Swing tool set, 141, 521-525
    abstractions, 504-505
    ButtonModel interface, 525-526
    ComboBoxModel interface, 526-527
    efficiency, 519-520
    events, 524-525
    list data event, 449-455
    ListModel object, 506-507
    MutableComboBoxModel interface, 526-527
    MVC support, 507-508
    SingleSelectionModel interface, 528
    TableModel interface, 528-529
    TreeModel interface, 529, 531
    TreeSelectionModel interface, 532-533
modelToView(int pos) method, 258
modes (Graphics class), 574-581
monitors (color), 593
mouse events (AWT), 415-419
mouseClicked( ) method, 384
MouseEvent class, 364-366, 410, 415-416
MouseInputListener interface, 376, 415
MouseListener Class (listing 9.2), 384
MouseListener Class As An Anonymous Inner Class (listing 9.7), 398
MouseListener interface, 375, 384-385, 406, 415
MouseMotionListener interface, 375, 415
MOVED constant (MouseEvent class), 416
moveToBack(Component c) method, 161
moveToFront(Component c) method, 161
multi look-and-feel package (JFC), 26, 30, 32
MutableAttributeSet getInputAttributes( ) method (JTextPane class), 281
MutableAttributeSet interface, 274
MutableComboBoxModel interface, 522, 526-527
MutableComboBoxModel model, 44
MVC (Model-View-Controller), 10-13, 41-46
abstractions, 503-504
    event listeners, 508-510
    synchronization, 508-509

application logic, 510
controller, viewer integration, 505
Swing model support, 507-508

N

NAME key, 494
Named Inner Class (listing 9.5), 389-390
named inner classes, 389-391
names
abstractions, 522
Component class, 76-77
Font class, 602
native graphics
AWT (Abstract Windowing Toolkit), 539-541
calling methods, 542
native peer objects (AWT), 18
native peers
AWT (Abstract Windowing Toolkit), 74
input events, 419-421
Swing tool set
lightweight components, 146
look-and-feel, 166
nested containers (AWT), 92-97
Nested Containers To Organize Child Components (listing 4.3), 92-95
Nested Containers with BoxLayout Layout Managers (listing 8.5), 326-327
nesting, 50
noneditable Swing combo boxes, 196
NORTH (BorderLayout class), 315
NORTH region (BorderLayout class), 313-317

O

Object cloneWithSource method, 476
Object getChild method (TreeModel interface), 530
Object getElementAt method, 507
Object getItemAt(int index) method (JComboBox class), 200
Object getLastSelected method (JTree class), 290
Object getPrototypeCellValue( ) method (JLabel class), 221
Object getRoot( ) method (TreeModel interface), 531

Object getSelectedItem( ) method
ComboBoxModel interface, 527
JComboBox class, 200
Object getSelectedValue( ) method (JLabel class), 222
Object getValueAt method (TableModel interface), 529
Object [] getSelectedObjects( ) method
AbstractButton class, 183
JComboBox class, 201
lists, 121
Object [] method
check boxes, 107
Choice Class, 110
object-oriented programming (OOP), 10
objects
AdjustmentEvent, 431
AWT (Abstract Windowing Toolkit), 18
BorderLayout, 314
BoxLayout, 322, 328
ButtonHandler, 383
CardLayout, 318-319
constraints (layout managers), 300
container classes, 22
DefaultListModel, 451
events, see events
Graphics (calling methods), 543
GridBagConstraints, 341
GridLayout, 311
IndexColorModel, 595
JComboBox, 510-512
JList, 512
JRootPane, 152
ListModel, 506-507, 513
ListSelectionModel, 519
MenuListener interface, 459
named inner classes, 391
plafComponentUI, 173
TreeModel, 284
views, 11, 503
Object[] getSelectedValues( ) method (JLabel class), 222
occluding windows (clipping graphics), 563-565
OOP (object-oriented programming), 10, 502
OPENED constant (WindowEvent class), 422
ordering containers (AWT), 98-99
origins (graphics), translating, 569-573
ovals (Graphics class), drawing, 558
OverlayLayout class, 301

P-Q

pack( ) method, 59
packages
   AWT (Abstract Windowing Toolkit), 17, 74, 85, 592
   color packages, 592
   JFC (Java Foundation Classes), 25-26
   Swing tool set, 140-141
      events, see Swing tool set, events
PackedColorModel class, 593
padding (internal), 351, 353
paint events (AWT), 422
paint mode (graphics), 574
paint( ) method, 82, 539-543, 583-584
   Component class, 582-583
   FontMetrics class, 614
   Swing Paint model, 585, 587
paint(Graphics g) method, 81
paintAll method, 582
paintComponent( ) method, 585-589, 609, 614
PaintEvent class, 366
painting, 538
   AWT Paint model, 582-584
   event causes, 582
   Swing Paint model, 584-590
Painting a Lightweight Component Incorrectly (11.11), 585-587
Palette layer (JLayeredPane class), 38, 161
Panel class (AWT), 20-22, 49, 85
Panel container, 54, 60-62
panels (BoxLayout class), 328-329
panes
   JFC (Java Foundation Classes), 35-38
      container classes, 35
      glass, 39
      layered, 38-39
   Swing tool set
      editor panes, 269, 271-273
      split panes, 244-249
      tabbed panes, 250-255
      text panes, 273-277, 279-282
parameters
   codebase, 64
   constraints, 301
   drawLine( ) method, 557
   GridBagConstraints, see GridBagConstraints
   height, 64
   width, 64

paramString( ) method, 364, 445
   JSlider class, 243
   JTextArea class, 269
   JTextComponent class, 258
parents, 50
parser package (JFC), 26
password fields (Swing components), 263-265
paste( ) method (JTextComponent class), 258
peers
   AWT (Abstract Windowing Toolkit), 18, 74
   input events, 419-421
   Swing tool set
      lightweight components, 146
      look-and-feel, 166
pens (graphics), 549-550
permanent focus transfers, 408
pixels
   alpha value, 593
   color, 593
   graphics, 549-551
   IndexColorModel class, 594
plaf (pluggable look-and-feel) package
   JFC (Java Foundation Classes), 25, 30-32
   Swing tool set, 29-32, 141, 166-174, 203
plafComponentUI object, 173
Platform's Default Look-and-Feel (listing 6.5), 169
platforms, 18-20
Point indexToLocation(int index) method (JLabel class), 222
point sizes (fonts), 603
policies
   application logic (selected indexes), 520-521
   layout managers, 298
polygons (Graphics class), drawing, 558-559
pop-up dialogs (JOptionPane class), 180
pop-up menus
   AWT (Abstract Windowing Toolkit), 108, 110
   combo boxes, 196
   Swing events, 464-467
Popup layer (JLayeredPane class), 39, 161
PopupMenu class, 49
PopupMenuEvent class, 464-467
PopupMenuEvent event, 370
PopupMenuListener interface, 377, 464-467
positioning
   graphics
      clipping, 568
      Graphics class, 549
      translating graphics origins, 569-573
   labels, 208, 210, 212-213

postActionEvent( ) method (JTextField class),
  262
preferredLayoutSize( ) method, 299
press events (keys), 410
PRESSED constant (MouseEvent class), 416
pressed events (key), 413
Pressed state (ButtonModel interface), 526
print package (AWT), 17
Printing the Names of the Looks-and-Feels
  (listing 6.6), 169-170
processComponentKeyEvent method
  (JTextArea class), 269
processEvent( ) method, 371-372
Program That Can Be Run As an Applet or
  Application (listing 3.4), 68, 70
Program That Demonstrates The Use of
  Multiple Fonts (listing 12.1), 604-605
programming
    abstractions, 8-10
    MVC, see MVC
    target audiences, 8-9
    user expectations, 8-9
progress bars (Swing components), 234-238
ProgressBarUI getUI( ) method (JProgressBar
  class), 237
properties
    Component class, 76
    Grphics, 538
    JComponent class, 147-148
    SMALL_ICON, 494
    SystemColor class, 600-601
protected Document createDefaultModel( )
  method (JTextArea class), 268
protected EditorKit method (JEditorPane
  class), 272
protected int getColumnWidth( ) method
  (JTextArea class), 268
protected int getRowHeight( ) method
  (JTextArea class), 268
protected ListSelectionModel
  createSelectionModel( ) method (JLabel
  class), 220
protected String paramString( ) method
    JFileChooser class, 206
    JPasswordField class, 265
    JProgressBar class, 237
    JSlider class, 243
    JTextArea class, 269

JTextComponent class, 258
JTextPane class, 281
JToolTip class, 284
protected StyledEditorKit getStyledEditorKit( )
  method (JTextPane class), 281
protected void consume( ) method, 364
protected void finalize( ) method, 364
protected void fireSelectionValueChanged
  method (JLabel class), 220
protected void fireStateChanged( ) method
  (JSlider class), 242
protected void init method (JMenuItem class),
  232
protected void paintBorder method
  (JProgressBar class), 237
protected void processComponentKeyEvent
  method (JTextArea class), 269
protected void setup (FileSystemView view)
  method (JFileChooser class), 207
protected void updateLabelUIs( ) method
  (JSlider class), 244
public void paint method, 582
public void paintAll method, 582
public void repaint method, 583
public void repaint( ) method, 583
public void repaint(long tm) method, 583
public void update method, 583

R

radio buttons
    JRadioButton class, 180-181
    JRadioButtonMenuItem class, 181
    Swing components, 192-196
RadioButton class (JFC), 29
read method
    JEditorPane class, 272
    JTextComponent class, 258
read-only fields (event listeners), 402
Rectangle getBoundsAt(int index) method
  (JTabbedPane class), 253
Rectangle getCellBounds method (JLabel
  class), 221
Rectangle getPathBounds method (JTree
  class), 291
Rectangle getRowBounds(int row) method
  (JTree class), 291

Rectangle modelToView(int pos) method
(JTextComponent class), 258

rectangles (Graphics class), drawing, 559, 561

redrawing damaged graphics, 564-566

regions (BorderLayout class), 313-317

registerEditorKitForContentType method
(JEditorPane class), 272-273

Registering a CaretListener With a JTextField
(listing 9.21), 436-437

Registering a ChangeListener With a JSlider
(listing 9.22), 438-442

Registering a HyperlinkListener With a
JEditorPane (listing 9.23), 441-442

Registering a ListDataListener With a
ListModel (listing 9.26), 452-455

Registering a Listener For WindowEvents
(listing 9.17), 423-425

Registering a ListSelectionListener With a
JList (listing 9.27), 456-458

Registering a MenuListener With a JMenu
(listing 9.28), 459-464

Registering a PopupMenuListener With a
JPopupMenu (listing 9.29), 465-467

Registering a TextListener With a TextArea
Component (listing 9.19), 428-429

Registering an AdjustmentListener With a
JScrollBar (listing 9.20), 431-432

Registering an InternalFrameListener With a
JInternalFrame (listing 9.25), 446-449

Registering Listeners For MouseEvents
(listing 9.14), 416-418

Registering Listeners For Tree-Related Events
With a JTree (listing 9.30), 469-473

RELATIVE constant (GridBagConstraints class),
341

relative locations (Component class), 76-77

RELEASED constant (MouseEvent class), 416

remove(AbstractButton b) method
(ButtonGroup class), 193

remove(Component c) method (JMenu class),
231

remove(Component component) method
JSplitPane class, 249
JTabbedPane class, 254

remove(int index) method, 161, 249

remove(int pos) method (JMenu class), 231

remove(JMenuItem item) method (JMenu
class), 231

removeActionListener method
JFileChooser class, 206
JTextField class, 262

removeAdjustmentListener( ) method, 430

removeAll( ) method
JMenu class, 231
JSplitPane class, 249
JTabbedPane class, 254

removeAllItems( ) method (JComboBox class),
201

removeCaretListener method
(JTextComponent class), 258

removeChangeListener method
BoundedRangeModel interface, 519
JSlider class, 243
JTabbedPane class, 254
SingleSelectionModel interface, 528

removeChoosableFileFilter method
(JFileChooser class), 206

removeElement(Object obj) method
(MutableComboBoxModel interface), 527

removeElementAt(int index) method
(MutableComboBoxModel interface), 527

removeHyperlinkListener method
(JEditorPane class), 273

removeIndexInterval method
(ListSelectionModel), 516

removeItem(Object item) method
(JComboBox class), 201

removeItemAt(int index) method (JComboBox
class), 201

removeListDataListener method, 507

removeListSelectionListener method
(ListSelectionModel), 516

removeMenuKeyListener method, 483

removeMenuListener(MenuListener) method,
458

removeNotify( ) method (JTextComponent
class), 258

removePropertyChangeListener method
(TreeSelectionModel interface), 533

removeSelectionInterval method
JLabel class, 222
JTree class, 292
ListSelectionModel, 516

removeSelectionPath method
JTree class, 292
TreeSelectionModel interface, 533

removeSelectionPaths method
JTree class, 292
TreeSelectionModel interface, 533
removeSelectionRow(int row) method (JTree class), 292
removeSelectionRows method (JTree class), 292
removeStyle(String nm) method (JTextPane class), 281
removeTabAt(int index) method (JTabbedPane class), 254
removeTableModelListener method (TableModel interface), 529
removeTreeExpansionListener method (JTree class), 293
removeTreeModelListener method (TreeModel interface), 531
removeTreeSelectionListener method
JTree class, 293
TreeSelectionModel interface, 533
removeTreeWillExpand method (JTree class), 293
rendering images
AWT package, 17
Component class methods, 81-82
drawing comparisons, 567-568
repaint( ) method, 81-82, 583-584, 587
replaceRange method (JTextArea class), 269
replaceSelection method
JEditorPane class, 273
JTextComponent class, 259
JTextPane class, 282
rescanCurrentDirectory( ) method (JFileChooser class), 206
resetChoosableFileFilters( ) method (JFileChooser class), 206
resetRowSelection( ) method (TreeSelectionModel interface), 533
resetToPreferredSizes( ) method (JSplitPane class), 249
RGB (Red, Green, Blue)
DirectColorModel class, 596
index color models, 594-595
RGBtoHSB method, 600
RIGHT alignment (FlowLayout), 305
RIGHT_ALIGNMENT constant, 213
rollover states
ButtonModel interface, 526
Swing buttons, 185, 188

root pane (JRootPane Swing container), 153-154
Root pane property (JComponent class), 147
RootLayout class, 301
rounded rectangles, 559-560
routines
drawString( ), 539
Graphics class, 551
RowMapper getRowMapper( ) method (TreeSelectionModel interface), 532
rows (GridLayout class), 310-311
rtf package (JFC), 26
Runtime Errors from Attempting to Add Components to a Heavyweight Swing Container Directly (listing 6.2), 157

S

screen locations (Component class), 76-77
Scrollbar class, 20, 49
scrolling (JScrollPane class), 180
ScrollPane class, 22, 49
scrollPathToVisible method (JTree class), 293
scrollRectToVisible method (JTextField class), 262
scrollRowToVisible(int row) method (JTree class), 293
select method (JTextComponent class), 259
selectAll( ) method (JTextComponent class), 259
selected index policies, 520-521
Selected state (ButtonModel interface), 526
selections (event listeners), 513-517
semantic events, 365-368
actions, 498
adjustment events, 429, 431-433
item events, 425-427
Swing tool set (change events), 437-440
Separator class (JFC), 29
setAccelerator method
JMenu class, 231
JMenuItem class, 232
setAccessory method, 206
setActionCommand method, 262
setAnchorSelectionIndex method, 516
setApproveButtonMnemonic method, 206
setApproveButtonText method, 206

setApproveButtonToolTipText method, 206
setArmed(boolean b) method, 232
setBackground(Color c) method, 597
setBackgroundAt method, 254
setBorderPainted(boolean b) method, 237
setBorderPainted(boolean s) method, 233
setBottomComponent method, 249
setCaret(Caret c) method, 259
setCaretColor(Color c) method, 259
setCaretPosition method, 259
setCellEditor method, 293
setCellRenderer method, 293
setCharacterAttributes method, 282
setClip( ) method, 568
setColumns method, 269
setColumns(int columns) method, 262
setComponent(JComponent c) method, 284
setComponentAt method, 254
setConstraints( ) method, 341 method,
  346-347
setContentType method, 273
setContinuousLayout method, 249
setCurrentDirectory method, 206
setCursor(Cursor) method, 80
setDelay(int d) method, 231
setDialogTitle method, 206
setDialogType method, 206
setDisabledIcon method
  AbstractButton class, 183
  JLabel class, 214
setDisabledIconAt method, 254
setDisabledSelectedIcon method, 184
setDisabledTextColor method, 259
setDisplayedMnemonic method, 214-215
setDividerLocation method, 249
setDividerSize method, 249
setDocument(Document doc) method
  JTextComponent class, 259
  JTextPane class, 282
setEchoChar(char c) method, 265
setEditable(boolean b) method, 259
setEditable(boolean flag) method
  JComboBox class, 201
  JTree class, 293
setEditorKit method, 273
setEditorKit(EditorKit kit) method, 282
setEditorKitForContentType method, 273

setEnabled(boolean b) method
  AbstractButton class, 184
  JMenuItem class, 232
  JTextComponent class, 259
setEnabled(boolean enabled) method, 201
setEnabledAt method, 254
setExtent(int extent) method, 243
setExtent(int newExtent) method, 519
setFileFilter method, 206
setFileHidingEnabled method, 207
setFileSelectionMode method, 207
setFileSystemView method, 207
setFileView method, 207
setFixedCellHeight method, 222
setFixedCellWidth method, 222
setFocusAccelerator method, 259
setFont( ) method, 605
setFont( ) method, 545
setFont(Font f) method
  JTextArea class, 269
  JTextField class, 262
setForeground(Color c) method, 597
setForegroundAt method, 254
setHelpMenu(JMenu menu) method, 234
setHighlighter method, 259
setHorizontalAlignment method
  AbstractButton class, 184
  JLabel class, 215
  JTextField class, 263
setHorizontalTextPosition method, 215
setHorizontalTextPosition(int align) method,
  184
setIcon(Icon defaultIcon) method, 184
setIcon(Icon icon) method, 215
setIconAt method, 254
setIconTextGap method, 215
setInverted(boolean b) method, 243
setInvokesStopCellEditing method, 293
setKeymap(Keymap map) method, 259
setLabel( ) method, 103
setLabelFor(Component c) method, 215
setLabelTable method, 243
setLargeModel method, 293
setLastDividerLocation method, 249
setLayout( ) method, 302
setLeadSelectionIndex method, 516
setLeftComponent method, 249

setLineWrap(boolean wrap) method, 269
setListData method, 222-223
setLogicalStyle(Style s) method, 282
setLookAndFeel( ) method, 171
setMajorTickSpacing(int n) method, 243
setMargin(Insets insets) method, 184
setMargin(Insets m) method, 259
setMargin(Insets margin) method, 234
setMaximum(int maximum) method, 243
setMaximum(int n) method, 238
setMaximum(int newMaximum) method, 519
setMaximumRowCount method, 201
setMenuLocation method, 231
setMinimum(int minimum) method, 243
setMinimum(int n) method, 238
setMinimum(int newMinimum) method, 519
setMinorTickSpacing(int n) method, 243
setMnemonic(char mnemonic) method, 184
setMnemonic(int mnemonic) method, 184
setModel method
    JMenu class, 231
    JProgressBar class, 238
    JSlider class, 243
    JTabbedPane class, 254
setModel(TreeModel newModel) method, 293
setMultiSelectionEnabled method, 207
setOneTouchExpandable method, 249
setOpaque(boolean o) method, 259
setOrientation method
    JProgressBar class, 238
    JSlider class, 243
    JSplitPane class, 249
setPage method, 273
setPaintLabels(boolean b) method, 243
setPaintMode( ) method, 574
setPaintTicks(boolean b) method, 243
setPaintTrack(boolean b) method, 243
setParagraphAttributes method, 282
setPopupMenuVisible method, 231
setPopupVisible(boolean v) method, 201
setPosition(Component c method, int
    position) method, 161
setPressedIcon method, 184
setPrototypeCellValue method, 223
setRangeProperties method, 519
setRightComponent method, 249
setRolloverEnabled method, 184
setRolloverIcon method, 184

setRolloverSelectedIcon method, 184
setRootVisible method, 293
setRowHeight(int rowHeight) method, 293
setRowMapper method, 533
setRows(int rows) method, 269
setScrollOffset method, 263
setScrollsOnExpand method, 293
setSelected method
    AbstractButton class, 184
    ButtonGroup class, 193
setSelected(boolean b) method, 231
setSelected(Component sel) method, 234
setSelectedComponent method, 254
setSelectedFiles method, 207
setSelectedIcon (Icon selectedIcon) method,
    185
setSelectedIndex method
    JLabel class, 223
    SingleSelectionModel interface, 528
setSelectedIndex (int anIndex) method, 201
setSelectedIndex(int index) method, 254
setSelectedIndices method, 223
setSelectedItem method, 527
setSelectedItem (Object anObject) method,
    201
setSelectedTextColor method, 259
setSelectedValue method, 223
setSelectionBackground method, 223
setSelectionColor(Color c) method, 259
setSelectionEnd method, 259
setSelectionForeground method, 223
setSelectionInterval method
    JLabel class, 223
    JTree class, 293
    ListSelectionModel, 516
setSelectionMode method
    JLabel class, 223
    ListSelectionModel, 516
setSelectionMode(int mode) method, 533
setSelectionModel method
    JMenuBar class, 234
    JTree class, 293
setSelectionPath method
    JTree class, 293
    TreeSelectionModel interface method, 533
setSelectionPaths method
    JTree class, 294
    TreeSelectionModel interface, 533

setSelectionRow(int row) method, 294
setSelectionRows method, 294
setSelectionStart method, 259
setShowsRootHandles method, 294
setSize(Dimension) method, 79
setSnapToTicks(boolean b) method, 244
setString(String s) method, 238
setStringPainted(boolean b) method, 238
setStyledDocument method, 282
setTabPlacement method, 255
setTabSize(int size) method, 269
setText(String t) method, 259
setText(String text) method
    AbstractButton class, 185
    JLabel class, 215
setTipText(String tipText) method, 284
setTitleAt method, 255
setTopComponent method, 249
setUI(MenuBarUI ui) method, 234
setUI(ProgressBarUI ui) method, 238
setUI(SliderUI ui) method, 244
setUI(SplitPaneUI ui) method, 249
setUI(TabbedPaneUI ui) method, 255
setUI(TextUI ui) method, 259
setUI(TreeUI ui) method, 294
setValue(int n) method
    JProgressBar class, 238
    JSlider class, 244
setValue(int newValue) method, 519
setValueAt method, 529
setValueIsAdjusting method
    BoundedRangeModel interface method, 519
    JLabel class, 223
    JSlider class, 244
    ListSelectionModel method, 516
setVerticalAlignment method, 215
setVerticalAlignment (int alignment) method,
  185
setVerticalTextPosition method, 215
setVerticalTextPosition(int textPosition)
  method, 185
setVisible(boolean) method, 79
setVisibleRowCount method
    JLabel class, 223
    JTree class, 294
setWrapStyleWord method, 269
Shape class (clip regions), 562
shapes (Graphics class), drawing, 551-557

showDialog(Component parent, String
  approveButtonText) method, 207
showOpenDialog(Component parent) method
  (JFileChooser class), 207
showPopup( ) method (JComboBox class), 201
showSaveDialog(Component parent) method
  (JFileChooser class), 207
Single and Multiple Selection Lists
  (listing 5.6), 118-119
SingleSelectionModel interface, 44, 522, 528
SINGLE_INTERVAL_SELECTION constant
  (ListSelectionModel), 515
SINGLE_SELECTION constant
  (ListSelectionModel), 515
size
    BorderLayout class, 315
    Component class, 76-79
    components (layout managers), 296-297
    containers
        CardLayout layout manager, 321
        FlowLayout class, 304
    fonts, 603
    glyphs, calculating, 609-612
    graphics pen lines, 549
    GridLayout class, 310-311
    index color models, 594
slider bars
    JSlider class, 180
    Swing components, 238-244
Slider class (JFC), 29
SliderUI getUI( ) method (JSlider class), 243
SMALL_ICON property, 494
source field (EventObject class), 364
sources (events), 364, 401-402
SOUTH region (BorderLayout class), 313-317
split horizontally view (JSplitPane class), 180
split panes (Swing components), 244-249
split vertically view (JSplitPane class), 180
SplitPane class (JFC), 29
SplitPaneUI getUI( ) method (JSplitPane class),
  248
Standalone Check Boxes and Grouped
  Checkboxes (listing 5.2), 105-106
start method, 66
start( ) method, 65
startEditingAtPath method (JTree class), 294
starting applications, 63
stateChanged(ChangeEvent) method, 437

states
   ButtonModel interface, 526
   Graphics class, 549
States of a Button (listing 5.1), 103-104
static Box createHorizontalBox( ) method, 329
static Box createVerticalBox( ) method, 329
static Color decode method, 599
static Color getColor method, 599
static Color getHSBColor method, 600
static Component createGlue( ) method, 329
static Component createHorizontalGlue( )
   method, 329-330
static Component createRigidArea(Dimension
   d) method, 329
static Component createVerticalStrut(int
   height) method, 330
static EditorKit method (JEditorPane class),
   272
static float constants (Component class), 213
static float[] RGBtoHSB method, 600
static int CONTENTS_CHANGED constant, 511
static int HSBtoRGB method, 600
static int INTERVAL_ADDED constant, 511
static int SINGLE_INTERVAL_SELECTION constant, 515
static int SINGLE_SELECTION constant, 515
static int X_AXIS method, 323
static int Y_AXIS method, 323
static Keymap addKeymap method, 256
static Keymap getKeymap method, 257
static Keymap removeKeymap method, 258
static String DEFAULT method, 490
static String LONG_DESCRIPTION method, 490
static String NAME method, 490
static String SHORT_DESCRIPTION method,
   490
static String SMALL_ICON method, 491
static void loadKeymap method, 258
static void registerEditorKitForContentType
   method, 272-273
stop( ) method, 65
stopEditing( ) method, 294
stopping applications, 63
String convertValueToText method, 289
String getActionCommand( ) method, 129
String getApproveButtonText( ) method, 205
String getApproveButtonToolTipText( )
   method, 205

String getColumnName method, 529
String getContentType( ) method, 272
String getDescription(File f) method, 205
String getDialogTitle( ) method, 205
String getItem(int index) method
   Choice Class, 110
   lists, 120
String getLabel( ) method
   Button class, 104
   check boxes, 107
   MenuItem class, 129
String getName( ) method, 130
String getName(File f) method, 205
String getSelectedItem( ) method, 121
String getSelectedText( ) method
   JTextComponent class, 257
   TextComponent class, 134
String getString( ) method, 237
String getText( ) method
   AbstractButton class, 183
   JEditorPane class, 272
   JLabel class, 214
   JTextComponent class, 258
   labels, 117
   TextComponent class, 134
String getTipText( ) method, 284
String getTitle( ) method, 114
String getTitleAt(int index) method, 253
String getToolTipText method, 253
String getTypeDescription(File f) method, 205
String getUIClassID( ) method
   JEditorPane class, 272
   JFileChooser class, 205
   JMenu class, 230
   JMenuItem class, 232
   JPasswordField class, 265
   JProgressBar class, 237
   JSlider class, 243
   JSplitPane class, 249
   JTabbedPane class, 253
   JTextArea class, 269
   JTextField class, 262
   JTextPane class, 281
   JToolTip class, 284
String paramString( ) method, 243
String toString( ) method, 308, 313
String [] getItems( ) method, 120
String [] getSelectedItems( ) method, 121
strings, graphical representation, 539-541

stringWidth(String str) method, 613
struts, 330-333
Struts to Specify Spacing In a Layout
  (listing 8.6), 330-332
Style addStyle method, 281
Style getLogicalStyle( ) method, 281
Style getStyle(String nm) method, 281
Style interface, 274
StyleConstants class, 274
StyleContext class, 274-275
StyledDocument getStyledDocument( )
  method, 281
styles
    fonts, 602
    text, creating, 275-276
Swing Buttons (listing 7.1), 185-187
Swing Check Box Menu Items and Radio
  Button Menu Items (listing 7.9), 229
Swing Check Boxes (listing 7.2), 189-191
Swing Combo Boxes (listing 7.4), 198-199
Swing Editor Panes (listing 7.17), 270-271
Swing File Chooser (listing 7.5), 202-203
Swing Labels (listing 7.6), 209-213
Swing Lists (listing 7.7), 216-219
Swing Menus (listing 7.8), 225-226, 228
Swing Password Fields (listing 7.15), 263-264
Swing Progress Bars (listing 7.10), 235-236
Swing Radio Buttons (listing 7.3), 194-196
Swing Sliders (listing 7.11), 239-241
Swing Split Panes (listing 7.12), 245-247
Swing Tabbed Panes (listing 7.13), 251-252
Swing Text Areas (listing 7.16), 266-267
Swing Text Fields (listing 7.14), 260-261
Swing Text Panes (listing 7.18), 276-280
Swing tool set, 16, 24-25
Swing tool set, 140-143
    abstractions, 502-503, 512
        event listeners, 508-510
        ListModel object, 506-507
        naming conventions, 522
        synchronization, 508-509
    AWT
        combinations, 141
        AWT/JFC comparisons, 40-41
    Box class, 329
        containers, 333-334
        methods, 329-330
        struts, 330-333

Component class, 143
containers, 145, 148-149, 301-302
    abstractions, 149-151
    heavyweight, 36, 63-64
    heavyweight/lightweight comparison, 162-165
    JDialogBox, 164
    JInternalFrame, 163
    JRootPane, 151-158
Delegation Event Model, 32-33
events, 363, 368-371, 433
    action events, 489-499
    adapters, 387
    ancestor events, 434-435
    AWT complements, 377-378
    caret events, 435-437
    change events, 437-440
    event listeners, 376-377
    hyperlink events, 440-444
    internal frame events, 444-449
    list data events, 449-455
    list selection events, 455-458
    menu drag mouse events, 486-488
    menu events, 458-464
    menu key events, 482-486
    pop-up menu events, 464-467
    tree expansion events, 468-476
    tree model events, 478-482
    tree selection events, 476-478
graphics
    component states, 543-546
    deleting instances, 548-549
    methods, 541-543, 546
heavyweight components, 27-28
JComponent class, 143, 145
    abstractions, 146-148
    methods, 148
    properties, 147-148
JLayeredPane class, 159-162
lightweight components, 25-29, 142-146, 178-181
    AWT classes, 179
    AWT events, 406
    buttons, 181-189
    AbstractButton class, 182
    check boxes, 189-191
    combo boxes, 196, 198-201
    file choosers, 201, 203-207
    labels, 208-215
    lists, 215-223
    JLabel class, 223
    menu bars, 233-234

JMenuBar class, 233
menus, 223-233
progress bars, 234-238
radio buttons, 192-196
sliders, 238-244
split panes, 244-249
tabbed panes, 250-255
tooltips, 282-284
trees, 284-294
look-and-feel configurations, 166-171, 173-174
    Look-and-Feel API, 18
    pluggable look-and-feel, 29-32
models, 521-525
    abstraction, 504-505
    ButtonModel interface, 525-526
    ComboBoxModel interface, 526-527
    creating, 534
    efficiency, 519-520
    events, 524-525
    MutableComboBoxModel interface, 526-527
    SingleSelectionModel interface, 528
    TableModel interface, 528-529
    TreeModel interface, 529, 531
    TreeSelectionModel interface, 532-533
MVC support, 507-508
packages, 140-141
Paint model, 584-590
text components, 255-260
    editor panes, 269, 271-273
    password fields, 263-265
    text areas, 265-269
    text fields, 260-263
    text panes, 273-277, 279-282
Swing Tool Tips (listing 7.19), 283
Swing Trees (listing 7.20), 285-288
SystemColor class, 592, 600-601

T

tabbed panes (Swing components), 250-255
TabbedPaneUI getUI( ) method (JTabbedPane class), 253
Table class (JFC), 29
table package (JFC), 26
TableColumn event, 370
TableColumnModel interface, 522
TableColumnModelListener interface, 377
TableModel interface, 522, 528-529

TableModelEvent event, 370
TableModelListener interface, 377
tabs (JTabbedPane class), 180
target audiences, programming for, 8-9
targets (events), 32
temporary focus transfers, 408, 410
text
    AWT (Abstract Windowing Toolkit)
        areas, 131-136
        events, 427-429
    Graphics class, drawing, 561-562
    styles, creating, 275-276
    Swing components, 265-269
Text Component Classes (listing 5.8), 131-133
text fields
    AWT (Abstract Windowing Toolkit), 131-136
    JPasswordField class, 180
    Swing components, 260-263
text package (JFC), 26
text panes (Swing components), 273-282
text Swing components, 255-260
TextArea class, 20, 49, 131, 135-136
TextArea( ) method (TextArea class), 135
TextComponent class, 20, 131, 134-135
TextEvent class, 367, 427-428
TextField class, 49, 131, 136
    AWT (Abstract Windowing Toolkit), 20
    input events, 421
    key events, 413
TextField( ) method (TextField class), 136
TextField(String text) method (TextField class), 136
TextListener interface, 375, 428-429
TextPane class (JFC), 29
TextUI getUI( ) method (JTextComponent class), 258
three-dimensional graphics (rectangles), 559
toggle buttons (JToggleButton class), 181
ToggleButton class (JFC), 29
ToolBar class (JFC), 29
toolbars (JToolBar class), 180
ToolTip class (JFC), 29
ToolTip property (JComponent class), 147
tooltips (Swing components), 141, 282-284
ToolTipUI getUI( ) method (JToolTip class), 284
TOP_ALIGNMENT constant, 213
toString( ) method, 363-364, 456, 476, 479
TRACK (AdjustmentEvent class), 431

TRAILING (FlowLayout), 305
translate( ) method, 569
translating graphics origins, 569-573
Translating a Graphics Origin (listing 11.9), 569-572
Tree class (JFC), 29
tree expansion events (Swing), 468-476
tree model events (Swing), 478-482
tree package (JFC), 26
tree selection events (Swing), 476-478
tree views (JTree class), 180
TreeCellEditor getCellEditor( ) method (JTree class), 290
treeDidChange( ) method (JTree class), 294
TreeExpansionEvent class, 370, 468-474, 476
TreeExpansionListener interface, 377, 468
TreeModel getModel( ) method (JTree class), 290
TreeModel interface, 284, 288, 522, 529-531
TreeModel object, 284
TreeModelEvent class, 370, 478-482
TreeModelEvent Listener Class (listing 9.32), 479-480
TreeModelListener interface, 377, 478-480, 482
TreeNode interface, 284, 288
TreePath getClosestPathForLocation method (JTree class), 290
TreePath getEditingPath( ) method (JTree class), 290
TreePath getLeadSelectionPath( ) method
    JTree class, 290
    TreeSelectionModel interface, 532
TreePath getPathForLocation method (JTree class), 291
TreePath getPathForRow(int row) method (JTree class), 291
TreePath getSelectionPath( ) method
    JTree class, 291
    TreeSelectionModel interface, 533
TreePath methods, 476
TreePath[] getSelectionPaths( ) method
    JTree class, 291
    TreeSelectionModel interface, 533
trees (Swing components), 284-294
TreeSelectionEvent class, 476-478
TreeSelectionEventListener Class (listing 9.31), 477
TreeSelectionListener interface, 377, 476-478

TreeSelectionModel getSelectionModel( ) method (JTree class), 291
TreeSelectionModel interface, 532-533
TreeWillExpandListener interface, 377, 468
try-catch block (Swing tool set), 168-169
two-dimensional graphics, 538
    AWT models, 538
        native graphics, 539-541
        Paint model, 582-584
    clipping, 562-566, 568
    component states, 543-546
    deleting instances, 548-549
    Graphics class, 549-551
        arcs, 560-561
        lines, 557-558
        ovals, 558
        polygons, 558-559
        rectangles, 559, 561
        shapes, 551-557
        text, 561-562
    graphics origins, translating, 569-573
    methods, 541-543, 546
    modes, 574-581
    painting causing events, 582
    strings, 539-541
    Swing Paint model, 584-590
type events (key), 411
typed events (key), 413
typesetting (FontMetrics), 606

U

UIDefaults class, 173
UIManager class, 173
UIs (user interfaces), 8
    abstractions, 9-10
    application logic, 10
    GUI, see GUI
    Look-and-Feel (Swing tool set), 141
underscore characters (Swing buttons), 188
undo package (JFC), 26
UndoableEdit event, 370
UndoableEditListener interface, 377
unidirectional communication, 12
UNIT_DECREMENT (AdjustmentEvent class), 431
UNIT_INCREMENT (AdjustmentEvent class), 431
update( ) method, 82, 585, 587

update(Graphics g) method, 81
updateLabelUIs( ) method, 244
updateUI( ) method
    JProgressBar class, 238
    JSlider class, 244
    JSplitPane class, 249
    JTabbedPane class, 255
    JTextComponent class, 260
    JToolTip class, 284
    JTree class, 294
updating hyperlink events (Swing), 440
URL getPage( ) method, 272
user program expectations, 8-9

V

validate( ) method, 298
valueForPathChanged method, 531
variables
    CLASSPATH, 57
    GridBagConstraints class, 337
        anchor, 348-349, 351
        fill, 347-348
        gridheight, 343-346
        gridwidth, 343-346
        gridx, 341-342
        gridy, 341-342
        insets, 351-353
        ipadx, 353-354
        ipady, 353-354
        vertical fill, 347
        weightx, 354-358
        weighty, 354-358
vertical labels, 208-213
vertical sizing (BorderLayout class), 315
vertically split view (JSplitPane class), 180
view object, 503
viewer (MVC), controller integration, 505
viewport (JViewport class), 29, 180
ViewportLayout class, 299
views, 11, 41, 43
viewToModel(Point pt) method, 260
visibility
    Component class, 76-79
    containers, 74
void add method, 83, 252, 360
void add(AbstractButton b) method, 193
void add(MenuItem mi) method, 128

void add(String item) method
    Choice Class, 110
    lists, 120
void add(String label) method, 128
void addActionListener method, 204
void addAdjustmentListener method, 430
void addChangeListener method
    BoundedRangeModel interface, 518
    SingleSelectionModel interface, 528
void addChoosableFileFilter method, 204
void addElement(Object obj) method, 527
void addHyperlinkListener method, 272
void addItem(Object anItem) method, 200
void addItem(String item) method, 110, 120
void addItemListener method, 425
void addLayoutComponent method, 298, 300, 308, 312
void addListDataListener method, 507
void addListSelectionListener method, 515
void addMenuListener method, 230
void addPropertyChangeListener method, 491, 532
void addSelectionInterval method
    JLabel class, 220
    JTree class, 289
    ListSelectionModel, 515
void addSelectionPath method
    JTree class, 289
    TreeSelectionModel interface, 532
void addSelectionPaths method
    JTree class, 289
    TreeSelectionModel interface, 532
void addSelectionRow(int row) method, 289
void addSelectionRows(int[] rows) method, 289
void addSeparator( ) method
    JMenu class, 230
    menus, 128
void addTab method, 253
void addTableModelListener method, 529
void addTreeExpansionListener method, 289
void addTreeModelListener method, 530
void addTreeSelectionListener method
    JTree class, 289
    TreeSelectionModel interface, 532
void addTreeWillExpandListener method, 289
void ancestorAdded method, 434

void ancestorMoved method, 434
void ancestorRemoved method, 434
void append(String str) method
    JTextArea class, 268
    TextArea class, 135
void approveSelection( ) method, 204
void cancelEditing( ) method, 289
void cancelSelection( ) method, 204
void changeToParentDirectory( ) method, 204
void clearSelection( ) method
    JLabel class, 220
    JTree class, 289
    ListSelectionModel, 515
    SingleSelectionModel interface, 528
    TreeSelectionModel interface, 532
void collapsePath(TreePath path) method, 289
void collapseRow(int row) method, 289
void consume( ) method, 364
void contentsChanged method, 450, 509
void copy( ) method
    JPasswordField class, 265
    JTextComponent class, 256
void cut( ) method
    JPasswordField class, 265
    JTextComponent class, 256
void deleteShortcut( ) method, 129
void deselect(int index) method, 120
void doClick( ) method, 182
void doClick(int pressTime) method, 230
void ensureFileIsVisible(File f) method, 204
void expandPath(TreePath path) method, 289
void expandRow(int row) method, 290
void finalize( ) method, 364
void fireHyperlinkUpdate method, 272
void fireTreeCollapsed method, 290
void fireTreeExpanded method, 290
void fireTreeWillCollapse method, 290
void fireTreeWillExpand method, 290
void first(Container parent) method, 319
void getAlphas(byte[] a) method, 595
void getBlues(byte[] b) method, 595
void getReds(byte[] r) method, 596
void hidePopup( ) method, 201
void insert method, 269
void insert(MenuItem, int index) method, 128
void insert(String label, int index) method, 128

void insert(String method item, int index), 110
void insert(String s, int pos) method, 230-231
void insert(String str) method, 136
void insertComponent method, 281
void insertElementAt method, 527
void insertIcon(Icon g) method, 281
void insertIndexInterval method, 516
void insertItemAt method, 201
void insertSeparator(int index) method
    JMenu class, 231
    menus, 128
void internalFrameActivated method, 445
void internalFrameClosed method, 445
void internalFrameClosing method, 445
void internalFrameDeactivated method, 445
void internalFrameDeiconified method, 445
void internalFrameIconified method, 445
void internalFrameOpened method, 445
void intervalAdded method, 450, 509
void intervalRemoved method, 450, 509
void invalidateLayout method, 300
void last(Container parent) method, 319
void layoutContainer method, 299, 308, 312
void makeVisible method, 292
void makeVisible(int index) method, 121
void menuCanceled(MenuEvent e) method, 459
void menuDeselected(MenuEvent e) method, 459
void menuDragMouseDragged method, 487
void menuDragMouseEntered method, 487
void menuDragMouseExited method, 487
void menuDragMouseReleased method, 487
void menuSelected(MenuEvent e) method, 459
void menuSelectionChanged method
    JMenu class, 231
    JMenuBar class, 233
    JMenuItem class, 232
void moveToBack(Component c) method, 161
void moveToFront(Component c) method, 161
void next(Container parent) method, 319
void paste( ) method, 258
void popupMenuCanceled method, 464
void popupMenuWillBecome method, 464
void postActionEvent( ) method, 262

void previous(Container parent) method, 319
void putValue method, 491
void read method
    JEditorPane class, 272
    JTextComponent class, 258
void remove (MenuComponent c) method, 130
void remove (MenuComponent item) method, 128
void remove method, 83
void remove( ) method, 84
void remove(AbstractButton b) method, 193
void remove(Component c) method, 231
void remove(Component comp) method, 298
void remove(Component component) method
    JSplitPane class, 249
    JTabbedPane class, 254
void remove(int index) method, 161
    JSplitPane class, 249
    MenuBar class, 130
    menus, 128
void remove(int pos) method, 231
void remove(int position) method, 121
void remove(JMenuItem item) method, 231
void remove(String item) method, 121
void removeActionListener method
    JFileChooser class, 206
    JTextField class, 262
void removeAdjustmentListener method, 430
void removeAll( ) method, 83, 298
    JMenu class, 231
    JSplitPane class, 249
    JTabbedPane class, 254
    lists, 121
    menus, 128
void removeAllItems( ) method, 201
void removeCaretListener method, 258
void removeChangeListener method
    BoundedRangeModel interface, 519
    JSlider class, 243
    JTabbedPane class, 254
    SingleSelectionModel interface, 528
void removeElement(Object obj) method, 527
void removeElementAt(int index) method, 527
void removeHyperlinkListener method, 273
void removeIndexInterval method, 516
void removeItem(Object item) method, 201

void removeItemAt(int index) method, 201
void removeItemListener method, 425
void removeLayoutComponent method, 299, 313
void removeListDataListener method, 507
void removeListSelectionListener method, 516
void removeNotify( ) method, 258
void removeProperty method, 491
void removePropertyChangeListener method, 533
void removeSelectionInterval method
    JLabel class, 222
    JTree class, 292
    ListSelectionModel, 516
void removeSelectionPath method
    JTree class, 292
    TreeSelectionModel interface, 533
void removeSelectionPaths method
    JTree class, 292
    TreeSelectionModel interface, 533
void removeSelectionRow method, 292
void removeSelectionRows method, 292
void removeStyle(String nm) method, 281
void removeTabAt(int index) method, 254
void removeTableModelListener method, 529
void removeTreeExpansionListener method, 293
void removeTreeModelListener method, 531
void removeTreeSelectionListener method
    JTree class, 293
    TreeSelectionModel interface, 533
void removeTreeWillExpand method, 293
void repaint method, 583
void replaceItem(String newValue, int index) method, 121
void replaceRange(String str, int start, int end) method, 136
void replaceSelection method
    JEditorPane class, 273
    JTextComponent class, 259
    JTextPane class, 282
void rescanCurrentDirectory( ) method, 206
void resetChoosableFileFilters( ) method, 206
void resetRowSelection( ) method, 533
void resetToPreferredSizes( ) method, 249
void scrollPathToVisible method, 293
void scrollRectToVisible method, 262
void scrollRowToVisible(int row) method, 293

void select method, 259
void select(int index) method, 121
void select(int method, 134
void select(int pos) method, 110
void select(String str) method, 110
void selectAll( ) method
    JTextComponent class, 259
    TextComponent class, 134
void setAccelerator method
    JMenu class, 231
    JMenuItem class, 232
void setAccessory method, 206
void setActionCommand (String command) method, 129
void setActionCommand method, 262
void setAlignment method, 308
void setAlignment(int alignment) method, 117
void setAnchorSelectionIndex method, 516
void setApproveButtonMnemonic method, 206
void setApproveButtonText method, 206
void setApproveButtonToolTipText method, 206
void setArmed(boolean b) method, 232
void setBackground(Color c) method, 597
void setBackgroundAt method, 254
void setBlockIncrement(int b) method, 430
void setBorderPainted(boolean b) method, 237
void setBorderPainted(boolean s) method, 233
void setBottomComponent method, 249
void setBounds method, 297
void setCaret(Caret c) method, 259
void setCaretColor(Color c) method, 259
void setCaretPosition (int position) method, 134
void setCaretPosition method, 259
void setCellEditor method, 293
void setCellRenderer method, 293
void setCharacterAttributes method, 282
void setCheckboxGroup method, 107
void setColumns method, 269
void setColumns(int cols) method, 313
void setColumns(int columns) method, 262
void setComponent method, 284
void setComponentAt method, 254

void setContentType method, 273
void setContinuousLayout method, 249
void setCurrentDirectory method, 206
void setDelay(int d) method, 231
void setDialogTitle method, 206
void setDialogType method, 206
void setDisabledIcon method
    AbstractButton class, 183
    JLabel class, 214
void setDisabledIconAt method, 254
void setDisabledSelectedIcon method, 184
void setDisabledTextColor method, 259
void setDisplayedMnemonic method, 214-215
void setDividerLocation method, 249
void setDividerSize method, 249
void setDocument(Document doc) method
    JTextComponent class, 259
    JTextPane class, 282
void setEchoChar(char c) method
    JPasswordField class, 265
    TextField class, 136
void setEditable (boolean b) method, 134
void setEditable(boolean b) method, 259
void setEditable(boolean flag) method
    JComboBox class, 201
    JTree class, 293
void setEditorKit method, 273
void setEditorKit(EditorKit kit) method, 282
void setEditorKitForContentType method, 273
void setEnabled( ) method, 129, 491
void setEnabled(boolean b) method
    AbstractButton class, 184
    JMenuItem class, 232
    JTextComponent class, 259
void setEnabled(boolean enabled) method, 201
void setEnabledAt method, 254
void setExtent(int extent) method, 243
void setExtent(int newExtent) method, 519
void setFileFilter method, 206
void setFileHidingEnabled method, 207
void setFileSelectionMode method, 207
void setFileSystemView method, 207
void setFileView method, 207
void setFixedCellHeight method, 222
void setFixedCellWidth method, 222
void setFocusAccelerator method, 259
void setFont( ) method, 130

void setFont(Font f) method
    JTextArea class, 269
    JTextField class, 262
void setForeground(Color c) method, 597
void setForegroundAt method, 254
void setHelpMenu(JMenu menu) method, 234
void setHelpMenu(Menu m) method, 130
void setHgap method, 308
void setHgap(int hgap) method, 313, 319
void setHighlighter method, 259
void setHorizontalAlignment method
    AbstractButton class, 184
    JLabel class, 215
    JTextField class, 263
void setHorizontalTextPosition method, 215
void setHorizontalTextPosition(int align)
    method, 184
void setIcon(Icon defaultIcon) method, 184
void setIcon(Icon icon) method, 215
void setIconAt method, 254
void setIconTextGap method, 215
void setInverted(boolean b) method, 243
void setInvokesStopCellEditing method, 293
void setKeymap(Keymap map) method, 259
void setLabel method, 104
void setLabel(String label) method
    check boxes, 107
    MenuItem class, 129
void setLabelFor(Component c) method, 215
void setLabelTable method, 243
void setLargeModel method, 293
void setLastDividerLocation method, 249
void setLayout method, 298
void setLayout(LayoutManager l) method,
    330
void setLeadSelectionIndex method, 516
void setLeftComponent method, 249
void setLineWrap(boolean wrap) method, 269
void setListData method, 222-223
void setLogicalStyle(Style s) method, 282
void setMajorTickSpacing(int n) method, 243
void setMargin(Insets insets) method, 184
void setMargin(Insets m) method, 259
void setMargin(Insets margin) method, 234
void setMaximum(int max) method, 430
void setMaximum(int maximum) method, 243
void setMaximum(int n) method, 238
void setMaximumRowCount method, 201

void setMenuLocation method, 231
void setMinimum(int min) method, 430
void setMinimum(int minimum) method, 243
void setMinimum(int n) method, 238
void setMinimum(int newMinimum) method,
    519
void setMinorTickSpacing(int n) method, 243
void setMnemonic(char mnemonic) method,
    184
void setMnemonic(int mnemonic) method,
    184
void setModal(boolean modal) method, 114
void setModel method
    JMenu class, 231
    JProgressBar class, 238
    JSlider class, 243
    JTabbedPane class, 254
void setModel(TreeModel newModel)
    method, 293
void setMultipleMode(boolean b) method,
    121
void setMultiSelectionEnabled method, 207
void setName (String name) method, 130
void setOneTouchExpandable method, 249
void setOpaque(boolean o) method, 259
void setOrientation method
    JProgressBar class, 238
    JSlider class, 243
    JSplitPane class, 249
void setPage method, 273
void setPaintLabels(boolean b) method, 243
void setPaintTicks(boolean b) method, 243
void setPaintTrack(boolean b) method, 243
void setParagraphAttributes method, 282
void setPopupMenuVisible method, 231
void setPopupVisible(boolean v) method, 201
void setPosition(Component c, int position)
    method, 161
void setPressedIcon method, 184
void setPrototypeCellValue method, 223
void setRangeProperties method, 519
void setResizable (boolean resizable) method,
    114
void setRightComponent method, 249
void setRolloverEnabled method, 184
void setRolloverIcon method, 184
void setRolloverSelectedIcon method, 184
void setRootVisible method, 293

void setRowHeight(int rowHeight) method,
293
void setRowMapper method, 533
void setRows(int rows) method, 313
    JTextArea class, 269
    TextArea class, 136
void setScrollOffset method, 263
void setScrollsOnExpand method, 293
void setSelected method
    AbstractButton class, 184
    ButtonGroup class, 193
void setSelected(boolean b) method, 231
void setSelected(Component sel) method, 234
void setSelectedComponent method, 254
void setSelectedEnd (int selectionEnd)
method, 135
void setSelectedFiles method, 207
void setSelectedIcon (Icon selectedIcon)
method, 185
void setSelectedIndex (int anIndex) method,
201
void setSelectedIndex method
    JLabel class, 223
    SingleSelectionModel interface, 528
void setSelectedIndex(int index) method, 254
void setSelectedIndices method, 223
void setSelectedItem method, 527
void setSelectedStart (int selectionStart)
method, 135
void setSelectedTextColor method, 259
void setSelectedValue method, 223
void setSelectionBackground method, 223
void setSelectionColor(Color c) method, 259
void setSelectionEnd method, 259
void setSelectionForeground method, 223
void setSelectionInterval method
    JLabel class, 223
    JTree class, 293
    ListSelectionModel, 516
void setSelectionMode method
    JLabel class, 223
    ListSelectionModel, 516
void setSelectionMode(int mode) method
    TreeSelectionModel interface, 533
void setSelectionModel method
    JMenuBar class, 234
    JTree class, 293
void setSelectionPath method
    JTree class, 293
    TreeSelectionModel interface, 533

void setSelectionPaths method
    JTree class, 294
    TreeSelectionModel interface, 533
void setSelectionRow(int row) method, 294
void setSelectionRows method, 294
void setSelectionStart method, 259
void setShortcut (MenuShortcut s) method,
129
void setShowsRootHandles method, 294
void setSize method, 297
void setSnapToTicks(boolean b) method, 244
void setState(boolean state) method, 107
void setString(String s) method, 238
void setStringPainted(boolean b) method,
238
void setStyledDocument method, 282
void setTabPlacement method, 255
void setTabSize(int size) method, 269
void setText(String t) method
    JTextComponent class, 135, 259
    TextField class, 136
void setText(String text) method
    AbstractButton class, 185
    JLabel class, 215
    labels, 117
void setTipText method, 284
void setTitle(String title) method, 114
void setTitleAt method, 255
void setTopComponent method, 249
void setUI method, 294
void setUI(MenuBarUI ui) method, 234
void setUI(ProgressBarUI ui) method, 238
void setUI(SliderUI ui) method, 244
void setUI(SplitPaneUI ui) method, 249
void setUI(TabbedPaneUI ui) method, 255
void setUI(TextUI ui) method, 259
void setUnitIncrement(int u) method, 430
void setValue(int n) method
    JProgressBar class, 238
    JSlider class, 244
void setValue(int newValue) method, 519
void setValue(int v) method, 430
void setValueAt method, 529
void setValueIsAdjusting method
    BoundedRangeModel interface, 519
    JLabel class, 223
    JSlider class, 244
    ListSelectionModel, 516
void setVerticalAlignment (int alignment)
method, 185

void setVerticalAlignment method, 215
void setVerticalTextPosition method, 215
void setVerticalTextPosition(int textPosition) method, 185
void setVgap method, 308
void setVgap(int vgap) method, 313, 319
void setVisible method, 297
void setVisibleAmount(int v) method, 430
void setVisibleRowCount method
    JLabel class, 223
    JTree class, 294
void setWrapStyleWord method, 269
void show( ) method, 114, 319
void showPopup( ) method, 201
void startEditingAtPath method, 294
void treeCollapsed method, 468
void treeDidChange method, 294
void treeExpanded method, 468
void treeNodesChanged method, 478
void treeNodesInserted method, 478
void treeNodesRemoved method, 478
void treeStructureChanged method, 478
void treeWillCollapse method, 468
void treeWillExpand method, 468
void updateUI( ) method
    JProgressBar class, 238
    JSlider class, 244
    JSplitPane class, 249
    JTabbedPane class, 255
    JTextComponent class, 260
    JToolTip class, 284
    JTree class, 294
void valueForPathChanged method, 531
void write(Writer out) method, 260

W

weightx parameter (GridBagConstraints class), 338
weightx variable (GridBagConstraints class), 337, 354-358
weighty parameter (GridBagConstraints class), 338
weighty variable (GridBagConstraints class), 337, 354-358

WEST region (BorderLayout class), 314-317
width, positioning graphics, 568
width parameter, 64
Window class, 22, 49, 85
Window container, 54
window events (AWT), 422-425
WindowAdapter interface, 400
WindowEvent class, 366, 422
WindowEvents class, 423-425
WindowListener interface, 400, 423-425
WindowListener to Your Frame (listing 9.9), 400
windows
    affect on graphics, 567
    container class, 34
write(Writer out) method, 260

X-Y-Z

x grids (GridLayout class), 335
XOR mode (graphics), 574-581
XOR Mode for Rubber-Band-Like Drawing (listing 11.10), 575-581

y grids (GridLayout class), 335

z-ordering (containers), 98, 150

Other Related Titles

Java 2 for Professional Developers
Mike Morgan
0-672-31697-8
$34.99 USA/$52.95 CAN

Pure JFC Swing
Satyaraj Pantham
0-672-31423-1
$19.99 USA/$28.95 CAN

Java Distributed Objects
*Bill McCarty and
Luke Cassady-Dorion*
0-672-31537-8
$49.99 USA/$71.95 CAN

**Java Thread
Programming**
Paul Hyde
0-672-31585-8
$34.99 USA/$52.95 CAN

**The Official VisiBroker
for Java Handbook**
*Michael McCaffery
and Bill Scott*
0-672-31451-7
$39.99 USA$59.95 CAN

**Developing Java
Servlets**
James Goodwill
0-672-31600-5
$29.99 USA/$44.95 CAN

SAMS
www.samspublishing.com

All prices are subject to change.